By the Same Author

I LOST IT AT THE MOVIES

KISS KISS BANG BANG

GOING STEADY

THE CITIZEN KANE BOOK

DEEPER INTO MOVIES

DEEPER INTO MOVIES

by Pauline Kael

CALDER & BOYARS LONDON

First published in Great Britain in 1975
by Calder & Boyars Ltd
18 Brewer Street, London W1R 4AS

ORIGINALLY PUBLISHED IN THE UNITED STATES BY
LITTLE, BROWN AND COMPANY, 1973
COPYRIGHT © 1969, 1970, 1971, 1972, 1973 BY PAULINE KAEL

ALL RIGHTS RESERVED

All the material in this book appeared originally in *The New Yorker*

ISBN 0 7145 0753 9   Casebound

Any paperback edition of this book whether published simultaneously with or subsequent to the casebound edition is sold subject to the condition that it shall not, by way of trade, be lent, resold, hired out, or otherwise disposed of, without the publisher's consent, in any form of binding or cover other than that in which it is published.

No part of this publication may be stored in a retrieval system, reproduced, or transmitted by any means, electronic, mechanical, photo-copying, recording or otherwise, except for brief extracts for the purpose of review, without the prior, written consent of the copyright owner and the publisher.

PRINTED IN THE U.S.A.
Bound in Great Britain

Contents

AUTHOR'S NOTE — XV

Part One

THE BOTTOM OF THE PIT — 3
Butch Cassidy and the Sundance Kid

WAITING FOR ORGY — 8
Bob & Carol & Ted & Alice

OFF WITH THE STATUES' HEADS! — 14
Oh! What a Lovely War
The Bed Sitting Room
A Walk with Love and Death
de Sade

HIGH SCHOOL AND OTHER FORMS OF MADNESS — 19
High School
The Royal Hunt of the Sun
The Madwoman of Chaillot

SOMEBODY ELSE'S SUCCESS — 26
Paint Your Wagon
Lions Love

PRIVATE WORLDS — 31
The Sterile Cuckoo
The Secret of Santa Vittoria
Duet for Cannibals
Coming Apart

THE ONCE AND FUTURE KING? — 37
Goodbye, Mr. Chips
Adalen 31
Hail, Hero!

BLOOD AND SNOW — 42
In the Year of the Pig
Downhill Racer

KAZAN'S LATEST ARRANGEMENTS   48
    The Arrangement

THE BOURGEOISIE AND THE RABBLE   53
    La Femme Infidèle
    Futz
    All the Loving Couples
    Popcorn

ELFSKIN   59
    The Comic

EXILES   63
    Z
    Alfred the Great

GLORIA, THE GIRL WITHOUT HOPE   68
    They Shoot Horses, Don't They?
    John and Mary
    Gaily, Gaily

AMERICANA   75
    The Reivers
    Tell Them Willie Boy Is Here
    Topaz

KEEP GOING   80
    Hello, Dolly!
    On Her Majesty's Secret Service
    Marooned
    The Damned

ENGLISH BULL   88
    Hamlet
    A Boy Named Charlie Brown

BLESSED PROFANITY   92
    M*A*S*H
    Anne of the Thousand Days

THE MAN WHO LOVED WAR   97
    Patton
    Hospital

DUDS   102
    The Milky Way
    The Molly Maguires
    The Kremlin Letter
    The Honeymoon Killers

TRENDS AND PAROXYSMS   107
    A Married Couple
    End of the Road

THE BEAUTY OF DESTRUCTION 113
   Zabriskie Point
   The Looking Glass War

RECOGNIZABLE HUMAN BEHAVIOR 119
   Loving
   The Only Game in Town
   Start the Revolution Without Me
   The Magic Christian
   Tropic of Cancer

FELLINI'S "Mondo Trasho" 127
   Fellini Satyricon

SCAVENGERS WITH COMPUTERS 132
   The Adventurers
   Airport
   The Boys in the Band

LUST FOR "ART" 138
   Women in Love

Part Two

NUMBING THE AUDIENCE 145

MOTHERS 153
   Trash
   The Baby Maker

CLOBBER-MOVIE 158
   The Great White Hope
   Monte Walsh
   First Love

KAMIKAZES 163
   Ice

MEN IN TROUBLE 169
   I Never Sang for My Father
   Goin' Down the Road
   This Man Must Die
   Little Fauss and Big Halsy
   C. C. and Company

MYTHMAKING 175
   Burn!
   The Twelve Chairs
   Cromwell
   WUSA

TEAMWORK 183
The Owl and the Pussycat
Where's Poppa?
The Private Life of Sherlock Holmes
Song of Norway

BOLT & LEAN 188
Ryan's Daughter
Perfect Friday

SLAPSTICK TRAGEDY 193
The Pizza Triangle
Bombay Talkie
Scrooge

WORLDS APART 197
Groupies
I Walk the Line

STALINISM 200
The Confession
The Act of the Heart

BEYOND PIRANDELLO 206
Gimme Shelter

EPIC AND CRUMBCRUSHER 212
Little Big Man
Love Story

MEGALOMANIACS 220
Investigation of a Citizen Above Suspicion
Husbands

SPAWN OF THE MOVIES 224
Alex in Wonderland
Brewster McCloud
There Was a Crooked Man . . .

NOTES ON HEART AND MIND 230

GENIUS 238
The Music Lovers

HOW BOYS GROW UP 243
Bed and Board
Promise at Dawn

BLOOD AND SAND 248
The Last Valley
Puzzle of a Downfall Child

VARIETIES OF PARANOIA 253
Little Murders
The Hour of the Furnaces

MISANTHROPIC MOVIES   259
   Doctors' Wives
   The Sporting Club
   The Garden of Delights

ERIC ROHMER'S REFINEMENT   264
   Claire's Knee
   Wanda
   A New Leaf

THE POETRY OF IMAGES   270
   The Conformist
   The Andromeda Strain

PIPE DREAM   277
   McCabe & Mrs. Miller
   Klute
   Carnal Knowledge
   The Anderson Tapes

Part Three

A MOVIE CLASSIC IS NOT NOTHING   289
   Sunday Bloody Sunday

MOVIES IN MOVIES   293
   The Last Picture Show
   The Last Movie
   Skin Game

HELEN OF TROY, SEXUAL WARRIOR   300
   The Trojan Women

LOUIS MALLE'S PORTRAIT OF THE ARTIST AS A YOUNG DOG   305
   Murmur of the Heart
   The Début
   T. R. Baskin

URBAN GOTHIC   313
   The French Connection

CHEATERS   319
   Long Ago, Tomorrow
   Is There Sex After Death?

A BAGEL WITH A BITE OUT OF IT   327
   Fiddler on the Roof

EL POTO — HEAD COMICS   334
   El Topo

WINGING IT 341
    Billy Jack

NOTES ON NEW ACTORS, NEW MOVIES 347
    Born to Win
    Going Home

PETER BROOK'S "Night of the Living Dead" 354
    King Lear
    Man in the Wilderness
    Bedknobs and Broomsticks

THE FALL AND RISE OF VITTORIO DE SICA 360
    The Garden of the Finzi-Continis

COUPLES 366
    Nicholas and Alexandra
    Made for Each Other

STANLEY STRANGELOVE 373
    A Clockwork Orange

PLEASING AND PUNISHING 378
    The Hospital
    The Boy Friend
    Such Good Friends

SAINT COP 385
    Dirty Harry
    Diamonds Are Forever

BABY MACHOS 390
    The Cowboys

PECKINPAH'S OBSESSION 393
    Straw Dogs

KILLERS AND THIEVES 399
    Macbeth
    The Hot Rock
    Le Boucher

THE MESSINESS OF LOVE 405
    X Y & Zee

GRINNING 409
    Cabaret

LITERARY ECHOES — MUFFLED 413
    Without Apparent Motive
    Outback
    Bartleby
    To Die of Love

ALCHEMY 420
The Godfather

COLLABORATION AND RESISTANCE 426
The Sorrow and the Pity
What's Up, Doc?

INDEX 435

Author's Note

This collection of my reviews from *The New Yorker* for September 1969 to March 1972 is also a record of the interaction of movies and our national life during a frantic time when three decades seem to have been compressed into three years and I wrote happily — like a maniac — to keep up with what I thought was going on in movies — which is to say, in our national theatre.

Right now, movie critics have an advantage over critics in most other fields: responsive readers. And it can help you to concentrate your energies if you know that the subject is fresh and that your review may make a difference to some people. I suspect that my reviews gain rather than lose from the speed and urgency of making deadlines and reaching the public before the verdicts are in on a film.

A word of explanation may be needed about the intent of "deeper" in the title of this book. It is twenty years since I first began to publish movie reviews, and I have come to see what a booby-trapped subject I'm involved in. I seem to have more to say now; I hope there's more depth to it because I think that's what is needed. I have become very uneasy about the widespread turn-on-to-the-excitement-of-film approach. I try to use my initial responses (which I think are probably my deepest and most honest ones) to explore not only what a movie means to me, but what it may mean to others: to get at the many ways in which movies, by affecting us on sensual and primitive levels, are a supremely pleasurable — and dangerous — art form.

I would feel like a fake if I dedicated a book to anyone, because I know I write because I love trying to figure out what I feel and what I think about what I feel, and why. But when the writing is any good, it's because three people wanted it to be good and I wanted them to feel some proprietary pride: William Shawn of *The New Yorker,* William Abrahams of the Atlantic Monthly Press, and my daughter Gina James, the hardest to satisfy and hence my ideal reader.

PART I

The Bottom of the Pit

A college-professor friend of mine in San Francisco who has always tried to stay in tune with his students looked at his class recently and realized it was time to take off his beads. There he was, a superannuated flower child wearing last year's talismans, and the young had become austere, even puritanical. Movies and, even more, movie audiences have been changing. The art houses are now (for the first time) dominated by American movies, and the young audiences waiting outside, sitting on the sidewalk or standing in line, are no longer waiting just for entertainment. The waiting together may itself be part of the feeling of community, and they go inside almost for sacramental purposes. For all the talk (and fear) of ritual participation in the "new" theatre, it is really taking place on a national scale in the movie houses, at certain American films that might be called cult films, though they have probably become cult films because they are the most interesting films around. What is new about *Easy Rider* is not necessarily that one finds its attitudes appealing but that the movie conveys the mood of the drug culture with such skill and in such full belief that these simplicities are the truth that one can understand why these attitudes are appealing to others. *Easy Rider* is an expression and a confirmation of how this audience feels; the movie attracts a new kind of "inside" audience, whose members enjoy tuning in together to a whole complex of shared signals and attitudes. And although one may be uneasy over the satisfaction the audience seems to receive from responding to the general masochism and to the murder of Captain America, the movie obviously rings true to the audience's vision. It's cool to feel that you can't win, that it's all rigged and hopeless. It's even cool to believe in purity and sacrifice. Those of us who reject the heroic central character and the statements of *Easy Rider* may still be caught by something edgy and ominous in it — the acceptance of the constant danger of sudden violence. We're not sure how much of this paranoia isn't paranoia.

Some of the other cult films *try* to frighten us but are too clumsy to, though they succeed in doing something else. One has only to talk with some of the people who have seen *Midnight Cowboy*, for example, to be aware that what they care about is not the camera and editing pyrotechnics; they are indifferent to all that by now routine filler. John Schlesinger in *Midnight Cowboy* and, at a less skillful level, Larry Peerce in *Goodbye, Columbus* hedge their bets by using cutting and camera techniques to provide a satirical background as a kind of enrichment of the narrative and theme. But it really cheapens and impoverishes their themes. Peerce's satire is just cheesy, like his lyricism, and Schlesinger's (like Tony Richardson's in *The Loved One* and Richard Lester's in *Petulia*) is offensively inhuman and inaccurate. If Schlesinger could extend the same sympathy to the other Americans that he extends to Joe Buck and Ratso, the picture might make better sense; the point of the picture must surely be to give us some insight into these derelicts — two of the many kinds of dreamers and failures in the city. Schlesinger keeps pounding away at America, determined to expose how horrible the people are, to dehumanize the people these two are part of. The spray of venom in these pictures is so obviously the directors' way of showing off that we begin to discount it. To varying degrees, these films share the paranoid view of America of *Easy Rider* — and they certainly reinforce it for the audience — but what the audience really reacts to in *Midnight Cowboy* is the two lost, lonely men finding friendship. The actors save the picture, as the actors almost saved parts of *Petulia;* the leading actors become more important because the flamboyantly "visual" exhibitionism doesn't hold one's interest. Despite the recurrent assertions that the star system is dead, the audience is probably more interested than ever in the human material on the screen (though the new stars don't always resemble the old ones). At *Midnight Cowboy*, in the midst of all the grotesque shock effects and the brutality of the hysterical, superficial satire of America, the audiences, wiser, perhaps, than the director, are looking for the human feelings — the simple, *Of Mice and Men* kind of relationship at the heart of it. Maybe they wouldn't accept the simple theme so readily in a simpler setting, because it might look square, but it's what they're taking from the movie. They're looking for "truth" — for some signs of emotion, some evidence of what keeps people together. The difference between the old audiences and the new ones is that the old audiences wanted immediate gratification and used to get restless and bored when a picture didn't click along; these new pictures don't all click along, yet the young audiences stay attentive. They're eager to respond, to love it — eager to *feel*.

Although young movie audiences are far more sentimental now than they were a few years ago (Frank Capra, whose softheaded populism was hooted at in college film societies in the fifties, has become a new favorite at U.C.L.A.), there is this new and good side to the sentimentality. They are going to movies looking for feelings that will help synthesize their experience, and they appear to be willing to feel their way along with a movie like Arthur Penn's *Alice's Restaurant,* which is also trying to feel its way. I think we (from this point I include myself, because I share these attitudes) are desperate for some sensibility in movies, and that's why we're so moved by the struggle toward discovery in *Alice's Restaurant,* despite how badly done the film is. I think one would have to lie to say *Alice's Restaurant* is formally superior to the big new Western *Butch Cassidy and the Sundance Kid.* In formal terms, neither is very good. But *Alice's Restaurant* is a groping attempt to express something, and *Butch Cassidy* is a glorified vacuum. Movies can be enjoyed for the *quality* of their confusions and failures, and that's the only way you can enjoy some of them now. Emotionally, I stayed with Penn during the movie, even though I thought that many of the scenes in it were inept or awful, and that several of the big set pieces were expendable (to put it delicately). But we're *for* him, and that's what carries the movie. Conceptually, it's unformed, with the director trying to discover his subject as well as its meaning and his own attitudes. And, maybe for the first time, there's an audience for American pictures which is willing to accept this.

Not every movie has to matter; generally we go hoping just to be relaxed and refreshed. But because most of the time we come out slugged and depressed, I think we care far more now about the reach for something. We've simply spent too much time at movies made by people who didn't enjoy themselves and who didn't respect themselves or us, and we rarely enjoy ourselves at their movies anymore. They're big catered affairs, and we're humiliated to be there among the guests. I look at the list of movies playing, and most of them I genuinely just can't face, because the odds are so strong that they're going to be the same old insulting failed entertainment, and, even though I may have had more of a bellyful than most people, I'm sure this isn't just my own reaction. Practically everybody I know feels the same way. This may seem an awfully moral approach, but it comes out of surfeit and aesthetic disgust. There's something vital to enjoyment which we haven't been getting much of. Playfulness? Joy? Perhaps even honest cynicism? What's missing isn't anything as simple as talent; there's lots of talent, even on TV. But the business conditions of moviemaking have soured the spirit of most big movies. That's why we may be willing to go along with something as strained and self-conscious as *Alice's Restaurant*. And it's an immensely hopeful sign that the audience isn't derisive, that it wishes the movie well.

•

All this is, in a way, part of the background of why, after a few minutes of *Butch Cassidy and the Sundance Kid*, I began to get that depressed feeling, and, after a half hour, felt rather offended. We all know how the industry men think: they're going to try to make "now" movies when now is already then, they're going to give us orgy movies and plush skinflicks, and they'll be trying to feed youth's paranoia when youth will, one hopes, have cast it off like last year's beads. This Western is a spinoff from *Bonnie and Clyde;* it's about two badmen (Paul Newman and Robert Redford) at the turn of the century, and the script, by William Goldman, which has been published, has the prefatory note "Not that it matters, but most of what follows is true." Yet everything that follows rings false, as that note does.

It's a facetious Western, and everybody in it talks comical. The director, George Roy Hill, doesn't have the style for it. (He doesn't really seem to have the style for anything, yet there is a basic decency and intelligence in his work.) The tone becomes embarrassing. Maybe we're supposed to be charmed when this affable, loquacious outlaw Butch and his silent, "dangerous" buddy Sundance blow up trains, but how are we supposed to feel when they go off to Bolivia, sneer at the country, and start shooting up poor Bolivians? George Roy Hill is a "sincere" director, but Goldman's script is jocose; though it reads as if it might play, it doesn't, and probably this isn't just Hill's fault. What can one do with dialogue like Paul Newman's Butch saying, "Boy, I got vision. The rest of the world wears bifocals"? It must be meant to be sportive, because it isn't witty and it isn't dramatic. The dialogue is all banter, all throwaways, and that's how it's delivered; each line comes out of nowhere, coyly, in a murmur, in the dead sound of the studio. (There is scarcely even an effort to supply plausible outdoor resonances or to use sound to evoke a sense of place.) It's impossible to tell whose consciousness the characters are supposed to have. Here's a key passage from the script — the big scene when Sundance's girl, the schoolteacher Etta (Katharine Ross), decides to go to Bolivia with the outlaws:

> ETTA *(For a moment, she says nothing. Then, starting soft, building as she goes):* I'm twenty-six, and I'm single, and I teach school, and that's the bottom of the pit. And the only excitement I've ever known is sitting in the room with me now. So I'll go with you, and I won't whine, and I'll sew your

socks and stitch you when you're wounded, and anything you ask of me I'll do, except one thing: I won't watch you die. I'll miss that scene if you don't mind . . . *(Hold on Etta's lovely face a moment—)*

It's clear who is at the bottom of the pit, and it isn't those frontier schoolteachers, whose work was honest.

Being interested in good movies doesn't preclude enjoying many kinds of crummy movies, but maybe it does preclude acceptance of this enervated, sophisticated business venture — a movie made by those whose talents are a little high for mere commercial movies but who don't break out of the mold. They're trying for something more clever than is attempted in most commercial jobs, and it's all so archly empty — Conrad Hall's virtuoso cinematography providing constant in-and-out-of-focus distraction, Goldman's decorative little conceits passing for dialogue. It's all posh and josh, without any redeeming energy or crudeness. Much as I dislike the smugness of puritanism in the arts, after watching a put-on rape and Conrad Hall's *Elvira Madigan* lyric interlude (and to our own Mozart — Burt Bacharach) I began to long for something simple and halfway *felt*. If you can't manage genuine sophistication, you may be better off simple. And when you're as talented as these fellows, perhaps it's necessary to descend into yourself sometime and try to find out what you're doing — maybe, even, to risk banality, which is less objectionable than this damned waggishness.

Butch Cassidy will probably be a hit; it has a great title, and it has star appeal for a wide audience. Redford, who is personable and can act, is overdue for stardom, though it will be rather a joke if he gets it out of this non-acting role. Newman throws the ball to him often — that's really exactly what one feels he's doing — and is content to be his infectiously good-humored (one assumes) self. He plays the public image of himself (as an aging good guy), just as Arlo Guthrie plays himself as a moonchild. Yet, hit or no, I think what this picture represents is finished. Butch and Sundance will probably be fine for a TV series, which is what I mean by finished.

•

One can't just take the new cult movies head on and relax, because they're too confused. Intentions stick out, as in the thirties message movies, and you may be so aware of what's wrong with the movies while you're seeing them that you're pulled in different directions, but if you reject them because of the confusions, you're rejecting the most hopeful symptoms of change. Just when there are audiences who may be ready for something, the studios seem to be backing away, because they don't understand what these audiences want. The audiences themselves don't know, but they're looking for *something* at the movies. This transition into the seventies is maybe the most interesting as well as the most confusing period in American movie history, yet there's a real possibility that, because the tastes of the young audience are changing so fast, the already tottering studios will decide to minimize risks and gear production straight to the square audience and the networks. That square audience is far more alienated than the young one — so alienated that it isn't looking for *anything* at the movies.

[September 27, 1969]

Waiting for Orgy

Bob & Carol & Ted & Alice has been widely attacked in advance: it opened the New York Film Festival, and the *Times* has had at it three times already, calling it a "sniggery" movie, and the news magazines have been jumping on it, too. *Time* was outraged that it was chosen to open "a presumably serious film festival." If one laughs at it, as I did (and I didn't snigger), one may suspect either (a) that even as good an American commercial comedy as this is *too* American and *too* commercial for the kind of fusty film-festival thinking that splits movies into art versus entertainment or (b) that there is something about the film that bugs people. It's both, I think.

When I see those ads with the quote "You'll have to see this picture twice," I know it's the kind of picture I don't want to see once. It's practically a penance to sit through some of these movies, and a new Pasolini or a "late" Bresson lasts one a long time. The movie press has not suddenly become avant-garde; it's just embracing the European cultural values it feels safe with. European films have not struck out in any major new directions this year; they've been rather dull — which can hardly be said of American movies at this time. When one considers some of what has been urged on us as "art" this last year — all those films that *look* like art

(*Teorema*) — it's clear that a commercial comedy doesn't fit into this framework of austere mortification of the audience. If you ever wanted to go see *Bob & Carol & Ted & Alice* again, it would be because it was funny, not because you didn't get it the first time. It's true it's not a work of depth that would yield up more with subsequent viewings, but it's almost schizophrenic for the movie critics to attack a movie for having just those entertaining qualities that drew them to movies in the first place. It's so damned easy to be cultured.

Bob & Carol & Ted & Alice is a slick, whorey movie, and the liveliest American comedy so far this year. It's unabashedly commercial, and in some ways it's the kind of commercial picture that succeeds with audiences by going just a little farther than they expect, but titillation is no longer easy, and this particular kind of titillation is so unconcealed that maybe it has earned the right to be called honestly comic. There is nothing hidden in this movie — the acrid commercial flavor is right there, out front. Because it's funny, and because it's marital-situation comedy and it's set in the middle-class southern California of so much tawdry Americana, it's easy to say this is DorisDayland, and those bothered by the acridity may use that as a way of putting the film down. Superficially, the picture looks like a Day, and the people live in the same style (they did in *The Graduate* also), but this movie is made up of what was left out of the optimistic Doris Day comedies. (What a perfect name. *Sui generis.*) This is the far side of middle-class marriage, after Doris Day fades out. The period is late 1969, when the concept of legal marriage is being undermined and the members of the middle class who are trying to be swingers are nervous — culturally uneasy about clinging to something square, and personally tantalized by thoughts of the sex possibilities they're missing. The movie works its way through cuteness and "sophistication" and out the other end of nowhere. It's tawdry, all right, but the tawdriness is *used*. This is the kind of movie in which a modern husband who has just had an affair comes home unexpectedly to find another man in bed with his wife and decides that the sensible new behavior is to have a friendly drink. This solution is hardly satisfactory; the tension is unresolved. The scene is badly played, but still it nags at one: Is there a better solution?

A sophisticated popular comedy isn't Hollywood's stock-in-trade anymore; the times are too volatile. This picture is a bit more unusual than it may seem, and it raises some of the problems that may plague actors in the next few years. Paul Mazursky and Larry Tucker, who wrote *Bob & Carol & Ted & Alice,* also wrote last year's *I Love You, Alice B. Toklas!,* which had some very funny dialogue but was directed (by Hy Averback) in a loose scat style that didn't give the movie much distinction. Mazursky has directed this time, and the material takes on a far more self-aware aspect. The occasional attempts at visual effects (such as a sex fantasy on a plane) are disastrously shoddy, but Mazursky, directing his first picture, has done something very ingenious. He has developed a style from satiric improvisational revue theatre — he and Tucker were part of the Second City troupe — and from TV situation comedy, and, with skill and wit, has made this mixture work.

During the past three or four years, many directors have tried to put revue humor on film, and, except for some of the early comedy sequences in *The Graduate,* it has failed, painfully — as in *Luv, The Tiger Makes Out,* the Eleanor Bron-William Daniels bits of *Two for the Road,* parts of *Bedazzled,* the Elaine May role in *Enter Laughing, The President's Analyst,* and so on. Revue theatre is a form of actors' theatre; even when the material isn't worked up by the actors — even when it is written by a Murray Schisgal (or, in England, transformed into more serious drama by Harold Pinter) — the meaning comes from the rhythm of clichés, defenses, and little verbal aggressions, and this depends on the pulse and the intuition of the performers. It would be as difficult to write down as dance notation. Typically, as in the Nichols-and-May routines, the satire is thin and the thinness is the essence of the joke. We laugh at the tiny, almost imperceptible hostilities that suddenly explode, because we recognize that we're tied up in knots about small issues more than about big ones, and that we don't lose our pretensions even when (or especially when) we are concerned about the big ones.

This style developed here (and in England) in the fifties, when college actors went on working together in cabarets, continuing and developing sophomoric humor. That word isn't used pejoratively; I *like* sophomoric college-revue humor, and one has only to contrast its topicality and freshness with the Joe Miller Jokebook world to understand why it swept the country. In revue, the very latest in interpersonal relations — the newest clichés and courtship rites and seduction techniques — could be polished to the point of satire almost overnight. Mort Sahl and the stand-up comics might satirize the political *them,* but cabaret, with its interacting couples, satirized *us.* We laugh at being nailed by these actors who are cartoons of us, all too easy to understand, and though there's a comic discomfort in listening to what our personal and social rituals might sound like if they were overheard, it's a comfortable form of theatre — the dishevelled American's form of light domestic comedy.

But it didn't work in the movies. A skit builds by the smallest of inflections, and each inflection becomes important because we construct the whole ambience from the performers — mainly from their voices. And that's what, in the past, killed this kind of acting on the screen: the performers did too much with voices and pauses, and when the director interrupted them with camera shifts and cuts, the performers lost their own rhythm and rapport. In relation to how it was being used, their acting was overdeveloped in a specialized way, and the result was, oddly, that they seemed ugly and rather grotesque and terribly stagy. And the milieu always felt wrong, because we didn't need it; instead of getting our bearings from the performers we looked at the sets and lost our bearings. This is still a problem in *Bob & Carol & Ted & Alice* — the houses the couples live in get in the way of our accepting the situations — but some of the other problems have been solved.

Mazursky has designed most of the picture in a series of sequences focussing on the actors, letting the rhythm of their interplay develop, and he has taken the series of revue sketches on the subject of modern marital stress and built them into a movie by using the format of situation comedy, with its recurrent synthetic crises. What is so surprising — and yet it should have been obvious — is that he has found useful dramatic elements in situation comedy. It's pleasant to stick to the same people throughout a movie, instead of wandering around and having the continuity broken into all the time, and it's relaxing to be in a form with controlled expectations, where there's no threat of violence, or even of direct assault on our emotions. This TV format is probably the best and most straightforward way to make revue material work on film, and it gives Mazursky a few small miracles (largely from Elliott Gould and Dyan Cannon), but, as a result of the long scenes, there's almost no way to conceal the failures.

Revue theatre has attracted actors of a different kind from ordinary theatre; frequently they are actor-writer-directors, literary satirists as well as satirical actors, and since their acting is so close to directing, they frequently become directors or comedians, but few of them have really become big *actors*. The kind of acting they've learned to do — which is both more demanding and, in some areas, less demanding than conventional acting — is *different*, and a basic trouble with *Bob & Carol & Ted & Alice* is that Natalie Wood can't do it. The design of the film is for two contrasting marriages — one a "good" marriage (Robert Culp, as a documentary filmmaker, and Natalie Wood), the other a mismatch (Elliott Gould, as a lawyer, and Dyan Cannon), yet a mismatch so recognizably common (she's bored and he's bewildered) that it's almost the typical perfect match. But there's no possibility of our believing in the good marriage. Natalie Wood doesn't seem to have any substance as a human being, so there's nothing at stake, as there would be with a fuller-dimensioned woman in the role. Her resources as an actress are skinny; she has nothing to draw upon but that same desperate anxiety and forced smile and agitation she's always drawn upon.

The whole area of screen acting is probably going to be a big can of worms in the next few years. We are already looking for closer identity between actor and role in many movies; we have become too acute about nuances (partly because of revue) to accept the iron-butterfly kind of star acting anymore. We never had the slightest illusion we were seeing Doris Day as she was offscreen, and that hardly concerned us. In the kind of acting now being required, it *does* concern us, partly because of nudity and sex scenes, the influence of non-actors in *cinéma-vérité* roles, and the effect of TV news and talk shows, but mainly because of a new interest in less structured and less stereotyped approaches to character than in past movies. I think it's almost impossible to watch *Bob & Carol & Ted & Alice* without wondering how much the actors are playing themselves. Natalie Wood is still doing what she was doing as a child — still telegraphing us that she's being cute and funny — and she's wrong. When she tries hard, she just becomes an agitated iron butterfly. An actress's armor becomes embarrassing when character armor is the subject of the movie — and it's the subject of this movie, as it has always been the basic subject of revue.

With this material — concerning how much people are hiding from themselves — we begin to ask questions about the actors, to wonder whether they are what they appear to be. The performances that work best force us to a speculative invasion of the privacy of the actors; what would have once seemed gossip is now central not only to the performance but to the conception itself. With the camera coming in closer and closer, the inescapable question is: Can you act it if you're *not* it? Playing the bitch who sets the mechanism of "Let's have an orgy" in motion, Dyan Cannon — who looks a bit like Lauren Bacall and a bit like Jeanne Moreau, but the wrong bits — is most effective (really brilliant), I think, just because you don't like her, and I don't mean simply the character she plays; we react to her in the way untutored people used to react to actors, identifying them with their roles. We don't think she's just playing a bitch. And, on the same basis, we *like* Gould — not just because of his performance but because of an assumption, which is probably false, but which this kind of acting imposes, that he is what he's playing. Culp, who has the most difficult role, is solidly competent, and yet he fails somewhat, because he is too much the conventional actor *type* — Robert Cummings crossed with Timothy Leary.

•

But there is something else in this movie that bothers people. I don't think it's because it's *conventional* that they're somewhat unnerved by it; it's because, though it *looks* conventional, it *isn't,* and it doesn't quite give them what they want. The press loved Woody Allen's *Take the Money and Run* — a limply good-natured little nothing of a comedy, soft as sneakers. And it would probably feel more comfortable with this if it were soft or if it *were* "sniggery"; then it could be put down more easily as just another commercial picture. Maybe, like Dyan Cannon in the movie, the press and the audience want an orgy — and think it's a cop-out when they don't get one. An orgy would be the simplest thing in the movie world to give us right now, but it wouldn't be consistent with the idea of this movie, which, as in revue, is the comedy of recognizing that we (those on the screen and we in the audience) are not earth-shakers or sexual new frontiersmen. This light domestic comedy no longer takes domesticity for granted, but after the characters begin to experiment sexually, they return for cover. Near the end, when the two couples go into one bedroom together, it's obvious that the movie could take a different turn — that if they went into two bedrooms instead of one, the cross-coupling would probably occur without any difficulty. But that would only *postpone* the return, or the movie would descend into romp and farce. The return makes perfect sense: they realize that they are about to go farther than they can handle, and they retreat to save something they still care about. Though the ending might have been better served by wit than by a "thoughtful" neo-Fellini walk, the point is clear. They need some home base and the safety of the old bourgeois traps. Forced to choose between decaying DorisDayland and Warhol Nowheresville, they go back to what is for them, if not the good life, at least the not-bad life.

Many people in the audience have probably done just what the people in the movie do (either before or after a little wife-swapping and a small orgy or two). Why, then, do they resent it in the film? I'll make the guess that the situations are so comically close to the people in the audience that they may reject the characters for doing what they themselves have done, because that retreat cuts them off from what they want to believe in. At the beginning, the film has some satirical passages on Esalen "encounter" techniques (satire that backfired because Natalie Wood looks as if the treatment might help her), and people around me became rather hostile — not just the young, who might be expected to, because the touching is very important to them (it's a form of "truth," of approaching without being afraid, of making non-aggressive, non-hostile, "human" contact), but older people, too, because they, too, are looking for healers. The atmosphere around me was as if the Church were being satirized before an audience of early Christians. In commercial terms, the opening, with its easy targets, may be a miscalculation, and it's loosely ambivalent — as if Mazursky and Tucker were unsure and were trying to play it safe. The audience reaction to the opening may be a clue to the later discomfort: People may be so desperate to be other than what they are that they resent a movie for dealing with bourgeois values even in disruption. They may consider these characters (so like themselves) not worthy even of comic attention. And they may resent still more the suggestion that an orgy *won't* expand their consciousness, and that they might risk losing something if they try everything. They don't believe they've *got anything*. The audience is still waiting for Godot, which in this context is salvation by orgy.

[October 4, 1969]

Off with the Statues' Heads!

Oh! What a Lovely War has a great deal of good will going for it. It's the kind of movie that is said to "make a statement," and some people will no doubt take it as a statement about Vietnam. Many of the great knights and ladies of the English theatre who appear in it brought their children along and worked at minimum scale. It was nevertheless very expensive, and an anti-war musical that must take in roughly eight million dollars just to break even is the kind of picture that needs critical help. Though I found the movie lethal, I hate to say so, because it gives comfort to the enemy: it encourages a policy of not taking chances like this again. It may seem unkind and snobbish to say it's *too* big, when one suspects that it probably couldn't have been financed if it were smaller — that it had to be big to get done at all — still, the scale is too impersonally large, and doesn't add anything, except perhaps the divertissement of detecting the famous actors and actresses under the makeup (as in *Around the World in 80 Days*). The conception is a music-hall revue in which the songs of the First World War are counterpointed with the battle statistics, to evoke the myths and facts of war. One guesses that the picture should have pathos and nostalgia, that it should be a mixture of jolliness and horrors, and that the music should be irresistible. We sit waiting to be affected, to be stabbed and be scalded by tears; as each song starts, we expect to be overwhelmed, but the music is all too resistible, and the emotions don't come. There's a suggestion of how things should go in an early music-hall number; the naïve young chorus girls luring the boys to do their patriotic duty have an authentic innocence — the purity of ignorance — and when Maggie Smith delivers a raucous patriotic song, she's startling and vivifying. But the movie lapses back into blandness and that brand of satire which has become the new convention in English movies.

Oh! What a Lovely War repeats the satirical forms already exhausted in Richard Lester's *How I Won the War* and Tony Richardson's *The Charge of the Light Brigade*. Although all three of these movies are presented as anti-war movies, their specific target is the follies of the upper classes, and their explanation of war is the British equivalent of the adolescent *Mad*-magazine approach: wars are made by the officers, who are homicidal imbeciles interested only in personal position and indifferent to the death of their men. At times, when these movies positively exult in imbecility (Gielgud in *Light Brigade,* Olivier harrumphing around in *Oh! What a Lovely War*), the satire is effective, because the actors can give these monster-ninnies such a glow that their stupidity has a real, Marx Brothers madness to it. But most of the time, particularly in *How I Won the War* and *Oh! What a Lovely War,* this tedious class stuff about dupes and dupers is so single-minded it has nowhere to go, no way of developing; it just keeps demonstrating the same proposition as outrageously as possible. The ritual exhumations of historical figures become as elaborate as their funerals once were. The satire becomes baroque. It's really just sport for a dispirited culture, and rather ugly sport. The English rouse themselves every few months to pick at their old dead leaders once more, pounding and jabbing — toreros trying to draw blood from stuffed toy bulls. After a few movies, we're connoisseurs; we observe that the capework was fancier in *Light Brigade*. Baroque satire is satire that has lost its purpose: the wit and the mockery become ends in themselves and serve to cut the movies off from their avowed targets. And when they're cut off, there's no life in the satire, just capework.

To an American, these movies with the upper class as enemy may seem horribly arch and upper-class-made. These movies like the *idea* of loving the common man, but moviemakers show their feelings in how they create their characters, and even the upper-class caricatures are more animate than the "good" common-soldier victims. This show-business Marxism, with its condescension toward the heroic, gullible working classes, becomes claustrophobic. *Oh! What a Lovely War* comes up with five boys named Smith, just like those Hollywood callow youths circa 1944 — the kind that made American soldiers shoot up the screens. For the beauty of the songs to pierce us, the movie needs to be, at *some* level, generous to the rich and the poor, the officers and the enlisted men — to all those who died believing in their country, or perhaps in their comrades, or in nothing. The small-mindedness of the approach destroys feeling, but the movie keeps trying different ways of moving us, from the leapfrogging, cavorting officers, who might have stepped out of *Duck Soup,* to the poppies and miseries of *All Quiet on the Western Front.* There's a stoical nurse (who is meant to be admirable, though she's even more prim than Anna Neagle used to be in those cool nursy roles), and there's much solemnity in the staging, especially in the exchange of Christmas presents between Huns and Tommies at the front. You watch this sequence knowing perfectly well it's supposed to get you *here,* in the chest, like Lassie making it home. And it's in Panavision, and overpoweringly *clean.*

Directing for the first time, Richard Attenborough is very careful. *Oh! What a Lovely War* is stately and measured — tightly *staged* — in the tradition of other "important" English pictures, like *Colonel Blimp, Stairway to Heaven, The Magic Box,* and *Gilbert and Sullivan,* and I longed to sneak away. This picture is almost an exact contemporary equivalent of the 1933 movie of Noël Coward's celebratory don't-the-English-break-your-heart *Cavalcade. Oh! What a Lovely War* is a blasphemous *Cavalcade,* with the old stiff-upper-lip attitudes now burlesqued, but it's still preoccupied with them, and the knights of the theatre are paraded in full twilight-of-empire style. This swollen, hollow anti-*Cavalcade* may seem to us much closer to the old model than it may seem to the English. They're still trying to break our hearts, and the style of their pathos is much the same. And, though the fight has gone out of them, they still enunciate to the death.

●

There must surely be a connection between the English tradition in painting and their moviemaking, which, visually, is weak and illustrative. The points are almost always made verbally, and the war satires, which are meant to be surreal and absurdist, are verbal-joke-crazy, chattering away like a radio that can't be turned off. Charles Wood, the Céline of gagwriters, had a hand in *How I Won the War* and *The Charge of the Light Brigade,* piling puns on atrocities, and though no writing credits are given for *Oh! What a Lovely War,* one may suspect his unsettled, joky hand (or influence) there, too. He is definitely present in Richard Lester's new *The Bed Sitting Room,* from the Spike Milligan-John Antrobus play, an apocalyptic farce. The time is after the Third World War; the twenty-odd straggling survivors in London wander in and out of blackout sketches, with Rita Tushingham giving birth to something unspecified and Ralph Richardson mutating into a bed-sitting room. In style, it's like *The Running, Jumping and Standing Still Film* extended to feature length, and the chaos becomes numbing. One laughs from time to time, but, as in so much modern English far-out satire, there's no spirit, no rage, nothing left but ghastly, incessant sinking-island humor. We end up blank, and in need of something we can connect with, to restore perspective, because this perpetual giggle almost seems to require a bomb. What this movie lacks is the simplicity of feeling that makes *Shame* so powerful, that made *All Quiet on the Western Front* effective despite its crudeness and naïveté. That simplicity is something that can't be faked, and without it this movie isn't a cautionary reminder of horror, it *is* a horror.

•

I wish John Huston had not moved to Ireland back in the early fifties, because, although he has gone on making "American" movies, even when they're good, they're not vital anymore. It doesn't matter if you miss them, the way it would once have mattered. It's a little like Mailer's trip to the moon: we wait for him to come back. But Huston's been gone a long time, and I suppose he's not coming back. *A Walk with Love and Death* isn't a bad movie; I rather like it. (But then perhaps I am by temperament drawn to much of Huston's work; I liked *Reflections in a Golden Eye* much better than most critics did.) Yet one feels that Huston is no longer doing what's close to him — that he's looking for subjects. *A Walk with Love and Death,* from the Hans Koningsberger novel, is a romantic, emotional story set in France in the Middle Ages, a tale of chivalry which is at times as brutal as *The Seventh Seal.* Though it's not so explicit, it's a much stronger anti-war movie than *Oh! What a Lovely War* or *The Bed Sitting Room.* It is set, specifically, during the Hundred Years' War (a name that no longer sounds as preposterous as it did when we were schoolchildren), and an almost unbearable touch is that this fable of two young lovers eager to live should be set *early* in that war — at the end of the second decade, when survival was even less possible than it seems to be now. Yet the movie lacks urgency. One fears it will be pretentious, but it isn't, and it's continually compelling. But it's too remote, and, maybe because it's so restrained — almost reserved — it never fully releases the lyricism of the conception. The lovers (Anjelica Huston and Assaf Dayan) aren't ludicrous like the ones in the recent *Romeo and Juliet,* except for one ridiculous high overhead shot of them making love. Dayan's hero has a good, sane quality, like a younger version of Gunnar Björnstrand's squire in *The Seventh Seal,* and Miss Huston, though her face doesn't open up to the camera and she might be more effective on stage than on screen, has unusual intelligence both in her face and in her readings. The script is rather literary — in a way I enjoyed, because Huston is one of the few directors who know that poetry needs to be tough-minded. But some of the casting is poor, and, like many directors as they get older, Huston seems to have lost interest in montage; the uprising of the peasants against the knights is shot too close in and is poorly edited. But the movie has at least one superb image — a great, clumping white horse, a dream horse, like the one in *The Sundowners* — and when this fairy-tale beast is slaughtered war becomes obscene the way it is meant to in those British films. *A Walk with Love and Death* has a feeling to it, and though the film doesn't quite come to enough, it has an unusual integrity of vision.

•

Sex on the screen puts critics in an even worse bind than inept anti-war satires. The whole legalistic "redeeming-artistic-merit" principle is asinine. (Should men be put in jail because they have no talent?) The only good part of *I Am Curious (Yellow)* is the rather amusing sex scenes, and it's a bad joke that in order to make a legal case for the film one should have to pretend that what's fun in it is redeemed by what's a bore — all that poorly done sociological stuff. It may be one of the last vestiges of American puritanism that entertaining sex is, in the courts, redeemed by poor sociology. The new American International Pictures' *de Sade* has no "redeeming" merits — and even the orgies aren't entertaining — yet I don't think it will corrupt and deprave, any more than I think other rotten movies corrupt and deprave. It sure is a rotten movie, though.

It took me many dutiful bursts of effort over a two-week period to get through Susan Sontag's essay on pornography, and when I finally thought I'd grasped it, it evaporated. I don't have any great thing for pornography. So I can't say how de Sade's life should have been done, but I'm pretty sure de Sade shouldn't have been played by Keir Dullea, and Dullea looks as if he knew it — at times the planes of his face collapse in utter misery. At best, he hardly has the face of a voluptuary, which is what de Sade is in this version, and Dullea licking jam off a girl's breast looks as if he'd rather be beaten. Poor Dullea did take rather a beating at the première. He had just come into the theatre and sat down when the lights went out and the picture started. There he was in the first shot, de Sade riding a horse, and as the next shot was a cut to his face in closeup the audience gave him a round of applause. But the very next cut was a closeup of the horse's face, and it was inevitable: the horse got a round of applause, too. Then the credits came on, with such names as Billy Strange (music), Richard Angst (cinematography), Alexander Ebermayer V. Richthofen (assistant director), and the whole picture began to seem a put-on. I wish it had been — and some in the audience chose to take it that way. At the end, there were satirical shouts of "bravo."

This porny swashbuckler has been staged like a high-school pageant, and it doesn't have a spark of real perversity, yet it dabbles in dangerous areas. There's a sequence in which three adults take their pleasure from the beating of a child, and there's a sequence in which de Sade uses a rapier to beat and disfigure a prostitute, and the movie treats her contemptuously. Her being a prostitute apparently justifies his cutting her up; somebody at A.I.P. seems to think like Jack the Ripper.

[October 11, 1969]

High School and Other Forms of Madness

Movies sometimes connect with our memories in surprising ways. My vocabulary loosened up during my freshman year at Berkeley, and I was quite pleased when my mother remarked that the more educated I got the more I sounded like a truck driver. When I was a sophomore, a group of us went on a trip to Los Angeles, and our car broke down in Oxnard; we were huddled there in the garage at night when two garage mechanics got into an argument and started swearing at each other. As the rhythm of their fury and venom built up, those words that I had been so free with sounded hideous. I hadn't understood their function as swearwords — hadn't understood that they were meant to insult the person receiving them, that they were a way of degrading another person. That night at Oxnard came back when I saw Frederick Wiseman's *Law and Order* on N.E.T.: the police were cursed constantly by thieves and drunks. I had assumed that the police, coming from stricter and more religious backgrounds, didn't understand that college kids use the words in that liberated way that empties them of degradation or any real power; I hadn't considered that they hear that kind of talk so much they probably just can't stand it anymore. They're drowning in obscenity. College students are sometimes contemptuous of the cops for fearing *words,* but in the film those words really *are* weapons — often the *only* weapons of angry, frustrated people — and they're directed against the police all the time. *Law and Order* was the most powerful hour and a half of television that I've seen all year, and, since it won an Emmy, one might suppose that it would stir up interest in Wiseman's other films, but the New York Film Festival, which featured so many mindless forms of "artistic" moviemaking in the main auditorium, tossed some of the best new American pictures into the two-hundred-seat hall, and among them was Wiseman's *High School,* in its first New York showing.

There's a good deal to be said for finding your way to moviemaking — as most of the early directors did — after living for some years in the world and gaining some knowledge of life outside show business. We are beginning to spawn teen-age filmmakers who at twenty-five may have a brilliant technique but are as empty-headed as a Hollywood hack, and they will become the next generation of hacks, because they don't know anything except moviemaking. Wiseman is a law professor and urban planner turned filmmaker, a muckraking investigative journalist who looks into American institutions with a camera and a tape recorder, and because he doesn't go in with naïve and limiting concepts, what he finds ties in with one's own experience.

Many of us grow to hate documentaries in school, because the use of movies to teach us something seems a cheat — a pill disguised as candy — and documentaries always seem to be about something we're not interested in. But Wiseman's documentaries show what is left out of both fictional movies and standard documentaries that simplify for a purpose, and his films deal with the primary institutions of our lives: *Titicut Follies* (Bridgewater, an institution in which we lock away the criminally insane), *High School* (a high school in a large Eastern city), and *Law and Order* (the Kansas City police force). Television has been accustoming us to a horrible false kind of "involvement"; sometimes it seems that the only thing the news shows can think of is to get close to emotion. They shove a camera and a microphone in front of people in moments of stress and disaster and grief, and ram their equipment into any pores and cavities they can reach. Wiseman made comparable mistakes in *Titicut Follies,* but he learned better fast.

High School is so familiar and so extraordinarily evocative that a feeling of empathy with the students floods over us. How did we live through it? How did we keep any spirit? When you see a kid trying to make a phone call and being interrupted with "Do you have a pass to use the phone?" it all floods back — the low ceilings and pale-green walls of the basement where the lockers were, the constant defensiveness, that sense of always being in danger of breaking some pointless, petty rule. When since that time has one ever needed a pass to make a phone call? This movie takes one back to where, one discovers, time has stood still. Here is the girl humiliated for having worn a short dress to the Senior Prom, being told it was "offensive" to the whole class. Here it is all over again — the insistence that you be "respectful," and the teachers' incredible instinct for "disrespect," their antennae always extended for that little bit of reservation or irony in your tone, the tiny spark that you desperately need to preserve your *self*-respect. One can barely hear it in the way a boy says "Yes, sir" to the dean, but the dean, ever on the alert, snaps, "Don't give me that 'Yes, sir' business! . . . There's no sincereness behind it." Here, all over again, is the dullness of high-school education:

> TEACHER: What on the horizon or what existed that forced labor to turn to collective bargaining? What was there a lack of?
> GIRL: Communications?
> TEACHER: Security, yes, communications, lack of security, concern for the job. The important thing is this, let's get to the beginning. First of all, there was the lack of security; second of all, there was a lack of communication. . . .

The same old pseudo-knowledge is used to support what the schools think is moral. The visiting gynecologist in a sex-education class lectures the boys:

> The more a fellow gets into bed with more different girls, the more insecure he is, and this shows up actually later in all the divorce statistics in America. . . . You can graph right on a graph, the more girls fellows got into bed with or vice-versa the higher the divorce rate, the greater the sexual inadequacy. . . .

And there's the beautiful military doubletalk when it's a question of a teacher's incompetence or unfairness. A boy protests a disciplinary action against him by a teacher, and after he has explained his innocence, the dean talks him into accepting the punishment "to establish that you can be a man and that you can take orders." The teachers are masters here; they're in a superior position for the only time in their lives, probably, and most of the petty tyrannies — like laying on the homework — aren't fully conscious. They justify each other's actions as a matter of course, and put the students in the wrong in the same indifferent way. They put a student down with "It's nice to be individualistic, but there are certain places to be individualistic," yet they never tell you where. How can one stand up against such bland authoritarianism? The teachers, crushing and processing, are the most insidious kind of enemy, the enemy with corrupt values who means well. The counsellor advising on college plans who says "You can have all your dream schools, but at the bottom you ought to have some college of last resort where you could be sure that you would go, if none of your dreams came through" certainly means to be realistic and helpful. But one can imagine what it must feel like to be a kid trudging off to that bottom college of last resort. There's a jolly good Joe of a teacher staging a fashion show who tells the girls, "Your legs are all too heavy. . . . Don't wear it too short; it looks miserable." And she's not wrong. But, given the beauty norms set up in this society, what are they to do? Cut off their legs? Emigrate? They're defeated from the legs up. Mediocrity and defeat sit in the offices and classrooms, and in those oppressive monitored halls.

We went through it all in order to graduate and be rid of passes forever, and once it was over we put it out of our minds, and here are the students still serving time until graduation, still sitting in class staring out the windows or watching the crawling hands of those ugly school clocks. So much of this education is part of an obsolete system of authority that broke down long ago, yet the teachers and administrators are still out there, persevering, "building character." *High School* seems an obvious kind of film to make, but as far as I know no one before has gone into an ordinary, middle-class, "good" (most of the students go to college) high school with a camera and looked around to see what it's like. The students are even more apathetic than we were. Probably the conflicts over the restrictions come earlier now — in junior high — and by high school the kids either are trying to cool it and get through to college or are just beaten down and sitting it out. We may have had a few teachers who really got us interested in something — it was one of the disappointments of the movie *Up the Down Staircase* that, treating this theme, it failed to be convincing — and, remembering our good luck, we could always say that even if a school was rotten, there were bound to be a few great teachers in it. This movie shows competent teachers and teachers who are trying their best but not one teacher who really makes contact in the way that means a difference in your life. The students are as apathetic toward the young English teacher playing and analyzing a Simon & Garfunkel record as toward the English teacher reciting "Casey at the Bat," and, even granted that as poetry there might not be much to choose between them — and perhaps Casey has the edge — still, one might think the students would, just as a *courtesy*, respond to the young teacher's attempt, the way one always gave the ingénue in the stock company a special round of applause. But it's very likely that high schools no longer *are* saved by live teachers, if hostility and cynicism and apathy set in right after children learn their basic skills. The students here sit on their hands even when a teacher tries. That's the only visible difference between this school and mine. I think we would have responded appreciatively to obvious effort, even if we thought the teacher was a jerk; these kids are beyond that. So the teachers are trapped, too. The teachers come off much worse than the police do in *Law and Order*. *High School* is a revelation because now that we see school from the outside, the teachers seem to give themselves away every time they open their mouths — and to be unaware of it.

At the end, the principal — a fine-looking woman — holds up a letter from a former student, on stationery marked "U.S.S. Okinawa," and reads it to the faculty:

> I have only a few hours before I go. Today I will take a plane trip from this ship. I pray that I'll make it back but it's all in God's hands now. You see, I am going with three other men. We are going to be dropped behind the D.M.Z. (the Demilitarized Zone). The reason for telling you this is that all my insurance money will be given for that scholarship I once started but never finished, if I don't make it back. I am only insured for $10,000. Maybe it could help someone. I have been trying to become a Big Brother in Vietnam, but it is very hard to do. I have to write back and forth to San Diego, California, and that takes time. I only hope that I am good enough to become one. God only knows. My personal family usually doesn't understand me.... They say: "Don't you value life? Are you crazy?" My answer is: "Yes. But I value all the lives of South Vietnam and the free world so that they and all of us can live in peace." Am I wrong? If I do my best and believe in what I do, believe that what I do is right — that is all I can do.... Please don't say anything to Mrs. C. She would only worry over me. I am not worth it. I am only a body doing a job. In closing I thank everyone for what they all have done for me.

And the principal comments, "Now, when you get a letter like this, to me it means that we are very successful at [this] high school. I think you will agree with me."

It's a great scene — a consummation of the educational process we've been watching: They are successful at turning out bodies to do a job. Yet it's also painfully clear that the school must have given this soldier more kindness and affection than he'd ever had before. There must be other students who respond to the genuine benevolence behind the cant and who are grateful to those who labor to turn them into men. For those students, this schooling in conformity is successful.

Wiseman extends our understanding of our common life the way novelists used to — a way largely abandoned by the modern novel and left to the journalists but not often picked up by them. What he's doing is so simple and so basic that it's like a rediscovery of what we knew, or should know. We often want more information about the people and their predicaments than he gives, but this is perhaps less a criticism of Wiseman's method than it is a testimonial to his success in making us care about his subjects. With fictional movies using so little of our shared experience, and with the big TV news "specials" increasingly using that idiot "Mc-Luhanite" fragmentation technique that scrambles all experience — as if the deliberate purpose were to make us indifferent to the life around us — it's a good sign when a movie sends us out wanting to know more and feeling that there is more to know. Wiseman is probably the most sophisticated intelligence to enter the documentary field in recent years.

•

The Royal Hunt of the Sun could turn into a classic of the hooting variety. Christopher Plummer, hissing and prancing, is a wickedly funny Inca king, and Robert Shaw, who, as Pizarro, has been running the show for the first half hour, is hilariously upstaged. Shaw has a strong screen presence, and he's fine as long as his Pizarro is a bastard, but when the script turns Pizarro into a sweetie-pie, Shaw's performance disintegrates along with the script. This adaptation of Peter Shaffer's play treats it like Shakespeare: people stand on rocks and make speeches. The script, officially blamed on Philip Yordan, has lines that a first-year screenwriting student should know enough to cross out, like "Let me understand you," preceding a recapitulation of an argument. The reason we need so many recaps is that the central situation doesn't make movie sense. Shaffer trumped up reasons for Pizarro and the Inca king to be trapped together, but this theatrical convention stops the movie cold. It's as obvious and silly as Leonard Whiting playing the boy-put-there-to-be-disillusioned.

(One can practically hear Brandon deWilde at the back of the theatre crying, "Look! He's playing me!") Irving Lerner's direction is erratic, but I don't know that anybody was wildly looking forward to another "distinguished" playwright's exercise in the heroic style of historical confrontation, and sometimes when things go terribly wrong in a movie it's more fun than if they'd gone right. The cinematography is very poor, and the editing is often of the kind that gives us the shot an instant before anything happens in it; as a result, we keep expecting Tony Curtis to ride in, stop, and speak, or Maria Montez to come into frame and walk across the sand. But Turhan Bey was never like Christopher Plummer — he wouldn't have *dared*. And as this may be the most outrageous, outlandish, and absurd performance that any major actor has given since John Barrymore swung on a trapeze with Mary Beth Hughes, it almost makes the movie worth seeing.

•

There's no madness in *The Madwoman of Chaillot*. Edward Anhalt's script is leaden-hearted; Jean Giraudoux's fragile play is doubtful screen material at best, and Anhalt's updating and message-mongering destroyed at the outset whatever chance it might have had. Although the movie isn't actually painful, nothing in it feels right. Bryan Forbes, a literal-minded director, hasn't the temperament or the artistic means to make a movie that must be all conceit, enchantment, and lunatic poetry. Katharine Hepburn is charming and lyrical when she's on the loose in the streets of Paris, but her essential sanity shines forth. Her sanity is rare among actresses; it is her gift, and it is perhaps the true poetry and eccentricity of her own character. Her "madwoman" is just Hepburn acting more charming than usual — *too* charming for the role. In the smaller role of Constance, Margaret Leighton has much more of the dottiness necessary for the fantasy conception, and she might have been relatively successful in the lead, but *The Madwoman of Chaillot* misses being anything by so much that it hardly seems apropos to discuss what it might have been. It may be a comfort to Edith Evans and Giulietta Masina that, having now given the worst performances in their careers, they can hardly go anywhere but up. Danny Kaye, on the other hand, has been even worse (though I will be kind and not recall the occasions), so some may mistake his performance for a good one. Whenever possible, Claude Renoir, shooting the outdoor scenes, tries to give the movie a magical radiance, and the editor has been dexterous at keeping things in motion, but there are indoor set pieces that are textbook examples of incompetence: the trial sequence, the execution, and that scene that reverberates through screen history and has always been a vomiter — when the dear old lady mistakes the young hero for her lover of long ago. Isn't there some way to toss it up for good? This movie keeps telling us that it's about the battle of evil and computerization against individualism and romance, but the movie itself is computerized. The cast, selected for appeal in many countries, includes Charles Boyer, Claude Dauphin, John Gavin, Yul Brynner, Donald Pleasence, Paul Henreid, Fernand Gravey, Gordon Heath, Richard Chamberlain, and Nanette Newman; there's a great big noisy score to promote, so that if the movie flops the records can still "generate" revenue; and the material has been rewritten in the forlorn hope of giving it an anti-Establishment appeal to "youth." The whole movie is a sham. The madness is behind the cameras.

[October 18, 1969]

Somebody Else's Success

*P*aint Your Wagon is not the sort of movie that people who read movie criticism are likely to go to, but it's one of the three or four most expensive musical films ever made, and I don't think it should just be ignored. It's probably one of the last of its breed — the super-gigantic blockbuster musicals, such as *Camelot* (fifteen million), *Sweet Charity* (eight million), *Star!* (fourteen million), and *Doctor Dolittle* (eighteen million), that have finally broken the back of the American movie industry. There is almost no way — short of a miracle — that it can recover its costs, and although there are several other movies of this kind waiting to be released or to be completed, and at least one of them is even *more* expensive, it is highly unlikely that any new ones will be scheduled for production in the years to come, or, perhaps, ever.

The movie companies have gone on bringing out these Edsels; this one cost twenty million, give or take a few, and the company makes a valiant attempt to turn its release into an event. Everybody goes through the motions, and just about everybody expects the picture to come down the ramp and sink. It won't be the critics' fault, though they'll get blamed, and there will be more of those high-level everybody-commiserating-with-everybody-else discussions about how you just can't tell what people want anymore. The director, Joshua Logan, did no better or worse than he usually does — he must have been hired for what he can do, and this is it. The stars — Lee Marvin, Jean Seberg, and Clint Eastwood — have never pretended to be musical-comedy stars, and they must have been hired for what *they* can do: Marvin to overact and cavort energetically, Jean Seberg to be lovely, Eastwood to be sensitive in that deadpan way that is supposed to have mysterious power at the box office. The financial failure won't be the fault of Frederick Loewe, some of whose music is very pleasant, or even of André Previn, whose additional music isn't. Nor can it be blamed on Paddy Chayefsky, even though he did the adaptation in short scenes that never give one a chance to get involved with the characters; he did what he can do. (Remember when Eddie Fisher wanted Chayefsky brought in to work on the script of *Cleopatra*? The bad jokes of yesterday come home to roost. But not to crow.) And, maybe, though we're getting warmer, it won't really even be the fault of Alan Jay Lerner, who produced the movie and did the screenplay and lyrics. In a certain sense, they're all responsible, but what they've all done is part of a rotting system in which mediocrity and skyrocketing costs work together to turn out films that would have a hard time making money even if they were good. If the pictures were good and lost money, there would be some glory in it, but it's financially disastrous and inglorious, too, to make these big movies in which the themes are modernized and the elements jiggled around until finally nothing fits together right and even the good bits of the original show you started with are shot to hell. *Paint Your Wagon* plays it so safe that it has been directed by a man whose qualification is having directed *Camelot,* which was also a failure, but *in the same financial class.* Here he is, making another big musical with stars who can neither sing nor dance; their qualification is that two of them appeared a year earlier on the lists of top box-office stars. The major studios are collapsing, but they're not being toppled over by competitors; they're so enervated that they're sinking of their budgetary weight.

The studios looked at the profits on a few big musicals and thought big musicals were a safe investment and tied up enormous sums of money in them — so much of a studio's total investment that two or three flops can actually mean that the studio changes hands. But to be successful a musical must give you a joyous feeling — a sense that it's good to be alive, a communion in the simple pleasures and the common emotions. Maybe those who made *The Sound of Music* got by with it because of their shamelessness. It was such a cornball enterprise that they threw in everything: the opening mountaintop exaltation out of Leni Riefenstahl, the draperies cut up for clothing out of *Gone with the Wind* — what did it matter? Ever since, the industry has been trying to calculate what made that picture a hit, trying to repeat the success. But the moviemakers are full of shame, and the pictures sicken from it. The musical is a stylized form for releasing and celebrating emotions through song and dance. When Fred Astaire sang a bit of verse to Ginger and then reached out his hand and whirled her into the dance, that dance and their whole series of dances together were the most exquisite courtship rites the screen has ever known. Astaire's happiness was contagious; it's obvious that it takes a performer who wants to give us something to make us happy that way. When Harve Presnell suddenly turns up in *Paint Your Wagon* and sings "They Call the Wind Maria," the movie comes to life for a minute, because he belongs here; he can *sing,* and he stands and breathes like a singer, with some pride in what he's doing. How can we watch Clint Eastwood in a musical? When he walks around in the great outdoors of a gigantic movie and sings "I Talk to the Trees," in his toneless, light little voice, he hardly seems to be in the movie. He's controlled in such an uninteresting way; it's not an actor's control, which enables one to release something — it's the kind of control that keeps one from releasing anything. We could stand the deadpan reserve of Nelson Eddy's non-acting because he gave of himself when he sang, but Eastwood doesn't give of himself *ever,* and a musical with a withdrawn hero is almost a contradiction in terms. His singing isn't bad in a rhythm number like "Gold Fever," but as the amiably nameless Pardner of No Name City he's only slightly more animated than as the Man with No Name of the Italian Westerns, and now he lacks even his wooden menace. We wait for him to shoot somebody, because that's all he can do, and he doesn't do it. He's a nowhere man, woodenly proper. Jean Seberg has become a pale, lovely, dimpled movie queen — a synthesis of Bibi Andersson and Stella Stevens, and with that worn, somewhat used look, like Ava Gardner's, which makes her more humanly beautiful than in her French films. But she's just barely alive in a musical: she can't sing or dance; she can hardly *move.* Her eyes are as coolly blank toward Eastwood as toward everyone else; why should we care if these two get together? They are so devoid of romance or passion they're like the unpeople at the end of *1984*. And so Lee Marvin comes on comical, as if he were something left over from *Cat Ballou,* and he works at it, doing double takes and backfalls and W. C. Fields imitations — because somebody has to give this show some charge — and he works so frenetically that it kills some of the quieter things he does rather well, such as his handling of "Wand'rin' Star." There's a stock bit involving a farmer boy's triple initiation into liquor, smoking, and sex that has a nice, warm, corny feeling; Logan is good at this kind of humor, as he demonstrated in *Bus Stop*. But the movie is a road show and it's meant to be *sustained* rousing, lusty Americana of the *Oklahoma!* and *Seven Brides for Seven Brothers* variety, so at intervals it simulates epic joy by throwing in a men's choir and turning up the sound. You come out smashed from the noise of it.

One of the reasons each blockbuster musical is such a gamble is that we need to build up familiarity with a voice and have our expectations satisfied from movie to movie, as we did with Astaire's dances. The dubbed voices (like Jean Seberg's) and the nondescript voices, like Eastwood's, don't carry over; the producers have spent twenty million dollars, and they haven't even developed a singing star for *another* picture. Their methods are practically suicidal; they make each picture as if it were the last. And therefore, because of the way they work and the financial pressures, the company needs a general, not an artist, and it wants a man with a broad "popular" approach. So it settles for a compromise figure. Logan tries hard, but there's no beauty of feeling when he does "pictorial" scenes, such as the miners coming from miles around to stare at a woman. A fortune has been spent constructing a gold-mining camp, yet the contrast between that transient, womanless life and what the heroine wants is fumbled, and so the big theme is lost and only the big scale remains. Logan doesn't aim for coarse effects, but his handling is coarse, and so there are crude, stupid scenes, such as Lee Marvin tearing open Jean Seberg's blouse just after she's been shown suckling an infant. Logan is looking for laughs, and so he caricatures people — like the farming family — at the expense of the remnants of the theme. A picture like this involves one emotionally in the moviemaking process, because one can see why they're doing just about every damn thing they're doing. They don't use the original plot because the thin little story about a young girl and a Mexican boy didn't sound very "in," so it becomes a *ménage à trois* instead — a "now" plot. Because they're afraid that the movie might be considered an operetta, they cast cool non-singers, like Eastwood and Seberg. Because they want to sound hip, the lyrics use rhymes like "Californy" and "horny." One can't help feeling sympathetic to all the effort and anxiety, but all the problems they're trying to solve are *business* problems. Broadway composers forage around for some old movie that can be made into a musical, and that's essentially what Lerner and Loewe are trying to do, too; though they reverse the procedure, and though *Paint*

Your Wagon is their own old property, they're trying to revamp it into a new commodity.

So many people in the movie business, as on Broadway, are trying to pump new revenue out of a few old songs or jokes or a piece of an old plot. But if a show can't be done the way it was written in the first place — if it has to be brought up to date — isn't that because it wasn't really very good in the first place? Wouldn't it be better to start fresh? And not just for the public but for the "artists"? If they have so few ideas that they've got to hoard the old ones and try to mold them into new shapes, are they still artists, or are they now just tired businessmen trying to get additional capital out of old investments of talent and effort? In the climax of *Paint Your Wagon,* No Name City collapses because the heroes have tunnelled under it to catch the gold dust that falls between the floorboards of the saloons. The studios are collapsing the same way on the Hollywood moviemakers who have been scrounging around for old gold dust. They take their old work off the shelf and try to get it rewritten to make it "youth-oriented"; they come out with a leering family picture that won't appeal to youth, and — what's worse — it doesn't honestly represent anybody anymore. Nobody believes in it; everybody just hopes that the beads on Lee Marvin will have magic, or that John Truscott's gold-rush hippie costumes will sweep the nation and save everything. At the high-level conferences, they'll say, "If only we hadn't had all that production trouble, if it hadn't rained, if only we'd finished sooner, when the hippie movement was still big . . ." They'll explain the bind they're in by saying, "We got it out too late." They'll be wrong, because they couldn't have made it with this picture last year or the year before or five years ago. There was never a right time for a picture that shifts around trying to find the secret of somebody else's success, yet that's the only kind of big picture the businessmen who now control the major studios really believe in.

•

Lions Love also features a sexless, passionless *ménage à trois,* and it would be beautifully symmetrical and ever so convenient if this first American feature by Agnès Varda, which cost less than a quarter of a million dollars, were an example of what can be done in movies. Visually, it's very pretty — much prettier than *Paint Your Wagon.* Steve Larner's lyric color cinematography gives Los Angeles a sunny Mediterranean enchantment, and Agnès Varda is a marvellous movie technician who knows how to compose shots, how to structure sequences, how to make a movie move. *Lions Love* is a much better-made film than *Paint Your Wagon.* But technique, which counts for so much when a picture doesn't have it, counts for very little when it's all a picture has. This movie, in which Viva cuddles in bed with Gerome Ragni and James Rado, the two authors of *Hair,* while they watch Robert Kennedy's assassination on television, is both silly and deeply offensive (because of that silliness). *Lions Love* has a graceful surface, but it lacks a sense of the fitness of things — and I don't mean empty proprieties but true sensibility. We really don't want to look at Viva — all done up as a stoned Pre-Raphaelite — as she makes vacuous little remarks about how sorry she feels for the orphaned Kennedy children. In this prankish context of a make-believe movie about moviemaking, with people spouting the usual about how they don't know movies from reality, we may experience some disgust that they *don't* have a sense of reality. The *lumpen* world of star worship that Andy Warhol featured was, in its narcissistic way, self-contained, and this movie is entertaining as a *jeu d'esprit* when the three principals improvise comic phone calls. Viva's deracinated version of ZaSu Pitts is sometimes funny, and Ragni occasionally suggests a Belmondo who has joined the Three Stooges. But their subculture and their little games are too cut off from political events for Miss Varda's vague and ambiguous points about television voyeurism to make sense. When she relates Kennedy's death to the attempt on Warhol's life, and to an awkward and rather cruel sequence involving the mock-suicide of Shirley Clarke, there is appallingly little intelligence at work. The chic superficiality of this view of American life is more offensive than anything in *Paint Your Wagon,* which — flailing around in all directions, as it does — is so painfully aware that it has missed out.

[October 25, 1969]

Private Worlds

Despite its title and an advertising campaign that seems designed to keep people away ("I'm 19, I want to be loved. Hurt me!"), *The Sterile Cuckoo* should — and will, I'm sure — be a great success. The production is on a minuscule scale — it's a somewhat *under*produced movie, which makes it almost a freak among recent American pictures. In addition, the print quality and the color are so poor that one experiences some visual discomfort — and some bafflement about *why*. But though the camerawork is barely adequate, at least the camera is placed where it should be in each shot to make the material clear, and in this kind of film that's what counts most. *The Sterile Cuckoo* is a small, delicate tragicomedy, beautifully written (Alvin Sargent did the adaptation of John Nichols' 1965 novel), and directed very simply, but with remarkable and sustained *tact,* by Alan J. Pakula. The movie has a modest range, and the technical ineptitude makes it appear square; the weak, blurry look softens the story and turns it all into part of some never-never rural past, which, I suppose, those who resist its charm will call "fifties" — the most contemptuous word around these days. That accusation was justifiably levelled at *Goodbye, Columbus,* because the language of romance has different nuances for each period and that story was a fifties romance as surely as *The Beautiful and Damned* was twenties. For people who read, movie versions of novels almost always seem to be in the wrong period, because the movies aren't made until the mass audience is prepared to accept the material. *The Sterile Cuckoo,* however, has not been bought late and then "brought up to date," like *Goodbye, Columbus.* What has happened, as I make it out, is the reverse. Lacking much expertise, Pakula (in his début as a director) probably tried to make things easier for himself by presenting the college setting in isolation from the world. But an insulated college is part of an old stereotype of college life, so the college seems to belong to an earlier era than the new, "activist" stereotype does. In order to cope with the material, he has instinctively dated it *back*.

Pookie Adams (Liza Minnelli) is a close relative of Holden Caulfield and of the boys in Lionel Trilling's "Of This Time, of That Place" and the Joyce Carol Oates story "In the Region of Ice." One of those brilliant, disordered, and dissociated kids, she is (possibly intentionally) a sister of Carson McCullers' Frankie Addams, but she doesn't grow up and join the world, like Frankie. The bright adolescent who is in pain and comes on freaky seems to speak to something in American life and has a special magic for us. It would have been easy to exploit the magic and wreck the character in the old Hollywood way — making Pookie, the imaginative, witty compulsive talker, into a madcap heroine and using her eccentricities and comic perceptions to turn her into a darling junior Auntie Mame. But Liza Minnelli's timing is so good that the charming, comic lines tumble out of her without sounding delivered, and we never forget that there's something else going on in that comic chatter. Miss Minnelli's sad, quizzical persona — the gangling body and the features that look too big for the little face — are ideal equipment for the role. She's very funny rattling on about the creeps and weirdos (i.e., everybody who conforms enough to function in the world), but one knows that even when everything Pookie says about them is right her reasons for saying what she does are bad. Anybody she doesn't know how to get along with, or anybody who grows impatient with her or fed up with her, automatically becomes one of the weirdos. Pookie is not just a delightful nonconformist in a world of conformists, or another cute Hollywood gamine, or one of those nonconformists who would fit right in at a progressive college; like her fictional counterparts and the nonfictional counterparts one may have known, Pookie turns family, teachers, friends, and lovers into betrayers.

The stories of those gifted, maddening losers who make impossible demands on other people are generally told in the first person — or else told by those who feel guilty for having failed them. The narrator of the novel, Pookie's boyfriend Jerry, has been reconceived for the movie. He's a placid, uncomplicated college freshman whom Pookie draws into an affair, and he squirms under her pressure. Jerry (Wendell Burton) is a soft and downy, protected boy who is vulnerable to Pookie because he's so totally, *childishly* conventional that he hasn't yet developed an adult outlook, with adult defenses. Wendell Burton, who was Charlie Brown on the stage in San Francisco, looks such a Charlie Brown of a kid that it's astonishing that he can also *act* it. He gives a flawless performance as a decent, limited kid who wants to get along in all the ordinary, middle-class ways. One watches what happens to them as Jerry tries to join in the college world and as Pookie, who can't function in it, tries to hold him in her private arena, which is supposed to be superior to that of the weirdos. Someone like Pookie generally makes other people feel guiltily conventional when they prefer worldly pleasures to the *folie à deux* that the brilliant, half-mad person wants to live in. Jerry never gets that involved emotionally; he's so simple and so *stable* that he loves Pookie without ever being taken in by her, the way a more complex person might be taken in and begin to share her fantasies. His very conventionality makes much of the movie a touching comedy of the absurd. (The movie gives Pookie a mother who died in childbirth and a father who was never close to her; this clinical background provides too facile a basis for sympathy — i.e., loneliness — and makes us think we understand more than we do. It's the kind of commercial device that closes off a subject in a way an artist wouldn't.) Though the screenwriter has taken a lot of the dialogue from the novel, he has placed it in a different, simpler structure, which looks as if it might have been conceived and thought out with Liza Minnelli and Wendell

Burton in mind. If the roles weren't tailored for them, the director found the actor and actress they fit beautifully.

One doesn't want to destroy *The Sterile Cuckoo* by building it up too much. If the movie has any major flaw besides the technical weaknesses and the insulated college setting, it is a certain cautiousness of spirit — almost as if Jerry were directing. It's a bit plodding; one senses that everything has been worked out in the script and that the director is following the blueprint. And Pakula's gentleness and control are so *steady* that one becomes too much aware of them; maybe because one senses his caution, one begins to watch to see that he doesn't spoil things and that the actors don't make a mistake. There are two or three scenes that put extraordinary demands on Liza Minnelli, and, maybe because of the general low-keyed cautiousness, we're too conscious of how she handles these big moments. She carries them off (and without going too far), but the tension has been deflected from Pookie onto whether Liza Minnelli is enough of an actress. We're as aware of *performances* as we are in the theatre, and this is probably the director's fault. Good as it is, the picture has a classical, neat, middle-brow banality to it; it doesn't soar, it lacks a sense of discovery, it doesn't have the elation or excitement of art. Pakula plays it safe and works within his limitations; if he doesn't begin to take chances, he's going to be a dull director. Still, *The Sterile Cuckoo* is blessedly free of false excitement. It's a nice little picture, a plain garden flower that smells very good among the big plastic ones.

Pookie is a created character, and there haven't been many in recent movies. More than that, she is, in her small but resonant way, an American archetype that has finally reached the screen, and archetypal roles make stars. Liza Minnelli is probably going to be acclaimed as a great actress, and I rather dread that. She's just about perfect here, and one fears that she will be typed in loser roles. She can be a lovely comedienne, but if she were to go on drawing on that emotional quality that is so close to the surface in her that one almost fears to see it exposed, she could become an awful pain. I mean, we don't want the movie companies to drag out *The Constant Nymph* and *The Enchanted Cottage* and *Escape Me Never* and all the rest of that wistful, suffering old muck now that they've got another actress with Keane eyes. If she's smart, she'll learn to wink.

•

When you see Anthony Quinn holding up a bottle of wine in the ads for *The Secret of Santa Vittoria,* you may think you've already seen the movie, and, of course, you *have*. Stanley Kramer has synthesized those other pictures coarsely and rambunctiously, and with confident bad taste.

It's *Zorba the Greek* and forties Hollywood combined into a horrible kind of picturesque anti-Fascist *opéra-bouffe* bacchanal that is so energetically gross that even while one cowers in one's seat one knows there's an audience for it. Quinn has often been a big bull of a hero, but never before has he been encouraged into such bullish buffoonery as coughing at the audience and rampaging around while a roaring Anna Magnani — her face a mask of bitterness — throws pots and pans and fruit and vegetables and pasta at him and bangs him with the biggest rolling pin in the history of bad movies. She seems to hate her role as his shrewish wife, Rosa, so much that she acts it with a malevolent fury that almost makes one fear for Quinn's skull. Quinn is Bombolini, the town drunkard, who finds his manhood and regains Rosa's respect when he stands up to the Nazis — and merely setting down this résumé makes *my* head hurt. He finds his "dignity," and we lose ours just sitting there.

You don't know what world you're in at this movie. The people of Santa Vittoria are all at work to save a cache of a million bottles of wine from the Nazis, and, except for the principal actors, they all have those hairy, warty old peasant faces so dearly beloved of visiting American directors, and the principals are encouraged to behave in a manner that is probably thought to be *ethnic*. The movie is done in some (intentional? unintentional?) movie-begotten mock-heroic style in which every personal exchange is ludicrous or repulsive. The Nazi commandant (Hardy Krüger) seems to be the only quiet, civilized person in the town. Ernest Gold has provided a score that one assumes — one prays — is intended to be mock Italian, but bad music does not a good parody make. The whole movie could be said to be parody, but that doesn't improve it.

•

We naturally expect — and hope — that new, young filmmakers will bring something new into movies and bring movies into contact with the modern world. It's understandable that Susan Sontag, making her first film in a foreign country — Sweden — should protect herself; still, it's disappointing that *Duet for Cannibals* is one more sealed-off-sex-games-and-guess-what's-real movie. Miss Sontag is often a thoughtful writer, but she has never had much dramatic sense — it's hard to think of an American writer with *less* dramatic sense — and she certainly doesn't get a lot of drama going here. The black-and-white photographic style is plain and handsome, but the author-director doesn't show much feeling for character, and the actors in the sexual foursome haven't been given enough to work with. They seem to be stranded on the screen, trying to fill in the slack of the dry, expository dialogue, and looking for some clues to what's wanted of them. There is a good bit — a psychotic old man eating in a restaurant and making everybody nervous; he, at least, has something to *do*. The pivotal figure is said to be a revolutionary; if it turned out that he was an impostor or a chef, no one in the audience would be surprised. Nothing in the movie has been made to count for anything. A hermetic game-world need not connect with ours, but it needs to have its own logic. We need to be involved in the aesthetics of how the game is played; this movie hardly seems to be aware of its own conceit. Miss Sontag solemnly calls our attention to a wall scrawled with the names of Simone de Beauvoir, Sappho, Hypatia, and Virginia Woolf. The publicity and some of the reviews say the movie can be interpreted many ways, but they don't offer them. The only question I came out with is: Who's Hypatia?

•

A worried psychiatrist named Dr. Glazer takes a bachelor apartment under the name Glassman and, in a mirror, photographs his own crackup. *Coming Apart* was written and directed by Milton Moses Ginsberg. (Ezra Pound said that he named his son Homer Shakespear Pound for the crescendo effect; Ginsberg's parents must have wanted the diminuendo effect.) When filmmakers start using three names, like the lady poets in the *Saturday Review*, it may be a sign of what's happening in movies. There have been glowing advance notices of *Coming Apart;* a sex-exploitation-plus-hangups movie, it seems to have that lacerating deep-truth and demonic-laughter *Faces* stuff for some people. Rip Torn is the psychiatrist, naked and spread-eagled, Christ-like, on his couch at the opening, and for the first fifteen minutes, as various girls threw themselves upon him, I hopefully took it as an Alfie-He-Was-Curious put-on and had a good time laughing, but it appears that this prelude was designed to seduce the viewer and make him accept Ginsberg's concern for our mental health and his supposedly searing visions of torment and hysteria and rot. The *Life* reviewer says, "I despise the current trend to abuse [traditional morality] for sensation's sake. And yet in honesty it must be recorded that *Coming Apart* does have a morally instructive dimension." As far as I'm concerned, I could do with a hell of a lot less of the moth-eaten misery of the morally instructive dimension, and the picture could use a few good sensations. Can't we have pornography without agony?

[November 1, 1969]

The Once and Future King?

An actor often comes to movies from the theatre with a big reputation, plays a big movie role, and is acclaimed as a great actor. After a string of bad movies, he no longer seems so great, his technique coarsens, and his face shows the dissipation of success. There were indications that this was happening to Peter O'Toole. In weak, characterless roles, such as the one he had in *How to Steal a Million,* he had become merely a pleasant, "stylish" leading man, a walking luxury item. It was all that the role required, but he certainly didn't burst its very obvious seams. Then, last year, in *The Lion in Winter,* he gave good evidence that he could be an actor of vitality and passion — an actor in the heroic mold. Some of the best English actors — Alec Guinness, Ralph Richardson, John Gielgud, Rex Harrison, Paul Scofield — lack the kind of animal presence, the threat of violence, that makes certain roles exciting. O'Toole did what Olivier almost alone of English actors could do (and what Nicol Williamson so feverishly overdoes). An actor who can make us feel that he has "heart" — that the feelings he projects are at the center of our lives — can hold a play or a film together and make it seem major. Richard Burton seemed to have it, but in such abundance that he began to toy with it and to devalue it. Perhaps it needs to be harder won (as Olivier won it over the obstacle of his young inconsequential charm, his lack of *weight*). It isn't so much a matter of talent or training, or even physique, as of temperament. O'Toole's king suggested physical strength and heroic power. He could bellow. (Can one imagine Gielgud bellowing?) He could be brutal. (Can one imagine Richardson as a brute?) The threat of violence in his king suggested that he was an actor of considerably greater range than his screen career had indicated — and of a different range. He has now taken on another role that calls for a heroic actor, though it's a quiet, unassuming role, which needs to be played at the other end of the keyboard from his roistering Plantagenet. Neither role is a great one, but O'Toole may be turning into something of a new phenomenon among movie actors — an actor who can transform lame vehicles the way great stage actors used to.

At a mere eighteen thousand words, James Hilton's *Goodbye, Mr. Chips* — an "affectionate" tribute to a small man's useful, uneventful life — was at least lightweight, and, despite its soggy gentility, it had the virtues of gentleness and modesty. It had come out as a story in 1933, but when it was put between covers the next year it looked like a novel, and it has gone through more than seventy-five printings in the United States alone. It was a durable tear-jerker and has the odd distinction of being probably the shortest best-selling novel known. The first time on the screen, in 1939, it was saved by Robert Donat's performance as Mr. Chips (which won him the Academy Award) and by a charming young actress named Greer Garson, who, however, quickly patented her charm and became one of the most richly syllabled queenly horrors of Hollywood. The weather is much rougher now, but *Goodbye, Mr. Chips* has been saved again — this time by O'Toole, by Petula Clark as his wife, and by an added character, played by Sian Phillips. The new movie is far from being a good one, but, despite its heaviness and length, and the *longueurs* caused by an atrocious, numbing score, the director, Herbert Ross (who was formerly a choreographer), has managed to keep it a gentle romance, and keep it fairly buoyant. What this all adds up to is that one can look at Peter O'Toole's performance without too much pain.

Goodbye, Mr. Chips had a core idea of immense popular appeal — the power of love to transform a person. The Chips of the story was a mild schoolmaster, a conservative bachelor of forty-eight, who, on vacation, suddenly met and married a twenty-five-year-old governess with radical-socialist sympathies. After his marriage, he won the love of his students, because he was "kind without being soft" — because he was a happy man. When his wife died in childbirth, two years later, he became an old man at fifty. But she had broadened his ideas and humanized him, and he was a mellow old man for the remaining thirty-ad-infinitum years of his life. Hilton had a commercial genius for domesticating "the impossible dream." This story must have spoken to millions of hearts: "You poor stick-in-the-mud, you may yet be saved by a Cinderella touch and have a long, wonderful, happy life and be loved by everyone."

Terence Rattigan, who did the adaptation for this new, demi-musical version, has made the young Chips a dry-as-dust martinet of a schoolmaster (much like the one in his own *The Browning Version*) who falls in love with a musical-comedy actress, marries, and is transformed (through fifteen years of marriage — a more comforting period of time) into a loving, lovable old man. The movie is a vernal romance, with a true-blue, good-to-the-last-drop heroine and an inert structure that spans Chips's unconscionably prolonged life. (His longevity must have been part of the story's appeal; Hilton immediately took perpetual life itself as the core idea for *Lost Horizon,* and made another fortune.) Rattigan promises much more than he delivers. At the beginning, when Chips says that he doesn't care if he's liked by his students as long as he can *teach* them, he suggests a genuine sense of vocation (rigid and misguided though it may be). Since the two great loves of his life are teaching and the girl he marries, we expect the crucial part of the movie to be his discovery, through his marriage, of how to be a good teacher instead of a deadly pedant. But the movie simply settles for showing how well liked he becomes, obviously on the assumption that we really don't care if he's a good teacher as long as he's popular. Nor do we discover how the young actress perceives the hidden qualities in Chips, because they are not revealed to us until much later. Flowers on the table — a token of domestic bliss — are made to stand for a happy marriage. The flowers are nice, but we want to know what the couple's life together is like. The movie gives us the courtship and the end of life, but the middle — the transformation that we've looked forward to — seems to happen offscreen. Yet even the *suggestion* that the movie is about what makes a good life is appealing. The idea of a peaceful, useful life and of a happy marriage is now almost more romantic and more desirable than Hilton's Shangri-La once seemed. It's dream enough for now.

If only we could be left alone with our feelings, we could practically entertain ourselves at this movie just mulling it all over, marvelling at the appeal of its pleasantly dowdy simplicities. But periodically, almost ceremonially, Leslie Bricusse's Muzak fills the air, as if to create a mystique of sentiment, and it inflates whatever one may have begun to feel, and makes it cheap and false. This Muzak is in some neutral neo-sentimental mode that makes you feel that it's programming you to be banal, putting a pacifier in your head. And while these pitiful songs (eleven of them, as distinct one from another as sections of beige wall-to-wall carpet) are being sung, mostly offscreen, you're treated to visual Muzak — "mood" visuals — providing enough redundancy to pad the movie out to two hours and thirty-one minutes plus intermission.

One's heart may sink every time a music cue starts up, and the picture lingers on long after it should end — and I haven't told *all* the worst —

but O'Toole and Petula Clark play together so well that one smiles, wanting to accept the romance, wanting to believe in this middle-class fairy tale. Miss Clark is not very good at the beginning, when she's supposed to be a young girl (she's done up in short curls and looks too much like Mary Martin), but she improves when the romance begins to take hold, although her role is a cut-rate version of one of those sickeningly intuitive James M. Barrie heroines. She has a lovely glow in the Second World War period of the film, when she's supposed to be the age she actually is. She relaxes then, and one begins to believe in her as a truly happy woman. One wonders why the adapter, in changing the character to provide an excuse for Miss Clark to sing, didn't eliminate the age difference. Before their marriage, when Chips was explaining to her that he was too old for her, I kept waiting for her to correct him. As Miss Clark is actually about the same age as O'Toole, the supposed difference puts a strain on our credulity and on her performance. If she were older, it would improve the movie, by explaining her willingness to give up her career. The *implications* of the change haven't been worked out, either. Surely it would not be difficult, in substituting an actress for a governess with progressive ideas who liberated her husband, to show how a more worldly wife might broaden a schoolmaster's outlook, but nothing is done with this, so one gets the impression that the actress is drawn to the safety and protective comforts of a narrow academic life. That leaves Chips's transformation to be a pure miracle of love, and it makes the movie more complacent toward Chips's stuffiness than the story was.

Though Chips's role isn't particularly well thought out in the writing, O'Toole gives an extraordinarily detailed performance. He stays in character, and he resists the temptation (which can easily be imagined) to patronize Chips. The reserves of strength within gentleness are not easy to demonstrate, but he does it; his Chips is diffident to the point of disappearance, yet you still know there's a man there. O'Toole treats that man with such extraordinary respect that Chips grows in stature as the character *must* grow if the movie is to succeed as romance. And when Chips stops growing, O'Toole manages, through what in an actor is heroic intelligence, not to make him an endearing, stomach-turning old codger. There is, of course, all too much precedent for praising an actor when he plays a role such as a crusty, crotchety, noble old schoolmaster, especially if he gets a chance to age onscreen and quaver a bit. But O'Toole plays the part without seizing all the depressing opportunities or puttying himself up with wrinkles and wattles. He plays the role from within, and the externals are kept to a minimum. It's a romantic performance, not a bathetic one — a "little" man played by a very large actor — and the finest performance I've seen on the screen this year.

There is a third star — one who isn't billed that way but is felt that way. Sian Phillips (she is Mrs. O'Toole), who has had unattractive roles, such as the wife in *Laughter in the Dark,* is cast as Ursula Mossbank, an actress friend of Mr. Chips's wife. Sian Phillips's Ursula is a Beardsley vamp — theatrical in that witty, stilted way that has already become one of the small but true treasures of the past — and she gives the movie a few desperately needed shots in the arm. *Goodbye, Mr. Chips* keeps going on what used to be called charm, but it's heaven to have Miss Phillips around to needle it. Here is the actress who might have played Gertrude Lawrence as the great camp-vamp star she was.

•

Bo Widerberg, the writer-director of *Elvira Madigan,* has made *Adalen 31* with great skill and artistry and intelligence, yet it's uninspired, and it misses, I think, by quite a lot. The movie re-creates a 1931 strike that was a major factor in establishing Sweden's Social Democratic Party, and Widerberg sets up a group of stereotypes as the participants — elegant and sensitive stereotypes, but stereotypes nevertheless, who fill in the historical picture illustrating the points he wants to make. It's an exquisite form of social realism — which is certainly an unusual form of social realism — but, lush and lyrical as it is, it's fundamentally didactic and academic. And because Widerberg seems to work best in vignettes and to have some architectural problems when he's working on such a large scale, his argument isn't clear. He makes the little points but not the big ones. We watch the evocations of the past and the little episodes for their beauty, as if they were a painter's still-lifes, and when the violence erupts we don't really understand its political significance, and we're left "appreciating" it, in a rather embarrassed way, for its pictorial values. He has framed it all so carefully in the past that it doesn't have the immediacy of action in the present tense that is the usual movie tense even when the movie is set in the past. *Adalen 31* feels like a "classic," and that's not how a new film that really speaks to us feels. This remote, alienated reaction is a terrible distortion of how we know we should react. We understand that we are meant to see the ironic contrast between the beauty of nature and the cruelty of men, but because Widerberg fails to involve us in the issues of the struggle, because his technique isn't *dramatic,* we are left with his visual artistry, and so we look at the bloodshed and at the men grouped in combat for their compositional values. I certainly don't mean to suggest that *Adalen 31* is a negligible picture, but Widerberg is far too gifted to be using film to give us textbook lessons, and his orthodoxy (the warmth and generosity of the worker's family contrasted with the mean-spiritedness of the affluent, etc.) is transparently an attempt to be "relevant." He's so gifted that there are beautiful moments all through the film. But there is also something dutiful about the experience of watching it, like looking at someone's color slides of the past.

•

If *Adalen 31* is a failure at a very high level, the week has also been marked by an American failure at the lowest level within recent memory. *Hail, Hero!*, a real succulent, is currently splattering its virtue at Radio City Music Hall. That's the right place for this conglomerate-made "youth" soap opera, which is supposed to be "the first motion picture to deal with the sensitive issues of the Vietnam war and its relationship to the Generation Gap." *Hail, Hero!* is so confused about what attitudes to take to please the maximum number of paying customers that it mixes them all up together. Michael Douglas is the saintly, barefoot young hippie who enlists for Vietnam and gives his clothes to the poor. Considering the kind of movies the Music Hall has been running lately, it may need to take up a collection for itself.

[November 8, 1969]

Blood and Snow

In the Year of the Pig is an assemblage of news footage and interviews that presents an over-view of the Vietnam war; Ho Chi Minh is the hero, and the theme is not, as might be expected, the tragic destruction of Vietnam but the triumph of Vietnam over the American colossus. The movie is not a piece of reporting: Emile de Antonio, who gathered the material, has never been to Vietnam; his footage comes from a variety of sources, not specified on the screen but elsewhere acknowledged to include East Germany, Hanoi, the National Liberation Front offices in Prague, Britain, and some American companies (A.B.C., Paramount News, U.P.I., Pathé News, Fox Movietone News), and there is a Russian-staged reënactment of the battle of Dien Bien Phu. But, taking this footage from all over, he has made a strong film that does what American television has failed to do. It provides a historical background and puts the events of the last few years into an intelligible framework. Though the television covage has often been covertly anti-war, and though watching the Americans behave like the bad guys in Hollywood war movies has undoubtedly helped turn the country against the war, the general effect of years of this has been a numbing one — constant horror but no clear idea of how each day's events fitted in, and growing uncertainty about the meaning of victories and defeats beyond the day's events. We now feel helpless to understand the war; we want to end it, and the fact that we can't demoralizes us. We seem to be powerless. Because this film makes sense out of what's been going on, even if this sense isn't the only sense to be made of it, de Antonio's historical interpretation becomes remarkably persuasive.

The movie does not claim to be "objective" (except in the way that every documentary implicitly claims to be, because it uses photographic records and, despite talk of media sophistication, "seeing is believing"). One could certainly argue that *In the Year of the Pig* (the title, I assume, does not refer only to the Chinese calendar) is merely restoring the balance by showing "the other side" — that if it attempted to be "objective" it would turn into another of those essays in confusion, like the network specials, that balance everything out until they get a collection of the disparate facts and platitudes that are considered "responsible" journalism. However, while the commentators' face-saving gestures and revelations have made us aware of the tacit commitment in that kind of coverage, we may be less conscious of the games being played with this footage. Some of them are obvious, loaded little tricks, like the film's crude beginning (a body in flames, still moving, followed by satiric glimpses of Hubert H. Humphrey, John Foster Dulles, President Johnson), and there are pranks (the insertion of a closeup of a toothy photo of Joseph P. Kennedy, and one of Arthur Schlesinger, Jr., looking like a lewd Dracula). This is schoolboy stuff: de Antonio's judgment is erratic. But in the main line of the narrative he plays a highly sophisticated game, using the pick of the archives and recent interviews, expertly (and often very sensitively) edited, and with unusually good sound-editing.

What de Antonio has done is to present the issues of the war and American policy and the American leaders as Hanoi might see them, and he has done it out of our own mouths. He has gone to what must have been enormous effort to put the film together so that the words of men like Dulles, Dean Rusk, Joe McCarthy, and Wayne Morse and of experts and journalists like Roger Hilsman, Paul Mus, Harrison Salisbury, Jean Lacouture, and David Halberstam tell the story. They provide his polemic, without any additional narration. This makes it more credible — and more of a feat. De Antonio calls the film "political theatre," and the counterpoint of words and actions involves so many heavy ironies it becomes too much of a feat. He's almost too clever, and his cleverness debases the subject; the method is a little obscene. But one tends to accept the line of argument, not just because it's a coherent historical view but because emotionally it feeds our current self-hatred.

The Americans make it so easy for de Antonio to build his case. When you listen to Mark Clark and Curtis LeMay, the war really sounds like a racist war. They're war boosters out of the political cartoons of an earlier era; their dialogue would make us laugh at how old-fashioned the satire was if we read it in a Sinclair Lewis novel. When one hears LeMay's vindictive tone as he talks about how every work of man in North Vietnam should be destroyed if that is what it takes to win, and when one hears Mark Clark say of the Vietnamese, "They're willing to die readily, like all Orientals are," it's hard to believe that the war they're engaged in is the same war that's still going on. I saw this film on the afternoon of Monday, November 3, and after sitting there and thinking how far away much of it seemed — Eisenhower with President Diem, the dragon lady Mme. Nhu, Dulles and the domino theory, the American leaders explaining how we were going to help the Vietnamese help themselves — I came home to hear President Nixon's speech, which seemed to belong to the same past as the speeches in the movie, though the new rhetoric is smoother and more refined. The continuity of the war that evoked the earlier crude justifications with the war that's still going on, even though hardly anybody believes in the justifications anymore, makes one susceptible to de Antonio's argument. In the context of the movie, even the casual stupidities of American soldiers sound meaningfully racist. When some American soldiers relaxing on a beach say that they miss girls, they're asked what's the matter with the Vietnamese girls, and a silly, grinning boy replies, "They're gooks. You know, slant-eyes. They're no good," and we're revved up to think, "The pig! And our leaders are trying to tell us he's there to keep the Vietnamese free!" In another context, we might simply think that this silly, lonely soldier was trying to find acceptable male slang for not being interested in girls he can't talk to. It might even mean that he wanted *more* than sex. In this context, America is represented by clips of our leaders at their most repellent, of an American soldier who stands by smiling as a helpless, bound prisoner is kicked in the groin, of Mark Clark and Curtis LeMay, and of young George S. Patton III saying of his buddies, "They're a bloody good bunch of killers" (also a line that would sound very different in the context of, say, a Second World War movie). De Antonio finds a soldier who likes defoliation work, because it seems a step toward ending the war; Morley Safer, it may be remembered, interviewed a G.I. who said that he didn't like "riding the people's gardens down." No doubt there are both kinds, and certainly they're both destructive, whether they like the work or not. But by selecting Americans who do like it, by selecting Curtis LeMay and the others, de Antonio obviously means to suggest a basic rottenness in Americans, and an America that is anti-life. After one watches the movie for a while, the Americans in it begin to look monstrously callow, like clumsy, oversized puppets.

De Antonio has not merely made a protest film documenting the "downward spiral" (as the North Vietnamese Pham Van Dong described it) of American policy, though that is the film's most valuable aspect. He has attempted to foreshadow the fall of the West — and not just in Vietnam — by presenting the Vietnamese as a people solidly behind Ho Chi Minh, who represents their goals and ideals, and as a people who have been ennobled by war and who must win. In his own way, de Antonio seems to support Mark Clark's view of Orientals; the movie suggests that the Vietnamese are willing to die because they are united in a common purpose, and that if they die, their dying still somehow stands for life, while we are dying though we live. The tone of the latter part of the film is almost mystical; the ability of the tiny country to go on fighting against a great power is not presented in practical terms of how much more difficult it is for a super-nation to fight in a divided, decentralized country than to incapacitate a modern, powerful, centralized state but, rather, in terms of our inability to defeat the mystical spirit, the will (and perhaps the destiny?) of Ho Chi Minh's people. It is, in other words, as patriotic and jingoistic and, in its way, as pro-war as American wartime movies used to be about *our* mission and destiny, and in this reversal it is the Americans who have become dehumanized.

•

Downhill Racer is about a poor American boy (Robert Redford) trying to become an Olympic skiing champion and succumbing to a sex parasite (Camilla Sparv), who deserts him when he loses a race. In other words, it's *Blood and Sand* on the ski slopes, with the addition of the team coach (right out of an old Pat O'Brien movie) who shakes his head over the boy's arrogance but trains him to become a true winner — which, as in old movies, still means a change of heart before the big match. The older versions' virtuous girl back home who really loved the boy is now the hometown girl who's good in the back seat of a Chevrolet. She doesn't make any demands, though she queries the hero on whether she should go away to become a dental technician or a waitress — a question the movie doesn't answer, though it's just about the only human question the movie raises. Nevertheless, *Downhill Racer* is a new movie in feeling and tempo, and it's not too bad. There's a sense of freedom in the way it's made (mixing 16-mm. with 35-mm. and moving fast), so even when it isn't good it isn't depressing the way a big, heavy, expensive movie is. There's no hemming and hawing; it isn't a drag. It's transient, which is right for the ski-race subject; it isn't meant to be art for the ages. Michael Ritchie, making his début as a movie director, uses too many *cinéma-vérité* clichés (especially at the beginning, one keeps backing away from the screen as the closeups keep hitting one like the Yo-Yos in 3-D movies), but he shows talent, and some wit, in handling the actors in the semi-documentary situations. He has a good feeling for short scenes and modern detail, and for movement, and his work is strengthened by the speed and shorthand style of the editing.

Just as the big companies have over-exploited optimism, the younger filmmakers have been exploiting hopelessness and despair. It's a relief to see the new, loose moviemaking techniques freed from the shallow miseries. But the techniques of *Downhill Racer* deserve a better script. The scenarist, James Salter, tries for the spare, taut, "masculine" style of Ernest Hemingway. Maybe the script had to be tacked together to fit the ski footage, which is the true excitement of the film; still, crucial scenes are so laconic they sound as if they'd been written by Calvin Coolidge, and they get unintended laughs. When the hero goes home to visit his farmer father, the old man (who, like fathers in the days of silent pictures, seems to be a half century older than his son) greets him with "Hello. I got your postcard. Your cousin said to thank you for the stamps." The movie fails to affect us because the son is just as tongue-tied. Not being able to express himself to his father could mean something, and not being able to express himself to anyone could also mean something, if the movie told us *what* it meant. But the movie has no center; it doesn't come into focus on what the meaning of a champion is. It is no more expressive than "Hello. I got your postcard." We never find out what it means to this boy to become a champion, or what is in him that makes him one, so we don't much care whether he gets broken up on the slopes or wins. This kind of thing doesn't require lots of exposition; Paul Newman did it mainly in one short speech in *The Hustler,* and it can be done non-verbally, too. The best dramatic moments in *Downhill Racer are* non-verbal (when Redford, sitting in a car — the front seat this time — with Camilla Sparv, drowns out her chatter about why she has been too busy for him by pressing his hand on the car horn; the smile of relief on Redford's face when his teammate gets up from a fall — a smile signalling us that he's good at heart and will be the winner). One gets the impression that the moviemakers are afraid to let the hero be "cocky," because that might be old hat, so he's nothing special — a little spoiled, maybe, and a little uncertain, and ludicrously terse, as if speech were what athletes are supposed to sublimate. The blankness and absence of consciousness in Redford's role suggest a misunderstanding of his appeal, and that is especially odd in a project he is said to have initiated. We like to see Redford because he doesn't make false, actorish moves; his humor and energy go beyond his roles and comment on them, indicating a stronger character — a man hiding as a juvenile. Redford has to go blank as an actor *not* to have that awareness that so many actors have to struggle to show. In a role in which we expect to see the intensifications of instinct and intelligence that set a champion off from his competition — and which indeed set Redford off from other, cloddish juveniles — he seems to be trying to turn himself into a young Robert Wagner or Rock Hudson. It appears that those who made this movie don't know the difference between a champion and a non-champion, in sports or in acting.

Ritchie has brought off one thing that takes skill, even though it isn't worth doing: he's kept the audience from howling at the coach's speeches. The coach, Gene Hackman, is such a sane, unassuming actor that he somehow makes it a pleasure to watch him as he delivers his ritual (though now quickie) sermons on moral fibre and sportsmanship; he does them with an earnestness befitting a saint. Ritchie also racks up some failures. The single worst sequence involves a woman journalist, who understands nothing of sports; it is condescendingly written and so excruciatingly directed that it stops the show cold — which serves the moviemakers right. Now that they're "sensitive" about Negroes, they're making women subhuman. Camilla Sparv, one of those girls who look better in stills than on the screen, plays her inscrutable-bitch role in the smiling, highborn, dragon-lady style of yesteryear.

[November 15, 1969]

Kazan's Latest Arrangements

In Elia Kazan's novel *The Arrangement*, the narrator-hero, while making love to the heroine, says "You're the only thing in the world I really care about, don't you know that?" and hits her. As he describes it, "I struck her with all my might, my open palm across her face, not in anger but to make her believe what I was saying, or was I making myself believe it?" Kazan's movie of *The Arrangement* keeps belting us the same way, to impress us — though I think it *is* in anger. In this autobiographical-fantasy movie, in which Kazan's voice cannot be separated from his hero's, anger at not being able to resolve the tensions of conflicting drives is scrambled up with anger at not achieving enough and not being taken seriously enough. Kazan once said that the artist should "force [people] to feel, since they do not want to or cannot discern any longer by themselves," and that "one must almost shock them, give them a turn, if one wants to make them aware that something deep can happen." There is an intensification in the movie of *The Arrangement* of Kazan's longtime confusion of the deep and the shocking, and there's a desperate, evangelical emptiness. One begins to suspect that he's looking for big truths to lacerate us with — something to justify all his punching and yelling and flailing about. *The Arrangement* is practically all played on one loud, self-important note, and the uninflected voices and unmodulated acting, plus Kirk Douglas's Steve Canyon look, call to mind the classic comic-strip big novel *The Fountainhead*. That, however, was about a strong man; this is about a weak man, with convictions or delusions of greatness. Kazan is not clear on this point, but one rather assumes that the decibel level of the man's agony is supposed to have some correlation with the size of his talent. But, if I may be forgiven, Kazan's "Howl" is bigger than his bite.

Under the picture of Kirk Douglas, the ad for the movie says, "You may go on lying to yourself after seeing *The Arrangement.* But it won't be easy," and, under the picture of Faye Dunaway, "Eddie Anderson had to face up to the truth. She nearly killed him." Oddly, these don't misrepresent the movie. That is pretty much what it's intended to be about. Eddie (the second-generation American, also known as Evans Arness and, to his father, as Evangelos) is a successful Los Angeles advertising man in his early forties who tries to kill himself, and as he recovers we begin to see the tensions that have made him self-destructive — on one side a girl (Faye Dunaway) who is contemptuous of his lucrative job and conventional life, and on the other a wife (Deborah Kerr) who wants security, and in the background his Greek immigrant father (Richard Boone), who measures worth in dollars. As a boy, the advertising man wanted to be a writer, and, sure enough, at the end Kirk Douglas goes off with Faye Dunaway into the sunset to write.

In the novel, the author was so involved in telling his story that he didn't seem to notice that it was full of clichés — or, if he did, to care. It was seriously written pulp, not just turned out for the market but torn out of the writer, and his apparent belief that the garish was the significant gave it a crude fascination. It was the kind of attempted epic that good American writers have abandoned to the mass market — the literature of "What went wrong and how do we find our way back?" Kazan is a good, energetic storyteller, so it reads better than it sits on one afterward. Even more blatantly than the book, the movie is a noisy glorification of anguish over selling out, with such an exaggerated evaluation of the loss to the world of the hero's wasted creativity that one does not know which way to look. No superstar of the underground fantasizes bigger. "You could have been — " Eddie's girl says, and he asks, "What?" "What you could have been," she replies, in an oracular, accusing tone that suggests Alexander the Great or Shakespeare at the very least. Yet one does not giggle at *The Arrangement,* because it's painfully bad in a way that isn't fun. But one also knows that Kazan is building up the pain as proof of the significance of his message, that he has always been a pain peddler, that he developed the school of theatre in which one screams when no more than a grimace is appropriate — until honest emotions are devalued, because who would notice them? If there has ever been a movie director whose cries of "Wolf" deserve to be ignored, it's Kazan. However, he also has a record of achievements which can't be ignored. Like so many other great figures in the theatre and the movies, he has always been a precarious mixture of the crude and the sensitive. When that mixture goes out of balance — when Kazan leans on us like an amateur — we want to know why. The misery in this film is flamboyant, but Kazan is so inept that the ineptness almost seems to be part of his misery. Kirk Douglas, made up to look gaunt and demonic, trudges through his disasters and guilts and memories like a Pop mixture of John Gabriel Borkman and Halvard Solness. Arthur Miller has taken off from the mundane, social-problem side of Ibsen; Kazan takes off from the wild, driven-to-greatness side. *The Arrangement* is a modern version of *The Master Builder,* with Faye Dunaway as the Hilda Wangel who comes to destroy the hero's complacent arrangements and spur him into setting out for the goals of his youth.

Most of us desire to be bigger than we are, so it's easy to understand grandiosity, which is the assertion that one *is* bigger than one is. The grandiosity of this film is an outgrowth of all that forcing of the audience to feel and that drive toward more and more intense "truths" to shock us with. In his earlier movie about the background of his family, *America America,* in which the hero was Eddie's uncle, Kazan attempted to show the fervor of the immigrant for a new life in which he would be free of grovelling under tyranny and of swallowing his honor. It was to be the first part of a trilogy, which, one can guess, would have demonstrated how the land of promise became corrupted by material values, but it was a flabby, overambitious epic, and an epic-size failure. He has jumped to the end of his family saga in *The Arrangement* (I sincerely hope, for his sake and everybody else's, that it *is* the final installment, and not the middle); this is the story of the hero's desire for a new life free of materialistic corruption. Kazan's dream of a new life in *The Arrangement* is as naïve as his analysis of the materialistic sellout. As a writer, Kazan is the same man who became a success in the theatre with "effectiveness" sold as drama. A writer works alone, not in the marketplace, but Kazan has internalized the popular market. He is a popular writer who made a popular success of his confessions about popular success. The novel *The Arrangement* was as commercial as hell, though it was written by a man who wasn't under any pressure to write commercially and who maybe didn't even know he was doing it. Kazan is as naturally commercial in his thinking as many good businessmen, and three million copies of the novel have been sold. He writes like an unlettered Mailer — tough-guy sex and gutsy-naïve psychodrama. And in writing *The Arrangement* he *didn't* sell out; he probably wrote just what he felt — startling truths of a kind that made the book reviewer in *Life* say, "No matter who you are, it will cause a falter in the rhythm of your days and nights, perhaps a defoliation of your life style." It was certainly meant to, and at the end the hero achieves his spiritual rebirth by returning to a simple life.

In making a big movie like this one about not whoring in the big-money mass market, one is forced into deals and compromises that are a truer reflection of how talented men sell out (at least in the theatre and in the movies) than Eddie's dramatic selling out through an advertising campaign for Zephyr, a "clean" brand of cigarettes. As a movie, *The Arrangement* is so self-contradictory it's no wonder Kazan is as noisy as he is. How can he talk to us about spiritual renewal and make a film that looks like this — a big, cliché-riddled, false-eyelashes-in-bed, star-stoned movie? It's like the slickest, ugliest, most exaggerated forties M-G-M movie, splintered for modernity. In the few opening shots before the hero leaves his palatial home for the office, there are glimpses of a white maid, a black cook, and two Oriental gardeners, and you immediately know what kind of movie it is, even if Kazan is fooling himself. Kazan is trying to make a "clean" — a noncommercial — commercial movie. The hard sell of integrity is as contradictory as the "clean" cigarette, but Kazan's salesmanship is much cruder than his hero's. This movie represents what successful people dissatisfied with themselves and their work are very likely to turn out when they want to show "truth" and their integrity. It's "personal moviemaking" by people who want a new life, who want to be cleansed, and whose idea of a personal statement is "Don't sell out."

Kazan may be destroying his talents by the intensity of his wish for greater moral stature. To an outsider, it appears that, far from finding himself, he has been losing his way ever since he tried to become the whole show — which isn't necessarily a *creative* drive. What to him seems a rebirth may seem to us a spiritual test he overdramatized and hence flunked. As evidence, one could point to the lack of feeling in this film. If one did not know that Kazan is a major figure in films, one would find nothing in the way this movie has been made to suggest it. The direction is tight and almost cruelly coercive of the actors. They have no life of their own as performers, no trace of invention; they're just shouting ciphers, acting out ready-made popular ideas about selling out. To use these accepted ideas is already a sellout, and for a man who aspires to seriousness to use them almost a decade after *L'Avventura* is a disgrace.

Kazan is not the first author-director to use actors merely as mouthpieces, but Kazan was a director (and an actor, too) before he was an author, and one does not expect even a self-preoccupied director (which I think he has become) to forget his obligation to his actors and constrict them into caricatures. Though the main narrative line in *America America* was badly flubbed melodrama, there were some fine images, such as the sealed, stifling, yet warm and inviting interiors of the rich merchant's home in Constantinople, and some memorable performances, such as

Paul Mann as the merchant and Linda Marsh as the daughter. *The Arrangement* has no quiet scenes that we can take away and savor; hardly any of the performances pass beyond mediocre TV level, and some are grotesque. Deborah Kerr is wrong in every nuance as a conventional Los Angeles matron (through she probably lives there). She's even less at home than she was as the adulterous Kansas housewife in *The Gypsy Moths*. The understanding-unloved-wife role she plays here (and she's hideously made up) wears out an actress's welcome faster than anything else; it just about convinced me that I didn't ever want to see her again. Miss Kerr used to play against her overemotional voice; now she lets it use her for a constant neurotic nagging that is revolting. In the book, Kazan painted the wife as a sanctimonious, dependent monster and kept telling the reader how lovely she was. In the movie, all that Deborah Kerr has to do is say her lines and she becomes a nightmare woman, and the author as director still doesn't seem to recognize that that's what he has made of her. He salts her speeches with "damn"s and "hell"s as if that would somehow turn her into a likable human being. As the life-force girl, Faye Dunaway drags her usual star-bundle of Theodora Van Runkle supposedly swell clothes around and yells on demand. In the novel, the girl used her you-should-have-been-great line on weak men as a way of drawing them to her; in the movie, Kazan has sacrificed even that bit of ambiguity. Ibsen understood that Hilda Wangel was goading Solness to climb higher than he could — that the dreams of his youth could not be carried out. Eddie gets away with it, but when Kazan tries to act on the dreams of his youth he comes crashing to the ground, like Solness. Kazan has taken forceful acting to the parody point: when Kirk Douglas and Richard Boone are on the screen together being intense — two manic, explosive specialists in the domineering-presence school of acting — two hams are trying to devour each other. How can Kazan be messianic about not selling out when he has coarsened and simplified whatever interest the novel — his *own* novel — developed? He has said that he wants to be in "at the birth of the film, instead of being, as before, the conductor of cadenzas and solos." Yes, one understands this desire. Since sound came in, however, there have been few directors who actually conceived and wrote their own pictures. Even those who do (and there have been more of them in recent years, though still fewer than one might suppose) are young and work differently, and on a different scale. They don't carry big stars and a big production on their back; they don't shape their material for the mass audience. I think Kazan has got to scale down his idea of the epic size of his talent and do something small, and do it right, for a change, whether it's his own material or somebody else's. We can't be forced to feel, only to react, and when we've been pushed around too much we don't even react. But Kazan used to know how to help us to feel. Perhaps he undervalues that gift, but it's his only true one. Is it really a penance for a big movie director to try to think small? In movies, the worst sellout has always been thinking big.

[November 22, 1969]

The Bourgeoisie and the Rabble

Claude Chabrol's *La Femme Infidèle* is an exquisitely detailed, impeccably acted, stunningly directed suspense story about adultery and passion among the bourgeoisie. I can't think of anything that's the matter with it; of its kind, it's just about a perfect movie. I only wish it were fundamentally more interesting. Yet to ask for a breath of life in this kind of quiet, civilized thriller would be to ask it to violate its own genre; "life" is as carefully excluded from this web of artifice as it is from certain kinds of detective fiction. A web of artifice is also the subject. Chabrol's hero is of the "comfortable" upper middle class that lives by forms and ceremony; for centuries it has deliberately excluded "life." This gentle bourgeois holds his emotions so thoroughly in check that a sudden access of rage turns him into a killer. You could try to make a case for the film as more than an expert, superbly wrought suspense story, but while you're watching it you don't really believe a second of it, except at the level on which a commercial thriller is gripping, and at the end the wife's "ironic" little smile of new respect for her husband when she realizes he has killed for her trivializes everything — reduces it to carriage-trade perversity.

The movie is "objective" in an odd way — much more direct and sure than Chabrol's earlier *Les Biches* but with that same voiceless quality. It can be seen as an attack on the bourgeoisie or it can be admired for its bourgeois subtlety and control. It is banality — the traditional elements of the triangle, and a few tiny ironies — carried to perfection of craft. From the first lines, about how the husband is putting on weight and not getting enough exercise, we watch each detail in the creation of a cuckold. He listens to classical music in bed while his languorously sensual wife, who can't sleep, lies, overheated, on top of the covers; the seducer, of course, listens to pop music. There's a kind of tired expertise in the writing; the details are as classical as the husband's taste. Yet this is also part of the conception — the symptoms of marital disturbance are intentionally the same old ones. Chabrol seems to have extracted from the performers exactly what was needed — Michel Bouquet's elegant little performance as the husband, the glossy beauty of Stéphane Audran (she looks like a rich, chic Jeanne Hébuterne), and Maurice Ronet's professionalism as the seducer.

When intentions like Chabrol's are perfectly achieved, is it enough? I admire Chabrol's total control of the medium for what he wants to do. The way the camera pans to make points and the way it backs away are truly remarkable; the camera never makes a false move. He's a sublime craftsman, the ideal conventional moviemaker, and the film is, in one sense, a graceful obituary of his own class values. But this kind of formal admiration is not the same as response to a work of art, even a failed one. *La Femme Infidèle* isn't a failure, but it isn't a work of art, either. One could respond with much more feeling to some of Chabrol's earlier movies *(Le Beau Serge, Les Cousins,* and even the rather doubtful *Les Bonnes Femmes)* than to this masterly, perfectly slick, humanly empty box. *La Femme Infidèle* is so carefully contained it leaves you with nothing; to enjoy it is probably bourgeois connoisseurship. (The audience gave off an aromatic blend of expensive perfume.) One enjoys not what it is so much as how well made it is. This is not a great pleasure but a minor one, and yet the pleasures of craftsmanship and fine detail are uncommon in movies, and to be savored.

•

"I wants to make your flesh creep," Joe the Fat Boy in *The Pickwick Papers* shouts to deaf old Mrs. Wardle before revealing that he has seen two people kissing and hugging. *Futz,* the movie version of Rochelle Owens' play, has the same impulse to excite and horrify us, but the director, Tom O'Horgan, has come some distance from hugging and kissing. *Futz* is the kind of movie in which as soon as you see a fat girl you're afraid her dress is going to be ripped off and, sure enough, it is. And then even your worst expectations are topped when she wallows in mud, with two men smearing it on her gargantuan breasts. By the end, what with the pulsating music and the rhythmic knife thrusts at the hero's genitals, *Futz* has been whooping and hollering so long it does make one's flesh creep. But not only in the way intended.

Futz is supposed to be about freedom and conformity; freedom is represented by Futz, who loves his pig Amanda, and conformity by the farmers who are outraged at this individualism and hound him down. (In the farming area where I was born, not far from where the movie was shot, their outrage would get more laughs than any of the jokes in the movie.) An allegory about personal liberty may be lodged in Miss Owens' poetic diction, but the incantatory style, which breaks the lines down into phrases, impedes comprehension, and the poor sound recording makes everything spoken fairly obscure. The O'Horgan rationale is to move us by "primal" fears and "ritual" (a word that has come to stand for much of what I could happily do without in the theatre). *Futz* is all performed in that revealing-everything style of acting that seems to reveal nothing. It is full of screaming and frothing at the mouth and nudity and the new, Kabuki style of sex, in which couples keep leaping into sportive positions, and the actors reveal less than an actor in another style can do with a pause in a line. There is often no decipherable relationship between the actors' words and their actions. O'Horgan sacrifices meaning for effectiveness so consistently that *Futz* is simply about the attempt to excite an audience. He works us over so much that the manipulation disgusts us even when we can't help being affected. The one arresting image, of Sally Kirkland, nude, arm flung up to heaven, astride a huge fat porker, gives the movie its only suggestion of freedom and celebration. The freaky abandon of this shot suggests that some of the material in *Futz* might possibly have worked as bucolic knockabout farce or as a comic revel, with the Village cast (the movie is performed by the La Mama stage company) playing mock-hayseeds — if O'Horgan weren't trying to rape the audience and if he weren't such a hayseed about moviemaking.

It is partly because of the movies' obvious superiority in presenting realistic material that the theatre has in recent years been returning to such anti-realistic techniques as chanting, choreographic movement, and "ritual." Most of this "advanced" theatre staging (as it used to be called) was tried in "avant-garde" and experimental films in the twenties and thirties, such as *Lot in Sodom,* and was generally disastrous, not just because stylization tends to look pretentious and absurd on the screen but because the screen exposes what was pretentious and absurd in the material to start with. On the stage, when non-dancers move rhythmically, we may have an empathic and kinesthetic response; when it happens on the screen, we simply observe, and it takes truly brilliant direction, camera placement, and editing to compensate for the loss of that response. O'Horgan takes a stylized theatre piece and sets it on a platform outdoors, and starts the howling and carrying on; he repeats the naïve mistakes of the worst avant-gardists of thirty years ago, and is noisier about it. Formalization on the screen is generally achieved by the most austere means, not by people screeching and bending in funny ways while they talk, and though one shouldn't rule out the possibility that formalization might be achieved by group movement if the director knew how to place the camera, surely it would have to be better movement than this. These are actors trying to behave like dancers, but they lack the formalized beauty of dance, or even of interesting choreography for non-dancers. And so we sit there observing this Dogpatch romp and passion play with, dear God, a Greek chorus that does recitations and with the kind of Village bucolic acting that makes one cower in one's seat (especially at Seth Allen's Obie Award–winning loony murderer). Nothing makes us more aware of staginess than actors reciting poetry outdoors — as directors of Shakespearean movies discover when they look at their first day's rushes. O'Horgan uses the movie medium and the outdoors mainly for their superior capacities for realistic mud and blood. And for a realistic pig — whose presence undermines the theatrical conceits, though our embarrassed knowledge that her participation is involuntary reinforces her position as the heroine.

I sat through *Futz* wondering why I was able to skip *Battle of Britain* with such an easy conscience but felt I should sit this damned thing out. I suppose the answer is that I'd been through that war too many times, but to walk out on *Futz*, as good sense dictated, seemed like cheating — for a critic, that is. A critic is supposed to be able to say not just that something is awful but why, so I sat there to the repulsive end. It's still not easy to explain why it's awful, and the problem probably isn't just a matter of how execrably it's been filmed. The *Times* reviewer said, "The scandal of this *Futz* has nothing to do with loving pigs, or your mother's breasts or the smell of your own two feet. It has to do with violating that sacred space between camera and subject, that dense and highly charged field of view that is in fact the 'medium' by which movies live." That has an impressive sound, but when the play was staged the *Times* drama critic took a similar way out: after explaining that some people were scandalized by the subject, he explained that he was "scandalized that such slovenliness should be permitted to masquerade as new art." Well, the performance is no longer slovenly but fairly precise (the La Mama company has by now had considerable practice in its roles), and it's still scandalous. Is poor placement of the camera really what's the matter? One reviewer wrote, "D. H. Lawrence defined obscenity as anything which is anti-life. The Christ which this movie continually mocks, along with everything else, wasn't life-denying. Not even Nietzsche in his *Anti-Christ* lays that blame on the man. *Futz* is. I am opposed to any form of censorship for adults. But *Futz* strains that conviction. It's a depraving movie — watching it one can only be sickened, or, I think, ashamed." That review appeared in the *New York Review of Sex & Politics,* and in those pages it may seem like flipping out. But though I think this view is overwrought and overstated (I don't consider the movie "depraving"), it may be a more honest response than to deal with *Futz* strictly at the level of technique. The production is gross and mean-spirited. The way O'Horgan uses the actors — their general cretinous, white-trash piggishness, with snouts and tongues and jaws thrust at the camera and the big girl in the mud like a sow — is mainly just ugly, and it speaks much louder than the supposed message about respect for the rights of individuals. The fact is that though we (particularly critics) may be a little uneasy about appearing to reject a *subject,* we're not really mad to see a play (or a movie) about a hillbilly who loves a pig, especially a verse play about a hillbilly who loves a pig, and this lack of enthusiasm (fully justified though it may be by past experience) is, psychologically, used against us. It's treated as inhibition, and hence the reason we need to be assaulted by this sexy romp and Shocking, Overpowering Experience. The subject certainly isn't appealing, but it's the assault — being subjected to battery by O'Horgan — that's the big offense. Despite the fancy parable-theme that surrounds the production with a liberal moral nimbus, O'Horgan tries to force us to respond to the juicy piggery of it. He treats us with contempt, and he gets back what he gives us.

•

Probably the most moralistic film around is the sex-exploitation film *All the Loving Couples.* It proselytizes for wife-swapping as a way of keeping the American home together. The villain is a young insurance salesman who tries to sully the purity of wife-swapping by getting into a group of Friday-night swingers for business reasons and thus "selling" his wife. The Friday-night regulars include a bush-jacketed Bircher who turns out to be impotent, and a Jew who looks mild but turns out to be a good, strong Indian wrestler and such a fine liberal humanist that he often seems to be addressing a Reform congregation. Because the sex-exploitation filmmakers now have their own association and their own self-policing code (in order to keep the law off), there's actually less nudity in this movie than in many current big-studio pictures; there are glimpses of breasts and rear-view shots of nude women, and that's it. What makes it a sex-exploitation picture is not what it shows but what it's about and the way it conforms to the blatant simple-mindedness of the genre. The casting is rather amusing — especially a very tall girl and a blond giggler and the inevitable refined girl who's there sort-of-by-mistake — and a comic stag movie within the movie has a very good sullen blonde who keeps up a traditional smoker-movie moaning about how hot she is. There are also parody commercials coming in at such regular breaks that you have to remind yourself that you're not watching television. Despite its subject, the movie has a television banality. *All the Loving Couples* domesticates vice. The whip that the amazonian girl displays turns out to be merely a tease. These are not sadists or perverts; they are plain American folks (befitting the company name, Cottage Productions). At times, *All the Loving Couples* lectures us like a government training film: "Orgy is just another name for group therapy," etc. It's message-coated sex — an exploitation film carefully plotted to make you feel you're getting something that's good for you as well as some eye-poppers. The big difference between this picture and old exploitation items like *The Immoral Mr. Teas* is that *Mr. Teas* (a much more inventive and entertaining movie) was still aimed at the old burlesque audience, and this is aimed at the general public — probably the same public that enjoys *The Beverly Hillbillies*.

•

There is a particular kind of shooting and editing that I despise, and *Popcorn* is, almost *in toto*, an example of it. The method is to film very close in, for "immediacy," so the movie is almost all closeups and details, without the "establishing" shots that show you where you are, where the people are in relation to each other, or even what a whole person looks like. When this kind of footage is put together, with details of rock singers and musicians intercut with details of brutality and poverty and death, it all becomes sensation. The kids around me at the theatre recoiled as I did; they had gone to see the Rolling Stones and a rock show, and it's a hell of a way to make a revue to show you animals being butchered in the middle of it. It's perfectly obvious that the "significance" stuff is just padding for the skimpy rock footage, and this makes including it a doubly lousy thing to do. It's bad enough to disappoint an audience without throwing in this pretension to significance. *Popcorn* is a trap: hardly enough footage of the Rolling Stones and a few other groups to make a short, stretched to feature length with surfing, shots of Twiggy, a disc jockey mugging for the camera, a sickeningly cheery singer named Johnny Farnham, a Western gundown, fictional shorts, travelogues, and documentary footage of a cremation in India. There is so little of the good performers, and they are photographed with such overreliance on the zoom and funny-house lenses, that you never get a chance to see them at their best — you hardly see them at all, under the jumping "strobe" cutting and the superimpositions thrown in to make the photography look more exciting. The sound, as you might expect, is post-synched, and rarely in synch. A boy sitting next to me said the picture was for "the uninformed teen-ager." I left before the threatened views of Vietnam and the atomic bomb. I'm told they came on schedule.

[November 29, 1969]

Elfskin

No doubt everyone has his own set of deterrents to moviegoing — subjects and players that make one reluctant to see a movie no matter how good it is reputed to be. Based on rotten experiences in recent years, I don't anticipate much pleasure from:

Brain-damaged heroes *(Charly, The Rain People)*.
Bestiality *(Futz, Pigpen)* and mutilation *(The Night of the Following Day,* recent Westerns).
Virgins driven mad (particularly when played by Sandy Dennis).
Aging virgins (particularly when played by Joanne Woodward).
Anything with Anthony Quinn as a peasant.
Christ figures.
Female self-manipulation *(The Silence, The Fox)*.
Writhing nudes *(Coming Apart)* and symbolic sex *(Hurry Sundown)*.
Labor pains and LSD trips.
Rape (particularly teen-age), robbery (jewels, bank), and spies (particularly comic).
That may suggest that I'm in the wrong job, but there are also promis-

ing subjects, and certain players and writers and directors who make me eager to see a movie no matter how bad it is reputed to be. And so I went to Forty-second Street to see Carl Reiner's *The Comic*, which opened there on a double bill. The life of a silent-film comedian is a potentially great subject, but *The Comic*, like Woody Allen's *Take the Money and Run* and other recent movies involving television performers and writers, is an emaciated little picture. As Billy Bright, Dick Van Dyke has the true manic feeling for the silent-comedy routines, and Mickey Rooney, as his teammate, Cockeye, creates a character out of almost nothing and lives it on the screen so convincingly that one fully expects to see him again after the movie is over, yet they don't have the kind of beauty that the picture should be *about*. I don't think it's their fault — it's Reiner's.

A moderately unbalanced visionary filmmaker once told me that he could see "elfskin," which he explained was "the white light emitted by all living creatures" — though, he said, some gave off more than others. I suppose that he was universalizing what Tolkien ascribes to elves ("They bore no lights, yet as they walked a shimmer, like the light of the moon above the rim of the hills before it rises, seemed to fall about their feet"). Whether or not all living creatures give off a white light, actors must, and, of all actors, comics, the elves of the theatre, must especially. What's depressing about *The Comic* is the total absence of elfskin, the glow that comics emit when they're giving of their best and when everything comes together right. Without it, you have at most a mild, disappointing little comedy; with it, you can have greatness.

When you see a good old comedy, you feel that the people involved gave you everything they had — rehearsing that split-second bit until it would look so perfectly, effortlessly funny that you would laugh every time you thought of it, for days, maybe for years, afterward. Carl Reiner has a prodigious gift for that kind of comic invention, for the details and bits of business that are comic in the greatest movie tradition — the comedy that unites the sophisticated audience and the mass audience. But he doesn't think his story through; he doesn't develop and sustain the characters; he tosses things together. And without a structure to give his bits meaning they don't have enough resonance to be memorable. As fast as they come and go, we forget them, and we're still starved for entertainment when the picture is finished.

Television has been destroying the old show-business belief in giving everything you have to an audience. With the skimpy material they're handed, performers can't give much. And as they go from a movie role or a TV series to the circuit of game shows and talk shows, they reach the peak of celebrity when they're such "big names" that, like Jack Benny and Bob Hope, they no longer need to do anything to be applauded. (The name, like the label on a can, is supposed to certify that the performer is great. The "guest appearance" has come to mean just a flash of the label.) The big-money writers and directors leap from medium to medium; they become so rich and their time is so valuable that they can't *afford* to keep working on a project until they get it right.

In *The Comic*, Reiner uses his subject in the way TV writers use subjects, as a peg to pin some skits and jokes on. He begins with Billy Bright's funeral, where Cockeye, carrying out Billy's instructions, throws a pie at the pontificating eulogist from the Motion Picture Academy. We expect the flashbacks to reveal a Billy consistent with this gesture; what we get is a narrow-minded, self-centered comic — television's idea of hard-hitting realism — and not a clue to what made him great. We see Billy's life fall apart into alcoholism when his wife and leading lady (Michele Lee) leaves him, though we never had any indication that he cared for her. We see him as a money-grubber who can't waste even the crowd at his wedding and photographs it for use. Later, poor and forgotten, he watches on TV a picture he produced and starred in. Reiner has confused the lives of the great comedians (like Chaplin and Lloyd) who retained control of their pictures, and who are rich, with the lives of those who didn't (like Stan Laurel and Keaton). And in thus eliminating the whole business background, and the role of the studios in breaking performers and dumping them, he has left out the factors that might explain the wasted, poverty-stricken lives of some of our greatest talents, discarded in their twenties or thirties. Billy Bright's drunken egomania is used to explain his decline; this is so far from what actually happened to the artists Billy resembles — Stan Laurel and Keaton, who loved what they were doing so much that they left the arithmetic to others — as to be an insult. It's the way Hollywood businessmen like to explain what happened to artists. Surely, of all people, Carl Reiner might have been expected to seize the chance to show how radio and talking pictures altered comedy, and to indicate the different kinds of people who prospered in the sound era, but he doesn't even *try*.

What makes the movie worth attention is Reiner's facility, which is both his vice and his phenomenal talent. Though he apparently hasn't learned anything about the technical side of moviemaking — visually the picture is dead — he has developed a controlled, light touch with the actors (who don't mug, as some did in his *Enter Laughing*). Michele Lee is charming — at times reminiscent of Mary Tyler Moore (and who would quarrel with *that?*) — and, as a mercenary stage mother, Pert Kelton, in her last performance, goes out in glory. But Reiner also throws in the worst kind of TV writing and acting; he uses Steve Allen and Cornel Wilde and himself like empty cans with fancy labels. One feels that if only he would give a movie his full attention and find collaborators who would do the same he could make great comedies — as great as the ones of "the golden era." We have the resources in actors and actresses. Television is full of brilliant performers wearing themselves out or stagnating, dying creatively though they go on performing. It doesn't do to say that they're reaching millions of people and that that's what counts, because they're not really reaching people in the *way* that counts — they're not really satisfying the need for comedy and entertainment that we all share; they provide a constant diet of hors d'oeuvres that sickens and starves us. Reiner is one of the greatest talents in television, yet he just tickles us, he doesn't touch us. He draws back from his subject here before he gets near it, just as he draws back from giving the audience anything it can feel and take away. He seems terrified of trying anything that might have any depth; he has, perhaps, accepted the too limited idea of entertainment that dominates television — an idea that, I think, is based on failure to believe in the audience. Elfskin comes not just from the pains — and the pleasure — that an author takes in working out his ideas but also from the director and the actors caring enough about what they're doing to make it shine. I think you must really *believe in the audience* to do that — believe, that is, that you owe the audience your best. And, given the underdeveloped tastes of the mass audience, you must believe that you owe the audience your best even if it is willing to "love" you for your second best or third best, or for your token presence. A man like Carl Reiner or Woody Allen spreads himself so thin that he may never discover his full self; there just isn't enough of him together at any time in any one place. Now that such men are making movies, they treat the movie audience like the television audience; their movies are as thin as skits.

Maybe I overestimate Reiner — maybe the talent he scatters is all he has. But even that is so great that if he husbanded it he could make comedies that people could really respond to. In the crumbling Forty-second Street picture palace, the people who had gathered there hoping for a little something came out with nothing — once again.

[December 6, 1969]

Exiles

Z is almost intolerably exciting — a political thriller that builds up so much tension that you'll probably feel all knotted up by the time it's over. The young director Costa-Gavras, using everything he knows to drive home his points as effectively as possible, has made something very unusual in European films — a political film with a purpose and, at the same time, a thoroughly commercial film. *Z* is undoubtedly intended as a political act, but it never loses emotional contact with the audience. It derives not from the traditions of the French film but from American gangster movies and prison pictures and anti-Fascist melodramas of the forties *(Cornered, Crossfire, Brute Force, All the King's Men, Edge of Darkness, The Cross of Lorraine,* et al.), and, like those pictures, it has a basically simple point of view. America stopped making this kind of melodrama (melodrama was always the chief vehicle for political thought in our films) during the McCarthy era, so Costa-Gavras has the advantage of bringing back a popular kind of movie and of bringing it back in modern movie style. *Z* has been photographed by Raoul Coutard, Godard's cameraman, in Eastmancolor used in a very strong, almost robust way, and although the photography is perhaps a little too self-consciously dynamic and, at times, not as hard-focussed as it might be, the searching, active style doesn't allow you to get away. Remember when the movie ads used to say, "It will knock you out of your seat"? Well, *Z* damn near does.

There hasn't been an exciting anti-Fascist suspense film around for a long time, and the subject of *Z* is so good that the audience is not likely to resent the use of melodramatic excitement the way it would now if the film were anti-Communist, like those Hollywood films of the early fifties in which our boy Gregory Peck was ferreting out Communist rats. *Z* is based on the novel by the Greek exile Vassili Vassilikos about the assassination of Gregorios Lambrakis, in Salonika, in May, 1963. Lambrakis, it may be recalled, was a professor of medicine at the University of Athens who was also a legislator and a spokesman for peace. He was struck down by a delivery truck as he left a peace meeting — a murder planned to look like an accident. The investigation of his death uncovered such a scandalous network of corruption and illegality in the police and in the government that the leader of the opposition party, George Papandreou, became Premier. But in April, 1967, the military coup d'état overturned the legal government. Z reënacts the murder and the investigation in an attempt to demonstrate how the mechanics of Fascist corruption may be hidden under the mask of law and order; it is a brief on the illegality of the present Greek government.

Jorge Semprun, the Spanish writer, who worked on the screenplay and wrote the dialogue, has said, "Let's not try to reassure ourselves: this type of thing doesn't only happen elsewhere, it happens everywhere." Maybe, but not necessarily in the same way, though some Americans are sure to take the conspiracy in Z as applying to our political assassinations, too. This movie has enough layers of reference without anyone's trying to fit the American political assassinations into it; our freaky loners, on the loose in a large, heterogeneous country, are part of a less tightly structured, more volatile situation. It's ironic that what apparently did happen in the Lambrakis affair should resemble the conspiracy fantasies of Mark Lane and other Americans about the death of President Kennedy. And to see how the network of crime and politics works to conceal the assassination in Z is aesthetically satisfying. One can easily recognize the psychological attraction, for both left and right, of spinning conspiratorial systems that make things grand and orderly. (Z opens with a witty treatment of right-wing paranoia.)

Z could not, of course, be made in Salonika; it was shot in Algeria, in French, as a French-Algerian co-production. The director, Costa-Gavras, is a Greek exile. (He was a teen-age ballet dancer in Greece before going to France, where he studied filmmaking and made his first picture, *The Sleeping Car Murder*.) The score, by Mikis Theodorakis, who is now under house arrest in Greece (where his music is banned), is said to have been smuggled out. Yves Montand, who is the Lambrakis figure here, was recently seen as the Spanish hero of *La Guerre Est Finie,* which Semprun, an exile from Spain, also wrote, and other actors from the Spanish setting turn up here, too. The Algerian locations, being the sites of actual tortures and demonstrations, add their own resonances; the hospital where injured men may be mistreated instead of treated plays its former role. The atmosphere is thus full of echoes, and the movie — consciously, I think — reactivates them. The subject touches off our recollections of Greece, of Algeria, of Spain, which combine to make us feel, "Yes — this is the way it happens," and to evoke images of and fears about all rightist terrorism.

On the one hand, there are the weak and corrupt and degenerate, the bullies and criminals — in a word, the Fascists. On the other, there are the gentle, intelligent, honorable pacifists — in a word, humanitarians. But Costa-Gavras gets by with most of this, because, despite our knowledge that he's leaning on us, he has cast the actors so astutely and kept them so busy that they miraculously escape being stereotypes. Some of them — particularly those who play the right-wing leaders, such as Pierre Dux in the role of a general — manage to suggest more than one notorious political figure. The cast of famous names and faces from the confused, combined past of many other movies forms a familiar, living background. I'm not sure exactly how Costa-Gavras has accomplished it, but in this movie — in contrast to so many other movies — the fact that we vaguely know these people works to his advantage, and enables him to tell the story very swiftly. It does not surprise us that François Périer, as the public prosecutor, is weak; that Renato Salvatori enjoys hitting people; that the magnificent Irene Papas is a suffering widow; that Charles Denner is half-Jewish; that Jean-Louis Trintignant is civilized and intelligent; and so on. All their earlier make-believe characters have merged in our memories; by now, when we see these actors they seem like people we actually used to know. I have sometimes found myself nodding at someone on the street before I realized that that was no old friend, it was David Susskind. There is the same sort of acquaintance with these actors, whom we have come to take for granted, and the ambience of known people seems to authenticate the case.

Not all the elements are convincing. The staging of the crowd at the peace rally and of the police lines surrounding it doesn't feel right; it's confusing that the leader who dies appears to be beaten less than a man who survives; the motives of one of the assassins, who turns himself in, are obscure. Marcel Bozzufi, the actor playing this assassin, gives the most flamboyant performance in the film; it's enjoyable, because the movie needs to be lifted out of its documentary style from time to time, yet you are as much aware of Bozzufi's performance — even though it's a good one — as you were in *Open City* when the Gestapo chief came on faggy. There are scenes, such as Georges Geret acting a shade too comic with an ice pack, and Magali Noel being excessively vicious as his vicious sister, that are too much in the standard Jules Dassin–Edward Dmytryk tradition. And, as in the Hollywood forties, the martyred man is such a perfect nondenominational Good Man — like Victor in *Casablanca* — that one never really understands his politics or why the police and the military want to get rid of him. This is an ironic element in the book, where a possible explanation is offered — that the Fascists were afraid not of the left but of liberals, like this man, who were beginning to coöperate with the Communists. In the movie, though, we get the impression that this pure peacenik-liberal and his friends *are* the left and that they are mistaken for Communists (who probably don't exist at all) by the paranoid right.

But the pace, the staccato editing, the strong sense of forward movement in the storytelling, and that old but almost unfailingly effective melodramatic technique of using loud music to build up the suspense for the violent sequences put so much pressure on you that these details don't detract much. There is a serious flaw at the end, however, where the wrap-up comes too fast. All the way through, Z stays so close to the action that it doesn't explain the larger context, and by the end we have been battered so much that we want to understand more, so that we won't have been riding this roller coaster just for the thrills. The explanations of what happened to whom and how this incident precipitated the change in government, and then the reversals of fortune after the military coup, go by at dizzying speed, and this is a psychological miscalculation. We have an almost physical need for synthesis from a movie as powerful as this. We want to know who was protected by the new rightist regime and who was sacrificed; we want to see the larger political meaning of the events. We don't want just to use the film masochistically, to feed our worst fears or to congratulate ourselves for being emotionally exhausted.

In a thriller, the director's job is to hold you in his grip and keep squeezing you to react the way he wants you to, and Costa-Gavras does his job efficiently — in fact, sensationally. Is it valid, morally, to turn actual political drama — in this case, political tragedy — into political melodrama, like Z? I honestly don't know. The techniques of melodrama are not those of art, but if we accept them when they're used on trivial, fabricated stories (robberies, spy rings, etc.) merely to excite us, how can we reject them when the filmmakers attempt to use them to expose social evils and to dramatize political issues? Yet there is an aesthetic discrepancy when the methods are not worthy of the subject; when coercive, manipulative methods are used on serious subjects, we feel a discomfort that we don't feel when the subjects are trivial. It's one of the deep contradictions in movies that in what should be a great popular, democratic art form ideas of any kind seem to reach the mass audience only by squeezing it. I anticipate that some people may ask, "What's the problem? The movie is telling the truth." And others may say, "Whether it's accurate or not, it's convincing, and that's all a critic need fret about." Neither of these arguments clears away my basic uneasiness about the use of loaded melodramatic techniques, particularly now, when they can be so effectively blended with new semi-documentary methods to produce the illusion of current history caught by the camera. Given the genre, however, the men who made this film have been intelligent and restrained. I don't think Costa-Gavras ever uses violence except to make you hate violence, and such humanitarianism in filmmaking is becoming rare.

Melodrama works so well on the screen, and when it works against the present Greek military government it's hard to think ill of it. People will say of the moviemakers not that they're "laying it on" but that they're "laying it on the line." The truth is, they're doing both. *Z* is a hell of an exciting movie, and it carries you along, though when it's over and you've caught your breath you know perfectly well that its techniques of excitation could as easily be used by a smart Fascist filmmaker, if there were one (fortunately, there isn't), against the left or the center.

•

Alfred the Great appears to be not about the king who burned the cakes but about a movie studio that has been burning money. It is set in the Dark Ages, and it seems to have been made in the Dark Ages of M-G-M. Alfred, it turns out, is another "reluctant" king. (Was there ever a hero-king on the screen who wasn't reluctant?) David Hemmings' Alfred is some sort of sword-swinging pacifist with a Gandhian anti-sex, self-deprivation twist. Hemmings performs much like Tony Curtis in his "Yonder lies da castle of me fodder" days, and Michael York clangs around in funny armor as wild Guthrum, the Danish barbarian who's all aglint for the pleasures of the flesh. When Alfred agrees to give this sexy pagan anyone in his kingdom as a hostage, there can hardly be a child in a movie house anywhere in the world who won't know what poor Alfred can't guess — that Guthrum will take Alfred's bride, Queen Aelhswith. Prunella Ransome, as the sadly neglected Aelhswith, wears lovely gowns and the latest hair styles, but, in the interests of some madman's idea of authenticity, the actors and actresses don't wear skin makeup. It's such a novelty that our attention becomes absolutely riveted on their blotches and blemishes. There isn't much else that's riveting, because the movie begins with murder, rape, and a bloody battle before we know why we should care, and it's execrably edited, as if it sought to keep us dislocated. It is all so terrible that after a while one sits back and counts the money going by on its way to the furnace; between five million and seven million dollars passes before the picture is charred to a halt. *Alfred the Great* is preposterously brutal, with such incidental details as the wholesale ravaging of nuns, but the movie has been made so incompetently that the violence doesn't shock one, as it does in *Z*. It's just director Clive

Donner's way of getting you to pay attention. Vivien Merchant plays a rather mysterious mute. My guess is that after she had read the script she simply refused to speak her lines. Which makes her the smartest person who had any connection with *Alfred the Great*.

[December 13, 1967]

Gloria, the Girl Without Hope

A movie of Horace McCoy's 1935 "classic" Hollywood novel *They Shoot Horses, Don't They?* was long overdue. Like Nathanael West's *The Day of the Locusts, They Shoot Horses* deals not with the movie business but with the people drawn to Los Angeles because that's where the movies come from. In the Depression years especially, it was a gathering place for the rootless and dispossessed, who hoped to find a new life in the movie sunshine. Robert, McCoy's hero, has been scrounging for work around the studios and hoping to become a director; and never doubting that he will, until he meets Gloria, who is young but looks old. Gloria, a would-be actress, got the idea of coming to Hollywood "from the movie magazines" while she was in the hospital recovering from having taken poison. She persuades him to enter a dance marathon with her, so that they can be spotted and maybe get a break in the movies. But in the hundreds of hours they dance together Gloria keeps telling him that she would be better off dead, and she's so bitter and so cruelly negative that she spoils things for everybody, so finally he's convinced that she *would* be better off dead, and when she asks him to shoot her he obliges — without malice or much feeling of any kind. He puts her out of her misery — a mercy killing, a murder from which he is totally estranged; the novel, which is in the American tough-guy tradition, is a home-grown, unassuming precursor of Camus's *The Stranger*. The story, which begins with Gloria's account of her suicide attempt and ends with her death, is narrated by Robert, presumably while the judge is sentencing him to be hanged.

McCoy, who worked as a scenarist on some seventy movies before his death, in 1955, had already written the scenario in the novel, as Dashiell Hammett had done even earlier in *The Maltese Falcon;* that whole school of hardboiled American writers who simplified fiction to the fast, objective narrative style of describing what the characters did and what they said were, whether intentionally or not, writing in scenario form. If the printers had laid out their novels a little differently, the job of "adaptation" would have been done. (One might have expected American fiction to become more introspective as the movies "took over" action and dialogue, but the tough-guy fiction ran on a parallel track.) Intermittently over the years, there had been talk of filming *They Shoot Horses, Don't They?* — as there has been talking of filming all the key Hollywood novels. But when Hollywood novels have been filmed, they have generally been badly done, and have done badly besides. *They Shoot Horses,* however, had a great photogenic thirties subject — the marathon dance contest — and in the movie the Hollywood-novel aspect of the story has been deëmphasized.

If the story needed to be changed for the movie, it needed, perhaps, to be lightened; instead, it has been adapted with a sledgehammer touch, and for cosmic reverberations. There are thudders like "The whole damn world's like one big Central Casting — and they got it all rigged before you ever show up," and at the finale the master of ceremonies describes the contest still going on: "These wonderful, wonderful kids still struggling, still hoping while the Clock of Fate ticks away. While the Dance of Destiny continues. While the Marathon goes on and on and on and on. How long can they last?" In the novel, the men running the marathon were reasonably fair, and when the police stopped the contest the promoter divided up the prize money among the contestants, and even threw in an extra thousand. In the movie, the marathon is rigged so that no one will get any money. The contestants are all pursuing an illusion, and the marathon is thus turned into a dance of death that *justifies* Gloria's feeling that no one can win. The added incidents, such as the heart attack of one contestant (Red Buttons) as Gloria carries him on her back, and the flip-out of another (Susannah York), are well played and are effective in themselves (though the latter reeks of old Isabel Jewell movies), but they confirm Gloria's hopelessness. McCoy's hardboiled story stayed within its small frame; that's what was clean and good about it. But the moviemakers want to be more significant and more symbolic. Their approach throws the plot mechanism out of balance — as their additions support Gloria's cynicism, she seems tough and hard in a knowing way, and a survivor rather than a girl who is driven to suicide. She seems stronger than anyone else. So when she quits the marathon, the movie collapses, and when she asks Robert to kill her we just don't believe it.

I have dwelt on the novel because I think some elements in the movie (particularly at the end) are incomprehensible if one doesn't know the original story. Obviously, moviemakers have a right to alter their material, but the material here has been altered so that it doesn't make sense. It doesn't even make good *commercial* sense; the moviemakers have sacrificed McCoy's plain story and his sane, balanced view of the marathon-dancing phenomenon for a banally "philosophic" microcosm-allegory that has already led some reviewers to make such remarks as "One of the phenomena of America's Depression days was the marathon dance, which turned into a national orgy of hunger, physical exhaustion, greed, despair, and downright brutality" and "Screenwriters James Poe and Robert E. Thompson and director Sydney Pollack convey the message that there is no justice." Sometimes it's hard to know what goes on in the heads of the moviemakers who labor to put in such deep-think messages and in the heads of the reviewers who so eagerly receive them. Marathon dancing was about as much of a "national orgy" as goldfish-swallowing or the roller derby.

Though it staggers under this heavy load, *They Shoot Horses, Don't They?* is a very striking movie, with vestiges of the hard sarcasm of thirties lower-depths humor — those acrid sick jokes that make one wince and laugh simultaneously. Sydney Pollack is not an imaginative director, or inventive, but he stages a big, macabre elimination-race scene terrifyingly well, and he keeps the grisly central situation going with that special energy and drive that often make American movies more exciting and more fun to watch than even the best European movies. Though in this picture Pollack doesn't rise much above a high level of competence, he doesn't botch things, either. He keeps very tight control of the actors, and they work well with him — in some cases, better than ever. The adapters have written a good role for Gig Young as the promoter-m.c.; he's a crude barker who in his pitches on the microphone cheapens every human emotion, but he's also sensitive and empathic, and he knows how to handle people in crises — partly, one gathers, because he has been among people in ugly messes all his seamy life. A contrasting character, a hopeful pregnant girl, is played by Bonnie Bedelia, who sings "The Best Things in Life Are Free" in a lovely voice that, in the harrowing relentlessness of this movie, fills one with gratitude — it's like a reprieve. Robert, however, needs to be defined in some way so that his *acte gratuit* makes sense to us, if not to him. The adapters may have thought they were making him an Existential hero by giving him no reactions or motivations, but instead they just made him a weak character — a vacuum in the picture. Michael Sarrazin, who demonstrated his abilities in earlier work, is lost. Robert wanders around looking calf-eyed and vaguely benumbed, and I wouldn't be surprised if some people take him for a mild psychopath.

Fortunately, Gloria, who is the raw nerve of the movie, is played by Jane Fonda, who has been a charming, witty nudie cutie in recent years and now gets a chance at an archetypal character. Sharp-tongued Gloria, the hard, defiantly masochistic girl who expects nothing and gets it, the girl who thinks the worst of everybody and makes everybody act it out, the girl who can't ask anybody for anything except death, is the strongest role an American actress has had on the screen this year. Jane Fonda goes all the way with it, as screen actresses rarely do once they become stars. She doesn't try to save some ladylike part of herself, the way even a good actress like Audrey Hepburn does, peeping at us from behind "vulgar" roles to assure us she's not really like that. Jane Fonda gives herself totally to the embodiment of this isolated, morbid girl who is determined to be on her own, who can't let go and trust anybody, who is so afraid of being gullible that she can't live. Gloria is not just without false hope but without hope; she's not an easy girl to like when she goads the pregnant woman to get rid of her baby or when she rebuffs all gestures of comfort or sympathy. Jane Fonda makes one understand the self-destructive courage of a certain kind of loner, and because she has the true star's gift of drawing one to her emotionally even when the character she plays is repellent, her Gloria, like Bogart's Fred C. Dobbs, is one of those complex creations who live on as part of our shared experience. Jane Fonda stands a good chance of personifying American tensions and dominating our movies in the seventies as Bette Davis did in the thirties; if so, Gloria will be but one in a gallery of brilliant American characters.

They Shoot Horses, Don't They? would be more compelling and give much more pleasure to the audience if the moviemakers had not employed a grotesquely inefficient storytelling device — the flash-forward. One reason people who are not forewarned may take the hero for some kind of nightmare-ridden nut is that we get flash-forwards of him behind bars and on trial; it's easy to mistake these for his past or for visions. The flash-forwards are a disgraceful example of *nouveau* artistry; they present material that we are not yet prepared to assimilate, and that many people are sure to misinterpret, because, in a melodrama like this, flash-forwards *feel* like memories or premonitions. With the whole movie looking strange and unrealistically dark (macabre lighting and a lot of brown tones), and the flash-forwards even more oppressive (in midnight blues), how can an audience reasonably be expected to understand that it's being given glimpses of the actual future? In the marathon dance, one sees the people deteriorating physically in the speeded-up continuity of a testing situation; the main body of the picture was apparently shot in continuity, and that helps to make the deterioration convincing. As a screen subject, the marathon dance is "a natural," not because of its corny allegorical possibilities but because movies are ideally equipped to show us what happens to people in unusual situations under incredible stress. To break into something like this with the latest devices that have some French cachet is to betray the kind of insecurity that is turning big-studio American movies into an embarrassment. And, to compound the folly, the movie opens with a flashback that is presumably triggered by an *implicit* flash-forward. This little madness is meant to act out the title metaphor for us — as if we needed it — though what we see is two people who seem to be hunting horses. They're following a stallion with a shotgun, waiting for him to need shooting. And when he falls down, they proceed to shoot him, although he may just have a pain in his chest or acid indigestion. And, oh, these movie men, with their misplaced romantic imagery, giving us a wild, beautiful stallion running free before it stumbles instead of Old Nellie, the plow horse that McCoy's hero remembered, who was hitched to the plow when she broke her leg and still hitched to the plow when she was shot.

•

Anyone who says anything against a trifle like *John and Mary* risks appearing ridiculous, for it's the merest gossamer of a movie, but that gossamer littleness, which is intended to be ever so appealing, leaves a bad aftertaste, because there's so much calculation involved in keeping this picture wispy-small. One can feel the presence of regiments of advisers and technicians hiding behind the butterfly's wing and trying to make it iridescent; we're so conscious of them that the movie never leaves the ground. *John and Mary* latches on to the latest imaginary life style and sells it back to the narcissists of "now" consumer goods — like selling the snake its own tail. It's so damned cleverly manufactured to be skimpy and insubstantial and to tie in with the very latest totally non-controversial commodities. It's about people whose highest aspiration is to cuddle, and the computerized formula includes American equivalents of the romantic ingredients that made *A Man and a Woman* such a misty-eyed, hand-holding, let's-go-to-bed hit. This time, it's the man (Dustin Hoffman) who has the block — not a sexual one but reservations about opening his life to feeling — and it's the understanding little girl (Mia Farrow) who sticks around until the block is overcome. And in case we didn't know that *John and Mary* is up-to-the-minute from the accoutrements and the people's chic jobs and nuanced attitudes, there's the new political quietism of the let's-get-away-from-it-all-and-cuddle generation. The source of the hero's suspiciousness and his fear of being "open" is that his mother was too busy demonstrating (for Biafran relief and other causes) to make a home for him.

Mia Farrow's eyes are like headlights, but she's adorable in a beautiful little sick-kitten way. Everyone understood that the old fragile heroines — the Depression waifs like Loretta Young in *A Man's Castle* — needed to get well, and it's rather frightening that this little rabbit looking for a hutch is presented as a modern ideal. The waif who has done it to herself — made herself a sprite and put herself outside the range of normal possibilities — may have a momentary appeal, but, like that other bizarre waif-actress, Luise Rainer, whose career was short-lived, Mia Farrow is beginning to strain her "delicious" mannerisms. Every tiny lick of the lips is just too vixenish; the inner-directed smile, the childlike movements, and the odd little voice are getting rather creepy. But Dustin Hoffman draws upon his astute knowledge of the audience's good will toward him and does well, and Michael Tolan is shrewdly personable as a senator — and particularly attractive here because he behaves like an adult. This movie is supposed to be about two people who have sex the first time they meet and whose *subsequent* romance we observe. But taking Peter Pan home to bed doesn't seem very sexual. Both John and Mary are far more infantile than the Johns and Marys in the old necking-only-until-marriage movies, and the super-subtleties of their "mating rituals" are childish. When she phones home, he feels she's broken the mood and spoiled everything. These hairbreadth nuances are like a childish parody of Nichols and May routines, yet the movie is selling just this brand of romantic infantilism — babes-in-the-wood in bed and in love. John Mortimer wrote the script with perfect market pitch, and Peter Yates directed with an infallible eye for success, so they can't really be faulted except for their intentions, and for their failure to make the film truly lyrical or magically romantic. It's fast and very deftly edited, however — a shrewdly contrived product. Reviewing this perfect nothing of a movie is rather degrading: it's like giving consumer hints on the latest expensive, worthless gift for the person who has everything.

•

Gaily, Gaily should be wonderful: Ben Hecht's reminiscences and fantasies about his early years as a Chicago newspaperman are marvellous movie material — evocative, good-humored, full of life. A good subject, a charming plot, and not too bad a script (by Abram S. Ginnes) have been lost along the way in this overproduced period re-creation that is only moderately entertaining. The director, Norman Jewison, tries hard, but he just doesn't have the feeling for Hecht's Chicago; he uses huge mobs and big locations, but the whole movie seems to be on a musical-comedy stage, and the joyous comedy of our corrupt past is turned into picturesque (non-denominational) Americana, overembellished, overplayed, and almost always off target.

As the young Candide-Ben, Beau Bridges has a smiling, engaging presence and, as an older reporter, Brian Keith is, as always, splendid. (The best reason to see the picture is for his timing, and for the way he can deliver an epithet like "You quack!") But the picture bustles around in all directions trying to be lusty, and never discovers how. The scenes of Carl Sandburg reciting a poem and the young hero screaming about political power are really inexcusable. Melina Mercouri is the madam of a bordello that looks as big as the Ritz; she seems to have been encouraged to act like a tempestuous drag queen of the forties, and she is allowed to sing in a post-Dietrich style. There's also a revolting, condescending performance as a politician by Hume Cronyn (who has become my least favorite actor now that Ernest Borgnine has improved somewhat). Jewison so consistently puts the camera in the ornately wrong place that the whole picture begins to be decorative and "artistic" — just what Ben Hecht, the greatest American screenwriter, hated most in movies. When Jewison opens a scene through jewelled droplets on a window, one can almost hear Hecht roaring obscenities. The man who wrote the final script of *Gone With the Wind* * without reading the book, the man who provided the classic comic descriptions of how the picture business falsifies material would have appreciated the joke of the 1910 demonstrators in this movie gathering outside the Chicago Board of Trade with placards calling for "Love."

[December 20, 1969]

---

* Officially the credit (and Academy Award) went (posthumously) to Sidney Howard, who had prepared the first treatment.

Americana

There was a moment early in *The Reivers* when I became rather apprehensive: Ned McCaslin (Rupert Crosse), Negro kin to a Southern white family, who hasn't learned to drive, takes the family's gleaming new 1905 Winton Flyer on a comically uncontrolled drive through town (Jefferson, Mississippi). It felt so much like those passages in old movies that embarrass everyone that I couldn't imagine what the moviemakers thought they were doing. But when the car comes to a halt, the family's white handyman and official chauffeur, Boon (Steve McQueen), is so beside himself with rage at Ned for endangering the car that he wants to kill him, and one can relax, because Boon, punching away at Ned, is furious without the slightest condescension. Then we remember that we are in William Faulkner country and that we need not have worried. Rupert Crosse's Ned is probably the best Negro character on the screen since Juano Hernández' Lucas Beauchamp in *Intruder in the Dust*. Not that there haven't been marvellous performances by black actors (Sidney Poitier has been one of the best reasons for going to the movies these last two decades), but there haven't been *characters* one remembers, like Lucas and Ned — multidimensional, with individual sensibilities and temperaments, the kind of characters who suddenly turn facets to you that you hadn't guessed were there. Ned is a man of sudden impulses who takes sublime satisfaction in carrying them out. Crosse makes him immensely likable: Ned seems to skip through life without a care, in some bizarre way that captures the imagination. He's like a living, walking sense of humor. I had the illiterate notion that the title of the movie had something to do with threshing, or maybe husking corn, but it turns out to be a variant of "robbers," and the picture is about how Boon and Ned and another McCaslin, twelve-year-old Lucius (Mitch Vogel), steal that same yellow Winton Flyer — a dream of a car, magical then and now — for a trip to Memphis, Tennessee, the nearest sin city.

When the director, Mark Rydell, isn't sure how to do things, he overdoes them. He's good with the actors and he obviously loves the material, but he grabs at our emotions with arch closeups and forces the incidents to be too beguiling, so at times *The Reivers* seems to be rogue Disney. And the movie is sweet enough and rollicking enough without the score's constantly reminding us to appreciate how darling everything is; the music is like a fungus that cheeps and chirrups. But the script, by Irving Ravetch and Harriet Frank, Jr. — who tapped this popular vein in Faulkner ten years ago, with *The Long, Hot Summer* — has great charm, of the *Our Town* and *Ah, Wilderness!* sort, though the narration, by Burgess Meredith, in a jocular-avuncular style, is dismaying. It's identifiably Burgess Meredith's voice — so distinctively his that the fiction that it belongs to Lucius as a grown man is unacceptably artificial. It is perhaps the true price of fame that one cannot lose one's identity when ones wishes to — though, indeed, Meredith carries on so characteristically that he hardly seems to be aware of any problem. As Boon's character never really emerges, it's fortunate that Steve McQueen is one of those rare modern actors whose presence carries the right kind of familiarity; he's ingratiating, and that's enough here. His harlot bride-to-be is played with a nice pungency by Sharon Farrell, who isn't afraid to give her role some contrasting elements. The madam of the Memphis whorehouse is played by the late Ruth White, and Juano Hernández himself turns up in a good small role as Uncle Possum.

The Reivers is marred by such instances of self-consciousness as Boon's saying to Lucius, "If you're going to reach your manhood, you have to say goodbye to the things you are and hello to the things you're not." It's as if they'd left in the "statement of theme" that's used to impress the money men. But the movie is a Faulkner tall-tale comedy celebrating the fun of storytelling, and it's epitomized by Rupert Crosse's slightly snaggle-toothed grin. I wish *The Reivers* were better done, but it does make one feel good.

•

Surely we've earned this bit of affectionate Americana; we have to have a little balance. If Americans have always been as ugly and brutal and hypocritical as some of our current movies keep telling us, there's nothing for us to do but commit genosuicide. That's what *Tell Them Willie Boy Is Here* suggests we should do. American self-hatred has reached such a point that the movies are selling it, and projecting it onto the American past as well as into present-day stories. The movie of *They Shoot Horses, Don't They?*, for example, a hardboiled story turned into a macabre fantasy of the thirties, belongs to the same nightmare world as *Midnight Cowboy*. At the movies this year, I've sometimes had the feeling that audiences respond so intensely and with such satisfaction to paranoid visions because they believe that America is collapsing and that they can't stop the apocalypse, so they might as well get it to happen sooner and get their fears confirmed and have it over with. They're on the *side* of apocalypse: since they feel it's all going down anyway, it seems to make them feel better to see these movies saying that it *should* go down, that that's *right*. And now here's a movie that goes all the way — turning white Americans into a race carrying blood guilt, a race whose civilization must be destroyed. *Tell Them Willie Boy Is Here* does not, however, use the currently fashionable idioms of America-the-horrible movies; it isn't in the fractured Modern Gothic style that is as sensational and overpowering as a trip through a madhouse. It is a solemnly measured Western with the thesis explicated by symbolic characters, allusions, and heavy ironies. In a very curious ideological way — more forties movie than late sixties — *Tell Them Willie Boy Is Here* attempts rationally to *prove* its apocalyptic message that we must all go down together in flames — because we deserve to. I think that for this message (which I find deeply questionable anyway) its technique is a mistake; when we're presented with an *argument* for the glories of Willie's self-destructive behavior, we reject it.

Onto the simple story of an Indian (Willie is well played by Robert Blake) in California in 1909 who kills another Indian, the father of his girl (she is not well played by Katharine Ross, though Lord knows what she should have done), the writer-director Abraham Polonsky has grafted enough schematic Marxism and Freudianism and New Left guerrilla Existentialism and just plain new-style American self-hatred so that every damned line of dialogue in the picture becomes "meaningful." There isn't a character who doesn't make points and stand for various political forces, and the sheriff (Robert Redford) is named Coop so that his actions will symbolize the ultimate cowardice and failure of the Gary Cooper hero figures. The movie is loaded with references to fears of a Presidential assassination, so we'll know that even in 1909 we were a bloody, brutal, violent, no-good nation, and the woman doctor (Susan Clark, whom I like less each time I see her, and I didn't like her to start with) who is superintendent of the reservation is a patronizing-to-Indians liberal — the ultimate villainess. Ashamed of her sexuality (like all liberals, in this schematic view), she is given such lines as — to Redford — "I use you the way you use me." (Most women in the audience will probably think, Lucky you.) The movie seems to be composed of a series of obligatory scenes: Willie goes to a bar in order to encounter racists and be insulted; the varieties of racists include Barry Sullivan, who tells us about the fun of stalking Indians and scalping them; and so on. While Willie is given a modern consciousness, the other characters are stuck with period attitudes and false postures that, in this symbolic context, make them seem like monsters, until, at the end, Redford, having shot and killed the unarmed Willie, has a big Lady Macbeth scene, trying to clean his bloody hands with sand. The picture is shot in an "artistic" style (color de-saturated for barren, dusty landscapes), and is paced deliberately, so that the meanings can sink in. The numbing hopelessness of an *Easy Rider* has emotional appeal; the irrationality and the cool, romantic defeatism are infused with an elegiac sense of American failure. It's easier to dismiss the programmed ideological negativism of *Willie Boy,* which stays on a conscious (almost abstract) level while attempting to demonstrate that we are a nation with bad *instincts*. There's no *regret* — not even the facile tone of regret that made Peter Fonda's Captain America such a sham hero. And one resents being trapped in a picture that says there is no place to go but down when one doesn't believe it, even in the terms of the picture. The message is that compromise is unmanly, that it's better to die — which makes you a hero. It also says that since a black man (the Indian pretense isn't kept up for long) can't trust any white man — not even Coop — there can be no reconciliation of the races, so he should try to bring everything down. That is the only way he can make them know he was here. A strange contradiction, because there won't be anybody around to remember. *Tell Them Willie Boy Is Here* may look impressive abroad; in this country it's not likely to be very satisfying except to black kamikazes and to masochistic white Americans — the kind who want to believe that the corollary of "Black is Beautiful" is "White is Ugly."

•

In the last couple of years, the *auteur* theory of the role of the movie director has, in the general press, evolved into its opposite. Originally, it was a defense of the studio system — and especially of such studio products as Westerns and action pictures — on the ground that those directors who were artists transformed their assignments into works with a personal vision, that they were *auteurs* who could fulfill themselves within the commercial system. It was on the basis of this theory of the superior hack as hidden artist that the movies of men like Raoul Walsh and Samuel Fuller were acclaimed. But people interested in film don't read theoretical articles, so they took the *auteur* theory simply to mean what the word *auteur* suggested — that the director should be the "author" of the film, which is to say, in creative control of the picture. That, of course, is what those of us who argued against the *auteur* theorists' defense of the studio system have always believed. In fact, it's what just about everybody except the studio heads — and the *auteur* theorists — has always believed. By now, the term stands for almost nothing except the idea that the movie director is an artist. But in the reviews of movies there's still a residue of the original theory and its defense of the directors who go on making the same kind of picture in the same way year after year.

The comic underside of the *auteur* theory is that if a man repeats himself unconscionably, his readily apparent tired old gambits can be acclaimed as proof of his great distinctive style. And if he repeats himself to the point of self-parody, then there is the joy of perceiving the old master's brilliant new strokes. I once complained of an obvious backdrop in a street scene in Alfred Hitchcock's *Marnie* to an upholder of the *auteur* theory, who immediately said, "But you missed the point. It's deliberately bad. That's what is so brilliant about it." Hitchcock's new film, *Topaz,* his fifty-first feature, is the same damned spy picture he's been making since the thirties, and it's getting longer, slower, and duller. *Topaz,* which is even worse than *Torn Curtain,* is in the same Red Menace genre, and though it is based on the Leon Uris book about the Cuban missile crisis, and is therefore said to have some basis in fact, I've seen more believable pictures set in Ruritania. The movie will probably be acclaimed as a masterpiece by those who think slow, awkwardly timed scenes and bad setups are deliberately bad; *Topaz* is full of them.

Alfred Hitchcock is an immensely successful, widely honored, rich, famous popular entertainer who has never aspired to be anything else. He used to be the master entertainer of the screen, because he could tease us so cleverly; we enjoyed being wittily manipulated to be tense and afraid and expectant. The plots were usually fantastic, and "the MacGuffin" — what the thieves or spies were after — was a mere pretext for the chases and excitations and thrills. He gave pleasure to the world. But now that he no longer gives pleasurable excitement there are no other dimensions to his work; there is not even "craftsmanship." What tends to happen in the case of commercial moviemakers is that they become deadened to their times and to new work in movies and the other arts; they repeat their old successful subjects and formulas, with diminishing visual interest and with less ingenious editing. A singer with almost no voice left can give a concert that is a triumph of "musicianship" over nature; even a pop singer who loses his voice has his "style" to draw upon — his timing and phrasing and showmanship. And this, though not in such a strikingly obvious way, is what happens to actors and actresses who have learned enough to sustain their careers after their youth and looks are gone; frequently they become better actors because they *must*. But successful movie directors generally deteriorate, not only because of physiological processes but because success has overprotected them, so they don't recognize how their work has declined. Rich, and cut off from the influences of their youth and the pressures to explore new ideas, they go on doing the same old things, which younger men have already taken from them. The embarrassment of *Topaz* is that Hitchcock is lazy and out of touch. I think he really expects us to identify with the waxwork Cuban rightists who are spying for the United States; he really expects us to accept the creaking late-late-show romances, and the Arrow-collar-shaving-cream-ad hero (Frederick Stafford), and all the people who look like cutouts and behave like drab, enervated versions of spies in his earlier, better films. Per-Axel Arosenius, Michel Piccoli, and Philippe Noiret have a few moments, and Roscoe Lee Browne, looking like a dark-skinned Richard Roud, does an amusing turn, but most of the others waste away in their roles. The ideal decent, dedicated American secret-service official is John Forsythe, Mr. Soft Voice himself, the incarnation of effortless, gutless acting. The actors seem to have been selected to be stereotypes, but what Hitchcock thinks they represent may be a long way from what they mean to us.

[December 27, 1969]

Keep Going

The size of *Hello, Dolly!* has a primitive appeal, like the rocket going off onstage in the Christmas show at the Radio City Music Hall. The picture cost over twenty million dollars, and you can see it all; it took gigantic effort, and you can see all of that, too. Like that rocket onstage, it makes one hold one's head and say, "I don't believe it!" It really is hard to believe that people have gone to all this staggeringly unimaginative effort and expense to bring you the biggest movie musical yet. After a noisy hour of amorphous music, frenetic dance, broad acting, and flat dialogue featuring "roguish" humor, Dolly — Barbra Streisand — is alone on a park bench singing "Before the Parade Passes By"; then, standing by a tree, she speaks to her dead husband, Ephraim, and, still alone, she begins to sing again, walking, then running toward us. At that point, with a person on the screen expressing some human feelings, the giant circus comes to life, and in the second half of the movie she energizes and transforms the prancing rubbish.

In *Hello, Dolly!* Streisand has almost nothing to work with. It's a star role, of course — a role that seems to release something triumphant in an actress — but the songs are dismal affairs, with lyrics that make one's teeth ache, and the smirky dialogue might pass for wit among not too bright children. (When Mr. Vandergelder — Walter Matthau — insults Dolly, her snappy retort is "Oh, Mr. Vandergelder, that's the nicest thing you've ever said to me.") The movie is full of that fake, mechanical exhilaration of big Broadway shows — the gut-busting, muscle-straining dance that is meant to wow you. This dancing, like the choral singing, is asexual and unromantic, and goes against the spirit of the little farce plot about the matching up of several pairs of lovers. At the center of all the asexuality, impersonality, and noisy mediocrity, there is Streisand, an actress who uses song as an intensification of emotion. She's not like the singers who are sometimes passable actresses if you don't push them beyond a small range. She opens up such abundance of emotion that it dissolves the coarseness of the role. There's no telling what she *can't* do. Almost unbelievably, she turns this star role back into a woman, so that the show seems to be about something.

Barbra Streisand has a protean, volatile talent that calls for a new era in movie musicals, and burial without rites for these routines designed to work up an audience to such a pitch that the arrival of the glorified-to-paralysis star will "kill them." It's a typical movie-career joke that she should be cast in *Hello, Dolly!,* which is a consummation of the old traditions. When the waiters sing "It's so nice to have you back where you belong" as she enters the Harmonia Gardens of 1890, they could not be more wrong. Streisand is a fine clotheshorse and she enters superbly; she makes this place her own. But she also explodes it. In *Hello, Dolly!* the whole archaic, structured production is surrounding a Happening. When, a moment after the big entrance number, she moves over to the leader of the band, Louis Armstrong, and they sing a duet, it's the true love match of the movie. There they are — immortals — and the "wow-wow-wow" scat sounds that come out of her throat are cries of relief from the restraints of the dumb, unsophisticated show and all those tight, square chorus sounds. Except for this one great scene, Streisand totally dominates the screen whenever she's on. She doesn't seem to have any limitations, but this dominance could become one. It's impossible to tell from her first two movies whether she can act *with* people, because that hasn't yet been required. Great personalities often don't have the gift that sometimes explains the staying power of lesser personalities — the gift of making others look better. Few have it to the degree of Dean Martin, whose ability to give himself over to bringing out the best in his partners is uncanny. Without it, stars operate in a vacuum and risk becoming domineering monsters. It's a good omen that Streisand works with Armstrong with pure love.

The use of the screen as a giant stage in *Hello, Dolly!* is an effective solution to the technical problems of transferring this property to the movies. And the exterior sets, in all their hugeness, are attractive. But the interior of the Harmonia Gardens is a gratuitously, vulgarly opulent set in beer-barrel rococo — full of upholstery and statues and fountains and chandeliers, like a storeroom of all the garbage left over from the Alice Faye–Don Ameche musicals. This set, redolent of every bad operetta ever written, makes all the action in it look unnecessarily ugly — and the director, Gene Kelly, and the choreographer, Michael Kidd, perhaps inspired by the set, have staged in it their most tasteless "show-stopping" dance. There were big, terrible production numbers in thirties movies, too, but they had redeeming qualities — a grandiose, crazy frivolity in the Piccolino and the Continental, and sometimes, as with Busby Berkeley's ambitious, strange ideas, a native American eccentric's invented form of surrealism, as perplexing in its way as the Watts Towers. It's apparent why Kelly and Kidd decided to avoid trick camera effects and the bird's-eye views that infatuated the thirties choreographers, and stay within the giant-stage concept, but the dancing itself needs some freedom and folly. The excesses of the thirties choreographers were naïve and funny (even at the time); the excess here is of anxiety and strain, and it's rather painful. The dances are monstrous feats of precision; they seem to have been choreographed by engineers with computer memories. This musical, with more dance than I've seen on the screen in years, has no real solos; it's as if a musical this size were considered too important for individual performers.

So much effort has been expended on the gut-busting things that don't *mean* anything, that have no feeling attached to them — the drilled dancers; the whopping parade; the sad imitations of Comden and Green ideas (and of "A Couple of Swells," from *Easter Parade*) in the number "Elegance" — and so little care has been given to the dialogue or to those supine lyrics, or to the characters. *Hello, Dolly!* is not just a farce about matchmaking; as a musical, it must be a celebration of an end to loneliness. But the three minor pairs matched up don't have any romantic chemistry; there is nothing to link them, and when Michael Crawford, his arms pinched tight to his scarecrow body, sings, in his adolescent-whose-voice-is-changing quaver, "My arms feel sure and strong," you expect his vis-à-vis, Marianne McAndrew, to laugh in his face. And Walter Matthau hasn't been given a hint of sexuality or charm — nothing to explain how Dolly perceives that there is a man for her to bring out from inside that rich miser. In the scene where Dolly arrives at the Harmonia Gardens and stands poised at the top of the stairs — in this entrance that she has planned as the moment to dazzle him, when even the children in the theatre are crying out, "Isn't she beautiful!" — the movie fails to show us Matthau's *response*. Even in terms of their own dumb material, the scriptwriter (the producer, Ernest Lehman) and the director fell asleep at the controls. Couldn't Streisand have been allowed more songs? Kelly is trying so hard for zest and verve; he tries to force it in every production number. But Streisand has it: her energy and exuberance aren't forced; one feels that she's in a straitjacket through most of the dialogue, trying to hold herself down. And when she's given a chance to let her energy out, she's great. She's a very sexy lady, which is what keeps this show from withering away on the screen.

Now that the studios are collapsing, the movie industry has finally recognized what everybody has been telling it for fifteen years — that big, expensive productions are insane, because the hits don't make enough to pay for the blockbuster flops. But now it has decided that since big, expensive movies are "dead" (there's no financing for future ones), the musical as a movie form is dead. Darryl F. Zanuck says you can't make little musicals, and the rest of the industry seems to concur. I think they're dead wrong. I love musicals, but I hate big, expensive musicals, because I have to wade through all the filler of production values to get to what I want to see, and I suspect there are millions of people who feel the same way. Do the moviemakers think we go to musicals for the *sets?* Or for those big orchestral arrangements? The great moments in this movie are not the big production numbers, and they rarely have been in other musicals. Big, expensive chorus lines serve mainly a camp function, and even this can be managed with a few performers, as the choreographer Danny Daniels demonstrated in *The Night They Raided Minsky's*. What we enjoy in *Hello, Dolly!* are the solo in the park; Streisand's "Hello, Dolly!" solo and the moments with Armstrong; her blazing, raucous "So Long, Dearie" song to Matthau, when she satirizes her own energy; and the lovely seconds near the end when they dance. In these moments, she makes you believe that she could bring warmth and life into a dull existence, because she does it for this Barnum and Bailey movie. And for these we endure the rest — to see her even in a bad role. We know that this bossy, overbearing woman, a role that has to be overdone to be done at all, is not what she should play — that, in fact, it feeds into what's rather unpleasing in her personality. It's obvious that she should have more delicately conceived roles, but then we've almost always had to settle for the great movie personalities in bad roles and be grateful for that much.

Somewhere along the line, Hollywood got the idea that musicals were "family entertainment" and had to be wholesome and overproduced and full of mugging actors and cloying ingénues and a processed plot and all the rest of the paraphernalia that has made so many people say, "I can't stand musicals." And, as the years went on, the big musicals drew more and more upon just what we liked least in the old ones. (The choreography in *Hello, Dolly!* imitates and draws upon what was worst in *An American in Paris* — the big ballet, which was what I enjoyed that movie *in spite of*.) What is great in musicals is to see talented people doing what they do best, as they used to do in those Paramount musicals in the thirties that cost about fifty cents — as any group of talented people can do on a tiny budget.

When Hollywood gets the kind of "impetuous, overwhelming, absorbing personality" (as Shaw described Ellen Terry) who brings audiences into theatres because she has so much to give, the studios just want her to apply artificial respiration to old Broadway properties. It's a bad joke for these moguls who star Barbra Streisand in a big musical to tell us that a small musical can't be made, when it's her kind of energy and vitality — what she brings to their decaying movies — that are the basic ingredients of the modern renaissance in pop music and rock and blues. Now, at the time when modern classical music, like much of modern theatre, has become enervated, but popular songs are alive, and the whole country is alive to their force — at just the time for great new movie musicals — the moguls who can't see any farther than the end of their cigars tell us that the form is dead. For them, a musical is something with a score by Leslie Bricusse or Jerry Herman. This should be the best time for movie musicals since the early thirties, when the talkies took up the great revue stars of the stage — Fanny Brice, Astaire, and the Marx Brothers and all the rest. But while the studios that tried to imitate *The Sound of Music* are preparing to destroy themselves again by imitating exploitation films and "wheelers" (*Easy Rider* and the Westerns on motorcycles, like *The Wild Angels*, that *Easy Rider* grew out of), the personalities and talents that could restore American movies are not available on film. Don't the studios know that there is an audience ready and waiting for Aretha Franklin and Grace Slick and Janis Joplin and Flip Wilson and dozens of others? American movies did less with Ray Charles in the fifties and sixties than they did with Fats Waller in the first years of talkies. College students keep going to old W. C. Fields films that cost *less* than fifty cents, and Jonathan Winters, maybe the most wildly imaginative comedian who ever lived, has yet to be really unleashed in a movie so that he can show what he can do. Of course, he'll be hard to use, but so was Fields; they had to let him take off and improvise.

Barbra Streisand needs to be liberated from period clothes and big-studio musical arrangements, so that her modern, urban, unpretentious humor can be fully let out. Obviously, she's already too big a star for shoestring movies, but a musical can cost two or three million instead of twenty plus. Streisand could inaugurate a new kind of musical, because she uses song as Astaire used dance, expressively, to complete a role and make it a myth. I can't think of any single greater waste of screen talent than there would be if, because of the new economic calculations about musicals, this actress-singer decided to turn to straight acting roles. She would be abandoning her true singularity — her ability to extend a character in song. Inexpensive musicals could use her talent and the talents of comedians, singers, and dancers — and, please God, new scenarists and new songwriters — and allow them some freedom, in a way that a blockbuster like *Hello, Dolly!* doesn't. When Louis Armstrong sings to Streisand, "You're still glowin', you're still crowin', you're still goin' strong," one wants them to dump the movie and just keep going. And that's what people could do in a small musical.

•

The latest episode in the super-serial of the sixties, the new James Bond thriller, *On Her Majesty's Secret Service,* is set mainly in Switzerland, and it's marvellous fun. It introduces a new Bond, George Lazenby, who's quite a dull fellow, and the script isn't much, either, but the movie is exciting anyway. The director, Peter Hunt, is a wizard at action sequences, particularly an ethereal ski chase that you know is a classic while you're goggling at it, and a mean, fast bobsled chase that is shot and edited like nothing I've ever seen before. I know that on one level it's not worth doing, but it sure has been done brilliantly. Diana Rigg is a tall, amusing Mrs. Bond; it's a shame they kill her off (in a bad "sincere" ending). A wife never hurt Nick Charles, and the Bond figure is beginning to need all the help he can get. Gabriele Ferzetti (the hero of *L'Avventura,* who is aging to look like Olivier) is an amiable gangster-tycoon; he and Ilse Steppat, the indefatigable villainess, help give the picture some tone.

Marooned, on the other hand, a sci-fi space epic, is total, straight Dullsville. John Sturges is becoming the most sedate director in the business; working with a script that sounds as if the author had never met a human being, he's out there in space, walking heavy. Who in his right mind would cast the three leads with Gregory Peck, Richard Crenna, and David Janssen, when anybody can see they're all the same man? At times, this picture seems like a straight-faced parody of nice-guy, concerned-American stereotypes, and the dummies in space have left dumdum wives below. The sanctimonious chitchat of these ladies gets the only laughs in the movie — horselaughs. The final few minutes, with a rescue operation somewhere in space, are fairly tense, but the picture has already died.

•

I have rarely seen a picture I enjoyed less than *The Damned,* a ponderously perverse spectacle by Luchino Visconti. There are, of course, people for whom anything to do with Nazi decadence pushes a button marked "True and Great," but still these rotten, scheming degenerates who look like werewolves talking politics while green lights play on their faces are rather much. When the young hero's impersonation of Marlene Dietrich is interrupted by the news that "in Berlin, the Reichstag is burning," he goes into a snit. Visconti is grimly serious about all this curling-lip-and-thin-eyebrow decadence. He has everything he needs for his centerpiece — the orgy and massacre of Roehm's homosexual Brown Shirts — including the gorgeous naked boys in black lace panties, but he can't seem to make up his mind why he's showing it all to us. My candidate for silliest lurid sequence of the year is the Krupp-Borgia Baroness (Ingrid Thulin) lying in bed with her lover (Dirk Bogarde), her face green and her eyes deeply shadowed in blue, while she talks rapturously of power — "all the power" — and the camera prowls around her body and settles on a giant closeup of her breast.

But I'm making *The Damned* sound like fun, and it isn't, though the depravity is borderline, and if the picture were speeded up a trifle it could be a camp horror film. Visconti is a major director who likes to work on a large scale, synthesizing ideas from the classics, but his work is frequently cold and flawed, and ambitious in ambiguous ways. It's easy to say that the decadence in this movie is a metaphor for Nazism, but it's a dubious metaphor, and I think people take it not as a metaphor but as an *explanation;* I think they really want to believe that German perversions and moral decay were what caused the Second World War. They want to believe in villains who shave their eyebrows and leer a lot — like humorless, Wagnerian Little Foxes. (They can always say that there *was* corruption in Germany and there *were* perverts and psychopaths — and of course there were, just as there are in situations that don't resemble Hitler's Germany.) Anyway, whatever Visconti's intentions are, I think he's not using decadence as a metaphor for Nazism but the reverse: he's using Nazism as a metaphor for decadence and homosexuality. The movie is being sold by a great ad campaign featuring a picture of Martin (Helmut Berger), the transvestite in Dietrich drag, and the words "He was soon to become the second most powerful man in Nazi Germany," but, despite the character given Martin and the fact that he is *played* as a homosexual, he does just about everything except sleep with a man. And the homosexual orgy and massacre are staged immaculately and reverentially, without comment. The movie never deals explicitly with any homosexual relationship, yet, for all the parallels with German history that the mad dynasty in this film goes through, the basic impulse and spirit of the film seem more closely allied to the use of Nazi emblems in *Scorpio Rising* and the wheelers than to political events. It seems to be not so much a political movie as a homosexual fantasy.

The Damned could be ludicrous politically (as I think it is), and a mixture of hatred of the Nazis and fascination with them, and still be emotionally effective. But Visconti, though drawn to excess, lacks the gifts of an F. W. Murnau or a Fritz Lang; he's *carefully* flamboyant. And when you don't have a talent for the grotesque but are nevertheless determined to tell the story of a fag-hag mother (Thulin) who turns her son into a dope-addicted transvestite who molests little girls and eventually beds down with mother — which is too much even for her and turns her into a zombie — it's grotesque, all right. To add to it, the sound and the dialogue are a complete disaster; though some of the actors speak their own English, *The Damned* has all the disadvantages of a dubbed movie — everything sounds stilted and slightly off. The characters are dressed and made up for the thirties, but they talk in a language that belongs to no period or country and sounds like translated subtitles. After the Baroness writhes around in bed, she persuades Bogarde to kill yet another member of her family. "Complicity," he announces, in his usual anguish. Visconti punctuates rapes and murders with dialogue like "I beg you, Konstantin" and "Keep calm, Konstantin, the coup d'état has failed." Martin, the creepy psychopath with two sets of eyebrows (his own and the painted thin ones), complains to his mother of "your will to subjugate me at all costs." It's really a story about a good boy who loves his wicked mother, and how she emasculates him and makes him decadent — the basic mother-son romance of homoerotic literature, dressed up in Nazi drag.

[January 3, 1970]

English Bull

Nicol Williamson is a violently self-conscious actor whose effect on the camera is like that of the singers who used to shatter crystal. And he had the bad fortune to enter movies just when new, strenuous forms of sexual freedom were coming in, so he's gone through more gyrations in a year and a half than most actors do in a long career. He has already run a gamut of sexual positions, plus such assorted Jacobean exertions as drooling, vomiting, murder, and suicide. He goes from being gracelessly virile to being repulsively masochistic, and, whichever it is, he's too much. His racked and tortured energy seems to be irresistible to the English directors he works with; as if in awe of his force, they stand back and let him rage and snivel and curse. They don't often get an actor with a powerful animal presence, and they probably hope Williamson's thumping virility will keep their movies from being dull, but he just flails around like a self-flagellating windmill. A little exhibitionism goes a long way on film; many of us probably flinch every time the ads promise another "tour de force." Williamson is always "brilliant" and "dazzling." He *is* brilliant, he *is* dazzling — yet he's awful. You feel as if he were trying to reach out of the screen and grab you and strong-arm you. The great movie actors know when to cool it and how to relax on camera and just *be*. During the same period, Robert Redford has become a star without ever having had a really good role, because he's an intuitive master of movie technique, of non-actorish readings and minimal gestures; he seems extraordinarily sensitive to the medium, and naturally wary about any inflation of feeling. He's the opposite of a ranter. Williamson is always at white heat. By his fifth movie, it's just about impossible to take his snarling and whining seriously; it's just the Williamson routine. He's so damned electrifying he burns us out.

One easily forgave Williamson the movie version of *Inadmissible Evidence,* because he had been so great in the role on the stage, and because the movie was so badly misconceived that he could hardly be blamed for not saving it. But after *The Bofors Gun, Laughter in the Dark,* and *The Reckoning* (which was made last year but has not yet been released) I walked out on his *Hamlet* and had to force myself to go back and see it to the end. Though much of the blame for the artistic failure of his films must fall on Jack Gold, who directed *The Bofors Gun* and *The Reckoning,* and on Tony Richardson, who directed *Laughter in the Dark* and *Hamlet,* Nicol Williamson is probably the worst major (and greatly gifted) actor on the English-speaking screen today.

The Bofors Gun was supposed to be about a weak upper-class corporal (David Warner) who out of cowardice fails to help an anguished, suicidal Irish serviceman (Williamson). But Williamson's self-destructiveness was so wildly, flamboyantly out of scale — his Irishman was such a drunken, satanic brute — that one simply couldn't imagine how *anybody* could help him, and one's sympathy shifted to the corporal. *The Bofors Gun* was an impossible venture anyway — a movie designed for no conceivable audience — and perhaps this distortion made the film more interesting (and less ideological) than it would otherwise have been. But *Laughter in the Dark* was a good, tawdry movie subject. Tony Richardson is, however, a strange mixture of intelligence and insensitivity, a director with terrible lapses of judgment, and *Laughter in the Dark* was full of them. One could never be quite sure what the tone was meant to be, or whether it was all right to laugh aloud at what appeared to be funny. Nicol Williamson was up there on the screen suffering away to the point of ridicule and beyond, and the director, apparently infatuated with all this great acting, couldn't see what was happening to the picture. Williamson *seems* so brilliant that in his first few movies I thought he would be great if only there were less of him and he could tone down a bit for the camera and get himself under control. I no longer think so; I think the problem is somewhat different, and much deeper.

Williamson has no center as an actor, no core to his characters, nothing one can trust and fall back on. You never have the sense of how his characters would be if things were going well for them; there's no indication of what their normal state would be, no suggestion that his Hamlet was different when the old king was alive. Williamson seems to be trying to find himself — acting-out, like the worst Method-driven American actors. He doesn't mumble inarticulately, like the Method actors; he's overarticulate. But since he reduces words to fast rant and gibberish, the result is about the same — an apparent distrust of language. The frightened eyes, the words sputtered out like tongue twisters from between the gnashing teeth are part of an anti-Establishment explosiveness in English theatre which dates back to Jimmy Porter in *Look Back in Anger* but is only now beginning to find its personification — in Nicol Williamson. That, I would guess, is why Tony Richardson was drawn to mount this *Hamlet* — because Williamson would bring the compulsiveness of the Osborne heroes into the Shakespeare "classic" and thus demonstrate a new, "revolutionary" spirit. If Americans have loved English actors, it has been in large part for their immaculate diction and quiet craftsmanship, in contrast to our own overwrought juveniles' sweating and straining, always *feeling* so much more than they can express. Williamson's surly *Hamlet* is more in the American spirit; his acting is all pathos and vituperation, snarls and tantrums. Yet he isn't really strong; he's such a weeper. Bearded, and with a nasal twang, he's deliberately, wretchedly unattractive. He stares so much he's in danger of wearing out his eyeballs; his Hamlet's troubles could be due to epilepsy as easily as to corruption in the royal house. When Ophelia describes him as having been the glass of fashion and the mold of form, she seems already mad; this Hamlet was *never* the glass of fashion.

The tension is gone, because this Hamlet is not a man who is destroyed by the events we see and by his own divided feelings; he is weak at the outset. He never had "a noble and most sovereign reason" to feign losing, and he is so teary and petulant with his mother that his anger over her remarriage seems a spoiled child's resentment. The play collapses not only as drama but as poetic drama. Williamson's morose, self-pitying Hamlet lacks heroism, and Hamlet's speeches, as Williamson delivers them, lack beauty. Williamson's is the least noble Hamlet imaginable, but if Hamlet is not a prince, what is he? The movie isn't a reinterpretation of *Hamlet* but an exploitation of what's worst in Nicol Williamson as an actor, and Tony Richardson hasn't worked out a conception to back him up.

This *Hamlet* is a claustrophobically enclosed production. The movie was shot in the Round House — the old London engine shed converted into a theatre — where Richardson also staged the play, and it is done almost completely in oppressive closeups, without concern for locating the players in terms of where they are or what they are to each other. The words and the faces are mostly divorced from action, and Richardson has had many of the actors speed up their lines and recite them as if they were worthless. From the darkness and candle flames, it appears to be always nighttime and in limbo, though the railway-shed backgrounds suggest that the action is taking place in tunnels or sewers. A few ramparts and castle sets need not cost very much, so one must assume that Richardson thought this dark-sewer staging would be more effective. Presumably, the other perversities and eccentricities (the lascivious, incestuous Ophelia, Osric as a drag queen, and so on) are also deliberate. There are a few good moments: Roger Livesey's entrance with the players provides the first touch of humanity in the movie; he is in beautiful cracked voice and fine music-hall spirit. Anthony Hopkins, though he is a very young Claudius, has a handsome, Burtonlike authority, but he's so much more appealing than Williamson that one rather wishes Claudius were left in peace to rule the country, since Hamlet is obviously unfit. This is a fundamentally damaged production of *Hamlet* — a great play made into a monotonous and incomprehensible movie. The desire to take the "beauty" out of *Hamlet* and make it abrasive and new is understandable, but this *Hamlet* isn't tragic or absurdist or interestingly modern. It's just cheap Jacobean-Mod, sexed up whenever possible.

•

A Boy Named Charlie Brown is a very sad excuse for a children's picture, a pathetically limp animation feature that barely taps the verbal wit or the great charm of the comic strip it's derived from. It's particularly inexcusable if one has seen the animation short *Windy Day,* which is so fresh in its treatment of childhood fantasies, and which *moves* so beautifully. This lumpy, padded-out feature doesn't even just ramble on — which might be engaging. It rambles and then tries for big effects. *Charlie Brown* is a parasitical film whose makers had no real idea of how to present the "Peanuts" material. Seeing the picture in an audience full of disappointed children is very depressing; it may be the first movie experience for many of them, and it doesn't show them what movies can be. After the first few minutes of eagerness and awe, the incompetence of the moviemakers takes its toll: the noise level (which is the indifference level) in the theatre begins to rise. Are there people who really think the unctuous optimism of the Rod McKuen songs (which are not even in the spirit of the "Peanuts" strip) will appeal to children, or are the songs just another example of cheating the children by appealing to that sickly condescension of fearful parents toward the young? The program at the Radio City Music Hall includes a long short, from Universal Pictures, glorifying the Air Force Academy, and the stage show features the planting of the flag on the moon, with a song about "The astronauts who called the tune/ And put Old Glory on the moon." This crude patriotism is the perfect complement to John Scott Trotter's musical direction in the movie and to the flabby icky-mindedness of McKuen's songs.

For the patient, loving parents who line up with their children — six thousand strong every few hours — hoping to give the children the pleasure of a big holiday show, the "showplace of the nation" is an American disgrace. Only a few blocks from the theatres where great American dancers perform, the sad, klutzy ballerinas of the Music Hall pollute children's first live experience of dance. The only redeeming element of the whole stage-and-screen spectacle is a bit of the pageantry of the stage show — a few pretty calendar-art designs and some trick effects. There was an intelligent letter in the *Times* last Sunday complaining of how young children (including busloads of schoolchildren from "underprivileged" homes) are kept waiting in the freezing cold outside the theatre and of the painful disappointment of those who don't get in. This, though bad enough, is perhaps not so serious in terms of their future lives as the disappointment of those who do get in, and the resulting apathy. Now that, by M.P.A.A. policy, admissions are restricted, children are not getting even the experiences that turned earlier generations into movie lovers. American movies are in an interesting period, but most of the best ones are not available to children. The children are cut off from "adult" entertainment, and nothing is offered in its place that provides comparable pleasure or excitement. It is really incredible that a great nation can be so culturally demoralized that the high point of children's entertainment for hundreds of thousands of people is a visit to a tourist trap. Apathy is one hell of a holiday gift for children, and it's the same gift they're offered all year long.

[January 17, 1970]

Blessed Profanity

*M*A*S*H* is a marvellously unstable comedy, a tough, funny, and sophisticated burlesque of military attitudes that is at the same time a tale of chivalry. It's a sick joke, but it's also generous and romantic — an erratic, episodic film, full of the pleasures of the unexpected. I think it's the closest an American movie has come to the kind of constantly surprising mixture in *Shoot the Piano Player,* though *M*A*S*H* moves so fast that it's over before you have time to think of comparisons. While it's going on, you're busy listening to some of the best overlapping comic dialogue ever recorded. The picture has so much spirit that you keep laughing — and without discomfort, because all the targets *should* be laughed at. The laughter is at the horrors and absurdities of war, and, specifically, at people who flourish in the military bureaucracy. The title letters stand for Mobile Army Surgical Hospital; the heroes, played by Donald Sutherland and Elliott Gould, are combat surgeons patching up casualties a few miles from the front during the Korean war. They do their surgery in style, with humor; they're hip Galahads, saving lives while ragging the military bureaucracy. They are so quick to react to bull — and in startling, unpredictable ways — that the comedy is, at times, almost a poetic fantasy. There's a surreal innocence about the movie; though the setting makes it seem a "black" comedy, it's a cheery "black" comedy. The heroes win at everything. It's a modern kid's dream of glory: Holden Caulfield would, I think, approve of them. They're great surgeons, athletes, dashing men of the world, sexy, full of noblesse oblige, but ruthless to those with pretensions and lethal to hypocrites. They're so good at what they do that even the military brass admires them. They're winners in the war with the Army.

War comedies in the past have usually been about the little guys who foul things up and become heroes by accident (Chaplin in *Shoulder Arms*, Danny Kaye in *Up in Arms*). In that comedy tradition, the sad-sack recruit is too stupid to comprehend military ritual. These heroes are too smart to put up with it. Sutherland and Gould are more like an updated version of Edmund Lowe's and Victor McLaglen's Sergeant Quirt and Captain Flagg from *What Price Glory* and *The Cockeyed World* — movies in which the heroes retain their personal style and their camaraderie in the midst of blood and muck and the general insanity of war. One knows that though what goes on at this surgical station seems utterly crazy, it's only a small distortion of actual wartime situations. The pretty little helicopters delivering the bloody casualties are a surreal image, all right, but part of the authentic surrealism of modern warfare. The jokes the surgeons make about their butchershop work are a form of plain talk. The movie isn't naïve, but it isn't nihilistic, either. The surgery room looks insane and is presented as insane, but as the insanity in which we must preserve the values of sanity and function as sane men. An incompetent doctor is treated as a foul object; competence is one of the values the movie respects — even when it is demonstrated by a nurse (Sally Kellerman) who is a pompous fool. The heroes are always on the side of decency and sanity — that's why they're contemptuous of the bureaucracy. They are heroes *because* they're competent and sane and gallant, and in this insane situation their gallantry takes the form of scabrous comedy. The Quirt and Flagg films were considered highly profane in their day, and I am happy to say that *M*A*S*H*, taking full advantage of the new permissive rating system, is blessedly profane. I've rarely heard four-letter words used so exquisitely well in a movie, used with such efficacy and glee. I salute *M*A*S*H* for its contribution to the art of talking dirty.

The profanity, which is an extension of adolescent humor, is central to the idea of the movie. The silliness of adolescents — compulsively making jokes, seeing the ridiculous in everything — is what makes sanity possible here. The doctor who rejects adolescent behavior flips out. Adolescent pride in skills and games — in mixing a Martini or in devising a fishing lure or in golfing — keeps the men from becoming maniacs. Sutherland and Gould, and Tom Skerritt, as a third surgeon, and a lot of freakishly talented new-to-movies actors are relaxed and loose in their roles. Their style of acting underscores the point of the picture, which is that people who aren't hung up by pretensions, people who are loose and profane and have some empathy — people who can joke about anything — can function, and maybe even do something useful, in what may appear to be insane circumstances.

There's also a lot of slapstick in the movie, some of it a little like *Operation Mad Ball*, a fifties service comedy that had some great moments but was still tied to a sanctimonious approach to life and love. What holds the disparate elements of *M*A*S*H* together in the precarious balance that is the movie's chief charm is a free-for-all, throwaway attitude. The picture looks as if the people who made it had a good time, as if they played with it and improvised and took some chances. It's elegantly made, and yet it doesn't have that overplanned rigidity of so many Hollywood movies. The cinematography, by Harold E. Stine, is very fine — full of dust and muddy olive-green tones; it has immediacy and the clarity possible in Panavision. The editing and the sound engineering are surprisingly quick-witted. When the dialogue overlaps, you hear just what you should, but it doesn't seem all worked out and set; the sound seems to bounce off things so that the words just catch your ear. The throwaway stuff isn't really thrown away; it all helps to create the free, graceful atmosphere that sustains the movie and keeps it consistently funny. The director, Robert Altman, has a great feel for low-keyed American humor. With the help of Ring Lardner, Jr.'s, script (from a novel by a combat surgeon), Altman has made a real sport of a movie which combines traditional roustabout comedy with modern attitudes. As in other good comedies, there's often a mixture of what seems perfectly straight stuff and what seems incredible fantasy, and yet when we try to say which is which we can't. *M*A*S*H* affects us on a bewildering number of levels, like the Radio Tokyo versions of American songs on the camp loudspeaker system. All this may sound more like a testimonial than a review, but I don't know when I've had such a good time at a movie. Many of the best recent American movies leave you feeling that there's nothing to do but get stoned and die, that that's your proper fate as an American. This movie heals a breach in American movies: it's hip but it isn't hopeless. A surgical hospital where the doctors' hands are lost in chests and guts is certainly an unlikely subject for a comedy, but I think *M*A*S*H* is the best American war comedy since sound came in, and the sanest American movie of recent years.

•

Anne of the Thousand Days isn't exciting, but it's fairly civilized entertainment — well acted and with much sharper dialogue than the original Maxwell Anderson play. The movie is a companion piece to *A Man for All Seasons,* dealing with the events that led Henry VIII to make himself head of the Church of England. As Henry, Richard Burton is rather good; he delivers his lines with considerable sureness and style, and yet his performance is colorless, with more craftsmanship than vitality. It's almost as if he *remembered* how to act but couldn't work up much enthusiasm or involvement. He seems too weary even for the way the role is conceived here. Henry in this version is a weak, tentative, somewhat apologetic monarch, a man willing to be deceived by his advisers if that will spare his conscience. This isn't unlikely, but it isn't dramatically satisfying. The whole point of historical drama is to make history spring to life by showing us the emotions of the people who determined the events. From line to line, *Anne of the Thousand Days* is intelligent, but the emotions that are supplied seem hypothetical and doubtful, and the conception lacks authority. Charles Laughton's image, in *The Private Life of Henry VIII,* will probably remain stronger (even for those who see it only on television) than Burton's. Laughton's Henry was a greedy, vain man who could act out his impulses because he was king. Burton's Henry is less vain and greedy but also less human, and not a very impressive king, either. Burton and Genevieve Bujold, as Anne, don't seem big enough — their passions are not strong enough — for the events that Henry VIII and Anne Boleyn set in motion. You don't believe that Henry is going to fight Rome for this little girl.

In this version, Anne Boleyn is a clever, wily, sexually experienced young girl who keeps the King waiting for her sexual favors for six years — until he can marry her and make their children heirs to the throne.

95

Genevieve Bujold works at the role with all her will and intelligence. Her readings are superb — really quite phenomenal when one considers that English is not her native language (and has been only recently acquired). She's a skillful actress, with remarkable technique, and she does wonders with the part, but she's too tight, too self-contained. One admires her as an actress, but one does not really warm to her. There is something lacking — that emotional, yielding, fluid, instinctive quality of the "born" actress that makes us want to see some actresses with much less technique, and often less intelligence, too. Irene Papas has a small, bad role in this movie, another of her suffering rejected wives, and her lines echo so many of her recent movies that she is almost ludicrous. Yet when Papas is on the screen one is drawn to her, and moved and carried away by her as one is never moved and carried away by Bujold. We are impressed by Bujold, but that's not what we go to movies for — to see a strong studied perforance. She also lacks certain physical tools. Nature simply did not cast this girl in the heroic mold; she doesn't have the nose for tragedy. Her little pug face and her own temperament (which is calculating rather than fiery) should point her in a different direction. I think Genevieve Bujold could become a charming comedienne, because she has a witty command of technique, but whatever it is that makes a great emotional screen star she doesn't have.

Though the dialogue is epigrammatic and often much crisper than one anticipates, the script has a structural weakness: it does not convince us that, after all those years of waiting for Anne, Henry would turn against her when she gives birth to a daughter. Up to then, his passion for a son has not seemed stronger than his passion for her. His hostile reaction to Anne at the birth of Elizabeth comes as a shock and a surprising eccentricity. The birth scene is the turning point in the events here, for in this version Anne is not guilty of the adultery for which she is executed but is framed by Cromwell in order to oblige Henry, and yet this turning point is not satisfactorily explained. If she was not an adulteress, why didn't he give her more time to produce a son? Why did he fall out of love so quickly? The heart of the picture — Henry's crucial dissatisfaction with Anne once he has defied Rome, risked war, and disembowelled his friends to get her — is not accounted for, and so his character and her fate don't make much sense. Henry seems to feel so little love for Anne once he's got her, and so little pain about killing her, that it's hard to believe he has much feeling of any kind. And that doesn't make for much of a historical drama.

Charles Jarrott, who directed, is inept at action and pageantry, and the picture is often static, but Jarrott is good with the actors and he keeps the issues and the dialogue intelligible. John Colicos, whose Cromwell is in the amusingly wicked tradition of Martin Kosleck's scheming Nazis, and Michael Hordern as Anne's father and Anthony Quayle as Wolsey all act away happily in their plummy roles. However, Jarrott's attempt at a big, lingering exit for Quayle fails to come off; it assumes that we feel more about Wolsey's loss of power than we do, and it's reminiscent of too many other fake "great moments" when the camera does for an actor what naughty hams all too often do for themselves on the stage. In this poorly lighted movie, there were times when I couldn't tell outdoors from indoors, or day from night; the last time I was similarly confused, the picture had been shot by the same cinematographer, Arthur Ibbetson.

The adapters did not eliminate all of Maxwell Anderson's glowing, fatuous hindsight. Miss Bujold is quite marvellous in some of those speeches that you know are supposed to make your skin tingle and your heart soar, such as Anne's speech of determination that Elizabeth will be queen and of pride that her own blood is well spent. At the end, there is an embarrassingly perfect visual equivalent of the Anderson "O bright ironic gods" style of dramaturgy: a final shot of Anne's posthumous triumph — the baby Elizabeth wandering about, deserted, as her foolish father, who doesn't know what *we* do, goes off to beget a male heir. You might try pinching yourself to work up a bit of tingle.

[January 24, 1970]

The Man Who Loved War

*P*atton runs almost three hours, and there is not a single lyrical moment. The figure of General George Patton, played by George C. Scott, is a Pop hero, but visually the movie is in a style that might be described as imperial. It does not really look quite like any other movie, and that in itself is an achievement (though not necessarily an aesthetic one). The movie was shot in 70-millimetre and in "Dimension 150"; I don't know exactly what that means, but technically the movie is awesomely impressive. It was directed by Franklin J. Schaffner, and it looks a little like the early huge landscapes in his *Planet of the Apes;* the images, typically, are incredibly long, wide shots, taking in vast areas, with the human figures dwarfed by the terrain, and with more compositional use of sky than I've ever before seen in a movie. There's so much land and air — and it's so clear — that we seem to be looking at *Patton* from God's point of view. When Patton is in an interior, the interior is usually that of a castle, with doors opening into rooms beyond rooms in an apparent infinity, and one perceives the necessity for this — the need to keep the interiors consistent with the scale of the exteriors. The landscapes are full of men; the cast must surely run into the tens of thousands. But they're all extras — even the ones that *should* be important. There's really nobody in this movie except George C. Scott.

The Patton shown here appears to be deliberately planned as a Rorschach test. He is what people who believe in military values can see as the true military hero — the red-blooded American who loves to fight and whose crude talk is straight talk. He is also what people who despise militarism can see as the worst kind of red-blooded American mystical maniac who *believes* in fighting; for them, Patton can be the symbolic proof of the madness of the whole military complex. And the picture plays him both ways — crazy and great — and more ways than that, because he's a comic-strip general and even those who are anti-war may love comic strips. I suspect that just for the reason that people can see in it what they already believe, a lot of them are going to think *Patton* is a great movie. I'm sure it will be said that the picture is "true" to Patton and to history, but I think it strings us along and holds out on us. If we don't just want to have our prejudices greased, we'll find it confusing and unsatisfying, because we aren't given enough information to evaluate Patton's actions. *Patton* avoids the clichés of famous men's personal lives by not presenting any personal life. Patton is treated as if he were the spirit of war, yet the movie begs the fundamental question about its hero: Is this the kind of man a country needs when it's at war? Every issue that is raised is left unresolved. Patton is a spit-and-polish disciplinarian and his men win battles. Do men fight better if their shoes are shined? (A boy near me whispered, "The Israelis keep winning victories.") Do men fight better, as Patton indicates, if they fear their leaders? Was Patton a great strategist or did he just follow classic theories? The movie shows us Patton's campaigns, which often seem to be undertaken for personal glory and with indifference to the possible losses, but then it balances this out with suggestions that his strategy was sound, and it doesn't give us enough data to evaluate one judgment or the other. Yet since the movie indicates that Patton can get his men to do more than the other generals can, it implicitly validates his ideas of discipline and of the value of instilling fear, even while showing him as an eyeball-rolling nut.

In approach, *Patton* is a synthesis of a satirical epic like Tony Richardson's *The Charge of the Light Brigade* and the square epic celebrations of the role of the Allies in the Second World War. It's a far-out movie passing as square, and finally passing over. I think the conception was to use Patton as if he'd been dreamed up by Terry Southern. (It's probably not altogether coincidental that Scott played General Buck Turgidson in *Dr. Strangelove*.) But Patton is so much stronger than anyone else that he has glamour and appeal, even for liberals who will take him as the confirmation of their worst nightmares of the military. It could, of course, be a very smart liberal ploy to make Patton a monster-man among mice — to surround him with nonentities and thus present this monster as the true embodiment of military thinking rather than as its distortion — but it backfires by turning him into a hero.

Patton is enormous in scale; it cost more than twelve million dollars. And, with the picture to himself, George C. Scott gives it all his intensity and his baleful magnetism. At the opening, standing in front of a giant American flag, he delivers a long, measured speech while holding the audience in a vise, and he continues to hold us whenever he's on the screen. He has practically all the good lines in the movie. Except for some briefly glimpsed Germans, who, naturally, have the most histrionic uniforms, and who are, by modern convention, elegant and epigrammatic, the movie is full of colorless, unattractive fourth-rate actors impersonating the English and American leaders. As Omar Bradley, Karl Malden is not as offensive as usual — he's merely negligible. If Bradley were presented as a contrasting kind of military leader — a brilliant but civilized officer — we might be able to get our bearings on what Patton is doing right and what he's doing wrong, but Karl Malden just stands around acting "restrained." Probably intentionally, the movie shows no *admirable* military leaders. The actors playing Montgomery and the others could be shoe clerks more easily than great generals. They have no class as actors, and their generals have no class; they're vain, small-minded competitors — mediocrities in drab uniforms. Scott's strength and scale as an actor make him the right hero for the imperial style of the picture, and since no one else has any star quality, the style itself validates him as a hero. It is an index to the oddness of this movie that Patton, the war lover, is so much more compelling than any other character that when Bradley is given the command Patton wants, it seems like injustice.

There are stylistic problems: the informal, dramatic conversations look a bit stiff and posed, as if Schaffner couldn't find a way to make the transitions from the implicit formality of the huge landscapes and horizons. (I point this out with full sympathy for what he was up against.) A larger problem is the continuity: the script doesn't follow through on the sequences presented. For example, the Germans guess Patton's strategy at one point, but we are never told whether they act on their guess or what the repercussions are. We are shown a great desert tank battle in which Patton's men are doing brilliantly until Nazi planes arrive, and then it is not made clear what the result is, or even whether Allied planes arrive, though Patton has been struggling with the British to get air cover for his men. And since we don't know how the scenes of war relate to the strategy of the campaigns, or even how this strategy works out, there is simply too much footage of exploding shells and burning tanks for its own beautiful sake.

The public-relations designation of this film is *Patton: A Salute to a Rebel*. Whom does Twentieth Century-Fox think it's kidding? What was Patton a rebel against except humanitarianism? The ads contain such lines as "*Patton* is a salute to a rebel *with* a cause," and "Patton was a rebel. Long before it became fashionable. He rebelled against the biggest. Eisenhower. Marshall. Montgomery. Against the establishment — and its ideas of warfare." One can scarcely blame the movie for the ads, but the movie is also busy trying to outsmart the public, presenting an arch-authoritarian as a rebel, the way one might present Spiro Agnew as a rebel against effete snobs. The pitch is, of course, that Patton is a straight-talking man opposing the stuffy bureaucrats, and that it's his uninhibited speech that scares them, because although they may agree with him they have to get along with the politicians. The movie is so manipulative that it flirts with the American jingo audience, which will probably agree with Patton even at his most rabid, when he wants to fight the Russians. (*That's* the kind of rebel he was.) And it flirts with the smart young audience, which may think the movie is really "tough" because it shows the military stripped of hypocrisy. The most treacherously clever bit in the movie comes when Patton is in disgrace for having slapped a soldier in a hospital. The Nazis (who throughout the film seem much smarter than the Allies) refuse to believe he isn't still in active command, because they can't imagine that the Americans would pull their best general out of the war for such a reason. It is an irony that will please every bully: See, the Nazis aren't weak and sentimental like us. We in the audience don't know any more about Patton when *Patton* is over, but we've had quite an exhibition of winking at the liberals while selling your heart to the hawks.

"There's nothing to be ashamed of," a woman doctor reassures an elderly man who is crying in misery because he thinks he has cancer and is too deeply humiliated by his symptoms to discuss them. In *Hospital*, a new documentary by Frederick Wiseman, the material does not appear to have been transformed in the editing process. Though Wiseman obviously selects, he does not select in terms of a prearranged structure or for a problem-solving approach, and so our responsiveness to what we see is not limited by an imposed point of view. You feel that the experience is totally naked, that there is no protective tissue between you and the people on the screen. It is as open and revealing as filmed experience has ever been. You look misery in the eye and you realize there's nothing to be ashamed of.

The movie was made at Metropolitan Hospital in New York, but although the hospital conditions are not pretty, it is not an exposé of man's inhumanity to man. The revelation of *Hospital* is the many surprising forms of man's humanity to man: the tenderness of a doctor as he examines an old man, or the doctor's awkward attempt to straighten the covers to make the old man more comfortable; the Puerto Rican who fights hospitalization because he's terrified of not being home to look after his children; the bewildered daughter of a woman who has had a cardiac arrest, trying to comfort her mother, bobbing up to peck her on the chin — the only part accessible for a kiss. It is a melting-pot hospital, and the film demonstrates that the melting-pot dream has to some degree been fulfilled. There are so many human gestures within the misery, such as the solemn "Thank you"s of aged poor patients for whom speech is no longer easy. The general decency of the staff toward the patients may shake cynics, because it is so basically disinterested. It would be pathetically easy to pull rank on these patients who are helplessly dependent on the attention and civility of the staff; the staff doesn't seem to, though. The doctors and nurses are not unctuous in that fake-"professional" fashion of private hospitals; they don't have time for fancy talk, and few of the doctors have the personal style for a bedside manner, or, one gathers, would want to. They sound fairly natural, as if they were people before they were doctors, and they talk to the patients — many of them shattered by isolation and deprivation — in a direct way, without visible condescension. Their occasional crudeness, even roughness, seems to be part of a recognition of the facts of life for the poor in a big city. Only rarely (as with a doctor treating a student on a bad trip) does one have any doubt that they're people of good will doing their damnedest.

In allowing the material to retain its complexity, Wiseman seems to put us back in contact with our common experience. I say "back in contact" because although a film like *Hospital* deals with basic material of our lives, most of us have probably lost sight of that material. At the beginning, *Hospital* seems almost a random view, but as the scenes and details begin to accumulate, the vision takes hold. By the end, we are so thoroughly involved — in a way I think we rarely are in conventional, guided documentary — that tears well up, because we simply have no other means of responding to the intensity of this plain view of the ordinary activities in Metropolitan Hospital. The habitual cant and concealments of most documentaries seem, by contrast, chintzy and puritanical and fundamentally insulting. Movies that spare our feelings assume that there are things we are ashamed to look at. *Hospital* doesn't spare our feelings, and — I don't know exactly how or why — it seems to clean away the shame. We've gone through the barriers of middle-class good taste, and it's better on the other side.

[January 31, 1970]

Duds

The new Luis Buñuel film, *The Milky Way*, is genial, and its tone of cool irony is charming and very distinctive, but an awful lot of Buñuel's little jokes are so clerical and enigmatic that although I could see where a joke was intended, I didn't hear myself laughing. After a while, watching it became a trifle wearisome — like listening to an amiable academician whose recondite anecdotes depend on a familiarity with ancient languages. Buñuel's story — a guided tour of heresies — concerns two pilgrim-tramps and their encounters with the Devil, the Virgin Mary, people who are arguing about Catholic doctrine, and assorted religious zealots. There are polished, witty scenes (such as a class of young girls reciting anathemas), but there are also many scenes that leave one blank — not, I think, because the dogmas being parodied are so difficult to penetrate but because Buñuel's sense of humor is. The absence here of a controlling dramatic logic is often tonic, but Buñuel's comic timing is so casual and eccentric that sometimes, as in a sequence involving two bedrooms at an inn, one seems to be expected to chortle over private, antiquarian jokes that never come off. And sometimes, as in an episode in which Jesus is about to shave until his mother persuades him to keep his beard, one seems to be watching a Catholic college revue, full of dud barbs and daring seminary humor. The film looks beautiful (the cinematography is by Christian Matras), and it moves along in a masterly way that is specifically, characteristically Buñuelian; it's all very simple — just one episode after another, with past and present joined without effort or fuss, and with occasional (and very odd) animal sounds on the track. It's interesting to see that Buñuel, at seventy, has abandoned surreal violence for this relaxed parody of religious doctrines and excesses. *The Milky Way* is more impudent than blasphemous. It's a rather mild movie — almost innocuous.

•

The Molly Maguires is a failure, nailed on its own aspirations to the tragic and the epic, yet it's an impressive failure. It's unusual for an American movie to be carried more by an elegiac feeling and by its visual qualities than by the story idea, and it would be wasteful to neglect the qualities that *The Molly Maguires* has because of those it lacks. It's not a movie one can work up much enthusiasm for, but it's not a negligible movie. One rarely sees a new movie that doesn't just try everything, that has a design and works within it. The cinematography, by James Wong Howe, which stresses abstract and geometric values, is integral to the stylized plan, and the basic compositional strength and the handsome use of space give the movie an imposing solidity. *The Molly Maguires,* which was directed by Martin Ritt, is too sombre and portentous for the rather dubious story it carries, but it feels like a reminder of a bitter, tragic past, and when you come away you know you've seen something.

The picture is set among the Irish immigrant coal miners in Pennsylvania in the eighteen-seventies. The Molly Maguires, a secret terrorist organization within the larger body of the Ancient Order of Hibernians, commit repeated acts of sabotage — dynamiting the trains carrying the coal they have just mined, and so on. It is never explained how they think these acts will get them the living wage they need. The picture is so beautifully made that its intellectual short circuit is puzzling: the violent Molly Maguires are treated as heroes because they have the courage to defy the mineowners and destroy things. One waits in vain for something resembling a plan of action or a rationale; instead, one sees them martyred after their secret organization has been infiltrated by a company spy. Since there is no strategy suggested behind their violence, one concludes that the movie is concerned not so much with its apparent subject as with presenting an analogy (a deeply sympathetic one) with contemporary black violence, and it all seems like a screenwriter's fancy. Maybe *The Molly Maguires* is more lifeless and more lugubrious than evocations of the past generally are because it's so basically artificial; it's a dirge, and not a dirge for people who actually suffered and died so much as a dirge trumped up for current relevance. And so it just doesn't connect with enough and doesn't add up right; we don't quite believe any of it, and we come out wondering what the people who made it thought they were doing.

But the movie not only has a look, it's acted with great intensity, and it focusses on a figure who is generally given only marginal treatment in this kind of material — the company spy. Richard Harris, whose devious, hangdog expression makes him a natural for the role, is wily and complex as a smart but weak man. Harris has a volatile edginess that draws us into the spy's divided spirit and contributes most of the suspense in the film. Sean Connery, who has admirable screen presence — grace as well as strength — gives a sure and intelligent contrasting performance as the leader of the Molly Maguires, even though it's an almost unwritten role and we never discover what's in his head or how he thinks his explosions will feed his family; and Samantha Eggar is surprisingly forceful as the girl who becomes the fiancée of the stool pigeon.

It was easy to see why the Swedish film *Adalen 31*, also a re-creation of labor strife in an earlier era, had a romantic feel to it; it's more difficult to grasp why *The Molly Maguires* seems romantic. I think maybe it's because Ritt takes his time in building the atmosphere and introducing the people, and lets an image stay on the screen until we take it in. There are bad scenes (like the overloaded one of Frank Finlay, the sadistic cop, talking to Harris, and the Judas routine at the end), but the movie has unusual dignity, and there's a fullness to it. It's good to see a movie now and then that allows time for scenes to be prepared — that doesn't just rush from one scene to the next. Ritt assumes (rightly, in this case) that a scene is worth lingering over, and this in itself makes the movie feel romantic. One person connected with it who certainly didn't behave romantically was the composer, Henry Mancini. When a movie costs over eleven million dollars, a composer who skimps must value his creativity very highly indeed; the music is so repetitive that it recalls those poor few themes that Max Steiner used to bring back over and over again. By the second hour of *The Molly Maguires*, Mancini's themes are an assault.

•

The publicity calls *The Kremlin Letter* "John Huston's cinematic exercise in amorality," which is an allusion to the fact that the methods of the American spies in it are as disgusting as those of the Russian spies, but the amorality that the film traffics in is the disease of commercialism — making a movie for no reason except to make a movie, making it without involvement in the subject or in the craft of moviemaking. Like the big Warner and M-G-M films of the late forties that seemed to have rotted in their tins before they were shipped, *The Kremlin Letter* reeks of money and lethargy. Though it's full of marquee names (Max von Sydow, Richard Boone, Patrick O'Neal, Orson Welles, George Sanders, Barbara Parkins, Bibi Andersson, and on and on), there don't seem to be any people in it. The actors can't find suitable expressions to go with lines like "Then in 1954 he was reported dead in Istanbul," so they mostly remain deadpan. With a couple of exceptions (Bibi Andersson and Nigel Green), the large cast is badly used or simply wasted. Patrick O'Neal has given amusing performances in the past (particularly as a psychiatrist in *A Fine Madness*), but as the central character here he has a deadpan so totally dead and a voice so unmodulated and ill-recorded that he seems to be walking through a rehearsal while suffering from the blahs. Richard Boone, as the other major character, chews up the screen in a meaninglessly self-serving way. The trouble with a "magnetic" actor like Boone is that when he's bad you can't take your eyes off him — he's magnetically bad. He scowls his malign smile and holds the audience, but his magnetism is like that of the domineering drunks who make scenes in bars. And Huston directs in the same way Boone acts — obviously and insensitively, as if all the gross, leering touches were signs of mastery.

The Kremlin Letter carries a foul load of script, full of exposition, and a complicated plot that loses one at the outset. The picture is visually undistinguished, and the sound is badly recorded. About midway, the picture begins to have an unpleasant kind of tension that is, I suppose, "gripping," but it isn't much fun to be clobbered and brutalized just so you won't be bored. I don't know who needs to receive the message that *we're* no better than *they* are, but if moviemakers are determined to tell us something via the thriller form, hadn't they better show enough dexterity to make us care about the corrupters and their victims? *The Kremlin Letter* has a trick, unresolved ending that is miscalculated, because we don't give a damn. The publicity says, "Be on time. . . . For, if you miss the first five minutes, you miss one suicide, two executions, one seduction, and the key to the plot." If you don't go at all, you can miss that and a lot more.

•

The Honeymoon Killers is terrible in such a primitive way that it has a strange sort of austerity and integrity (qualities notably lacking in *The Kremlin Letter*). Based on the lives of the multiple murderers Martha

Beck and Raymond Fernandez, who met their victims through Lonely Hearts clubs, and who were put to death at Sing Sing in 1951, the movie is so literal-minded that it resembles a *True Detective* account of the case — so faithful to its tawdry crime-exploitation genre that it seems almost like a documentary. It is dedicated realism governed by a vision of life drawn from pulps. It's as if someone re-created the Grade Z movies of the forties and did it in absolute seriousness. Is *The Honeymoon Killers* uncompromising in its unromantic approach or is it so limited in its artistic means that it accidentally becomes something resembling "minimal art"? I think maybe a little of both. The movie goes through the chronicle of the Beck-Fernandez crimes with pedestrian relentlessness; it's paced as if the actors were walking in lockstep. Probably the writer-director, Leonard Kastle, whose first film this is, confuses the forties low-budget realism that he imitates with "honesty" but isn't certain enough about what he's doing to stick to it. He puts excerpts from Gustav Mahler on the sound track and at one point tries to be expressively artful with some fast cuts.

The beginning of the movie is a shambles, with holes in the continuity, and Shirley Stoler, who plays the two-hundred-pound Martha Beck, is much too shrill, reminding one of the gorgons in *Caged,* of twenty years ago. The picture never explains what Ray sees in fat Martha, but Miss Stoler quiets down and improves as the movie plods on, and after the almost incredible lack of depth of the first half hour the movie begins to acquire a sort of fascination *because* of the total superficiality. Watching it is like looking at the work of a Sunday painter and wondering if he knows how two-dimensional it is. In this case, I suspect not, but a movie made without the conventional skills can, by its very limitations, become a real one-of-a-kind thing, like a castle built of toothpicks or clothespins. Since a movie has duration, we see each stick being put in place. We know exactly what's coming in every scene in this movie — when to expect an old lady to get suspicious, when to expect a child to scream. It's so banal it isn't even lurid; the black-and-white images are as neat as the nice old ladies' living rooms. The picture is so brightly lighted and so exactly planned and worked out that every ugly detail is in place — the hammer blow on the head, the trickle of blood, the ludicrous tongues sticking out of dead faces. As the sleazy charmer Ray Fernandez, Tony LoBianco, who looks a bit like Charles Aznavour, is almost alarmingly authentic to the pulpy genre, and the woman victims are a fine group of actresses, each of whom could have been convincing if the director hadn't let them set their own rhythms. Since they try to milk their opportunities, they frequently pace themselves as if they were on daytime TV, and to the banality of their characters is added the banality that undirected, uninterrupted performances usually have on the screen. But these actresses do good things — particularly Marilyn Chris, Barbara Cason, and Mary Jane Higby (who would make a great Mamie Eisenhower). It's such a terrible movie (with only one line clever enough to break the monotony: when Martha suggests going back to nursing and Ray says he won't live off a woman) that I can't recommend it to anybody. I would not have sat through it for my own pleasure. Yet it can't quite be overlooked, either; it's simple-minded in such a nagging, insistent way that this anachronism — a primitive version of old Republic pictures — is a true curiosity. People hostile or unresponsive to the subtleties and the difficulty of many modern movies may even *enjoy* it.

[February 7, 1970]

Trends and Paroxysms

Allan King's "actuality drama," *A Married Couple,* was made by a camera crew that moved in on a Canadian advertising man and his wife for ten weeks and photographed their marital conflicts. Recording the antagonisms in an actual marriage yields much less decisive revelations than conventional dramatic techniques do, and to the question of whether the quality of these revelations is such as to outweigh the tediousness and the unresolved complications the answer in this case, I think, is no. However, I've discovered that *A Married Couple* is the kind of movie that you can't say you dislike without having people jump to the conclusion that you're "fighting" it. People who like it tend to talk in terms of how much good it did them, and they assume that you disliked it because it was "too much" for you — that you rejected the experience because it was too disturbing, too tough, too close. Observing the bickering of Billy and Antoinette Edwards may help the people who say they're helped, but I think that's a rather specialized reaction. *Cactus Flower* is said to have done wonders in improving the self-image of dentists and dental assistants, but I wouldn't recommend it to others because of that. *A Married Couple* is not too much, it's too little. Like certain forms of modern theatre, it has been praised for its supposed liberating or therapeutic effect on the participants as well as on the audience. Are the Edwardses trying to "cure" themselves by performing for us? Allan King shot seventy hours of film and then edited it to the ninety-seven minutes we see, and it is said that the Edwardses, who saw all seventy hours, benefitted greatly from the experience and that possibly it was making the film that saved their marriage. But even if we presume to judge the film as therapy, we don't know whether group therapy, or perhaps joining a little-theatre company, might not have done them as much good.

For the Edwardses, *A Married Couple* must be a fantasy made actual: having one's life recorded as one lives it, and then being able to see what one did and what the other people did — not, as in Freudian therapy, by recalling it but by having it brought back through mechanical techniques. The catch is that it is lived for the camera, and living for, and with, the camera overcomplicates the relationships. The Edwardses make a transference to us, the audience (or to the filmmakers with the camera and tape recorder, who stand in for us), and so we're involved in a knotty new kind of transference situation, with elaborate games of role-playing, and we don't have the training (or the interest, necessarily) to sort it out. Our attempts to do so, if they were caught by a tape recorder, would probably sound as feeble as Billy's and Antoinette's efforts at self-analysis. It could be said that actors always project onto the audience their need for love and approval, but when they are acting roles, they ask for approval of their acting, which we can easily grant or withhold. Our relationship to them is relatively simple compared to our relationship to the Edwardses as they act "themselves" being "natural" and try to get approval for this concocted version of themselves. The role of amateur psychiatrist that is forced on us is messy, and it leads us into a morass. For example, when Antoinette doesn't want sex with Billy, are we to assume that she doesn't like him sexually, or that she's cold, or that she's reacting to the presence of the camera crew, or that she's trying to make a more dramatic scene, or that she's trying to humiliate Billy on camera, or what? Or, for another example, we try to figure out why their three-year-old son seems to have tuned out, but we can't be sure that he isn't just upset by the filmmaking process. All we can do is guess, and our guesses set us up for more guesswork, about why we thought what we did, which can go on and on, in an infinite regression. And, really, the emotions and maneuvers are not that interesting; they're the raw material that has already been refined not only in drama but even in soap opera, and certainly in the skits of satiric revue.

We assume that the couple here want to bring us into their act. (And their new, improved relationship may be the result of their success in bringing the public into their act.) The Edwardses are the kind of hip couple who, although they live in an attractive house, with flowers on the dining-room table, and although they modulate their voices with love when they talk to their son, are deliberately crude with each other. Their coarse language may have helped to bring them together; it was probably a unifying rejection of social "hypocrisies," as the long hair of a younger generation is, but they no longer use it just against the world. They use it against each other, and the lack of civility becomes exhausting, because their language limits their expressiveness. We're awkwardly aware that their gracelessness to each other is a theatrical routine — that they're trying to shock us in order to make their scenes more "honest" and explosive. They act for us, and then, of course, Allan King selects the most "dramatic" moments — when they celebrate or when they quarrel and then reconcile — so the material resembles fictional drama. But the "dramatic" moments don't serve the function they do in drama; they don't heighten or resolve anything. As in *The Dance of Death,* one cannot tell if the marriage was made in Heaven or in Hell, but whereas in Strindberg that is the brutal, comic point, here it seems to be because we don't know enough about the Edwardses' forms of faking or about King's methods of selection.

People improvising seriously seem to turn themselves into a parody of Method acting. The Edwardses' behavior does not have the spontaneity that is sometimes claimed for "found" drama; rather, it has the pattern of self-conscious improvisation, full of pauses, that is already the familiar sound of *cinéma-vérité* films. Professional actors can, by a gesture or a look, involve us from the start, and can spare us all this embarrassment of speculating on whether they would have done this or that if the camera weren't there. The Edwardses have both had previous connections with acting (Mrs. Edwards was a disc jockey, acted in summer stock, and was Shelley Winters' private secretary; Edwards was an actor in Montreal and a stage manager Off Broadway), and the picture would probably be much duller if they hadn't. Clearly, they want to give us a good show, but they don't have the personalities for it. A major reason *cinéma-vérité* films have thus far been commercially successful only when they featured stars or other major personalities is that those personalities brought some vitality to the films. Even *Lonely Boy,* a documentary on the pop singer Paul Anka that satirizes his success story, succeeds largely because Paul Anka, ridiculously untalented as the movie makes him out to be, is enough of a star to dominate it and hold it together. *The Most,* on the other hand, though it has good footage, never quite takes off, partly, I think, because its subject (and target), the editor Hugh Hefner, doesn't project like a performer; what the movie reveals is that Hefner is hard-edged and tight and colorless, and this is ironic and fascinating, but centering on a constricted personality keeps the movie flat. A film like *A Married Couple* might have some spark if the people in it were the rare sort of people who open up to the camera, but the Edwardses don't hold us the way star personalities in a documentary can, or the way good actors with written scripts can. There is a lot of talk about how movie stars don't count anymore, but when they're not there you certainly feel their absence. To conclude that the public has lost interest in stars merely because an occasional film with Steve McQueen or Paul Newman may fail is to misunderstand what stars are. Clark Gable appeared in numerous flops; just about every big star has had flops. The point is that in a role that's right a star can contribute something more to a movie than an ordinary actor can. The appeal of stars isn't part of some outworn studio system; it's as basic to movies as it is to theatre or opera or pop music. Whether through talent or through training (usually both), some people are more exciting to see on the screen than others. Yet even the greatest star-actors may fall into the "actuality" trap. On television talk shows, stars, trying to be serious and natural, are often embarrassingly banal, just like the non-actors in *cinéma vérité;* even their famous faces are boring, and they appear to be far less spontaneous than they do in a well-rehearsed role. When they're "themselves," they usually bring us not more but less.

A Married Couple is based on an approach that, even though it has little public appeal (unless the subject is sensational), is bound to be attractive to filmmakers. It must appear to them to be a way of finding art in the midst of life, and young filmmakers, who are rarely writers but are hooked on technology, love an approach in which the thinking out in advance is minimal — an approach in which you shoot a lot of footage and then try to find your film in it. Young filmmakers generally know almost nothing about how to handle actors, but probably *all* filmmakers have unhappy or "unfulfilled" friends eager to have a movie made of their lives; fame is probably the cure they seek. We're going to get some awfully dreary pictures out of this, because non-actors don't know how to exhibit the best in themselves — only the worst, which they tend to equate with "truth." What is abandoned in this kind of filmmaking is imagination. The filmmaker looks for the drama in life, and may occasionally find some, but he has to pan a lot of earth for a little bit of gold. Imaginative writers and moviemakers and actors intuitively know what a marriage in crisis is like, and bring the "truth" out of themselves.

•

Life's nine-page spread began, "More than a movie, *End of the Road* is a two-hour paroxysm — the intensely personal plea of Aram Avakian against pervasive violence in America." A paroxysm, according to the Random House Dictionary, is "1. any sudden, violent outburst; a fit of violent action or emotion: *paroxysms of rage.* 2. *Pathol.* a severe attack or an increase in violence of a disease, usually recurring periodically." Though I don't think its status as a paroxysm makes *End of the Road* more than a movie, I do think the movie it is fulfills both the first definition and the pathological one. It is not a plea against "pervasive violence in America," and it's as intensely personal as wearing a maxicoat is for a teen-age girl, but it *is* an increase in the violence of a disease among filmmakers — a fever to pound us with significance and shatter us with truths. *End of the Road* is an apocalyptic message movie, and perhaps I can convey its tone best by another quotation from *Life* — this one from the director's wife, Dorothy Tristan, who also plays the heroine: "A lot of people will hate the film. They'll think it's a desecration of the American flag — and it's just the opposite. It's a cry to the American people — a cry in the dark. I don't think it will do any good." The film was made by people who don't seem to know that a picture like this doesn't get seen by many people likely to think it's a desecration of the flag, and maybe they don't even know that the country is crawling with filmmakers crying, "Repent of your violence, America!" When I saw the movie, I was handed this synopsis:

> *End of the Road* is a baroque and pointedly absurd adaptation by Dennis McGuire, Terry Southern and Aram Avakian of the classic novel by John Barth, in which a young man, in an attempt to escape his own violence, falls into the violence of others in a plot that plays like an animated collage of a bizarre madhouse, a weird doctor, an absurd college campus, a gun fetishist professor and his rebelling wife, adultery, abortion and death.
>
> It is an experience, not a movie, a cinematic assault on the audience, the individual and the senses, a trip without drugs. With many aspects of comedy, it is about as funny as history.

I don't know what can be done about this kind of self-inflation and hysteria; it is becoming a standard kind of filmmakers' smugness, and it results in excruciatingly bad attempts at art. The filmmakers throw in every fancy trick they can steal or dream up and every shock effect they think they can get away with, and then they tell us the whole damp bag of fireworks and hysteria is an attack on the American psychosis of violence. And they're so self-righteous they believe it. If in *End of the Road* the mushroom clouds and the moon shot and the atrocities and the mixed-media effects and the overlay of voices of the Kennedys and Martin Luther King and everybody else you'd expect don't all tell you less than you want to know, there are the special shticks. Guns and American flags are the running jokes of the movie. The hero (Stacy Keach) wears a flag, his colleague (Harris Yulin) sucks gun barrels as if they were lollipops, and so on. It's camp paranoia.

The John Barth story, about a triangle in an academic setting in the early fifties, was published in 1958. The conceit of the movie is that the hero is catatonic because he's stoned by Hiroshima, L.B.J., napalm, etc., but Avakian destroys this conceit by the connections he tries to make, such as cutting from the heroine's choking on her own vomit during an abortion to the flag to the astronauts to Nixon moving forward and backward via reversed film. The movie is full of asserted connections so opportunistic that if their equivalent were tried by a reactionary — say, cutting from flower children littering Central Park to fish dying in polluted waters to Mick Jagger on a platform laughing to Stalin, and so on — the movie would be howled out of theatres. The few relatively good scenes are the quiet ones that are closest to the spirit of the novel (the hero's job interview, his put-on defense of prescriptive grammar). Avakian was formerly a film editor, and though the movie is encrusted with effects that are meant to be "relevant," the key relationships aren't clear, and the actors are badly served. Harris Yulin has a few good moments, and Keach isn't bad when he's funny, but there are too many closeups of him with his eyes bugging out and his mouth open, and we never quite relate to him. The funny-farm stuff, with James Earl Jones as the doctor, is painfully misdirected, so that it isn't clear what the doctor represents, and Jones is photographed as if he were a leftover pig from *Futz*. The camerawork, by Gordon Willis, is often beautiful, the optical effects are sometimes quite elegant, and the sets and details are often remarkably fine. It's intelligence that's missing, as it is in paroxysms.

[February 14, 1970]

The Beauty of Destruction

When Michelangelo Antonioni made his first American public appearance, late in 1968, at the San Francisco Film Festival, *Variety*'s Rick Setlowe reported that before Antonioni arrived "a chicklette with lank, flowing hair turned to her bearded companion and pronounced with wide-eyed awe, 'He's flying in from Death Valley.' 'Wow! Where else?' he answered softly." There is an inevitability about it, and that's part of what's the matter with Antonioni's *Zabriskie Point*, which is a rather pathetic mess. Death Valley is the perfect Antonioni location, because his infatuation with desolation has become his defining characteristic. He wore out his material in his Italian films, and he has not renewed himself; instead, he has gone to new places — England, in *Blow-Up*, and now America — to reproduce the same material. His early style (influenced, possibly, by Cesare Pavese's *Tra Donne Sole*, which he turned into *Le Amiche*) reached its climax in *L'Avventura*, a masterwork in which the postwar alienation of the prosperous classes and his negative prognosis for them seemed perfectly expressed by long, open rhythms and by a generalized sourness. But then, having distilled that sterile atmosphere, he kept going back and trying to re-create it. I've been frantically restless at all of Antonioni's films since. Beginning with *La Notte*, they turned stagnant and essentially repetitive, and it seemed to me that the moralism he more and more injected into them had become obligatory — a way of justifying his style, which was formed in death valley. Even those of us who had lost interest in Antonioni's mind looked forward to his vision of America. But he doesn't offer an outsider's view that illuminates what we had never seen for ourselves or what we had taken for granted — he plants and arranges every loaded bit of banality about our sins and vices. Working outside the studio and on a huge scale, he winds up with an America as false and unconvincing as if it had been manufactured in a studio by foreign craftsmen. Though he uses actual locations, *Zabriskie Point* is as far off America as the Italian Westerns shot in Spain.

It was possible for people who got caught in the Mod alienation and the mystery of *Blow-Up* to ignore or misunderstand Antonioni's moralism. In *Zabriskie Point,* it saps his style. He has rigged an America that is *nothing but* a justification for violent destruction, and the only distraction — love in the desert sands — is inane. The story is about a semi-political boy who wants to live dangerously and an uncommitted girl, and how everything they encounter of American life is cruel and rotten. The boy steals a plane because he needs "to get off the ground" and the girl drives to the desert to meditate, and they meet there and fall in love. When he is (implausibly) killed by a "pig," she sees what must come: the destruction of America. It is a very odd sensation to watch a message movie by a famous artist telling us what is wrong with America while showing us something both naïve and decrepit; if it weren't for this peculiar sense of dislocation and the embarrassment one feels for Antonioni, *Zabriskie Point* would be just one more "irreverent" pandering-to-youth movie, and (except photographically) worse than most.

But the dislocation is crucial: *Zabriskie Point* is a disaster, but, as one might guess, Antonioni does not make an ordinary sort of disaster. This is a huge, jerry-built, crumbling ruin of a movie. At the opening, he tries briefly to capture the ambience of revolutionary youth, but he soon returns to his own kind of apparently aimless scenes in his own kind of barren landscape. He can't animate the young performers — he can't, it seems, truly connect with them. It's as if he were baffled by America and it all got away from him, and so he, like other filmmakers, picked up the youth mythology so popular in the mass media; but he uses it as a rigid, schematic political point of view, and it doesn't fit his deliberately open-ended, sprawling style. Antonioni has always been a clumsy director, and has never had much luck at solving the mechanical problems of how to get his characters in and out of the places where he needs them and still keep his open construction, but it didn't matter too much when the characters were supposed to be suffering from lassitude and indifference about what they did. However, when a scene is planned to be loose, as if the characters were being observed at random, and then the characters make their politically pointed remarks, the effect is ludicrous.

Zabriskie Point is pitched to youth — that is, to the interests and values of the rebellious sons and daughters of the professional and upper middle classes — the way the old Hollywood movies used to be pitched to lower-middle-class values. The good guys (youth) and the bad guys (older white Americans) are as stiffly stereotyped as in any third-rate melodrama, and the evil police have been cast from the same mold as the old Hollywood Nazis. Antonioni has dehumanized them, so that they can be hated as pigs, but since he has failed to humanize the youth, it's dummies against dummies. Antonioni's specialty has always been "exposing" dehumanization in a dehumanized way; he has never before fallen into the trap of trying to show people with energy and vitality, and he simply doesn't have the temperament for it. The young in this movie don't communicate, any more than those earlier characters of his whose problem was supposed to be that they *couldn't*. When the people in his earlier films were zombies, this could be interpreted as upper-class enervation or working-class despair, but when activist youths are the zombies it is the director who appears to be alienated. If an artist's style is his content, Antonioni's style gives the lie to his own political message, because in this movie the young are lifeless. There's more energy in little visual details: the composition with a flag outside an executive's windows; the satires of billboards; the parody TV commercial that seems so strange and foreign, and is fun for that reason. If it is fair to judge an artist's involvement and his true convictions by what he does well and what he does badly, then from the evidence Antonioni doesn't believe in "revolutionary" youth — he doesn't understand them and they bore him — but he does have a feeling for Pop commercialism and enjoys devising his own versions of it.

The romance is a washout. Antonioni has frequently used actors as if they were non-actors, but when he used Jeanne Moreau and Alain Delon that way they still had the intensity and the expressive qualities of experienced performers, and they held the eye. This time, his hero, Mark Frechette, and his heroine, Daria Halprin, really are non-actors, and it makes a fatal difference. Frechette has a movie-star face — he looks like a cross between Warren Beatty and Peter Fonda — but he's a nothing on the screen: all profile and chin, and no projection of intelligence or emotions. Daria Halprin has a lovely figure but no way of coping with her excruciating lines, and she's rather clumpy, in a well-fed, middle-class way that inadvertently reveals far more truth about "revolutionary" youth than anything Antonioni has deliberately put in the movie. Partly because of atrocious sound recording and crude post-synching, their voices are so toneless and their readings so amateurishly flaccid that their most serious lines (which, as in nearly all message movies, are, of course, the worst) are greeted by ripples of laughter. Until the aestheticized fantasy of blow-ing up America at the end, the only alive sequence is the entertaining boy-meets-girl episode, as he, in the stolen plane, buzzes her car and, after her initial fear and anger, she begins to dig it. (It's fairly typical of Antonioni's clumsiness that this central erotic sequence is so poorly introduced that the boy has no way of knowing there's a girl in the car when he buzzes it; apparently, his Cessna fell in love with her Buick.)

As with the films of rank amateurs, one cannot always be sure what is deliberate ambiguity and what is the result of ineptness — a problem that sometimes arose in earlier Antonioni films but was never central. There are implausible plot details (such as the galaxy of police waiting at the airport for the hero to come back) that seem to be the result of wildly incompetent planning, and there are what appear to be planned mysteries and ambiguities (a paint shop in the desert, a pack of children out of nowhere who molest the heroine). Antonioni's grasp of the milieu is so shaky that the deliberately implausible scenes are rather reassuring — his mannerisms being more familiar to us than his exotic America. There is no clear relationship between the story line and the characters; what they do always seems to come out of Antonioni's head, not theirs.

It's a dumb movie, unconsciously snobbish, as if America should be destroyed because of its vulgarity. We're embarrassed for Antonioni not because he insults America — everybody does that, and we're used to it — but because he insults our intelligence. For a man who has so little insight into America and so little rapport with Americans to make a film of social criticism is an almost incredible *gaffe*. We have such a lot to choose from that we've become connoisseurs of anti-Americanism, and his is trivial and off-target. There is no force in his political analysis; even when he gets on to something like the real-estate developers, he turns them into straw men. What he exposes is not America but the class basis of his own tastes and reactions. He gets an easy laugh out of a family of tourists in the desert — out of their garish clothes and their materialistic equipment; he himself is an upper-middle-class tourist with aristocratic tastes.

At the end, when America is so lusciously destroyed, is the sequence deliberately beautiful because Antonioni thinks America is so evil that destroying it is a beautiful act or because Antonioni is such an aesthete that, like Mussolini's son Vittorio, who wrote poems about the beauty of the bombs exploding in Ethiopia, he cannot resist the photogenic glories of destruction? He aestheticized the factory smoke in *Red Desert,* and it has never been quite clear whether he was sacrificing meaning to beauty or whether he himself understood the confusions his aestheticism led him into. It is perhaps a true sign of his aristocratic aesthetics that in the final sequence, when America blows up, there are no bloody bodies, no people at all; only our material objects go up. And, even here, one cannot tell if this is because he wouldn't be so crude as to show bloody bodies or because he is being satiric and saying that America is nothing but garden furniture and books and the contents of our freezers — that we are a nation not of people but of objects. (It would be a charming satire on youthful fantasies if it were Daria's idea that she could burn the evil in America and get in her car and drive away, but the movie isn't that playful.) *Are* we nothing but material objects, or is it that Antonioni can't connect with us and so, like his alienated protagonists in earlier films, turns us into objects? I think the deadness of *Zabriskie Point* comes from his own inability to respond to America and his falling back on treating everyone in it as an object in a demonstration. In the ending, when Antonioni makes extraordinarily pretty pictures of chaos, isn't he doing just what he attacked the "decadent," "irresponsible" photographer in *Blow-Up* for doing? (He used the title *Blow-Up* on the wrong movie.) I doubt if he's much interested in his theme of revolutionary action; I think it's the other way around — politics provides the excuse for photogenic explosions.

It is one of the insanities that grow out of the photographic nature of the movie medium that a great deal of the death and destruction now being so moralistically flung in our faces is probably a response not so much to a political situation as to the dramatic problem of finding images powerful enough for a flash finish. Much of the hopelessness in movies like *If . . .* and *Easy Rider* and *Medium Cool* and the new thrillers that kill off their protagonists is probably dictated not by a consideration of actual alternatives and the conclusion that there's no hope but simply by what seems daring and new and photogenic. The moviemakers, concerned primarily with the look of their movies, may not even realize that audiences are — rightly, I think — becoming resentful of the self-serving negativism. The audience is probably just as much aware of the manipulation for the sake of beautiful violent imagery as it was of the manipulation when Hollywood gave it nothing but happy endings, and it probably knows that these apocalyptic finishes are just as much of a con.

•

The Looking Glass War — a youth-oriented spy film — has some painful similarities to *Zabriskie Point*. Directed by Frank R. Pierson, who adapted it for the screen from a John le Carré novel, it is a handsome, relatively sophisticated production that also fails at the primer level of drama — basic involvement. Christopher Jones plays a runaway Pole who is offered sanctuary in England if he will perform a mission in East Berlin for

British Intelligence, represented here by Ralph Richardson, Paul Rogers, and Anthony Hopkins, Pierson, who goes in for cryptic, stylish dialogue that obviously does more for him than for the audience, doesn't make key points clear. We can't follow the story well enough to know what the plan is or when things are going right or wrong, and one really becomes frustrated and angry when a thriller plot doesn't make sense — it's like starting a jigsaw puzzle and then discovering the pieces don't fit. In a movie like this, it doesn't take us long to know we've been had — that instead of engaging us and building the suspense the director is going for images. After a series of episodes, the hero and his girl (Pia Degermark, who looks like Lewis Carroll's Alice) are murdered, and the blame is pinned on the cynical older generation at British Intelligence. The title is an allusion to Lewis Carroll, and the horrid old Intelligence men have their tea party while the young innocents die, but Pierson hasn't directed the film in a Lewis Carroll spirit; he has directed it for gloom and brutality and startling images, and after Jones, who is the only personable character, is killed off for no apparent reason except to make the director feel like a serious "realistic" artist, and the audience is depressed because it's been cheated and flung down the generation gap, the references to Lewis Carroll seem ill-advised. When the vicious game of the old cynics is revealed, a young man charges, "It's better than monkey glands for you old-timers." And one winces, knowing that this anti-Establishment slanting is the monkey glands of Hollywood. But it's not going to rejuvenate the industry, because it doesn't fool the audience. It fools only the industry.

Increasingly, movie directors are making their choices not in terms of the situations or the characters in their movies but in terms of the images. Sometimes, as with young filmmakers (this is particularly true in the colleges), the directors think only in terms of the camera, and they go for the image without preparing the situation or getting into it, and then they wonder why they lose the audience so fast. In watching films by older directors, one often has the feeling that they're afraid the situations they've set up are too banal (they may be right), so they throw them out and retain only the most striking images. In both cases, vital links are missing. The results are as heady for the artist and as unsatisfying for the public as the Imagist school of poetry became. In movies, this concentration on images is becoming a new kind of formalism, in which characters and meaning and narrative interest are sacrificed to camera techniques and shock editing. This is a sign not of a superior craftsman but of an inferior one. What it means is that the moviemakers are not fully in control of their camera techniques or their material, and settle for the lucky accidents and the handsome effects.

[February 21, 1970]

Recognizable Human Behavior

Loving is an unusual movie — compassionate but unsentimental. It looks at the failures of middle-class life without despising the people; it understands that they already despise themselves. Although it doesn't try to spare the characters, and it is sometimes rather wry in its humor, there's a decency — almost a tenderness — in the way that the director, Irvin Kershner, is fair to everyone. He shows the lives of mediocre people for what they are, but he never allows us to feel superior to them.

Kershner is a director who has been on the verge of broad recognition for over a decade. Among Hollywood legends are the stories that people tell of seeing Kershner's *The Hoodlum Priest* before the studio reëdited it, and of how Jack Warner suddenly got the point of *A Fine Madness*, discovered that it was "anti-social," and ordered it recut. Despite everything, Kershner generally managed to bring some intelligence to the screen in at least a few sequences of each film, and traces of his original intentions would also shine through now and then. There was the ravenous energy of Sean Connery as the artist-hero of *A Fine Madness*, walking across a bridge in a way that told us the world was his; and the friendless young ex-convict of Keir Dullea in *The Hoodlum Priest,* so tense and pale that his fear of society was a justified neurosis. And in the film that Kershner made in Canada, *The Luck of Ginger Coffey*, Robert Shaw and Mary Ure, skilled professionals in other films, were suddenly — maybe for their only time on the screen — believable human beings. *The Luck of Ginger Coffey* was a picture that one knew — even while watching it and admiring the love and craftsmanship that had gone into it — wouldn't be a commercial success, no matter how much reviewers praised it. Not only was it the story of a loser but structurally and dramatically it ran downhill, and further down than the material really warranted. Though *Loving* is emotionally very similar, it doesn't drag one down that way; it's a more playful film, and the time may now be right for Kershner's temperament and talent. In 1964, concern for the lives of losers like Ginger Coffey was considered depressing, but, the way the world has changed, what seemed too downbeat five years ago may seem hopeful now. And movies have been on such a crash course of shock and depersonalization that concern for people, whether they're winners or losers, may in itself be inspiring — almost healing. Back then, Kershner's subtleties and his balanced approach to character didn't stand much chance with the mass movie audience, which wanted entertainment that was easier to respond to. In most big movies, responses were built into the product; you were signalled when to be afraid, when to swallow the lump in your throat, when to be awed, as clearly as if cue cards were being held up for you. In essence, they were. But it is no longer true that no one ever went broke underestimating the intelligence of the American public; look at the figures on *Doctor Dolittle*. The European moviemakers who became popular at the art houses helped to break down the acceptance of predigested entertainment, and during the last year talented Americans who in the past were frustrated and crushed by the studio heads have finally been making contact with audiences who are willing to work out their own responses.

The company releasing *Loving* has been publicizing it as if it were for the older audience; I think the young audience will respond, too, because it's a good movie: not a great movie but a good one — better than one expects, and different from other movies. It isn't callous, and it isn't bitter; though more sophisticated in its comedy, it resembles the Czech movies that have been giving American audiences the pleasure of seeing recognizable human behavior. I think the young audience will discover it; unlike the movie companies, the young don't all swallow the mass-media line about youth's being interested only in youth. *Loving* may be a key film, even a turning point in films, because it assumes (I hope rightly) that we will care about its characters although they are just the kind of people it is currently so easy to treat with contempt — the people from whom the educated young audience that now talks of reverence for life sprang.

Kershner is fortunate in having as his middle-class anti-hero George Segal, an actor with a core of humor and a loose, informal sense of irony, and one who radiates human decency and likable human weakness. He has perhaps the warmest presence of any current screen actor. I don't know anyone who doesn't like Segal — not just Segal the actor but Segal the person who comes through in the actor — and this is an immense advantage to the movie, because even though he plays a mediocre, failed artist, we like him to start with and can't dismiss him without dismissing almost all of humanity. Segal gives what I think is his best performance. The story is of the artist's dissatisfaction with his life. He's a free-lance illustrator, plodding along from one grubby job he hates to the next, making good money but never making enough money, fighting off decisions until they're made for him. There's no word for the defeats of a limited man; one can't quite call *Loving* a tragicomedy, any more than one could quite call *L'Avventura* a tragedy. Segal's hero never rises high enough for a classic fall, but he's aware of his stumbling. He's a bit of a clown, but he's not a fool; he's a poor bastard trying to make a living, do right by his wife and children, and keep the possibility open that he could yet be a dashing, gifted artist. The new girl he longs to run away with is not very different from his wife — only younger, and not bound down by his children. As the wife, Eva Marie Saint gives a stunning performance in what might have been a cliché role (and what she herself has played in the past as a cliché role). It's wonderful to see what reserves of talent performers can sometimes draw upon when they get the chance. Miss Saint lets us see that the wife doesn't have many illusions about her husband or herself. She knows what will happen to her if he leaves; there's not much she can do except try to hang on, and it's a humiliating position. But she's not just a hanger-on; she's a tough, gallant woman who will somehow manage to take care of her children whatever her husband does. As for the hero, his life is a mess, but it's not a tragic, austere mess, and, unlike Antonioni's hero-failures, he manages to blot out his troubles and have a pretty good time. The movie keeps a sane — often funny — perspective on his wriggling this way and that.

The script, by Don Devlin, is somewhat sparse, and this seems rather negligent, since in the novel it's based on — *Brooks Wilson Ltd.*, by J. M. Ryan — there is material that might have given the movie a richer substance and more of the resonances of American middle-income life. Because the script isn't full enough, we become too mindful of every action and vocal inflection; we get the feeling that the director is trying to stretch the material and make it count for more than it's worth. Nevertheless, *Loving* is Kershner's best-sustained film. From start to finish, it's a demonstration of his sensibility and his superb craftsmanship. It's a relief to see such a harmonious, beautifully rhythmed piece of moviemaking, and a special pleasure to see an American movie that's so quietly detailed. The score, by Bernardo Segall (who also scored *Ginger Coffey*), is unusually delicate for an American movie score, and Gordon Willis's camerawork serves the conception gracefully and unostentatiously. This is a modest and somewhat obviously controlled picture. It doesn't reveal the exuberance or the liberated, explosive intelligence that has sometimes broken through in bits of Kershner's other films, but there are remarkably fine moments: domestic scenes between Eva Marie Saint and the children; Segal just standing and looking at his two daughters through the window of a dress shop — exceptionally unsentimentalized children, who are simultaneously alien to their father's life and at the center of it.

Sensibility has become so rare in movies that to see people on the screen whom one can relate to is a gift of feeling. The characters in *Loving* seem to have believable human reactions and conversations, for a change. Kershner doesn't strike attitudes; he opens up these people's lives to the camera and reveals that they don't really mean to hurt each other, that they do it out of carelessness — or, sometimes, when they do what they want, it just goes wrong for other people and they can't help it. After so many movies that come on strong with big, flamboyant truths, a movie that doesn't pretend to know more than it does but comes up with some small truths about the way the middle class sweats gives us something we can respond to; it gives us something we desperately need from the movies now — an extension of understanding.

•

To paraphrase Groucho's "Either this man is dead or my watch has stopped," either Frank D. Gilroy (of *The Subject Was Roses*) has a barely visible talent or I have a blind spot. His script (based on his own play) for George Stevens' *The Only Game in Town* has the wrong kind of simplicity, and his attempts at sprightly badinage have that leaden jocularity which makes you know you should respond, though you can't for the life of you figure out how. You can feel your facial muscles trying to settle on something — like those people on TV talk shows trying to laugh politely at bad jokes without making fools of themselves. George Stevens' attentiveness to the actors might have shown to some advantage if the script weren't so transparent; there's nothing behind the dialogue, no sense of the texture of people's lives. It's a movie that should never have been made, because everyone will see through it. After the initial pleasure of finding Elizabeth Taylor looking prettier than she has looked in years, and watching Warren Beatty's attractively relaxed style, it turns into a sluggish star vehicle of the old, bad days. This love story of a gambling musician and a chorus girl is set in Las Vegas, but it was shot mainly in Paris, and there are long sequences of such blinding banality that you begin to wonder if the credit to Henri Decae, one of the world's great cinematographers, could be some kind of joke. Miss Taylor has a sweetness and, despite her rather shapeless look, a touching quality of frailty (like some of the women stars of an earlier era, as she gets older she begins to have a defenseless air about her), but the plot makes her ridiculous. Beatty is obviously younger than she is, and he's in fine shape, so when she prolongs this pokey, drowsy movie by stalling on his honorable marriage proposal, the audience gets so impatient you half expect to hear that old movie-house cry "Say yes so we can all go home!"

•

Start the Revolution Without Me, a spoof of swashbucklers, begins bouncingly, with some neat parodies and with the birth of Donald Sutherland and Gene Wilder as two sets of identical twins, mismatched by a harried obstetrician — one mismatched pair to be raised as peasants, the other pair as aristocrats. But the script doesn't hold up, Bud Yorkin's direction is flaccid, and Sutherland smirks and mugs through his dual role. The picture turns silly, but at least it doesn't turn sour. It's worth mentioning mainly for Hugh Griffith, who is oddly poignant as a befuddled Louis XVI, and for Wilder. Wilder has a fantastic shtick. He builds up a hysterical rage about nothing at all, upon an imaginary provocation, and it's terribly funny. It's the sort of thing one wouldn't expect to work more than once, but it works each time and you begin to wait for it and hope for it — it's a parody of all the obscene bad temper in the world. Wilder's self-generated neurasthenic rage could become a lasting part of our culture, like Edgar Kennedy's slow burn.

•

Unfunny camp is contemptible. *The Magic Christian,* Terry Southern's novel, relocated in England and directed by Joseph McGrath, has been made into such an inert collection of bad jokes that even the mean-spiritedness of the original fails to come through. There were occasional flashes of vicious wit in the book; the movie is merely unpleasant. The cast of stars and guest celebrities who act out the demonstration that every man has his price appear to be the venal rich insulting the venal poor.

•

Joseph Strick's movie version of Henry Miller's *Tropic of Cancer* is an entertaining little sex comedy — a trifling series of vignettes and sex fantasies about Americans abroad, with bits of Miller's language rolling out, happy and bawdy. The movie is so much less than the book that it almost seems deliberately intended to reduce Henry Miller — probably the funniest American writer since Mark Twain — to pipsqueak size. I'm sure this isn't deliberate, however. Having seen several Strick adaptations by now (Genet's *The Balcony* and Joyce's *Ulysses* preceded *Tropic of Cancer* to the block), I think the diminution is an all but inevitable result of Strick's methods. He adapts "daring" literary classics the way a Broadway playwright adapts a successful Parisian farce; that is, he picks out the scenes and lines and characters he thinks will travel (to the movie medium). Since he gives no evidence of independent imagination and doesn't invent, his adaptations can be called "faithful" to their sources. Though Strick's approach hasn't changed, his *Tropic of Cancer* doesn't have the respectful library worminess of his flat, unfunny *Ulysses;* that was really a sobering experience. At least, this movie of *Tropic of Cancer* — careless and slipshod though it is — makes one laugh, and, unlike his *Ulysses,* it won't be mistaken for a classic. (I have already heard *Tropic of Cancer* panned by a television reviewer as a "filthy picture." That probably means he had a good time at it.) I enjoyed the movie and I think others will, too, though there's something rather tacky and second-hand about it that prevents us from laughing very deeply. One could hardly guess from this thin trickle of jokes that Henry Miller is the closest an American has come to Rabelais. It's rather discouraging to read in *Variety,* "The fault, however, may not be Strick's at all, because, stripping away the once-shocking dialogue which formerly made 'criminals' out of many a returning American tourist, what is there left? A few philosophical truisms, little more. This wouldn't be the first film to show up an established book writer." I have an uncomfortable feeling that the movie may have come out at a time when some members of the press are eager to prove that they draw the line *somewhere,* so this harmlessly amusing movie (and the sublimely funny book it derives from) may take an unjustified trouncing.

The movie doesn't begin to suggest the American tradition that Miller belongs to — or, more exactly, belonged to, because it is by discounting his work after the thirties that one can clearly see him as the link between *Leaves of Grass* and the beats, and, of course, as the precursor of Mailer. Since the movie doesn't bother to keep the book in its period, Miller loses his place in history and, with it, his originality. We lamented the time change in *Ulysses,* yet had to forgive it, because we recognized the difficulty and expense of re-creating Dublin as it was in 1904, but there's no good excuse in this case. Moviemakers who modernize books usually say that the period doesn't matter, that the work is "universal," but what makes Miller's book "universal" is that it is the story of the bum as writer at a particular period, which made him a particular kind of bum. Earlier or later, he might have been a thief or a professor; in his time, he was the Joe Gould who wrote. Taken out of the bohemian Depression milieu of rootless Russian and American expatriates scrounging around Paris in the early thirties, the anecdotes are no longer parts of life stories. They don't connect with anything; they're just small jokes. Because American moochers abroad are younger now, the characters all seem tired and over-age, and we never really know what these people are doing there. When the story is made timeless, the characters are out of nowhere, and the author-hero is not discovering a new kind of literary freedom in self-exposure, he's just a dirty not-so-young man hanging around the tourist spots of Paris. Strick tosses in so many starts of parades and tourist views that at times the movie feels like a travelogue (and one that isn't particularly well shot, either); luckily, the fast edit keeps the action from sagging.

George Orwell said that Miller treated English as "a spoken language, but spoken *without fear*," and Orwell was referring not just to the fact that Miller's language rode right over the taboos but to the fact that it was "without fear of rhetoric or of the unusual or poetical word" and was "a flowing, swelling prose, a prose with rhythms in it." One hears Miller's prose as one reads him; in the early forties, when a friend of mine got hold of a smuggled-in copy of *Tropic of Cancer,* our immediate impulse was to read him aloud. But when that same prose is used in the film as a voice-over narration, it doesn't have the drive of common speech, it has the static fake poetry of cultivated literary language. Somehow, Strick has performed a reverse miracle — a feat like turning bread into stones.

When I saw the movie and started to think about the book again, I realized that I remembered it filtered through the Orwell essay "Inside the Whale." Orwell clarified the feelings we had about Miller; in a sense, he authenticated our excitement, not just by agreeing with us but by helping us to understand why we felt as we did. *Tropic of Cancer* is now easily available for ninety-five cents, but it comes with an introduction explaining enthusiastically, "If one had to type him [Miller] one might call him a Wisdom writer, Wisdom literature being a type of literature which lies between literature and scripture; it is poetry only because it rises above literature and because it sometimes ends up in bibles." This was not what drew us to Miller — Wisdom literature is what I can do without. Miller's later writing, full of boozy mysticism about his creativity and lyrical bulling about his sexual prowess, is what Orwell anticipated in 1940 (there was already plenty of evidence) when he said Miller might "descend into unintelligibility, or into charlatanism." *Tropic of Cancer* had a liberating spirit, because it seemed *totally* without hypocrisy. This basic appeal of the book doesn't emerge in the movie, owing to something so obvious one might not think of it. In the book, Miller sees friends in terms of the possible meal or bed he can cadge from them, women in terms of their sexual possibilities. Miller seems to bring us closer to "reality," seems to bring art closer to truth. But when we're reading him we don't think of his sexual hyperbole as objective description; we don't assume, for example, that all the women Miller meets are sexy sluts visibly panting for what he can give them. In the movie, however, Strick has made the outer circumstances correspond to the inner vision. This disintegrates the meanings; the levels of comedy collapse, and the narrator-hero's character collapses, too. In the book, the hero is amazing because he takes such joy in the diversity of possible pleasures; one imagines him as a mild little man with all-embracing tastes, a man eager to try whatever he can get, being excited by even the most unlikely ladies. In the movie, no eye for hidden possibilities is necessary. Joseph Strick's fantasy life being more limited than Henry Miller's, the women are the same bundles of lust that they are in the dull porny pix all over town. Not only are they the same easily available and badly used type, they're nearly all around the same age.

The whole movie lacks contrasts, depth, surprises. It succeeds best with two characters, Fillmore (James Callahan), whose essential American innocence is really lovely, and Carl (David Bauer), who has a sizable discrepancy between his surface character and what we see of his self-deceptions and lies. But Miller, one of the great characters in American literature — Huck Finn as a starving expatriate — is just a straight man for Fillmore and Carl. Considering that Rip Torn is almost completely wrong for the role of Miller — that he's cast against his usual type, and even against his own physical tensions — he does quite well. Miller the hero of the book is a joyful coward who will always sneak away rather than face an unpleasant scene. Torn is a tight actor whose face can split in a mean grin or a satyr's crooked smile. Miller needs not a satyr's smile but the satyr's soul of an ordinary man. Torn manages to kill the hostility that had become his stock in trade, and he's quite amiable, but he is never really loose or passive or relaxed, never the hero whose heroism is his acceptance of whatever comes his way, never really *friendly*. And that may be another reason the narration — which is about openness to experience — sounds so phony.

With the actual Henry Miller available, the director couldn't think of anything to do with him but to plunk him into a shot, just standing in front of a church. The poverty of imagination represented by that shot haunts me. I've been torturing myself thinking of the ways that Strick would probably use other authors if they were around. If he made a film of *Hamlet*, he might stuff Shakespeare into a seat at the Globe watching the performance; in his *Don Quixote*, Cervantes could be planted among the guests dining at an inn; and so on.

[March 7, 1970]

Fellini's "Mondo Trasho"

Fellini Satyricon uses the pre-Christian Roman world of debauchery during the time of Nero as an analogue of the modern post-Christian period. Like Cecil B. De Mille, who was also fond of pagan infernos, Fellini equates sexual "vice" with apocalypse; in *La Dolce Vita* he used the orgies of modern Rome as a parallel to ancient Rome, and now he reverses the analogy to make the same point. The idea that sticks out in every direction from *Fellini Satyricon* is that man without a belief in God is a lecherous beast. I think it's a really bad movie — a terrible movie — but Fellini has such intuitive rapport with the superstitious child in the adult viewer that I imagine it will be a considerable success. If it were put to members of the foreign-film audience rationally, probably few of them would identify the problems in the world today with fornication and licentiousness, or with the loss of faith in a divine authority. But when people at the movies are shown an orgiastic world of human beasts and monsters it's easy for them to fall back upon the persistent cliché that godlessness is lawlessness. De Mille, whose specialty was also the photogenic demonstration that modern immorality resembles the hedonism of declining Rome, used to satisfy the voyeuristic needs of the God-abiding by showing them what they were missing by being good and then soothe them by showing them the terrible punishments they escaped by being good. Fellini is not a sanctimonious manipulator of that kind; he makes fantasy extravaganzas out of tabloid sensationalism, but he appears to do it from emotional conviction, or, perhaps more exactly, from a master entertainer's feeling for the daydreams of the audience. He seems to draw upon something in himself that many people respond to as being profound, possibly because it has been long buried in them. When he brings it out, they think he is a great artist.

Fellini's pagans are freaks — bloated or deformed, or just simulated freaks with painted faces and protruding tongues. This is not the first time Fellini has used freaks in a movie; he has been using them, though in smaller numbers, to represent mystery and depravity all along, and especially since *La Dolce Vita*. Often they were people made up freakishly, as if in his oddly sophisticated-naïve eyes decadence were a wig and a heavy makeup job. His homosexual boys with gold dust in their hair were the "painted women" of naughty novels. It's the most simple-minded and widespread of all attitudes toward sin — identical with De Mille's. And so it wasn't surprising that some enthusiasts of *La Dolce Vita* took it as "a lesson to us" — a lesson that Rome fell because of high living and promiscuity, and we would, too. The labors of Gibbon and other historians never really permeated people's minds the way banalities about retribution for sin did. The freak show of *Fellini Satyricon* is a grotesque interpretation of paganism, yet I think many people in the audience will accept it without question. When we were children, we may have feared people wth physical defects, assuming that they were frightening to look at because they were *bad*. In our fairy tales, it was the ugly witches who did wicked deeds, and didn't we pick up the idea that if we were good we would be beautiful but if we did forbidden things it would show in our faces? Some of us probably thought that depravity caused deformity; at the most superstitious level, ugliness was God's punishment for disobedience. Many of us have painfully learned to overcome these superstitions, and yet the buried feelings can be easily touched. Fellini's popular strength probably comes from primitive elements such as these in a modern style that enables audiences to respond as if the content were highly sophisticated. Perhaps the style enables some viewers to think that the primitive fantasies are Jungian, or whatever, and so are somehow raised to the status of art. But there is no evidence that Fellini is using them consciously, or using them *against* their original impact; they're not even fully brought to light. In Fellini's films, buried material isn't jabbed at and released in obscene jokes, as in Buñuel's films. Our primitive fears are tapped and used just as they are by a punishing parent or an opportunistic schoolteacher who's unaware of what he's doing — except that Fellini does it more playfully.

Like a naughty Christian child, Fellini thinks it's a ball to be a pagan, but a naughty ball, a *bad* one, which can't really be enjoyed. In *La Dolce Vita*, Fellini's hero was a society reporter who got caught up in the life of the jaded rich international party set; in *8½*, the hero was a movie director who lived out the public fantasy of what a big movie director's life is like — a big, swirling party; in *Juliet of the Spirits*, the hero was some sort of official greeter and partygiver whose wife dreamed of fruity, balletistic parties. In *Fellini Satyricon* the party scenes are no longer orgiastic climaxes. Fellini uses Petronius and other classic sources as the basis for a movie that is one long orgy of eating, drinking, cruelty, and copulation, and he goes all the way with his infatuation with transvestism, nymphomania, homosexuality, monsters.

Fellini Satyricon is *all* phantasmagoria, and though from time to time one may register a face or a set or an episode, for most of the film one has the feeling of a camera following people walking along walls. The fresco effect becomes monotonous and rather oppressive. It's almost as if the movie were a theatrically staged panorama, set on a treadmill. At first, while we're waiting for Fellini to get into the material and involve us, there's a sequence on an ancient stage which seems to promise that the movie will be a theatrical spectacle in the modern theatre-of-cruelty sense. But Fellini never does involve us: we seem to be at a stoned circus, where the performers go on and on whether we care or not. And though there's a story, we anticipate the end a dozen times — a clear sign that his episodic structuring has failed. Afterward, one recalls astonishingly little; there are many episodes and anecdotes, but, for a work that is visual if it is anything, it leaves disappointingly few visual impressions. Giton, the adolescent boy whom the two heroes battle over, *is* memorable, because Max Born makes him a soft, smiling coquette full of sly promise; he's the complete whore, who takes pleasure in being used. The one charming episode is a sweetly amoral Garden of Eden sexual romp of the two heroes with a beautiful slave girl in a deserted house. Except for Giton's scenes and the slave girl's, and perhaps a shipboard-rape-and-marriage sequence, the picture isn't particularly sensual — though one assumes that carnality is part of its subject matter, and though Fellini has previously shown a special gift for carnal fantasies, as in the harem sequence of *8½*. Some of the set designs (by Danilo Donati) have a hypnotic quality — a ship like a sea serpent, a building with many stories and no front wall, so that we look into it as if it were a many-layered stage set — but the photography isn't very distinguished. It's a tired movie; during much of it, we seem to be moving past clumsily arranged groups and looking at people exhibiting their grossness or their abnormalities and sticking their tongues out at us. If you have ever been at a high-school play in which the children trying to look evil stuck their tongues out, you'll know exactly why there's so little magic in Fellini's apocalyptic extravaganza. It's full of people making faces, the way people do in home movies, and full of people staring at the camera and laughing and prancing around, the way they often do in 16-millimetre parodies of sex epics, like *Mondo Trasho*. Fellini's early films had a forlorn atmosphere, and there were bits of melancholy still drifting through *La Dolce Vita* and *8½*; if the people were lost, at least their sorrow gave them poetic suggestions of depth. There was little depth in *Juliet of the Spirits,* and there is none in this *Satyricon*. Perhaps Fellini thinks Christ had to come before people could have souls, but, lacking emotional depth, the movie is so transient that elaborate episodes like Trimalchio's banquet barely leave a trace in the memory.

Somewhere along the line — I think it happened in *La Dolce Vita* — Fellini gave in to the luxurious basking in sin that has always had such extraordinary public appeal. He became the new De Mille — a purveyor of the glamour of wickedness. And, though he doesn't appear in them, he became the star of his movies, which are presented as emanations of his imagination, his genius; he functioned as if the creative process had no relation to experience, to thought, or to other art. As this process has developed, the actors, and the characters, in his movies have become less and less important, so at *Fellini Satyricon* one hardly notices the familiar people in it — it's all a masquerade anyway, and they are made up to be hideous, and they come and go so fast — and one hardly knows or cares who the leads are, or which actor is Encolpius, which Ascyltus. (Encolpius, the blond Botticelli-angel face, is an English stage and TV actor named Martin Potter; Ascyltus, the goatish brunet, is Hiram Keller, an American who was in *Hair*. Encolpius and Ascyltus look as if they might be found among the boys cruising the Spanish Steps, and that is certainly right for the ancient-modern parallel Fellini makes, but Potter appears uncomfortable in his role.) I feel that what has come over Fellini is a movie director's megalomania, which has not gone so far with anyone else, and that part of the basis for his reputation is that his narcissistic conception of his role is exactly what celebrity worshippers have always thought a movie director to be. His idea of a movie seems to be to gather and exhibit all the weird people he can find, and one gets the feeling that more excitement and energy go into casting than into what he does with his cast, because, after the first sight of them, the faces don't yield up anything further to the camera. People coming out of *La Dolce Vita* and *8½* could be heard asking, "Where do you suppose he found them?" — as if he were a magician of a zookeeper who had turned up fabulous specimens. This increasingly strange human zoo into which he thrusts us is what people refer to when they say that there is a Fellini world. The partygoers of *La Dolce Vita*, with their masklike faces of dissatisfaction and perversity, have given way to this parade of leering, grinning cripples. And these primitive caricatures of what depravity supposedly does to us are used as cautionary images. In interviews, Fellini frequently talks of the need to believe in miracles, and of how "we have not the strength" to do without religion or myth. My guess would be that Fellini, as a Catholic, and a notably emotional one, has small knowledge of or interest in any forms of control outside the Church. As an artist, he draws upon the imagination of a Catholic schoolboy and presents us with a juvenile version of the Grand Inquisitor's argument.

Fellini's work has an eerie, spellbinding quality for some people which must be not unlike the powerful effect the first movies were said to have. Perhaps the opulence and the dreamlike movement of his films and the grotesques who populate them are what some people want from the movies — a return to frightening fairy tales. Following the Kubrick line in selling pictures, Fellini, in an interview, says, "Even the young ones not smoking, not with drugs — they grasp the picture, they feel the picture, eat the picture, breathe it, without asking, 'What does it mean?' This film — I don't want to sound presumptuous, but it is a very good test just to choose friends with, a test if people are free or not. The young kids, they pass the test." I should say that emotionally his *Satyricon* is just about the opposite of "free"; emotionally, it's a hip version of *The Sign of the Cross*. There's a certain amount of confusion in it about what's going on and where, so some people may take it "psychedelically" and swallow it whole, though the audience at *Fellini Satyricon* is already on to part of the con: there was a big laugh when Encolpius identifies himself as a student. But this new selling technique of congratulating youth for not thinking — which is also a scare selling technique to reviewers who are afraid of being left behind "free" youth — puts the audience at the mercy of shrewd promotion. "The young, they just love and feel," says Fellini, "and if there is a new cinema, pictures such as *2001* — and, yes, *Satyricon* — it is for them." Sure it's for them, because they constitute about fifty per cent of the paid admissions, and so poor old *Fantasia* has now been reissued as a trip movie, and the ads for *Zabriskie Point* say "It blows your mind," and so on. When Susan Kohner, sobbing, clutched the flowers on her black mother's casket in *Imitation of Life,* you might have felt the anguish in your chest even as you laughed at yourself for reacting. Maybe if Fellini personally didn't impress people so much as a virtuoso they'd become as conscious of the emotional and intellectual shoddiness they're responding to in *his* films. The usual refrain is "With Fellini, I'm so captivated by the images I don't ask what it means." But suppose it's not the "beauty" of the images they're reacting to so much as that step-by-step intuitive linkage between Fellini's emotions and their own almost forgotten ones? I'm sure there are people who will say that it doesn't matter if Fellini's movies are based on shallow thinking, or even ignorance, because he uses popular superstitions for a poetic vision, and makes art out of them. The large question in all this is: *Can* movie art be made out of shallow thinking and superstitions? The answer may, I think, be no. But even if it's yes, I don't think Fellini transformed anything in *Fellini Satyricon*.

[March 14, 1970]

Scavengers with Computers

I recommend *The Adventurers* only to the officials of the universities who have bestowed honorary degrees upon its producer, Joseph E. Levine. Mr. Levine and Paramount Pictures are said to be cutting a half hour from the version I saw; they should keep cutting until there's nothing left. The film is potentially profitable, but if the major motion-picture companies can survive only by making pictures like this, they don't deserve to survive. The question the businessmen ask is whether a picture will make money, and if it does they feel vindicated as well as richer; they regard themselves as heroes and arrange honors for themselves. The question they don't seem to ask is what the picture will mean to people throughout the world. A picture like *Airport* will, I think, mean nothing; it's too conventionally dull and stupid for anybody to be moved by it. *The Adventurers,* however, is conceived in a way that coarsens one's perceptions, and it has been made on a scale that gives it the status of an event. We talk about how the old pictures live on, and the industry likes to sentimentalize the memories it has given us, but it doesn't accept the blame for the callousness and crudeness and the whore's thinking that have also affected us. James Agee once wrote of a movie called *I Walk Alone* that, except for a few scenes, "the picture deserves, like four out of five other movies, to walk alone, tinkle a little bell, and cry 'Unclean. Unclean.'" Harold Robbins' books tinkle for all to hear, but a little bell isn't enough now for *The Adventurers* — a hugely expensive movie with an international cast, a computerized production designed to blanket the globe and then circle it by satellite. It's an alarming case of global pollution, and sirens need to be sounded.

At the beginning of *The Adventurers*, a boy gambols on the hills with his dog. Bang! — and the dog is a bloody corpse. The boy runs home, and in the next scenes he watches as soldiers attack his home and rape and kill his mother, along with the family servants. Right from the start, with the juicy pictures of the rapist-murderers among breasts, limbs, bloody knives, and so on, *The Adventurers* produces a queasy nervous apprehensiveness that is a clod's notion of suspense. The ominous anticipation of horror that affects us in the gut keeps the audience from being bored, but this nervous stomach is not the same as the pleasurable excitement of aesthetically devised suspense. Nor are the tensions resolved dramatically. The orgies of killing subside, but they start up again whenever the picture runs out of steam. The boy takes refuge in another village and watches while everyone *there* is murdered. The director, Lewis Gilbert, has almost no technique, and he stages one scene as indifferently as the next, but he knows what business he's in: there's carnage or a sex scene every fifteen minutes or so to keep you from losing interest in the slack story and Harold Robbins' philosophical gems.

The reason given for the violence in a number of recent pictures is that it's there to make you see that violence is bad. As things work out, the matter isn't all that simple. There are many of us who hate violence so much that we can't bear to see it, even on the screen, and there are others who go to violent movies because they don't mind the violence particularly (often they're quite sophisticated about the tricks and don't take the violence seriously) and they find violent movies exciting. And though the moviemakers claim to hate violence — and maybe some of them do — they *want* the audience to find it exciting. In *The Wild Bunch*, Sam Peckinpah thought that by making violence realistically bloody and gruesome he would deglamourize warfare and enable the audience to see how horrible it is. This approach isn't new; almost every anti-war movie has tried to make the fighting and dying more "realistic," in order to shock people out of their illusions, and sometimes, as in *All Quiet on the Western Front,* the movies have been relatively successful in this. But Peckinpah started his anti-violence movie in the framework of a Western, and he got in over his head. He pushed his violence theme so far that the Western structure could no longer contain his own, obviously complicated emotions or the statements he was trying to make about modern life. And he got so wound up in the aesthetics of violence that what had begun as a realistic treatment became instead an almost abstract fantasy on violence; the bloody deaths, repeated so often and so exquisitely, became numbingly remote. One no longer knew how to react and stopped reacting. *The Wild Bunch* was a beautiful self-destroying machine; it got so intricately involved in the problems of violence that it tore itself apart. A brilliantly directed and photographed study in confusion, it played to audiences who apparently didn't take it as an attack on violence but simply enjoyed it as a violent Western. In a recent television talk show, there was evidence of how a director's convictions about what he's doing can be undermined by the genre he works in and by his own unresolved feelings; members of the audience told Peckinpah that they had liked *The Wild Bunch,* and — as if they were justifying the movie against charges of excessive violence — that it hadn't bothered them at all.

I am conceding that *The Wild Bunch* was possibly enjoyed by some people for its violence, but I think there is still an important distinction between the violence in *The Wild Bunch* and the violence in *The Adventurers.* The violence in *The Wild Bunch* was out of control, but for honest reasons: Peckinpah got caught in the trap of discovering that he was no longer sure what he was trying to do. When artists are dealing with basic, complex situations, we can respect failures, and sometimes an art form advances because of the problems the artist couldn't solve — Peckinpah, by getting into something bigger than the story he was telling, raised crucial issues for future artists working on action films. What we have a right to ask of those who treat such themes is that they have some awareness of what they're doing, that they care about what they're doing, that there be some fundamental intelligence and honesty at work. The men who made *The Adventurers* appear to have had no object in mind but to excite people in order to make money, and the "ideas" about violence, political revolution, childhood traumas, and the rest were merely exploitable material. These men are businessmen who use the idea of showing the horrors of violence the same way Robbins uses the lives of celebrities — as a convenience, for ready-made excitement. What's at issue isn't simply that a Peckinpah or an Arthur Penn is a man of taste and doesn't offend one aesthetically, while those who made *The Adventurers* aren't and do. Conceivably, a clumsy, "tasteless" man could still make an honest movie, in which he struggled to tell some kind of truth. But no one is struggling to get at anything in *The Adventurers,* no one is trying to make anything beautiful; everyone is just doing a passable job. And the banal treatment of violence is sickening; men who are insensitive to pain are playing with it.

Lewis Gilbert's squareness about Harold Robbins' sleaziness makes you feel you're looking at dry rot. There was not one moment in *The Adventurers* when I felt that anyone in it was trying to do a single honest thing. And in the whole movie, a swinger's tour of primitivism and decadence which cuts back and forth between the massacres and upheavals of a mythical poor country in South America and the tortured sex lives of the international celebrity set in Europe and America, there are only a couple of amusing scenes — a nice moment when Thommy Berggren, as the gigolo Sergei, tips his doorman father, and a stylishly villainous moment or two by Alan Badel, as the Trujillo-style dictator. A star cast has been assembled for international box-office appeal, but movies that are made with contempt for the mass audience don't give actors a chance to act, so a good many of them must feel degraded by this whorehouse work, which they presumably took because of the money and "the exposure." They don't provide any leavening; even Claude Renoir's cinematography, which keeps the movie looking pretty good, doesn't hide the coldhearted sluggishness. This picture can't be passed off as fun or camp: some of it is unintentionally funny, because of the improbable dialogue and the unconvincing acting, but Lewis Gilbert doesn't have the crude dynamism that Edward Dmytryk brought to the Robbins material in *The Carpetbaggers* and that made it entertaining in a tawdry, bad-movie way. Gilbert plods along, depending totally on the intrinsic grossness of the material to carry the picture.

The dependence on brutality in *The Adventurers* is such an aesthetic offense because it is part of a computerized mass-medium package that makes everything, including life itself, cheap. The movie is based on Robbins' law of eternal human corruption. The message is that nothing changes. The poor suffer and die, the rich are sated and empty, revolutionaries will be as bad as the oppressors they overturn, and so on. When Anna Moffo sings, those listening to her in the movie are bored, and so are we. The picture is so dispiriting that one does not perceive any beauty even in an aria; we wait for the next shock. Although it was probably inevitable, the moviemakers were right to have the aria boring: artistic achievement of any kind would explode the thesis of this movie, and expose the way it was made.

I've seen a lot of rotten movies, but this is the most disgusting of them all, because there's so much of it and it's on such a spectacular scale — it cost over ten million dollars, and it's going to get a promotion commensurate with its budget. The violence is supposed to explain why the hero — Bekim Fehmiu, playing a character obviously modelled on Porfirio Rubirosa — "does not feel" when he makes love to women. A lot of people can thus be killed to explain a lot of lovemaking. The people who made this movie didn't feel, either, and maybe movies can't do violence of this kind to us for very long without our ceasing to feel. *The Adventurers,* by the way, is not X-rated — no picture with a big budget has ever been X-rated — so you can take the kiddies. Here and abroad, all over the world, for generations to come, people can have the shared memory. Harold Robbins, via Levine and pals, is affecting the emotions of the world. That's obscenity.

•

By contrast, the vacuity of the Ross Hunter–George Seaton ten-million-dollar *Airport* has the dull innocence of an accounting error.* Arthur Hailey, the author of the novel on which *Airport* is based, has publicly explained his methods of work — the number of hours of research per character, the time spent on plotting, etc. There appears to be perfect harmony in the matching of his businessman's approach with that of Ross Hunter, the producer, who bought a No. 1 best-seller that sold over four million copies, assembled a cast with twenty-three Oscars among them, and played everything safe. But it doesn't work. The publicity lulls one into imagining that *Airport* might be slick and fun — the kind of movie of a book-that-one-wouldn't-ever-think-of-reading that can be relaxing in a dumb, enjoyable way. But *Airport* flops even on that *Hotel* or *The V.I.P.s* minimal-entertainment level. There's no electricity in it, no smart talk, no flair. The director and scriptwriter, George Seaton, who is a past president of the Motion Picture Academy, is reputed to be a very nice man, but he has never made a good movie. (The high points of his career are *Miracle on 34th Street, Little Boy Lost, The Country Girl, The Counterfeit Traitor.*) *Airport* is bland, predigested entertainment of the old school; every stereotyped action is followed by a stereotyped reaction — clichés commenting on clichés. The actors play such roles as responsible,

* An error from my point of view only; the film was, in fact, one of the most financially successful of all time.

harried executive (Burt Lancaster), understanding mistress (Jean Seberg), spoiled, selfish wife (Dana Wynter), man who needs to care for someone (Dean Martin), and the someone (Jacqueline Bisset), with Helen Hayes doing her lovable-old-trouper pixie act; the only person in it who suggests a human being is Maureen Stapleton, who manages to bring some intensity out of herself — it certainly isn't in the lines. This is the kind of movie in which Miss Hayes tries to get a laugh by saying that her late husband was so good a violinist he could play the "Minute Waltz" in fifty-eight seconds. Uggh.

•

"*The Boys in the Band* . . . is not a musical," say the ads. Next time around, it probably will be. In the theatre, *The Boys in the Band* was a conventional play about a "shocking" subject — a gathering of homosexuals at a birthday party. It was enlivened by giddy gay-bar humor and actors carrying on onstage as actors often do backstage, but it was also full of lachrymose seriousness about the miseries and heartbreaks of homosexuality. It was like *The Women,* but with a forties-movie bomber-crew cast: a Catholic, a Jew, a Negro, one butch type, one nellie, a hustler, and so on, and, in place of the bomber crew's possible homosexual, a possible heterosexual, who acted like great-lady Norma Shearer herself. They didn't want to be the way they were, the characters kept telling us. The gist of the play was "We homosexuals may talk like bitches, and give you a laugh by degrading ourselves, but we have feelings, too" — and those feelings turned out to be the same old need-to-be-understood and need-to-be-loved. On the screen, as on the stage, *The Boys in the Band* is full of exposition — that straight fellow from the Victorian era is there so he (and we) can get a crash course in homosexual problems — and of such venerable devices as the host of the party taking a swig of gin and turning from Jekyll to Hyde. Not an awful lot has been changed in the movie version — even the cast is the same — but it's a theatre piece that has lost its theatrically satisfying form, and what was bad is now worse, while what was passable because it "played well" doesn't play so well on the screen. Maybe because the author, Mart Crowley, is the producer, the text has been preserved as if the quips were ageless and pure gold (and they're delivered with knee-whacking emphasis), and the director, William Friedkin, brings out the worst of the play with guilt-ridden pauses and long see-the-suffering-in-the-face closeups. Every blink and lick of the lips has its rigidly scheduled meaning, and it's all so solemn — like Joan Crawford when she's thinking. The actors sweat so freely that the movie seems to have moved the party to the baths. The fun of the homosexual vernacular and the interaction of the troupe of actors onstage helped a little to conceal the play's mechanics, in which each reveals "the truth" about himself. But the actors are no longer fresh in their roles, and Friedkin, by limiting the number of actors in the frame to those directly involved in the dialogue and by the insistence of his closeups, forces our attention to the pity-of-it-all. When the camera slowly moves in for the emotional kill as Emory-Emily talks about how the kids at school made fun of him, one's thoughts drift back to *East Lynne* and other works of cool sophistication.

[March 21, 1970]

Lust for "Art"

Ken Russell's movie of *Women in Love* could perhaps be described as a Gothic sex fantasy on themes from D. H. Lawrence's novel. Visually and emotionally, it's extravagant and, from time to time, impressive; Russell is no ordinary, uncertain-of-himself filmmaker. He goes for what you've never seen anything quite like before; he pours on the décor and startling camera positions. Russell has a purple style of filmmaking, and by that I mean just what we mean when we say an author writes purple prose: he goes for grand effects, but his meanings are wildly imprecise. The picture practically wallows in "style," which is to say, in excess; he overreaches so consistently that one comes out without any clear idea of what was supposed to be going on among the characters. Because Lawrence was one of the most (perhaps the most, though rivalled by Conrad) purple of all great writers, Russell's style might deceive one into imagining that he was providing a film equivalent to Lawrence's prose. But Lawrence's passionate imprecision is what's bad in his writing. It's unforgivable in a pulpy novel like *The Plumed Serpent,* but the overwriting is easy to pass right through in *Women in Love,* because Lawrence was reaching for clarity; he might make a fool of himself groping around his characters' psychosexual insides like a messianic explorer, but he *was* opening up new terrain. Russell, on the other hand, heads right for the purple, and does it not for character revelation, or for clarity about how sexual relations are affected by character, but for virtuoso tableaux "inspired" by Lawrence: the domineering Gerald (Oliver Reed) forcing his terrified horse toward a roaring train, whipping and kicking the bleeding animal; Gerald and Rupert Birkin (Alan Bates) wrestling nude by firelight in a gloomy mansion; the discovery of the entwined bodies of a drowned newlywed couple; Gudrun (Glenda Jackson) dancing defiantly in front of a herd of bullocks, their long horns swaying rhythmically to her movements; and so on. Russell's baroque, romantic period evocations are never static — he treats period material with the speed of *cinéma-vérité* techniques — but the overheated scenes are piled on for our admiration, not for our understanding. The movie is a series of lavish caricatures, bursting with intensity that isn't really grounded in anything. It might seem that Russell confuses being gorgeously lurid with capturing the essence of the novel. More likely, however, this is not confusion as much as it is the drive of Russell's temperament; he takes off from Lawrence's novel in the way that Kurosawa in *Throne of Blood* takes off from *Macbeth*, and he does it with great assurance, even though *Women in Love* does not have the kind of structure that is intelligible when it's treated this way. Russell, I think, is after a highly colored swirl of emotional impressions that is more Brontë sisters than Lawrence. He makes Lawrence's period romantically *exotic*, the way a movie like *Black Narcissus* was exotic, so even when he's most effective it's a fruity falsification of Lawrence's work. Vulgarisms like "With Ken Russell for a friend, Lawrence doesn't need an enemy" come to mind. Yet some instinct tells one that Russell is indifferent to all that — that he sees himself not as an interpreter of Lawrence but as a free artist, using past art as material to make something new. And he has not merely a lust for art but a lust for "art" — for visual effects that are strikingly "artistic." His movie is purple because his idea of art is purple pastiche.

Superficially, in its use of words and scenes from the text, the movie stays close to Lawrence, but in a way that makes little sense — and certainly doesn't make *Lawrence's* sense — unless you know the book. Richard Aldington wrote, "The less you know about Lawrence the more baffling and irritating you will find *Women in Love*. . . . Was it his knowledge that he put so much of his mysterious self into it which made him so often claim it as his best?" To extend this, the less you know of the book the less you'll understand of the movie, and I think maybe to see the movie before reading this particular book is desecration. The novel is a staggering accomplishment — the sort of book that leaves one dumbfounded at how far its author got — and since there are few English novels of this stature, we shouldn't jeopardize our vision of it by reading it in terms of the actors and images of the movie. Movies affect us so powerfully that if you pick up the book afterward Lawrence seems to be lying or to have got things all wrong. There's an even worse danger. The movie is full of "big scenes," which churn up a lot of emotion, but they're not great scenes; they're not fun, and not good to watch. If one tries to view this movie as *sui generis* in what one assumes are Ken Russell's terms — as one big violently sensuous experience — it's disturbing and unresolved and anti-erotic. One feels uneasy when it's over; it's an opaque, unsatisfactory movie — the experience of it is rather like Lawrence's accounts of bad sex. You feel so confused you don't even want to talk about it. Those who don't know the book (and there are many) might take being overpowered by Russell's knockabout passion as the equivalent of reading *Women in Love*, and, since the after-emotions of the movie are so turgidly unpleasant, never open the book. They not only will never know what the movie is about but will have lost out on something much bigger.

In the movie, there's so much rumbling from the unconscious that we begin to feel we need seismograph readings on the people. That, of course, was what Lawrence — investigating our "subterranean selves" — provided: he showed us the hidden mechanisms of the characters that explained what they said and did. The script — by Larry Kramer, who is also the co-producer — retains some of Lawrence's dialogue, but without supplying clues to the motives behind it. Kramer has an aberrant gift for selecting the dialogue in which Lawrence sounds like a prizewinning television dramatist and changing it slightly to make it even worse.

> BIRKIN: You can't bear anything to be spontaneous, can you? Because then it's no longer in your power. You must clutch things and have them in your power. And why? Because you haven't got any real body — any dark sensual body of life! All you've got is your will and your lust for power.

And there are serious pre-coital conversations that make one squirm:

> GUDRUN: Try to love me a little more and want me a little less.
> GERALD: You mean you don't want me?
> GUDRUN: You're so insistent. You have so little grace. So little finesse. You are crude. You break me and waste me and it is horrible to me.

In the novel, we are told *why* the characters talk such drivel. Since the movie doesn't tell why, it's hardly surprising that reviewers are praising

Russell but commiserating with him for being stuck with poor old Lawrence's "dated" material. According to one, the film is *too* faithful, and "The trouble with *Women in Love* is D. H. Lawrence." Since various movie reviewers also blamed what they didn't like about *Far from the Madding Crowd* on dated old Thomas Hardy, one wonders who is hip enough for them to read, or if they're catering to "the film generation," for whom, they believe, all books are dated. But it's a gross deception to pretend that you can get the same things out of a movie that you can get out of a great novel, and the movie of *Women in Love* isn't even *interested* in the same things.

The women in love are sisters, educated women trying to be free women — the unimaginative Ursula, based on Frieda Lawrence (though Jennie Linden in the role suggests Debbie Reynolds), and Gudrun, Lawrence's glittering, poisonous portrait of Katherine Mansfield. Glenda Jackson is an odd, tense, compelling actress, and her Gudrun dominates the movie. However, except for occasional glimmers of humor, Miss Jackson isn't — so far, at least — a very likable actress; she's not someone an audience is likely to identify with or feel with. She interests us, but she puts us off; if you know the book, you can see that her interpretation of an unyielding, castrating woman is original and bold and a considerable feat, but her Gudrun is so self-contained and remote from the audience that without that knowledge of the book you can't figure out what she is meant to be. Russell is flamboyantly gifted, but where human beings are concerned he may be a little obtuse. Either he takes too much for granted or he's indifferent to meaning; he doesn't compensate for what is left out or for his casting. Miss Jackson has a stony, artificial quality that is like an Expressionist study of Gudrun's soul. In Lawrence's portrait, this was on the inside of a soft, desirable woman; now that it's outside, any man could spot it and beware.

Birkin, Lawrence's autobiographical hero, marries Ursula, while the destructive Gudrun torments to death his friend Gerald. The movie doesn't enable us to understand the contrasting chemistries of these two couples. Oliver Reed isn't bad as Gerald, but nothing clues us in on what sort of man he is, and there isn't enough shading in the portrait. He just seems to be rather glum and bilious — a masochistic Rochester — and we don't see why this suffering lump is drawn to Gudrun. The worst failures are with subsidiary characters — especially Eleanor Bron's disastrous Hermione, a character so repulsively misconceived and satirized that one feels sorry for the actress. Russell gives us effects without causes: a flashy scene showing Gerald's mother's hatred of beggars, but without Lawrence's brilliant, Dostoyevskian analysis of why. As a human observer, Russell fails all along. In a schoolroom sequence, with Birkin explaining about the long danglers that produce pollen to fertilize the little seed-producing flowers, the kids in the class don't burst out laughing — they don't respond at all. And however we are meant to react to the nude-wrestling sequence, what we do react to is the fact that Oliver Reed's genitals are clearly visible, while the lighting and the photographic angles obscure Bates's; we are thrown right out of the movie, to consider the actors, not the characters.

Despite the visual sophistication of this film, in some ways its techniques are primitive. We know more about the sex lives of the characters played by Trevor Howard and Wendy Hiller in *Sons and Lovers,* because as performers they had mastered ways to represent emotions that included sexuality. The movies don't really have any iconography for a direct representation of what goes right or wrong in sexual relations. For actors, trying to stay in character and to act sexual abandonment and unselfconsciousness is like trying to swim on land — they go through the motions, but it's a dry run. The movies used to use symbolic substitutes for sex acts — a blazing fire or the embers dying, trains and tunnels, exploding fireworks, and so on — or else indicate how the act had gone by a pussycat smile of satisfaction (Scarlett O'Hara) or a hostile look of frustration or just a bored expression. Now, when the performers are naked and are either simulating or actually having intercourse, the directors clue us in by the same old methods. And it becomes ludicrous to watch two people thrashing around if, in addition to that, we have to wait for acted closeups or some symbolic action to tell us how it is. Sometimes the heightened realism in *Women in Love* is grotesque: when Gerald and Gudrun are together and the activity is bed-bangingly violent, Russell seems to be staging a love match and a boxing match simultaneously. There was one marvellous bed scene in *Room at the Top,* in which Simone Signoret talked to Laurence Harvey and one got a sense of sexual passion — one believed in her pleasure in sex, and her fears. There is nothing comparable in *Women in Love* — we never believe that either girl is in love. Lawrence's fervor was for knowledge of what love and sex mean in our lives; Birkin said it for him in the novel: "I only want us to *know* what we are." Ken Russell wants merely to excite the senses — to make a bash of a movie. A great movie artist must, I think, care about both; and perhaps a movie director can't excite the senses pleasurably and satisfyingly unless he does care about both.

[March 28, 1970]

PART II

Numbing the Audience

Early this year, the most successful of the large-circulation magazines for teen-age girls took a two-page spread in the *Times* for an "interview" with its editor-in-chief, and after the now ritual bulling (Question: "You work with young people — what is your view of today's generation?" Answer: "My faith in them is enormous. They make a sincere attempt at being totally honest, at sharing. They're happily frank about their experiences. They're the most idealistic generation in history. . . . When you consider the vast problems confronting us, their optimism and activism is truly inspirational"), and after the obeisance to the new myths ("They are the best-educated and most aware generation in history"), the ad finally got to the come-on. Question: "Is it true that your readers don't differentiate between your ads and your editorials?" Answer: "Yes, that's true. Our readers are very impressionable, not yet cynical about advertising . . . eager to learn . . . to believe." The frightening thing is, it probably is true that the teen-agers don't differentiate between the ads and the editorials, and true in a much more complex sense than the delicately calculated Madison Avenue-ese of the editor's pitch to advertisers indicates. Television is blurring the distinction for all of us; we don't know what we're reacting to anymore, and, beyond that, it's becoming just about impossible to sort out the con from the truth because a successful con makes its lies come true.

A lot of the "film-generation" talk is, of course, business-inspired — an attempt to create a new youth market to replace the older audience lost to television — and, via the schools, the businessmen are making it true. The textbook *The Motion Picture and the Teaching of English,* financed by a grant from Teaching Film Custodians (an affiliate of the Motion Picture Association of America) to the National Council of Teachers of English, heralded the push into the schools, and teachers who want to be hip have taken up movies as what's happening. Publishers have rushed to prepare books to take advantage of the new film courses, and conglomerates have bought up the 16-mm.-film-distribution companies in expectation of educational funds' being poured into film rentals. Everywhere in the media, one has begun to hear of the wonderful new "visual literacy" possessed by the young — how, without effort, they have acquired a magical new kind of education from television. Teachers who couldn't get their students to do any work and couldn't think of anything else to do with them have begun to see the virtue of bombarding them with images, and so across the country the schools are acquiring the hardware of "visual literacy." According to the pamphlet handed out at the recent New York Film Festival to encourage donations to the Film Society of Lincoln Center, "Once they were just 'the movies.' Now movies are the core language of the young. More than that . . . suddenly films have become the meaningful way for all generations, all nations, to really talk each other's language."

After a half century in which movies were indeed a medium that linked people, and gave us, for good and for ill, common experiences, we get this public-relations "suddenly" stuff when the bulk of American movies are being aimed directly at the young audience and are sold to it on the basis that it's different from all previous audiences. In its small way, the pitch is as delicately calculated as the teen-age-magazine ad (the two are even dotted the same way). By the time the media men, with the teachers at their heels, have finished indoctrinating school kids to be the film generation, that "core language" — whatever it is — may be the only language they've got left. The joker in this stacked deck is that school kids and college students go to movies less frequently than earlier generations did. Although students are saturated from watching television at home (which may be a major factor in why they expect to be passively entertained at school and turn off when they aren't), movies are being pushed in the school systems because the number of paid movie admissions per year is about a fourth of what it used to be. Movie companies are trying to develop new customers, like the tobacco companies when they sent free cartons to the soldiers in the Second World War, to get them hooked on cigarettes.

Actually, something has gone terribly wrong with movies. I think it can be said that the public no longer goes to them with much expectation of pleasure, and, as a result, many people have stopped going to any but the most highly praised and publicized films, and often regret going to those (such as *Catch-22*). Even college students, who do seem to make intense contact with a few films each year, don't go to many new movies. Often they prefer old movies on television to the less publicized of the new films (they say they have a better time watching old movies), and they don't go regularly to whatever is playing, as students used to. In fact, they, like the people in their thirties and forties, tend to go to the same few big hits — to *Easy Rider* and *Midnight Cowboy* and *M*A*S*H* — the difference being that they tend to go repeatedly. Most movies these days are made for nobody; the proportion of movies that fail commercially is at an all-time high, and now when they fail they often fail mercilessly — sometimes on the opening day of a first-run movie a theatre does not sell a single ticket — so that investing money in movies is becoming a fantastic long-shot gamble against public apathy. Movie companies try to cut their losses by not releasing some of their less promising completed films; that way they save on advertising and the cost of making prints.

Laments for the entertaining movies of the past are pointless; with rare exceptions, those movies are still around to be seen and enjoyed at revivals or on television, but we cannot imitate them successfully now, nor should we try. Hollywood did try, and for far too long. The conventions of those movies were years ago drained of energy, and the movies that stick to them now, such as *Airport,* appeal to the sort of people who get their juices flowing by denouncing pictures like *Candy* and *Myra Breckinridge* and *Beyond the Valley of the Dolls* as morally subversive. We can't, unless we're stupid, ask film people to make movies the nice, stodgy way they (or their predecessors) used to. I can't even review the twenty-five-million-dollar *Tora! Tora! Tora!* After a half hour, I fell into a comatose state; reprieved by the intermission, I sneaked away. It was always too late for a movie that thinks it's being fair to the Japanese by having Japanese actors behave like slit-eyed Americans. The cast of non-Japanese — Leon Ames and Neville Brand and George Macready and James Whitmore and Wesley Addy and Leora Dana and E. G. Marshall, ad infinitum — has all the charisma of a veterans' convention. With that weary bunch of second-string actors, the war seems to have been caused by American enervation, and with lines like "I must get back to the fleet. There is a lot to be done" who needs bombs? I do recall one joke, though an inadvertent one, when some poor historical facsimile of an actor stands by a window and cries, "For God's sake, man, that's not a paper fleet out there!" — and the view is so pathetically fake that one's first thought is: Well, if it isn't paper, what is it, an oil painting? This kind of moviemaking never carried any conviction; only in the heat of battle — and Vietnam isn't that kind of battle — could audiences deceive themselves about its quality. Richard Fleischer's direction has no bite, no tension, no beauty. One can't get angry at the lack of depth, or at the pedantry about acts of treachery on one side and acts of incompetence on the other; this movie is too weakly uncertain of itself to be the occasion of anger. One merely dozes, knowing that *Tora! Tora! Tora!* is one of the last of its kind; the only question it raises is whether it will finally sink the oft-bombed Twentieth Century-Fox.

But, except for the big hits, the newer kinds of movies mostly don't satisfy *anybody*. After the breakdown of the studio system, the good side of the chaotic situation got attention first, with the looser, more individual-in-style films of Sam Peckinpah, Mazursky and Tucker, Dennis Hopper, Robert Altman, and others; but the bad side is becoming overpowering, and that regular weekly audience, decimated by television, is being shrivelled by too many nights at movies like *End of the Road, The Looking Glass War, Futz, Duffy, The Legend of Lylah Clare, The Bed Sitting Room, The Magus, Coming Apart, The Happy Ending, The Adventurers, The Magic Christian*. Why should people submit to more? The answer is they don't, and almost all the films released this summer have been box-office bummers. I don't think it's anything as simple as lack of talent; one does not have to be supremely talented to do entertaining work in films, and many of the men whose work has given enduring pleasure were probably less gifted than some of the men now making intolerably insensitive films. The problem may lie in the attitudes that permeate new films; even when they're relatively clever and fast-moving, one is likely to come out depressed rather than refreshed, feeling disagreeable or angry from having so much unsorted-out material and gratuitous technique flung in one's face. Is this perhaps because the moviemakers don't have the respect for the audience essential to the creation of satisfying theatrical experiences?

Many of the men who have been quickest to take advantage of the flux since the conglomerate takeovers and failures are those with the low cunning to exploit the current mood of the young movie audience (as in *Joe*) or with the strong, shallow egos to convince the shaken-up studio heads that they know what the youth market will buy. The rising hacks now making deals have taken over some of the coarsest attitudes of the moguls and have left out one vital ingredient of old picture-making. It used to be understood that no matter how low your estimate of the public intelligence was, how greedily you courted success, or how much you debased your material in order to popularize it, you nevertheless tried to give the audience something. That was the principal excuse for all the story conferences and the gimmicks and restrictions inflicted on the writers and directors by the producers, and even though this excuse was the basis for crippling men of talent and presenting garbage to the public, the excuse wasn't *totally* false. It seems a little silly to have to point this out, but the assumption that a movie was supposed to do something for the audience was a sound one. The greatest moviemakers — men like Griffith and Renoir — were the men who not only wanted to give the audience of their best but had the most to give. This is also, perhaps, the element that, combined with originality of temperament, makes the greatest stars and enables them to last — what links a Louis Armstrong and an Olivier and a Streisand and maybe, with luck, a Flip Wilson. In the new, fluid movie situation, with some of the obstacles gone, it should be easier for artists to give everything they have; that's what freedom means in the arts. Working at one's peak capacity, going beyond one's known self, giving everything one has, makes show business, from time to time, art.

Good hack work could be done under the old system, because even when you worked beneath your full capacity — grinding your teeth in frustration — you could still do an honest job, respectful of the audience's needs, and some fine American movies were made as plain, honest jobs of hack work. But the American audience outgrew the conventional genre films. What new wine could be poured into the bottle of the Western? (The new wine of *The Wild Bunch* explodes the bottle.) The myths of the Old West, with the heroic figures of authority and the coming of law and order, no longer touch off the right reverberations in an audience. The familiar patterns whose unfolding once gave the audience such anticipatory pleasure and such nostalgic satisfaction in the formal closing began instead to turn the surfeited audience derisive, and so the Western heroes became camp figures who grew old and fat (as in *True Grit*) or Freudian-freaky (as in the Burt Kennedy Westerns), or escaped to other countries (as in *Butch Cassidy and the Sundance Kid*). The strength had been sapped from the old genres; they belonged to the studio system, and the attempt by the nervous, unimaginative studio heads to cling to them sapped the studios.

But substituting the clichés of Madison Avenue militancy for the formulas and the middle-class banalities is a disaster at every level; in Europe a movie like *The Strawberry Statement* may be considered politically daring, but we here can recognize it for what it is — the twin of that teen-age-magazine pitch for the youth market. The puerile old romances may have been bourgeois, but at least they bound us together by reminding us of our common fantasies. Exploitation "message" movies like *The Strawberry Statement,* the brash, confident *Getting Straight,* and the new *R.P.M.* are more offensive. No contemporary American subject provided a better test of the new movie freedom than student unrest. It should have been a great subject: the students becoming idealists and trying to put their feelings about justice into practice; their impatience at delays; the relationship between boredom and activism; and what Angus Wilson has called "the mysterious bond that ties gentleness to brutality, a bond that has made our times at once so shocking and so hopeful." Instead, we've been getting glib "statements" and cheap sex jokes, the zoomy shooting and shock cutting of TV commercials, plus a lot of screaming and ketchup on the lenses. These movies took the recently developed political consciousness of American students, which was still tentative and searching and (necessarily) confused, and reduced it to simplicities, overstatements, and lies. In the standard Hollywood vulgarizing tradition, the theme of student revolution was turned into a riot-movie fad, polished off now by Stanley Kramer's grandstanding liberalism in his *R.P.M.* Though Anthony Quinn, as an acting college president, is the hero, and the movie is meant to show primarily the Kramer old-warrior-liberal side, the movie, for all its jabber of hating violence, nevertheless heads right toward it, just like *Getting Straight* and *The Strawberry Statement*. The directors present violence as the students' only courageous course of action, not because it arises out of the given issues but because of their crudeness as moviemakers — because they want the smash finale of a big-production-number violent confrontation. They change their rhetoric but not their styles: Richard Rush's carnage in *Getting Straight* is just like his carnage in the wheeler *The Savage Seven;* Stuart Hagmann is still making commercials in *The Strawberry Statement*.

In an article in the *Times,* Israel Horovitz explained that he didn't write the screenplay of *The Strawberry Statement* for radicals. "We sit in New York," he said, "and reek of sophistry." From his ideas ("Isn't it strange that man could invent wealth but never find a way to spread it around?"), he seems to be a sophistic Andy Hardy. He wrote the movie, he tells us, to radicalize a typical fifteen-year-old girl in his home town. His article could almost be a classic New Left parody of the old Hollywood explanations of why movies had to be made for twelve-year-old minds. How is it that, unlike the writers on the Andy Hardy pictures, who knew they were hacks when they wrote down to the audience, Mr. Horovitz does not know? How is it that Richard Rush and his scriptwriter, Robert Kaufman, do not know that when they reject criticism of *Getting Straight* (as they did in the *Times*) by appealing to the superior court of those "lined up every night in record numbers" they are giving the same old Hollywood answer, and that when they gild it with the information that these queues are composed of "the new generation of moviegoers who have taken film as their own medium, as their personal art form and instrument of communication" they are talking the Hollywoodspeak of Louis B. Mayer and Darryl F. Zanuck? Horovitz didn't appeal to the court of the public, because *The Strawberry Statement* was a flop, but Rush and Kaufman had a hit, so they followed mogul tradition and claimed that the public knows best, or, as they put it, "There are other more demanding and uncompromising critics who will instantly reject a fraud. These critics are the new generation."

The avowed aim of most of the new film men is to shatter the complacency of the audience. Michael Sarne, the director of *Joanna* and *Myra Breckinridge,* threatens us with more of the same until "some compromise is achieved between the generations and races, classes, and warring factions." He and the others justify everything in their movies with slick revolutionary catch phrases; they are, they tell us, attacking the bestiality of our time by making brutal movies, attacking the shoddiness of American culture by shoving shoddiness down our throats. Their movies become our punishment, and the worse their movies turn out, the more self-righteously they explain that it was just what we deserved. They're shaking up Middle America — us, the fifteen-year-olds in Israel Horovitz's home town.

The weathercocks of movie business are the press releases. Here is one from last year:

> Stirling Silliphant will launch his first multiple-picture screenplay agreement by writing the film script for Harold Robbins' forthcoming novel, *The Inheritors,* it was announced today by Joseph E. Levine, president of Avco Embassy Pictures. Silliphant will also write the scripts for two more films for the company: *All the Emperor's Horses* and *America the Beautiful,* and he will produce the latter....
>
> *America the Beautiful* is a satiric comedy about sex, security, and the "easy buck," and is based on a series of essays published by David White.
>
> The press reception at which the announcement was made was Silliphant's first in New York since he left the helm of the Twentieth Century-Fox publicity department in 1953. "This time," he quipped, "I'm on the other side of the fence."

He isn't; he's still in the same business, whether he writes publicity or makes movies, whether he writes the script for *The Inheritors* or a script attacking men just like himself. Madison Avenue sells attacks on Madison

Avenue the same way conglomerate-appointed studio heads grow beards and serve up the terrorist, utopian thinking that they hope will appeal to young ticket-buyers.

•

While students don't go to many movies (they read even less, and perhaps *that's* why they've been named the film generation), the few movies each year that they do care about they seem to take more *personally* than earlier generations of students did. It's the jackpot of turning out one of those few that the new moviemakers aim for. The movies that are popularly considered the best movies at any given time may or may not be good movies — they may be important bad movies — but they touch a nerve, express a mood that is just coming to popular consciousness, or present heroes who connect in new ways. They not only reflect what is going on in the country but, sometimes by expressing it and sometimes by distorting it, affect it, too — such movies as *The Wild One, Rebel Without a Cause, Blackboard Jungle, On the Waterfront, Morgan!, Bonnie and Clyde, The Graduate, Midnight Cowboy, Easy Rider,* the new *Joe,* and probably the new *Five Easy Pieces.* Movies like these enter the national bloodstream, and, at the moment, the few big movies seem to do so faster than ever before, and more directly — maybe because that "best-educated" generation in history is so nakedly vulnerable to whatever stirs it emotionally. This susceptibility, rather than "visual literacy," is the distinctive trait of the "film generation"; the young go back to reëxperience the movies they identify with, entering into them with a psychodrama involvement. *Easy Rider* tapped a vein of glamorous suicidal masochism, and *Joe,* a real main-liner, rushes in all the way. This picture is so slanted to feed the paranoia of youth that at its climax (a reversal of the Sharon Tate case), when the young hippies are massacred by the "straight" adults — the blue-collar bigot Joe and a liberal advertising man — members of the audience respond on cue with cries of "Next time *we'll* have guns!" and "We'll get you first, Joe!"

The apprehensiveness that one feels throughout *Joe* — the sense of violence perpetually about to erupt — makes it effective melodrama but also makes it an anxious, unpleasant experience. I had some doubts about the use of melodramatic techniques on the serious political theme of *Z,* but the director seemed reasonably responsible; in *Joe* the manipulation of the audience is so shrewdly, single-mindedly commercial that it's rather terrifying to sit there and observe how susceptible the young audience is. Since the assassinations, there's been a general feeling of powerlessness, and what gives *Joe* some of the validity that the audience reacts to is that the television and teen-age-magazine advertising-editorial lies have finally resulted in many young people's not knowing how to sort things out, not caring, and not believing *anything.* They go numb, like the young girl in *Joe* looking vaguely for some communal Eden where those without hope can cling to each other, and they accept and *prefer* the loser self-image, not wanting to believe that anything good can happen to them. They don't make it happen; they won't even let it happen. *Joe,* written by another former advertising man, preys on this stoned hopelessness and martyrdom in a congratulatory way, and feeds the customers a series of tawdry clichés about the hypocrisy and hostility and rottenness of the straight world. Its message is that it's all crap — the same message that gets shouts of approval and applause at *Five Easy Pieces.* The few new movies that the "film generation" responds to intensely are the most sentimental (about youth) and the most despairing (about America). It's a bad combination.

[October 3, 1970]

Mothers

The up-to-the-minute title *Trash* is perhaps the cleverest ploy of the movie season; it has the advantage of that self-deprecatory humor that makes criticism seem foolish. But (although *Trash* apparently claims nothing for itself) when people are trashing the cities there are sure to be those who will take the poor white trash of the movie as a metaphor for what the city has made of the people in it. The movie, like the Warhol films that preceded it, winks at the concepts of victimization and futility. *Trash,* an Andy Warhol production but written, photographed, and directed by Paul Morrissey, who was known as the factotum of the Warhol factory until his emergence as a separate figure last year, is now being given a major-art-house release. The assumption is that after the limited success of Warhol's *Lonesome Cowboys* and Morrissey's *Flesh* in the exploitation market the Warhol underground style will finally make contact with a large audience, and Don Rugoff, whose previous releases were

Z, Putney Swope, Elvira Madigan, and *The Endless Summer,* is handling the picture.

The basic Warhol style was to let the camera run and neither to direct nor to edit what was recorded; since Warhol's friends spent a lot of time loitering in front of the camera while trying to think of something to do and were, by and large, exhibitionists who sought to make themselves interesting by shocking the viewers, the results were acclaimed four years ago as "a searing vision of Hell, symptomatic of the corruption of the Great Society," and all that. But, despite the media buildup and the celebrated review in *Newsweek* acclaiming *The Chelsea Girls* as "the Iliad of the underground," few could sit through the passively recorded, lethargic pictures. A value was claimed for the boringness, but it was not a value audiences responded to. Warhol's movies were not movies to go to; they were conversation pieces, and were soon worn out in talk.

Though *Trash* isn't as torpid as *The Chelsea Girls,* and one can sit through it, Morrissey's work raises some of the same issues as Warhol's about why one should. The Warhol "superstars" generally did the sort of caricature imitations of Hollywood sex goddesses that female impersonators do in night clubs for homosexuals and slumming tourists, and added a backstage view of their own lives, so that one got not only grotesque comedy but the fullest sordidness they could dredge up. Though the media, in their constant appetite for the new, acclaimed it as satire, it really wasn't focussed enough for that. The performers didn't put the old movie myths down so much as they put themselves down, acting out a value system in which all that matters in life is to be a glamorous, sexy movie queen. They became what was worst in the old stars, but more so; they tried to become stars by exhibiting their narcissistic self-hatred and spitefulness. They were counterfeit stars willing to mock their failure to pass for genuine but nevertheless hoping that the travesty would make them a new kind of star. Actors in Hollywood needed the break of good roles and a good director, but Warhol was a director only in a nominal sense, and as he let the performers do whatever they wanted, the performers were limited only by their own resourcefulness. Their bitchiness was sometimes witty, their cruelty sometimes vivid, but it was not accidental that, though they became names in the media, they didn't become stars. Stars give the public something that feels new, and they draw us toward them; the superstars were exhibitionists getting their gratification from being part of that Warhol world on the screen, and the audience, reduced to onlookers, judged them — rightly — as people, not as actors. And as people they were like the self-disgusted, gregarious, quarrelsome people in bars and street fights — people to be avoided. A popular hit like *Tobacco Road* might employ the humor of degradation, but it was understood that we were watching actors, and though the ostensible purpose was to call attention to the degradation, the real purpose was to present comedy. In Warhol's bohemian Tobacco Road, the people flaunted their own dishevelment and their own nausea, and it was all so depressing that even when they did funny things, one didn't feel much like laughing.

The aesthetic that some discerned in Warhol's films — that he was purifying cinema by taking it back to simple, static recording — cannot be claimed for Morrissey. Though the visual interest in *Trash* is negligible and the sound is abysmal, the explanation is surely poverty and incompetence, because Morrissey, while he has kept the Warhol films' ambience of exhibitionism and degradation, has joined this to the techniques of the Theatre of the Absurd and the Theatre of the Ridiculous in a relatively conventional narrative. *Trash,* which appears to be semi-improvised, is a classically structured porno comedy about an impotent junkie (Joe Dallesandro) whose sort-of-wife (Holly Woodlawn) is trying to get them on welfare. She pretends to the welfare office that she is pregnant, and plans to take her pregnant sister's unwanted child. Morrissey knows exploitation possibilities, and he has a dramatic sense of shock; the movie opens on the hero's bare, blemished behind, and then the camera moves around to reveal that, despite the best efforts of a girl who is working on him, he is indeed, and graphically, impotent. The movie proceeds by a series of rather familiar absurdist revue-style sequences: other women try, unsuccessfully, to rouse the hero, and the wife's hopes of welfare fade (because the welfare investigator wants the fabulous-forties shoes that the wife found in a garbage can, and she refuses to give them up). As the wife's highest aspiration is to get on welfare, and as the wife isn't even a woman (Holly Woodlawn is a female impersonator), the element of the grotesque is certainly present. *Trash* is steeped in a sense of grotesque parody, but of what isn't clear. Mostly, it seems to be the knocked-out couple doing a put-on of marriage; we are invited to laugh at their outcast status and their meaningless lives, and to feel sorry for them. The tone is absurdist pathos about a make-believe lower depths that one assumes is meant to suggest a true lower depths of homosexuals and junkies; Morrissey lingers over needles going into flesh and puts a nimbus around the messiest head of hair.

Unlike the Warhol superstars, with their suggestions of forties M-G-M-personalities, *Trash* suggests the Depression films and the over-the-hills-to-the-poorhouse silents, with the limp penis substituted for the empty cupboard, and, like the plays of recent years set in basements and rooms full of debris, it wrings humor from the general dejection. When the action moves into a different atmosphere — when the hero is caught burglarizing a modern apartment and is persuaded to remain as a guest — the listlessness that could pass for appropriate in the dirty-kitchen-sink settings is revealed as directorial ineptness. The caught-burglar situation, so familiarly Shavian and once standard in polite comedies, is treated as a wild, far-out idea, in a long, self-contained skit, but there isn't enough dramatic energy to sustain it, and it dribbles along to its contrived climax. Badly timed improvisation on camera can result in the deadest kind of movie: every pause can seem endless, the excremental language is like baby talk, and the viewer falls into a stupor. The inertia of *Trash* is almost certain to evoke comparisons with Beckett, but the inertia is what's *bad* in *Trash* and it's what Morrissey tries to fight off. The *outré* face and voice of Jane Forth as the indolent housewife in the modern apartment are a throwback to Warhol's predilection for plastic ghouls. Morrissey is at his best with weirdly unlikely animal high spirits, like those of the warm, lively go-go dancer who tries to entice the hero in the first sequence. He attempts to keep *Trash* going on the humor of degradation and the comic shocks of breaking taboos: the hero is excited by his wife's nude seven-months-pregnant sister, Holly Woodlawn fakes masturbation with a Miller High Life bottle, and so on. Yet even what may not have been done before is of too low an order of invention to be original; the shocks are without resonance. The humor in the improbable tends to be a quick, forgettable jolt, and when improbabilities become predictable, they're just tedious. The movie is filmed Off Off Broadway theatre, and its style of freakishness was old upon arrival.

Trash depends on our finding camp sordidness both true and funny, but, because of the sluggish rhythm of the picture, we are dependent, as in the Warhol films, on the vitality of the performers. Holly Woodlawn acts up a storm, and though he doesn't quite have the incredible strength of insolence with which Mick Jagger, his hair lewdly slicked down, spews out his big number in *Performance,* Woodlawn does hold you — he belts out his goofy pathos like a snaggle-toothed witch you can't take your eyes off. Like Jagger (and, for that matter, like Marilyn Monroe), Woodlawn defies normal acting categories. Jagger is horrifying, repellent, yet a star presence, and I think we feel something new in him that draws us to him — he's surly and self-involved, and he doesn't clean up and try to ingratiate, and when that shocking power bursts forth, it seems to come out of his not being Mr. Nice Guy. The fascination of Woodlawn is that, in this quasi-Warhol ambience that is so depressing because the human spirit is diminished, his intensity is startlingly, crazily *incongruous*. But it's not much praise to say that the high points of the movie are when people are bizarrely alive rather than just vacuous; and that limp hero is at dead center. The attractiveness of utter cool passivity has been a factor in the success of some of the homosexual-exploitation films — the ads for *Flesh* featured Dallesandro with the words "Can a boy be too pretty?" — and I guess we're supposed to find his blotchy, beat-out quality, the big muscles and the lice in the hair, both attractive and funny, but his apathy enervates this movie. He isn't just impotent; he's barely alive. That's supposed to be the point, but it isn't enough point, and the joke of watching him drag himself around while advances are made to him runs down like a stale burlesque show. What is sometimes called decadence may be just lack of energy.

•

The heroine is named Tish, and the men in her life are named Tad and Jay; that's one of the ways that James Bridges, who wrote and directed *The Baby Maker,* keeps things moving in this perfectly slick, manufactured tearjerker. It's about a woman (Collin Wilcox-Horne) who loves her husband (Sam Groom) but can't have a baby; she wants to raise one that is, as the ads say, "at least half theirs," so she arranges for a young hippie girl (Barbara Hershey) to have a baby by the husband. Shades of Bette Davis and Anita Louise in *That Certain Woman,* and Mary Astor and Bette Davis in *The Great Lie.* Pale shades. This one is all decorative pesudo-seriousness about the development of the fetus, cellophane-wrapped little insights into everybody's feelings, and total evasion of the moral problems implicit in the gimmicky idea. The heroine dehumanizes herself and makes herself the ultimate whore, selling herself unto the second generation, but the movie never takes notice of any of that. The running time is padded out with diversionary tactics and enough poignant touches and discreetly meaningful facial expressions to cover the director with medals for sincerity. Typical of the novelettish approach to issues: when someone asks how the hippie girl can turn her baby over to be raised by bourgeois squares, everyone is satisfied by the answer that a bourgeois-raised child might revolt and a hippie-raised child might grow up to be President. It's like having your head stuffed with feathers. Though we never believe the heroine's reasons for consenting, Barbara Hershey does well with some of her opportunities in the second half of the picture, and it's probably not Miss Wilcox-Horne's fault that she is required to be the most sickeningly banal understanding wife since Norma Shearer. *The*

Baby Maker is the first picture James Bridges has directed, and it is customary to be kind on the occasion of a directorial début, but this débutant has, with his first step, entered the old Hollywood society of commerce. There is not a single one of the carefully planted "sensitive" nuances in the picture that I felt meant anything to James Bridges or told the truth about any emotion he has ever had.

[October 10, 1970]

Clobber-Movie

It is perhaps in the nature of theatre for audiences to be hypnotized by a startling performer, and if a play is performed at noisy fever pitch and gives them the kind of fireworks that the modern theatre is starved for, people may be so carried away by this rare experience of being emotionally moved in the theatre that they confuse great theatre with great drama. This is by way of explaining the honors and awards heaped upon the Howard Sackler play *The Great White Hope*. Although the play, which has a huge cast and has scenes set in many cities and countries, reads like a movie, the movie version, directed by Martin Ritt, clunks along like a disjointed play. The movie is composed of a series of obvious stage scenes; Ritt breaks into them with gigantic closeups, but each scene stays in a given place, and the actors come into it and leave it, making stage entrances and exits. The effect is sometimes very odd — as when the protagonist, Jack Jefferson (James Earl Jones), has a scene, before his championship fight, with a group of religious Negroes who can't get in to the fight but have come to pray for him. When he finishes talking to them, we don't follow him into the arena but, instead, are cut right into the celebration scene after the fight. At the movies, we don't expect to be left waiting outside, like the audience at *Carmen* when Escamillo goes in to the bullring, and since a movie cut does not acknowledge an omission (as a stage blackout does), the effect is almost as if the projectionist had skipped a reel.

One wants James Earl Jones to be a legendary spellbinder; one wants the big performance to work and to hold the epic intentions together by sheer full-bodied epic power, and Jones starts with a great thundering, capering presence, so one can see how when the performance was live he might have accumulated so much force that he swept the audience up. But in a movie the actor can't set the curve and arch of his performance, and there isn't the dynamism — the raw charge — of seeing an actor build a character in a few hours. His stage power can wreck him if the director and the editor don't provide the curve for him, by modulating the other elements and piecing together the bits of film so that the big performance seems to grow organically out of the material. Ritt makes the most obvious mistakes: he keeps the camera close while Jones is projecting with all his might, and whole scenes, such as the one when Jefferson sends his girl away, are disasters because of the stage yelling. In many ways, Jones might have been better served if the movie had been simply a photographed version of the stage production, on the order of the film record of Olivier in *Othello;* then we would make allowances. In this wasteful big (roughly eight-million-dollar) production, Jones's talent is dashed against the movie's scrappy construction. I don't understand how Sackler's hit-them-with-everything dramaturgy got by on the stage. Did audiences really accept that beware-the-ides-of-March-type doom crier and the rag-doll-Ophelia finish of the heroine? At the movie, one squirms at the grandiosity.

It's strange to see crowds being pushed this way and that, as they used to be in the patriotic parades and celebrations of those forties musicals with John Payne and June Haver that you went to in desperation when you'd seen everything else in town. It's all so stagy that when Ritt splurges and shows us thousands of people at the final match, counting time with the referee (so it obviously isn't stock footage), we are moved not by any meaning in the shot but by its pathetic extravagant exhibitionism. It's there to prove they could afford it. I don't know what happened to Ritt between *The Molly Maguires* — which, despite its flaws, was a beautifully designed film, with crowds that were moved by a sure, if heavy, hand — and *The Great White Hope.* Perhaps James Wong Howe, who was the cinematographer on *The Molly Maguires,* was largely responsible for its fine compositions, and certainly the camerawork here, by Burnett Guffey, is flabby and characterless, but still how can one explain the cramped and congested staging, the actors moving in terms of a stage audience, the groups milling about on cue? One can tick off the missed opportunities as they go by; for a crucial example, the triumphal procession of the bloody white winner at the end, which is surely meant to be ironic and ominous and is just a cluttered mess. Given the chest-beating neo-Brechtian script, there was, obviously, no easy way to treat the material — but imagine a reputable director in 1970 thinking he could turn a play into a movie by filling it up with extras.

In Sackler's screen adaptation, only slightly altered from the stage version, the pieces of sociology — like a pedantic little speech about the threat of blacks' moving into the cities — stick out, because we can see that they are an attempt to force wider ramifications upon Jefferson's drama. The core of the drama is psychological: Jefferson is brought down because of white men's fear of the strength and sexuality of blacks and because of their need to have their own prowess reaffirmed by a white champion. This psychological meaning is strongly implicit in the situation, and if the author had concentrated on the principal character and his story, this element might have taken care of itself. But Sackler has so little sense of humor and so little sense of the theatrical chic of fairness that he's even false to his own premises. Though the material gets the credibility benefit of the resemblance of Jack Jefferson's career to Jack Johnson's, Jefferson is never allowed to be brazenly successful with white women. The whole point of the play is that he infuriates the American whites by flaunting his black virility, but the movie, like the play, is so afraid of letting its hero antagonize the audience that instead of having a blonde tucked under each arm, like the actual Johnson, Jefferson is allowed only one dowdy brunette, whom he tries to protect from the limelight. So there isn't even a spring for the mechanism of the action. And the lack of adequate motivation makes it very perplexing that in whatever country Jefferson travels to there are white Americans who have come all that way to trap him and destroy him — conspiratorial monsters pulling strings to bring down the black colossus.

The program given out to the press summarized the theme: "The Establishment — government, industry, labor unions, the boxing racket itself — feared that the spectre of a black man wearing the heavyweight crown might inspire the mass of blacks to rebel. A way had to be found to rid him of his halo, his championship title. Hence, the great conspiracy and the search for a 'Great White Hope.' " And that's how the movie treats the material — as an ambitious melodrama of the sneaky, rotten whites plotting against one noble black. The Jefferson-Johnson life could have provided a clear example of unconscious mistreatment — for surely the whites must have rationalized what they did to him, and found legal ways to justify their actions, just as they did with Muhammad Ali — but the *conscious* conspiracy is, in movie terms, banal. When the whites' ignorance and their unconscious fears and resentments (plus some dirty pool by interested parties) are turned into an overt conspiracy to keep the blacks down, we're in Fakesville. Every time the camera moves in to demonstrate the impassivity and fear and meanness in gloating, villainous white faces, we go back to the world of Westerns and cops-and-robbers, where the guilty man's face gives him away. There isn't a white man or child in the movie with a healthy skin tone or with flesh that isn't stony or wrinkled or rotting, and we just don't believe it. The camera lingers on poor Chester Morris's rheumy eyes and swollen lids as if all our guilt were reflected there, but we know it's just sickness and age. It's a disgustingly insensitive movie cliché that the aged, the ugly, and the deformed are evil; in a movie that's festooned with modern attitudes about race, it's a pitiful anachronism.

What this bad production of *The Great White Hope* does is to expose the material. In his very first scene, when he's asked if he's fighting to free his race, Jefferson answers, "My mama tole me Mr. Lincoln done that — *ain't that why you shot him?*" We're supposed to take this not as Jefferson's distorted view but as a shrewd and deeply disturbing riposte — though all whites did not seek, and collaborate in, the death of Lincoln, any more than all blacks bear the responsibility and guilt for the murder of Malcolm X. This is the kind of all-purpose accusation and rhetoric that has become familiar in Black Panther arguments — and one can perceive its freewheeling effectiveness in those arguments. The intention is to build up a sense of injustice and rage, and to make what the black accuser says that the hateful white man really wanted to do more true than the facts of what white men actually did. But when this kind of argument is used as the basis for a Brechtian demonstration-drama — a clobber-drama — what can be its intention? There's no way for an audience to work off guilt for what it didn't do, and that's the kind of guilt this play specializes in. Whether consciously or unconsciously — probably both — this play is designed to intensify white guilt, and the wildness of the national-conspiracy charges, which makes the guilt so engulfing that the audience is surrounded, permeated, and helpless, was probably part of the play's effectiveness in the theatre.

There used to be bewildered figures in fiction who, as in *Crime and Punishment,* confessed to crimes they hadn't committed; in American movies such characters were more often treated satirically, and the nuts who rushed forward to expiate crimes they'd read about in the tabloids were given the bum's rush by movie cops. But we are developing a beat-me-for-everything-bad-that's-ever-happened kind of serious movie that drowns the audience in helpless misery and is turning *us* into nuts.

•

Monte Walsh is another tombstone for the graveyard of the Western. This one is so solemn about the bygone days of the cowboys that the elegiac intentions are not polluted by suspense. A melancholy hour passes before you discover that there's actually going to be some sort of story, and then all the principal characters die off except Monte (Lee Marvin), who is left a senile derelict, talking to his horse. *Monte Walsh*, which cost six millon dollars, will be lucky to play to so large an audience. Directed by William A. Fraker (the cinematographer on *Bullitt*), it is a handsome-looking film, but it's paced as unvaryingly as a funeral march, and scored (by John Barry) to sustain the illusion of an epic for the movie company, if not for the audience. The music is about all you hear in the movie. Moviemakers seem to have been confusing the strong, silent Western heroes of silent motion pictures with history, and *Monte Walsh* follows the tradition of recent earnestly "authentic" Westerns in keeping speech to an absolute, monosyllabic minimum — apparently on the theory that people in the West didn't learn to talk until the automobile was invented. The only advantage of this quaint, taciturn, unwritten script is that in the role of the hero's buddy Jack Palance, who usually rivals the elocutionary style of Victor Jory, is preternaturally subdued. The picture might as well have been called *Lee Marvin*, because Marvin is given nothing else to play. The others are dumb sufferers. Mitch Ryan starves, steals, and gets killed; Palance goes into the hardware business to avoid starvation but gets killed anyway; and Jeanne Moreau makes her American début as a whore who can't earn a living during the bitter winter and dies because "she just didn't want to hang on." It's a Nixon-era Western.

•

First Love is full of words — recitations, poems, stories, and even a bit of narration from its source, the Turgenev novella. But, because the members of the cast, who include the English John Moulder Brown, the French Dominique Sanda, the Austrian Maximilian Schell, the Italian Valentina Cortese, and assorted actors like Marius Goring and John Osborne — all playing Russians — share no language, the movie is elaborately and cleverly dubbed and post-synchronized. We're never really certain whether the slightly disembodied voices are issuing from the people we're looking at. (At times, as when John Osborne, in a big black hat, recites "How Do I Love Thee?" to a gathering of sows, we may prefer to think we're not looking at the real person, either.) We're not certain of much in this movie, which confuses mystification with lyricism, but it was superbly photographed by Sven Nykvist, one of the world's master cinematographers. His craftsmanship is usually at the service of a master director, Ingmar Bergman; here Nykvist's beautiful pictures are just beautiful pictures. That's a lot, but it doesn't make a movie. Turgenev's story (about an adolescent boy's crush on his father's mistress) is set in 1833; Maximilian Schell, who participated in the adaptation and directed, retains the dialogue and characters but opts for "timelessness," which he apparently thinks can be achieved by a jumble of periods. The movie includes the Russian Revolution, but in most ways it's a nineteenth-century variant of the summer-I-grew-to-be-a-man Brandon de Wilde special. As the boy, John Moulder Brown is pink-cheeked and inoffensive, and has one lovely, original moment (when, after he has been kissed behind an ostrich fan, he comes out bobbing his head with joy at his good fortune). The princess he falls in love with (Dominique Sanda, a sumptuous blond former model with a big mouth, who looks like a depraved Valkyrie) becomes, in Schell's strenuous pursuit of the fashionably enigmatic, some sort of high-strung nympho, and the movie is all romantic madness and moth-eaten passion and decadence. In between the poetry readings, people visit a crypt or play with daggers and shriek and laugh. Simplicity seems to be the first casualty now when a director doesn't know what he's doing. Schell chops up the scenes with shock cuts, and throws visions and premonitions, a burning forest and distant gunfire into the lush summer imagery; he piles Chekhov and Marx onto Kahlil Gibran. The sensibility of the film is so mediocre that at the end, when what should have been the theme is summed up by the narrator in Turgenev's own words, the precise intelligence of what his story was about comes as a complete surprise. Apparently, Schell has so little self-critical sense that he doesn't realize that the few sentences by Turgenev wipe out the movie.

[October 17, 1970]

Kamikazes

Ice is a surprisingly honest, comprehensive view of the life style of young American revolutionary terrorists; though nominally set in the indefinite near future, when the Vietnam war has been superseded by a war in Mexico, it is simply an extension of current urban-guerrilla attitudes and activities. However, the film generates far more interest when you talk about it afterward than while you're seeing it. As a piece of moviemaking, it is gray and grainy and painfully stagnant, and when you strain to make out the overlapping mumbled conversations you discover that nothing in particular is being communicated. Though it's an acted film, it has a hazy semi-documentary style, as if a stoned anthropologist were examining his own tribe and were so indifferent to the filmmaking process that he hadn't learned how to read a light meter or bothered to work out a continuity. It's a film about political commitment that is made not only without commitment to film as an art form but without any enthusiasm for its own political commitment.

The director, Robert Kramer, has perhaps the least ingratiating style imaginable. In *Ice* as in his 1968 film *The Edge*, the viewer is likely to get the characters confused, because they're not introduced to us or individualized; we are left to sort them out for ourselves, if we care about the particulars. Obviously, Kramer doesn't, because he doesn't follow such elementary theatrical principles as not casting look-alikes, or costuming people so that they can be readily distinguished. The only care in *Ice* seems to have gone into the violent scenes, and then only into their staging, not into their dramatic function. The film offers a cross-section of guerrilla activities, without explanations. We are plunked into the middle — into receiving guns and hiding them, into meetings, killings, sabotage — without being informed why someone is being killed, or who he is, or why someone else is being tortured. When things go wrong, we don't know why, or even which side they're going wrong for; we're not sure who the opposition are — whether they're police or right-wing groups or left-wingers with a different ideology. And since the scenes don't build out of each other, you get the feeling that the significant parts must be missing, and you become impatient — you feel you're getting the fringe details and mumbo-jumbo of conspiratorial organization rather than the heart of revolutionary activity. It all seems pointless and utterly unreal as you watch kids playing at being guerrillas in their parents' tasteful apartments in the Belnord and other upper–West Side bastions of the middle-class left. When they go out to liberate a luxury high-rise, the nuttiness of it all may make you groan.

But these weaknesses in the movie as plausible dramatic entertainment are just what make it such a revealing account of the anomalies in this movement that *is* concerned with immediate destructive actions rather than a vision or a long-range plan, this movement whose participants do indeed look alike, and talk tonelessly, as if anesthetized, and who are indeed likely to be upper-middle-class kids whose parents support them and, in varying degrees, agree with them and coöperate. It's obvious that some parents made their homes available to Kramer, and some appear in the film. *Ice,* though it cost only twelve thousand dollars (from the American Film Institute), has a cast of two hundred and fifty. Kramer gives a remarkably accurate picture of the world he is part of, and, in a very peculiar way, which I think rarely occurs, his style as a moviemaker — which is to say his *weaknesses* as a moviemaker — is part of the style of life he chronicles. This long, ambitious picture is passive and demoralized and mechanical; it's as alienated as its characters. I don't think Kramer has merely projected his own alienation onto them; I think he shares in their absence of goals, and that's why his movie is so paralyzingly boring.

Ice is the cold, dank side of the youth consciousness; it is concerned primarily with life-taking and with routinized self-sacrifice. *The Edge* was a chronicle of the disillusion of a group of once active civil-rights workers living together in a community; one of them made plans to assassinate President Johnson, failed, and committed suicide. In *Ice,* the actions planned seem just as senseless and suicidal, and are presented that way. The movie is a kind of aging New Left self-examination, a where-we-are-now — a record of random violence and grubby, inane discussions. The movie appears to be coldly objective, and one may think that it is almost obsessively introspective and self-critical until one recognizes that the objectivity is a matter of tone, not of method. Television has accustomed us to thinking that objectivity lies in not evaluating the facts, and this movie, which does not interpret what it shows, and which is so diffuse that the shots don't even appear to be framed, carries "objectivity" so far that the picture seems to be visually decomposing while you're watching it. But though it is not a propaganda film in any obvious sense, there can be no doubt that the presentation is made from inside. *Ice* takes a despondent view, but it believes in the revolutionary actions it shows. It doesn't believe in them *much,* but it believes in them more than it believes in anything else. The commitment is implicit not only in the fact that the movie finds nothing strange about this way of life but in what it takes for granted by starting at the point where all other possibilities have been excluded — which is why it seems totally nondramatic. The characters have already resigned themselves to becoming bodies to be put not just on the line but over it. Kramer doesn't sentimentalize details, any more than he dramatizes situations, but he does sentimentalize at the most basic level in presenting this communal-guerrilla mode of living, on behalf of the poor and victimized (whether they want it or not), as a necessity. And the slight pretense that we're in a future police state makes the underground guerrilla network seem inevitable. However, there's little doubt that some, perhaps many, believe it's inevitable now, and the participation in terrorism by young, privileged, well-educated people is not likely to disturb the younger movie audience, who may accept *Ice* as where things are — and conceivably even as an affirmation.

The extremists are not colorful, emotional, wild-eyed revolutionaries. They go about their plotting and bombing as if revolution were an unpleasant business they were engaged in — a dangerous business that was going to turn out badly for them but that they must go on with. Though the characters are not stereotypes in the Hollywood sense, they nevertheless seem stereotypes rather than people, and this is, I think, part of the revelation of the film — the revolutionaries' interchangeability. They have accepted their roles as cogs in the revolution, and, being devoid of strong personality or flamboyant passions, they *are* alike. They seem to believe they are rational political beings because they are not romantic in style; they have managed to make nihilism banal. They are like the mild, affectless terrorists making bombs in their parents' Village town house; their voices are as low-keyed and lacking in ardor as the Bernardine Dohrn tape. They don't really choose violence; they acquiesce in it. In the movie, they're trying to bring about an apocalyptic change that they don't expect to survive, but they go about their tasks methodically. They have rationalized their irrationality, and they have domesticated their alienation in communal living. (They do not lose their alienation in communal living; instead, they reinforce it, because their alienation becomes the life style that links them.) One could almost say they carry out their tasks like the anonymous workers on a cathedral — for the greater glory of the poor.

They seem to be wiped out as people, but though their dreariness and their acceptance of the self-obliterating life go together, we can't tell which came first. The movie isn't illuminating on this point, yet from the evidence in the film (and elsewhere) I infer that this depersonalization is not distressing to the depersonalized. Maybe their acceptance of conspiratorial action gives them a mission that justifies the depressed state they were in anyway — gives them a definition as people that they hadn't had before, a *reason* for losing the lives that they'd never fully found. They may feel less depersonalized in the movement because they no longer feel the need to express themselves individually. The fact is that within the last couple of years well-educated students have accommodated themselves to terrorism with startling ease. *Ice* shows them to be as blandly programmed as they do indeed seem to be in newspaper accounts. One begins to see the movie as part of a phenomenon, and to look into it for clues to how it is that some of the most freely brought-up children in our society — the children of poets and professors and analysts and successful businessmen — are so personally depressed about "Amerika" and so affectless about violence that they have turned into Kamikazes. In the movie, the guerrillas talk about their regional offensive as part of a spontaneous revolution that, by the meshing of many groups like theirs, will overthrow the warmaking establishment, and yet nihilism is their normal, everyday outlook. They have commitment but not conviction.

They are conspirators in violence, but they aren't like revolutionaries as we've traditionally thought of revolutionaries, because they don't seem to be carriers of revolution — they don't have any revolutionary *spirit*. The film itself raises this question, as it raises so many others, only to drop it in, like the TV producers who think that when they mention something they have covered it, though they have only covered themselves against the charge of having omitted it. The characters in *Ice* relax with drugs or sex, and there is never a hint of intellectual excitement or of any pleasure in thought. They are a joyless, unhappy group, and one gets no sense of how they want society to be, of what their dream of the good life is. Even their despair is neutral. One looks at them and thinks, What kind of revolution could they conceivably make? What kind of life do they visualize? From the evidence, they have no sustaining vision beyond smashing the state. They speak of better conditions for the poor, but they speak of nothing for themselves — not even survival.

Self-abnegation pervades the movie. One can only surmise that these people don't really believe in a liberating revolution — that they believe only in the repression they constantly expect. With the specifically modern look of being faintly blocked emotionally that is as common in the faces in suburban supermarkets as it is in the faces of the girl defendants in the Tate case and the girls sought for bombings, they accept a conspiratorial role, as if everything political had been settled except the details. They carry out their actions like the girl in *La Chinoise* who, having got the hotel-room numbers mixed, assassinates the wrong man, curses herself for her mistake, and goes back into the hotel and shoots the right man — a bureaucrat whose crime is that he carries out orders mechanically. The depressed state of the conspirators suggests that mechanized equality is their goal. One gets the strong impression that it is not politically but psychologically that the terrorists have lost interest in nonviolent alternatives, and that they *prefer* this conspiratorial, terrorist nonpolitics, in which they don't have to believe in anything or try to make actual contact with blacks or the poor, who might rebuff them.

They don't have to leave their own middle-class group. The mechanical solutions of terrorism — the simple acts of destruction — can satisfy their desire for accomplishment. When they blow something up, they have tangible results — not the frustrations they heard about from those who worked in the South or in the ghettos or in the McCarthy campaign. Terrorism is the ultimate materialism. Functioning this way, they don't develop as people; they become like guns.

The atrophy shows in the filmmaking process: Kramer throws in flaccid derivations from Godard — agitprop statements, some revolutionary "theatre," some war toys, a documentary montage. The political slogans that are recited might be a comment on left-wing sterility, but who can say? In this spongy atmosphere, sterility and comment on sterility are not distinguishable. Kramer's work has an ill-defined self-consciousness; almost anything one can perceive in the film might have been put there deliberately or might have found its way in and been accepted as belonging there. The title itself may refer to the frozen rigidity of the movement as it waits for mass support, and it may indicate a recognition that to live just to "smash the state" is not enough. The director, disengaged from filmmaking while engaged in it, is also disengaged from the results: his name isn't even on the picture. All through the ambiguousness and gloom of *Ice*, Kramer seems to be saying that the movement is doomed and maybe the movie isn't worth doing; his pessimism is a deeply offensive form of face-saving sentimentality, since it is used to justify everything from killing to taking pictures out of focus.

In *One Plus One*, Godard's alienation devices backfired. He put down intellectuals, but he did everything in the movie for intellectual reasons; he used black actors as worker-guerrillas and had them recite political lessons inexpressively. Panthers, even when they sound programmed, convey the emotional basis for what they are saying, but in *One Plus One* there was no connection between the words and any revolutionary impulse. And since the words carried no emotional force — not even hate — audiences got bored and stopped listening. Without emotional charge, the revolutionary rituals were like parodies of what Godard himself apparently believes in. The black workers were just blank, and the demonstration-lecture style was so dehumanized that you couldn't even grasp why they'd get involved in a revolutionary struggle. But what you couldn't believe about his black workers you can believe about the educated young middle-class. In *Ice*, the characters appear to get involved in guerrilla action *because* they are blank.

[October 24, 1970]

Men in Trouble

Never Sang for My Father is a drama of a middle-aged man's unresolved relationship with his father. The dramatist, Robert Anderson, keeps things on that truthful level where no solutions are really satisfactory, and the director, Gilbert Cates, doesn't cheat — he accepts the risks of being solidly obvious. Like "creditable" serious TV drama (the genre to which it basically belongs), the movie goes thumping along making points, each scene performing its necessary function, each character working his way to his key lines. The structure is barren of detail; the language is plain and repetitive. It's the kind of drama that is indistinguishable from an outline. And yet, for all one's awareness of how blunt and ingenuous it is, one is held by the plain, prosaic strength of the film — by the immediately recognizable applicability of its observations. By its refusal to offer false reassurances, by its decency in not pulling sloppy feelings out of us, *I Never Sang for My Father* develops valid emotion and so transcends its genre.

One does not expect this sort of bargain-basement dramaturgy to be used to such powerful effect, but in this case the very familiarity of routine "serious" problem drama serves to provide a base for a popularly shared unsentimental emotional experience. Perhaps — ironically — Anderson's screenplay is able to reach and unite the movie audience *because* it is not a great drama but a basically banal and limited work. The one truly great American play on the same theme, *Long Day's Journey Into Night*, is perhaps too complex to reach a large audience the way this movie does just by being perfectly commonplace — so commonplace that the surprisingly austere tough-mindedness has extraordinary impact. It's easy to be snobbish about this kind of unimaginative playwriting, but if art can be made of junk (as it has been), isn't it possible that something authentic may come out of middlebrow seriousness? The TV audience used to be regularly castigated for preferring mindless entertainment to dull worthwhile plays, but in the last few years the mindlessness has been so unentertaining that the lacklustre problem plays have gained a large, respectful audience. That audience is prepared, I think, to accept the conventions in this film and to perceive the authenticity that, this time, comes out of them.

The immaculately false prosperous setting and the ugliness of the production may work in its favor: the movie *looks* like a TV play. The cinematography is a mixture of old, bad studio lighting and too bright color; the sets are overdecorated, and one sculpture-filled room for an "available" woman is the sort of garish concoction one would expect an artistic fallen woman in a bad thirties movie to live in; the music is noisy and banal at the start and then soft and sentimental. In all technical ways, the movie is worse than mediocre, and it's not helped by little flash reprises that show us what the son (Gene Hackman) is thinking of when he has already made it clear. Yet Cates displays a good, discreet feeling for what counts: in general, he keeps the camera at the right distance from the actors for their lines to have the maximum effect.

Each line is too firmly stated, but the line readings are stunningly precise, and this becomes reassuring; one knows exactly what kind of drama it is. Gene Hackman has his best screen role thus far; he's a fine naturalistic actor, and though he isn't particularly handsome, he has an interestingly expressive face. He's believable and compelling in what could be a drag of a role. Estelle Parsons, his wife in *Bonnie and Clyde,* plays his sister with appropriate restraint, but Anderson must have soaked up decades of bad plays and then dried out circa 1945 to have written the character the way he did. And, as the father, Melvyn Douglas *uses* the infernal self-righteousness that made him a pain in movies like *Billy Budd.* He gives the role a marvellous mixture of elements, so one responds to him without hatred and without false sympathy. *I Never Sang for My Father* is in a different league from O'Neill, nor does it come near the dramatic dexterity of that wizard of the banal, George Kelly, but in its own dumb, plodding way it has a very moving integrity.

It may seem a small point, but the movie contains some semi-documentary footage in homes for the aged where despairing, deteriorating people are engaged in leather crafts and other keeping-the-hands-busy activities, and I wish to protest the obscenely narrow interpretation that is offered by a doctor (and sanctioned within the film) — that "this is the other side of our miracle drugs . . . we keep them alive." The aged in our society are the victims not of modern medicine, which eases their pains, but of the changes in how we live that have made them superfluous objects. In the past, they would have been useful — telling stories, mending their grandchildren's toys, sewing, and repairing household objects. Now they are given useless, made-up tasks, and the futility of their displaced, concentration-camp lives encourages senility and that horrible vacant staring at the television box.

•

There is scarcely a false touch in *Goin' Down the Road*; Don Shebib, who directed it, is so good at blending actors into locations that at times while watching it one forgets that it is an acted film. Since it is in color, and is sensitively shot (blown up from 16 mm.), and the total cost was $82,000, it can stand as a model for film students of the kind of craftsmanship that can be achieved on a shoestring. Shebib, a young Canadian who took his Master's in film at U.C.L.A., started this film on a small grant from the Canadian Film Development Corporation and apparently finished it on jawbone and by deferring processing costs. Its base is obviously in the documentary tradition, though Shebib's fusion of documentary and fiction suggests a kinship with such work as Francesco Rosi's *The Moment of Truth*. He has a delicate feeling for the nuances not of traditional "class" but of the class feelings that come from different educations, and he uses this gift to put in social perspective the lives of two totally unhip boys from Nova Scotia (Doug McGrath and Paul Bradley) who come to Toronto for the legendary opportunities of the big city. The picture deals with what they find; it deals always in particulars — the two boys have remarkably well-differentiated characters and responses — and yet the particulars add up to a general social picture. The film is, however, a somewhat hollow triumph of craft over an insufficient idea: the story is too familiar, though the two prodigious, unactorish central performances and Shebib's feeling for detail keep the familiar fresh. But, with a technique like his, Shebib should be working with a more original substance. I don't mean to suggest that he should go the usual route. (In this period of movies, and with openings like *Little Fauss and Big Halsy* and *C. C. and Company*, it would be madness to say, "Go thou and do likewise.") A fine documentarian who knows how to use actors is doubly touched with grace; Shebib has the technique for a new kind of sociological observation on film, and I hope he finds his way.

Goin' Down the Road, which is perhaps the most uncorrupt movie in town, and a movie that will probably suffer at the box office because of its gentleness, has been rated R (or restricted) by the Motion Picture Association of America. The hypocrisy stinks. The rating system is, of course, designed to keep the heat off the industry (and in this, and this only, I hope it succeeds), but since the heat comes from women's clubs and other organizations obsessed by the dangers of carnality and unconcerned about violence, pictures so brutal one can no longer look at the screen get unrestricted ratings, while a thoroughly decent picture with a trace of unsalacious nudity is restricted. One does not have to be a cynic — only informed — to know that if *Goin' Down the Road* had come from an American company and cost millions, it would have been unrestricted.

•

This Man Must Die, adapted from Nicholas Blake's *The Beast Must Die,* is one of Claude Chabrol's lesser films. Even the bourgeois formalism of his previous film, *La Femme Infidèle* — an aestheticized version of the "civilized" entertainment that people used to go to foreign films for — seems to have broken down in this one. After the powerful opening, one looks forward to the storytelling of a celebrated technician, famous for the elegance of his perfectly controlled camera movement, but Chabrol's technique sags, and the movie is so hush-hush quiet, so unoriginal, and so unhurried that it dies on the screen. The film is not even highly distinguished visually; the exterior shots are handsome, but just about any halfway competent cinematographer can get beautiful exteriors. It's knowing how to do the interiors that is the test, and the interiors here are nothing special.

The father (Michel Duchaussoy) who sets out to avenge the hit-and-run death of his son is a pasteboard profile that never suggests a capacity for hatred (or even for fatherhood), and the characteristically unpopulated, stripped-to-essentials screen of Chabrol makes the plot absurd; when we hear that the quest for the child's murderer is like looking for a needle in a haystack, we want to giggle, because practically the only other man in the movie is the hit-and-run driver. In the repressed, stiff characters that Chabrol now favors, aggression can come out only at one remove, in fabricated detective-fiction crimes of violence. This means that if the performers don't manage to convey some emotions beneath the repression, there's not much going on — just the usual shallow suspense story. When the story is as attenuated as *This Man Must Die,* it's not even good pulp. Surely it's not intentional that the picture gets a breath of life when the uncouth villain (Jean Yanne) comes on, yet the beast is the only person in the film who has any vitality. The flourishes — Brahms, and allusions to classical legends — are the ornaments so common in classy detective fiction. But this classy nothing of a movie isn't really even so classy: Chabrol might have done a more subtle job introducing the names of restaurants. In a movie in which every detail is supposed to speak delicious, ambiguous volumes, this suggests payola.

I have nightmare visions of the American movie companies' trying to play it safe by turning to Ross (*Airport*) Hunter to find out how he does it, because they just don't know how to structure the value system for the good guys and the bad guys in youth movies. Two new major-studio motorcycle pictures are indications of the crassness of confused merchandisers. In *Little Fauss and Big Halsy*, which has been synthesized from *Bonnie and Clyde, Hud, Easy Rider, Butch Cassidy and the Sundance Kid,* and *Downhill Racer,* Robert Redford is symbolically wounded, and has a great big scar running down his spine to prove it. The scar is much in evidence, because Redford, playing a swaggering oaf, rarely wears a shirt. (This will not, however, do as much for his career as it did for Paul Newman's.) Redford can't seem to keep his pants up, either, and he's constantly fiddling with his zipper and juggling his genitals (on one occasion, in what is possibly a movie first, in a close shot). Trying to be cute and raunchy, Redford also flashes his teeth like Kirk Douglas, keeps a toothbrush stuck in his mouth, wears funny hats, and wiggles his behind. Was it only a few months ago that he seemed a promising actor? He's already an overripe star, smirking on lines like "Cycles is a mean toy, lady." As his sidekick, Michael J. Pollard does an extended version of his runty, nasal pixy bit. The girl, Lauren Hutton, enters naked, running toward the camera for no particular reason except to make a flash entrance, and she reaches her finest moment when she's carrying a copy of Burroughs' *The Naked Lunch* tucked into her belt, at the rear. This movie, directed by Sidney J. Furie (who has seen better days on motorcycles), is a wheeler crossed with a bucolic romp crossed with a morality play. The boys are professional motorcycle racers, but you never get to see a good race, and you wouldn't know who it was you were supposed to root for if you did, because the runt takes over the vicious attitudes of the wounded stud and this seems to be what enables the runt to become a winner. The picture is interlarded with Johnny Cash singing messages like "It takes nerve to take a curve," but the script, despite much cornpone philosophizing, treats the heroes as aberrant jerks. And when they're doing their buddy-buddy stuff on their cycles, frightening sheep by aiming at them, are we supposed to react with anything but contempt? The ads say Little Fauss and Big Halsy are not your father's heroes. Does Paramount really expect them to be *anybody's* heroes?

C. C. and Company, directed by Seymour Robbie, is a simpler sort of porno-wheeler, with Joe Namath saving Ann-Margret from rape by his outlaw motorcycle gang. Namath has a light, high voice, and when it breaks he sounds a bit like Aldo Ray, and he's generally mild and camera-shy; his physique isn't especially photogenic. But he's rather sweet. (He might become a sub-teen favorite.) The thing we can't figure out in this movie is what this clean-cut fellow is doing among the Hell's Angels–American International pack, or why it's all right for Namath to be civil and decent while the cyclists' whores who steal from straight people are funny and cool and their victims are made ridiculous, and so on. The *machismo* of the cyclists is exploited, but as soon as Namath falls in love and leaves the gang the other cyclists become villains. In *C. C. and Company*, everything finally depends on whether you're nice or not. The gang's girls approach the men sexually, and their sexual bouts lead to quick dissolves, but when Namath lands hard-to-get Ann-Margret they roll and roll while the camera makes lyrical hay. So it turns out to be a boy-meets-girl wheeler about sacred and profane love. The confusion of point of view, plus the crudeness in humor and gestures that it shares with the Redford film, doesn't satisfy the audience even on a fantasy level.

These two movies feature grown men behaving like adolescents, and try to sell this behavior and condemn it at the same time. Moviemakers used to know what made a hero romantic: the actor had to incarnate a personal code of honor and a personal sense of freedom; he had to have the strength to be "his own man" and yet the sensitivity that is attractive to women. (John Wayne, for example, who lacked that sensitivity even when he was young and handsome, rarely had romantic appeal for women.) On the level of idle distraction in action-entertainment movies, this hasn't really changed, except in *style*, as the successes of Paul Newman and Steve McQueen have indicated. Redford seemed destined to be a new, modern version of the romantic mythic hero. But don't the moviemakers ever go to the movies? You must really have had to pull the jacks out of your connections to cast Robert Redford as a cruddy blowhard loser and Ann-Margret as a refined high-fashion writer who needs protection from rapists.

[October 31, 1970]

Mythmaking

Gillo Pontecorvo's *Burn!* is an attempt to tell the story of a mid-nineteenth-century slave uprising on a fictitious Caribbean island from a neo-Marxist, Frantz Fanonian point of view, so that it will become *the* story of black revolution and a call to action. No one, with the possible exception of Eisenstein, has ever before attempted a political interpretation of history on this epic scale, or attempted to plant an insurrectionary fuse within a historical adventure film. The 1952 *Viva Zapata!*, which also starred Marlon Brando, and which *Burn!* somewhat resembles, merely imposed the then current American liberalism on the Mexican revolutionaries. If Pontecorvo's film is flawed throughout, it is nevertheless an amazing film, intensely controversial even in its failures. The audience seems to be grooving to the emotionally charged imagery (which has some of that quality that Buffy Sainte-Marie and the Missa Luba and classic blues have of hurting while giving pleasure) and yet, at times, arguing about political points, and I think this mixed reaction is a valid one. *Burn!* is primarily a celebration not of Black Is Beautiful but of Black Is Strong, and the strength Pontecorvo celebrates has a far deeper beauty than we are accustomed to at the movies. Nevertheless, the movie goes wrong. Maybe it was one of those ambitious ideas that look great until you try to carry them out; if there was a way to make it work, Pontecorvo didn't find it.

Pontecorvo can show brutality without giving the audience cheap shocks, and he doesn't arrange suffering in pretty compositions. He has a true gift for epic filmmaking: he can keep masses of people in movement on the screen so that we care about what happens to them. They're not just crowds of extras; they're the protagonist. And *Burn!* is perhaps the least condescending film that has ever dealt with slavery. No doubt the dignity of the slave victims is ideological, but, clearly, Pontecorvo is not distorting his vision to fit his ideology; when he endows them with nobility, it rings aesthetically true.

The film is large-spirited, and sometimes it really soars with the imaginative force of art. Movie imagery rarely overwhelms us with such a mixture of sorrow and anger as the sequence near the opening in which the widow of an executed insurgent pulls a cart bearing her husband's decapitated body. The film, though political, is by no means Spartan; it's luxuriant and ecstatic. When black rebels ride white horses that prance to what sounds like a syncopated Gregorian chant, the sequence is so shimmering and showy that one knows that Pontecorvo and his cinematographer, Marcello Gatti, couldn't resist it. Wasn't it this kind of thing that drew the director to the theme? *Burn!* shows the violation of rapturous beauty, and this is the emotional basis for whites to believe that blacks should destroy white civilization. (It may be a tragedy for whites that their culture and traditions are not so photogenic.) In his feeling for crowds and battles, for color and imagery, and for visual rhythms, Pontecorvo is a sensuous, intoxicating director, and he gives his island (which has been synthesized from locations in Colombia, Africa, and the Caribbean) physical unity and, by the use of moving figures in the background of the compositions, a volatile, teeming population. In the last two years, Pontecorvo's *The Battle of Algiers,* a reconstruction of the violent death of a colonial regime, has become known as the black militants' training film. Pontecorvo appears fully committed to the idea of killing and being killed for your principles; in *Burn!,* however, the whites have no principles. *Burn!* is unquestionably intended to arouse revolutionary passions, but the racist-Marxist plot is too schematic to structure the heroic fall and rise of a people.

Some of the flaws in the film are not the director's fault. *Burn!* was originally called *Quemada*, which means "burned" in Spanish, and which was the name that Pontecorvo and his scriptwriters (Franco Solinas and Georgio Arlorio) gave to their sugar-producing island. They also gave it a history of having been burned by the Spaniards in the sixteenth century, because the Indians were rebellious, and then repopulated with African slaves. The movie was to show how, in the 1840s, the English fomented a new rebellion to wrest power from the Spanish. However, the current Spanish government, sensitive about Spaniards' being cast as heavies even in a period piece, applied severe economic pressures against the producers, who, remembering what the Spanish government had done when it was displeased by Fred Zinnemann's *Behold a Pale Horse* (the losses from the Spanish boycott of Columbia Pictures ran to several millions), capitulated. Parts of the film were deleted, others reshot, and the Spaniards who had historically dominated the Antilles were replaced by the Portuguese, who hadn't, but aren't a big movie market. The European title was changed to *Queimada* — the Portuguese for "burned." After the delays and extra expenses, the picture has still not been released widely; United Artists, which has probably been financially burned in the deal, has rather touchingly altered the American title to the opportunistic *Burn!* In addition, the American version has lost twenty-odd minutes at the hands of a New York "film doctor" whose previous experience was in editing movie trailers. These cuts are, I assume, responsible for some of the non sequiturs in the action and some of the lacunae. Finally, the movie was "dumped" — opened without the usual publicity and advance screenings. This ordinarily means that a company doesn't expect a movie to do well, and such a lack of faith usually insures that it won't do well, because magazine reviews will come out two or three months late, and even reviewers who might have been enthusiastic have their spirits dampened by the general feeling that it's a bomb and will close before they get into print. I'm reasonably certain that this film has been dumped not because of its incendiary potential but because of the company's evaluation of its box-office potential. I think that the company miscalculated and that *Burn!* could have been a hit, because it plays right into the current feelings of the young movie audience. But now we'll never know, though the picture may do well in revivals. Such are the business conditions in the background of a revolutionary movie, but the larger irony is that white men made this movie that says black men should never trust white men.

Despite its visual sophistication, *Burn!* has an unmistakable tang of the old heart-stirring swashbucklers in which Errol Flynn risked all for liberty, or Tyrone Power (*Son of Fury*) abandoned the corrupt life of the English nobility for an island, a dream, and a native girl (Gene Tierney). Although Pontecorvo's feeling for the slaves is that of an artist, his treatment of the vacillating, cowardly white colonial officials and their mulatto accomplices is exactly that of the more conventional seafaring adventure films. In scenes involving these officials, one might as well be at *Lydia Bailey* or *Anthony Adverse,* and Marlon Brando's cynical, daredevil Sir William Walker seems a direct development from his foppish Fletcher Christian in *Mutiny on the Bounty.*

Considered politically (rather than dramatically), the plot is an ingenious synthesis. (You don't appreciate *how* ingenious until you think over what has been left out.) Sir William is an *agent provocateur* sent by the British Admiralty to instigate a revolt of the slaves against their Portuguese masters. He tricks a band of slaves into committing a robbery in order to make them outlaws, arms them, turns them into killers, and trains a black leader, José Dolores (Evaristo Marquez), who defeats the Portuguese and tries to seize power for the slaves. Sir William is reluctantly preparing to eliminate him when José Dolores, unable to run the government without advisers, relinquishes power to the British and their mulatto puppet ruler. Having accomplished his mission and obtained sugar for a nation of tea drinkers, Sir William leaves the island. So far, he appears to be a super-cool C.I.A.-type mastermind crossed with Lawrence of Arabia. Brando's impersonation of a languid British gentleman is amusing and decorated with linguistic conceits, and since Sir William helped to liberate the slaves and tried to convince the businessmen of the economic advantages of free workers, one assumes he is personally on the slaves' side, and so does José Dolores, still his friend, who accompanies him to the ship to say goodbye. When José asks him where he's going, he replies, "I don't suppose you've ever heard of a place called Indo-China? Well, they're sending me there."

Ten years pass offscreen. José Dolores has been fighting the British all these years, and he has organized a new rebellion. Sir William has left the Admiralty and (like Lawrence?) has sought obscurity. The sugar company's agents go to look for Sir William in London, find him brawling in a cheap dive, and report that he is "like another man," but they make him a lucrative offer to return to Queimada to deal with José Dolores, and he accepts. His hopes are gone, he says, and the ten years have revealed the century's contradictions. He tries to establish contact with José Dolores but is rebuffed. Then, although he gives evidence of believing in what the rebels are doing and despising the whites, he organizes the slaughter of the blacks, burns native villages that help the guerrillas hiding in the mountains, and, when the puppet tries to regain control in order to end the suffering, has him executed. Sir William explains why the blacks will eventually win — a guerrilla can do fifty times as much as an ordinary soldier, because the guerrilla "has nothing to lose," and so on. Yet Sir William brings in British troops and destroys the island. It is shelled and shelled and then burned again, so that the British businessmen are left asking what good his actions have done them, since now there's no sugar for anybody. He says that he doesn't really know what he's doing but that he must do it. And so he comes to represent the murderous, self-destructive folly of colonialism—the whites' irrational determination to destroy everything rather than share with the blacks — and when he's killed there's a happy heavenly choir.

There's a contradiction between Brando's role as the personification of colonial manipulative policies (as well as, by implication, of the American involvement in Vietnam) and Brando's style, because, the way he plays his role, he's the comic relief in a tragedy. The oppressor as cynical clown is an entertaining idea, and perhaps the audience needs his foppish foolery, the contempt with which he addresses the English businessmen, his sophistic explanation that he's merely an instrument of government policy and if he didn't carry it out the Admiralty would send someone else, but he seems to have wandered into the wrong movie. He causes starvation and death, yet he's also slapping his horse and drawling "Giddyap, you fool." If Sir William were played impersonally as a historical force, the movie would be heavy and didactic; a more conventionally villainous interpretation would probably turn it into Grade B melodrama. But when the role is played with Brando's bravura, so that Sir William becomes a daring white loner who loved and betrayed the blacks, it's a muddle, because we simply don't understand his motives or why he is so zealous in crushing the rebellion, or why no one else understands anything.

When you personify a deterministic theory of history and don't stylize it but, rather, do it in natural settings, the leaders seem to be all that matter, so the method distorts the theory. It seems as if history were a melodrama made solely by heroes and adventurers. This movie really becomes a swashbuckler — a romantic, glamorized view of black struggle — but a swashbuckler engaged in a cute game of slipping in historical parallels and of scoring textbook points. Almost every line jogs us to fit it into the scheme. "Ah, yes," we say to ourselves, "Sir William is a liberator of the blacks only when the English interests and theirs coincide," and so on. When Brando warns the English of the danger of making José Dolores a martyr — "Think of his ghost running through the Antilles!" — we see it as another point racked up, and when Brando thinks it's madness for José Dolores to sacrifice his life, we know we're being prodded to see that whites are incapable of understanding the blacks' true passion for freedom, and we're being prodded to see that it is this passion that makes the blacks superior, and will make them win.

The end is clearly meant to be only the beginning. The spirit of the film is one of triumph, for José Dolores, who preferred death to compromise, has set an example for the survivors and for the slaves on other islands. "Ideas travel," Sir William has explained, and dead heroes become myths. The message of the film is that freedom is worth all the suffering it takes. After we have seen the blacks tricked and maneuvered and crushed over and over again, this simplistic encouragement to die for your principles seems rather cavalier, as if the film had been made by a new incarnation of Sir William, who still doesn't know what he's doing. José Dolores' visionary speeches about lighting the flames for whites to burn in are fashionably modern, and his last words are "Civilization belongs to whites. But what civilization? Until when?"

There's something painful and disturbing about movies that fail on as high a level as *Burn!*, but mixing art and politics has always had its difficulties. Still, if you can't force human suffering into an ideological diagram without having it all look phony, that could be a blessing.

•

Mel Brooks has given himself only a small role at the beginning of his *The Twelve Chairs*, and the picture never quite recovers from the loss of him. The movie also needs more from Mel Brooks as writer and director. This comedy-fable, based on the same Ilf-and-Petrov novel as the 1945 Fred Allen picture *It's in the Bag*, is about three men hunting for a fortune stuffed into one of twelve chairs — a good, loose comedy plot that allows for invention, but Brooks hasn't come up with enough. The story is set in post-revolutionary Russia, and this gives Brooks an opportunity to show his nostalgic affection for the slapstick and mugging and innocent nuttiness of earlier periods — such as burlesque and the mad Russian accents of early radio — but, gifted as he is, he still doesn't go beyond gag comedy. His worst failure is with the witlessly written handsome juvenile, played by Frank Langella in a supercilious, self-satisfied manner; he seems to be meant to be the romantic lead in a musical, but since there's no girl and no singing, he just cavorts narcissistically. And there's too much Dom DeLuise: he's funny, as low comics go, but a little of his Three Stooges–Abbott & Costello stuff is already much. Ron Moody is the lead — the once wealthy nobleman whose mother-in-law hid the jewels — and he suggests so much more talent than is tapped here that it becomes frustrating to watch him. His *idées fixes* are glittering, but manic intensity isn't enough to create a character; he needs material to make his melancholia more than just a look in his fine eyes, although in a scene toward the end, broken-hearted and clutching a piece of chair, he gives us a glimpse of a great comedian. The exteriors, which were shot in Yugoslavia, have a sprightly, picturesque Grandma Moses atmosphere that is appropriate to this souvenir-tribute to the primitive folklore of radio and B-movie comedy. It's a bit forlorn, this attempt to make comedy out of old comedy that has lost its satirical bite. When Brooks is on-screen, he brings a fervid enthusiasm to his own nonsense; when he isn't around, there's no comic tension. He has made a movie about greed, but the forms of greed here are cozily antiquated.

•

Cromwell is a dry spectacle, written and directed by Ken Hughes with dedicated stodginess. Was there ever a period of history when the clothes were less photogenic? The actors waddle around in their barrels and bloomers, then stand still to make speeches at each other. Richard Harris, of the hangdog expression, who is a star not by virtue of public appeal but simply because he's such a domineering powerhouse that he seems a natural for important roles, plays Cromwell with glum, frowning righteousness, using his weird straight eyebrows like punctuation marks. England seems a large country to have had only one just man, and surely Cromwell must have been more than this sullen prig who hates power, or he couldn't have obtained it. One rather wishes the film would explain him a bit instead of deifying him. If Cromwell wasn't brilliant and wasn't eloquent, what *was* he? By what force did he condemn and behead a king of England and become ruler? If his righteousness was his only weapon, he must have had it to a frightening degree, and combined with incredible energy. One doesn't have to know anything about Cromwell to disbelieve the movie. *Cromwell* doesn't make basic sense: this sturdy, honest reformer stalks in and tells the corrupt Parliament what to do, and it proceeds to do it. Why? Just because he's so right? Alec Guinness barely wiggles a few facial muscles and manages to make an acting showcase out of his restrained performance as King Charles I, and the Battle of Naseby is well staged, but that's not enough. Shakespeare spoiled us for this sort of thing: we wait for great speeches and witty remarks, for rage and poetry, and we get nothing but a relentless academicism. And not only are Harris's lines flat but there is no music in his voice. Is this a movie about a great national *hero*? If virtue is as toneless as this Cromwell, who wouldn't prefer vice?

•

Stuart Rosenberg, the director of *WUSA,* made his movie reputation with a contemptible success, *Cool Hand Luke,* a film that pretended to have something to say and was full of touches designed to make the audience feel "knowing" — such as a girl teasing a bunch of convicts by washing her car seductively, playing with the nozzle of a hose and squeezing fluid out of a sponge. That is, he transferred a commercial hack's sexual innuendo onto a young girl, just for effect. Rosenberg's "touches" don't grow out of his material — they're stuck on; his movies are full of signals to us, but the signals don't direct us anywhere. The road gang in *Cool Hand Luke* went through a lot of waste motion just to satisfy the director's desire for a rhythmically edited sequence, and in *WUSA* Joanne Woodward hangs herself by a chain so that Rosenberg can have the camera travel along the links. He did show some comedy talent in the sequences with Harvey Korman and the errant commuters in *The April Fools*, but with the overwrought melodramatics of *WUSA* he aces out Frank Perry as the most flat-footed director around.

In *WUSA*, Rosenberg's pushing and pummelling destroy what might have been good performances (despite implausibly baroque roles) by Joanne Woodward and Tony Perkins. There wasn't much he could do to Paul Newman that the script (by Robert Stone) hadn't already done. *WUSA* continues in the movie tradition of liberal hysteria on the theme of Southern right-wing hysteria. In Hollywood, this form of exhibitionism is called "making a statement" (and when the picture fails they think it's because it told too many hard truths). *WUSA* is a whopper, with some of the gaudiest dialogue since *The Oscar,* though in a superior style of gaudiness that is less fun. Paul Newman is Rheinhardt, a gutless, non-involved failed artist (he used to play the clarinet) who goes to work as a newscaster for WUSA, a right-wing radio station in New Orleans. He is hyperverbal and is given to self-lacerating bitter tirades that upset his girl, Geraldine (Joanne Woodward), an honest tart who hasn't learned how to be servile. (She calls him "Rheinhardt" and he calls her "friend.") After much narrative fumbling and many garish Gothic scenes about a highly opaque welfare swindle, it all culminates in a big patriotic rally, with the Christlike madman Tony Perkins trying to assassinate the top Fascist (Pat Hingle, of course) and causing a bloody riot, after which Geraldine hangs herself by that chain in a prison cell, after which Rheinhardt visits her grave — in potter's field, no less — and savagely addresses the departed lady: "I'm a survivor and I'm leaving these flats for the mile-high city. When I get up there, baby — when I look down — I'll have a few regrets." There's also Laurence Harvey as a bogus clergyman, and Cloris Leachman as Philomene, a crippled newspaper peddler. As if all this weren't more than enough, there's a score by Lalo Schifrin. My favorite line: In the midst of the panic caused by the assassination attempt, with people being crushed and stomped on and beaten, the fleeing Newman looks at us and says sagely, "If that's the way people want it, that's how it's going to be."

•

Crippled newsies are back, and the business of making movies hasn't changed as much as some people say. Jules Dassin has announced that he will make a movie on the life of Rosa Luxemburg, starring his wife, Melina Mercouri. And Paramount has just sent out this press release:

> *Brother Sun and Sister Moon,* Franco Zeffirelli's first project for Paramount Pictures since his *Romeo and Juliet,* is scheduled to go before the cameras in

January, 1971, it was announced by Robert Evans, Paramount's Senior Vice-President in charge of worldwide production.

Based on an original story about St. Francis of Assisi, the drama with music will be directed by Zeffirelli and produced by Luciano Perugia. Dyson Lovell will be the associate producer. A coproduction with Paramount and Euro International Productions, *Brother Sun and Sister Moon* will be filmed on locations in Italy.

Suso D'Amico, Lina Wertmuller, and Zeffirelli wrote the original story, which bears a striking parallel to the current youth movement all over the world.

St. Francis, the son of a wealthy merchant, returned from war shattered by his experiences and saw a vision which caused him to embark on a different life in which material objects were of no use to him. He and his friends formed what could be described as the first commune and lived with nature, earning their keep by working in the fields.

Casting for *Brother Sun and Sister Moon* will be announced shortly.

[November 7, 1970]

Teamwork

Barbra Streisand's delicate snarl is the voice of New York tuned to a parodist's sensibility. It's the sound of urban character armor; she rattles it for a finely modulated raucousness. In *The Owl and the Pussycat*, her clipped diction is so full of controlled tension that her lines never go slack; the words come out impetuously fast and hit such surprising notes that she creates her own suspense. She's a living, talking cliff-hanger; we're kept alert catching the inflections, hoping that the laughter in the theatre won't make us lose anything. Though she doesn't sing in this picture, she's still a singing actress; she makes her lines funny musically, and she can ring more changes on a line than anybody since W. C. Fields, who was also a master of inflection. (I'm not forgetting Mae West; her specialty was innuendo — a more limited comic field.)

The Owl and the Pussycat, directed by Herbert Ross, is a cheering, satisfying romantic comedy about a self-deceiving would-be writer, played by George Segal, who works in a bookstore, and a hooker, played by

Streisand. Bill Manhoff's play, which had only the two characters, has been well adapted by Buck Henry (who has added a neat little role for Robert Klein). The material is far from first-rate, but it's functional. Like some of the thin and totally concocted screwball comedies of the thirties, it draws its life from the performers. Streisand, self-conscious and self-mocking, combative but wistful, is an intuitive actress who needs someone to play against. In her last picture, with Yves Montand, there was no contact; their scenes together looked as if the two had been photographed separately and matched in the editing room, and she was stranded on the screen. But she and Segal have the temperamental affinity that makes a romantic comedy take off. Their rapport has a beautiful, worked-out professionalism. Were Hepburn and Tracy this good together, even at their best, as in *Pat and Mike*? Maybe, but they weren't *better*. Segal is a very unusual actor: he never does anything wrong. You never catch him out in a false gesture or doing things his character wouldn't do. He's a superlatively "human" actor, who can play a timid, pretentious phony without making him a weakling or an utter fool.

Built into all urban humor are the derisive acceptance of oneself as part of a mass and techniques for bringing down those who would deny their membership in that mass. This coincides with the theme of the movie — the hooker, a pretender herself, is trying to bring the book clerk back to his humanity — and in American romantic comedy there's love behind swapping wisecracks. The ideas in the play and the script are not fresh, and sometimes they're really wobbly — as in having the book clerk throw away his typewriter — but the basic impulse of the comedy is sound. And though it's getting rather pathetic that moviemakers can't think of anything else for good, lively broads to be but prostitutes, Streisand's hooker is an updated version of the smart working girl (like Ginger Rogers in comedies such as *Vivacious Lady*). Movie romances used to come in two flavors — the ones featuring frail, duped, suffering, meek-cow heroines who had to be rescued, and the more specifically American ones featuring good-bad, tough, comic heroines (starting with Pearl White) who used their wits. We've lost the first flavor, with few regrets, but the second has come back in a modernization that is, perhaps, a good joke on us. The abrasiveness, the insults and strong language make it possible for us to enjoy a love story in a venerable American tradition without feeling square. The comic heroines wake the heroes up. Streisand and Segal energize each other; he plays second fiddle to her, and it's still probably his strongest comic performance.

There's an air of festivity about this kind of teamwork. Streisand and

Segal charge right through the "lonely little people" stuff; they bull their way through the bad spots (though no one could redeem one sour sequence in Central Park, in which Segal is called upon to humiliate her). Their energy and Herbert Ross's sense of pace just about overcome the principal dramatic weakness of the material — that it starts high. This takes a while to get used to; then one doesn't want it to let down. Ross does a fine job of keeping things moving, so that one adjusts to the subsequent more romantic tone and tempo. The picture is a bit crude at the outset, but it has a good spirit — perhaps the one essential for comedy, and the one most often missing in recent American attempts at comedy. What's funny about the scene in which the hero and heroine are bombed out of their heads in a bathtub together is that it really is *romantic. The Owl and the Pussycat* isn't in any way an important picture — it's just a doodle — yet it's probably the most enjoyable comedy since *M*A*S*H*.

It's good to see Streisand get out from under the archaic production values of large-scale movies — especially after *Hello, Dolly!* and the thudding dialogue of *On a Clear Day You Can See Forever,* that huge picture with only one redeeming sequence, when Streisand, gowned by Cecil Beaton, toyed with a glass of champagne. She has a more simple memorable moment in this one, when she mimes the sun coming up over the bedcovers. She may never again look as smashing as she did in that high-style champagne bit, but if the price of that glamour is the paralysis of talent, it isn't worth it. Streisand, who is easily the best comedienne now working in American movies, is better when she isn't carrying all that dead weight. She can be trusted when she cuts loose, because she has the instinct and the discipline to control her phenomenal vitality. She is like thousands of girls one sees in the subway, but more so; she is both the archetype and an original, and that's what makes a star.

•

George Segal shows different facets of his talent as the star of Carl Reiner's *Where's Poppa?* Like the sly younger Alec Guinness, Segal can carry amiability right up to the surreal and reveal the furtive, quirky ideas that lurk in the heads of very ordinary-seeming men. He is also an actor with a special sort of romantic folly about him — a gift of silliness — that could be used for a true comic persona. This particular gift is barely visible in *The Owl and the Pussycat,* but in *Where's Poppa?* he has an opportunity for some lovely comic riffs. The high point of the movie is perhaps its quietest moment: when Segal, in a near-trance of romantic longing, sings "Louise" to Trish Van Devere — a charming comedienne, despite that terrible name.

The movie is full of talent — Reiner's and Segal's — and worth seeing, though it goes down the wild, freaky drain. Robert Klane's script (from his own novel) is about two brothers (Segal and Ron Leibman) who promised their dying father they wouldn't put their mother (Ruth Gordon) in a home for the aged and are stuck with this senile psychopath. His face still shrouded in his Owl mustache, Segal now walks in a stooped position, under an oedipal load; his role is a series of skits, and they have considerable vitality, but often their only point is to go further than is permitted on television. When Ron Leibman rapes a woman in Central Park who turns out to be a cop dressed to decoy rapists, the payoff — the cop sends him roses — is too cute. Even if we laugh, we know that a skit like this has been set up for no reason except that payoff, and we can see that the movie will go any which way for a gag. Though it is planned for the new "youth" market, *Where's Poppa?* is the furthest reach of Broadway's anything-for-a-yock humor. Some of the noisiest sequences (such as a courtroom scene with a mad militarist) are a bit smug in the way they seem to congratulate the audience for being hip. Others, like a visit to an old-age home that has lost count of the neglected inmates, are *Mad*-comics ideas that probably sounded funny in a story conference but were never thought through. The trouble with this sort of unlimited, omni-destructive humor is that there's nothing for our laughs to bounce off, nothing to hold on to — not even an idea behind the movie, or a dedication to the craft of comedy. This isn't a matter of wanting something to be kept sacred, or clinging to taboos; it's that these skits have nowhere to go. They don't shape up into full routines but tend to fall apart for want of *aim*.

Probably there are no subjects that can't be made funny, but some require more artistry than others, because the associations they evoke aren't normally funny. These are the "daring" ones, and when they're handled poorly the audience feels a discomfort — it feels "offended." The moviemakers will probably think this is because the audience is inhibited, but more likely it's because *Where's Poppa?* has walked right into the trap of being "daring" without having the vision or the skill to bring it off.

•

Though *The Private Life of Sherlock Holmes* is a Billy Wilder film, it's rather like the second-class English comedies of the fifties; it doesn't have enough bounce, and it isn't really very interesting, but it would be quite pleasant if it didn't dawdle on for over two hours. I was looking forward to seeing Robert Stephens, who had been so impressive in a few small roles (*A Taste of Honey*, *The Prime of Miss Jean Brodie*), as Holmes, but his face is all crumpled up, as if he were ill or exhausted, and this interferes with the fabled Holmesian stylishness. Though his readings are very deft, and Wilder and his long-time script collaborator, I. A. L. Diamond, have given him some archly amusing lines, Wilder's sense of comic timing has run down, so we don't laugh as often as we should.

Worse, Wilder has made a detective picture that fails to whet our curiosity. The picture is meant to be a put-on of the Sherlock Holmes mythology, concentrating on a case that Holmes fouls up. But for this idea to be comic and have suspense we need to see the clues and draw our own inferences, so that we can spot where Holmes is going wrong and enjoy his booboos. And for it to be somewhat romantic, as it's meant to be, we need to see much more of how he's being distracted by the charming treachery of the lady played by Genevieve Page. The script doesn't accomplish the minimal feats necessary for a fashionable exercise — we have to wait until everything is explained to Holmes — and the actors aren't well directed, so one must content oneself with the occasional wit, the handsome Victorian décor, and Christopher Challis's lovely, if somewhat dark, tinted-looking cinematography. It's a graceful picture, even though it grows dull.

•

Self-parody is built into operettas and is part of their innocent, campy charm. But Andrew Stone's *Song of Norway* isn't authentic kitsch of the Wiener-schnitzel variety, it isn't a dated crowd-pleaser squeezed for the remaining box-office juice; it's second-generation kitsch — an imitation operetta, on the joys and tribulations of Edvard Grieg's life, that combines the worst of *The Sound of Music* with the worst of *A Song to Remember* and *Song Without End*. I had expected the hills to be on fire again, and had been prepared for dirndls and roguish smiles, but who would have anticipated the distorted sound, the pasty, pudgy faces, and the bewildering use of dance as if it were mood music? (When the picture isn't showing you waterfalls, flaxen-haired dancers go leaping by — a few frames at a time — to maintain a frolicsome Norwegian mood.) The movie is of an unbelievable badness; it brings back clichés you didn't know you knew — they're practically from the unconscious of moviegoers. You can't get angry at something this stupefying; it seems to have been made by trolls.

[November 14, 1970]

Bolt & Lean

Virginia Woolf wrote that the cinema was a case of the savages' beginning not with two bars of iron and working up to Mozart but with grand pianos and nothing to play. David Lean makes pictures — like *Doctor Zhivago* and the new *Ryan's Daughter* — that consume years and involve enormous physical effort as well as enormous expense. As a director, he is a supertechnician, and probably he doesn't really have anything he wants to do in movies except to command the technology. He probably enjoys working in his characteristic gentleman-technician's tasteful-colossal style. But tasteful and colossal are — in movies, at least — basically antipathetic. Lean makes respectable epics, and that's a contradiction, and self-defeating. Humorlessly meticulous, his epics have no driving emotional energy, no passionate vision to conceal the heavy labor. The painstakingly constructed streets, the antiqued houses, a field of perfect daffodils or of quivering lilies waiting to be fructified, even a flight of sea-gulls — when we see them, we know they were put there to be photographed. The style of the sets is like the style of Lincoln Center — Monumental Temporary.

At the opening of *Ryan's Daughter,* with cosmic vistas of sand and seashore in impeccable focus, and the actors seen from above and at a great distance, as if photographed from the moon, one's first thought may be that the moviemakers are trapped. What spectacle could they give an audience this jaded? What story could they tell that could conceivably be commensurate with this technology? Lean was the savior of the previous regime at M-G-M when the sluggish but romantic *Doctor Zhivago* rather inexplicably became one of the half-dozen biggest financial successes in movie history; now Kirk Kerkorian and James Aubrey, who head the new regime, are hoping Lean will rescue *them.* Lean has been to the mountaintop, and seen a big mountain; that's what is in his pictures, and the mountains keep getting bigger.

Everything in *Ryan's Daughter* is familiar, but it was previously on a smaller scale. The movie is about a yearning Irish girl, Rosy Ryan (Sarah Miles), who marries a widowed schoolteacher twice her age (Robert Mitchum), has a rapturous affair with a war-shattered British officer assigned to duty in Ireland (Christopher Jones), and is punished by the villagers, who strip her and cut off her hair. It's *Ecstasy* blown up to the proportions of *The Decline and Fall of the Roman Empire*. The setting — and it is never more than that, because it's not organic to the love story — is the Irish "troubles" during the First World War.

Despite Lean's reputation as a storyteller, his movies have a way of falling apart on him. His Zhivago often looked as if he just happened to be around when some big events were taking place, and the themes that should have bound character to event kept evaporating. Robert Bolt, who wrote the adaptation of *Doctor Zhivago* and an original script for *Ryan's Daughter,* has understandable difficulties with prestige-epic construction: it really isn't easy to write literate dialogue for credible characters and still place them in the huge, photogenic predicaments that the genre requires. The game of superspectacles is a big-money, big-prizes game. Bolt and Lean are doing something essentially crazy and extravagant without a craziness in themselves to match it; they're working on a gargantuan scale with *restraint*. Bolt, too, is a technician; his "literacy" is another form of expensive technology. In *Ryan's Daughter,* he's trying for a wild, lyrical spirit, and he just doesn't have the temperament for it; the script trudges on with carefully calculated excesses. He comes up with a mute, crippled idiot who tears a claw off a live lobster and who is himself tormented by the morally crippled Irish villagers. The idiot loves Rosy the way Quasimodo loved Esmeralda, and Bolt must be pleased with his creation, because he throws him into damned near every sequence in the movie, with Maurice Jarre providing a Felliniesque idiot-gambolling tune.

The camera swoops in on people from a heroic distance, but the characters are small — they're "pawns of fate" rather than heroes — and the only possible justification for the scale of the picture is the heroine's passionate nature as she walks on deserted beaches or, with her lover, lies in a fairy-tale forest, made magical by desire. Unfortunately, Sarah Miles (Mrs. Bolt) is not a passionate performer. She's a good, modest actress, and occasionally a fine one, but the role requires a star. In a sense, every star is a freak: Sarah Miles isn't unusual enough. One can barely remember what movies she has been in before, or be positive that it was she, and not Susannah York. In *Ryan's Daughter,* there is nothing in her personality that links in with the Gothic effects that Bolt and Lean pile on; she isn't so much more intensely alive than other people that her yearning could find an equivalent expression in waves and storms and flowers and stars. This girl simply does not move the heavens, and that's what this picture needed to get up to the level of entertaining-daydream trash.

After we have gone through her disappointing wedding night with her, we wait for a lover to appear, and after an hour or so Lean deposits Christopher Jones on the giant screen like a maimed sun god arriving on earth. He stands there alone for an eternity, with a limp and a scar and a permanently pained expression; soon he begins to shake uncontrollably. Lean has made him such a romantic wreck that the picture never recovers from his landing. The sex-starved colleen falls for the shell-shocked hero when she sees his anguished twitching, and soon there are shots of her lying in bed awake next to her husband while, back at the barracks, the solitary Jones lies in his bed, sweating. This routine was already a gas when Rossano Brazzi was a youth; David Lean was once a famous film editor — where are those skills now? When Jones starts looming up on the horizon like Heathcliff but dragging a leg, the picture is a comedy, beyond salvage. (No doubt some of the laugh-provoking shots will be trimmed. Too bad, because they might alert the credulous.)

In this movie, everyone is trying to be something he isn't — not only Bolt and Lean and Miss Miles. Robert Mitchum is trying to be unsexy and self-effacing; at first he just naturally livens up the movie, but then he becomes as dull as his role. Why cast Robert Mitchum as a gentle schoolmaster who pores over students' notebooks and presses wild flowers? Obviously, to suggest strength within. But Mitchum has such immense camera presence not just because he's a natural and original actor but because his cynicism is there in the drooping eyelids and the great, reptilian face. To use him in a Herbert Marshall–John Forsythe-type role is to cancel him out. Sure, we'd rather watch him than Forsythe, but Bolt and Lean ought to recognize that if they have to try to make a role more interesting by casting an actor against the grain, it's because of a failure in conception — because they're trying to trick a stereotype into life. The characters in this movie are all just detailed stereotypes, worked up to fit the giant screen and the mass market. Christopher Jones has been drained of vitality and remade into a synthesis of exhausted romantic clichés. In addition to the scar and the limp, he has been given a green complexion and dark hair, like the soulful, sickly Sharif of *Zhivago;* the doomed look sits on his wily James Dean face like enamel. John Mills is the idiot, and Trevor Howard is a wise old darlin' of a priest. Everybody (with the possible exception of Leo McKern, whose role as the publican Ryan would fit right into any old *Gunsmoke*) is cast against his natural appearance and aptitudes, so one is always aware of the acting. (This is the kind of thing that gets people Academy Awards, because the acting is so conspicuous.)

There is no artistic or moral rationale for this movie — only expediency. It is amoral to put Emma Bovary back into the romantic Gothic tradition from which Flaubert took her — permanently, one had hoped. Bolt and Lean have given us an Emma Bovary without Flaubert's irony. This girl dreams of bliss, and the bliss she gets is beyond her dreams. Her orgasms are recorded in glinting star-shaped patterns in the heavens; the sun itself has become a strobe light blinking in rhythm with Rosy's pleasure. And the picture puts Lady Chatterley's lover back into the pseudo-aristocratic pulp romanticism from which D. H. Lawrence wrested him. The upper classes were the masters of the art of love in those pre-Lawrentian fictions; this frightfully noble British officer is right out of the pitiful nonsense of aristocracy-crazed silent pictures. Bolt must have recognized this, because Jones has been given almost nothing to say; what could this figment of soggy romanticism talk about?

At the beginning, we see the dreamy Rosy reading a cheap romance. Many of the novels that a girl in that period would have furtively enjoyed must have been very like this movie: illicit bliss with a classy lover, ruin and suffering, forgiveness from the devoted, ever-loving betrayed husband, and, at last, losing one's uppitiness and finding redemption. At her wedding party, Rosy refuses to kiss the idiot; we wait for the final cliché, knowing that the picture can't end until Rosy is chastened and humbled enough to deliver the kiss that means her salvation. That, I am afraid, is what Bolt's craftsmanship has come down to.

Ryan's Daughter is an expensive movie, but it's a cheap romance. Lean and Bolt are probably the leading exponents of bourgeois romanticism — gush made respectable by millions of dollars "tastefully" wasted. When a David Lean movie takes five years and fourteen million dollars, there is the presumption of perfectionism, but the technology he commands is really only in the set construction and in the perfectly focussed, salon-quality cinematography. Those crafts give Lean's movies their distinctive look of impersonal, glorified realism — like a face-lift of the world. Even the sun and the moon look reconstructed, and Ireland didn't have beaches big enough, so a stretch of African coast was grafted on.

There is enjoyment to be had from the smooth unfolding of a story, and at the beginning *Ryan's Daughter is* smooth, but despite the years Lean puts in on his films, *Ryan's Daughter* (like *Doctor Zhivago*) looks as if he'd been rushed and hadn't had time to complete the editing or tie up loose ends. (A constable is murdered at the beginning and his body is hidden, but apparently he's never missed, because he isn't mentioned again.) Literal-mindedness may be passing for craftsmanship. The big sequences are just unrelated set pieces that don't function in the story. Lean featured the sun in *Lawrence of Arabia* and the snow in *Doctor Zhivago,* and now he gives us the sea. This picture has the biggest (and loudest) Gothic storm ever photographed, but the spirit is missing. Bolt has failed to get the principals into the storm, or even emotionally involved in it, so it's antiseptic. On the other hand, Lean works up such a frenzy when the villagers come to punish the adulteress that one expects her to be stoned or beaten or mutilated, and seeing her afterward with her hair cut is as anti-climactic and absurd as the few little scratches on Tippi Hedren's face after she was attacked by that roomful of Hitchcock's birds.

The only reasons for placing this story in 1916 were to legitimatize the fact that every idea in it is shopworn, and to build sets. For years, during the making of a Lean film, publicity people send out photographs of the handsome director standing in the cities he has built, and then the movies arrive and he never seems to have figured out what to do in those sets. They have a gleaming pictorial look, a prepared look — everything is posing for a photograph. Do people who rave about Lean's "professionalism" ever *look* at his movies? What do they *think* when they see the Russian revolution come marching neatly down that perfect street in *Zhivago?* In *Ryan's Daughter,* the villagers never for an instant convince you that they live in that perfect village. And when they mill about, you can practically see the invisible assistants directing their movements. The villagers are treated as sheep, with the priest their only shepherd. Trevor Howard keeps rounding them up and telling them they've been bad again while they bleat apologies. The exigencies of the silly plot lead Bolt and Lean to be condescending to the Irish — a stuffy mistake when they're flogging themselves trying to whip up some of the wildness that the Irish are rich in. They don't have it in them to create Irish characters; there isn't a joke in all the hours (three and a half, including intermission) of *Ryan's Daughter,* except maybe the idea that an Irish girl needs a half-dead Englishman to arouse her.

There's no point in asking "What's it all for?" We know what it's for; it's to try to repeat the financial success of *Doctor Zhivago.* The question is "Can they get by with it?" Will the public buy twinkling orgasms and cosmetic craftsmanship? The emptiness of *Ryan's Daughter* shows in practically every frame, and yet the publicity machine has turned it into an artistic event, and the American public is a sucker for the corrupt tastefulness of well-bred English epics. One begins to feel like a member of a small cabal, powerless to fight this well-oiled reverence.

•

Perfect Friday is a modish trifle — a suspense film about how an amoral trio (Ursula Andress and David Warner, her husband, and Stanley Baker, her lover) rob a bank. The only reason to see it is that the Swiss actress Ursula Andress, who has always been sensational-looking and has indicated a certain amount of good humor, has improved her English and has turned into a witty deadpan comedienne. With her face and figure, the addition of technique makes her dazzling. The picture is a bit humdrum, despite an attempt to be jazzy with flash-forwards, and the director, Peter Hall, doesn't do much to set Ursula Andress off, but, even without the elegant trimmings, she's seductive and funny, like the larcenous Dietrich of *Desire*. Unfortunately, without the trimmings she doesn't leave one with that fine afterglow of remembered images. The picture holds one's attention, but the memory is starved.

[November 21, 1970]

Slapstick Tragedy

Halfway through Marcello Mastroianni's superlative comic performance as a sleepy bricklayer in *The Pizza Triangle*, I suddenly remembered the scrupulous intelligence and concentration with which his Meursault in *The Stranger* tried to understand the world, and I stared back hard at the flaccid moon face of his violent, foolish, suffering Oreste, the bushy-haired bricklayer who doesn't always smell good. Mastroianni is an astonishingly versatile actor, who seems to get better and better. Despite the stale American title (the Italian title was *A Case of Jealousy*), *The Pizza Triangle* is an original — a true plebeian, extroverted comedy, a modern romantic satire with jokes about the pollution in Rome and modern sex mores, with sight gags and slang and topical references. The director, Ettore Scola, doesn't seem to be anxious; the picture is spotty, and some of it goes way off, but nothing is forced, so one can relax even when the ideas misfire.

It's a genial mutt of a movie — a comic-strip parody of operatic passion. Mastroianni's Oreste is married to an old battle-axe, a fat hag with a topknot, whose name one expects to be Katisha. (She's like the woman Chaplin was married to in *Pay Day*.) He falls in love with Adelaide, a young flower seller, whom Monica Vitti plays with a soulful silliness that is a parody of generations of comic waifs and neo-realist heroines. When she betrays him with his best friend, a Tuscan pizza cook, the movie turns into a delicate cartoon of tragedy that is not altogether funny, or meant to be. It's a slapstick tragedy, loose and openhanded in its comic invention. The lovers meet on deserted piles of rubble; after a tender love scene, they pick debris out of each other's hair like monkeys cleaning out lice. The picture is punctuated with little motifs and routines, as in comic strips: people bang their heads when one least expects it; the slob hero has a blowfly who is his spirit; a careering ambulance marks the end of various episodes. This kind of folklore became so slack and repetitive in American movies that many of us could no longer respond, but it has sprouted in fresh ways here, with that mixture of simplicity and sophistication that our silent comedies sometimes had. The picture keeps shifting ground. When Oreste and Adelaide are in an amorous embrace and she says she loves him so much she'll do anything he wants, he pulls back happily and says, "Vote Communist," and we're in a Punch-and-Judy world. Later, when she's unfaithful, he becomes a crank, obsessed with the idea that there's a class basis for her betrayal. He tries to pin his misery on the class struggle, and, as in a libretto, jealousy drives him out of his mind and he commits a crime of passion. Oreste, the great *stupido*, whose face reflects a mind that has been emptied of everything but fluky ideas, becomes an operatic figure — the crazed lover.

The color is warm and bright, the music is light and nostalgic, like the score for *Mr. Hulot's Holiday*, and the quick rhythm of the cutting again suggests a comic strip. The interrogation about the crime goes on during the action; there are voice-over transitions in which the characters explain matters to the police while they are in the events that they're commenting on. It's a more extended use of a technique that goes back to Sacha Guitry's films and the early sequences of *On Approval*; it's done so deftly that moving back and forth begins to seem perfectly natural and one forgets what a complicated time-juggling stunt it is. There are probably a good many jokes that depend on knowledge of the conventions of the *fumetti*, and others that are dependent on understanding the vernacular — and maybe that neat, compact Tuscan pizza cook seems funnier in Italy than here — but Noelle Gillmor has provided ingenious subtitles, and even if one misses out on specifically Italian references, there is enough to keep one giggling through most of the movie.

You need a bit of tolerance for some of it, but Mastroianni holds it all together. Monica Vitti, with her supple, humor-filled face, is adorable as the Raggedy Ann buffeted by her emotions, but it's Mastroianni's gift for getting inside his slob and then just *behaving* as that slob that lifts the picture above its makeshift genre. Oreste cracks before our eyes. I don't think I fully grasped what a sensitive actor Mastroianni is until I saw him in *Il Bell'Antonio;* perhaps he really stretched himself in that performance (the way Laurence Olivier stretched himself after his early career as a charming juvenile). He keeps growing. He has that gift that the greatest screen actors (as distinguished from stage actors) have of seeming to live the role so fully that we assume the character goes on about the business of living whether the camera is on him or not. This isn't a flashy gift — this gift for simply living as the character on the screen — and it usually isn't remarked on as much as more ostentatious acting. It can be exciting to watch a Vanessa Redgrave burn up the screen with a stage type of performance, but more often the overpowering performer becomes a movie-wrecker, while the easy, unassuming performer quietly develops. Without Mastroianni, *The Pizza Triangle* would be clever; with him, it has heart — and not just the heart that Italian comedies wear on a sleeve. But that heart worn on a sleeve is worth something, too. This movie tries to please the way a Mack Sennett film tried to please — not playing down to the mass audience but not taking itself altogether seriously, either. It's in touch with the audience without condescension, and that's still the open secret of comedy.

•

James Ivory, who directed *Shakespeare Wallah* and last year's *The Guru*, has now made *Bombay Talkie*, which is about a bored, sensation-seeking English woman novelist (Jennifer Kendal) who destroys the life of a young Indian film star (Shashi Kapoor). The glimpses of the confusion of cultures in modern India are ironic without unnecessary underlining, and the picture is full of wonderful marginal details: the preparations for a musical film, with plump-bottomed Indian girls dancing on giant typewriter keys; a guru preaching gibberish to his assortment of Eastern and Western followers and showing them color slides of his conquest of Los Angeles; a night club with an Indian chanteuse singing an

American song. The atmosphere is like a Hollywood thirties movie, and this kitschy datedness, along with the exotic flavor, makes one feel affectionate and nostalgic. Everything is fine except for the maundering central story, which seems to belong in an old De Mille picture and is told in too artlessly simple a style. No doubt some of the melodramatic clichés are deliberate clichés, intended to comment on the way currently popular Bombay movies resemble old Hollywood movies and on the way the characters' lives echo cheap melodrama, but Ivory's technique is too naïve to sustain these conceits. His bead-stringing narrative method is appealingly innocent, but nothing *develops,* and when he attempts to use banality for his own purposes, the banality proliferates. The movie star's beautiful young wife shows her jealousy and impending suffering from her very first reaction shot, people signal their indifference by looking away from the person talking to them, and so on. The director may be doing all this consciously, but he's still doing it. Shashi Kapoor is enchantingly handsome, like an Indian version of the radiantly eager young John Gilbert, but the story of his ruin is tiresome. When the wife is being threatened by creditors, one knows to expect the scene in which the hero squanders his wealth on the mistress. Ivory must mean us to expect it, but that doesn't help, since the chemical change that would make it new doesn't take place. When the hero takes his decadent inamorata to a fortune-teller, the fortune-teller reaches for the woman's hand and looks at it, and then, a shadow crossing her face, refuses to tell what she sees. And a shadow crossed my face, too; I knew this picture would come to a bad end.

•

Leslie Bricusse is the name of a form of instantly disposable music; your mind flushes it away while you're hearing it. Bricusse is hired to compose a big score for *Scrooge* for the same reason that Ronald Neame is hired to direct it: they are both innocuous. And when you're planning to get yourself an annuity by making a musical version of *A Christmas Carol* (which is conveniently in the public domain), you don't take risks. If you make it tastefully dull, you stand a very good chance of coming out with a picture that will be acclaimed a screen classic. People without kids won't go to *Scrooge* anyway, and, there being so few "holiday" pictures to take kids to, people with kids will probably be trapped this year and for years to come. Will children enjoy it? I doubt whether they will, much. Bricusse also did the careful, uninspired script, and it preserves the Victorian melodrama without Dickens' buoyancy. Albert Finney plays Scrooge glumly and *realistically,* which is a terrible mistake. The gloom doesn't lift until the last twenty minutes, when Scrooge's cheerful repentance is accompanied by some bumptiousness and dancing in the streets. Alec Guinness camps up Marley's ghost a bit, and one is grateful for that, but the production is dim and humorless. When Finney sings "I Hate People," there's no verve, no spirit. When Kenneth More, as the Ghost of Christmas Present, sings "I Like Life, Life Likes Me," the words are so banal they contradict what they're saying. *Scrooge* smells of mothballs.

[November 28, 1970]

Worlds Apart

The first groupie to reach the screen was probably Shelley Plimpton's Reenie, in *Alice's Restaurant;* she was the sniffling, flat-chested thirteen- or fourteen-year-old girl who wanted to make it with Arlo, " 'cause you'll probably get to be an album." Earlier generations of teen-age fans slept with pictures of movie stars over their beds; groupies sleep with rock stars and, it would seem, anybody connected with them they can get. Though groupies attach themselves to rock groups, in the film *Groupies* they seem much the same as the little celebrity-lovers who rolled on the lavender paper with the photographer in *Blow-Up*. They're not sad, lost little girls like Reenie, they're a spooky bunch of junior hookers and hardened name-droppers.

Like the documentary *The Queen,* about the Miss All-American beauty contest for female impersonators held in New York City in 1967, *Groupies* reveals a way of life that has shock and curiosity value for the audience. The subject of baby band-molls is such a good one that it holds one's speculative interest even though this is a slight, badly made, and uninformative documentary. The girls who come on for the moviemakers are juvenile variants of Warhol's performers, swearing and showing off, trying to be daring and unusual; they describe everything as "fantastic." Because of their extreme youth and brazen parasitism, they themselves seem fantastic; they're gutsy little girls, but, like all hangers-on, they're depressing. Their specialized shallowness is what makes them a fascinating subject, but the filmmakers don't bring enough skill or depth to the project.

The crew spent nine months photographing their prey in various cities; however, the camerawork wanders affectlessly and the images are poorly framed. The cameramen obviously didn't know when they had something worth photographing and when they didn't. The material has been padded out with footage of homosexual groupies in San Francisco and a party scene at a swank apartment, and encumbered with unrelated rock numbers, to make it a feature.

Some of the girls are falling apart and already half dead from drugs (a beat-out girl talking about past good times as she dries herself after a bath has the shrivelled belly of a scrawny old woman); some are obviously just precocious drabs — tough, cheerfully foul-mouthed baby prostitutes, unappetizing but not yet the abject streetwalkers they will probably become. Others look as if their lives might not be very different from those of earlier generations of movie-star worshippers-from-afar (who sometimes got fairly close through fan clubs and autograph collecting). Are their mothers and grandmothers those hard-faced witches who line up to get into the audience for afternoon TV shows? The plaster-casters (who make mementos of their heroes' genitals) suggest that in some ways they may be not so different from the girls who used to go out for the drudge jobs in little theatres. These girls, whose proudest possession is their plaster statue of Jimi Hendrix's phallus, still have their baby fat and seem only a couple of years past reading *Little Women*. Did they skip that and go right to *The Love Machine,* or do they watch the box? Do they have part-time jobs, or do their parents support them? Are groupies just the latest style in how girls become prostitutes or, sometimes, stars or mistresses or wives of stars — or do some of the groupies represent a whole new thing?

The central weakness is that we never see the girls listening to music. It's understandable that we rarely see the girls in the same backstage-life shots as the musicians (that would present legal problems, because so many of the girls are under age), but since we don't actually see them responding to any performance or to a record, or even talking about the music, we can't tell whether this music is the mechanism for changing their lives. There is one good musical number in the movie — Joe Cocker singing "Delta Lady," in which, as in his other screen appearances, the jerky movement of his hands suggests an orgiastic helplessness. This is a long way from the clean, powdered pretty-boy crooners who made fans swoon; he looks like the Three Stooges impersonating Beethoven having a fit — yet this spastic desperation is now accepted, without surprise. One wonders why the filmmakers didn't have enough feeling for the scaffolding that holds a movie together to *use* this sequence to integrate the film. For what we still want to know when we come out of the movie is whether rock music means something more exciting to some teen-agers than they can handle in the context of education and family life — in which case the phenomenon of groupies is not just the latest fashion in dislocated kids' latching on to big-name free-spenders but something new. Are groupies a world apart, like the female impersonators in the Miss All-American contest, or are they the coming center? *Groupies,* unfortunately, exhausts the commercial interest in a good subject without getting into the subject.

•

One of the abiding problems of movies is that success cuts off the directors and stars from contact with the audience. When they try to find their way back, they begin to think about doing something on a simpler scale — making a small, honest movie about real people. But success seems to have cost them their capacity for self-mockery. They don't think in terms of the kind of movie that made them famous (not that they should, necessarily) but in self-important, dated, penitential terms. When they actually do make these films, the results usually are either urban-elemental (typical, natural poor people crushed in the hostile city) or rural-elemental (typical, natural poor people crushed in a stark farming environment). The new John Frankenheimer film, *I Walk the Line,* which stars Gregory Peck, is rural-elemental. The movie is half over while you're still wondering when it's going to start, and finally it's over but never did get started. *I Walk the Line* has gone so far in deglamorizing everything that it forgets to give you a reason for watching it. Peck, a weather-beaten, gaunt-faced Tennessee sheriff, married to well-meaning Estelle Parsons, gets tragically involved with a young girl (Tuesday Weld), the daughter of a moonshiner (Ralph Meeker). The people are homespun and dirt-poor. They look at each other expressionlessly, hopelessly, and talk in hillbilly dialect, with a pause after every line so you'll know their lives are arid.

What was good about Frankenheimer's early films was a straightforward, ingenious approach to pace and craft and entertainment values. But the man who directed the workmanlike *The Manchurian Candidate* and *Seven Days in May* now loiters over every shot trying to squeeze art into it. One might have hoped after *The Fixer* that Frankenheimer had done enough for mankind and might try to pull himself together. A director shouldn't be put down for trying to extend himself, and I don't mean to say that Frankenheimer should be a happy hack. But he needs to build on what he's good at, and use it in new ways. He was a smart, sophisticated director; he isn't developing through these anti-audience films, he's just becoming a bore. *I Walk the Line* oozes sanctimoniousness, like his *The Gypsy Moths,* and the technique is as clumsy as it was in *The Fixer.* When Peck has a line of dialogue to speak, he isn't allowed just to say it; the camera has to discover him sitting on a staircase, with a piece of the banister carefully cut out to provide a frame for his haggard misery as he talks. The audience isn't suffering from success, but we're forced to do penance with the director when we have to watch a slobbering bully force himself on the lovely young heroine and shoot the dog who's guarding her. This is about as elemental as a movie can get; it's almost the primal movie scene.

There's always been a tendency for movie directors to think that the more dismally uninteresting the characters, the more honest the movie. *I Walk the Line* has a laconic hero and a girl in calico and the same kind of solemnly virtuous seriousness that famous movie directors flopped with in the twenties and thirties. Frankenheimer has persistently fallen into a big-director-trying-to-find-himself trap. There are changes in the movie business, but the persistences tell us something, too. The news magazines go on dreaming up those cover stories on how there are no stars any longer or on how the new star is utterly unlike previous stars in that he doesn't really care about stardom. Shirley MacLaine crinkles up her face and grins like Louise Fazenda, Paul Newman is getting more and more like Richard Arlen, and there is David Frost asking movie stars the same old fan-magazine questions: Who is your ideal? What would you say if your daughter wanted to follow in your footsteps and become an actress? What does love mean to you? What is the biggest thing in your life? At least, the plaster-casters would give him a plain, graphic answer.

[December 5, 1970]

Stalinism

Costa-Gavras's *Z* was a complex detective story, investigating how a political crime had been concealed; the new Costa-Gavras film, *The Confession,* is almost the opposite — the story of how men are made to confess to imaginary crimes. There has been no American movie about the new form of theatre that was invented under Stalin — the show trials by which Communist leaders were eliminated. *The Confession* is based on one of the major show trials — the Slansky trial of 1952, in Czechoslovakia, in which fourteen leading Communists, most of them Jewish, were accused of Trotskyism, Titoism, espionage for the West, and Zionism. The movie plays it very close and stays with the particulars, and at first the semi-documentary look and the bureaucratic realism have a counter-effect — the film seems to be non-involving. For the first half hour, I thought that it was too late for this film, that in America it was part of a consciousness that is in the past, when people were discussing *Darkness at Noon*. But the movie has been made out of an absorption in politics, and it catches us up as we begin to see its scope — an examination of how Stalinism works. There is a distinct possibility that young American audiences aren't familiar enough with recent political history to have heard of the Slansky trial, or to understand why most of those purged were Jewish, or to know how the procedures, modelled on the Moscow trials, were perfected in Hungary, or, indeed, how these vast frame-ups served Stalin's policies. But the movie fills us in so thoroughly on this specific case that even those who don't know anything about the trials can hardly fail to grasp the meaning of the central situation, or the final demonstration that Stalinism didn't end with the death of Stalin.

The characters in the movie are all Communists, and the victims and the victimizers are interchangeable; the chief exhibit at the trial, Rudolph Slansky himself, Secretary-General of the Party and then Deputy Premier, helped to arrange the arrest of the other victims, not knowing he was slated to join them. Those who are forced to confess are compromised people, whose belief that the Party must be right has in the past led them to acquiesce in the false confessions of others. All fourteen of the defendants at the Slansky trial confessed. Eleven were executed; three were given life sentences. After Stalin's death and Khrushchev's denunciation of Stalin's policies, the survivors were released. In 1968, the Dubček government officially exonerated all fourteen — the living and the dead.

Despite the historical importance of these carefully staged trials, and their innate drama, the subject is not one that would appeal to Hollywood. Hollywood right-wingers are generally too crude in their approach to be interested in such events, which are of supreme concern only to the left, since the victims — unlike Cardinal Mindszenty, whose trial stirred the general press, and on whom the film *The Prisoner* was based — are themselves Communists. But among the Hollywood leftists, who suffered unduly for their political sympathies, open criticism of the policies of the Soviet Union is still considered Red-baiting or washing dirty linen in public; the classic movie-colony reason for covering things up is that "it's the wrong time."

When you came out of the high-pressure *Z*, you may have asked yourself if you'd been conned into accepting something phony, because the staccato technique seemed a potentially dangerous one that might be used to sell almost anything. Costa-Gavras has scrupulously avoided such danger in *The Confession*. He's fast; the experience of seeing *The Confession* is like a fast read — at times, almost a speed test. One has to pay careful attention, because Costa-Gavras whips through the data and nothing waits. The pace doesn't allow for much thought while you're watching. Yet Costa-Gavras doesn't put on the squeeze, and the film depends not on visceral impact but on the viewer's adding things up; the director has adapted his technique to the subject of political orthodoxy. The film never falls below a certain level of excitement, but it doesn't rise and explode the way *Z* did. He has used the same screenwriter, Jorge Semprun; the same cinematographer, Raoul Coutard; the same leading actor, Yves Montand, who appears this time with his wife, Simone Signoret, playing his wife. But the people aren't melodramatically clear-cut here, and the propagandistic aim — to argue for a more humane socialism — is not so simply stated. The subject is closer to European experience than to ours, and the movie is not likely to stir American audiences the way *Z*'s attack on American-supported fascism did, but it's a great, neglected movie subject.

The Confession is a thoughtful, intelligent demonstration of how strong, idealistic men of character are turned into pawns of history, who confess publicly to imaginary crimes, and not just to the crime of treason but to the degrading petty crime of bribe-taking — a crime devised to satisfy the common citizens who have no mind for the big issues. The men who make the confessions are the sort of idealists who have covered up what shouldn't be covered up. One of the three survivors of the Slansky trial, Artur London, wrote the book on which this film was based. According to London, "The very day that I arrived in Prague with my wife in order to give my manuscript to the Union of Czech Writers publishing firm, I witnessed the invasion of my country by 600,000 men and 6,000 tanks of the Warsaw Pact armies." The book was nevertheless published. Plans that had been made to shoot the movie in Czechoslovakia as a Czechoslovak-French co-production were cancelled, however, and the film was made in France.

Unlike this exact, factual movie, *The Prisoner,* with Alec Guinness's intense performance as the imprisoned cardinal, had originally been conceived as a play, and it treated the process of Mindszenty's confession to trumped-up charges (of treason, currency racketeering, spying for the United States, and conspiracy to restore the Hapsburg monarchy) in terms of impassioned rhetoric and psychological subtleties. The intransigent Mindszenty, whose actual crime had been opposition to the Communist drive to nationalize the Hungarian church schools, was arrested in 1949 and was brought to confess in thirty-eight days. Artur London was worked over for twenty-two months, in a systematic, far less dramatic process. Costa-Gavras, by his cumulative method of building the film, conveys how this time-passing doggedness, rather than specific tortures, leads to the disintegration of the prisoners. The postscript to the London story — the 1968 invasion — is included in the film. *The Prisoner,* which came out in 1955, missed its own postscript: in 1956, a small band of Hungarian revolutionaries broke into the building where Cardinal Mindszenty was kept under armed guard and freed him; four days later, the Russians swept into Hungary.

Artur London is not like those disillusioned Communists who go to work for the F.B.I.; nor is he like those who become left-wing anti-Communists. He is, in fact, still a Communist, and when, this year, after the film opened in Paris, the Czech government under Husák provided an additional postscript by accusing London of spying and stripping him of his citizenship, even *L'Humanité,* the French Communist paper, protested. At the end of the film, during the Russian invasion, Czech students are seen writing in giant letters, "Wake up, Lenin. They have gone mad." Artur London still wants Russia to stop betraying his dreams. It may be a limitation of London's point of view that he's still seeking democratization from within the Party, but that is nevertheless the film's point of view. It is anti-Stalinist, but it still looks back to Lenin. Within those terms, it's a solid, strong movie, but it never raises larger issues, as, for example, Milosz's book *The Captive Mind* does — or as Rosa Luxemburg did when Lenin was still awake.

Costa-Gavras has an urgent, pushing-forward narrative sense, and though he sometimes pushes so fast he doesn't give us a chance to get our bearings (at one point a hallucination is edited right into a flash-forward to the period after the trial), his shorthand narrative style holds everything in check and keeps a great many elements moving without clumsy exposition. His way of handling the actors prevents the material from getting sticky; the brief scenes simply don't allow the actors time for emotional pirouettes, and he keeps reaction shots, which are usually the purest proofs of fakery, and without which TV might not survive, to a minimum. He doesn't permit the actors to show much in a reaction shot, and so a certain subtlety and dignity replace the usual eyebrow-wiggling telegraphy.

There was so much speculation in the press, particularly when priests were tried, about how some new drug must be involved in inducing the confessions that even after the plain explanations came out many people couldn't accept them and went on believing that there was some unsolved mystery. It's remarkably simple, and perfectly convincing when you see the steps. The interrogators don't have to be the diabolically cunning figures that fictional accounts have sometimes made them out to be; they're probably considerably less intelligent than the men they're grilling and training. They may even be rather opaque, which is how Gabriele Ferzetti plays Artur London's chief interrogator; after leading London to confess, he's still bewildered when he himself is imprisoned. You don't have to be smart when you hold all the cards; it may actually help to be a little stupid, or, like some of the other interrogators in the movie, so young that you're ignorant of history and full of zeal for the Party — so young that you don't know enough not to believe.

In a sense, the performers, many of them from earlier Costa-Gavras films, are merely standing in for the historical characters. This, I assume, is the reason that the people in this movie, as in Z, are rarely named but are instead identified by their function or rank, and the reason that the red-haired actor who plays Slansky (who isn't identified as Slansky) is, except in one quick shot, seen from the back (as actors impersonating American Presidents or famous generals are sometimes seen from the back, so the illusion won't be dispelled by our recognition that this is not Roosevelt or MacArthur but only an actor). The method has certain disadvantages — it's hard to sort out the unnamed characters, and in discussing a Costa-Gavras movie it's maddeningly difficult to refer to the individuals — but it ties in with a highly objective style of acting that takes one's mind off personalities and into the events themselves. Yves Montand gives a remarkably non-egotistic performance as London (called simply Gérard in the movie). It's unusual to see a big movie star become an instrument; Montand's personality disappears into the role, which is played without pathos. Signoret, too, gives a performance, instead of the star turn other directors have been using her for. One wants to say "Welcome back!" when one sees performers give themselves over to roles this way.

Even though *The Confession* is subdued, Costa-Gavras's work has tremendous zing, but it's not until the movie is almost over that it gains resonance. He has sacrificed viewing pleasure to a full development of the material. This is certainly virtuous, but a greater artist might possibly not need to make such a sacrifice. Costa-Gavras doesn't quite have the intellectual toughness to bring out the latent meaning in some of the scenes. He's too intelligent to make them cheaply melodramatic, but he lacks the gift of, say, a cool political ironist like the late Polish director Andrzej Munk, who could have made certain of these scenes tragically funny without losing the look of objectivity. The sequence in which one of the defendants mocks the Party's conception of justice by dropping his pants is not done well, and the scene that is potentially a great, revealing climax — when the defendants, after being tricked in court, cry out for their interrogators like children deserted by their mothers — is somewhat flat. Because the emotional support that the inquisitors represent isn't made funny, it doesn't really seem tragic, either. Only if one recognizes how far these once mighty political leaders have fallen is their clutching at their last links to the Party a tragicomic climax. Perhaps the scene is underplayed because the filmmakers themselves don't quite see its implications; they're still hanging on, too. But probably Costa-Gavras just isn't the kind of director who can take imaginative leaps. One respects his fairness but misses those leaps. However, there are some exquisitely edited memory scenes (involving shots from revolutionary epics) and some extraordinarily elegiac scenes of the Russian invasion of 1968 (involving stills as well as motion-picture footage).

By now, certain aspects of Costa-Gavras's style are becoming apparent: He appears to be facile, because the camera never seems to be looking for the action or moving toward it. The camera is always *there*. You're zipped along to just what you need to see, which is never held, never lingered on. You don't pay much attention to the camerawork in *The Confession;* it's so even — so smooth and consistent — that you're not caught by particular images. The distinctive feature of Costa-Gavras's style is that nothing is held for the possible emotions in an image or a scene to sink in. As a result, the edited-in stills and motion-picture footage — which *are* held for a specific emotional response — become so lyric that we're suddenly overwhelmed and suffused with feeling. It's a very strange and ambiguous testimonial to the complexity of the ways in which film can be used that Costa-Gavras's fictional re-creations of history seem prosaic, while bits of old film and photographs of the actual invasion of Czechoslovakia become the poetry that lights up *The Confession.*

•

The Act of the Heart is about flaming hearts, priestly vows, and self-immolation. It's one of those passionate, spiritual jobs about a girl who is "different" — Genevieve Bujold, doing her Peter Pan–Joan of Arc specialty. She's not a bad actress, but in this film, which was written for her and directed by her husband, Paul Almond, there's nothing for her to do but fall back on the old fragile, incandescent child-woman shtick. This is one of the staples of fake-"sensitive" theatre; the big-wet-eyed-crying-when-she's-laughing-and-vice-versa routine used to be very popular at matinées. It's a sickly show-business game, and Miss Bujold ought not to play it. A few silly, casual bits in the film are rather nice, but Almond goes for obsessions and fatalities and an elliptical style — he's very high on portents. The overload of scrambled, whopping emotions is dreadful — a masochistic feminine fantasy gone berserk. The heroine sings the solo with the church choir; she suffers while singing in a night club; she even — God help us — makes love with an Augustinian monk (in the unlikely, affable person of Donald Sutherland) at the foot of the altar. When, after hours of fire symbolism, she finally poured kerosene on herself to create a new sacrifice for a world that has forgotten Jesus, I rummaged in my bag for a match. I sat through this picture as a matter of professional discipline, trying to figure out why the other people in the crowded theatre didn't leave. I imagined they must be going mad, like me, but at the end I heard murmurs of "What a beautiful movie!"

[December 12, 1970]

Beyond Pirandello

The young movie audience will want to see Altamont on film, because even if it went bad it's still their scene. They will go to *Gimme Shelter* for Mick Jagger — the most incredible of all rock stars, the man you hate to love — and death on film. The cinematography is highly variable, but it's good enough to show what is going on. The editing of the images to the music is very good, but the film's structure is a bit confusing. The filmmakers, Albert and David Maysles and Charlotte Zwerin, obviously wanted the suspense factor of the violence to come at Altamont but also wanted to use their best stuff on Jagger from earlier concerts, so after you've been prepared to expect Altamont they've thrown numbers in without telling you where they were performed. However, you don't expect clarity in this kind of film, and you don't think to worry about where you are when you get tough little Jagger in a silvery Uncle Sam hat, or with a Marlene Dietrich–style breeze rippling his shining hair and his draperies. His effects are brilliantly insolent. Jagger's new form of show-biz can seem anti-show-biz because it's so openly corrupt it appears incorruptible. And what other movie has dozens of freak-outs and a death?

But how does one review this picture? It's like reviewing the footage of President Kennedy's assassination or of Lee Harvey Oswald's murder. This movie is into complications and sleight-of-hand beyond Pirandello, since the filmed death at Altamont — although, of course, unexpected — was part of a *cinéma-vérité* spectacular. The free concert was staged and lighted to be photographed, and the three hundred thousand people who attended it were the unpaid cast of thousands. The violence and killing weren't scheduled, but the Maysles brothers hit the *cinéma-vérité* jackpot.

If events are created to be photographed, is the movie that records them a documentary, or does it function in a twilight zone? Is it the cinema of fact when the facts are manufactured for the cinema? The Nazi rally at Nuremberg in 1934 was architecturally designed so that Leni Riefenstahl could get the great footage that resulted in *Triumph of the Will;* in order to shoot *A Time for Burning,* William C. Jersey instigated a racial confrontation that split an Omaha church. It is said to be a "law" that the fact of observation alters the phenomenon that is observed — but how can one prove it? More likely, observation sometimes alters the phenomenon and sometimes doèsn't. In Gerald Temaner's and Gordon Quinn's *Home for Life,* the principal character — a woman entering a home for the aged — is so disoriented that she may accept the camera as just one more factor in her confused situation; in parts of Fred Wiseman's *Law and Order,* the police are in such routine but taxing situations that they may go on doing what they usually do. There is no reason to think the freaked-out people in *Gimme Shelter* paid much attention to the camera crews, but would the event itself have taken place without those crews? With modern documentarians, as with many TV news cameramen, it's impossible to draw a clear line between catching actual events and arranging events to be caught; a documentarian may ask people to reënact events, while a TV journalist may argue that it was only by precipitating some events that he was able to clarify issues for the public — that is, that he needed to fake a little, but for justifiable reasons. There are no simple ethical standards to apply, and because the situations are so fluid and variable, one has to be fairly knowledgeable not to get suckered into reacting to motion-picture footage that appears to be documentary as if it were the simple truth.

A *cinéma-vérité* sham that appeals to an audience by showing it what it wants to believe may be taken as corroboration of its beliefs, and as an illumination. Would audiences react to the Arthur Miller–Eugene O'Neill overtones in the Maysles brothers' earlier film, the "direct-cinema" *Salesman,* the same way if they understood how much of it was set up and that the principals were playacting? One should be alert to the questionable ethics in *Gimme Shelter,* to what is designed not to reveal the situation but to conceal certain elements of that situation. *Gimme Shelter* plays the game of trying to mythologize the event (Altamont) and to clear the participants (the Rolling Stones and the filmmakers) of any cognizance of how it came about.

When Mick Jagger is seen in *Gimme Shelter* pensively looking at the Altamont footage — run for him by the Maysles brothers — and wondering how it all happened, this is disingenuous moviemaking. One wants to say: Drop the Miss Innocence act and tell us the straight story of the background to the events. What isn't explained is that, four months after Woodstock, Stone Promotions asked the Maysles brothers to shoot the Stones at Madison Square Garden. The Maysles brothers had done a film on an American tour by the Beatles, and Albert Maysles had shot part of *Monterey Pop.* When, as a climax to their American tour, the Stones decided on a filmed free concert in the San Francisco area, the Maysles brothers made a deal with them to film it and rounded up a large crew. Melvin Belli's bordello-style law office and his negotiations for a concert site are in the film, but it isn't explained that Porter Bibb, the publicist of *Salesman,* was the person who brought in Belli, or that Bibb became involved in producing the concert at Altamont in order to produce the Maysles film. The sequence in Belli's office omits the detail that the concert had to be hurriedly moved to Altamont because the owners of the previously scheduled site wanted distribution rights of the film. *Gimme Shelter* has been shaped so as to whitewash the Rolling Stones and the filmmakers for the thoughtless, careless way the concert was arranged, and especially for the cut-rate approach to keeping order. The Hell's Angels, known for their violence, but cheap and photogenic, were hired as guards for five hundred dollars' worth of beer. This took less time and trouble than arranging for unarmed marshals, and the Hell's Angels must have seemed the appropriate guards for Their Satanic Majesties the Stones. In the film the primary concern of the Angels appears to be to keep the stage clear and guard the Stones.

The Hell's Angels, whose rigid, scary faces are already familiar movie faces from the wheelers — a genre they inspired and appear in — are made the villains in *Gimme Shelter,* and though I don't wish to suggest that the Hell's Angels should have been made the heroes, the fact is that the Angels — who don't have any share in the profits of the film — are made the patsies, while those who hired them are photographed all bland and sweet, wondering how it happened. When the self-centered, mercenary movie queen of *Singin' in the Rain* talked about bringing joy into the humdrum lives of the public, we laughed. Should we also laugh at Melvin Belli's talk in *Gimme Shelter* about a "free concert" for "the people" and at the talk about the Stones' not wanting money when the concert is being shot for *Gimme Shelter* and the Rolling Stones and the Maysles brothers divide the profits from the picture? One of the jokes of *cinéma vérité* is that practically the only way to attract an audience is to use big stars, but since the big stars coöperate only if they get financial — and, generally, artistic — control of the film, the *cinéma-vérité* techniques are used to give the look of "caught" footage to the image the stars are selling.

Mick Jagger, the most polymorphous-perverse star since Marilyn Monroe, is hypercharged and narcissistic; when he performs he's close to sadistic in the way he holds audiences and dominates them. Even those who loathe him — and it is said that many young girls do — acknowledge that he's a spellbinder. One half expects him to be sacrificed to the audience at the end of the concert. Offstage, he seems tranquillized and wan and pale. A hip, Mod zombie, he pouts prettily, and smiles with the meaningless sweetness of an earlier type of popular singer — not unlike the skinny young Sinatra, whom he resembles. In the movie, as in *Performance,* when Jagger is offstage it's as if he were offscreen; he doesn't have an actor's presence — he becomes a private, non-communicative person. It make sense that someone who performs so totally burns himself out onstage, but the near-catatonic figure of Mick Jagger wearing saucy little hats and mumbling mild platitudes gives plausibility to the view of him as demon-possessed when he sings in that harsh, abrasive voice and prances like a witch doctor.

This film has caught his feral intensity as a performer (which, oddly, Godard never captured in *One Plus One,* maybe because he dealt with a rehearsal-recording session, without an audience). It has also captured his teasing, taunting relationship to the audience: he can finish a frenzied number and say to the audience, "You don't want my trousers to fall down now, do you?" His toughness is itself provocative, and since rock performers are accepted by the young as their own spokesmen, the conventional barriers between performer and audience have been pushed over. From the start of *Gimme Shelter,* our knowledge of the horror to come makes us see the Rolling Stones' numbers not as we might in an ordinary festival film but as the preparations for, and the possible cause of, disaster. We begin to suspect that Mick Jagger's musical style leads to violence, as he himself suggests in a naïve and dissociated way when he complains — somewhat pettishly, but with a flicker of pride — to the crowd that there seems to be trouble every time he starts to sing "Sympathy for the Devil." He may not fully understand the response he works for and gets.

The film has a very disturbing pathos, because everybody seems so helpless. Many of the people at Altamont are blank or frightened but are in thrall to the music, or perhaps just to being there; some twitch and jerk to the beat in an apocalyptic parody of dancing; others strip, or crawl on the heads of the crowd; and we can see tormented trippers' faces, close to the stage, near the angry Angels. When Grace Slick and then Jagger appeal to the audience to cool it, to "keep your bodies off each other unless you intend love," and to "get yourselves together," they are saying all they know how to say, but the situation is way past that. They don't seem to connect what they're into with the results. Mick Jagger symbolizes the rejection of the values that he then appeals to. Asking stoned and freaked-out people to control themselves is pathetic, and since the most dangerous violence appears to be from the Hell's Angels, who are trying to keep their idea of order by stomping dazed, bewildered kids, Jagger's saying "Brothers and sisters, why are we fighting?" is pitifully beside the point. Musically, Jagger has no way to cool it, because his orgiastic kind of music has only one way to go — higher, until everyone is knocked out.

Mick Jagger's performing style is a form of aggression not just against the straight world but against his own young audience, and this appeals to them, because it proves he hasn't sold out and gone soft. But when all this aggression is released, who can handle it? The violence he provokes is well known: fans have pulled him off a platform, thrown a chair at him. He's greeted with a punch in the face when he arrives at Altamont. What the film doesn't deal with is the fact that Jagger attracts this volatile audience, that he magnetizes disintegrating people. This is, of course, an ingredient of the whole rock scene, but it is seen at its most extreme in the San Francisco–Berkeley audience that gathers for the Rolling Stones at Altamont. Everyone — the people who came and the people who planned it — must have wanted a big Dionysian freak-out. The movie includes smiling talk about San Francisco as the place for the concert, and we all understand that it's the place for the concert because it's the farthest-out place; it's the mother city of the drug culture. It's where things are already wildly out of control. The film shows part of what happened when Marty Balin, of the Jefferson Airplane, jumped off the stage to stop the Angels from beating a black man and was himself punched unconscious. After that, according to reporters, no one tried to stop the Angels from beating the crazed girls and boys who climbed onstage or didn't follow instructions; they were hit with leaded pool cues and with fists while the show went on and the three dozen cameramen and soundmen went on working. There were four deaths at Altamont, and a cameraman caught one. You see the Angel's knife flashing high in the air before he stabs a black boy, who has a gun in his hand. You see it at normal speed, see it again slowed down, and then in a frozen frame. But is it simply a news event? In the bright stage lights, surrounded by cameras, Mick Jagger is the apotheosis of star. He's the new Mr. Show Business — a moth sizzling in his flames. However, the Maysles brothers' approach to moviemaking is much too callow to cope with the phenomenon of people who are drawn to Mick Jagger's music in order to lose control — except at the level of attracting them and then exploiting the disastrous consequences.

It's impossible to say how much moviemaking itself is responsible for those consequences, but it is a factor, and with the commercial success of this kind of film it's going to be a bigger factor. Antonioni dickered with black groups to find out what actions they were planning, so that he could include some confrontations in *Zabriskie Point*. M-G-M's lawyers must have taken a dim view of this. A smaller company, with much to gain and little to lose, might have encouraged him. Movie studios are closing, but, increasingly, public events are designed to take place on what are essentially movie stages. And with movie-production money getting tight, provoked events can be a cheap source of spectacles. The accidents that happen may be more acceptable to audiences than the choreographed battles of older directors, since for those who grew up with TV careful staging can look arch and stale. It doesn't look so fraudulent if a director excites people to commit violent acts on camera, and the event becomes free publicity for the film. The public will want to see the results, so there is big money to deodorize everyone concerned. What we're getting in the movies is "total theatre." Altamont, in *Gimme Shelter*, is like a Roman circus, with a difference: the audience and the victims are indistinguishable.

[December 19, 1970]

Epic and Crumbcrusher

A few years ago, I asked the director of a sprawling, flattened-out epic what had gone wrong. He said that so many years had elapsed between his initial impulse to buy the property and the actual shooting of the picture, and there had been such a mammoth effort involved in the production — handling the huge crew and moving to locations in the snow and the heat — that by the time he was in the middle of the movie he no longer remembered why he had wanted to do it. He wasn't even sure any longer what it was about — the script had been rewritten so often — and he was so damned tired of the whole thing that it died on him, and when he and the editor finally tried to put the pieces together it just wouldn't take off. That's the danger of expensive epics, and I suspect that this — or something like it — is what happened to Arthur Penn on *Little Big Man*.

Little Big Man is a film one wants to like. It's Arthur Penn's big one — a hip epic that, though it stays fairly close to the Thomas Berger novel, also seems to represent Arthur Penn more fully than his earlier pictures did, since this time he is free to bring to the center the social consciousness that appeared before in disguised and fragmentary form. He has earned great good will, and because this film comes at the end of a terrible year for American movies, and because he was robbed of prizes for *Bonnie and Clyde,* and because *Alice's Restaurant,* despite its weaknesses, was an attempt to get at something, one wants to see him come into his own. Still, it takes great moral authority as well as great aesthetic authority to place white murderousness at the heart of a comic, picaresque narrative about the events that led up to Custer's Last Stand, and here, somehow, the different kinds of authority that are necessary don't merge to make one feel, Yes, that's it. You wind up disappointed, wishing you'd liked it better. It goes wrong in a subtle way — the wrongness seeping into your bones, so that when the movie is over, you don't really feel like talking about it. I think part of what happens is that we overreact to the charm and comedy of the farfetched, tall-story beginning, savoring the one-thing-after-another yarn, like adults rediscovering the taste of ice cream, and when the film turns messagey we are dismayed. That is what we liked it for not being. When the movie goes into the first of its three big massacre sequences, we can see that the change was prepared for, but we had been rejecting that preparation. We didn't want *Little Big Man* to turn into *another* movie that shows us how we should be against ourselves.

Dustin Hoffman has the leading role — Jack Crabb, an American Candide whose adventures take him back and forth between the red man's culture and the white man's culture. Hoffman is mannered and maybe a little cute, but at the outset that seems fine, because although he's the star, Jack Crabb is a peripheral character — an observer on the edge of the events. For roughly an hour, the comic tone is pleasantly askew. Amusing characters turn up and disappear and turn up again throughout the film: Faye Dunaway as a preacher's wife; Jeff Corey as Wild Bill Hickok; Martin Balsam as a swindler getting cheerfully dismantled limb by limb; Chief Dan George as an Indian chief who is part patriarch, part Jewish mother. But after the first hour the massacres start coming, and the speeches, too. Thomas Berger had suggested that the Indians looked like Orientals, but when you notice that Jack Crabb's lovely Indian bride looks Vietnamese you start waiting uneasily for more slaughter. And long before you get to Custer's Last Stand — and the madness-of-military-leaders bit, just the way you got it in Tony Richardson's *The Charge of the Light Brigade* — you've heard the little click in your brain that says, "Enough."

For the tall tale to function as an epic form, the violence must be wry and peculiar, or surreal and only half believable — insane, as it is in the book, and not conventionally bloody like this. For the mock-heroic, picaresque mode to make sense, the big scenes — the climaxes — must be funny or weird. What is the point of the naïveté and mock-innocence if Penn drops them when he's emotionally engaged? To be successful, the picture should deepen by comic means, and when Penn goes for seriousness he collapses the form of the movie, and it's obvious that the jokes and the relaxed episodes are just filler for the violence. In the past, Penn has demonstrated a talent for making violence both lyrical and startlingly comic, but this time he loses the touch that might have made the movie's burlesque ramble through American history culminate in a burlesque vision that said something fresh. The picture needed to get hipper; instead, it goes from hip to straight, and one cancels the other out. The picture goes really bad just before the first massacre — a raid on an Indian camp full of unprotected women and children — when a soldier says that if his wife had been captured by the Indians he wouldn't want her back after she'd been with an Indian, and a moment later one of the leaders of the raid leers with genocidal delight as he goes in for the killing. In scenes like this, Penn loses any claim to sensitivity; this is just crude, ideological filmmaking. The tone of the film gets sombre, and after the second massacre the pace goes slack and solemn, as if to impress us with the film's intentions. Penn's greatest effort is, ironically, wasted, because by the time he gets to his full-scale climax he's lost us; it's a dull anticlimax, and we observe the slaughter without caring about it. He's better on individual acts of violence; he doesn't handle the large crowds at Little Big Horn well. Somehow he has got himself into a situation in which he rarely uses his own special gifts and he doesn't have the skills that are needed. The picture is weak in both the epic and the comic.

The truth is that even while we were laughing at the early part, we were aware that the scenes were likable enough, indifferently genial, not more — the preacher's makeup was a stock-company job, and so was his performance; Faye Dunaway's long false eyelashes stuck in the spectator's eyes; and so on — and we couldn't tell if this was stylization or just a mistake, or a mixture of the two. But we have become so eager to enjoy ourselves at the movies that we giggle at almost anything, even at the dumb joke about a young girl who's disappointed because she isn't raped by the Indians (right after Indians have killed her family). We giggle hopefully at a clumsy scene in a tent with Jack Crabb giving his all, in turn, to three beckoning Indian girls. We try to find it funny when he is tarred and feathered by his long-lost sister. We smile at a stupid bordello scene and at two-bit homosexual gags. But it's clear that Penn's comic intuition is faulty. When Jack Crabb becomes a gunfighter, the parody of silent comedies is a high spot in the film, and one can make a case for the slow, offbeat timing in the gunfighter's saloon scene with Jeff Corey (who gives one of the few bright performances). But how can one make a case for the timing of the scene in which Jack's sister leaves him because he can't stand shooting people, or the timing of the sequence in Custer's tent when Jack comes to kill him, or the timing of the sequence with the homosexual Indian and the contrary Indian? Many scenes are heavily ill-timed, larded with the extra seconds that kill comedy. The not very funny jokes don't matter much as long as the director stays within the shaggy, relaxed framework. But as the full ambitiousness of the picture develops, all those ragged ends come back to mind. It may seem unfair to judge a talented man trying to do something major so much more harshly than one judges a lesser talent on an easy project, but a man trying to do something big takes a big risk. Whereas previously we saw Penn's gifts, we see his faults as soon as he attempts more than he can handle. We start thinking about all the bum details because the movie is bloody but banal. And we know that if the film didn't have its aspirations and some of Penn's characteristic details, if we just viewed the comedy as comedy, we'd rate it very ordinary.

Unfortunately, *Little Big Man* represents the ascension of Arthur Penn. This is his big one in the way *Catch-22* was Mike Nichols' big one. Arthur Penn stays within a smaller range, but you come out of this ten-million-dollar movie feeling that Penn, like Nichols, got into something complex he couldn't bring off. Psychologically, for the audience the picture ends in the second big massacre — a lyrical massacre set in the snow — which is truly horrifying and is the only visually effective sequence in the movie. Specifically, the picture ends — because we can't take any more — when the hero's Oriental-looking bride is killed and her newborn baby's head is blown off. Penn follows this by bringing up the faint sound of the fife-and-drum corps playing a military air, and when the music rises and swells, the movie is diminished. Penn has pushed it into political-ironic terrain when it has gone beyond that; he has cheapened the death he has just shown us.

The hip epic is a tricky form, because it functions without heroes, and when the leading character in a movie doesn't have heroic dimensions, when we don't really believe in him and aren't emotionally drawn to him, we try to fill the void by fixing our hopes on someone who will make us feel good. Hoffman, with his hopping walk and his nasal vocal tricks, is a good character actor, but one wearies of Jack Crabb's openmouthed bewilderment. One begins to accept handsome old Chief Dan George playing Old Lodge Skins as the central character, because his face draws the camera in a way Hoffman's doesn't; the chief has a radiance that the movie is starved of. (This was also part of the problem with *Alice's Restaurant;* Arlo Guthrie's face didn't invite the camera, either.) The movie lacks richness and audacity, even in its handling of its targets. Custer (Richard Mulligan) is used the way the military leaders in *The Charge of the Light Brigade* were used, only more crudely; he's paper-thin — good for a cartoon or a few jokes. But an epic requires larger figures.

The picture is about genocide — about the Indians and about Vietnam — and what Penn forces us to look at is too horrible for the pious nonsense of the movie's messages. The massacres of the helpless Indians on the screen are, of course, like the massacres of Vietnamese villagers, and this makes a powerful emotional connection. But when Penn tries to use the violence to stand in for a demonstration that white Americans have been racists throughout history, he wants to say something messianic but has nothing clear to say. The new racial interpretations of history that have come up in the last few movie years have become an insult to the audience's intelligence. The old chief tells us that his people "believe everything is alive . . . but the white man, they believe everything is dead." When Jack Crabb asks the old chief why the white soldiers kill women and children, the chief replies that the white creatures "do not seem to know where the center of the earth is" and that "the white man tries to rub things out." This is offensively simple, as is the melodramatic genocidal speech that Custer makes before ordering the butchery of the women and children in the snow massacre. It's Stanley Kramerism, and one expects something different from Penn. Custer — "the Devil" — is like the Germans or the Japanese in Second World War movies, but in this movie, as in others now, we in the audience are also supposed to be the Devil. This reversal is no more honest than putting us with the angels, and we experience the discomforts of guilt, confusion, and disbelief.

•

The book *Love Story*, by Erich Segal, represents a first in American letters: *Love Story* is the first novelization of a movie to make it to the top of the best-seller lists. The novelization of a movie is a new subliterary genre, an expansion from the "stories" of the movies which used to appear in fan magazines such as *Screen Stories;* as far as I can determine, novelizations appeared only in paperback until 1966, when *Fantastic Voyage* was the first to cross the barrier into hard-cover. But nothing like the promotion for — or the success of — *Love Story* has been seen before. (One can be sure that movie companies will now take a new interest in the script-into-novel market.) *Love Story* has also been reported to be the most popular hard-cover book in France and England, and the new paperback edition in this country is said to have sold over five million copies. Allowing for hyperbole and halving the figure, that is still one hell of a pile of pulp. The movie's star, Ali MacGraw, is the wife of the head of production of the movie company, and that is not a first. In fact, Miss MacGraw's husband, Robert Evans, became the head of production at Paramount after being selected by Norma Shearer to impersonate her late husband, the producer Irving Thalberg, in a movie. Mr.

Thalberg's pictures frequently starred Miss Shearer, sometimes as unfortunately as *Love Story* stars Miss MacGraw.

Mr. Segal's little golden movie book runs to about twenty-five thousand words. According to *A Black Glossary*, by Hermese E. Roberts, blacks refer to small children, or shorties, as "crumbcrushers." *Love Story* is a perfect example of a literary crumbcrusher. It's a generation-gap variant of a neo-Victorian heart-wringer in the movie tradition of *Madame X, Imitation of Life,* and *Magnificent Obsession,* with maybe a little *Dark Victory;* it is written in a snappy, tear-jerking, hard-soft style synthesized from *A Farewell to Arms* and *The Sun Also Rises.* Even allowing for the fact that Paramount helped it to the top of the best-seller lists, it has been there for an unconscionably long period, and there can be little doubt that it has been read by many people who rarely read anything in hard covers. One would like to find a positive side to this, but I doubt whether those who buy and love *Love Story* will be spurred on to become readers of other books. What could they follow it with that wouldn't be a disappointment? I doubt whether even the breathless, gosh-gee-whiz-can-all-this-be-happening-to-me TV-celebrity-author himself could cap this shlock classic with another.

The book is narrated by a rich Wasp boy who breaks with his family when he marries a poor Italian Catholic girl. Their love is near-perfect, but then he learns she is going to die. Here is our hero addressing God on the subject of his Jenny's leukemia before she learns about it:

> I don't mind the agony, sir, I don't mind knowing as long as Jenny doesn't know. Did you hear me, Lord, sir? You can name the price.

But she finds out, just after he has planned to take her on a last whirl to Paris:

> "I don't want Paris. I don't need Paris. I just want you—"
> "That you've got, baby!" I interrupted, sounding falsely merry.
> "And I want time," she continued, "which you can't give me."
> Now I looked into her eyes. They were ineffably sad. But sad in a way only I understood. They were saying she was sorry. That is, sorry for me.
> We stood there silently holding one another. Please, if one of us cries, let both of us cry. But preferably neither of us.

I doubt if a cynic could fake this. I don't mean to suggest that Segal is as gaga as this book — only that a part of him is. The book has curious lapses suggesting that the author sometimes slipped from his fantasy-hero into a fanciful self-infatuation, as in the passage in which the hero resolves "to tell nobody, to shoulder the entire burden" himself. He lies to his boss, Mr. Jonas, in order to stay close to his dying wife, and then speculates, "Oh, Christ, Mr. Jonas, when you find out the real reason!" Since the real reason is his nobility, how extraordinary that he should be anticipating his boss's future recognition of it. Slips like this make one think that Segal isn't a total fake, that he really does fantasize on this level.

His unworldly-worldly fantasy provides the movie business with a rare opportunity for a killing, at a minimum in production costs. On the screen, it can satisfy the desire for a 1944 movie which seems to afflict television watchers; that is, a movie that reflects an orderly world — one devastated by war but one in which Americans still felt like a moral people and could luxuriate in virtue. That desire for a reassuring moral universe is probably behind the acceptance of *Ryan's Daughter,* and *Love Story* — which takes place as if the outside world *were* still 1944, but without a war — may satisfy a national (perhaps international) longing. It deals in private passions at a time when we are exhausted from public defeats, and it deals with the mutual sacrifice of a hardworking, clean-cut pair of lovers, and with love beyond death.

This thing is so instinctively, plus manipulatively, engineered to leave 'em crying that it could hardly fail commercially even if the actors were programmed by Terry Southern to make obscene gestures at the audience at ten-second intervals. The weeping audience probably wouldn't notice, any more than it cares that just about every detail in the movie is phony and off — from having the boy's Brahmin father live and speak in a style that was already a comedy convention in the thirties to the way the hero stands with his girl during his Harvard Law School commencement exercises, from the cutie-pie strong language she uses when she's talking to the children's choir in church to the way she, a brilliant music major at Radcliffe, mispronounces "Köchel" on her deathbed. Those who are susceptible to this sort of movie may not even notice that Ali MacGraw is horribly smug and smirky, though if you share my impulses, whenever she gets facetious you'll probably want to wham her one. It's a role that the young Katharine Hepburn might have redeemed by her eccentricity and intensity; Miss MacGraw has neither. It might have been better if she hadn't tried to act at all; she didn't try to act much in *Goodbye, Columbus,* and that was fine, because she was supposed to be an insensitive bitch anyway, and she looked beautiful. She isn't supposed to be a bitch this time, and from some angles she doesn't look so good, either (though she used to be a marvellous model), and her attempts at classy repartee are destroyed by nose-flaring, lip-curling amateurishness. As the hero, Ryan O'Neal, the Rodney Harrington of TV's *Peyton Place,* holds the picture together — somewhat. His performance is not the kind I care much about — sincere, vulnerable movie heroes generally not being equipped for much besides trite suffering — but O'Neal knows how to be emotional without being a slob, and in this unskilled, mediocre piece of moviemaking (Arthur Hiller directed) his professionalism shines. *Love Story* will not be the first disgraceful movie that has laid waste the emotions of a vast audience, though it may be one of the most ineptly made of all the lump-and-phlegm hits.

Yet even if Ryan O'Neal were as incompetent as Miss MacGraw, *Love Story* would probably still have the smell of a winner. Those who sob away can flatter themselves that the picture must have been beautifully done — or they wouldn't have been so affected. *Love Story* is lucky in its timing, and a lot more than luck went into the timing. The book has been promoted from the start as an antidote to dirty books and movies, as if America were being poisoned by them. Erich Segal (in another compartment of his life a translator of Plautus) used as his sales pitch an attack on *Portnoy's Complaint* and Henry Miller's novels; this picture employs its few shock words repeatedly, but in that old blue way that Broadway does — so, of course, Segal isn't considered foul-mouthed. The movie has been pushed to attract the audience for the "clean and wholesome," the way *The Sound of Music* did, and to attract the kids who loved Zeffirelli's *Romeo and Juliet,* because this is a "contemporary" R. & J. story. It has been acclaimed by *Variety,* in a review that might have been written by the Vice-President himself, as a "rare breath of fresh air in the smog of contemporary cinema psychoneurosis." The review goes on, "And not just because Arthur Hiller's sensitive and restrained direction tells a story so touching that tears may be shed without any embarrassment whatsoever. But rather because this gentle romantic tragedy succeeds in conveying some timeless universal human ideals of emotional commitment in a contemporary frame of reference."

The original-soundtrack recording (on a Paramount label) includes such compositions as "Theme from *Love Story,*" "Snow Frolic," "The Christmas Trees," "Skating in Central Park," and "Bozo Barrett." Bozo Barrett is the name that the hero suggests for the child he and his doomed Jenny never have. The picture represents what one had hoped might have been laughed off the screen forever, and it heralds something worse. An audience that's swimming in tears, drowning in seas of virtue, can be a very self-righteous audience. Sentimentality and repression have a natural affinity; they're the two sides of one counterfeit coin.

Strangely, since the book was written after the script, the movie omits the emotional climax of the book, the climax that turns even some hardened, laughing readers to jelly — when, after the wife's death, the hero falls into his father's arms and cries. This was the reconciliation that the dead girl sought, the only thorn in their perfect love having been his refusal to try to understand his father. In the book, it is a Freudian generation gap, and the son has been as helplessly at fault as the father (who in the book is the head of the Peace Corps). Significantly, although the book seemed as opportunistic as is possible, the finished film goes a step further. In order (I assume) to flatter the young movie audience, the reconciliation scene is left out, and the hero ignores his father and remains alone with his memories. The movie thus posits a hopeless, unbridgeable gulf between the generations, even though no basis for conflict is presented, since the son becomes a respectable lawyer and gives no indication of having values that are different from his father's. The movie plays it every which way with the mass audience. A generation gap for the young audience, but no changed values that might upset the *Airport* crowd. It's calculation like this that earns a movie praise for being pure and fresh and idealistic.

[December 26, 1970]

Megalomaniacs

If in the theatre satire is what closes on Saturday night, in movies parable is what shows at film festivals and never opens. Kafka and Borges may appear to be very cinematic authors, but their epigrams and enigmas don't seem to supply enough sense of life or much texture. Godard and Bertolucci have had their flirtations with Borges; Elio Petri, a movie critic on an Italian Communist paper and then a scenarist, became a director a decade ago, and has from the start shown the influence of Kafka — particularly of *The Trial* and *The Castle*. Petri is distinctively unsentimental, and his indirect method of telling a story — which gradually takes the form of a paranoid fantasy — makes the viewer apprehensive. Typically, Petri, who uses Kafka politically, has worked with Marcello Mastroianni or Gian Maria Volonte as his trapped hero. In the remarkably intelligent thriller *We Still Kill the Old Way,* Volonte was a foolish professor innocently trying to solve a crime in a land where there was no justice. In that film, derived from *A Man's Blessing,* by Leonardo Sciascia, though one anxiously expected the worst at every moment, one feared for the hero and cared about what happened to him; it was a humane thriller. Petri's new *Investigation of a Citizen Above Suspicion,* based on a screenplay he wrote with Ugo Pirro, is a more sophisticated and somewhat perverse political film, and I think it may be too nasty and kinky for the political parable to be effective.

Starting with Kafka's cryptic "He is a servant of the law and eludes judgment," Petri sets out to demonstrate the proposition that those in authority are above the laws they are supposed to serve. He chooses for his demonstration the chief of Rome's homicide squad (Volonte), just promoted to a new post, in which he is to deal with political dissidents. This mad big-shot cop believes he has a license to kill. The theme is fascinating, but the queasy, tense atmosphere derives not from the horror of the proposition itself but from the kinkiness of the details, such as the use of jangly music when the cop slits the throat of his mistress (Florinda Bolkan) and then plants the incontrovertible evidence that he did it. Petri has a fun-and-games approach to chic perversity — like a cold, soured Vadim — and this makes one so jumpy that it distracts one from the meaning of the film. Though the megalomaniac's view of the world proves correct — he is not prosecuted for the murder, even though everyone knows he committed it — Petri doesn't develop this cosmic political joke. Instead of moving forward into a view of how power creates invulnerability, the movie goes backward into flashbacks about the cop's bizarre sex life.

The movie left enjoys the complacent — and photogenic — notion that people seek power because they are sexually inadequate, and that authoritarian personalities can be explained by impotence, repressed homosexuality, and so on. (Didn't Swift make fun of this idea a few centuries ago when he said that Alexander had to conquer the world because all his unused semen had gone to his head?) The thread of the film's argument gets lost when Volonte is revealed to be a sexual weakling and begins cracking up all over the place. Petri fails to take the parable to its conclusion and have the maniac revel in his victory. The end is fumbled, and the point of the film isn't made clear. It's easy to see why: the parable form is short on details, while the vicious thriller is full of possibilities for nervous excitation. The movie is extremely dislikable. Petri doesn't use suspense pleasurably, he doesn't resolve the tensions, and so the film leaves one in rather a foul mood. And, by the way, I'm not at all convinced that Kafka's elusive remark meant what Petri took it to mean.

•

If you resist the aggression of a certain kind of loudmouth, he is quick to tell you that you're afraid of life. And no matter how dispassionately you analyze what's the matter with *Husbands* — which is just about everything — those who made it and those who love it will insist that if you didn't like it, you're hung up or uptight, or some other "up" or "tight" construction. I think I gave my all by sitting through it. The film, which ran two hours and eighteen minutes when I saw it, had already lost sixteen minutes; if I were cutting it, I don't think there would be much left except one shot of Ben Gazzara coughing, a sequence of an actor named John Kullers singing "Brother, Can You Spare a Dime?," a short scene of John Cassavetes' little daughter crying when he comes home, and a few scenes involving two charming English actresses — a tall blonde named Jenny Runacre and a medium-sized blonde named Jenny Lee Wright. Maybe twenty minutes in all, and that's stretching it.

Husbands, directed by Cassavetes, extends the faults of his last film, *Faces;* one might even say that *Husbands* takes those faults into a new dimension. It is, as *Faces* was, semi-written by Cassavetes and semi-improvised by the actors. This time, the film is about three suburban husbands — Cassavetes (a dentist), Gazzara (a Peter Max sort of commercial artist), and Peter Falk (profession unspecified) — who go on a bender after attending the funeral of a fourth. The three buddies are boy-boy American males taking flight from their marriages and responsibilities, and, for the period in which we observe them, more emotionally involved with sports and each other than with their professions or their families. One assumes they are meant to be searching for themselves, their lost freedom, and their lost potentialities — and one can guess that Cassavetes believes that their boyishness is creative. But the boyishness he shows us isn't remotely creative; it's just infantile and offensive.

The three leads are like performers in a Norman Mailer movie, role-playing at being lowlifes. Despite the suburban-commuter roles they have chosen, they punch and poke each other like buffoonish hardhats. When one cries, "Harry, you're a phony," the riposte is "Nobody calls me a phony" — and this sort of exchange may be followed by gales of laughter. In fact, they act very much like Gazzara, Falk, and Cassavetes doing their buddy-buddy thing on the *Dick Cavett Show.* They horse around, encouraging each other to come up with dialogue like "The man is right. When the man is right, he's right." Since their performances don't have enough range for a full-length film, they become monotonous; Cassavetes apparently deceives himself and others into taking this monotony for fidelity to life. He replaces the exhausted artifices of conventional movies with a new set of pseudo-realistic ones, which are mostly instantaneous clichés. As a writer-director, he's so dedicated to revealing the pain under the laughter he's a regular Pagliacci. To put it in the puerile terms in which it is conceived, Cassavetes thinks that in *Husbands* he has stripped people of their pretenses and laid bare their souls.

Cassavetes' method was originally, back in the *Shadows* days, to combine a group of actors' improvisations into a loose story; now he writes and stages sequences to look improvised. *Husbands,* which went considerably over its initial million-dollar budget, is a fairly elaborate shot-in-color production that was planned to look like grainy caught "reality." The dialogue — written to sound unwritten — is deliberately banal; the timing is agonizingly slow, to simulate spontaneity; and there are inexplicable sequences (such as one involving a Chinese girl) that are staged to look crazily accidental.

His approach to filmmaking is an actor's approach, and when it's effective it has certain resemblances to Harold Pinter's approach to theatre. The three men interacting onscreen are like the basic Pinter stage situation. We don't know anything about the supposed characters or their connections to the world — when they're throwing up their past lives we don't know what they're throwing up — but the actors have occasional intense and affecting moments, going through emotions that they set off in each other. We're glued to the acting in this movie, because that's really all there is, and maybe the best clue to the chaos of Cassavetes' method comes from the subsidiary players. The three leads are, after all, successful actors who have chosen to do what they're doing; they seem to be having a good time, and it's their psychodrama and their picture. But there are a couple of dozen New York and London professionals in the cast, and it's troubling to watch them. There is a long sequence in a New York bar in which a bunch of drinkers are sitting around a table, and the three men tell each in turn to sing, and proceed to torment the person singing. And all we can see are actors and actresses trying their damnedest to do what is wanted because they need the work. When a middle-aged woman (who looks as if she'd be a wonderful movie mother for Tuesday Weld) sings a song beginning "It was just a little love affair" over and over — at their insistence — while they bait her and tell her they hate her and then kiss her, we're acutely conscious of discomfort. She isn't playing a role, she's being *used,* and yet she's also coöperating as an actress. Are Cassavetes and his buddies aware of how hostile their role-playing is, how much of it is just a form of picking on people on camera?

Husbands is a messy synthesis — a staged film with a documentary-style use of professional performers. We don't know what to react to: we can't sort out what we're meant to see from what we see. We know that the people around the table in the bar wouldn't sit there while these clowns bully them unless they were paid for it, but we also know that the sequence is supposed to reveal something that "ordinary" movies don't. But what does it reveal except the paralysis and humiliation of the bit players? Kullers and the two English girls triumph over *Husbands* by their talent and looks and style, but characteristically the camera gloats on hysteria or dismay or aging flesh. Cassavetes' camera style is to move in for the kill, like those TV newsmen who ask people in distress the questions that push them to break down while the camera moves in on the suffering eyes and choking mouth. In the past, Cassavetes has given some erratic evidence of being a compassionate director; I think he forfeits all claims to compassion in *Husbands*. A long closeup scene in a London gambling club in which an elderly woman is approached by Peter Falk and coyly propositions him is perhaps the most grotesquely insensitive movie sequence of the year. It's hideous not because this is truth that the spectator seeks to evade but because this is bad acting and a gross conception. It reveals nothing more than a sensitive director would reveal by a look or a gesture, and at a discreet distance. Since Cassavetes conveys no sense of illusion — since he's after the naked "reality" — we don't think about the role, we think about the actress, and we wonder if she could ever get enough money to compensate for what is being done to her.

[January 2, 1971]

Spawn of the Movies

Alex (Donald Sutherland), a movie director, has made only one movie, which has been previewed but has not yet been released; his fretting and fantasying over his next project are the subject of *Alex in Wonderland*. It's too bad that the writers, Paul Mazursky (who directed) and Larry Tucker (who produced), never chose to reveal what sort of first movie it was that Alex had directed, because if it was anything like *Bob & Carol & Ted & Alice*, the début film that made Mazursky's and Tucker's reputation, Alex's Felliniesque fantasy sequences might have gained some badly needed comic resonance. But since Mazursky and Tucker don't make the joke, it's a joke on them that men with a talent for situation comedy and revue humor, men who are best when the camera barely moves, are busily creating fiery apocalyptic visions for their hero. It's a bad joke, because their small satirical-comedy gift is rare.

If the imitation of *8½* were used for self-parody — as Alex's way of putting himself down — the fantasies might reverberate in his everyday life, but as it has been done the fantasies don't work on enough levels to be suggestive. Alex's fantasy life has no intensity — it's a series of emotionally antiseptic reveries, staged like the big production numbers in a musical. The flattery of Fellini is so sincere and single-edged that after Mazursky and Tucker went through God knows what machinations to get Fellini himself to appear in this film, they failed to provide him with good material. They must have thought his presence would work magic, but he adds nothing — he's very tight, very dull.

Mazursky and Tucker had been on to something fresh — an affectionate, ambivalent way of observing the contradictions in how we live. Fortunately, some of that observation still shows in the nonfantasy sections of *Alex in Wonderland:* in the domestic scenes of Alex, his wife (Ellen Burstyn), and their two daughters; and in the ambience of the new Hollywood. The film comes out of a true wonderland — the chaotic new Hollywood, where the anti-Establishment filmmakers have become the Establishment and the Establishment executives pose as anti-Establishment. In this wonderland, some studio heads may actually have been appointed to make movies, but others appear to have been appointed to dismantle the studios. During the auction of M-G-M artifacts last spring, *Alex in Wonderland* and Roger Vadim's *Pretty Maids All in a Row*, starring Rock Hudson, were the only movies in production on the lot. The ads for *Alex in Wonderland* show Sutherland's great, hairy head in the M-G-M lion's niche, and *Alex in Wonderland* captures for the first time on the screen the palmy-hip look of the new Hollywood. The sixties swingers have now adopted the prophetic-saintly style, which is super-relaxed. Bearded producers come out of their Polynesian-Tudor homes wearing Indian headbands and talking revolution with the fashionable pauses and non sequiturs of their Beverly Hills High stoned adolescents.

Mazursky and Tucker, with their background in improvisational revue, slip into the new idioms and rhythms and wriggle around in them comfortably. M-G-M is cuddling vipers, and the vipers love being cuddled. Mazursky doesn't overdo the waggish architecture of Los Angeles; the Spanish house that Alex considers buying is by some standards an atrocity, but it's probably heaven to live in. The movie doesn't put down the unbuttoned look of movie people; it accepts their adaptation to the sun. And it tries to do justice to the curious situation of talented Jews' raising their children to believe in Martin Luther King and Gandhi while they themselves are harboring fantasies of an armed uprising of blacks taking over Beverly Hills, and are so divided against themselves that they are, of course, for the blacks.

The satire of Hollywood is exact, and it's loving without losing its bite, though the film's only real triumph is malicious — a long revue skit in which Alex goes to lunch with a producer, Hal Stern, played by Mazursky. Mazursky pulls the picture together in this sequence the way Mel Brooks' brief appearance onscreen turns *The Twelve Chairs* into what it should have been. Mazursky's Hal Stern, in his Richard III haircut, and with his shirt hanging out over his roll of flab, struts like a baby boy whose parents patted him on the head for every step he ever took; his personality is so clearly defined that we know his phony new "openness" to any idea as soon as we see him. The propositions he offers Alex — a script on a heart transplant, Don Quixote as a Western — *are* the projects that directors have been getting offered. If this level of satirical accuracy had been sustained, the movie might have been a classic. Even written as it is, if Mazursky had played Alex and played him as a sharp, tough hipster who's making it big in Hollywood, Alex's dreams of directing art films might have been exposed as the current Hollywood fashion in dreams. But Sutherland's Alex is nebulous and glamorous, and his dreams seem to be intended as expressions of creativity. Sutherland isn't bad — he's loose and he has a soft-spoken way with dialogue — but we get no sense of a person there, or of what kind of drive or talent is hidden in his flowing beard and picture hats. He's wonderful when he leans back in fatuous satisfaction as Jeanne Moreau (who appears briefly as herself) sings to him. But he's so cool he drifts away while you're watching him.

One of the dangers of Mazursky's casual style is that if a scene doesn't come off, it's really dead — like the supermarket scene here, or the hand-held-camera sequence in the empty Spanish house. But for a dithering film *Alex in Wonderland* has a surprising number of good things: a long travelling shot of the baroque ceiling of an old picture palace, ending at the popcorn counter; a vision of Alex and Jeanne Moreau in a carriage drawn by white horses on a Hollywood overpass; the offhand performance of Mazursky's daughter Meg as Alex's intelligent, sensible twelve-year-old; the accuracy of Ellen Burstyn's tight-jawed portrait of the competent yet distraught Hollywood wife — one of those wives whose jaws get a hard set from the nights when they sit soberly at parties waiting to take their sloshed geniuses home. (Hollywood wives often seem to have been chosen because they're great drivers.)

But, good as he is on the new Hollywood, Mazursky can't get a satirical grip on the old Hollywood. When the voice of a very young Doris Day is heard singing "Hooray for Hollywood" over a satirical fantasy of guerrilla violence on Hollywood Boulevard, the device backfires, because at least she knew what she was doing and Mazursky doesn't. When a free-style conversation is going on in Alex's bedroom while Harlow and Tracy are on the TV screen in *Riff Raff*, we want to listen to the voices on the box, because there isn't enough conviction on Mazursky's part or on Sutherland's part that Alex's conversation is worth listening to. The film's informality is promising, but it's almost as if the modern disintegration of drama and conventional movie structure had disoriented precisely those who might have been expected to use the flux creatively. The hacks go on as if nothing much had changed, while the talented people are so afraid of failing to be unconventional enough that they fall apart.

It is right, in a way, that Alex's ideas are not much better than the projects Hal Stern offers him; it is right that he is despondent, because all he has is the instinct to know how crummy Stern's ideas are. But this irony — that directors who finally get into a position to do what they want to do don't know what they want to do — which is potentially the biggest joke in the new Hollywood, isn't developed. It isn't developed even though *Alex in Wonderland* is a reflection of it. Afraid that any subject they might select would be considered square, student filmmakers (using *8½* as their model) often begin with a spoof of their own dilemma — their search for a great subject. The subject of the film thus becomes their own empty-headedness. And that's the subject of Mazursky's and Tucker's *Alex in Wonderland*.

•

Brewster McCloud, directed by Robert Altman, whose last film was *M*A*S*H*, opens with a derisive remark coming in over the M-G-M lion's roar. In *Alex in Wonderland*, movie-colony schoolchildren sing "Over the Rainbow"; in this one the Wicked Witch herself, Margaret Hamilton, sings "The Star-Spangled Banner" off key at the Houston Astrodome, and dies in her ruby slippers. *Brewster McCloud* is almost as full of movie quotes and references as *Alex in Wonderland,* but they're not linked to a director figure; they're not really linked to much of anything. The picture is irreverent and parodistic — like a Road Runner cartoon, though it doesn't have the clear pattern or the established characters of a cartoon. The conception is amorphous; there's no frame of reference beyond the general notion of the life of the imagination (represented by Brewster, building wings to fly with) versus the rude, soulless materialists (Stacy Keach as a miserly old billionaire; the patriotic, croaking witch; a racist-sadist narcotics agent; and so on). Gentle Brewster (Bud Cort) is a weird conceit: a boy Phantom of the Astrodome who is also the imperilled virgin — a sort of mad, murderous Peter Pan or Rima the bird boy. It appears that he would be able to fly, with the help of his fairy godmother-guardian angel (Sally Kellerman), but she deserts him when he loses his virginity. She has lost her own wings; we are not told whether from the same cause, or why in this liberated atmosphere sex and taking flight are mutually exclusive — as in a Victorian fable. We should be able to grasp intuitively what Brewster is meant to represent, but whatever Altman had in mind doesn't emerge in Brewster's disconsolate baby face.

The picture has a demoralized, melancholy, yet silly tone; it isn't noisy, but it's somewhat manic. It's disconnected in a way that could be explained as social comment or as a new, free style, but I don't think it is either. Altman has a distinctive easygoing use of overlapping sound, and the track sometimes has an independent life; and he has a distinctive sense of film rhythm. But the individual sequences don't reveal what they're for — they can be taken in almost any way — and when they're all put together the picture has no driving impulse and no internal consistency. The ambiguities (such as whether Brewster or the fallen-angel-lady or a mysterious crow commits the murders) seem more like a form of indecision than like purposeful ambiguity. And yet it all appears to be done with considerable directorial confidence — as if Altman didn't know that the gags were schoolboy humor, the characterization vague, and the dialogue a shambles. Most of the members of the cast are weak — probably because they are playing almost unwritten roles, and the gaps haven't been plugged by improvisation. When an actor is supposed to parody a Steve McQueen hot-shot San Francisco police detective but is given almost nothing to work with except the repeated exclamation "Jesus Christ!" the effect isn't parody and it isn't comedy. It's like a rehearsal, with the actors just saying anything while waiting for the script to arrive.

•

The new Western *There Was a Crooked Man* . . . seems to have been written by an evil two-year-old, and it has been directed in the Grand Rapids style of filmmaking, but it's a movie pastiche, too. Everything in it is stolen from old movies and stood on its head. The clichés are just as stale upside-down, and are presented as leering realism. While the traditional Westerns gradually settled into the John Wayne mold — the strong, silent man of action for the silent majority — in the sixties the form began to be used in a new spirit of cynicism, as in the spaghetti Westerns and such American hits as *The Professionals*. *There Was a Crooked Man* . . . represents a new low in cynicism. Joseph L. Mankiewicz, who directed, and David Newman and Robert Benton, who wrote the script, would probably say that it merely mirrored the meaninglessness of a corrupt, polluted world, but the sophisticated amorality of this picture, which glorifies a mercenary killer (Kirk Douglas) and makes cheap fun of prison reform, is fundamentally ugly, and the more so because it is done in such a self-satisfied, aren't-we-clever style. This picture is far more reactionary than the John Wayne pictures, since it ridicules any beliefs or ideals beyond gratifying one's own greed.

Kirk Douglas — red-haired this time, as if he weren't flamboyant enough — is a smart, wisecracking robber-killer who is sent to a territorial prison in the Arizona desert in the eighteen-eighties; he becomes the leader of the prisoners and, for his own purposes, coöperates with Henry Fonda, the warden, in changing the prison from a brutalizing place into a decent one. The film, however, wouldn't dream of being square and standing for any kind of decency; it plays murderous double-crossing games until any characters with a decent impulse are dead fools or have become crooked. There's nobody to root for but Douglas, the charmer-jokester who cold-bloodedly wipes out all his buddies and most of the rest of the prison population. Kirk Douglas is maybe the least relaxed and least subtle of enduring screen stars. He's *on* all the time; he holds your attention without really interesting you. But he's a commanding presence, and Mankiewicz uses him for that cocky magnetism. The picture just keeps chugging along — but it has Douglas, and a group of actors working to steal as many scenes as possible (Hume Cronyn, playing a homosexual in the worked-up style that makes you certain he's played a homosexual on the stage recently; Martin Gabel; Burgess Meredith; Warren Oates; John Randolph). It isn't altogether boring, but it does seem as if the only rationale Mankiewicz and Newman and Benton had was to make a movie that wouldn't be boring.

Would the story have emerged as a spoof Western, kidding the heroic clichés, if it had been directed in a lighter spirit? I don't think so. The cynicism goes very deep: as flies to wanton boys are the characters to Newman and Benton. When the implications of a plot are not considered, when the writers and the director don't take the responsibility for the meaning of what they're working on, they are defining themselves as hacks. I thought it a despicable movie, not because I believe that audiences will take its commercialized nihilism very seriously but because of its clay heart. Is it naïve to ask how, when our prisons are packed with the uneducated, the addicted, and the retarded, thinking men can make such a picture? Look under the amorality and you'll find the true amorality.

[January 9, 1971]

Notes on Heart and Mind

Is anyone surprised that the critics and journalists who only a few weeks ago were acclaiming the new creative freedom of young American moviemakers are now climbing aboard the new sentimentality? The press may use the term "romance" for this deliberately fabricated regression in recent movies, but in Hollywood the businessmen talk more crassly. They say, "We're going back to heart." The back-to-heart movement is accompanied by strong pressures on reviewers, who are informed that they have lost touch with the public. Reviewers are supposed to show *their* heart by puckering up for every big movie.

•

As part of the Pop impulse of the sixties, movies have been elevated to a central position among the arts — a dominant, almost overwhelming position. Those who grew up during this period have been so sold on Pop and so saturated with it that they appear to have lost their bearings in the arts. And so when they discover that, of course, Pop isn't enough, and they want some depth and meaning from movies, they head right for the slick synthetic. Those who have abandoned interest in literature except for the à-la-mode mixture of Pop and sticky, such as Vonnegut, Hesse, Tolkien, Brautigan, and a little I Ching, are likely to have comparably fashionable tastes in movies. To the children of *Blow-Up* movies that are literary in the worst way — movies that superficially resemble head books and art films — can seem profound and suggestive. Every few months, there is a new spate of secondhand lyrical tricks. Robert Redford is impaled, like a poor butterfly, in frozen frames at the end of picture after picture. Directors have become so fond of telescopic lenses that any actor crossing a street in a movie may linger in transit for a hazy eternity — the movie equivalent of a series of dots. The audience accepts this sort of thing in movies that not only are without the vitality of Pop but are enervated and tenuous — like the worst of what earlier generations of college students fled from when they went to the movies. If you don't have that sense of the range of possibilities and pleasures which is developed from reading, from an interest in drama and the other arts, or even from a longer span of moviegoing, it's easy to overrate the fancy, novelettish alienation of a *Five Easy Pieces*. But while it's perfectly understandable that those without much to compare such a movie to may think it's great — just as a child's judgment of a movie may be ingenuous and droll because he has so few previous experiences to relate it to — this inexperience provides the opening for the media-hype. There is probably more insensate praise in movie reviews now than in any other field, including writing on rock. The new tendency is to write appreciatively at the highest possible pitch, as if the reviewer had no scale of values but only a hearsay knowledge of the peaks. And everything he likes becomes a new peak.

•

If one opens a newspaper to the movie pages and reads the quotes, one is confronted with a choice of masterpieces, but I didn't write a column last week because the new movies defeated me — I couldn't think of anything worth saying about them. You come out of a movie like *There's a Girl in My Soup* or *I Love My Wife* feeling that your pocket has been picked and your mind has been stunted.

Movie critics have always had to become acrobats, jumping from level to level, trying not to attack the timid amateurs the way we attack the successful hacks. The danger in this act is that one may fall into the trap of condescension. This used to take the form of that horrible debonair style which was once the gentleman-critics' specialty. They were so superior to the subject that they never dealt with it. Now it more frequently takes the form of a wisecracking put-down. And that's the bottom of the trap, because, as all critics know, the worst danger of the profession is that one may sink to the level of what one is reviewing. What sustains a critic from falling to the level of an *I Love My Wife* and making shrivelling bad jokes about its shrivelling bad jokes? Last week, I couldn't find anything sustaining; rage isn't condescending, but one wears oneself down, and these films weren't worth it.

Though sinking to the level of the work is a danger to the critic, to movies the more serious danger, of course, is that critics may not *rise* to the level of what they're reviewing. And, even with movies as bad as they are now, I think this is often the case, because those who stoop to review become insensitive.

•

I don't trust critics who say they care only for the highest and the best; it's an inhuman position, and I don't believe them. I think it's simply their method of exalting themselves. It's not always easy to analyze what is going wrong in movies, what is going right — even if only in small ways — and why. One might think this an exercise in futility, but, ideally, the regular reviewer provides a touchstone for movie lovers — so that they have a basis for checking themselves out — and for all those actively involved in movies. The regular reviewer knows he will not effect a radical transformation of movies, but he may be able to help us keep our bearings. Movies, far more than the traditional arts, are tied to big money. Without a few independent critics, there's nothing between the public and the advertisers.

•

Movie executives often say critics should be the same age as the average moviegoer; sometimes they say reviewers shouldn't go on for more than three years or they won't have the same enthusiasm as the audience. The executives don't understand what criticism is; they want it to be an extension of their advertising departments. They want moviegoers to be uninformed and without memory, so they can be happy consumers.

•

In most cases, the conglomerates that make the movies partly own the magazines and radio stations and TV channels, or, if they don't own them, advertise in them or have some interlocking connection with them. That accounts for a lot of the praise that is showered on movies. Then, too, many critics, knowing that the young dig movies, are afraid of being left behind. Besides, the critics don't get quoted in the ads unless they rhapsodize over a picture (or are willing to accept being misquoted and distorted), and each time they get quoted, their bosses are happy and their names become better known. There are critics whose reviews hardly anybody ever sees but who are widely known for their ecstatic quotes. The radio and TV boys get the point: their reviews *are* quotes.

•

A reviewer delivering quickie reviews at the end of a radio or television news program typically reacts to a picture "strictly on its own merits"; that is, he tells the theme, he praises or pans the structure, he says a few words about the acting, the photography, etc. He reviews a movie in a cheerful vacuum, and he is generally perfectly sincere when he tells you that he says exactly what he thinks.

To be the movie critic for a network, no training or background is necessary; "too much" interest in movies may be a disqualification. Novices are thought to speak to the public on the public's own terms. They age, but, like the critic on your home-town paper, they remain novices in criticism, because there is no need for them to learn; they understand that their job is dependent on keeping everybody happy, and they are generally not the kind of people who learn anyway. They can say "what they think" with more sincerity if they're the kind of people who don't realize they can say what they think because they don't think.

•

It is often said that it doesn't matter how bad a reviewer is as long as he stays in the job, because people learn how to read him. It's true they may learn how to interpret his enthusiasms, but what about the young practitioners of an art form? Bad notices — or being ignored — are death to them. In this mass medium, in which big-budget productions are hugely advertised — they're like epidemics spreading over the media — a new artist or a young artist working on a small budget doesn't stand a chance unless he gets the help of the press. A writer or a painter can generally keep going even if he fails to reach an audience; even a dramatist may be able to keep going, though he is creatively crippled if his plays aren't staged. But if a movie director fails to reach an audience, he simply can't get the money to go on making pictures.

The industry and many established actors on talk shows love the idea that the public doesn't need the critics; the young filmmaker knows different. Most of the new pictures that try to break the molds risk confusing audiences, and just about all the pictures that express new social impulses or that are critical or rebellious are small-budget pictures. If a few critics don't go all the way for them, the public doesn't hear about them in time to keep the directors working and to keep the art of film alive. It cannot be kept alive by pictures like *The Odd Couple, Cactus Flower,* or *Airport;* those are the ones that don't require the help of the press (though they often get it). The audience finds its way to them with the help of the advertising.

The casual moviegoer is often drawn to new versions of what he used to enjoy — the TV watcher to *Airport,* the aging art-house patron to the latest Chabrol. One can't quarrel with his enjoyment of them, only with his evaluation of them. A critic's point of view is likely to be somewhat different from the casual moviegoer's. The successful second-rate will probably anger him more than the fifth-rate, because it represents the triumph of aesthetic senility.

●

Since a critic may cost his publication advertising revenue — and no longer just from the loss of movie advertising but from records and whatever else the conglomerate is into — independent, disinterested criticism becomes rarer than ever just at the time when, because of the central importance of movies, it is needed most. The pressure is so strong on reviewers to do what is wanted of them that many of them give in and reserve their fire for pathetic little sex pictures — cheap porny pix — which they can safely attack because there's no big advertising money behind them. That way, the reviewer can keep his paper happy and at the same time get credit for high-mindedness in his community. Most of the people who give him credit never go to the movies anyway. Middle-aged people, particularly women, often use pornography as a self-congratulatory excuse for not reading and for not going to the movies. It becomes a righteous form of abstention for those who prefer *Hee Haw* or *The Beverly Hillbillies*.

●

In some ways, last week's movies probably aren't worse than movies of a decade or two or three ago, but there is something dead and nerveless about them; they don't know how to connect with the audience, and they have lost the simplicity and the narrative strength that used to pull one through bad movies. TV has destroyed the narrative qualities of older movies, but the restlessness one feels while watching a chopped-up movie on TV is mitigated by the fact that one isn't necessarily paying much attention. In a movie theatre, with nothing else to do, one is likely to become depressed. We've been told for some years now that visual excitement is what matters, but even the rare movie that is extraordinary to look at may be demoralizing. When it's obvious that the picture is going nowhere, there's an awful letdown of expectations, and for most people there seems to be nothing left but dumb submission; walking out may be too positive an act for the depressed state one falls into.

●

Yet even those who go enough to know how awful movies have been this year say, "But what else is there? Bad as they are, movies are better than the theatre." However, the thing that has happened to the theatre in the past decade is happening now to movies. On the average, Americans go to only seven movies a year. And as there were scarcely seven halfway good American movies for them to go to last year (and few from abroad), chances are they'll go to even fewer in 1971. *There's a Girl in My Soup* reminds you of why you stopped going to Broadway comedies. One never even knows what the principal characters are meant to be; it's not merely that this movie has no connection with any people who ever lived but that it doesn't sustain its own artifices. It's like going to see *Swan Lake* and finding that no one knew the dancers should be trained to get on their points.

When movies were bad a decade ago, it wasn't such a serious matter; despite the greatness of some films, movies in general weren't expected to be more than casual, light entertainment. You weren't expected to get your ideas of artistic possibilities from movies. I remember seeing *To Have and Have Not* the night it opened, in 1944, and I remember how everyone loved it, but if anyone I knew had said that it was a masterpiece comparable to the greatest works of literature or drama, he would have been laughed at as a fool who obviously didn't know literature or drama. Now, by and large, even the college-educated moviegoer isn't expected to, and the media constantly apply superlatives to works that lack even the spirit and energy of a *To Have and Have Not*.

•

What must it be like for those who know and love only movies, and not literature as well? Even if they don't consciously miss it, surely the loss of the imaginative ranging over experience is irreparable.

There's been almost no fight for it. Fiction has been abandoned casually and quickly. There haven't even been journalists to defend it. On TV talk shows, the hosts have generally given up even the pretense of having read the books that are being plugged. There are several cooking celebrities on TV but no TV personality who discusses books. If you ask college students to name half a dozen movie critics, they have no trouble supplying names. If you ask them to name three book critics, they flounder, and finally one of them may triumphantly recall the name of a critic who abandoned regular reviewing before they were born.

•

If a movie is a bowdlerization of a book and the movie's director is acclaimed for his artistry, surely something has gone askew. In some cases, directors add virtually nothing, and diminish and cheapen what was in the original, and yet the fraction of the original they manage to reproduce is sufficient to make their reputations.

Film theorists often say that film art is, "by its nature," closest to painting and music, but all these years movie companies haven't been buying paintings and symphonies to adapt, they've been buying plays and novels. And although the movies based on those plays and novels have visual and rhythmic qualities, their basic material has nevertheless come from the theatre and from books.

When a movie based on a book goes wrong but one isn't sure exactly how or why, one of the best ways to find out is to go to the book. The changes that have been made in the course of the adaptation frequently upset the structure, the characterizations, and the theme itself.

Generally speaking, when people become angry if you refer to the original novel or play while you're discussing a movie, it means they haven't read it. Twenty years ago, they hadn't always, either, but they didn't feel they didn't need to. McLuhanism and the media have broken the back of the book business; they've freed people from the shame of not reading. They've rationalized becoming stupid and watching television.

And television has become the principal advertising medium for movies. Even the few talk shows that held out against the show-biz personalities for a while are now loaded with movie people plugging away and often inflicting pain and embarrassment by trying to sing. Talk shows are becoming amateur hours for professionals.

•

Although good movies have often been made from inferior books, in the last few years I've been embarrassed to discover that even when movies have been made from books that aren't especially worth reading, the books are still often superior. That is to say, even our second- and third-string writers have more complex sensibilities than the movies that cannibalize them. A very minor novel like Ken Kolb's *Getting Straight* is a case in point. And I think reading Thomas Berger's *Little Big Man* — which is almost a major novel — is probably stronger than the movie even as a visual experience. American fiction seems to have reached a fairly high plateau at the very time when college students were deciding movies were more interesting. They didn't make that decision without encouragement from the media. *Would* they have made it without encouragement? I don't know. But the new dominance of Pop is the culmination of processes that have been at work in the mass media for many years. Gradually, as the things people used to fear would happen happened, ways were found to refer to the changes positively instead of negatively, and so "the herd instinct" that mass culture was expected to lead to became "the new tribalism."

If some people would rather see the movie than read the book, this may be a fact of life that we must allow for, but let's not pretend that people get the same things out of both, or that nothing is lost. The media-hype encourages the sacrifice of literature.

Movies are good at action; they're not good at reflective thought or conceptual thinking. They're good for immediate stimulus, but they're not a good means of involving people in the other arts or in learning about a subject. The film techniques themselves seem to stand in the way of the development of curiosity.

Movies don't help you to develop independence of mind. They don't give you much to mull over, and they don't give you the data you need in order to consider the issues they raise.

•

A young film critic recently told me that he needed to read more books than he did before he got the job — that he felt empty after seeing films daily. I don't have any doubts about movies' being a great art form, and what makes film criticism so peculiarly absorbing is observing — and becoming involved in — the ongoing battle of art and commerce. But movies alone are not enough: a steady diet of mass culture is a form of deprivation. Most movies are shaped by calculations about what will sell; the question they're asking about new projects in Hollywood is "In what way is it like *Love Story*?"

A teacher writes that "literate students are getting into the terms of film and the history of film in the same way that they have always got into the terms of literature, for example, and the history and evolution of that art form." If movies had become what they might be, this would make sense, but to study mass culture in the same terms as traditional art forms is to accept the shallowness of mass culture. It could mean that the schools are beginning to accept the advertisers' evaluations; the teachers don't want to be left behind, either.

•

The Faulkner who collaborated on the screenplay for *To Have and Have Not* is not commensurate with the Faulkner of the novels. Faulkner's work for hire is fun, but it's not his major work (though, as things are going, he and many other writers may remain known only for the hackwork they did to support the work they cared about). Yet until writers as well as directors can bring their full powers to American movies, American movies are not going to be the works of imagination and daring that the media claim they are already.

•

Writers who go to Hollywood still follow the classic pattern: either you get disgusted by "them" and you leave or you want the money and you become them.

Allowing for exceptions, there is still one basic difference between the traditional arts and the mass-media arts: in the traditional arts, the artist grows; in a mass medium, the artist decays profitably.

From indications in the press, the new line will be that the moviemakers have had too much freedom; the unstated corollary is that the businessmen know what's best. Moviemakers need more freedom, not less, or they'll never work through the transitional stage that American movies are in. If Hollywood tries to return to its childhood via romantic slop, movies will just get worse and worse. But if the advertisers and the media can blur the distinction between movies that are made in freedom as collaborative forms of expression and movies that are packaged, how many moviemakers will be strong enough to fight against success?

•

The film medium is too expensive for the kind of soft, sweet college students who want to work in it. Some of the most talented are lovely innocents; they will be the first to fall.

The great men of the screen have had to be tough; perhaps because of this, the great men of the screen have been crazy men. Jean Renoir is the only proof that it is possible to be great and sane in movies, and he hasn't worked often in recent years.

[January 23, 1971]

Genius

Are bad ideas in the arts like those border disputes that flare up when everyone had thought they were settled? Ken Russell is establishing a reputation based on a profusion of bad ideas, a richer mix of the same ideas that used to make Hollywood biographies of artists such campy drivel. Once again, the movies are exploiting romanticism and explaining art by "genius": some poor bastard gets a nod from Heaven and a prod from Hell, and out comes art. In musical biographies in the movies, all music is treated as program music, to be explained by events in the composer's life. The assumption that the man's joys and miseries are what went into his compositions is the basic crime of the genre; those who are interested in music are driven up the wall when they see a composer's life turned into the libretto for his music. It's the same romantic fallacy that popularizing biographers used to indulge in — often on the convenient, naïve basis that they would stir interest in the artist's art by involving readers in the artist's beautiful, suffering soul.

Ken Russell (who directed *Women in Love* and has made British television films about such artists as Delius and Dante Gabriel Rossetti and Richard Strauss) takes this process several steps further in his new film, *The Music Lovers,* with Richard Chamberlain as Tchaikovsky and Glenda Jackson as Nina, Tchaikovsky's mad wife. Russell and his scenarist, Melvyn Bragg (who had a hand in *The Loves of Isadora*), create an imaginary world of violent sexual extravagance to explain Tchaikovsky's music, and then somehow use this *against* both the art and the artist. *The Music Lovers* is so full of high spots that before the title comes on, you may think you're seeing a trailer for a coming attraction. Because of the deep volcanic purple of Russell's style, it's obvious that it's he who believes in sensual excitement above all.

For much of the movie, the characters slide in and out of fantasies that seem not so much theirs as Russell's. Whose pornographic fantasy is it that all the women in the movie have yellowish teeth — threatening, irregular teeth — while the men have gleaming white ones? Whose fantasy are we in when Glenda Jackson writhes in torment in a blue-green madhouse and, in one sequence, is seen deliberately lying across a grating, spread-eagled, while the madmen locked below reach up under her skirt? It's unlikely to be Tchaikovsky's fantasy, because his wife (whom he lived with for only a few weeks) wasn't confined in bedlam until three years after his death. How can things that didn't happen have "inspired" his music — which is how they are used? When Tchaikovsky's patroness, Mme. von Meck, licks a peach that he has just taken a few bites from, when Nina is brutally raped by an officer she has romantically invited to see her, when chains are put across a door to keep Tchaikovsky out of a house, and when fields are set on fire, whose fantasies are we in? The central plot mechanism of the movie — Mme. von Meck throws Tchaikovsky out when Count Chiluvsky, his castoff lover, reveals that Tchaikovsky is homosexual, and so he is forced to become a conductor to support himself — is a concoction. *The Music Lovers* has about as much to do with

Tchaikovsky's actual life as *A Song to Remember,* starring Cornel Wilde, had to do with Chopin's.

Though it rarely is, one has a right to expect that a movie biography, like a literary biography, will be an interpretation of how and why the people went from one known historical episode to the next. One realizes that the interpretation depends on who is making it and when, and one expects omissions because of reticence or ignorance. With new literary biographies featuring the homosexuality that used to be omitted or glossed over, it was to be expected that the movies would catch up. *The Music Lovers* does so with a vengeance, but, as usual in movies, it's a fictional biography. When the facts were falsified in the old Hollywood bios, it was generally to soften and simplify the characters and to make everything inspirational. The facts in *The Music Lovers* are just as deliberately fabricated as in any old Hollywood stinker, but Russell's motives are not so transparent.

If one compares the movie, peopled by monsters using Tchaikovsky for their own greedy or sensual purposes, with the known facts about his life — he was sustained by a large and loving family and devoted friends, who, along with Mme. von Meck, helped him to escape from his disastrous marriage and to live and work — the inevitable question is "Why?" Why use whatever discreditable impulse one can discover in historical characters as their entire motivation? Why use their sensual desires as the whole person, so that the sensuality becomes pathological? It is puzzling to find Anton Rubinstein, Tchaikovsky's teacher, and Nicholas Rubinstein, who introduced most of Tchaikovsky's compositions, combined into one person, called "Rubinstein," who is not much more than a sycophant. Why is the intelligent Mme. von Meck, a mother of twelve and an extraordinary woman who helped plan and run railroads, made into an amorous creep, attended by ghostly twins? She isn't allowed to love his music; she's turned on by it, and in this movie everything sensual is corrupt. Why is Tchaikovsky made a suicide? Russell's intention in all this must be to show that no one really cared about Tchaikovsky's art: how *could* anyone when this is what it's all about?

Will those who are impressed by the climactic style — everything caught *in flagrante delicto* — exonerate Russell for his disdain for facts on the basis that he, too, is a genius, so his artistic truth is superior to facts? But there is no higher truth than respecting facts. If Russell is driven to make a movie with this hyper-Hollywood vision of life, he should not impose it on Tchaikovsky or other historical characters. He's doing a kind of Protocols of Zion transferred to the arts.

What's on the screen reveals Russell's baroque vulgarity — *The Music Lovers* is Ken Russell's *Futz* — and his opportunism. From the evidence of this film, Ken Russell is one of the most reckless movie directors who have ever lived. To take an example of his method, there's a sequence in which Tchaikovsky, hearing a woman sing, thinks it is his dead mother, traces the voice to its source, and enters a steaming bathroom, where the singer, a stranger to him, lies in the tub. The film then intercuts his wild grappling with the nude woman to pull her out of the water with a flashback of the child Tchaikovsky grappling with the men who are immersing his mother, dying of cholera, in a hot bath. It's an intense, frenzied sequence, which we see through the child's hysteria in his efforts to save his emaciated mother, her ravaged face hideous with the marks of cholera, her breast exposed, in the steaming room. The moviemakers have created a situation — Tchaikovsky's hearing a woman whose voice he mistakes for his mother's — in order to tie it in with a biographical falsification. (Actually, Tchaikovsky's mother died not when he was a little boy but when he was fourteen.) Even if the data were accurate, is the scene there to help us understand anything about Tchaikovsky or is it there to jolt us and horrify us? The whole movie is made up of such conceits, and, piled together, they add up to the impression that Tchaikovsky's life was a bravura horror story. And Russell uses what the movie says was horrible and violent and sadistic in Tchaikovsky's life as a form of stimulus for the audience.

It is perhaps a cause for rejoicing that in this movie Russell's rash technique is self-defeating. The infatuation with shock and decay often turns into unintended self-parody. When Tchaikovsky plays the solo part in the first performance of the Concerto in B Flat Minor, the music is so familiar that we can't accept the convention that it has just been written, and instead of dispensing with the stale movie device of cutting away from the stage to the faces of those in the audience involved with the composer, Russell extends it to the rubbishy surreal. While the concerto is being played, there's a kind of visual rotten opera about incest and homosexuality and lust going on in a confusion of heads. The tumultuous emotions and sneaky passions are on the same level of revelation as in old Hollywood, except that now the dreaming lovers in the forest are incestuous, the lurking villain is a discarded homosexual lover, and so on. When the response to the concerto is "I felt as if all of last summer was in it," it hardly matters whether the girl saying it is a radiant Hollywood ingénue or, as in this case, a pale, vampirish sister, though in this movie it isn't funny and enjoyable, as it used to be — it's rather repulsive.

Russell's excesses are laced with imagery from the experimental "symbolic" films of the thirties, such as Watson's and Webber's *Lot in Sodom* — the old smoking-plains-and-tongues-of-fire school of filmmaking. He has a distinctive way of using effects borrowed from Expressionist painters (especially Schiele) for erotic horror — bony, wasted bodies, red mouths and red underclothes, and so on. These effects tone things up, but there's no rationale in Russell's use of Expressionist techniques and there's nothing, apparently, he won't throw in; he includes bits of imitation *Ivan the Terrible* and a picturesque use of children as dolls to be flung in the air. The surreal sequence with everyone the hero knows clutching at him and the fame-fantasy with colored streamers flying around him would look chichi even in a forties musical. Russell might have given anyone just about the same treatment. Of why Russian music flourished in that period or of what made Stravinsky say "Tchaikovsky was, of all of us, the most Russian" there isn't an inkling. The movie — which treats music as a Victorian aphrodisiac — uses Tchaikovsky's most frequently heard compositions, almost as if to destroy whatever reputation he has left (which is, I think, smaller than he deserves).

Even when you can't help being affected by a sequence in this movie, you know that the sequences don't come together into anything you can accept. And you don't like the way you're being moved — it's not the goose bumps of pleasure, it's more like the flesh-crawling of dismay. There are a few really good moments, such as Glenda Jackson's self-conscious grin when she first goes to meet Tchaikovsky. It's quite scary to watch this crazy girl snaring him, and this part of the movie has some suspense. Miss Jackson is a hard, compelling actress, but, unfortunately, her role (almost totally invented) is a compendium of her previous roles, and has so much *Marat/Sade* in it that it comes dangerously close to self-caricature. Richard Chamberlain is a handsome figure, and his alabaster anguish compares favorably with Cornel Wilde's. It's embarrassing to ask what Russell had in mind with Christopher Gable's Count Chiluvsky; Chiluvsky, who speaks such lines as "You must . . . know why I'm here," is a treacherous, snobby faggot — and totally gratuitously, except in terms of the homosexual *Song of Norway* plot that Bragg has cooked up. Russell's treatment of homosexuality is far more reactionary than simply omitting it. Tchaikovsky's homosexuality is made to seem the result of the invented traumatic horrors, and to accept one's homosexuality seems to mean becoming a flaming fop like Chiluvsky. The film is homo-erotic in style, and yet in dramatic content it's bizarrely anti-homosexual. When the Tchaikovskys and Chiluvsky witness a performance of the Black Swan pas de deux in *Swan Lake,* the libretto is compounded into a fantasy, with Chiluvsky as the evil sorcerer. (This isn't merely stupid; it's also anachronistic, as the Black Swan pas de deux was added after Tchaikovsky's time.) So many composers have been homosexual that one might have hoped to gain some understanding. I don't know anybody who'd be bothered by an account of Tchaikovsky's homosexuality, but Russell's damned panache makes *everything* shameful and unclean.

[January 30, 1971]

How Boys Grow Up

François Truffaut can seem to be inside one's head in some movies and a total stranger, who barely interests one, in others. It would, however, be arrogant to assume that the Truffaut films one really loved (in my own case, *Shoot the Piano Player, Jules and Jim,* and *The Wild Child*) were works he had done for himself, while films one cared for not at all (in my case, say, *The Bride Wore Black*) and films that seemed pleasantly, charmingly negligible (in my case, *Stolen Kisses* and the new *Bed and Board*) were simply potboilers. I don't think that's true; I think that Truffaut must be more complicated than one at first assumes, and that even the featherweight films are not intended to be merely commercial. He's a very special case: Godard's films grow out of each other, Chabrol's films have become like silvery sardines in a row, but Truffaut follows the rigorous simplicity of *The Wild Child* with *Bed and Board,* a flimsy, conventionally "beguiling" picture.

Probably there isn't an American director who could do this sort of blithe marital comedy and keep his head above water. Truffaut's *touch* — which is what this film depends on — is intuitively gentle, restrained, and unsentimental. There's nothing cheap or mean in the *manner* of the picture, and nothing is overdone. And yet *Bed and Board* left me unmoved and in the strange situation of feeling cut off from a cheerful, responsive audience. As this series of Antoine Doinel films has gone on, Truffaut has had less and less to say about his once semi-autobiographical hero, and

Jean-Pierre Léaud, who has played Antoine since *The 400 Blows,* has grown away from the role. Léaud has lost not only the exuberance of *The 400 Blows* but the child's mutinous intelligence. He keeps his feelings to himself and is without an actor's concentration, so he has no intensity. Léaud appears to have developed a dogged resistance to acting; he almost seems to be protecting himself against our invasion of his privacy. His manner is deadpan, with occasional quick changes of mood; it's like a non-actor's imitation of Buster Keaton — an imitation that doesn't comprehend how Keaton's body did everything for him, so the blank face was contrapuntal. And in Keaton's kind of comedy the gags *built.* Truffaut's visual humor is like Antoine's deadpan humor — the jokes are eccentric, and they dry up fast.

In great comedies, the mechanics are themselves funny, and a routine doesn't end with one joke. In *Bed and Board,* when you get the snapper, you understand why the seemingly random elements that went into the gag were introduced. In bad American comedies, one often sees the gag planted and waits for it to go off, but it isn't really so good to see the unfunny mechanics retrospectively, either, especially when the joke is a highly reminiscent one. The snappers are often not good enough to make one forgive the limp preparation. When an enigmatic neighbor whom everyone calls "the strangler" turns out to be a TV comedian doing a *Marienbad* impersonation, it isn't much of a payoff. The running joke about Antoine's sponging friend is dispirited, and jokes like Antoine's meeting his father-in-law at a bordello and engaging in a polite, "humane" exchange are exactly what one used to groan at in the pre-New Wave "Gallic" comedies. Scene by scene, the picture is *underdone,* but Truffaut's weakness in comic timing may be what saves the material from looking crude and familiar. For example, Antoine's ineptness at disposing of a bouquet of flowers his mistress has given him is inseparable from Truffaut's ineptness — he doesn't make it seem comically inevitable that Antoine can't get rid of the telltale flowers — and the relaxation of the sequence may prevent the audience from recognizing it as an old routine. Truffaut's gentleness turns his attempted thrillers into something else, and his gentleness here makes old jokes seem like casual, nice, unforced sophisticated humor. *Stolen Kisses* had incidental amusements — throwaway bits like the sequence of the *pneumatique* — and some wry characters. This time, the incidents are uninspired and the characters are imitation René Clair. The casting is dull, except for Claude Jade, as Antoine's bride. Now blond and thus looking even more like a younger sister of Catherine Deneuve, she has a less ethereal, more practical, but lovely quality. She suggests the solid middle-class feeling that would be attractive to an impractical young man. But you wonder what she sees in Antoine — perhaps some trace of the boy he used to be?

The problem in the Doinel series started, I think, when Truffaut stopped seeing Antoine as a surrogate. What had begun in *The 400 Blows* as a portrait of the artist as an impetuous, driven young boy turned into wayward vignettes of a tame, odd, somewhat withdrawn young man seeking conventional happiness — Antoine getting comic jobs and losing them in fluky ways, Antoine's marriage and baby, Antoine's infidelity, and so on. When Antoine arrives at the limited view of life and the gag humor of *Bed and Board*, the viewer may ask, "But is this where that marvellous child was heading? Is this dry insularity all that's left of his strength? Why isn't he outgoing anymore?" Despite the comic surface, it's a sad progression — a contraction of Antoine's possibilities.

When, in this film, Truffaut introduces the idea that Antoine wants to be a writer, it doesn't ring true. Antoine no longer has that kind of consciousness. We can't believe he's capable of sustained feeling, because he has become dispassionate and inexpressive. Antoine is out of it; he's a marginal, fringe character, like Hulot in *Mon Oncle*. It isn't just that Truffaut doesn't have much to say about Antoine anymore but that one doesn't believe what he says. Léaud is not convincing as an aspiring bourgeois, but Antoine is no longer convincing as a potential artist, either. I wish Truffaut hadn't shown Antoine writing a novel with loose sheets scattered all over the room; treating him as a foolish, fumbling budding writer seems like having it both ways. The texture of the movie is false. I never for a minute believed in Antoine's jobs; I didn't believe in the bluff, loud American construction executive who hired him or in the Japanese mistress who bored him. And, what's worse, I didn't respect Truffaut's reasons for setting up these flabby situations. The sureness of the director's style in *The Wild Child* is in such contrast to the infelicities of *Bed and Board* that the contrast suggests that Truffaut may be a greater artist than he wants to allow himself to be — that he values conventional success (on past models) so inordinately that instead of making his own distinctive works he tries to master the popular thriller and comedy genres of the past.

•

Promise at Dawn starts from a clever commercial premise: to use Romain Gary's autobiographical memoir for an anti-Freudian movie — a hero celebrating the memory of his wild, wonderful Jewish mother. The story is of how a Russian-Jewish actress (Melina Mercouri) who has had an affair with the famous stage and screen star Ivan Mosjoukine and borne him a son, Romain, makes a life for herself and the boy by grit and con as they go from Russia to Poland to France. However, for a director who used to know how to be forthright, if crude, Jules Dassin tells the story remarkably badly. The film is narrated back and forth in time; but Dassin's feeling for the different periods isn't strong enough to clue us in on where we are and when, so the different parts of the past run together in a blur, as if his time machine had got too oily. The production is elegant and prettily photographed, but this is the sort of attempt at shameless nostalgia that requires emotional warmth and a delicate feeling for detail — qualities that the director is notably lacking in. Instead, he relies on the latest fashions in mechanized lyricism — slow-motion sequences and freeze frames. The techniques keep saying, This moment should be treasured. But, like children told to remember too much and not allowed to discover anything for themselves, we feel nothing and remember nothing.

And there's a big problem: Melina Mercouri. It's not that you can't believe her as a Jewish mother but that you can't believe her as a human being. She's not a person, she's a star. It's one thing for a little boy to see his mother as bigger than life; it's another for her to *be* bigger than life. With Mercouri in the role, the movie has almost nothing to do with the common experience of looking back and perceiving the differences between our childish projections of our parents as giants and what our parents must actually have been like. Mercouri more than lives up to the projection, so there's no contrast; it's as if this boy's fantasies of his mother were true. It's perhaps a classic case of how miscasting alters meaning; the story of a devoted mother turns into the story of a great broad. In her dramatic scenes and in her closeups, Mercouri is more subdued than in her other recent appearances, but that's like saying Anthony Quinn is more subdued. She's amazing and likable but she's got so much presence she can't play a role — she overpowers it. Whatever she does becomes a *tour de force* and, soon, a self-caricature. Mercouri has always seemed too virile to be sexy. Like Quinn, she's terrifyingly energetic; just looking at her, you feel as if you're being whomped on the back.

Mercouri was splendid seen for the first time, in *Stella* (perhaps not coincidentally, directed by Michael Cacoyannis, who directed Quinn in *Zorba the Greek*), but the fortified presence that makes stars like this so exciting in their first big roles is what wrecks them when they attempt a quiet performance. Mercouri has only to appear for us to receive the impact of that contagious, tempestuous personality, and, whatever she does, she always seems to be trying to play a normal hearty, hot nymphomaniac. The place for stars like this is, of course, on the musical-comedy stage. But what if, like Melina Mercouri, they can't sing and can't dance? I don't know the answer to how she can be used, and neither, obviously, does her director-husband, Dassin. She's like one of those faces that Fellini flashes on — one look is enough. The second time around, she eats up the camera. Quinn, who is probably more talented than she is but who has been in many more star roles, has become an abomination; he needs a personality transplant.

One feels that there is a genuine love for and admiration of Mercouri behind the production, but Dassin hasn't expressed it in terms of the boy's love for his mother. And Mercouri isn't convincing as a mother. This isn't a matter of whether an actress in private life has or has not had children; Lauren Bacall, who has children, probably couldn't play a convincing loving mother, either. It's a matter of a particular kind of personality-star's emotional range. Mercouri doesn't have the patience a mother develops. Mercouri (even that name!) is always agitated and restless; she's never at peace, so we can't see what a child means to her. The boy's nurse assumes the maternal role. Roaring around with the boy, whacking people with her handbag, scowling and wheezing and making deep throaty noises, Mercouri is more Auntie Mame than adoring mother. And Auntie Mame is essentially a transvestite, not a woman. Mercouri is too strident; she projects more than one needs to project to one's own child. Even a tigress fears for her young, but there is no fear in Mercouri's maternity. The same restless indomitability that makes her unconvincing as a loving mother prevents her from being a great screen actress; the absence of the quality of repose is fatal. She does too much and it means too little, because it's obvious that she's acting out her own temperament.

Those of us who loved our mothers remember the many times we didn't love them, but the movie is all on one adoring level, so there's no sense of truth in it. And there's no irony in the film's point of view. If this tornado of a woman is a boy's only parent and he survives unscathed, that is, of course, remarkable. But if the boy Romain (François Raffoul) doesn't turn into something more definite and more unusual than the decent young fellow (Assaf Dayan) we see, then the movie undercuts its own anti-Freudian premise. In comparison with Mercouri, normality isn't much of anything; it suggests that he *has* been crushed. (I kept thinking, This is the life story of Romain Gary, the man who made *Birds in Peru*.)

The film is rather inert; the wartime sequences are singularly amateurish; and in the welter of accents it hasn't been made clear who's meant to be Jewish and who isn't. Yet there are moments of energy and humor—though they're all related not to the mother-love theme but to love of theatre and films. In one sequence, Mercouri, at home in Cracow, plays Marguerite Gautier to her little son's Armand, and when Armand leaves, after contemptuously slinging banknotes at her, she moans peerlessly; Mercouri does have a fine free-style sense of farce. Most of the best scenes are, surprisingly, from Dassin as an actor. He has appeared in his own films before, adequately as the Italian safecracker in *Rififi*, inadequately as the earnest, stuffed American in *Never on Sunday*, but as Mosjoukine he does several satires on "subtle" acting that are like good revue skits. Probably the movie works best in these stylized sequences because, without an actress who could reveal to us the feelings that the child doesn't perceive, the material is basically musical-comedy material.

[February 6, 1971]

Blood and Sand

Big, ambitious historical-adventure movies used to be overrated; now they're more likely to be underrated. *The Last Valley*, made by James Clavell, a novelist turned movie director, certainly isn't a work of art, but it's not really a bad movie, either, and one gets involved in how it develops and how it's going to work out. The setting is Germany during the Thirty Years' War. Omar Sharif, a Heidelberg professor running away from war and plague and starvation, stumbles into a hidden valley, an Eden where life is green and tranquil, and the peasants might, as is all too evident, have posed for Bruegel (the elder — I think). Michael Caine, the leader of a band of brutal mercenaries, discovers the valley, too, and prepares to pillage and destroy it, but he is persuaded by Sharif to stay there with his men and live peacefully through the winter. It's as if the soldiers from Kurosawa's *The Seven Samurai* had moved into Shangri-La. The interest in the film is in the details of the adjustment of the villagers to the soldiers — how the villagers are persuaded to provide whores for the soldiers, and so on — and the suspense factor is: What will happen when spring comes?

Caine, who holds most of the movie together, has the gift of conveying what his character is thinking without excess motion. He plays his role with a slight, tricky Germanic but not quite identifiable accent, which he uses to ironic effect. At first, it seems just a star turn, because many of the actors are unaccented, but it gives Caine a style in which to play the role (as Brando's accent gave him one in *The Young Lions*), and I suspect that the role wouldn't work at all without it. We need the faint foreignness in his voice to be able to accept the convention that we're in the seventeenth century. It's a distanced performance, not intended to be taken realistically; the character who is seen against the fields and the open landscapes speaks as a voice from the world that has already lost this fertile valley. Clean air these days has the ambience of a polemic. Caine and Sharif play intelligent, essentially modern men — our representatives — looking at the conflicts in the world outside the valley and the quality of the life of fat burghers and bigots inside the valley. Clavell is less successful with the inhabitants of the valley; they seem guided by plot necessities rather than by their own drives. Sadistic priests are becoming a movie cliché, and Per Oscarsson's role as the local Savonarola is overdrawn and too theatrically intense; Nigel Davenport is unnecessarily cold as the peasant leader. As a burgher paterfamilias, Arthur O'Connell is unmistakably an actor in makeup, even at a distance in a crowd. Are there awards for negative achievement? Rarely has an actor been so conspicuous in such a small role.

Sharif is a great sufferer: he seems to get more beautiful when he looks vaguely ill. What a Camille he'd be! Even in this setting, in which the greenish hue of his skin makes one fear he's about to topple over with plague, he's handsomely *spiritual*. He's more convincing in his loner role than in his usual lover role, because he isn't a very outgoing performer. But we never find out what has made the professor a survivor, and when he stands by and does nothing while a woman suspected of witchcraft is tortured, the picture disintegrates, because we no longer know what Clavell intends the professor to represent. Is Clavell saying that no humane course of action is possible unless one has sufficient power to back it up, and that power is obtained only through inhumanity? That's a hell of a message. The movie is an allegory without a point, finally, because Clavell doesn't seem clear about whether this last refuge will survive, or whether it should. He has got himself into a fix by making the last valley both Vietnam and Switzerland. In the past few years, movie people have been raiding history for analogies with Vietnam. Understandably, they feel they must say something about it in their movies, but who knows what to say anymore? Clavell comes out better than most, because he's a storyteller and he doesn't push the analogy, but he's caught in the same bind as the others: the attempted historical parallels are never really parallel, and so the meanings are befuddled. At the end of *The Last Valley,* a series of implausible events wipe out the movie instead of resolving it. Increasingly, adventure-epics have come to reflect a sense of hopelessness.

I haven't heard a good movie score in such a long time that it seems rather odd for me to complain of this score, by John Barry, but it has that infatuation with one theme that separates movie-business composers from composers, and it's the kind of mood music that tells you it's a big mood up there on the screen. The thick, rich musical sludge makes the movie seem more self-importantly middlebrow and old-fashioned than necessary. Audiences have begun to laugh now when movies open with the promotional ballad during the titles, because the unconcealed cynicism of the song-plugging provides a wry contrast to the counter-culture lyrics. But, at least, crassness doesn't inflate a movie. This score is in the old Hollywood tradition of grandiose scoring for big movies: it says "Listen to me"; it practically says "Reserved-seat hard ticket." There is a core of feeling in *The Last Valley,* so that even when the picture is platitudinous, it's still often powerful; it deserves a simpler score.

The film's brutality got too much for me a few times, and too much for the people around me. There were gasps and a whispered "Oh, Jesus!" The Motion Picture Association Rating Board gave the picture a wholesome family GP, of course — apparently on the assumption that if women are raped and torn apart and men are impaled and threatened with castration, kids will find it harmless entertainment, but that consensual sex is obscene. Well, there's a crazy logic to it.

•

Puzzle of a Downfall Child — the title is enough to warn one that this is going to be literary in the worst way. Once the movie gets started and it turns out to be about a movie being planned about the anguished life of a high-fashion model (Faye Dunaway), it's hard to know what's worse — that she calls herself Lou Andreas Sand or that her real name is Emily. When Lou Andreas Sand goes to her isolated beach house in the off season, one prepares for bogus desperation. She's a lapsed Catholic, striving for grace and sleeping with strangers. (Lapsed ladies strive for grace in the damnedest places.) Lou Andreas–Emily was molested by old men, or perhaps she enticed them; as a teen-ager, she was in love with a priest. She has nervous breakdowns and fantasies; she slashes her wrists; she lives on medication. In fact, her life could be the one described in the book-jacket copy for Joan Didion's *Play It As It Lays:* "Immediately and deeply recognizable as a young woman of our times . . . an emotional drifter who has become almost anesthetized against pain and pleasure . . . set in a place beyond good and evil . . . figuratively in the landscape of the arid soul . . . probing into the lives of the affluent, disoriented people." Lou Andreas has everything that that girl has except a neurally damaged daughter. Hasn't Carol Burnett already played this role?

From what we can piece together (out of teaser-flashbacks of traumas and messy relationships), Lou Andreas seems to have been prematurely alienated. But then why is the movie so obsessed with the sins of the brittle, empty, cruel people who (it says) surround a gorgeous, successful high-fashion model? If she wasn't destroyed by this high-pitched decadence, why doesn't the movie show us what did destroy her? (I know the answer, and so do you.) I have a constitutional aversion to movies about beautiful women whose souls have been lost, stolen, or destroyed, especially when it isn't made clear — and it never is — whether the heroine had a soul in the first place.

After looking at the heroine's teeny marble features for almost two hours — with the camera hardly ever leaving her face — we're offered the conceit that perhaps she's an empty wreck because every time someone takes a picture of her she loses a piece of her soul. (At twenty-four frames a second, this movie must have devastated Miss Dunaway.) There is a sense in which that primitive concept of soul-stealing is very important in modern life — the sense that John Grierson, the Scottish documentarian, gave it when he said, "You may take a part of a man's soul away by making a picture of him. You may take a part of his privacy away." But the movie doesn't descend to this level of sanity; its true concern is the high-flown chic of soullessness. Carol Eastman's scripts — she wrote *Five Easy Pieces* under the name Adrien Joyce and *Puzzle of a Downfall Child* under the name Adrian Joyce — are *tributes* to alienation. The smart cues for the knowledgeable are there just to make us feel we're getting something really hip. Miss Eastman cleverly puts the blame for selecting the name Lou Andreas on the girl herself. But why would a girl take the name of one of the most neurotic women in modern history — a woman whose most lasting accomplishment is that she persuaded Rilke to change his first name from René to Rainer? The film isn't designed so that we can see into the Dunaway character — it's designed so that we *can't*.

Obfuscation is the aim (as obfuscation was also, I think, at least partly the aim with the Nicholson character in *Five Easy Pieces*). The tipoff to the misery-glorifying process in the Eastman scripts is that the protagonists are sadder than anyone else but are not subject to ordinary human motivation; they're too special to have motives — they're way beyond that. They're out of control; doomed, like Miss Didion's heroine; beyond help and beyond our understanding. The model has been psychologically mutilated by life. And, as in *Red Desert,* the mystery of damaged beauty — in *Five Easy Pieces* it's damaged talent — is what is supposed to engage us.

I speak of the scenarist here rather than the director, Jerry Schatzberg, because, even though he initiated the project, this script is so similar to the script of *Five Easy Pieces.* Aaron (Barry Primus), the photographer who's planning the movie about Lou Andreas, is taping her story first; the script is primary here, too. It's a script that tries to be deep with toy ideas. If one discovered that this script had been written by consulting astrological charts, it would come as no surprise. The soul-stealing photographs are on the same level as the dimpled chin as the mark of God's disfavor in *Five Easy Pieces.* Unmotivated misery is another dimple. *Five Easy Pieces* depended heavily on Bergman's *Wild Strawberries* for its structure and several of its episodes, and, to a much lesser degree, on *East of Eden.* This time, Miss Eastman has borrowed primarily from Bergman's *Summer Interlude* (about an aging ballerina who goes to the island where she grew up) and Bergman's *Dreams* (about a fashion editor and a model who take a trip) and *Citizen Kane.* Miss Eastman combines suggestions, cross-references, and little borrowings from old movies — not only as the French directors do, for homages and inside jokes, but for a fancy cultural *tone.* If a movie could become a work of art by association, *Puzzle of a Downfall Child* would be one. But it's not enough to take your characters to remote islands; you must also have talent. The hysterical, fractured style of the film bears an unhappy resemblance to *The Arrangement;* this is hardly likely to be intentional.

Yet, despite the frenzy, the movie is bloodless and inbred. The characters seem to be the walking dead from old movies, echoing old dialogue. Is the character of the vicious photographer Falco (Emerick Bronson) changed if one catches the reference to Tony Curtis's Falco in *Sweet Smell of Success?* Perhaps Schatzberg and Eastman are hedging their bets, and *Puzzle of a Downfall Child* is designed to succeed as a movie-memory game if it flops as a movie. When Viveca Lindfors, as a super-rich photographer, trips and falls down, it's the only moment in the film that looks spontaneous, and it's the only good moment.

Faye Dunaway plays the neurosis rather charmlessly; she lays it on too thick. And she has developed some dotty vocal mannerisms. She says every line the same affected way she spoke in *Little Big Man* — stretching the line with pauses, never contracting short words, clinging to syllables. It sounds neurotic, all right, but it's as tedious as a neurotic narcissist off-screen. What Aaron and the others see in Lou Andreas isn't so mysterious, though. It's the same thing that causes Faye Dunaway to get cast in so many movies: Faye Dunaway is a perfect, almost archetypal *shiksa*, and so, to many, as remote in her own way as the unreachable heroines Godard used to use. She has the right quality for the role; the "model" in advertising art is the Jewish (and other ethnic groups') dream of the American princess. But the potentially interesting subject is the comedy of why they are drawn to her.

[February 13, 1971]

Varieties of Paranoia

Jules Feiffer's 1967 play *Little Murders* was a wisp of a satirical comedy about living between assassinations — on the national level and on the level of local snipers. The movie version, which he also wrote, and which has been directed by Alan Arkin, has lost the play's bit of dramatic logic and has become rather gross. Feiffer's dialogue has comic authority, and the movie has volatile moments of rabid farce, yet the humor keeps sliding into something ugly and slightly rancid. The material overlaps *Weekend*, Godard's surreal parable of bourgeois violence, but it's specifically and eccentrically American. The American adjustment to random violence in the movie is only a slight exaggeration; the setting is New York, but Chicago may have got there faster, and other cities aren't far behind. Though the Newquist family, who talk in sunny banalities and slogans wholly inappropriate to the facts of their lives, are meant to be middle-class, perhaps their musicales of huffy talk are closer to working-class *Reader's Digest* rococo. However, speeches in the movie like Patsy Newquist's determined refusal to let the horrors of the day ahead spoil her good temper, and her father's explanation of how he gets through each day in planned segments, are psychologically true (although I think hers is stated falsely). We do, increasingly, view the day ahead as an obstacle course, and when we hear ourselves describing the madwoman who jabbed at us with an umbrella, or the screams in Central Park, or the muggers on both sides of the street on warm nights divvying up the passersby, we know that we probably sound paranoid. Normal life does seem to have gone mad, and since the newspapers and the television news show us daily that in large areas of the world things are even worse, we hardly complain anymore. Our lives have become a psychopathic comedy, so we are prepared to laugh at Feiffer's jokes — perhaps even overprepared; we're willing to laugh at Freudian family gags and freaked-up vaudeville turns. At first, despite many misgivings, one thinks Arkin may be able to bring it off, but though in most movies the good parts help one over the bad, they don't this time.

The movie begins with an ingenious comic hook: Patsy (Marcia Rodd) saves Alfred Chamberlain (Elliott Gould) from a gang of boys who are beating him; rescued, he walks away while the boys beat her. Patsy runs after him, crying, "I helped you! Why didn't you help me?" It's a good question, and when they begin going together we ask ourselves, Will Patsy change Alfred, and if so will it be for better or worse? Having got us interested in where he's going to take us, Feiffer dumps everything by killing Patsy off with a sniper's bullet. This spares the movie from sorting out its attitudes toward Patsy's get-up-and-go involvement and Alfred's apathy; Alfred Chamberlain may be a cousin to Neville, but he is played straight — as a saner figure than Patsy, or her family, or his own parents. The movie encases the apathetic, catatonic hero in a protective hip saintliness, and it has nothing to put in the place of the comic situations it abandons except Alfred, covered with blood, on a long subway ride, Alfred on a cinematic stroll in the Park, Alfred, with his slack jaw, looking like an elongated Harpo Marx turned into a Morgan gorilla. We're into the fashionable new movies in which politics and subversion have become a matter of style and of what jokes one laughs at, and apathy is the new heroism and the new chic. (The middle class still gets attacked for *its* apathy; middle-class people just can't do anything in the right style.)

The cinematographer, Gordon Willis, helps things by keeping the action *looking* lyrical, but Arkin may be too honest to direct some of the sequences. When there isn't enough comic truth in them — and there's none at all in Alfred's visit to his cold-hearted old-radical parents — Arkin can't seem to think of any way to cover up. He's best on the Newquists and in one great revue sketch set in a Village church, with Donald Sutherland in a wickedly funny performance as the all-accepting minister. The frenzied-family situation and the characters talking at cross-purposes are reminiscent of Preston Sturges, and Vincent Gardenia's squalling, combative Newquist is in the garrulous Sturges tradition; we begin to feel punchy as soon as he begins to talk. But Sturges's comedies stayed free of ideology, whereas Feiffer's work is a collection of ideological points.

Feiffer's attempt to show that the middle class has created the violent situation it's caught in isn't convincing. (We all know that there are stable bourgeois societies and that there are some remarkably violent societies without much middle class.) He seems to be pushing on this point, trying to convict the middle class of self-destructive lunacy, and this works against the theme: because he takes pleasure in its follies, there's no enveloping horror about what's happening to this way of life. The movie misses on the mood — the sense of helplessness Americans feel at the way the chaos accelerates and fresh insanities seem a natural development. Did the newscaster reporting on the nun who was killed by a sniper actually say that there were a hundred murders this year in Detroit, or did we hear him wrong? A hundred in two months? By now, we can believe anything, true or false. But the movie doesn't concede the middle class enough humanity — or any grace — so it isn't much more than a domestic farce with intellectual pretensions.

That funny but falsely worded speech Patsy makes about not letting the city destroy her spirit goes, "Alfred, do you know how I wake up every morning of my life? With a smile on my face! And for the rest of the day I come up against an unending series of challenges to wipe that smile off my face," and so on. Patsy is the All-American cheer-leading, castrating female, the sort of woman who makes up a questionnaire for her husband's parents to fill out about his eating habits and his toilet training. You miss Patsy, the aggressive girl-clown, after she's gone (and recognize that she has the only force and spirit in the film), but while she's there she stands for square values and speaks lines like "Alfred, do you have any idea how many people in this town *worship* me?" When, at the end, the Newquists, having lost two children to snipers, are so frustrated and forlorn they themselves become snipers, there's no grisly humor in it, and no true despair, either. One feels that the movie enjoys saying that America is psychopathic; the shooting spree at the end isn't a comedy of horror, it's a disaster-bash.

Little Murders is not an ordinary bad movie, and it's disturbing in some difficult-to-define ways. It goes out of kilter quite early, when a gasbag judge (Lou Jacobi) delivers a long harangue. This is a cleverly written tirade about how hard his immigrant parents worked and how their faith in God sustained them — it's like a Lenny Bruce routine. The judge reminds you of the hardhats who use God and the struggles of their parents and their own lean years to justify their hanging on to everything they've won and keeping black people and new immigrant groups down. But as the speech goes on, the movie turns sour, and invites the audience to laugh as if the immigrants had *not* suffered to raise and educate their children in freedom. This sequence becomes part of the new retroactive anti-Americanism. I think many of us want to giggle whenever anyone launches into one of these speeches, because we know the person is really talking not about the past but about his hatred of the present; still, our past isn't all rotten just because rotten people use it as a self-serving mythology. If this sequence were meant to be an attack on sanctimoniousness and the perversion of American principles — if it were the self-righteous old son of a bitch we were supposed to react against — the judge would be played as a character, not as a booming-voiced symbolic figure standing under a flag in a courtroom. There's another monologue, delivered by a police lieutenant (played by Alan Arkin), which is intended to show the breakdown and corruption of police authority. At the outset, it's a very funny speech — a sort of *Catch-22* speech about how unmotivated homicides are a plot to destroy faith in the police — but as Arkin gets hysterical and turns into a gibbering idiot it becomes just embarrassing.

We're doubly embarrassed to have the police lieutenant who spins a paranoid fantasy turn into a spitting, drooling maniac in front of our eyes, since only a little while before, when our hero spun an anti-Establishment paranoid fable, his eyes were clear and the camera kept him in adoring closeup, as if he were unravelling a tale from Kafka. Nothing else on the screen is as grandiloquent as a long closeup of a person making a quiet speech; it's like saying "Listen to this — it's pure gold." The movie's reverential attitude toward Alfred's fable about how he turned the tables on the government spy who was reading his mail is just as crazy as the police lieutenant's attitude. How can a movie attack inflated, false piety and present the ascension of Elliott Gould, the saintly dropout? There's hip cant, too; Feiffer and Arkin have their own false piety about fashionable anti-Establishment attitudes. Feiffer's ideological attitudes are just as inappropriate to the theme of this movie as the sunny slogans the characters mutter in the midst of chaos. He's writing about the collapse of order and authority, and he still can't resist making anti-Establishment statements. He's attacking "the system" and at the same time satirizing the collapse of the system. He seems to be angry that it's so contemptibly weak that it hardly merits his anger. And he's satirizing the middle class, who, by the evidence in this film, brought it all on their own heads by tipping their doormen or trying to protect themselves against muggers and robbers, or maybe just by their vulgar desire to survive. His point of view is as hysterical as the Newquists', since he winds up saying that there are no choices except apathy and violence. The ads have always told us that a Jules Feiffer cartoon was "an act of aggression camouflaged by humor." The camouflage fails in *Little Murders*.

•

The Argentine film *The Hour of the Furnaces* takes its title from Che Guevara's rallying cry (a quotation from José Martí): *Esta es la hora de los hornos. Y lo unico que se ha de ver séra la luz*" ("It is the hour of the furnaces. And all that need be seen is their light"). The film is designed to be the movie equivalent of a revolutionary manifesto, and to serve those who cannot read. Made between 1966 and 1968, it is perhaps the most spectacular example of agitprop moviemaking so far, and it demonstrates in a classic way the problems that seem to be inherent in propaganda movies. It is painfully affecting, since it shows the diseases and miseries of the poor, but it is also upsetting and maddening, since it throws facts and figures at us that we cannot evaluate while we're watching it, and calls for revolution as if the case for it had been made on plain, objective grounds. But though the methods of the director, Fernando Solanas (and his co-scenarist, Octavio Getino), may undercut the film's effectiveness with skeptical viewers, it is conceived on an epic scale and it flings so much powerful material at the audience that, even for the skeptical, viewing it is like trying to sort out an avalanche. You don't know whether to give up or give in.

The film was planned as a revolutionary seminar — to be shown in sections, with discussions between — and that's how it's used at illegal, "underground" showings in Argentina. The entire film — or, more properly, teaching course — is four hours and twenty minutes long; Part I, which is being shown in New York, is a ninety-five-minute section of widely varying quality called "Neocolonialism and Violence." This section is informed by revolutionary-puritan fanaticism and by an anti-Americanism so strong that even Argentines having a good time dancing to rock music are intercut with images of deprivation, as if American decadence had turned them into Neros fiddling while the city burned. At first, it's difficult for us to understand the way Peronism, which we still think of as a Fascist movement, is treated as the beginning of the mass struggle for liberation from foreign powers, but gradually it becomes apparent that the Frantz Fanonian left (of which Solanas and Getino are part) hope to seize power with the help of the Perónistas, and that the big issue which unites them is anti-Americanism. (Perón, whose policies were inimical to United States interests, was deposed with the help of the United States.) I think it's easier for us to believe the film's statistics about American and British domination of the economy, and the statement that the Pentagon trained and financed the anti-insurrectionist force that occupies parts of the country, than it is for us to accept the case the film makes against American mass culture and advertising and European culture as calculated elements of deception — as the aesthetic forms by which capitalist societies keep their old colonies enslaved. The film construes the work of the Peace Corps as a deliberate attempt to corrupt the national consciousness that it considers a necessary prelude to revolutionary struggle in Argentina and other Latin-American countries. Even non-violence is considered a technique of bourgeois repression. Perhaps it is the elation of producing this unified vision of systematic oppression that leads the moviemakers to their mystique that death in the revolution isn't death.

The film is an emotional assault, punctuated with quotations from Fanon, and including a long still shot — held for minutes — of the dead Guevara. At times, the narration says so much more than the images show that the contrast is risible, as when the sound track unloads data about the exploiting class while one sees people playing golf, but despite such crudeness it is a highly sophisticated assault. In modern films, it's no longer easy to separate documentary footage from "re-created" documentary footage; violent sequences that are staged look startlingly "caught." And when rhythmic editing is used to overwhelm one with misery while the sound track punches home statistics and slogans, it's clear that the propaganda potential in movies is finally being exploited.

It's ironic, of course, that Solanas rejects European art and makes his film in the style of Buñuel and Eisenstein. But even to notice this sort of contradiction seems like a form of bourgeois decadence when you're looking at sickness and starvation. One knows that a comparable picture of poverty, sickness, and slaughterhouses could be made in the United States or almost anywhere else, that similar images could be used to make a case for any political theory, and that when a documentary film uses the track not to explain what one sees but to assert what one doesn't see, the images have been chosen merely to illustrate a thesis. But that is what one *knows* — and is on a different level from how one experiences starving children begging for coins. A movie like this *is* a gun in a struggle, and a far more effective gun than Godard's revolutionary movies, because though it may aim at both the heart and the mind, it strikes the heart.

[March 6, 1971]

Misanthropic Movies

During parts of that Jacobean soap opera *Doctors' Wives*, I watched the audience rather than the screen — I wasn't worried about missing anything — and I would guess that only a small fraction of the audience, perhaps one person in fifteen, looked away from the blood and gore and the flesh being cut and the steel pin being driven into a child's skull. *Doctors' Wives* gets into the pornography of surgery — blood used to give color and juice to pale-blue soap opera. I don't quite understand the attraction of surgery for the audience — whether it's the porno appeal or whether the audience is so bored with untalented moviemaking that this gory life-and-death surgery provides a dramatic jolt, a substitute for the emotional involvement in life-and-death conflicts that movies once provided. I don't mean to suggest that surgery is in itself pornographic; I have judged a competition of medical-surgical films without ever getting the slummy, scummy sensations I got from *Doctors' Wives*. This strung-together soaper uses surgery to excite and horrify, on the model of that infamous scene in *The Proud and the Beautiful*, with Gérard Philipe and Michèle Morgan, when a king-size hypodermic is inserted so slowly that the movie becomes fixated on the metaphor; it uses pink, pulsating blobs the way sci-fi horror films do. There's an incredible whorish innocence to this literal blood-and-guts approach: the moviemakers throw in surgery at regular intervals, like the sex acts in a porny picture. And it doesn't even get an X rating; it can play all over, and you can take the kids — if you're breeding vampires. Yet the surgery spoils the fun of laughing at the souped-up sex problems, so *Doctors' Wives* fails to become a lubricious howler like *The Oscar*.

Dyan Cannon, who plays the husband-poaching chief bitch, has tantalizing comic-pornographic qualities; she's the latest in a classic Hollywood funny-dirty-girl tradition. But these moviemakers aren't skillful even at the low trade they're plying. How could Mike Frankovich, who produced this surgico-porno curiosity, and George Schaefer, who directed it, and Daniel Taradash (the president of the Motion Picture Academy!), who wrote the script, kill off this sexpot-tease in the first reel, and have nothing left but Richard Crenna and a troupe of bland surgeons with sexually distraught wives? (Sex in the movie is treated as some sort of hysterical affliction that attacks only women.) One knows exactly why a picture like this was made — it is a major studio's bid for the skin-flick trade — but not why some of the performers consented to be in it. John Colicos plays in such a traditional unpleasant, smart-rotter villain style that he disengages himself from the proceedings. A male actor can absent himself more easily than an actress, because he's not as likely to be called upon to strip; it's difficult for Janice Rule writhing in drug-induced lust or Diana Sands playing her big dramatic scene in a see-through blouse or Rachel Roberts confessing, in closeup, to a lesbian affair (it began when the seductress removed a cinder from her eye . . .) to pretend she isn't there.

•

Larry Peerce's last film, *Goodbye, Columbus,* was best in the simple and romantic human relationships and when the actors spoke the Philip Roth badinage in long, unbroken scenes that made us feel melancholy about a period so newly past; it was poor whenever the director tried to be visually hip and satiric, not just because those sixties banalities were wrong for the mood of Roth's story but because the director was inept at visual satire and hopeless when he tried to stage big sequences. His Jewish wedding supper was disastrous. A man who has a crude visual style cannot successfully satirize vulgarity; he must be able to supply another dimension — one that suggests what's missing in his subject's way of life. This sequence threw one right out of the movie to speculate on whether a dimension of sensitivity wasn't missing in the director who so grossly showed people overeating so grossly. Surely people who have been hungry in their youth might be treated with a little more humanity, and even some affection, when they proudly put on a spread for their children. Peerce simply joined the ranks of the middle-class moviemakers who love peasants but consider it repulsive when middle-class people show the gusto of peasants. Upward mobility is an unfortunate drive in one who hopes to be an artist.

Once again, Peerce has taken a novel by a good writer: Thomas McGuane's *The Sporting Club* is a surreal woodland comedy in which the "aristocracy" of Michigan revert to base animality and turn their private deer park into Bosch's *The Garden of Earthly Delights*. But this time there are no simple human relationships — or performances — to save the movie, and the viewer never gets into it. The movie of *The Sporting Club* is *all* in Larry Peerce's worst range; he's trying to do exactly what he doesn't know how to do — short takes, crowds, lots of violence. It's *all* in the style of his wedding-eating sequence; there is not one good scene or one good performance in the entire movie, and the audience (me included) reacted to it with boos and hisses. Movie directors customarily explain audience hostility by saying that's what they wanted — to shock people out of complacency. Peerce would be wrong to think this; it's not that the audience isn't hip enough, it's that his film is loathsome — a word I don't think I've ever before applied to a movie.

Being puzzled as to how the novel — which is booby-trapped, like *The Manchurian Candidate* — would be adapted, I asked to see a copy of the script, by Lorenzo Semple, Jr. It is, I think, a borderline script — brilliant but also impossibly self-conscious and literary. It's all bitter bravura, and I doubt whether anyone could have made a good film out of it, yet it could hardly have fallen into worse hands than Peerce's, because it requires a daring, sophisticated style. (Semple is a nephew of Philip Barry, and he may have been drawn to the McGuane novel because it gave him an opportunity to take the rich Americans of *The Philadelphia Story* several steps further into witty decay.) The hero, Vernor, is in his mid-thirties, a wild but noble decadent, a spoiled millionaire but also a soured idealist contemptuous of his own class; he is determined to destroy the northern-Michigan hunting-and-fishing club to which he belongs by inherited membership, and the script (which clarifies the climax of the novel) records the chaos caused by his overripe college humor. Vernor's schoolboy tricks include baring his bottom to the crowd at the inauguration of a dam; nasty, idiotic duels with wax bullets; and a truly imaginative final jest. At the centennial celebration of the club, the members are to dig up a time capsule put in the earth by the club founders. Vernor gets there first and provides an inspired prankish forgery — an elaborate pornographic photograph of the founders in a daisy chain.

Peerce has managed to miscast the movie so outlandishly that one can barely guess what the principal characters are meant to be. Vernor, whom one visualizes from the script as the Robert Walker of *Strangers on a Train* or a smart Robert Vaughn, is played by Robert Fields, who bounds about sneering, with beetle brows and so much eye-liner he seems to be a cross between Johnny Downs and a Nazi played by Maximilian Schell. For the smaller roles — and it's painfully obvious that they're meant to be Fascists — Peerce has also picked relative unknowns, but he has used them in ways drawn from old movies; if you're going to use an actor to play the George Macready–Walter Pidgeon role, you might as well get one of them. This way, most members of the cast seem to be stand-ins. What in ideal hands might have been a weird, exuberant satiric fable of the self-dramatizing self-hatred of a rich American has become one more excuse for a series of rancorous attacks on American Gothic faces and American flag-waving Babbittry, joined to an equally repulsive series of scenes of a vile redneck-barbarian hippie gang. Peerce doesn't seem to understand that he hasn't earned the right to contempt the only way an artist can earn it — by the understanding he reveals. Since every detail and action seems inaccurate, our reaction is revulsion. In the film, the pornographic photograph that is dug up is not a forgery, and in context this isn't surreal — it becomes the movie's idea of the truth about the American past. It's followed by repulsive super-Jewish-wedding scenes of middle-aged debauchery, and watching moviemakers devour their elders isn't any more attractive than watching people devour their young.

Why would anybody go? Well, of course, nobody will. (Even *Doctors' Wives* isn't doing as well as the moviemakers calculated; maybe most of the people in the theatre don't object to the porno surgery, but there are probably many at home who do.) The brutality in *The Sporting Club* includes closeups of men shot in the mouth and splattering blood and teeth as they speak, and a screaming old man covered with smoking-hot tar and feathers. There's a rock song blasting on the track while he screams, but one could still hear the piping voice of a child in the theatre asking what was the matter; that small voice was the final sickening touch. I don't know any adult who has seen this film and hasn't been repelled by it, but, like *Doctors' Wives,* it's an expensive big-studio production and you don't see pubic hair — not in closeup, anyway — so it isn't X-rated. Brutality is so self-righteously employed in this movie that it doesn't make you hate brutality, it just makes you hate going to the movies.

It has always been assumed that the mass movie audience enjoys violence, but I think recent movies have gone way past the audience's pleasure threshold. When we are not expected to feel pity for the victim

— not even when his flesh is smoking — the whole experience of movie-going becomes ugly. The movie audience is now a minority audience (it fell from seventy-eight million people a week in 1946 to seventeen and a half million in 1970; admission prices are scandalously high because the industry is trying to get as much revenue as before from the reduced audience), and I suspect that a lot of people stay away for the excellent reason that they don't like being bludgeoned. Recently, I've noticed that some of us critics express more disgust with the brutality of movies privately than publicly; in our columns we tend to ignore the gore or to be rather jocular about it, as if only quaint old folks could react the way we ourselves actually reacted. I think we're afraid of being thought oversensitive and uncool. But really it's sordid sitting there looking at people's innards spilling out in cherry and maroon. No doubt the violence in movies reflects changes in our national self-image, but the empty theatres tell us we don't like what we see. This isn't necessarily because we can't face the truth but, more likely, because most of the time now the movies' attitude toward violence is, as in *The Sporting Club,* gloatingly exploitative.

•

The Spanish film *The Garden of Delights* doesn't come very close to Bosch, though it's a good try at the dramatic use of misanthropy. This story of an amnesiac industrialist whose relatives act out grotesque psychodramas from his childhood, trying to shock him into remembering and telling them the number of his Swiss bank account, lacks impetus, however. As the movie goes on and the worm never turns, we lose interest. For a political parable of Spain, it may be satirically valid that the whole family end in wheelchairs, but the drama has ground to a halt. If the director, Carlos Saura, involved us in the other characters, there might be some compensation for our diminishing interest in the central figure, but there's nobody to care about. Visually, the movie is elegant in a dark, heavy-lidded sort of way. But it's odd that a movie having to do with lust and greed should be so tightly controlled, and Saura has a maddening habit of cutting away in the middle of a sequence just when we've got interested in where it's going (as in the reënactment of the industrialist's confirmation ceremony).

Though Saura works in the tradition of Buñuel (with perhaps some derivation from Pasolini, too), he has a sedate, measured style; this gives the film an air of authority and intelligence, but after a while the whole enterprise begins to seem rather stilted. The director isn't an instinctual Surrealist, and that, given the nature and drive of Surrealism, is really the only kind there is. He's an academic Surrealist, and this is something of a contradiction in terms as well as a key to the tameness and respectability of the movie. Saura's images don't come from the hidden and unadmitted; they're impeccably planned to be "Surreal." When he brings a pig into a house, it's not something dirty being released from the unconscious, it's an emblem and an homage. We're not shocked by Saura's academic Surrealism, we "appreciate" it.

The movie has one brief gloriously redemptive sequence: the beautiful, voluptuous Lina Canalejas enters the industrialist's Art Deco bedroom, opens the French windows, and lets the breeze waft through the curtains and her chiffon gown before going over to flirt with the man in bed, and for a moment or two the film has a trace of magical reminiscence — of all the sexy, elusive movie stars who ever wafted through our imaginations. This is, I think, the only moment of sensuous beauty in all these hours of movies.

[March 13, 1971]

Eric Rohmer's Refinement

Claire's Knee is a charming, serene, sun-bright movie; it calls up lazy memories of adolescence, and makes one long for summer holidays and months in the country. It's a lovely film and an unusually civilized film — if one uses "civilized" to describe a particular blend of harmony and restraint — and I enjoyed it very much. However, I don't think it's a great film; it has a type of formal perfection, in the sense that it works out its own logic, but, dramatically speaking, this logic is very thin. The chief character, Jérôme (Jean-Claude Brialy), who is in his mid- or late-thirties, is a diplomat stationed in Stockholm; he's about to marry a woman he has lived with for six years, and before the wedding he returns to his childhood home in Annecy. There he visits an old friend, a Rumanian novelist, Aurora (played by the Rumanian novelist Aurora Cornu);

Aurora, obviously standing in for Eric Rohmer, the writer-director, proposes that Jérôme become a character in her fiction. She is staying with a divorcée, who has a daughter, Laura, who is sixteen, and a stepdaughter, Claire, probably about eighteen. Though Jérôme tells Aurora that he doesn't look at women anymore, because he's getting married — that he "can't even tell one from another" — Aurora informs Jérôme that Laura says she is in love with him, and suggests that if he allows himself to be involved, he will soon move of his own volition, and Aurora, following his movements, will have her novel.

The first half hour is quietly entrancing. We accept the novelistic conceits and the leisure-class atmosphere and the way the situation has been abstracted from normal living; we accept it all in a spirit of anticipation, as part of a fresh movie-novel game. We're carried along, I think, because we get a sense of pleasurable discovery from Laura's chameleon character; and since her character is a triumph of preciousness, we accept the precious atmosphere. Beatrice Romand, who plays Laura, is an exquisitely gawky dark young beauty who looks like a Pisanello princess. Her Laura is a prodigious and daring flirt, and while she tests her newly developed wiles on Jérôme, the film is on exhilarating high terrain, and Rohmer seems to be a master of intrigue without cruelty or innuendo — a chaste Choderlos de Laclos. But Laura, despite her pride and insolence, is still physically a tomboy, and Jérôme isn't interested; the sensual spark is missing. For the remainder of the film, Laura retreats into her own age group, and when she becomes a subsidiary character the excitement and originality of the film wane. Rohmer's psychology of attraction is impeccable, but the other characters — as characters — are pallid after Laura.

Jérôme has told his confidante, Aurora, that he doesn't believe in love without friendship, and that women's looks don't matter to him — only their intelligence counts. The movie now shifts into a demonstration of Aurora's thesis that "the heroes of a story are always blindfolded." Jérôme is drawn to Claire's golden, lithe sensuality. Claire, who has a tawny, muscular young boyfriend, ignores Jérôme, and he becomes preoccupied with her — especially with a desire to caress her knee: the knee her boyfriend casually rests a hand on. Laurence De Monaghan (what a name!), who plays Claire, could not be more nearly perfect for the role, and one understands exactly what the director has in mind. Claire's indifference to Jérôme is polite and total; she lives at a distance — in a frieze. But Rohmer doesn't fulfill the Proustian suggestions, and Jérôme's conquest of Claire's knee never involves us with the same humor and intensity that Laura's propositioning does. The excitement dies out partly because

Jérôme — through no fault of Brialy's that I can detect — is weakly formulated, so his achievement of his erotic goal and the contemptible method he uses to achieve it don't signify much to us. Brialy *embodies* Jérôme by moving and smiling in a faintly world-weary way, but he isn't given enough character to play so that we know how to interpret the moral danger that Claire represents to Jérôme's scheme of life — or is she perhaps just a challenge to his vanity? From what Jérôme says and does, he's a sententious stick, but Brialy is (perhaps of himself?) so likable that we can't tell if the character is supposed to be a nonentity or an engaging, superior sort of fellow, or both.

The film looks simply beautiful — the sunlight has a palpable richness in Nestor Almendros's color cinematography, and the air seems thick with summer and leisure — and the narrative method that Rohmer uses is very pleasing. But he also has some peculiarities (which I think are weaknesses). Despite the summery richness, the film has no emotional steam when it gets to the subject of sensuality and compulsive attraction; this may make it seem super-civilized, but there's a price. What keeps the movie from being the corny melodrama of a secure man whose life is suddenly disrupted by an unsuitable grand passion is the smallness of Jérôme's impulse. He doesn't have a passion; he has an "undefined desire." Claire "troubles" him a little, he tells Aurora — "so little I wouldn't mention it if you were not so interested in the little." His delicate urge is meant to be ironic, of course — just enough impulse to reveal that everything he said about himself was false, and that he's blinkered, like everyone else. But this irony doesn't have enough style; it's too mild. Aurora says, "One can write a good story with banal characters," but Rohmer's movie comes alive only when the characters *aren't* banal.

Despite the ambience of moral awareness, there's surprisingly little elucidation of what actually happens or of how we're meant to feel about it. Jérôme is smugly pleased at feeling *anything;* he says that the emotion Claire arouses in him "gives me a sort of right to her." He cheats, like a dirty old man, and he carries tales; he informs Claire that her boyfriend is unfaithful to her, reduces her to tears, and then sneaks his hand onto her knee under the guise of comforting her. And he not only feels "fulfilled by the gesture" but deceives himself into believing that it was virtuous of him to open her eyes about her boyfriend. He says he "could not have experienced such a perfect pleasure without this idea of a good deed." Jérôme judges himself more kindly than Rohmer appears to. The contrast between the high-flown talk and the unscrupulous "good deed" isn't discussed, but Rohmer provides a borderline O. Henry finish by showing us that Claire's boyfriend is innocent of Jérôme's charge. The movie thus deals in self-deception, and all that articulation of moral distinctions was just a series of setups — the hero making fatuous statements about himself before revealing the opposite. The method is somewhat defeating, because we keep hanging on all that love-and-will-and-choice dialogue that threatens to turn epigrammatic, expecting it to clarify the characters' morality. Instead, we get genteel counterpoint: Jérôme, who has said he doesn't make girls cry, makes Claire cry; the ponderous, enigmatic Aurora, who has said there is no man in her life, turns out to have a fiancé; and so on. The movie has the manner of precise intelligence, but often it seems to be Rohmer who is deceiving himself, as when the novelist says, for Rohmer, "I never invent; I discover." (That epigram of Picasso's is elegant because of its perfect arrogance: it's the sort of remark an artist should wait for others to make about him.)

All this is why it isn't a great film; what's harder to get at is what makes the bourgeois placidity of the film's surface so pleasing. The film is *all* surface; it has no depths, and I think that Rohmer's contentment with this surface (he may have nothing he wishes to say that he can't put on the surface) makes us — for the duration of the film, at least — content, too. The formal manner and structure are in themselves like a vacation interlude for moviegoers, and the absence of "action" is so deliberate that I think we look to find something profound going on in the inaction. The movie is a Q.E.D. demonstration of something very traditional (and Catholic): that even the most sober and cultivated people don't have control over their erotic impulses — that when you come down to it people do what "nature" dictates. Yet by featuring, instead of a strong sexual drive, the rarefied impulse to touch a girl's knee, Rohmer seems to be saying something more subtle, more intellectual. He is playing such a quiet, complacent, adult game that I think we may wish to pretend to ourselves that this neutral, controlled surface is a higher form of art than it is.

•

There is much to praise in Barbara Loden's film *Wanda* — especially in the way she stays in character as a grimy Polish-American mining-town girl who has never known how to live except by attaching herself to men, and in Michael Higgins' originality as a bitter, nervous small-time crook — but it's such an extremely drab and limited piece of realism that it makes Zola seem like musical comedy. Wanda is a passive, bedraggled dummy. We've all known dumb girls, and we've all known unhappy girls; the same girls are not often, I think, both dumb and unhappy. Wanda is a double depressant — a real stringy-haired ragmop. That makes her a sort of un-protagonist; generally you'd have to have something stirring in you to be that unhappy, but she's so dumb we can't tell what has made her miserable. We don't know why she has become a drifter instead of staying home with her hair in curlers, watching soap operas and game shows, and maybe even looking after her kids. She's an attractive girl but such a sad, ignorant slut that there's nowhere for her and the picture to go but down, and since, as writer-director, Miss Loden never departs from the misery of the two stunted characters, there are no contrasts. The movie is very touching, but its truths — Wanda's small voice, her helplessness — are too minor and muted for a full-length film.

To select as one's heroine a girl with no spark at all is perhaps a shortcut to noncommercial integrity. A social-minded realist of the old school might have explained how Wanda's spirit was crushed and why the crook is a reject from the middle-class life he aspires to, and we would have experienced the forces that destroyed them. *Wanda,* despite its technical primitivism, represents an "artistic" kind of nihilistic neo-realism; it starts when the girl is already a hopeless loser, and it's practically a rise in her station when she and the crook drive through desolate small towns committing petty robberies. The slag heaps and highways and the urban sprawl around Scranton make us feel we should react to these displaced persons as part of something larger, but they are such extreme cases that one would really have to lose one's sense of humor to go tootling off into explaining them as products of the ugliness of the semi-industrialized landscape. I think one can accept the film only as two character sketches and an odd sort of minimal love story; Wanda's one poignant smile when the crook tells her she "did good" in a stickup provides the barest flicker of relief for the audience. By the time you hear the line of dialogue "You gave me a wet cigarette," you're ready to think, Yeah, that's what the movie is saying—that life is like a wet cigarette.

And yet Miss Loden has a true gift for character — there is not a moment when Wanda or the gangster is unconvincing. The movie was shot in 16-mm., and the color frequently has that pale watery green one gets from shooting without adequate light; though it's an unresourceful and monotonous movie visually, there is a sequence in a movie house where Miss Loden shows a gift for imagery. And there are eloquent touches. There's a moment when Wanda, looking at the clothes in a store window, resembles the mannequins, except that her clothes are sweat-stained; physically, she's the American dream girl, and one knows that it can do nothing for her, since she's too numb even to be a competent hooker. And although Miss Loden is too honest to descend to anything actressy or glamorous, when Wanda is in her hair-curlers they form a sort of five-and-ten-cent-store nimbus that has both pathos and beauty. Miss Loden is a beginner, and the film is rough on an audience, but it's rough for some good reasons — there's nothing coy or facile in her approach, and she's doing things the hard way rather than falling back on clichés. It's an exploratory first film, and one respects the director's strength.

•

A New Leaf, which Elaine May adapted and directed, is commercial in a rather bizarre way. It is an attempt at a type of harmlessly commercial comedy so doddering that — especially since the film is so weirdly cast — it may pass for something unusual. It's a long time since we've had a movie about a rich, aristocratic American playboy (of British extraction) who loses his money and must marry a fortune in six weeks. To have cast Walter Matthau (who frequently delivers his lines like W. C. Fields) in this role, with James Coco as his equally British-ancestored uncle, Jack Weston as a Wall Street lawyer, and the director herself as a Lowell is of such dazzling lunacy that one can scarcely wait for the announcement of Elaine May's next picture. Perhaps David Niven and Deborah Kerr as a family in the Bronx?

The picture is almost implausibly bad — and it's an unusually ugly major-studio production — yet it isn't offensively bad. Somehow — and this may be a feminine contribution — there is a sweetness about its absence of style, about its shapeless, limp comic scenes. One hopes that the difficulties the director had with the studio executives (who have apparently altered some of her intentions) account for some of the worst episodes, such as the inept handling of the heroine's thieving servants. Miss May herself is rather appealing, like a frail Joyce Grenfell; there's a good wedding-night scene in which she can't master the intricacies of a Grecian-style nightgown. William Redfield has a fine bit, and George Rose restores the butler-valet role to its most glorious days. He outclasses the rest of the cast, but is it intentional or unintentional? In this picture one can't be sure that much of anything was intentional.

[March 20, 1971]

The Poetry of Images

What makes Bernardo Bertolucci's films different from the work of older directors is an extraordinary combination of visual richness and visual freedom. In a Hollywood movie, the big scenes usually look prearranged; in a film by David Lean, one is practically wired to react to the hard work that went into gathering a crowd or dressing a set. Bertolucci has been working on a big scale since his first films — *La Commare Secca*, made when he was twenty, and *Before the Revolution*, a modern story derived from *The Charterhouse of Parma*, made when he was twenty-two — and his films just seem to flow, as if the life he photographs had not been set up for the camera but were all there and he were moving in and out of it at will. Most young filmmakers now don't attempt period stories — the past is not in good repute, and period pictures cost more and tend to congeal — but Bertolucci, because of the phenomenal ease of his sweeping romanticism, is ideally suited to them; he moves into the past, as he works in the present, with a lyrical freedom almost unknown in the history of movies. He was a prize-winning poet at twenty-one, and he has a poet's gift for using objects, landscapes, and people expressively, so that they all become part of his vision. It is this gift, I think, that makes *The Conformist* a sumptuous, emotionally charged experience.

Bertolucci's adaptation of the Alberto Moravia novel about the psychology of an upper-class follower of Mussolini is set principally in 1938 (Bertolucci was born in 1941), and I think it's not unfair to say that except for Jean-Louis Trintignant's grasp of the central character — it's an extraordinarily prehensile performance — the major interest is in the way everything is imbued with a sense of the past. It's not the past we get from films that survive from the thirties but Bertolucci's evocation of the past — the thirties made expressive through the poetry of images.

Trintignant, who has quietly come to be the key French actor that so many others (such as Belmondo) were expected to be, digs into the character of the intelligent coward who sacrifices everything he cares about because he wants the safety of normality. Trintignant has an almost incredible intuitive understanding of screen presence; his face is never too full of emotion, never completely empty. In this role, as an indecisive intellectual, he conveys the mechanisms of thought through tension, the way Bogart did, and he has the grinning, teeth-baring reflexes of Bogart — cynicism and humor erupt in savagery. And, playing an Italian, he has an odd, ferrety resemblance to Sinatra. Everything around him seems an emanation of the director's velvet style — especially the two beautiful women: Stefania Sandrelli, an irresistible comedienne, as Trintignant's deliciously corrupt middle-class wife, and Dominique Sanda, with her swollen lips and tiger eyes, as the lesbian wife of an anti-Fascist professor he is ordered to kill. (She's rather like a prowling, predatory stage lesbian, but she's such an ecstatic erotic image that she becomes a surreal figure, and Bertolucci uses her as an embodiment of repressed desires. She also appears, only slightly disguised, in two other roles — conceived to be almost subliminal.) The film succeeds least with its ideas, which are centered on Trintignant's Fascist. I think we may all be a little weary — and properly suspicious — of psychosexual explanations of political behavior; we can make up for ourselves these textbook cases of how it is that frightened, repressed individuals become Fascists. In an imaginative work, one might hope for greater illumination — for a Fascist seen from inside, not just a left view of his insides. Yet though the ideas aren't convincing, the director makes the story itself seem organic in the baroque environment he has created, and the color is so soft and deep and toned down, and the texture so lived in, that the work is, by its nature, ambiguous — not in the tedious sense of confusing us but in the good sense of touching the imagination. The character Trintignant plays is by no means simple; when he says "I want to build a normal life," it's clear that he needs to *build* it because it's not normal for him. He shows a streak of bravura enjoyment as he watches himself acting normal.

Bertolucci's view isn't so much a reconstruction of the past as an infusion from it; *The Conformist* cost only seven hundred and fifty thousand dollars — he brought together the décor and architecture surviving from that modernistic period and gave it all a unity of style (even with the opening titles). Visconti used the thirties-*in-extremis* in *The Damned* — as a form of estrangement. Bertolucci brings the period close, and we enter into it. His nostalgia is open; it's a generalized sort of empathy, which the viewer begins to share. You don't think in terms of watching a story being acted out, because he provides a consciousness of what's going on under the scenes; they're fully orchestrated. Bertolucci is perhaps the most operatic of movie directors. I don't mean simply that he stages movies operatically, in the way that other Italians — notably Zeffirelli — do, but that he conceives a movie operatically; the distinction is something like that between an opera director and an opera composer. Visconti in *The Damned* was somewhere in the middle — composing, all right, but in a single, high-pitched scale, as if the music were to be howled by wolves. *The Damned* was hysterical; *The Conformist* is lyrical. You come away with sequences in your head like arias: a party of the blind that opens with the cry of *"Musica!"*; an insane asylum situated in a stadium — a theatre-of-the-absurd spectacle of madness; a confession-box satirical duet between priest and non-believer; a wedding-night scherzo, the bride describing her sins, to the groom's amusement; the two women on a late-afternoon shopping expedition in Paris; a French working-class dance hall (a *Bal Populaire*) where the women dance a parody of passion that is one of the most romantic screen dances since Rogers and Astaire, and where the crowd join hands in a farandole. The political assassination in the forest — an operatic love-death — is the emotional climax of the film; Trintignant sits in his car, impotent — paralyzed by conflicting impulses — while the woman he loves is murdered.

Two years ago, Bertolucci made *Partner,* an inventive but bewildering modernization of Dostoyevsky's *The Double,* in which the hero, a young drama teacher (Pierre Clémenti), had fantasies of extending the theatre of cruelty into political revolution. This basic idea is shared by many young filmmakers, including, probably, Bertolucci, but Clémenti never conveyed enough intellectuality for us to understand the character, who seemed to be a comic-strip Artaud. Despite the fascination of *Partner* (I recall one image in particular, in which books were piled up in heaps on the floor of a room like the Roman ruins outside), the film was shown here only at the 1968 New York Film Festival. It was a political vaudeville for the movie generation bred on Godard's *La Chinoise;* the meanings were lost in the profusion of images and tricks of his original, daring high style. Bertolucci seemed to have forgotten the story of his own *Before the Revolution,* in which his Fabrizio discovered that he was not single-minded enough to be a Communist — that he was too deeply involved in the beauty of life as it was *before* the revolution. Bertolucci, like Fabrizio, has "a nostalgia for the present." This may seem a bourgeois weakness to him (and to some others), but to be deeply involved in the beauty of life as it is is perhaps the first requisite for a great movie director. (And, far from precluding activity for social change, it is, in a sense, the only sane basis for such activity.) It's a bit ironic that the young director who has the greatest natural gifts of his generation for making movies as sensual celebrations should have sought refuge for this talent in the Fascist period.

After *Partner*, Bertolucci made a television film about a plot to murder Mussolini during a performance of *Rigoletto* — *The Spider's Stratagem*. Based on a Borges story, it was attenuated — it didn't have enough content to justify the atmosphere of mystification. *The Conformist* is his most accessible, least difficult film from an audience point of view. I don't put that accessibility down; despite the intermittent brilliance of *Partner*, it *is* a failure, and trying to figure out what a director has in mind is maddening when it's apparent he hasn't worked it out himself. *The Conformist*, though in some ways less audacious, is infinitely more satisfying. One may wish that Bertolucci had been able to integrate some of the Godard influence, but no one has been able to do that; Bertolucci has simply thrown the discordant notes out of his system and gone back to his own natural flowing film rhythm. (Is it perhaps an in-joke that the saintly bespectacled professor who is murdered faintly resembles Godard?) In this film, one knows that Bertolucci knows who he is and what he's doing; young as he is, he's a master director. Except for the unconvincing and poorly staged concluding sequence, the flaws in *The Conformist* are niggling. It's very tempting for young filmmakers, through cutting, to make their films difficult; the filmmakers look at their own footage so many times that they assume an audience can apprehend connections that are barely visible. Bertolucci uses an organizing idea that puts an unnecessary strain on the viewer: the film begins with the dawn of the assassination day, and the events that led up to it unfold while Trintignant and a Fascist agent are driving to the forest. The editing at the outset is so fast anyway that cutting to and from that car is slightly confusing, but as one gets caught up in the imagery that slight confusion no longer matters. In a Bertolucci film, in any case, there are occasional images that have no logical explanation but that work on an instinctive level — as surreal poetry, like the piles of books in *Partner* or the desk here, in a Fascist's office, that is covered with neatly arranged walnuts. However, I don't think *The Conformist* is a great movie. It's the best movie this year by far, and it's a film by a prodigy who — if we're all lucky — is going to make great films. But it's a triumph of style; the substance is not sufficiently liberated, and one may begin to feel a little queasy about the way the movie left luxuriates in Fascist decadence.

One of the peculiarities of movies as a mass medium is that what the directors luxuriate in — and what we love to look at — has so often been held up as an example of vice. Except for the sophisticated comedies of the past and occasional thrillers about classy crooks, we get most of our views of elegance under the guise of condemnation. Our desire for grace and seductive opulence is innocent, I think, except to prigs, so when it's satisfied by movies about Fascism or decadence we get uncomfortable, because our own enjoyment is turned against us. One wants modern directors to be able to use the extravagant emotional possibilities of the screen without falling into the De Mille–Fellini moralistic bag. There are some sequences in *The Conformist* that suggest the moralistic extremism of *The Damned* — that party of the blind, for example, and the blue light on Trintignant's and Sanda's faces in the cloakroom of a ballet school.

The old puritanism imposed on moviemakers is now compounded by the puritanism of the left which coerces filmmakers into a basically hypocritical position: they begin to deny the very feelings that brought them to movies in the first place. The democratic impulse that informed the earliest screen masterpieces was to use the new medium to make available to all what had been available, through previous art forms, only to the rich and aristocratic. It was the dream of a universalization of the best work that could be done. As this dream became corrupted by mass culture produced for the lowest common denominator, the young filmmakers had to fight to free themselves from mass culture, and the fervor of the earlier democratic spirit was lost. Most young American filmmakers, in college and after, now think of themselves as artists in the same way American poets or painters do — and the poets have long since abandoned Whitman's dream of the great American audience. Filmmakers often talk as if it were proof of their virtue that they think in terms of a minority art. American movies have now reached just about the place the American theatre did a decade or so back, when, except for the rare big hits, it had dwindled into a medium for the few.

The radicalized young are often the most antidemocratic culturally, and they push radical filmmakers to the point where no one can enjoy their work. Any work that is enjoyable is said to be counter-revolutionary. The effect may be to destroy the most gifted filmmakers (who are also — not altogether coincidentally — mostly left) unless the young left develops some tolerance for what the pleasures of art can mean to people. These issues become central when one considers a Bertolucci film, because his feeling for the sensuous surfaces of life suggests the revelatory abandon of the Russian film poet Dovzhenko. If anyone can be called a born moviemaker, it's Bertolucci. Thus far, he is the only young moviemaker who suggests that he may have the ability of a Griffith to transport us imaginatively into other periods of history — and without this talent movies would be even more impoverished than they are. The words that come to mind in connection with his work — sweeping, operatic, and so on — describe the talents of the kind of moviemaker who has the potential for widening out the appeal of movies once again. But movies — the great sensual medium — are still stuck with the idea that sensuality is decadent. If Bertolucci can break all the way through this barrier — and he has already broken through part way — the coast is clear. But if he uses his talent — as "commercial" directors so often do — at half-mast, and somewhat furtively, to celebrate life under the guise of exposing decadence, he'll make luscious, fruity movies. When "period" becomes more important than subject, the result is often decorator-style — as in the worst of Minnelli. Bertolucci has such a feeling for detail that one fears he could go this route into empty, gorgeous filmmaking. That would be one more devastating blow to the art of motion pictures; sensuality is what they have lost. Except for *The Conformist* (and *Claire's Knee*), the new movies in New York have — for what I think must be the first time in decades — sunk below the level of the theatre season (which happens to be an unusually good one). People say you have to psych yourself up to go to a movie these days, and that's not far from the truth.

•

The new Robert Wise production, *The Andromeda Strain,* is a gigantic, expensive (over six million dollars) version of the unpretentious, modestly budgeted sci-fi thrillers of the fifties (*The Thing, Invasion of the Body Snatchers,* etc.). The suspense is unusually strong for the biological-invasion-from-outer-space genre, and, coming after the landings on the moon, the movie seems less farfetched than its precursors. But Wise has overemphasized this new commonplaceness by employing the impersonal style of "official" documentaries — which is nobody's idea of a good time. It goes wrong in ways so obvious that one wonders: While they were constructing sets, didn't anybody consider the structure of the story?

A space satellite falls to earth, and in a nearby desert town all the inhabitants but two (an old wino and a baby with colic) suddenly die. Then, in one of the most preposterously ill-calculated pieces of moviemaking yet, what seems like a full hour is spent on assembling and decontaminating the team of four scientists who will examine the satellite (which is covered with some sort of rapidly spreading green muck). The decontamination process takes over the movie for so long that we practically forget the menace to the world outside. (It's fragmentarily dealt with in rather confusing brief cuts to a mysterious plane crash over the desert and to congressmen discussing the crisis, which the President takes in as desultory a fashion as the director.) Nothing matters, apparently, except decontaminating the dull team (Arthur Hill, James Olson, David Wayne, Kate Reid); one can only assume that Wise and his associates were so awed by the underground-station set they built that they tried to get the maximum use out of it, showing it five times, supposedly level by level (all five levels alike except painted in different colors, like an impacted banana split). The inadvertent comedy of this film is that after the hour of showing us how this decontamination installation works they don't show us what goes wrong when it becomes contaminated. Worse, the movie (following the Michael Crichton novel, I suppose) makes an almost unbelievably stupid dramatic mistake: the team turns out not to need to solve the problem of the biological menace that is about to destroy the world — the Andromeda Strain — because the substance somehow disposes of itself. The suspense of the movie shifts from stopping the cosmic menace to shutting off a bomb mechanism set to destroy the building — accomplished by James Olson's shinning up a pipe and inserting a key in a lock.

Actually, we have lost interest in the Andromeda Strain even before it evaporates (or disappears, or whatever it does), because it has become so abstract and hypothetical that it's visually dead anyway. There is one pure-horror sequence of a monkey's death; it perfectly illustrates how effective movies can be when horror is visualized. As long as the greenish slime seems to be pulsating like a growing organism — as if a frog's eye were expanding to take over the universe — it's terrifying, and the tension is enough to give one palpitations, but when the scientists examine it more closely and it becomes crystalline, or something, it's a bore. We can't assimilate the information about what it can and can't do fast enough to understand how it ceases to be a threat. Olson's getting up that pipe in time to stop the bomb is, in movie terms, Saturday-afternoon kid stuff — without any of the humor that would surround it in a Bond film. Isn't science fiction meant to have some fun to it — some imaginative playfulness? The fanatical realism of all that decontamination suggests nothing more than an obsession with cleanliness.

[March 27, 1971]

Pipe Dream

McCabe & Mrs. Miller is a beautiful pipe dream of a movie — a fleeting, almost diaphanous vision of what frontier life might have been. The film, directed by Robert Altman, and starring Warren Beatty as a small-time gambler and Julie Christie as an ambitious madam in the turn-of-the-century Northwest, is so indirect in method that it throws one off base. It's not much like other Westerns; it's not really much like other movies. We are used to movie romances, but this movie is a figment of the romantic imagination. Altman builds a Western town as one might build a castle in the air — and it's inhabited. His stock company of actors turn up quietly in the new location, as if they were part of a floating crap game. Altman's most distinctive quality as a director here, as in *M*A*S*H,* is his gift for creating an atmosphere of living interrelationships and doing it so obliquely that the viewer can't quite believe it — it seems almost a form of effrontery. He has abandoned the theatrical convention that movies have generally clung to of introducing the characters and putting tags on them. Though Altman's method is a step toward a new kind of movie naturalism, the technique may seem mannered to those who are put off by the violation of custom — as if he simply didn't want to be straightforward about his storytelling. There are slight losses in his method — holes that don't get filled and loose ends that we're used to having tied up — but these losses (more like temporary inconveniences, really) are, I think, inseparable from Altman's best qualities and from his innovative style.

There's a classical-enough story, and it's almost (though not quite) all there, yet without the usual emphasis. The fact is that Altman is dumping square conventions that don't work anymore: the spelled-out explanations of motive and character, the rhymed plots, and so on — all those threadbare remnants of the "well-made" play which American movies have clung to. He can't be straightforward in the old way, because he's improvising meanings and connections, trying to find his movie in the course of making it — an incredibly risky procedure under modern union conditions. But when a director has a collaborative team he can count on, and when his instinct and his luck both hold good, the result can be a *McCabe & Mrs. Miller*. The classical story is only a thread in the story that Altman is telling. Like the wartime medical base in *M*A*S*H*, the West here is the life that the characters are part of. The people who drop in and out and the place — a primitive mining town — are not just background for McCabe and Mrs. Miller; McCabe and Mrs. Miller are simply the two most interesting people in the town, and we catch their stories, in glimpses, as they interact with the other characters and each other. But it isn't a slice-of-life method, it's a peculiarly personal one — delicate, elliptical. The picture seems to move in its own quiet time, and the faded beauty of the imagery works a spell. Lives are picked up and let go, and the sense of how little we know about them becomes part of the texture; we generally know little about the characters in movies, but since we're assured that that little is all we need to know and thus all there is to know, we're not bothered by it. Here we seem to be witnesses to a vision of the past — overhearing bits of anecdotes, seeing the irrational start of a fight, recognizing the saloon and the whorehouse as the centers of social life. The movie is so affecting it leaves one rather dazed. At one point, cursing himself for his inability to make Mrs. Miller understand the fullness of his love for her, McCabe mutters, "I got poetry in me. I do. I got poetry in me. Ain't gonna try to put it down on paper . . . got sense enough not to try." What this movie reveals is that there's poetry in Robert Altman and he *is* able to put it on the screen. Emotionally far more complex than *M*A*S*H*, *McCabe & Mrs. Miller* is the work of a more subtle, more deeply gifted — more mysterious — intelligence than might have been guessed at from *M*A*S*H*.

The picture is testimony to the power of stars. Warren Beatty and Julie Christie have never been better, and they *are* the two most interesting people in the town. They seem to take over the screen by natural right — because we want to look at them longer and more closely. Altman brings them into focus so unobtrusively that it's almost as if we had sorted them out from the others by ourselves. Without rigid guidelines, we observe them differently, and as the story unfolds, Beatty and Christie reveal more facets of their personalities than are apparent in those star vehicles that sell selected aspects of the stars to us. Julie Christie is no longer the androgynous starlet of *Darling*, the girl one wanted to see on the screen not for her performances but because she was so great-looking that she was compelling on her own, as an original. She had the profile of a Cocteau drawing — tawdry-classical — and that seemed enough: who could expect her to act? I think this is the first time (except, perhaps, for some of the early scenes in *Doctor Zhivago*) that I've believed in her as an *actress* — a warm and intense one — and become involved in the role she was playing, instead of merely admiring her extraordinary opaque mask. In this movie, the Cocteau girl has her opium. She's a weird, hounded beauty as the junky madam Mrs. Miller — that great, fat underlip the only flesh on her, and her gaunt, emaciated face surrounded by frizzy ringlets. She's like an animal hiding in its own fur. Julie Christie has that gift that beautiful actresses sometimes have of suddenly turning ugly and of being even more fascinating because of the crossover. When her nose practically meets her strong chin and she gets the look of a harpy, the demonstration of the thin line between harpy and beauty makes the beauty more dazzling — it's always threatened. The latent qualities of the one in the other take the character of Mrs. Miller out of the realm of ordinary movie madams. It is the depth in her that makes her too much for the cocky, gullible McCabe; his inexpressible poetry is charming but too simple. An actor probably has to be very smart to play a showoff so sensitively; Beatty never overdoes McCabe's foolishness, the way a foolish actor would. It's hard to know what makes Beatty such a magnetic presence; he was that even early in his screen career, when he used to frown and loiter over a line of dialogue as if he hoped to find his character during the pauses. Now that he has developed pace and control, he has become just about as attractive a screen star as any of the romantic heroes of the past. He has an unusually comic romantic presence; there's a gleefulness in Beatty, a light that comes on when he's onscreen that says "Watch this — it's fun." McCabe pantomimes and talks to himself through much of this movie, complaining of himself to himself; his best lines are between him and us. Beatty carries off this tricky yokel form of soliloquy casually, with good-humored self-mockery. It's a fresh, ingenious performance; we believe McCabe when he says that Mrs. Miller is freezing his soul.

A slightly dazed reaction to the film is, I think, an appropriate one. Right from the start, events don't wait for the viewers' comprehension, as they do in most movies, and it takes a while to realize that if you didn't quite hear someone's words it's all right — that the exact words are often expendable, it's the feeling tone that matters. The movie is inviting, it draws you in, but at the opening it may seem unnecessarily obscure, perhaps too "dark" (at times it suggests a dark version of Sam Peckinpah's genial miss *The Ballad of Cable Hogue*), and later on it may seem insubstantial (the way Max Ophuls' *The Earrings of Madame de . . .* seemed — to some — insubstantial, or Godard's *Band of Outsiders*). One doesn't quite know what to think of an American movie that doesn't pretend to give more than a partial view of events. The gaslight, the subdued, restful color, and Mrs. Miller's golden opium glow, Leonard Cohen's lovely, fragile, ambiguous songs, and the drifting snow all make the movie hazy and evanescent. Everything is in motion, and yet there is a stillness about the film, as if every element in it were conspiring to tell the same incredibly sad story: that the characters are lost in their separate dreams.

The pipe dreamer is, of course, Robert Altman. *McCabe & Mrs. Miller* seems so strange because, despite a great deal of noise about the art of film, we are unaccustomed to an intuitive, quixotic, essentially impractical approach to moviemaking, and to an exploratory approach to a subject, particularly when the subject is the American past. Improvising as the most gifted Europeans do has been the dream of many American directors, but few have been able to beat the economics of it. In the past few years, there have been breakthroughs, but only on sensational current subjects. Can an American director get by with a movie as personal as this — personal not as in "personal statement" but in the sense of giving form to his own feelings, some not quite defined, just barely suggested? A movie like this isn't made by winging it; to improvise in a period setting takes phenomenal discipline, but *McCabe & Mrs. Miller* doesn't look "disciplined," as movies that lay everything out for the audience do. Will a large enough American public accept American movies that are delicate and understated and searching — movies that don't resolve all the feelings they touch, that don't aim at leaving us *satisfied,* the way a three-ring circus satisfies? Or do we accept such movies only from abroad, and then only a small group of us — enough to make a foreign film a hit but not enough to make an American film, which costs more, a hit? A modest picture like *Claire's Knee* would probably have been a financial disaster if it had been made in this country, because it might have cost more than five times as much and the audience for it is relatively small. Nobody knows whether this is changing — whether we're ready to let American moviemakers grow up to become artists or whether we're doomed to more of those "hard-hitting, ruthlessly honest" American movies that are themselves illustrations of the crudeness they attack. The question is always asked, "Why aren't there American Bergmans and Fellinis?" Here is an American artist who has made a beautiful film. The question now is "Will enough people buy tickets?"

•

Jane Fonda's motor runs a little fast. As an actress, she has a special kind of smartness that takes the form of speed; she's always a little ahead of everybody, and this quicker beat — this quicker responsiveness — makes her more exciting to watch. This quality works to great advantage in her full-scale, definitive portrait of a call girl in *Klute*. It's a good, big role for her, and she disappears into Bree, the call girl, so totally that her performance is very pure — unadorned by "acting." As with her defiantly self-destructive Gloria in *They Shoot Horses, Don't They?*, she never stands outside Bree, she gives herself over to the role, and yet she isn't *lost* in it — she's fully in control, and her means are extraordinarily economical. She has somehow got to a plane of acting at which even the closest closeup never reveals a false thought and, seen on the movie streets a block away, she's Bree, not Jane Fonda, walking toward us.

The center of the movie is the study of the temperament and the drives of this intelligent, tough high-bracket call girl who wants to quit; she tries to get modelling jobs, she wants to be an actress, she is in analysis, yet she enjoys her power over her customers. It is the life surrounding her profession that frightens her; the work itself has peculiar compensations. Though there have been countless movie prostitutes, this is perhaps the first major attempt to transform modern clinical understanding into human understanding and dramatic meaning. The conception may owe some debt to the Anna Karina whore in *My Life to Live*, but Bree is a much more ambivalent character. She's maternal and provocative with her customers, confident and contemptuously cool; she's a different girl alone — huddled in bed in her disorderly room. The suspense plot involves the ways in which prostitutes attract the forces that destroy them. Bree's knowledge that as a prostitute she has nowhere to go but down and her mixed-up efforts to escape make her one of the strongest feminine characters to reach the screen. It's hard to remember that this is the same actress who was the wide-eyed, bare-bottomed Barbarella and the anxious blond bride of *Period of Adjustment* and the brittle, skittish girl in the broad-brimmed hat of *The Chapman Report;* I wish Jane Fonda could divide herself in two, so we could have new movies with that naughty-innocent comedienne as well as with this brilliant, no-nonsense dramatic actress. Her Gloria invited comparison with Bette Davis in her great days, but the character of Gloria lacked softer tones, shading, variety. Her Bree transcends the comparison; there isn't another young dramatic actress in American films who can touch her.

Klute is far from a work of art, but it's a superior thriller-melodrama, well written, by Andy and Dave Lewis, and directed tactfully and intelligently, by Alan J. Pakula, so that it provides a framework for the pivotal character. Donald Sutherland's Klute, a straight, country-town policeman who has come to Manhattan to investigate the disappearance of a man said to have been one of Bree's Johns, is a supporting role, and Sutherland plays him with becoming modesty. The movie founders, however, on the conventions of the murder-mystery genre. Of course, everyone longs to see a good murder mystery, like the ones of the forties, but how can you make one now? Pakula is as much aware of the problem of square conventions as Altman, but, unlike Altman, who throws out as many as he can, Pakula compromises by trying to soft-pedal them. However, the mechanics of suspense — the lurking figures, the withheld information, the standard gimmick of getting the heroine to go off alone so she can be menaced by the big-shot sadistic sex fiend, the improbable confessions and last-minute rescues — are just claptrap, overused and inevitably associated in our minds with B pictures and TV fodder. That doesn't prevent us from being scared, but we're aware of what a synthetic sort of reaction we're having. There's no conviction in these devices anymore; they're hokum, and the movie's awful, repetitive horror-tingle music emphasizes the fancy excesses of the photography; the shadows and angles are as silly as a fright wig. Would a simpler, more documentary approach to the look of the film have worked better? A little, perhaps, but simplicity is far more difficult, and probably somewhat more hazardous commercially, and it wouldn't really solve the basic problem of fraudulent suspense. Nevertheless, *Klute* is a powerful, scary melodrama, and only once does the discreet director intrude on Miss Fonda's performance. In a scene between Bree and a customer, there is a cut to her looking at her wristwatch while feigning passion. A businesslike look at the watch *before* her ecstatic cries, or even after, might possibly be consistent with the character — Jane Fonda is just naturally in a hurry — but this is a crummy, cute nod to the audience for a laugh. The bit sticks out, because Miss Fonda has moved beyond working the audience.

•

Carnal Knowledge, the nifty title of the new Mike Nichols picture, from an original screenplay by Jules Feiffer, leads the viewer to expect a comedy (maybe because it's what the viewer *wants*), and I was psychologically prepared for a comedy, too, because it seemed the least that Nichols owed the movie audience after *Catch-22,* and I assumed he knew that. But he knew something else. *Carnal Knowledge* turns out to be a grimly purposeful satire about depersonalization and how we use each other sexually as objects, and, in Mike Nichols' cold, slick style, it is like a neon sign that spells out the soullessness of neon. This movie doesn't just raise a problem, it's part of it, and, aesthetically, it makes the problem worse. It's as if *Playboy* had suddenly seen the error of its ways and now sold its remorse in the same crusading format. The effects are almost all achieved through the line readings, and the *cleverness* is unpleasant. It's all surface and whacking emphasis. The controlled hysteria of this desperate, surefire, hit-it-on-the-button comedy style has about the same relationship to humor that belting has to singing.

Feiffer had what sounds like a promising idea: to take two college roommates in the mid-nineteen-forties (Jack Nicholson, who becomes a tax lawyer, and Arthur Garfunkel, who becomes a doctor) and follow their sexual attitudes and activities through to their middle age, in the early seventies. But Feiffer has rigged the case in order to write a tract on American romantic legends versus the unmitigated rotten "truth." Glowering Jack Nicholson is a jock Heathcliff with a big-breast fixation, and we watch him over the years yelling at Ann-Margret (who appears to be fitted out with giant plastic mammaries) and exploding in frustration as he becomes more and more impotent. Garfunkel is a mild drip who goes from a dull, proper marriage with Candice Bergen to an affair with a metallic mistress (Cynthia O'Neal, who looks like Helen Gurley Brown) and winds up with a curly-haired teen-ager who looks as if she might be his daughter. It's a parallel history of dissatisfaction and emptiness. The men have nothing to give, and they never learn anything; their aging is a process of becoming more nakedly ugly and corrupt, and the movie sours as they age, scoring off them repeatedly and never letting them win a round. There's an element of punishment in the movie's social criticism.

If you were surprised that in *Catch-22* some relatively harmless sex acts seemed to be included among the scourges and horrors of war, you may be even more surprised at the disgust heaped on sex in this movie. In the new, politicized morality, if well-heeled Americans do it sex must be vile, because how could they possibly know anything about love? (The bohemian left used to tweak the middle classes for their stuffy sexual morality and for taking sex too seriously; now the middle classes are flayed for having learned their lesson and wanting to play.) This show-business fundamentalism is probably perfectly timed: what *The Graduate* was for the generation gap, *Carnal Knowledge* can be for Women's Lib sex-gap arguments. A movie doesn't have to be good to be taken as a controversial, extremely important moral statement. People can use the movie against each other, and that sells tickets. Women can say "See!" and men can confess "Yes, I, too, have been guilty." And since the characters are of Benjamin's *parents'* generation, the movie audience is already prepared to believe that they never could feel, never could relate.

The movie replaces the old romantic stereotypes with new lecherous-decadent stereotypes. People can say, "It's all true, I know people just like that" — men who see women only as sex organs, and so on. There probably are some men like these two, just as there probably *still* are women like the chirrupy mothers and widows Spring Byington used to play, but truth in movies relates to something more than the existence of examples. This movie says not merely that there are some people like these but that this is *it* — that is, that this movie, in its own satirical terms, presents a more accurate view of men and women than conventional movies do. That may be the case, but the movie isn't convincing. It proceeds by duologues — conversations between the two buddies discussing their women, and man-woman conversations. Though *Carnal Knowledge* somewhat resembles *Husbands,* the women here are as vacuous as the men. This is, I think, where the movie first tips its mechanical hand: in the college scenes, when Candice Bergen is dating both men, her blank, smiling superiority and her refusal to give us a clue to her sexual behavior suggest merely incompetence until we realize that no one else in the movie is going to be comprehensible, either. Since we know nothing about their feelings, the steps they take and the patterns of their lives have no internal logic. The characters are depersonalized from the start through the elimination of all the possibilities in their lives except sex drives — not only love and work and family and affection are eliminated but even eroticism, even simple warmth — and then the two men are indicted as a monster and a weakling because the "truth" of their lives is not love but this depersonalized sex. The movie starts out by splitting sex from love as a satirical device and getting laughs from the separation. By the end, the movie is using its own device as "reality."

The actors are badly served; they're served up, really. Candice Bergen, who elsewhere has suggested some bright possibilities as a comedienne, is given scenes of emotional stress that are probably unplayable (since they don't make sense), and rises to the heights of middle-period Lana Turner. Garfunkel is pleasantly non-actorish at the start, but since he has no projection he becomes such a limp presence that you forget he's on the screen. Nicholson, on the other hand, acts up such a tormented, villainous squall that even his best scene — a well-written monologue about the perils of shacking up — seems to be delivered in full voice against cliffs and crashing seas. What with the big-band records and the now obligatory watching-a-movie-on-TV scene (Dick Powell singing "I'll String Along with You" in *Twenty Million Sweethearts*), what with Cynthia O'Neal's bitchy snootiness and Ann-Margret's simp pathos and Rita Moreno as an anxious-to-please prostitute and a scene of Miss Bergen laughing, laughing, laughing in closeup, it's all rather like a Ross Hunter production that has been sitting on the stove too long.

There is a small point that may get lost in all this: To contrast the American dream of true-love-forever with this cold sexual usage as if to clear away lies is — in some ways — being awfully silly. Audiences used to know better than those old romantic illusions, which were entertaining *romances,* while the current movie audience is so softened by repeated lacerations that the narrow view in *Carnal Knowledge* may pass for realism. It's true we can no longer sustain pleasant illusions; the realities at this time have made them intolerable. But this swing over to an illusion system in which we're worms just makes us more helpless to deal with facts.

●

The Anderson Tapes is a broadly played, slovenly crime-caper melodrama with enough crude energy to satisfy people who are looking for a dumb summer show that will kill a couple of hours. That is how I interpret the long lines and the packed theatre and the laughs. The movie is made up of just those crummy shoves at the audience that *Klute* slipped into that once. Sean Connery manages to rise above the material, but he succeeds only in making the rest of the cast look as bad as it is. I've rarely seen so many small, sleazy performances in one movie. The only distinction of *The Anderson Tapes* is the amount of time spent on a gimmick — everybody's conversations are being recorded — which turns out to be totally irrelevant to the plot. Some may be willing to call this irony.

[July 3, 1971]

PART III

A Movie Classic Is Not Nothing

Seeing *Sunday Bloody Sunday* was for me like reading a novel that was very far from my life and my temperament, and that yet when I finished it had me thinking, It all adds up; it has a vision and sticks to it — and, yes, there's something there, there's truth in it. The movie, which is about the ways in which people learn to compromise, spans ten days in the lives of three Londoners and the breakup of their love affairs. A homosexual doctor in his forties, played by Peter Finch, and an employment counsellor in her thirties, played by Glenda Jackson, are both in love with a boyish, successful kinetic sculptor, played by Murray Head, who casually divides his time and affections between them. He isn't a bitch, but he isn't quite a man, either; with youth and looks and a talent for success all on his side, he is not yet (and perhaps never will be) fully human in the way they are. Nothing has ever struck him down. He does what he pleases, avoids any kind of pressure, and can't see why other people's lives should be confused or messy. He has no special sexual preferences and doesn't understand what upsets the two older people about sharing him, since he loves them both.

The cool sculptor just has to *be,* and Murray Head seems effortlessly right in the role — a hip angel who has never heard of Hell — but the others suffer, and so Peter Finch and Glenda Jackson are required to act. (It's possible to see the characters as representing generations, though I should certainly prefer not to.) In terms of its own split-shift scheme, the movie goes somewhat out of balance, because the doctor's role is better conceived and also better played than the woman's. Peter Finch's Dr. Daniel Hirsh is possibly a movie first — a homosexual character who isn't fey or pathetic or grotesque. He is one of the most simply and completely created characters in recent films. Finch wears a yarmulke well but he never overdoes being Jewish, and he doesn't overdo being homosexual.

One is always aware of how faultless and polished and intelligent Finch's acting is, and, as with other characterizations of his, there's nothing for us to fill in, nothing spills over, there's no grit to complain of. We don't usually remember his characters or care about him as an actor the way we sometimes care about even sloppy, rather stupid actors who trust to instinct. Finch is lifelike without much life. Maybe greatness eludes him as an actor because he stays in character so perfectly he's a little boring. This time, however, his subtlety and modesty are memorably right, for the urbane Dr. Hirsh, resigned to loneliness, doesn't have much life in him. He has some guilt about his homosexuality, but not very much; what he feels is closer to occasional social embarrassment. The Doctor is a competent, intelligent man, more tidy than deep, and he doesn't ask much more from life than the half a loaf he gets from his young friend. Perhaps he doesn't really want the involvement of more.

The woman, however, does. Alex Greville is a divorcée, taut and well-born, with a "piercing, educated mind," a pill-popping woman who doesn't know what to do with herself. (In the theatre of the twenties, she would have been gallant Lady Alex.) But why is she anguishing over this boy? Alex's neo-Bankhead baggage of rue and harsh tenderness and a refusal to stoop to conventional feminine wiles doesn't provide much understanding of what Alex wants. (Surely not "all" of this innocuously blank boy — what could that do for her? And surely not merely a more conventional lover, either?) The boy is meant to be only a catalyst, but we can't see what elements in her are affected by him, or what possibilities crushed by her not having more of him. Glenda Jackson gives the picture a needed tensile strength, and yet the bile and violence in her seem wrong for the role; a scene in which she yells at a child feels totally out of character, and when you see Alex with her mother (Peggy Ashcroft) you just don't believe they could ever be mother and daughter. The director, John Schlesinger, hasn't helped Miss Jackson's performance by shooting her constantly in closeups in which she indicates her thoughts and emotions by movements of her tongue to her lips or against her teeth. Her specialty seems to be a slightly repellent hardness; it's erotic, all right, and she has a definite appeal — all edge and challenge — but she doesn't show many new facets in this role. Seen close, an actress really needs softness and some shadings; in the movies an intense actress without a soft side can easily become inexpressive and unlikable. (Bankhead herself didn't become a popular movie star until she returned to the screen in middle age as a raucous, lecherous comedienne.) Miss Jackson really is a bit hard-nosed. Katharine Hepburn had this glittering hyperconsciousness but could transform it into sheer radiance; Glenda Jackson is no chameleon. Alex's most likable moment comes near the end when she says something wryly self-depreciating to Dr. Hirsh; it's as if she felt free with him, since she has nothing to gain. But we never find out why Alex is such a Brillo pad with her mother and everybody else — or whether Glenda Jackson is simply miscast.

Though in the scheme of the film Alex, who rejects compromise, is the insurgent, her activism rings rather hollow, because the whole vision and attitude of the movie go the other way. The pervasive atmosphere is of a generalized quietism; *Sunday Bloody Sunday* is a curious sort of plea on behalf of human frailty — a movie that asks for sympathy for the non-heroes of life who make the best deal they can. This plea will, I think, help the picture find an audience; people can receive solace from it. It is probably the movie that educated people have been waiting for and longing for — a movie that says they should stop castigating themselves and that yet leaves them mourning for everyone's lost hopes.

It's an unusual film — one of a kind — and unquestionably the most sophisticated weeper ever made. (*Brief Encounter* was relatively middle-class.) The three principals are friends with a left-wing intellectual couple whose children giggle and drop little needling remarks indicating hidden layers of gamesmanship and complicity that make the quick of one's nails ache. The type of elegant, stylized novel that this movie resembles pays for its style with a certain bloodlessness, and the movie does, too. There is maybe a little too *much* sensibility; compassion is *featured*, and it's difficult to separate this compassion from masochism. "People can manage on very little," the Doctor says to relatives of an incapacitated patient. "Too late to start again," a sad, heavy-lidded woman who looks like Virginia Woolf says of her miserable marriage. And Alex's mother says to her, "You keep throwing in your hand because you haven't got the whole thing. There *is* no whole thing." Of her life with Alex's father the mother says, "You think it's nothing, but it's not nothing." This is what all our mothers told us and what we went to the movies to escape from, and so it's an unexpected message for a movie — that we should extend sympathy to those who live on the little margin that constitutes "not nothing." If I may borrow a term from Elizabeth Hardwick, the picture is "willfully vulnerable." It's even insistently vulnerable. All this hanging on may seem a little wan or rather noble, I suppose, depending on the viewer's psychological bent. I don't find it noble, but I was held and affected by the intelligence and skill and conviction that make the movie emotionally all of a piece.

Movies have bypassed this cultivated kind of sensitive fiction, and for reasons — not only because it used to be considered impossible for a large enough movie audience to take to heart emotional problems that are as refined and civilized as these (the characters here are all *coping,* they're not falling apart) but because it's extremely difficult to sustain the literary tone on the screen. It has never been done before — not successfully, that is — and so this movie is instantly recognizable as a classic. It will, I think, have a special lasting value, and it is certainly John Schlesinger's finest work to date. In the past, he has scored what I thought false points and hideously obvious points, and the fact that I could sense that his flash was effective with the audience made it worse for me. I walked out after a half hour of my first Schlesinger film, and I wanted to at the second. I always feel distant from his work; I see him putting it together and I hear it go tick, scratch, tick. In *Sunday Bloody Sunday,* Schlesinger — inspired, one may assume, by the delicate substance of Penelope Gilliatt's screenplay — has lost his stridency. The stresses and tones are adjusted just right, but his new modulated understatement is almost as mechanical as the old overstatement. This movie is superlatively well made. But though I can recognize how good it is, and though I was moved by it, *Sunday Bloody Sunday* is not my kind of movie. Its extreme refinement is capped by a recurrent inexpressibly sad fragment from a Mozart opera, an emblem of culture and restraint. The music didn't have me banging on the walls of my head the way the score for *The Go-Between* did, but it kept me aware of how little rapport I have with the movie's conception of culture.

This picture wouldn't be instantly recognizable as a classic if it weren't in a classic, immaculate style of filmmaking; that is, the preordained, fitted-together modern mosaic. Schlesinger's method of work is so pat it's almost a form of self-deprivation; there's no looseness or flow in this way of working, and no true freedom. *Sunday Bloody Sunday* bears some resemblance to *The Pumpkin Eater* (which also closed in on sensibility), but you weren't always sure what was going on in that movie; it was a very murky picture. And that murkiness was suggestive compared to this set of planted insights. You can practically count the watts in the illuminations.

The scenes are so tight and utilitarian that when the Doctor goes to his nephew's bar mitzvah and the movie lingers on the episode, at first you think "Why is this here?" When this sequence was over, I felt that it was richer in meaning than anything else in the film, *because I didn't know exactly why I was seeing it.* I'm afraid I liked this sequence best because I felt that the prolongation wasn't for a plot point but for its own sake —

because the director wanted it. I liked it because it loused up the dumb symmetry.

Schlesinger has it all — a gift for pacing, the energy to bring all the elements of a movie together — but he uses his technique so that it's just about impossible for you to have any reaction to *Sunday Bloody Sunday* that he hasn't decreed you should. Yet if Schlesinger doesn't stir the aesthetic sense, he does know how to make people feel something, and that's not nothing. This movie is a novel written on film — but truly written on film, in a pungent, slangy style that sounds accurate, not bookish, and with differentiated voices (the Doctor's "frankly"s and "How does that grab you?" are a class away from Alex's "Pack it in"). The movie itself, however, speaks with one voice: the director appears to have blended his own voice with that of the writer. Penelope Gilliatt has done what few people who write for the screen think to do: she has kept her self-respect as a writer, and written not down but up. She has trusted the audience. Miss Gilliatt and I are ships that pass each other in the night every six months. It is a pleasure to salute her on this crossing.*

[October 2, 1971]

Movies in Movies

A lot of people put the blame for the recent rotten pictures on the directors' having too much creative freedom, but what's probably closer to the truth is that the worst pictures have come about because they represent what the movie businessmen think the young audience wants. In the movie-factory days, the studio heads understood how to make acceptable trash; now the businessmen try to imitate the modern and free and avant-garde. They get hacks to imitate artists, and creative freedom is blamed for the results. I stress this point now because I want to praise a movie that is in some ways, and good ways, very old-fashioned — Peter Bogdanovich's *The Last Picture Show*, from the Larry McMurtry novel

---

* Penelope Gilliatt covers movies for *The New Yorker* from April through September; I cover them from October through March. (I filled in for her the week of July 3, 1971.)

— and I want to make sure that this praise for what will probably turn out to be a huge success with both critics and audiences isn't interpreted as a put-down of the talented people whose movies have been chaotic disasters.

The Last Picture Show arrives just when it seemed time to announce that movies as pop culture were dead. The few movies for the mass audience that succeeded were — artistically speaking — so macabre that it was best to forget about them, and the new, smaller movie audience was becoming used to looking for sparks of talent and was learning to reconcile itself to messy, semi-boring, promising failures. I think that maybe everyone who has kept going to the movies has understood that the explosion of forms *is* messy, and has felt the excitement of what was happening. The old commercial crust was being cleaned away. Fiascos like *Drive, He Said* weren't *dead,* in the way that fiascos like *The Last Run* were. And now Bogdanovich has made a film for *everybody* — not just the *Airport* audience but the youth audience and the educated older audience, too. The danger is that *The Last Picture Show,* which is a story about growing up in a small town in Texas in the early fifties — the kind of straightforward, involving, narrative picture that doesn't often get produced anymore — will turn into a bludgeon to beat other filmmakers with.

What makes Bogdanovich's movie about small-town life different from earlier films of the genre, such as *Kings Row* and *Peyton Place,* is an unexpectedly cool naïveté that carries conviction, so that the movie has the effect not of a slick, worked-up, raunchy melodrama about tangled lives but, rather, of something closer to common experience. Even *Kings Row* had the quality of a shocking exposé, though far less than *Peyton Place;* their selling point was that they showed you what was hidden under the surface of a nice clean town. *The Last Picture Show* presents almost as much of the material of standard melodrama, but simply, indicating that in this town it's all visible on the surface. The movie isn't exploitative of human passions or miseries; it doesn't work them up. Bogdanovich is so plain and uncondescending in his re-creation of what it means to be a high-school athlete, of what a country dance hall is like, of the necking in cars and movie houses, and of the desolation that follows high-school graduation that the movie becomes a lovingly exact history of American small-town life. It's a town that could never be mistaken for a wholesome place to grow up in. It's the smallest, bleakest, boringest kind of flatlands town — the kind that has only one street with businesses on it. McMurtry also wrote *Horseman, Pass By,* on which the movie *Hud* was based, and this new movie is set in the same dust-and-oil Texas. But *Hud* was written by Hollywood pros, cast with star personalities, and directed for "meaning" and charge. This time, the author did the script together with the director, and McMurtry's storytelling sense and his feeling for authenticity have been retained. The dialogue is so natural an emanation of the characters that you're hardly aware of it as dialogue. Our recent fiction films — especially those dealing with an earlier America — have become so full of self-hatred that, ironically, it has been only in documentaries, such as Fred Wiseman's, that one could see occasional decent and noble human gestures. This picture doesn't use the past merely to project current attitudes on it. McMurtry's truth is a small one, but Bogdanovich has been faithful to it: the nostalgia of *The Last Picture Show* reflects the need to come to terms with one's own past.

The movie is concerned with adolescent experience seen in terms of flatlands anomie: loneliness, ignorance about sex, confusion about one's aims in life. Sonny (Timothy Bottoms) and Duane (Jeff Bridges) grow into manhood without much in the way of models. The one person they look up to is Sam the Lion (Ben Johnson), a somewhat romanticized father figure, whose three businesses — the all-night café and the pool hall and the movie house — are the source of the only fun in town, and Sam dies just when Sonny needs him most. *The Last Picture Show* has a basic decency of feeling, with people relating to each other, sometimes on very simple levels, and becoming miserable when they can't relate. This is difficult to do now without seeming square or foolishly naïve. It's wonderful to see a movie that is unsophisticated in this sense; Bogdanovich isn't afraid of sentiment, and this lack of fear results in the finest moment in the movie — at the end, a long look at Sonny's suffering face. Though the older women in the town are dealt with sympathetically, the young girls are not; I hope no one tries to make a Women's Lib hanging case out of this. The girls are seen only from the boys' point of view; this is perhaps an indication of McMurtry's and Bogdanovich's limited understanding rather than a deliberately chosen perspective, but truth to one's experience is far more important in a writer and a director than a hollow "fairness" doctrine.

The Last Picture Show is in black-and-white, startlingly eloquent in the exterior views of the town; the black-and-white silhouetting — so that we seem to be looking at a map of life as it was — helps to clarify and stylize the subject matter. It badly needs this stylization, because, of course, this kind of subject matter — a shallow overview of town life — is dangerously close to TV, and especially to the *Peyton Place* TV series.

The proximity is emphasized by the fact that Timothy Bottoms often suggests Ryan O'Neal, but Bottoms is not so self-aware an actor, not so knowing about the effects he's producing; he gives himself over to the role with a beautiful unself-conscious openness. And so, just as most of the material in the movie escapes being cliché, Bottoms escapes being a standard sensitive juvenile. There are other resemblances and reminiscences: Ellen Burstyn, as the town bitch's mother, seems to be playing the Dorothy Malone role; the slutty girl (Cybill Shepherd, a familiar face from magazine covers and commercials) belongs to the world of Gloria Grahame movies; Eileen Brennan, as Genevieve, the waitress, has echoes of many an old-movie good broad. Bogdanovich is effective in using a variety of performers without milking their differences, though I have reservations about the casting of Cloris Leachman as the sex-starved woman — not because she doesn't play it well but because it's such a Cloris Leachman role. The movie is perhaps what TV soap opera would be if it were more honest — if it looked at ordinary experience in a non-exploitative way, if it had observation and humor. It is perhaps an *ideal* TV show.

There is one change in emphasis from novel to movie that fails, maybe because the director was overreaching a bit. In McMurtry's novel, the closing down of the movie theatre represented the end of a way of life. It marked the transition from the few hours at the movies that kids daydreamed on all week to the age of television. (I think one could say it was a transition from — mostly — tinny dreams to no dreams. TV watchers keep it going; there's no interlude for dreaming. And so TV watchers are not romantics.) Part of the authenticity of McMurtry's vision was that the kids lived on whatever movies came to town, because if you spent your youth in a remote small town in a huge, sprawling country the local picture show was all there was. In the novel, when the boys and girls went to the theatre to neck, the picture on the screen was *Storm Warning*, with Doris Day, Ronald Reagan, Steve Cochran, and Ginger Rogers, and Sonny's date fantasized about Sonny's looking like Cochran while Sonny waited for Ginger Rogers to take off her dress, because outside the theatre there was a still of her in her slip. When the movie house closed down, the last picture that was run was an Audie Murphy job called *The Kid from Texas*, with Gale Storm; it was a dog, and the boys — restless because Duane was leaving for Korea — walked out on it. In the film, however, the dating picture is *Father of the Bride*, with Elizabeth Taylor, and there's a coming-attraction poster for John Ford's *Wagonmaster* (with Ben Johnson). And when the theatre closes down, the final picture, from which we see a stirringly heroic clip, is Howard

Hawks' *Red River*. This clip is only a small part of *The Last Picture Show*, but it has a lot of metaphorical weight to it. Sam the Lion, who seems to belong to the stalwart world of movie epics, has already delivered one portentous line that sticks out: "You wouldn't believe how this land has changed." The effect is to suggest a big ironic contrast between the heroism in the movie clip — which appears to stand for an earlier, epic America — and the shoddy, meagre possibilities in the lives of the characters.

But movies don't have this resonance in the lives of the characters. The movies they grew up on were an escape from boredom; even the boring movies were an escape. Looking at Elizabeth Taylor might well make anyone dissatisfied with his lot — she really *was* the most beautiful girl in the world. But to be disconsolate when you're watching *Storm Warning* and waiting for a forty-year-old actress to get down to her slip — well, maybe you have to have seen *Storm Warning* to realize the poignancy of that level of dissatisfaction with your life, and that level is part of the truth of American experience. For several decades, the generally tawdry films we saw week after week contributed to our national identity — such as it was. Now only the counter-culture uses movies (and only a few, key movies) this way — for new heroes, new styles, new attitudes. *The Last Picture Show* is set in the right period; the early fifties marked the beginning of the change. But to use old movies as great heroic myths contrasting with drab lives is to simplify the nature of our moviegoing past.

•

The directors of a few big hits have also become counter-culture heroes, and perhaps the most interesting question posed by Dennis Hopper's *The Last Movie* is not aesthetic but sociological: Is Hopper enough of a hero (because of *Easy Rider*) to get by with this movie? "Last" in the title appears to be used apocalyptically; I think Hopper means to say that there must be no more movies. He seems to have shot several epics. One is about an American film crew (with Sam Fuller as director and Hopper as stuntman) shooting a Western in the Andes of Peru; the natives imitate them and turn moviemaking into a ritual game — the camera is made of bamboo, but the bullets and blows are (maybe; we can't be sure) real. This epic also becomes a Passion movie, with Hopper as the Christ victim of the natives' game. (His Christ looks like William F. Buckley gone hip.) Intercut is a story about a search for gold by Hopper and a buddy, and this story involves a profusion of native whores, plus some rich Americans, an amusingly hokey chanteuse, some sex exhibitions, and a very funny put-on about learning to find gold from *The Treasure of Sierra Madre*. Straight and lampoon blur: Is it a joke when Hopper turns into James Dean? I don't know, and I'm not sure he knows. Smashed together, the themes seem to form a gigantic classic paranoid fantasy, although that is clearly not what the director intended. He intercuts to destroy credibility, and throws in alternate scenes and occasional titles, such as "Scene Missing," so that viewers will not be able to sit back and be "carried away" by a story. Finally, he fractures whatever seemed to be left of the themes. His deliberate disintegration of the story elements he has built up screams at us that, with so much horror in the world, he refuses to entertain us. It would be stupid to deny that there are reasons for screaming, but I doubt if Hopper knows what he wants to do, except not entertain us, and I'm afraid he will interpret the audience's exhaustion from his flailing about as apathy and complacency. This knockabout tragedy is not a vision of the chaos in the world — not a *Weekend,* not a *Shame* — but a reflection of his own confusion. Hopper as Christ is maybe partly put-on, but only partly; Hopper doesn't seem to have a face anymore, only a profile, and he can't take the camera off it. The most embarrassing thing about his Christ bit is not that he has cast himself in the role but that he has so little visual interest in anyone else. The Peruvians in the film are an undifferentiated mass of stupid people; not a face stands out in the crowd scenes except Hopper's — the others are just part of the picturesque background to *his* suffering.

One would have to be playing Judas to the public to advise anyone to go see *The Last Movie.* Hopper may have the makings of a movie (perhaps more than one), but he blew it in the editing room. If he was deliberate in not involving the audience, the audience that is not involved doesn't care whether he was deliberate or not. That there's method in the madness doesn't help. The editing supplies so little in the way of pace or rhythm that this movie performs the astounding feat of dying on the screen in the first few minutes, before the credits come on. *Easy Rider* was heavily indebted to its varied songs, which changed the moods and rhythms; this time Hopper has used lugubrious songs that drag everything down to a standstill. And yet he has an amazing, distinctive visual style; if he could throw away his chop-chop scissors and stop disrupting the flow of images in order to make stupid points about what's real and what's unreal, he might be able to bring something new to movies. This film was shot by Laszlo Kovacs, and perhaps I'm giving Hopper undue credit for Kovacs' work. But I've seen a lot of Kovacs by now, and — though I'm guessing, of course — I think there's also a director's eye at work in these setups and in the palette, which is unlike any movie color I can recall. There's a faint but (I think) fully conscious primitivism in the shots; the color is a cross between the Sierra Club books and Mexican picture-postcard style — greens lush but slightly painted-looking, and with a hint of patterning. It's like exquisite calendar art, and reminiscent of early Miró and of the Juan Gris giant-postcard landscapes. The one thing of value in the movie is Hopper's way of looking at the countryside. But why are we in Peru? His message appears to be about the violence and evil caused by movies. (*Movies?*) But it would be hard to find a place with less evidence of corruption by movies than the Peru he shows us. The people on the Peruvian plains are probably as bored as the people in McMurtry's Texas, but they get few movies. There *is* a good subject in the effects of movies on remote cultures, but Hopper doesn't show the slightest interest in that subject; he's trying to be a social critic without providing any specific social content. It's hysterical to blame the violence in the world on American movies. Hopper seems to have worked up a big head of steam about nothing; with all the horrors there are, he has cooked up fake ones.

Yet I hope this won't actually be Hopper's last movie. He has cast himself as a scapegoat; I hope he doesn't become one. If Bogdanovich replaces Hopper as the hero of the industry — if, to the industry, he becomes the new hot director that everyone should imitate — the most talented moviemakers may be in trouble. Even Nixon could like *The Last Picture Show*. And though it's marvellous to have pictures like that for everyone to enjoy, most of the talented people don't work that way and can't make that kind of movie. But the businessmen seem able to keep only one idea in their heads at a time.

•

Warner Brothers is honoring itself for the release of its fifteen-hundredth motion picture (who's going to count?) with a picture fittingly entitled *Skin Game*. It turns out, however, to be charming — utterly unimportant, but another movie that almost everybody can enjoy. The director, Paul Bogart (a TV veteran), makes no distinctive contribution except for his unlabored, loose approach, but the movie is well written, the whole thing has a good fluky spirit, and the color is sometimes lovely. It's a casual series of jokes about three bunco artists in the Old (pre-Civil War) South — reminiscent of *The Scalphunters* but not as lively. (It lacks those two dynamos Burt Lancaster and Ossie Davis.) The casting is a bit lacklustre. Lou Gossett is pretty good as the Northern city-slicker Negro outwitting the Southern whites, but James Garner carries a TV actor's lassitude into his screen roles; he isn't bad, but his mild pleasantness just isn't enough to command one's full attention. I guess Susan Clark is better than usual (she has some comedy sense), but her attraction — if, indeed, anybody besides movie moguls considers her attractive — eludes me. This example of tall-story Americana, with its punning title, is not much more than an entertaining time killer, but you get a good feeling when you're in an audience that spontaneously breaks into applause for outrageously silly jokes.

[October 9, 1971]

Helen of Troy, Sexual Warrior

The flaws in the Michael Cacoyannis film of Euripides' *The Trojan Women* seem unimportant compared to the simple fact that here is a movie of one of the supreme works of the theatre, and not a disgraceful movie, either. The play is not just the first but the one great anti-war play. What Euripides did was to look at war's other side, and the view from the losing side was not pomp and glory but cruelty and pain. The Trojan women are powerless, defenseless. As Andromache, Hector's widow, says, "I cannot save my child from death. Oh, hide my head for shame . . ." The shame of these captive women is that they can do nothing but yield to the victors. When the play opens, their children have been taken from them and sent to unknown destinations, and the women are waiting to be shipped into slavery; it closes when they have all been consigned and the city is burned. *The Trojan Women* is the greatest lament for the loss of freedom ever written, the greatest lament for the suffering of the victims of war. An Athenian, Euripides staged this profoundly radical play in Athens in 416 B.C., during a long war, only a few months after Athens had conquered a small island in the Aegean that was trying to stay neutral, killing the men and enslaving the women and children. The play might be called *Woman's Fate*. The dramatist's vision of the women whose husbands and sons have been slaughtered is austere and controlled and complete, so that, in a way, he said it all, and for all time. And because he said it all, and yet said it simply, the play is inexorable; we go from step to step until it is all there and the full effect has us by the throat. We knew about the miseries of war before. The play does more than confirm what we knew: it lays it out so clearly that we feel a deeper and higher understanding. Euripides has put it into words for us; he distills the worst that can happen. ("The gods — I prayed, they never listened." "Count no one happy, however fortunate, before he dies.") Despite the makeshift style of the film, one may come out grateful for this clarity, grateful to be caught by the throat, because it has been achieved by the most legitimate of all means — by a drama that states its case, and achieves nobility, through simplicity.

Katharine Hepburn, always forthright, starts as a fine, tough Hecuba, plainspoken and direct, but she comes to seem pitiful and mummified. Too many "O sorrow"s and references to her old gray head, and your mind begins to wander, asking vagrant questions such as "Why are all the women listening to the Queen — don't they have troubles enough of their own?" That is to say, you stop accepting the classical stage convention of the chorus and ask the questions you normally ask at movies. Actually, Euripides was so acutely sensible that within the convention of the chorus he provided the answers to one's natural questions. But in the movie the chorus, instead of going through their own hells, appear to be passive witnesses to Hecuba's, and she, instead of expressing the emotions of all of them, seems to be speaking of her own grief only, and her voice begins to seem thin and querulous. Hepburn is splendid when she's angry — when she has an antagonist. Perhaps our awareness of her as Hepburn makes us a little impatient with the weak, resigned side of the character.

A false nose (a trifle pale but very becoming) gives Genevieve Bujold's mad seeress Cassandra. a classical look, and Bujold is becoming a daring and fascinating actress. She stretches the traditional sensitive-young-actress effects with a bursting conviction that they are good effects, and by strength of will, makes some of them work. That her performance doesn't come off is probably not entirely her fault. The role is the least modern, and the hokiest, in the play — Cassandra's virginal oaths and her prophecies don't mean much to us — and Cacoyannis has staged it with Ophelia-like flutters and with so much camera and chorus commotion that the narrative line goes out of whack. Bujold makes a stunning try, however, especially in her final fit. This performance is a leap in her career; her ambitiousness in tackling a role like this suggests prodigies ahead.

As Andromache, Vanessa Redgrave — that great goosey swan of the screen — fares better. Andromache is not as showy a role as Cassandra; it is written in a no-frills, clear-purpose style that pushes the narrative forward, and Redgrave's Andromache is magnificently uncomplicated. There are those who think that Vanessa Redgrave is a bad screen actress — that she jumps out of the screen at you, that she's always acting and does not allow you to *discover* anything in her performances. I think she *is* always acting, always "on." Though many moviegoers would probably be happy just to bask in her goddess image, she insists on doing something for them, on giving them the most imaginative performance she can. It's true one could look into Garbo, whereas Redgrave often seems to be staring one down, but there's a marvellous romantic excitement about this woman, because one never knows what audacity she will attempt, what heights she'll scale. This may prevent unconscious involvement, because we are always conscious of a *performance,* but our conscious involvement in the tension she creates has its own kind of excitement. She seems to act with her whole soul: you don't see her as a woman trying to play a role — the woman has been consumed by the determination to give the role all she has. Vanessa Redgrave never does the expected, and is never sloppy or overexpressive. Her Andromache is being freshly thought out while we watch — a dazed, pale-golden matron, unflirtatious, enough like Hepburn to suggest that Hector chose her because she was as free from guile and as naturally regal as his mother. Redgrave holds us by the quiet power of her concentration; she does odd little things — a tiny half sob gurgles from her throat. As an actress, she is such an embodiment of the idealistic, romantic spirit that I find myself rooting for her when she reaches for something new and difficult. There is a long meant-to-sound-wild cry when she is told that her child is to be slaughtered. She brings the cry to a sensational screaming finish; I realized I was hoping that others hadn't noticed how carefully it had begun. (Only once have I stopped rooting for her: I thought her dancing in *The Loves of Isadora* unforgivable, because she lacked the fluidity and lyricism to transform calisthenics into dance.)

Vanessa Redgrave gives the finest performance in the movie, but Cacoyannis demonstrates his love of the material, and his right to film it, in casting her as Andromache, and not in the obvious role for her — Helen. Because it is Irene Papas as Helen of Troy who cancels out the clichés of the legend and lifts the movie right out of the women's-college virtuous cultural ambience that plagues stage productions. *The Trojan Women* is not just a plainsong elegy disguised as a play. Euripides gave it one great melodramatic stroke. Helen, the adulterous wife of King Menelaus of Sparta, she whose flight with Paris, Prince of Troy, precipitated the war, is among the Trojan women survivors. The women would kill her if she were not protected from them by guards. Papas's Helen is a force of nature — a greedy woman who wants what she wants and who means to live. She has the vitality of a natural aggressor. She is first introduced prowling behind the slats of the stockade that protects her, and all we see are her brown-black eyes, as fiercely alive as a wolf's. While the other women mourn their dead, Helen uses all her animal cunning to survive. Cacoyannis makes the point that she is not defenseless — that the ruthless have weapons that the righteous don't have. Irene Papas is on her own turf in this play, and her Helen is a great winner — right there in the flesh. This Helen breathes sexuality; she is not merely a beauty but the strongest woman one has ever seen, and the more seductive because of her strength. You can *believe* that men would kill for her. She is not merely the cause of war, she is the spirit of war. When Hecuba says, "Fires comes from her to burn homes," it is perfectly plausible. The words of Andromache that seem like rhetoric on the page are given body:

> O Helen,
> many the fathers you were born of,
> Madness, Hatred, Red Death,
>   whatever poison
> the earth brings forth — God curse
>   you,
> with those beautiful eyes that
>   brought to shame and ruin
> Troy's far-famed plains.

The phrasing of the speeches is not always satisfying, however, and ends of phrases get swallowed when the characters are especially upset or are in motion. These variations in audibility may make the play superficially lifelike on the screen, but we regret not hearing all the words. And why oh why was the movie shot in the kind of muted dark color that dummies think is right for tragedy? The drained, gloomy spectrum looks like stage lighting. An even more fundamental problem is Cacoyannis's sense of movement and place. In a movie, before characters enter a room we are customarily shown their arrival on the street and at the house and sometimes in the foyer or a passageway. This isn't mere filler. In the live theatre, we know exactly where the characters are — they're on that stage right in front of us. But at movies we seem to need to get our bearings — to know where people are coming from and where they're going and where things are happening. Most of the time, movies provide this information and we take it in unconsciously. When we don't get it, the movie appears to be impoverished and *stagy*. When people enter and leave an area that we cannot locate in terms of surrounding areas, the area is, inescapably, stage space, and we become even more aware of this when the area is outdoors — and therefore unconfined — than when it's indoors. Everything in *The Trojan Women* is outdoors, and yet the movie is claustrophobic, because the locations — the harbor, Cassandra's cave, a field of corpses, and so on — have no more connection with each other than if they were stage sets replacing each other. I would guess that Cacoyannis was working on a relatively small budget and had to piece his Troy together from bits of Spain. But, with all consideration made for the problem, the fact is that he didn't solve it. And he doesn't seem to know how to use the ground he's got. You're not sure where the people are in relation to each other even when they're in the same shot.

It obviously took extraordinary dedication and talent to make this movie — to inspire the actresses to test themselves, and to coach them and blend their voices so that an American, a French-Canadian, and an Englishwoman become acceptable as a family. Yet I question whether a director with so little feeling for the most basic elements of moviemaking can ever be a good movie director. A director with a "film sense" knows where to put the camera so that you don't question the shot; for others every setup looks arbitrary. This play demands a plain, consistent cinematic style, with no flourishes — a style as supremely matter-of-fact as Euripides' language. Cacoyannis tries to make the movie impressive — there's embalming fluid in the images — and the tragic line breaks down into sequences. Some are derivative, such as the whirling camera when Cassandra spins about, the cacophonous music and fast cuts when the chorus is distraught; some are effective in an overly prestigious way, such as the freeze frames in the opening sequence while the narrator speaks — like the breaks for words in Stravinsky's *Oedipus Rex*. These are the attempts of a man without a film sense to make a drama cinematic; it winds up an anthology of second-rate film styles.

One may long for the ideal — for a great play transformed by a great movie artist into a great movie. But great movie artists are not often tempted to tackle great plays, and when they do, it sometimes turns out that they don't have the right skills. Short of the ideal, what it comes down to is whether in seeing a movie version one can still respond to what makes the play great. By that standard, I count the Cacoyannis film a success. Even if one is aware of everything the matter with it, the emotion of the play gets to you, and the emotion of Greek tragedy has a purity that you *can't get from anything else.* That's a very good reason to make a movie — to bring people the emotions that only a few in our time have experienced in the theatre. (And the productions they see are flawed and stilted, too — though, of course, in different ways.) Beautiful as the Edith Hamilton translation is, the movie has something you can't get from a reading: Irene Papas's Helen is a demonic illumination of the text. I think one would have to be maybe a little foolish to let aesthetic scruples about the movie's mediocrity as cinema deprive one of seeing *The Trojan Women* with a cast that one could never hope to see on the stage. The actresses come from different cultures, but they bring intensity of life to the screen; that's what makes them stars. If a movie releases that intensity, it hasn't bungled what matters most.

[October 16, 1971]

Louis Malle's Portrait of the Artist as a Young Dog

Murmur of the Heart is mellow and smooth, like a fine old jazz record, but when it's over it has the kick of a mule — a *funny* kick, which sends you out doubled over grinning. Assured and unflamboyant in technique, it is yet an exhilarating film — an irresistible film, one might say if one had not heard word of some resistance, especially by the jury at Cannes, which chose to ignore it, managing even to pass over Lea Massari's full-scale portrait of the carelessly sensual mother of a bourgeois brood of sons in favor of Kitty Winn's drab, meagre-spirited performance in *The Panic in Needle Park.* Massari's Clara is a woman without discretion or calculation; she's shamelessly loose and free, and she's loved by her sons because of her indifference to the bourgeois forms, which they nevertheless accept — on the surface, that is. What makes this movie so different from other movies about bourgeois life is that the director, Louis Malle, sees not only the prudent, punctilious surface but the volatile and slovenly life underneath. He looks at this bourgeois bestiary and sees it as funny and appalling and also — surprisingly — hardy and happy. It is perhaps the first time on film that anyone has shown us the bourgeoisie *enjoying* its privileges.

From the way Malle observes the sex education of the youngest, brightest son of the family, fourteen-year-old Laurent (Benoit Ferreux), one knows that the movie is a portrait of the artist as a young dog. It comes after a succession of Malle films, but in its subject, and in the originality and the special sure-footedness that the director (who also wrote the script) brings to the material, it is, clearly, the obligatory first film. The picture is set in Dijon — also the setting for Malle's *The Lovers* — in 1954, at the time of Dien Bien Phu (which must have been only a few years after the director's schoolboy days), and before the children of the bourgeoisie became radicalized. Though the film itself reveals the sources of Malle's humor, this story probably wouldn't have been nearly so funny or, perhaps, so affectionate if Malle had told it fifteen years ago. It is a film by someone who doesn't have to simplify in order to take a stand, who no longer needs to rebel; he has come a distance, and the story is additionally distanced by the changes in French student life that Godard recorded in *Masculine Feminine* and *La Chinoise*. In 1954, the sons of the successful gynecologist (Daniel Gélin) and the Italian-born Clara could still enjoy their wealth as their due. Seen with the vivacity of fresh intelligence, they're a family of monsters, all right, but normal monsters — no more monstrous than other close-knit families — and they're happy hypocrites.

I'm not sure how the picture was sustained and brought off so that we see the stuffiness and snobbery of the privileged class on the outside and the energetic amorality underneath, but the story moves toward its supremely logical yet witty and imaginative conclusion so stealthily that the kicker joke is perfect. Advance word had suggested that the picture was a serious, shocking view of incest, but the only shock is the joke that, for all the repressions these bourgeois practice and the conventions they pretend to believe in, they are such amoral, instinct-satisfying creatures that incest doesn't mean any more to them than to healthy animals. The shock is that in this context incest *isn't* serious — and that, I guess, may really upset some people, so they won't be able to laugh.

I can't remember another movie in which family life and adolescence have been used for such high comedy. The details are as singular, as deeply rooted in the period and the place, as the details in Truffaut's *The 400 Blows,* and the picture has that kind of candor. But no one in the film requires sympathy. Malle's approach has some of Buñuel's supple objectivity and aberrant humor. Malle satirizes the family from inside as Buñuel satirizes Catholicism from inside. The boys casually loot their own home, turn the dining room into a tennis court with a ball of spinach. Members of the family tease and squabble, but they enjoy the squabbling, because it is part of their intimacy and their security. Home is chaos; the three boys are not subdued even when there are guests. The vinegar-face father, severe and disgusted, though in a sort of ineffectual, ritualistic way, is tolerant — perhaps even, like the old family servant, proud that his boys are such irresponsible, uncontrollable *boys*. They're expensive pets, expected to commit outrages, and also expected to shape up eventually. In a poor environment, the boys would be brats, or even punks and delinquents; here they're the young masters. Papa's distaste is amusing, and the boys goad him; the grumblings of a put-upon father are a reassuring sound. And when you're furious with a brother, he's still a brother, and you have the pride and safety in that that you can never feel when you quarrel with those outside the family. This movie catches the way people care about each other in a family, and the feeling of a household in which there's no discipline. Which I think is probably generally the case but is something that movies like to lie about. The mixture of contempt and affection that the boys feel toward the old servant is so accurate — even if one has never been near a fuddy-duddy family retainer — that it sweeps away all those false, properly respected movie servants.

The only quality common to the films of Louis Malle is the restless intelligence one senses in them, and it must be this very quality that has led Malle to try such different subjects and styles. A new Chabrol or a Losey is as easily recognizable as a Magritte, but even film enthusiasts have only a vague idea of Malle's work. Had Malle gone on making variations of almost any one of his films, it is practically certain he would have been acclaimed long ago, but a director who is impatient and dissatisfied and never tackles the same problem twice gives reviewers trouble and is likely to be dismissed as a dilettante. Malle, though he is still under forty, predates the New Wave, and has made amazingly good films in several styles. Born in 1932, he was co-director with Cousteau of *The Silent World,* then assistant to Bresson on *A Man Escaped,* and then, in

1957, at twenty-five, he made his first film, the ingenious, slippery thriller *Lift to the Scaffold* (also called *Frantic*), with Maurice Ronet and Jeanne Moreau, and a Miles Davis score. The following year, he had his biggest American success — *The Lovers*, with its flowing rhythms and its Brahms, the message of woman's desire for sexual fulfillment and the wind rippling through Moreau's white chiffon. It was facile movie-poetry but erotic and beautifully made. In 1960, he did a flipover to *Zazie dans le Métro*, from the Queneau novel — a fiendishly inventive slapstick comedy about a foulmouthed little girl, which was too fast and too freakish for American tastes, so that Americans did not credit Malle with the innovative editing, and later gave the credit instead to Tony Richardson's *Tom Jones* and to Richard Lester and others. *Zazie*, a comedy that owed a debt to Tati but carried Tati's dry, quick style to nightmarish anxiety, included satirical allusions to *La Dolce Vita* and *The Lovers*. After the wild *Zazie* came *Vie Privée*, with Brigitte Bardot and about her life as a sex-symbol star. *Le Feu Follet*, in 1963, the film that first convinced me that Malle was a superb director, shows the influence of Bresson but is without the inhuman pride that I think poisons so much of Bresson's later work. *Le Feu Follet* (sometimes called *The Fire Within*) has been seen by few people in this country. It received some generous reviews (especially in *The New Yorker*), and no one appears to be very clear about the reasons for its commercial failure — whether it got snarled in distribution problems or whether the film was simply "not commercial" in American terms. An elegy for a wasted life, adapted by Malle from a thirties novel, it dealt with the forty-eight hours before the suicide of a dissolute playboy (Maurice Ronet again) who, at thirty, has outlived his boyish charm and his social credit. It is a study of despair with no possibility of relief; the man has used up his slim resources and knows it. He does not want to live as what he has become; his taste is too good. It was directed in a clean, deliberate style, with a lone piano playing Satie in the background. Genêt wrote of the director, "He has effected something phenomenal this time, having turned literature into film, photographed the meaning of an unsubstantial, touching, and rather famous book, and given its tragic intention a clarity it never achieved in print." And Brendan Gill said, "Between them, Malle and Ronet have composed a work as small and vast, as affecting, and, I think, as permanent as Fitzgerald's *Babylon Revisited*." It was a masterly film, and it seemed almost inconceivable that a director still so young could produce a work about such anguish with such control. *Le Feu Follet* should have made Malle's reputation here — in the way that *L'Avventura* made Antonioni's. After that painful, claustrophobic film, Malle did another flip, to the outdoors and the New World — to the frivolous, picaresque *Viva Maria!*, set in the Latin America of La Belle Epoque, with Moreau and Bardot. At the opening, the child who will become Bardot helps her imperialist-hating father dynamite a British fortress in Ireland, and the contrast between the father's act and the child's blooming, innocent happiness as she plays in the fields planting explosives is rapturously comic. *Viva Maria!* was lavish and visually beautiful, but the subsequent bombings and shootings weren't so funny; the central conceit involved in the pairing of Bardot and Moreau didn't work out, so the slapstick facetiousness was just left there, with nothing under it. But Bardot — not because of any *acting* — has never been more enchanting than in parts of this movie. When Malle put her into boys' clothes, with a cap and a smudge on her cheek, she was a tomboy looking for fun: Zazie grown up but still polymorphously amoral. After *The Thief of Paris,* with Jean-Paul Belmondo, Malle went to India, where he shot documentaries, the most famous of which, *Calcutta,* has never opened in New York.*

The director travelled a long road before looking into his own back yard; now, when he goes back to it in *Murmur of the Heart,* we can see in that gleeful, chaotic household the origins of the radiant prankishness of *Zazie* and *Viva Maria!* and of those riffs that don't stop for breath, and we can see the sources of the studied, overblown romanticism of *The Lovers,* and also of the caustic view of romanticism in the great *Le Feu Follet.* I don't think *Murmur of the Heart* is a greater film than *Le Feu Follet,* but in excluding all joy that film was a very special sort of film: getting so far inside a suicide's attitude toward himself can really wipe viewers out. This is a joyous and accessible work, and so the anguish of *Le Feu Follet* begins to seem youthful — like an early spiritual crisis that has been resolved. Although *Murmur of the Heart* is obviously semi-autobiographical, it's a movie not about how one has been scarred but about how one was formed. You can see that Malle is off the hook by the justice he does to the other characters. (The only character that seems to me a failure and no more than a stereotype is the lecherous priest, played by Michel Lonsdale.)

Lea Massari (she was the girl who disappeared in *L'Avventura*) has, as Clara, the background of a libertarian father — reminiscent of Bardot's background in *Viva Maria!* Clara says she grew up "like a savage," and

---

* *Calcutta* was shown on Channel 13 in New York early in December, followed by *The Impossible Camera* — the first in a series of seven films that make up *Phantom India.* All eight later opened in a theatre.

when she smiles her irregular teeth show her to be a spiritual relative of the impudent Zazie. Malle's films have swung back and forth between the eroticism of the Moreau characters and the anarchic, childish humor of the Zazies; Massari's ravishing Clara combines them. Her relaxed sensuality is the essence of impropriety. There is a moment when Clara, who has blithely remarked to her sons as they watch her changing clothes, "I simply have no modesty," catches Laurent peeping at her in her bath. She instinctively slaps him; he is deeply offended, and she apologizes and says he should have slapped her back. This many-layered confusion of principle and hypocrisy and instinct and injustice is one of the rare occasions when a movie has shown how knotted the ties of family life really are for most of us. Clara comes alive because of that freak bit of Zazie in her; she will never grow up and become the mature mother of simplified fiction. She is not one of those Fay Bainter mothers, born at forty full of wisdom and christened "Mother."

As for Laurent — or Renzino, as Clara calls him — Benoit Ferreux probably is only about fourteen, but, without being fey, he looks enough like the Lauren Bacall of an earlier era to hold the camera in a vise, and he appears to have an impeccable sense of what's wanted. You're never quite sure how you feel about Laurent. His musical tastes — Charlie Parker and the other jazz greats we hear on the track — are irreproachable, and, in their irreproachability, marks of fashion and caste. He's extraordinarily clever, but he's also an arrogant, precocious little snot who thinks that people were put in the world to serve him; he despises a snob Fascist boy because the boob hasn't mastered the right tone — the acceptable amount of snobbery. The movie is about the childhood and growing into manhood of those who are pampered from birth, and at every step it shows what they take for granted. It defines the ways in which the rich are not like you and me, and the ways in which they are. Malle resembles Fitzgerald, but a Fitzgerald with a vision formed from the inside, and with the intelligence for perspective. His is a deeply realistic comic view — free of Fitzgerald's romantic ruined dreams. In pulling his different styles together in *Murmur of the Heart,* Malle finds a new ripe vein of comedy: believable comedy; that is to say, life seen in its comic aspects. There's a sequence in which smart Laurent outsmarts himself: he attempts to disrupt a meeting that his mother is having with her lover, and his intrusion results in her going off with the lover for a few days. When it comes to family ties and basic affections and how to lose one's virginity, even the smart and the dumb aren't so very far apart.

•

The Russian film *The Début*, about a plain girl who is desperately determined to become an actress and is selected to star in a movie about Joan of Arc, is pleasant, though not a complete success. The script doesn't go far enough in developing the possibilities we see in the girl. As Inna Churikova plays Pasha, who is as intense when she goes after a man as she is about having a career, Pasha is the stuff actresses are made of — actresses like Helen Hayes and Julie Harris, who are transformed onstage, some by will and energy, others by will and talent. But, as the story turns out, she isn't *meant* to be a girl who becomes that appealing-mouse kind of actress — she's meant to be a sad-sack factory girl deluded about her talent. The story declines into implausible, none too lucid ironies — contrasts between Pasha's love life and Joan of Arc's suffering — and then into the bewildering notion that Pasha can't get work after her starring role. What happened? Was the film a success or a failure? In the clips from *Joan of Arc* that are intercut, Pasha is a spellbinder; we can't believe that nothing results from her performance. The sequence of events doesn't add up right, and at the end the audience is left to invent explanations for the confusion. But the picture (which is of some mild sociological interest, in the views of living arrangements, clothing, makeup, and so on) is worth seeing as a showcase for Inna Churikova. Pasha's face tells you everything and yet is totally, mysteriously closed, and her toothy, gummy smile is peculiarly mirthless. She's rather an awful girl, and you don't want to take your eyes off her. In one sequence, at a dance, Pasha stands among the girls waiting for partners; although her feet are still, her head and shoulders are already dancing in anticipation, and her yearning grace makes this scene perhaps the best of its kind since Katharine Hepburn in her organdie sat eager and desperate at the party in *Alice Adams*, trying to get rid of her wilted violets. That's probably enough reason to see *The Début*, though the picture, directed by Gleb Panfilov in rather grayish black-and-white, is padded out with so much of the *Joan of Arc* spectacle that you may begin to wonder if it wasn't concocted to use the footage of a misbegotten epic.

•

T. R. Baskin is ludicrously bad, and since the fault starts with the preposterously literary, essentially idiotic script, the first questions that come to mind are: Did anybody read it? How could it possibly have been produced — and in the glossy, impersonal style of a handsome budget? Since the writer was also the producer, I doubt if there was anything the director, Herbert Ross, could have done that would have made a measurable difference, though he certainly isn't given much help by its star, that toothpaste-goddess Candice Bergen, in clothes by Sacher-Masoch, playing a misunderstood girl.

The movie is about depersonalization — women's department, this time. (I should hate to think that some women might take this film for an *advance*.) T. R. Baskin (Miss Bergen) leaves her family, in a small town in Ohio, and moves to Chicago, where she gets a typing job in a giant corporation and encounters dimwitted human robots and rich reactionary creeps. The howler is that Miss Bergen (she is no actress and T. R. Baskin is not a character anyway, so let's drop the fiction) spouts — and that is how she delivers her lines, pell-mell, as if vastly pleased that she remembered them — a fully articulated women's-liberation position. And since (except for a one-night stand with a publisher, played by James Caan) she has no contact with anyone who thinks as she does, or thinks at all, she appears to be alienated not because of the quality of urban life but because she is so much smarter and more liberal than anyone else. She appears to be alienated because she's a liberal and a women's liberationist in a world with no others. You keep thinking, If she could just get away from those dumb girls at the office (doing jobs that one suspects have actually been taken over by computers) and get a job on a newspaper or at a college, or latch onto a women's-liberation group, she'd be fine. She simply seems to be in the wrong place. And how she worked out her advanced, left position all by herself, without contact with books or magazines, or even TV, is an enigma. It's the equivalent of making a movie about an ordinary black boy from Mississippi who arrives in Atlanta, gets a job as a busboy at the Regency Hyatt House Hotel, and, although there is no civil-rights movement, talks like an epigrammatic Julian Bond. Nobody understands what he's talking about, and so he's lonely and alienated.

Since there's not one believable moment in the artificial situation, probably the best thing the director could have done would have been to play the script for some sort of screwball-comedy effect. But for that you need players. I was never a devotee of the arch style of Irene Dunne, who always cued the audience on what lines were meant to be funny, but in this movie we could use that kind of cueing. The dialogue is one-easy-piece dialogue — pinhead alienation and, even worse, alienation *feminized* — turned into whimsey. The milieu of the picture is not the urban crisis but mechanization of the kind that playwrights like Karel Čapek and Elmer Rice wrote about — the kind that turns people into units. The Chicago of the movie is so shiny and prosperous and works so perfectly that one would think that the old sci-fi vision of the sanitized future had actually come about. Peter Boyle, of *Joe,* is Mr. Sad Middle America, the man who lives to retire; he owns lots in Florida in this one, too. Miss Bergen, vacuously superior and cool and expensively turned out, spends most of the movie pitying him. Boyle's performance is grotesquely earnest, while she is so odd when she tries to act that you don't know if the character is meant to be loused up, or what is going on; hysterical laughing scenes are becoming her specialty, and when she has a hysterical laughing scene, it's hysterical, all right.

This is, I believe, Miss Bergen's ninth picture; she is playing the *lead.* It is the worst starring performance I have ever seen. In an acting contest between her and Ali MacGraw, Ali MacGraw would win. Candice Bergen gives evidence of intelligence and humor in print and on television; she probably has more of each than most actresses have. But what she does in *T. R. Baskin* is an embarrassment to the audience. And the attempt to dress up her perky movements and lopsided lope in a sexually ambiguous wardrobe — camel's-hair coats and glorified Peter Pan collars — as if to turn her into a Hepburn or a Garbo, just makes one aware of how immense the distance is. She comes closer to being a starched Lizabeth Scott — a stiff.

[October 23, 1971]

Urban Gothic

When Mayor Lindsay began his efforts to attract the movie-production business, it probably didn't occur to him or his associates that they were ushering in a new movie age of nightmare realism. The Los Angeles area was selected originally for the sunshine and so that the movie-business hustlers — patent-violators who were pirating inventions as well as anything else they could get hold of — could slip over the border fast. As it turned out, however, California had such varied vegetation that it could be used to stand in for most of the world, and there was space to build whatever couldn't be found. But New York City is always New York City; it can't be anything else, and, with practically no studios for fakery, the movie companies use what's really here, so the New York–made movies have been set in Horror City. Although recent conflicts between the producers and the New York unions seem to have ended this Urban Gothic period,* the New York–made movies have provided a permanent record of the city in breakdown. I doubt if at any other time in American movie history there has been such a close relationship between the life on the screen and the life of a portion of the audience. Los Angeles–made movies were not *about* Los Angeles; often they were not about any recognizable world. But these recent movies are about New York, and the old sentimentalities are almost impossible here — physically impossible, because the city gives them the lie. (I'm thinking of such movies as *Klute, Little Murders, The Anderson Tapes, Greetings, The Landlord, Where's Poppa?, Midnight Cowboy, Harry Kellerman, Diary of a Mad Housewife, No Way to Treat a Lady, Shaft, Cotton Comes to Harlem, The Steagle, Cry Uncle, The Owl and the Pussycat, The Panic in Needle Park, Bananas,* and the forthcoming *Born to Win.*) The city of New York has helped American movies grow up; it has also given movies a new spirit of nervous, anxious hopelessness, which is the true spirit of New York. It is literally true that when you live in New York you no longer believe that the garbage will ever be gone from the streets or that life will ever be sane and orderly.

The movies have captured the soul of this city in a way that goes beyond simple notions of realism. The panhandler in the movie who jostles the hero looks just like the one who jostles you as you leave the movie theatre; the police sirens in the movie are screaming outside; the hookers and junkies in the freak show on the screen are indistinguishable from the ones in the freak show on the streets. Famous New York put-on artists and well-known street people are incorporated in the movies; sometimes they are in the movie theatre, dressed as they are in the movie, and sometimes you leave the theatre and see them a few blocks away, just where they were photographed. There's a sense of carnival about this urban-crisis city; everyone seems to be dressed for a mad ball. Screams in the theatre at Halloween movies used to be a joke, signals for laughter and applause, because nobody believed in the terror on the screen. The midnight showings of horror films now go on all year round, and the screams are no longer pranks. Horror stories and brutal melodramas concocted for profit are apparently felt on a deeper level than might have been supposed. People don't laugh or applaud when there's a scream;

---

* After two and a half months, the five major companies signed an agreement with the unions and production in New York was resumed.

they try to ignore the sound. It is assumed that the person yelling is stoned and out of control, or crazy and not to be trifled with — he may want an excuse to blow off steam, he may have a knife or a gun. It is not uncommon now for fights and semi-psychotic episodes to take place in the theatres, especially when the movies being played are shockers. Audiences for these movies in the Times Square area and in the Village are highly volatile. Probably the unstable, often dazed members of the audiences are particularly susceptible to the violence and tension on the screen; maybe crowds now include a certain number of people who simply can't stay calm for two hours. But whether the movies bring it out in the audience or whether the particular audiences that are attracted bring it into the theatre, it's *there* in the theatre, particularly at late shows, and you feel that the violence on the screen may at any moment touch off violence in the theatre. The audience is explosively *live*. It's like being at a prizefight or a miniature Altamont.

Horror is very popular in Horror City — old horror films and new ones. The critics were turned off by the madness of *The Devils;* the audiences were turned on by it. They wanted the benefits of the sexual pathology of religious hysteria: bloody tortures, burning flesh, nuns violated on altars, lewd nuns stripping and orgying, and so on. Almost all the major movie companies are now, like the smaller ones, marginal businesses. The losses of the American film industry since 1968 are calculated at about five hundred and twenty-five million dollars. Besides Disney, the only company that shows profits is A.I.P. — the producers of ghouls-on-wheels schlock pictures, who are now also turning out movies based on Gothic "classics." I don't believe that people are going to shock and horror films because of a need to exorcise their fears; that's probably a fable. I think they're going for entertainment, and I don't see how one can ignore the fact that the kind of entertainment that attracts them now is often irrational and horrifyingly brutal. A few years ago, *The Dirty Dozen* turned the audience on so high that there was yelling in the theatre and kicking at the seats. And now an extraordinarily well-made new thriller gets the audience sky-high and keeps it up there — *The French Connection,* directed by William Friedkin, which is one of the most "New York" of all the recent New York movies. It's also probably the best-made example of what trade reporters sometimes refer to as "the cinema du zap."

How's this for openers? A peaceful day in Marseille. A *flic* strolls into a boulangerie, comes out carrying a long French bread, and strolls home. As he walks into his own entranceway, a waiting figure in a leather coat sticks out an arm with a .45 and shoots him in the face and then in the torso. The assassin picks up the bread, breaks off a piece to munch, and tosses the remainder back onto the corpse. That's the first minute of *The French Connection*. The film then jumps to New York and proceeds through chases, pistol-whippings, slashings, beatings, murders, snipings, and more chases for close to two hours. The script, by Ernest Tidyman (who wrote *Shaft*), is based on the factual account by Robin Moore (of *The Green Berets*) of the largest narcotics haul in New York police history until the recent Jaguar case. The producer, Philip D'Antoni, also produced *Bullitt*, and the executive producer was G. David Schine, of Cohn and Schine. That's not a creative team, it's a consortium. The movie itself is pretty businesslike. There are no good guys in this harsh new variant of cops-and-robbers; *The French Connection* features the latest-model sadistic cop, Popeye (Gene Hackman). It's undeniably gripping, slam-bang, fast, charged with suspense, and so on — a mixture of *Razzia* and *Z*, and hyped up additionally with a television-thriller-style score that practically lays you out all by itself. At one point, just in case we might lose interest if we didn't have our minute-to-minute injections of excitement, the camera cuts from the street conversation of a few cops to show us the automobile smashup that brought them to the scene, and we are treated to two views of the bloody faces of fresh corpses. At first, we're confused as to who the victims are, and we stare at them thinking they must be characters in the movie. It takes a few seconds to realize that they bear no relation whatsoever to the plot.

It's no wonder that *The French Connection* is a hit, but what in hell is it? It uses eighty-six separate locations in New York City — so many that it has no time for carnival atmosphere: it crashes right through. I suppose the answer we're meant to give is that it's an image of the modern big city as Inferno, and that Popeye is an Existential hero, but the movie keeps zapping us. Though *The French Connection* achieves one effect through timing and humor (when the French Mr. Big, played by Fernando Rey, outwits Popeye in a subway station by using his silver-handled umbrella to open the train doors) most of its effects are of the *Psycho*-derived blast-in-the-face variety. Even the expert pacing is achieved by somewhat questionable means; the ominous music keeps tightening the screws and heating things up. The noise of New York already has us tense. The movie is like an aggravated case of New York: it raises this noise level to produce the kind of painful tension that is usually described as almost unbearable suspense. But it's the same kind of suspense you feel when someone outside your window keeps pushing down on the car horn and you think the blaring sound is going to drive you out of your skull. This horn routine is, in fact, what the cop does throughout the longest chase sequence. The movie's suspense is magnified by the sheer pounding abrasiveness of its means; you don't have to be an artist or be original or ingenious to work on the raw nerves of an audience this way — you just have to be smart and brutal. The high-pressure methods that one could possibly accept in Z because they were tools used to try to show the audience how a Fascist conspiracy works are used as ends in themselves. Despite the dubious methods, the purpose of the brutality in Z was moral — it was to make you hate brutality. Here you love it, you wait for it — that's all there is. I know that there are many people — and very intelligent people, too — who love this kind of fast-action movie, who say that this is what movies do best and that this is what they really want when they go to a movie. Probably many of them would agree with everything I've said but will still love the movie. Well, it's not what I want, and the fact that Friedkin has done a sensational job of direction just makes that clearer. It's not what I want not because it fails (it doesn't fail) but because of what it is. It is, I think, what we once feared mass entertainment might become: jolts for jocks. There's nothing in the movie that you enjoy thinking over afterward — nothing especially clever except the timing of the subway-door-and-umbrella sequence. Every other effect in the movie — even the climactic car-versus-runaway-elevated-train chase — is achieved by noise, speed, and brutality.

On its own terms, the picture makes few mistakes, though there is one small but conspicuous one. A good comic contrast of drug dealers dining at their ease in a splendid restaurant while the freezing, hungry cops who are tailing them curse in a cold doorway and finally eat a hunk of pizza is spoiled because, for the sake of a composition with the two groups in the same shot, the police have been put where the diners could obviously see them. It is also a mistake, I think, that at the end the picture just stops instead of coming to a full period. The sloppy plotting, on the other hand, doesn't seem to matter; it's amazing how much implausibility speed and brutality can conceal. Hitchcock's thrillers were full of holes, but you were having too good a time to worry about them; *The French Connection* is full of holes, but mostly you're too stunned to notice them. There's no logic in having the Lincoln Continental that has been shipped from France with the heroin inside abandoned on a back street at night rather than parked snugly in the garage of its owner's hotel; it appears to be on the street just so the narcotics agents can spot it and grab it. There's an elaborate sequence of an auction at an automobile graveyard which serves no clear purpose. And if you ever think about it you'll realize that you have no idea who that poor devil was who got shot in the overture, or why. For all the movie tells you, it may have been for his French bread. But you really know what it's all in there for. It's the same reason you get those juicy pictures of the corpses: zaps.

Listen to Popeye's lines and you can learn the secrets of zap realism. A crude writer can give his crummy, cheap jokes to a crude character, and the jokes really pay off. The rotten jokes get laughs and also show how ugly the character's idea of humor is. Popeye risks his life repeatedly and performs fabulously dangerous actions, yet the movie debases him in every possible way. Hackman has turned himself into a modern Ted Healy type — porkpie hat, sneaky-piggy eyes, and a gut-first walk, like Robert Morley preceded by his belly coming toward us in those BOAC "Visit Britain" commercials. Popeye (the name is out of Faulkner, I assume) has a filthy mouth and a complete catalogue of race prejudices, plus some "cute" fetishes; e.g., he cases girls who wear boots. He is the anti-hero carried to a new lumpenprole low — the mean cop who used to figure on the fringes of melodrama (as in *Sweet Smell of Success*) moved to the center. Sam Spade might play dirty, but he had a code and he had personal style; even Bullitt, a character contrived to hold the chases and bloodshed together, was a super-cop with style and feelings. This movie turns old clichés into new clichés by depriving the central figure of *any* attractive qualities. Popeye is insanely callous, a shrewd bully who enjoys terrorizing black junkies, and the film includes raids on bars that are gratuitous to the story line just to show what a subhuman son of a bitch he is. The information is planted early that his methods have already cost the life of a police officer, and at the end this plant has its pat payoff when he accidentally shoots an F.B.I. agent, and the movie makes the point that he doesn't show the slightest remorse. The movie presents him as the most ruthlessly lawless of characters and yet — here is where the basic amorality comes through — shows that this is the kind of man it takes to get the job done. It's the vicious bastard who gets the results. Popeye, the lowlifer who makes Joe or Archie sound like Daniel Ellsberg, is a cop the way the movie Patton was a general. When Popeye walks into a bar and harasses blacks, part of the audience can say, "That's a real pig," and another part of the audience can say, "That's the only way to deal with those people. Waltz around with them and you get nowhere."

I imagine that the people who put this movie together just naturally think in this commercially convenient double way. This right-wing, left-wing, take-your-choice cynicism is total commercial opportunism passing itself off as an Existential view. And maybe that's why Popeye's determination to find the heroin is not treated unequivocally as socially useful but is made obsessive. Popeye's low character is used to make the cops-and-robbers melodrama superficially modern by making it *meaningless;* his brutality serves to demonstrate that the cops are no better than the crooks. In personal style and behavior, he is, in fact, deliberately shown as worse than the crooks, yet since he's the cop with the hunches that pay off, the only cop who gets results, the movie can be seen as a way of justifying police brutality. At the end, a Z-style series of titles comes on to inform us that the dealers who were caught got light sentences or none at all. The purpose of giving us this information is also probably double: to tell us to get tougher judges and to make tougher laws, and to provide an ironic coda showing that Popeye's efforts were really futile. A huge haul of heroin was destroyed, but the movie doesn't bother to show us that — to give a man points for anything is unfashionable. The series of titles is window-dressing anyway. The only thing that this movie believes in is giving the audience jolts, and you can feel the raw, primitive response in the theatre. This picture says Popeye is a brutal son of a bitch who gets the dirty job done. So is the picture.

[October 30, 1971]

Cheaters

During what is said to be a period of nostalgia — or maybe it's just nostalgia for nostalgia — Channel 13-WNET has committed the worst crime ever perpetrated against our movie inheritance: running movie classics of the silent period speeded up. Twelve movies have been shown to the largest audiences Channel 13 has ever had, and most of these twelve have been reduced to garbage. People who have watched *The Silent Years* may have gathered the impression that the greatness of such films as *Intolerance* and *Orphans of the Storm* is a legend created by sentimental film critics. Those who don't know the movies simply have no idea of the enormity of the crime. Some of the movies are run at one and a half times their original speed. *Intolerance,* which I am not alone in regarding as the greatest film ever made in this country, is run at close to double time. Everything in it is destroyed; it has no emotional power — it's just a curiosity. Others, such as the exquisitely designed *The Thief of Bagdad,* were never great, but whatever qualities they had are gone. There is no technical reason the movies cannot be exhibited at their original speeds; * this would require some care and a little more expense — that is all. (The series is subsidized by a grant from the Bowery Savings Bank.) Instead, they have been transferred to tape at modern sound-movie speed, and generally with a maddeningly incongruous tinkling piano on the track. Theatres used to engage full orchestras to play the specially prepared symphonic scores; now, when the music can be put directly on tape with the film — and it need be done only once — the producers of this series don't bother with more than a chintzy piano or an organ. The reasons appear to be convenience and indifference. When one considers the dedication that went into the making of some of these films, it is almost incredible that men who can't provide a projection machine with a governable motor to run them properly ** are now mucking up some of the finest art ever produced in this country and taking bows for it. If there has been no public outcry, the reason is partly that some of those who know the movies are so disgusted they turn them off, while some others in "the film community" who might be expected to speak out do not because in one way or another they or their friends are implicated in this swindle. When I asked one eminence whose name appears in the credits how he felt about what was being done, he said, "Oh, I never watch movies on television." Collaborating in this mutilation provides a mite of profit; besides, there are professional associations, personal commitments, grants, jobs.

This series is comparable to presenting the children of America with miniature sets of the greatest classics of American literature from which a third or more of the words in every sentence are omitted. The children could get an idea of what the books were about but not of what made them great. And since what viewers have seen is obviously not great, and since few of the viewers realize the trick that has been played on them, why would they ever seek out the originals? They think they have already seen the movies. For these viewers, the whole tradition of the American silent film has been destroyed. When I protested this disgrace to executives of Channel 13 this summer, I received assurances that the second series, which is in preparation, would be projected as correctly as pos-

---

* On tape, that is.
** While transferring them to tape.

sible. But meanwhile the first series is being shown over and over and sent out across the country. If this package becomes the standard package from now on, it will mean that these films will be destroyed for future generations as well. The only way to get them withdrawn is through public protest. One official who assured me that the second series would be treated differently said contemptuously, "So we'll do it for you and the three other people who care." There must be others. Perhaps they have been fooled into thinking that some insuperable technical obstacle causes the films to look like "flicks" on television; perhaps, even worse, they no longer trust their memories. If they go to see silent movies at any showing where the films are treated with respect, they will find that the pictures are still big; it's the people who got smaller. Non-commercial television is proud of the fact that this series has brought it its highest ratings. Its pride should be changed to shame. Protests might be enough to get that first series retired permanently, so that even if the films have been destroyed for our children, at least our children's children will not be cheated.

•

I delayed going to see *Long Ago, Tomorrow* as long as possible — first, because I kept forgetting the title, and, second, because I knew it was about the love affair of two paraplegics, and who wants to go sit to watch people sitting? Despite a heavy rain, there were long lines at the theatre, and after seeing the movie I can make a few guesses why. The picture is more mobile than I had anticipated — the director, Bryan Forbes, who also adapted the autobiographical novel, by Peter Marshall, keeps it active — but it is just what I had dreaded. Those with instinctive self-warnings are quite right: this sort of thing could *conceivably* be done for other purposes than to mulct you emotionally, but it never really is, is it? The distributor, Don Rugoff, has put a big campaign behind the picture, and in this case his commercial instinct is shrewd.* *Long Ago, Tomorrow* is a highly skilled *Love Story*, understated and sincere, which means the goo is tasteful. It also has an extra ingredient: Since the tragic lovers are so badly crippled that they must go through considerable wheelchair wiggling even to kiss, and since the once rough and healthy boy learns tenderness when he loses the use of his legs, and since the girl dies happy after a fulfilling sex experience, it's probably a fantastic make-out movie.** It's got some of that

---

* Not really. Despite Rugoff's efforts, the picture didn't take off. That rainy day crowd deceived me.

** It didn't catch on for this either; maybe it was just too dreary. The make-out movie of the season was *Summer of '42*.

A Man and a Woman appeal (the non-threatening male) working along with the star-crossed bit. When you see the desperate need these lovers have for physical contact, and when you see how beautiful sex is for the poor, doomed girl, surely the message is: Count your blessings and make out, but gently. People go to be turned on by the sadness of it.

Malcolm McDowell and Nanette Newman (don't those names look like the perfect pairs on the marquees in *Singin' in the Rain*?) are well-trained pros, and they keep acting away, playing contrasting confections. He does working-class energy, restless impatience, bitterness and rage, and subtle maturing; she does the understanding heart, luminous eyes, and compassion. Though this quality goo actually *does* what *Love Story* only tries to do, I'm not sure I count that an achievement. Audiences longing for a good cry don't mind the feeble craftsmanship of *Love Story;* the superior craftsmanship here — the way the picture ladles on the sensitivity — only makes it easier for people to deceive themselves that it's not the same genre. But when the girl suddenly dies, you know it's just why Jennifer Cavilleri died — because without a big fat tragedy there would be no movie. Up to the girl's death, you could be fooled about what you were watching, but when the director slips in that hook, you know you've been had.

Long Ago, Tomorrow is the sort of movie that is sometimes called honest, but what it features is soft honesty. The selfish, cocky paraplegic hero is taken care of sympathetically in a lovely country-club atmosphere, so that his only problem is to "find himself" and to undergo the spiritual conversion that will uplift the audience: he must learn to care about someone else. Though it may seem a small point, it makes a big difference that, unlike Brando and the other paraplegics in *The Men*, who were crippled by war, these characters are crippled by fortune. Because, of course, it means that the hero's rage is just something he has to work out of his system. There he is, getting good treatment in a fine permanent home for the disabled, though the church people who run it are a bit smug about their charity, and he lambastes them showily for that piddling fault. He has nothing to complain of but an unhappy fate. A movie can't get into much trouble complaining of fate.

The audience can sniffle comfortably because it's not the audience's fault; it's nobody's fault. This gusher is as painless as *Love Story:* the things that go wrong are all beyond anyone's control. Blighted dreams. That's why, I think, a movie like this is so *respectable* — why *Variety*, for example, can say that it "could be the type of pic needed at a time when many people are getting sick of ultra-permissiveness." The assumption behind this is that a "permissive" movie is one that attacks social institutions or tries to challenge old ideas of entertainment. This movie won't sicken those people, because the hero's angry-young-man speeches have no real targets: they are there for a veneer of toughness — modern décor, like Jennifer Cavilleri's cute four-letter words. His anger is what he must conquer rather than what society must answer for. He is the angry young man domesticated into a Mod hero for a sentimental movie; they didn't need to castrate him — they just put him in a wheelchair, and his anger plays on your heartstrings. Though the movie ends in "tragedy," this is the opposite of the unhappy endings in recent American movies which are a reflection of the state of political hopelessness in this country. Our heroes die because we are no longer sure how to live honorably. While heroes who reject all the Crap are generally adolescent sentimentalists who don't define what needs rejecting, and while success stories in reverse, like *Harry Kellerman,* don't sort things out any more than the old straight success stories did, the messy pictures reflect a genuine, tragic confusion. This tragedy comes from England, but it's a whiff of old Hollywood, with the old square value system intact: You're sad, but you know it had to be, and consolation is provided. The girl did get her one night of love, and the boy has grown into a man. It's a *nice* cry.

Bryan Forbes' smooth, professional style (one thinks of the movie as having been executed rather than directed) has been intermittently effective in the past — when, for example, Leslie Caron in *The L-Shaped Room* or Edith Evans in *The Whisperers* brought such strong individuality to her role that she gave it a suggestion of mystery. This happens just once, I think, in *Long Ago, Tomorrow*: when the girl, having gone to her parents' home, complains that her mother does everything for her, that "she takes what's left away." For that second, Miss Newman's plaintiveness goes beyond the movie's surface. Forbes is a man of many talents, and yet in this film they add up to conscientious mediocrity. He has been quoted as saying, "In the last analysis, performance is everything." Well, it isn't, you know. His concentration on performance, though not the most exciting way to approach moviemaking, could be an acceptable way if the performers had good roles and could take off in them, but when the role is pasteboard, how much can a performer do? Sometimes an actor can give so much of himself to a sketchy role that he fills it in — like Warren Oates in *The Hired Hand,* or Bruce Dern as the coach in *Drive, He Said* — but the two star roles here are completely written, and there is nothing in them but conventional notions of what's "deep." The director has also said, "I think everything should be subordinate to the performance, and that's why I'm not highly regarded in the more esoteric cinema magazines." That's not why: it's not because he subordinates everything to performance but because he subordinates everything to a certain *kind* of performance — the pseudo-serious performance. The background roles are, as usual, the ones that expose Forbes' limitations — and not only of technique. He keeps cutting to the sort of fixated glimpses that are meant to tell you "everything" about the minor characters — shots of people being complacent or being sympathetic. One quality at a time. The frequent shots of the vicar being prissily evasive belong to a different age of filmmaking — and it was a bad age. The other paraplegic patients in the home are cut to for cute stock responses, like the family pets in a Disney movie. At the end, the Ping-Pong game, with Michael Flanders helping the hero over his crisis, is classic stiff-upper-lip — it might have been directed by Colonel Blimp.

Forbes' belief in decency of feeling is so black-and-white simple that it's an enshrined attitude — more suitable to statesmen than to artists. I guess what bothers me most about this picture is that though it's conventional it's never vulgar. It lacks the pop vitality that can make much more stupid pictures entertaining. I can enjoy a sleazy, silly old movie that presents a woman like Rita Hayworth as a super-dish, but something in me rebels against Forbes' tremulous, glowing heroines who are supposed to be "natural." This picture is so refined that the girl even has a refined orgasm. Though *Long Ago, Tomorrow* speaks for young love and for understanding, it's a deeply reactionary movie. Its refinement is a form of cant; the whole picture is cant. You feel as if you'd seen it all long ago, tomorrow in Radio City Music Hall.

•

Is There Sex After Death? — such a good title for *Long Ago, Tomorrow* — is, instead, the title of a new American porno-spoof, produced, directed, and written by Jeanne and Alan Abel. The genre has already established certain conventions. Abel plays an inquiring reporter-doctor, head of the Bureau of Sexological Investigation, who travels about in a Sexmobile; this permits the usual loose, revue-style structure — skits, interviews, candid-camera material. Photographically, the picture (which cost two hundred thousand dollars) is unusually good for the genre; it was shot in 16-mm. color, and this is one of the best jobs of 16-mm.-blowup-to-35-mm. I've ever seen. Partly because of the visual quality and the use of pastels, you don't get that depressed, crummy feeling that usually settles in with the first shots of porny pictures. Some of it is quite funny, like a college revue gone wild — especially the put-ons and one-liners by Buck Henry (who seems more relaxed here than in his other screen appearances) and Jim Moran — and there's one almost brilliant sequence with Marshall Efron as an ecstatically happy dirty-movie maker. But the genre has some problems, too. The directors in this field can kid themselves that, as this film claims, they're making "a spoof on the current wave of sexual frankness in America and much of the hypocrisy which lies behind it all." But while you're watching such pictures as *Guess What We Learned in School Today?* and *Cry Uncle* and *The Telephone Book* and *Is There Sex After Death?* you're perfectly well aware that, despite the claims of sophistication, the success of the films depends upon crudeness and plenty of sex and hefty amounts of teasing by women willing to act cute and dumb. And though the absence of solemnity about sex in porno-spoofs is a relief, and the sex jokes can have a fizzy, liberated humor that is *Mad*-magazine sophomoric in the best sense, after a while it isn't enough that they're being done; you want them to be done with some comic polish and style. You want the foolishness to be inspired, not to be just a series of repetitive jokes — jokes that are interchangeable from one film to the next. Since there is no story line or structure that isn't just a pretext, the only suspense is in hoping for a good skit or a bright one-liner; one sits apathetically, knowing that nothing will build, that a laugh will be followed by boredom. And here's where the problem comes in: People who wouldn't ordinarily go to pornos go to porno-spoofs, which always have an adolescent anti-establishment air about them. (A favorite gimmick is a fornication scene to the tune of "The Star-Spangled Banner.") But can the porno-spoofs improve and still attract this audience? If a porno-spoof were better, it would be a sex comedy, and the difference is a matter not only of talent but of attitude.

I think the audience for porno-spoofs likes the square coarseness of *Cry Uncle* — the fat hanging down from the comic slob (Allen Garfield), the clown of burlesque who has finally lost his baggy pants — and it likes the whorishness of the women, the same way burlesque patrons enjoy looking at "dogs." They couldn't laugh at beautiful young girls. Porno-spoofs, like pornos and like burlesque shows, make the patrons feel they could have any of that if they cared to — it's easily available. The genre is based on the idea of inviting you to laugh at sex — as if you were watching a dirty sit-com on TV. What's built into the genre is the economic fact that unless you treat sex as ridiculous or gross — as a schoolboy joke — you lose your audience. An artist who made sex comedies would probably have to find a different audience, although Woody Allen just might be able to make a porno-spoof that was sufficiently sustained to be a sex comedy.

Is There Sex After Death? stays within the funny-off-and-on porno-spoof genre. It provides the sex scenes, including five couples copulating simultaneously in an International Sex Bowl, and, unlike most of the other movies of the genre, it provides considerable naughty-bawdy comedy, but the filler is flat. The Abels are known as hoaxers: he was the founder some years back of a society to clothe all naked animals, and Mrs. Abel sometimes poses as "Yetta Bronstein," a Bronx housewife who runs for high political office. I suspect that few of us find these hoaxes as funny as the Abels must in order to work them up and sustain them for so long. Probably you have to convince yourself that if people are taken in, you're really proving something. This picture has the same sort of plodding persistence. As the sexologist interviewer, Abel has one of the dullest personas in recent movies; he behaves like a sexologist.

The film loses potential laughs because the lines aren't timed quite right and the scenes aren't shaped. Skits are set up, they're poised on the borderline of funny and unfunny, and you wait for them to go right, and they don't, they just die away. And in this kind of film, in which the actors and actresses can so easily be degraded, the bad timing can make one uncomfortable. Then you may begin to wonder about the people in the movie — about the mixture of politics and prankishness and perhaps exhibitionism that has led so many people to offer up their bottoms and bellies and breasts and genitals to the camera. Unlike the credits for most films of this type, the credits here carry long, carefully categorized lists of names, so that you can tell who was doing what to whom in each scene. I imagine that the Abels regard this as part of a crusade for frankness — to unclothe human animals. But the people who are unclothed are not often funny in that condition, except as nature is responsible. And so, like burlesque patrons, we're put in the position of laughing at fools and "dogs" — or not laughing much.

[November 6, 1971]

A Bagel with a Bite Out of It

I can't talk about Hollywood. It was a horror to me when I was there and it's a horror to look back on. I can't imagine how I did it. When I got away from it I couldn't even refer to the place by name. "Out there," I called it. You want to know what "out there" means to me? Once I was coming down a street in Beverly Hills and I saw a Cadillac about a block long, and out of the side window was a wonderfully slinky mink, and an arm, and at the end of the arm a hand in a white suède glove wrinkled around the wrist, and in the hand was a bagel with a bite out of it.
—*Dorothy Parker, in 1956,
in an interview in the Paris Review.*

Everyone may have a different view of what that bagel represents, but if it is the symbolic ordinary Jewish food that the show-business *nouveaux riches* cling to, it may also symbolize a vulgar strength that repelled Dorothy Parker — and in which she did not share. Hollywood Jews overdressed like gypsies who had to carry it all on their backs, and they clung to a bit of solid, heavy food even when they were no longer hungry, because it seemed like reality. Vulgarity is not as destructive to an artist as snobbery, and in the world of movies vulgar strength has been a great redemptive force, cancelling out niggling questions of taste. I think *Fiddler on the Roof,* directed by Norman Jewison, is an absolutely smashing movie; it is not especially sensitive, it is far from delicate, and it isn't even particularly imaginative, but it seems to me the most *powerful* movie musical ever made.

Musical comedy is one of the American contributions to world theatre; it is also primarily an American Jewish contribution. There would be a theatre in America without Jews, and perhaps it would be not much worse than it is — though it would certainly be different — but, as William Goldman has pointed out, "Without Jews, there simply would have been no musical comedy to speak of in America. . . . In the last half century, the only major Gentile composer to come along was Cole Porter." What separates *Fiddler on the Roof,* which is set in Czarist Russia, from other Broadway shows and from such movie musicals as *West Side Story* and *The Sound of Music* and *My Fair Lady* and *Hello, Dolly!* and *Camelot* and *Paint Your Wagon* and *Star!* and *Doctor Dolittle* is that it is probably the only successful attempt to use this theatrical form on the subject of its own sources — that is, on the heritage that the Jewish immigrants brought to this country. The only other big movie musical of recent years with any explicit Jewish material was *Funny Girl,* and although essentially a blown-up show-business bio, it also got some of its drive from that explicitness. *Fiddler on the Roof* finds its theme in the energy and gusto and the few remnants of moldy traditions — the religion of the bagel — that have resulted in such wonders as the American musical theatre as well as in the horrors of a pandering theatre full of Jewish-mother jokes. But *Fiddler on the Roof* is a celebration of a Jewish *father,* and Tevye, the dairyman pulling his wagon, is a male Mother Courage, not a male Molly Goldberg. Maybe because its means are utterly square and plain, the movie succeeds in doing what Elia Kazan, for all his gifts and despite some fine scenes, failed to do in *America America* (which dealt with the persecution of his Greek ancestors in Turkey and the dream of the new country). Though it is a musical, *Fiddler on the Roof* succeeds in telling one of the root stories of American life: as Tevye's daughters marry and disperse and the broken family is driven off its land and starts the long trek to America, Tevye's story becomes the story of the Jewish people who came to America at the turn of the century — what they left behind and what they brought with them.

It is not a movie about "little people," though it seems so in the first five minutes — a "hearty" pre-title sequence featuring the song "Tradition," which is show-business Jewish-Americana, a gruesome romp that makes one wince in expectation of more of the same. But then the credits come on, and Isaac Stern plays the theme (as he does in the solo parts throughout the movie) with startling *brio* and attack; Isaac Stern's energy and style carry us into a different realm. His harshly sweet music clears away the sticky folk stuff, and the movie takes off. It never again sinks to the little-people-at-their-simple-tasks level, because Topol's Tevye has the same vitality and sweetness and gaiety as Isaac Stern's music; he's a rough presence, masculine, with burly, raw strength, but also sensual and warm. He's a poor man but he's not a little man, he's a big man brought low — a man of Old Testament size brought down by the circumstances of oppression. The crooked, ironic grin when he gestures to God and the light in his eyes after a love song with his wife tell the story of a dogged man who can be crushed again and again and still come back.

Topol is a broad actor, but not in the bad sense of broad; Clark Gable, though incapable of registering much suffering, was a broad actor, and so is Sean Connery. I mean not an actor who lacks finer shades (although Gable certainly did, and it may turn out that Topol does, too) but, rather, an actor with a heroic presence, a man's man, an actor with *male* authority — a Raimu, a Jean Gabin. Typically, these actors play earthy, working-with-their-hands roles and look out of place when they are cast in the upper class. They are almost totally physical actors — deep-voiced men who dominate the stage or screen by energy and power, actors with a gift for projecting common emotions and projecting them to the gallery. Anna Magnani is the last woman star of this type — the actors and actresses of the people. Anthony Quinn's Zorba was a comparable large-spirited role. It's easy for small-spirited people to put down this kind of acting, but when a director has enough taste and control to keep an outsize performer within limits, the emotional effects can be satisfying and rich in a way that other kinds of acting never are. Topol (rather too broad for his role in *Before Winter Comes*) was a superb choice for the movie Tevye, because his brute vitality makes Tevye a force of nature — living proof of the power to endure. Tevye is the soul of *Fiddler on the Roof*; Topol, a giant dancing bear of a man, embodies the theme, and, big as the movie is — and it's *huge* — he carries it on his back.

Topol has a fine speaking voice, low and resonant but also cracked and playful; he can twist a word right up to a high register. The humor in Tevye's role is not only in the jokes themselves but in the playing; they don't stale, because a good performer reactivates them. Such folk humor as a man talking about a girl while the man he's talking to thinks the conversation is about a cow is so primitive one watches it ritualistically; it's the beginning of vaudeville. Perhaps because Topol is an Israeli, not an American Jew, he plays with a strength that is closer to peasant strength than to an American urban Jewish image. If his heroic strength overpowers the original qualities of the character, his backbone is what this big musical-comedy movie needs. His is a Sabra Tevye, and I suppose this may disconcert those who saw the first Broadway Tevye, Zero Mostel, who I understand was much funnier. Mostel is a brilliant, baleful, sad-eyed buffoon, weirdly inventive, and with his freak specialty — the surprise of how light he is on his toes — but on the screen he could no more embody the Jewish Everyman than W. C. Fields or Jonathan

Winters could be the Wasp Everyman. He is a clown, and, like many great clowns, he creates his own atmosphere. Topol is handsome, which is a blessing in movies, and, though bigger than life, he's still in the normal human range — his bigness is an intensification of normal emotions.

Norman Jewison's movie is astonishingly square — astonishing not only in how square his approach is but in how joyously square the results are. Never having seen *Fiddler* on the stage, I can't judge what has been lost, but, on its own terms, the movie has an over-all, ongoing vitality that is overwhelming. It is a show that reveals not what made Jewish writers or thinkers but what has made American Jewish show business. It is an attempt to bring joy out of basic experience; the hero is a myth-size version of a limited, slightly stupid common man. Jewison has a sound instinct for robust, masculine low comedy; he showed it in the way he handled Rod Steiger in *In the Heat of the Night* and Alan Arkin in *The Russians Are Coming, The Russians Are Coming*. (On a small scale, Arkin's Russian was a warm-up for Tevye.) The producers were probably wise — or maybe lucky — when they selected a Gentile director, because Jewison (an exotic name for a Methodist) doesn't let the movie slip into chummy Jewish sentimentality. In the movie, to be chosen for suffering is a joke that Tevye and the other Jews in the Ukrainian village are in on. The Jews are a chosen people the way blacks are beautiful. Those who suffer may need to believe there is a higher meaning in their suffering, just as those whose beauty has not been sufficiently recognized may need to rediscover it and emphasize it. The irony that the chosen of God seem to have less access to Him than others do is, in fact, the source of Tevye's comedy in the movie, as it is in the Sholom Aleichem stories on which the musical is based. Tevye is a religious man but also a realist — because he can't get God's ear. Younger members of the audience — particularly if they are Jewish — may be put off the movie if their parents and grandparents have gone on believing in a special status with God long after the oppression was over, and have tried to prop up their authority over their children with boring stories about early toil and hardship (as the superpatriot judge in *Little Murders* does). Too many people have *used* their early suffering as a platitudinous weapon and so have made it all seem fake. And I suppose that *Fiddler on the Roof* has been such a phenomenal stage success partly because it can be used in this same self-congratulatory way — as a public certificate of past suffering. And perhaps the movie can be, too. But this movie is far from a Jewish *The Sound of Music* and is infinitely less sentimental than the youth rock musicals.

Jewison treats the Jews as an oppressed people — no better, no worse than others — and this sensible attitude, full of essential good will, and yet not self-conscious, as a Jewish movie director's attitude might easily have been, keeps the movie sane and balanced, and allows it to be powerful. The movie is not a celebration of Jewishness; it is a celebration of the sensual pleasures of staying alive, and of trying to hang on to a bit of ceremony, too — a little soul food. Jewison does not permit the Jewish performers to be too "Jewish"; that is, to become familiar with the audience with that degrading mixture of self-hatred and self-infatuation that corrupts so much Jewish comedy. Only one of the leads — Molly Picon, as Yente, the matchmaker — gets away from him and carries on like a stage Jew, with a comic accent. Why do Jewish performers like Molly Picon have to overdo being Jewish when they play Jews? What do they think they are the rest of the time? They're like those Hollywood actresses who, when they got past forty and the time came for them to play the parents of teen-age children, did themselves up like Whistler's mother. It is an anomaly of American entertainment, in which Jews have played so major a role, that it is not the Gentiles but the Jews who have created the Jewish stereotypes, and not to satisfy any need in the Gentiles but to satisfy the mixed-up masochism of Jewish audiences. (Black performers put on comic black masks for black audiences, too; it could conceivably be argued that the comedy is in showing their own people the masks they wear for whites, but this argument certainly doesn't carry over to the Jews.) It's this kind of cheap courting of favor with the Jewish audience that one may fear when one goes to see *Fiddler on the Roof*, and Jewison keeps the movie about ninety-nine per cent pure.

As the timid tailor who loves Tzeitel, Tevye's oldest daughter, Leonard Frey is as innocent of heart and tangled in his limbs as a young Ben Blue, and as the daughter Rosalind Harris, a tall, slender young actress, looks just enough like Frey for the marriage to have been made in Heaven; they're a lunatically sweet pair of Shakespearean lovers — funny, pastoral, perfect. Paul Mann, with his winged eyebrows and ruddy, button-nose face, is a marvellous camera image — a true St. Nick. His wealthy butcher, like his rug merchant in *America America*, is a lived-in character. You look at him and you see a whole way of life — groaning boards loaded with meat, the pleasures of materialism. The butcher's and Tevye's explosions of temper at Tzeitel's wedding are possibly the truest moments of folk humor. (The movie is most false, I think, in the reaction shots of the constable when he and Tevye talk; these shots seem to come out of a Second World War movie — they make dignity-of-man points.) Michele Marsh is a bit too conventional an ingénue as the second daughter but redeems the performance with her farewell song; the third daughter, Neva Small, very young and with long red hair, has a special comic spark in her early scenes. The Golde (Tevye's wife) of Norma Crane is physically suitable, but the character, regrettably, never emerges.

The movie is highly theatrical, but it isn't stagy. Joseph Stein, who wrote the stage show, also did the movie script, and it's a serviceable adaptation. Jewison has managed to keep the whole production, including the out-of-doors scenes, somewhat stylized, so that the simple transitions in and out of the songs and dances are not jarring but just a further step in stylization. And since, as the stage show was conceived (mostly by Jerome Robbins, from all accounts), the songs and dances are meant to be not "professional" but heightened expressions of emotion by the characters, the numbers are in any case not so different from the somewhat formalized theatrical scenes they grow out of. Jewison's devices to get from one scene to the next are so naïve that they can easily be accepted, because they serve the material. The vastness of fields with only a few figures is a simple conversion from a bare stage. These fields may then be dissolved into an abstraction to end a scene, or the camera may move from the figures in a field to a landscape. Some of the devices don't serve good purposes. Though the picture seems to ride right over its own faults, it *is* irritating that the direction and editing so often go for obvious effects — a shift, say, from the candles' being lighted in one home to the candles' being lighted all over the village. Jewison fails at certain scenes because of a kind of nondenominational blandness: the revolutionary from Kiev (Michael Glaser) becomes just an attractive juvenile, and the scene in which he tries to teach radical ideas to Tevye's daughters is insipid. The third daughter's Gentile suitor (Raymond Lovelock) is a walking example of Hitler-youth-movement calendar art. However, the worst flaw in the film except for the unrealized Golde is that the best dance scenes are all but wrecked by the whirlybird attempt to create dazzle and speed with a camera amidst the figures instead of letting the dances build by choreographic means. You want to see the whole figures and the steps, not blurred faces and bits of bodies. Dance has greater power than filmmakers may realize, and the wedding dance of four men with wine bottles on their heads is the high point of the film. I don't know if it's traditional or a Jerome Robbins contribution — perhaps it's a blend of both — but it's a beautiful ritual dance, and beautifully performed. It comes as a gift of art, like Isaac Stern's violin songs.

I fear that people of taste have been so indoctrinated now with a narrow conception of cinematic values that a movie in a broad popular style will be subject to a snobbish reaction. But square can be beautiful, too. It can be strong in a very direct way, and the theme of *Fiddler on the Roof* justifies this large-scale (nine-million-dollar) production. One doesn't go to a big American movie musical expecting impeccable ethnic nuances or fine brushwork; that's not what this particular genre provides. What it does offer is the pleasure of big, bold strokes — and spirit. *Fiddler on the Roof* is American folk opera, commercial style. So was *Porgy and Bess*. And though the score, by Jerry Bock (the music) and Sheldon Harnick (the lyrics, functional but uninspired), isn't in the Gershwin class, it isn't *bad*. No other American folk opera (certainly not *Porgy and Bess*, which has a rather unfortunate libretto) has ever been so successfully brought to the screen as *Fiddler on the Roof*. Its great advantage on the screen is its narrative strength; the material builds and accumulates meaning, until, at the end, when the Jews who have left their homes huddle on a raft, Tevye's story becomes part of the larger story, and the full scope of the movie is achieved. Though the techniques and simplifications are those of musical comedy, when they are put to work on a large emotional theme that is consonant with the very nature of American musical comedy — is, in fact, at its heart — the effect on the large screen is of a musical epic. The music is certainly not operatic, but the movie of *Fiddler on the Roof* has operatic power. It's not a soft experience; you come out shaken.

Dorothy Parker, so apt and so funny, was also so *wrong*. She was right, of course, in seeing Hollywood as a mink-and-bagel story; that's what anyone researching movie history comes up against, and it must be what anyone researching the musical theatre comes up against, too. And it's the easiest thing to patronize. But that bagel with the bite out of it should have cheered her. Imagine that arm without the bagel and you have cold money. Didn't it tell her that the woman in the mink in the Cadillac didn't quite believe in the mink or the Cadillac? Didn't it tell her that movies, like musical comedies, were made by gypsies who didn't know how to act as masters, because they were still on the road being chased? Couldn't Miss Parker, split down the middle herself — a Jewish father and a Gentile mother — see that that bagel was a piece of the raft, a comic holy wafer?

[November 13, 1971]

El Poto-Head Comics

The atmosphere in the theatre is enough to inform you that *El Topo* is a head film, but while I was watching Alexandro Jodorowsky's horror circus I was nevertheless puzzled about why the mostly young audience sat there quietly — occasionally laughing at a particularly garish murder or mutilation — while the few older people staggered out in disgust. At one point, I drew in my breath sharply at the prospect of another slaughter scene, and a pretty, blank-faced girl sitting in front of me with her boyfriend's arm on her shoulder turned her head slightly toward me, as if to say, "What's the matter with her? Is she taking it seriously, or something?" And I realized that I and those older people who left — I would have joined them if I had not had a professional interest in seeing the film — were responding on a different level from the rest of the audience, part of which had probably already seen the film before its official opening last week, during the six months it played at midnight screenings, like a Black Mass. This film that they return to over and over doesn't need reviews (not in the overground press, anyway) to lure an audience, but maybe it's up to reviewers to try to explain why that audience is being lured.

Jodorowsky, born in Chile in 1930 of Polish-Russian-Jewish parentage, was once a member of Marcel Marceau's company and composed some of Marceau's pantomimes; he is now a theatre director in Mexico, and a cartoonist as well, whose weekly comic strip "Fabulas Panicas" (or "Panic Fables") appears in a major Mexico City newspaper. *El Topo* (it means "The Mole") was made in Mexico, and it resembles the spaghetti Westerns. It begins with a bearded stranger in black leather (Jodorowsky) riding on a sandy plain; the color looks cheap and overbright, unreal in that gaudy way that unsophisticated attempts at realism often produce — it's like Kodacolor, with aquamarine skies. But the stranger rides with his naked son sitting behind him, and it is immediately apparent that the nakedness is symbolic — the more so when the father says, "Now you are a man. You are seven years old. Bury your first toy and your mother's picture," and the burial ceremony consists of propping the symbols up in the sand. And when the father and son come to a town, the town is a scene of more than usual spaghetti-Western carnage. It is a town of corpses and entrails; animals, children — everyone has been butchered, and the waters literally flow red. The bearded man in black becomes the gunfighter, the avenger; he tracks down the murderous bandits and castrates their warlord. Then, with the words "Destroy me. Depend on no one," he leaves his son with a group of young monks whom he has liberated, and takes up with the warlord's mistress. Up to this point, the carnage has been steady, and with quantities of fetishism and perversion. (As captives of the brigands, used for sexual sport, the young monks had bloodstained bare bottoms.)

In the next section, the picture becomes more occult, and more like a fairy tale, as the man in black and the woman, whom he christens Mara, go into the desert, where she persuades him that he must conquer the four masters who dwell there. The masters being different varieties of holy men, each of the four contests is enigmatic, and in this section the characters converse in high-flown riddles — a sort of Zen, Confucius-say talk ("The desert is a circle"). The hero wins his contests by trickery and realizes too late that he has truly lost, and cries out to ask why God has forsaken him. Meanwhile, Mara has been joined by a sadistic lesbian in butch black couture, and as he thrashes about in guilt for his crimes, battering himself against walls that crumble, the lesbian comes at him, like Mercedes McCambridge in *Johnny Guitar*, and pumps lead into him; he keeps walking, arms outstretched and with stigmata on his hands and feet, until Mara shoots him down. The women kiss — tongues extended — and leave him for dead. A group of dwarfs and cripples lug his body off. Can it be the end? No, there is a third section.

Years have passed — perhaps twenty. He sits as a holy man in a cave in a mountain, tended by a worshipful dwarf woman. Spiritually reborn, with his beard and head shaved in penitence, he pledges himself to liberate the tiny, shrivelled cave people, who are now trapped in the mountain, imprisoned there by the people of a nearby town, so that the townspeople will not have to see the deformed results of their generations of incest. The holy man begins work on a tunnel; because of his height, he himself can scale the walls of the cave, and he comes and goes, taking the woman dwarf with him. When they go into the town, we are once more back in a Western. The town is a synthesis of the gambling, whoring saloon towns of American movies, with a cartoon catalogue of evils:

blacks are sold as slaves and branded, accused of rape by lecherous women, lynched, and so on. The penitent cleans toilets in the town jail and becomes a clown — God's fool — in order to buy dynamite to blast the mountain open. When he and his little woman (the only good woman in the entire film, and good by virtue of her total selfless devotion to him) go to the church (where the parishioners normally play Russian roulette) and ask to be married, the priest turns out to be the abandoned son. The three of them go back to the mountain to free the cave people; once free, however, the crippled, helpless little monstrosities — they're like deformed Munchkins — rush to see the wonders of the town, and the townspeople meet them with rifles and shoot them down. The holy man arrives too late; they have all been massacred. He yells and is shot, and is shot again and again, but he keeps coming toward the townspeople, like a Golem. Full of holes (like Toshiro Mifune's porcupine Macbeth full of spears in *Throne of Blood*), he picks up a gun and, once more the avenger, retaliates by slaughtering the townspeople. Seated then, cross-legged, he soaks himself in kerosene from a Western lamp and immolates himself (successfully). A new holy family — his son, bearded and dressed in black, and his dwarf widow, carrying his newborn baby, ride away into the whatever the movie began from.

Blood-soaked and piled high with deformity, the film is commercialized Surrealism. *El Topo* has been called a Zen Buddhist Western, but in terms of its derivations it's a spaghetti Western in the style of Luis Buñuel, and tinsel all the way. The avant-garde devices that once fascinated a small bohemian group because they seemed a direct pipeline to the occult and "the marvellous" now reach the new mass bohemianism of youth. But the marvellous has become a bag of old Surrealist tricks: the acid-Western style is synthesized from devices of the once avant-garde — especially *L'Age d'Or* and the whole lifework of Buñuel, with choice lifts from Cocteau's *The Blood of a Poet*, too. In *El Topo*, a brigand out on a rocky terrain sucks a woman's pink slipper, and then a collection of women's slippers are set up on the rocks as targets for shooting practice. An armless man and a legless man he carries on his shoulders function as one person — stumps exposed, of course; when shot apart, the helpless sections writhe on the ground. A man cuts a banana with a sabre. Crowds in the Western town applaud murders as if they were theatrical events. The lesbian lashes Mara's back, licks and kisses the wounds, and then offers her blood-smeared face for Mara to kiss. Even the dwarf woman is forced into a sex show by the lewd townspeople, and must remove her blouse and expose her pathetic little body. And not just to them but to us.

Bizarrely complicated though it is, one can follow the story without difficulty. The movie may seem bewildering, however, because the narrative is overlaid with a clutter of symbols and ideas. Jodorowsky employs anything that can give the audience a charge, even if the charges are drawn from different systems of thought that are — *as thought* — incompatible. For example, he gets a lot of mileage out of the viciousness of lecherous, sex-starved fat old women gloating over murders, pawing a young black boy to the accompaniment of pig noises on the track, and taking up rifles to mow down helpless, stunted children on crutches; it's a further distortion of the conventional distortions of Freudianism in American movies. But the movie is not a Freudian movie; if it were, the saintly love between the hero and the selfless, crippled dwarf might look pretty funny, but for *that* Jodorowsky shifts gears to penitential piety. One enthusiast of the film, who characterized it in an article in the Sunday *Times* as "a monumental work of filmic art," described Jodorowsky as "a man of passionate erudition in matters religious and philosophical, which he draws on with the zest of the instinctual thinker for whom ideas are sensuous entities." Well, of course, you don't need erudition to draw on matters religious and philosophical that way — any dabbler can do it. All you need is a theatrical instinct and a talent for (a word I once promised myself never to use) *frisson*. Jodorowsky is, it is true, a director for whom ideas are sensuous entities — sensuous toys, really, to be played with. By piling onto the Western man-with-no-name righteous-avenger form elements from Eastern fables, Catholic symbolism, and so on, Jodorowsky achieves a kind of comic-strip mythology. And when you play with ideas this way, promiscuously — with thoughts and enigmas and with symbols of human suffering — the resonances get so thick and confused that the game may seem not just theatre but labyrinthine, "deep": a masterpiece. I used the term "enthusiast" deliberately; the same writer describes the worshipful audiences and is himself among the worshipful, who treat *El Topo* as if it were the movie equivalent of a holy book. It is taken to be deep in the same sense that *The Prophet* used to be; "a work of incomprehensible depth," another enthusiast called it, and, still another, "an indescribable masterpiece." *El Topo* is really "The Bloody Prophet."

At the beginning, when the gunfighter in black is asked, "Who are you to judge me?," he replies, "I am God," and after punishing those who are not good enough to live he immolates himself because of the evil in the world. Unlike Buñuel, whose Surrealist techniques cracked open conventional pieties, Jodorowsky uses those techniques to support a sanctimonious view: Man-God tempted by evil, power-hungry woman abandons righteous ways and then, with the love of a good woman, becomes spiritual man, only to learn that the world is not ready for his spirituality. The movie uses Catholic symbols for "depth" much the way symbols were used to deepen *On the Waterfront*, or the way the directors of American-made Westerns hang a cross around the neck of a poor Mexican whore. Catholics may be losing belief in the magical power of artifacts, but moviemakers still squeeze crosses for the last drops of superstitious thrill. Titles flash on the screen — "Genesis," "Prophets," "Psalms," "Apocalypse" — like "Powie!" in a cartoon. They inflate the meaning of what you actually get. The Eastern riddles and prophetic utterances are used the same way, only they're cute — lisping profundities. But, of course, those who are drawn to the movie can say, "What's the matter with putting it all together? Everything is Everything." Or, as someone actually wrote, "*El Topo* is the all-inclusive myth, the Jungian archetypical dream of love/death, power and glory, body and spirit."

What makes it a head hit? Jodorowsky is not totally untalented; he has some feeling for pace and for sadistic comedy, and he seems to get the performances he wants. But he wouldn't be called a great master if he were being judged simply as a film director; enthusiasts think of him as a visionary, and even as a saint. Jodorowsky doesn't treat horror seriously as horror but, rather, treats it as both commonplace and somewhat funny — and, in a way, reversible. People in cruel comics who have their heads cut off sometimes put them right back on. The movie has a comparable buffoonishness about death — as, indeed, the spaghetti Westerns often have, but there is more of it here. It's a death romp, and the young audience appears to accept the film as no more "real" than the experiences they have in their skulls on drugs. That's why the blood doesn't bother them; that's why they don't gasp at knife thrusts or castrations, and why they're not repelled, either. I don't mean to suggest that this film appeals only to heads, or only to the pot generation (roughly, those who use marijuana frequently and trip out occasionally); there are others — probably some of the parents of the pot generation — who share in the sensibility, and still others who try to in order to feel in touch with youth. But *El Topo* has the right properties for a head film — the glaring color, the excesses and anomalies, the comic-strip jumble of periods and places, cacophonous music alternating with camp music and screeching bird sounds, women who speak with men's voices, primitive settings, nameless universal characters, porno eroticism, prophecies, transformations, rituals, miracles, and a sacrificial, somewhat paranoid vision. *El Topo* is all freaked out on love and mystery. And it's *violent*.

The confusion in talking about this film with someone who thinks it's a masterpiece comes from the fact that many heads consider their actual drug trips to be aesthetic experiences, and their only criterion for judging certain movies — head movies, especially, but some others, too — has become the intensity with which the movies hit them. I do not believe they would flock to *El Topo* and return to it if it were not for the violence. And, although I'm certainly not an authority on marijuana or on drugs, it seems obvious why: If the intensity of your sensations is what you judge a movie by, then the more shocks and dislocations and bloody thrills the better. On the one hand, the violence doesn't bother the heads, because they don't take it for real — it's a trip, a fantasy experience, separate from day-to-day living. On the other hand, the violence is what blows their minds. Devices from the theatre of cruelty are used to set off kicky fantasies. The cruelty becomes delectable, like the gore. I look at the screen and I know that the animals being slaughtered aren't plaster — not in Mexico, they're not — and I look at the cripples exhibiting their sores and shrunken limbs, which aren't plaster, either. And I react to the brutality, because I still associate violence with pain. But my guess is that for the head-movie audiences violence is dissociated from pain and is the richest ingredient of fantasy. It's the violence that turns them on.

I would not presume to guess whether there are dangers in this; I just don't know enough. But I do think this is at the core of why some of us want to walk out while others are having a big experience. One enthusiast wrote that the audience was "intoxicated" by the blood, another that "*El Topo* runs RED, with castrations, beheadings, shootings, and mass murders which make the Sharon Tate scene look like kindergarten fare." Jodorowsky uses violence, just as he uses the collection of cripples, to excite the audience, to help it fantasize, and I don't imagine that the young audience drawn to this film sees anything wrong with that, since indeed it does excite fantasies in them, and that is basically their criterion for a great movie. But I do see something wrong with it, and I feel it the more strongly because Jodorowsky's fundamental amorality isn't even honest amorality. He's an exploitation filmmaker, but he glazes everything with a useful piety. It's the violence plus the unctuous prophetic tone that makes *El Topo* a *heavy* trip. The filmmaker-star says, I am God and I sacrifice Myself for your sins; I am Christ-turned-killer for your sins. The whole movie is an act of self-worship, a narcissist's

Mass, and it sells mystical violence at just the moment when the counter-culture is buying mystical violence. Who would have thought that in the twentieth century Americans would become Spaniards?

Exploitation filmmakers have always specialized in sex or shock (or a combo), and their greatest virtue — their only virtue, really — has been how nakedly they sold it. Hollywood might titillate and pour on the sentimentality, but the exploitation men weren't such hypocrites; besides, they didn't have the means to pour on sentimentality. Jodorowsky has come up with something new: exploitation filmmaking joined to sentimentality — the sentimentality of the counter-culture. They mix frighteningly well: for the counter-culture violence is romantic and shock is beautiful, because extremes of feeling and lack of control are what one takes drugs *for*. What has been happening, I think, is that the counter-culture has begun to look for the equivalent of a drug trip in its theatrical experiences. I think it still responds to non-head movies if there's a possibility of direct identification with the characters, but increasingly movies appear to be valued only for their intensity. In the Arts and Leisure section of the Sunday *Times*, which has become a gathering place for euphoric critics, one can see that even the critical prose attempts to evoke psychedelic experience: "At moments [Ken] Russell achieves a kind of cinematic synesthesia, a dizzying, disorienting experience in which all senses — visual, aural, even tactile — seem to blur," and so on. The worst blows to the art of motion pictures in the past have come from the businessmen who primed everything for the tastes of the conformist mass audience; the worst blows now (and maybe not just to films) could come from the businessmen priming everything for the counter-culture — if the biggest successes turn out to be head movies. (*El Topo* is being distributed by the manager of three of the Beatles.) Head movies don't have to be works of art — they just have to be sensational. For heads, there appears to be no difference.

[November 20, 1971]

Winging It

There was an unusual sequence in *Christopher Strong*, an arch, highstrung, sickeningly noble Katharine Hepburn movie back in 1933. Hepburn played a famous record-breaking aviatrix, obviously modelled on Amelia Earhart, who fell in love with a distinguished political figure, a married man (Colin Clive), He was drawn to her because, unlike his conventionally feminine wife (Billie Burke), she had audacity and independence; he said that that was what he loved her for. But as soon as they went to bed together, he insisted, late on the very first night, that she not fly in the match she was entered in. There were many movies in the thirties in which women were professionals and the equals of men, but I don't know of any other scene that was so immediately recognizable to women of a certain kind as *their* truth. It was clear that the man wasn't a bastard, and that he was doing this out of anxiety and tenderness — out of love, in his terms. Nevertheless, the heroine's acquiescence destroyed her. There are probably few women who have ever accomplished anything beyond the care of a family who haven't in one way or another played that scene. Even those who were young girls at the time recognized it, I think, if only in a premonitory sense. It is the intelligent woman's primal post-coital scene, and it's on film; probably it got there because the movie was written by a woman, Zoë Akins, and directed by a woman, Dorothy Arzner.

I thought of it when I saw *Billy Jack* last week, because after the heroine (Delores Taylor), a Southwestern woman who runs an experimental "freedom school" on an Indian reservation, is raped by the son of a right-wing bully, she describes her emotions in terms of a specific feminine anger at the violation of her person. She may appear to be making too much of what happened; certainly the boring insistence of her tone is, by normal dramatic standards, a drag. Yet her reactions have some truth to women's feelings and to women's difficulties in articulating these feelings. The sequence doesn't have the high gloss of the crucial scene in *Christopher Strong*, which was accomplished in a few seconds — a line or two of dialogue, and that was it. The specifically feminine material in *Billy Jack* isn't slick at all; the movie just stops and lets the woman try to analyze her feelings. She speaks haltingly in a singsong monotone — as if she were working it out — and the scene is more affecting when you think about it afterward than when she's talking.

Movies have featured rapes and attempted rapes from the beginning of movies; rapes, after all, have both sex and violence. But I can't remember another movie in which the rape victim explained what the invasion of her body meant to her or how profound the insult and humiliation were. This woman isn't young — a woman of indeterminate age, she looks like a Dorothea Lange photograph of a hungry mountain woman; it's never suggested that she's a virgin, and she hasn't been beaten or injured. This kind of rape might be treated jeeringly, as of no consequence. Yet the film pauses for these emotions, which were perhaps improvised by Delores Taylor, who also narrates the story in her plain, non-actressy voice. Squinting, and talking out of the side of her mouth, she really looks like what she plays — a hard, dedicated pacifist. The schoolmistress is a heroine by virtue of what she does and how she thinks, not how glamorous she looks. Throughout the film, the girls in her charge — even the young beauties — are non-flirtatious, straight-talking girls, and as independent as the boys. One girl wears false eyelashes and comes on, but she's treated as a case.

The credits read, "Directed by T. C. Frank. Screenplay by Teresa Cristina and Mr. Frank. Produced by Mary Rose Solti." Those credits are as fake as they sound. Actually, there is no Mary Rose Solti, nor is there a T. C. Frank, and Teresa Cristina (T.C.) is the name of one of the children of Tom Laughlin, who plays Billy Jack, and his wife, Delores Taylor, who made the picture together. They wrote it and produced it jointly; he was the director. I don't know the reason for the pseudonyms (perhaps simply to augment the size of the team?), but the Laughlins played the same game in their first picture — a wheeler, *Born Losers*, released by A.I.P. in 1967 — though in that one the fake names they threw in were masculine. That film, which they began on their own and then sold to A.I.P., is one of the three or four most profitable A.I.P. films. The character of Billy Jack, the half-Indian war veteran who has become a loner, has been carried over from *Born Losers,* in which he came to the aid of a boy beaten by an outlaw motorcycle gang. The Laughlins started *Billy Jack* on their own again, inadequately financed; they began shooting in Prescott, Arizona, then had to close down for three months, and finally finished the film in New Mexico with a different cinematographer. (The changes show.) Then they sold it to Warner Brothers. Despite initial bad luck (and poor handling) in the big cities this summer, it has turned into a huge success, especially with teen-agers in the "heartland," but not only with them; I saw it on Forty-second Street with a very happy audience. It's one of Warner's top-grossing films of the year.

In plot and structure, *Billy Jack* is a shapeless mess. You feel as if the movie could expand or contract at any point, or add another theme or drop a couple; this is frequently the way one feels when moviemakers have shot a lot of footage without thinking it out and then tried to pare it down in the editing room. The story is about how the long-haired, racially mixed students of the workshop school are persecuted by the vicious bigots of the neighboring town. The movie sets this situation up like a Grade B melodrama, and you find yourself smiling at a lot of it, yet the smile is a sympathetic one, because even when the Laughlins' writing is terrible, their instincts are mostly very good. There's a sweet, naïve feeling to *Billy Jack* even when it's atrocious, and in the funny scenes and those involving the hip children of the school (the students appear to be of all ages, and the school is like a big encounter group) it's good in an unorthodox, improvisatory style. As a director, Laughlin shows an ingenuous, romantic talent in these scenes. I'd never before seen comic improvisations turn a movie audience on like this. The audience on Forty-second Street laughed at a street-theatre mock robbery and cheered at one sequence, involving the children's attendance at a Town Council meeting, which they break up. Though the setting is Southwestern and the hero out of a Western, the picture rather resembles *To Sir, with Love*, which was also a surprise success. But *Billy Jack*, a mongrel movie, isn't cloyingly simple like *To Sir, with Love*. When *Billy Jack* moves by feeling — when the scenes keep going because everybody's winging it together — it's like a good jazz session. The trouble with this approach is that you need a freshly thought-out core story to take off from and to go back to. That's where the movie fails — at its center. But in movies this isn't necessarily fatal. The good things in *Billy Jack* create an atmosphere that helps blot out the dumb plot about a deputy sheriff's teen-age daughter who gets pregnant, takes refuge in the school, and falls in love with an Indian boy. Some of the appeal is very basic. On Forty-second Street, when Billy Jack said there was no place people could get a square deal — not in this country, not in the world — a voice bellowed "New York!" and the theatre shook with laughter, and with solidarity.

Very young audiences, who are becoming repeaters, may like the picture because it has a hero, rather than the now customary anti-hero. Laughlin wears his cowboy hat flat across his forehead, like William S. Hart, and, except for a comic slow burn of disgust at examples of revolting behavior, and an occasional smile, his acting is similar, and it's not bad. I'm not sure how the tradition got started of the Westerner's having a poker face (was it carried over from the card table?), but Billy Jack, a folk hero who rights social injustices, is a throwback to this mode. He personifies the good, and he doesn't need to be expressive. And for the very young he not only is a hero, the idealist armed, but is armed on *their* behalf, since he protects Indians, children, and horses. You don't even have to go looking for him: he has mystic powers — he's in touch all the time and is there when you need him. It sounds silly, it *is* silly, but it's also innocent. The Laughlins seem, partly through their inexperience as writers, to have stumbled on a winning combination. For several years now, the heroes of hip American movies have been heroes not by virtue of anything they attempted or accomplished but by virtue of having rejected the possibility that anything could be done and of turning inward. In the pop arts, those who were *first* to start searching for themselves became culture heroes. To be hip has meant to feel that nothing external could be changed, and the movies have been ending in violence or failure or death. The character of Billy Jack combines the good man of action with the soul-searching mystic. He appears to be armed, rather than disarmed, by his studies with an Indian holy man. (In a ceremony in which a rattler strikes him repeatedly, he becomes "brother-to-the-snake.") He doesn't need weapons; in one sequence he K.O.s a gang of toughs by karate. Also, the movie restores the — by now welcome — tradition of the (relatively) happy ending. And in a new way: unlike the Westerns in which the hero shoots the villains and thus demonstrates to the schoolteacher that her pacifism won't work, it is the schoolmistress and her principles of nonviolence that carry the day.

Billy Jack gets by with most of its nonsense (even the new cliché of the director-star as savior) because the kids (a mixture of professionals and non-professionals) and some of the hip comics (from San Francisco's The Committee) are so loose and charming that they really do inspire hope. You can believe that the world isn't all gloom and corruption, because, despite the rigged polarity of adult psychopathic fools versus the free, happy, loving kids, the acting of the kids really is so free, happy, and loving — and so funny. The kids' fast, offhand semi-improvisations incarnate the hopeful theme and give the fairy-tale picture a surprising validity. The happy ending isn't the family-picture seal of approval that it is on Disney products or on a newly made antiquity like *Kotch*, because, in a primitive and original way, *Billy Jack* is hip. It's probably the first hip movie for teen-agers (and sub-teen-agers) since the Beatles' films, which were also hopeful. I don't mean that it was intended for children; I mean that it's so naïve that they respond to it as a hip fairy tale. ("How do you find Billy?" "We just want him and he shows up.") The school is the sub-teen Con III, where baby rock composers sing their condemnations of prejudice and war, and where there are no ambiguities, only right and wrong. We may have learned to resist the adorableness of Disney-style kids, but this infant counter-culture is harder to resist, because the kids are *like our own* — they scatter tough phrases and four-letter words, and their fresh faces take all the obscenity out. This infant idealism is widespread in the country; the Laughlins have put it on the screen, and the kids must be overjoyed to see themselves there.

Considering the material, there's one rather strange and implausible detail. The town's leading citizen and chief bigot, played by beefy Bert Freed, seems to be Jewish and is given a Jewish name; he and his son, the rapist, appear to be the only Jews in the town. I would guess that this is an expression not of anti-Semitism but of the frustrations and anger that build up when moviemakers are torn to shreds while trying to make deals with tough producers — who often physically resemble Bert Freed. The same sort of thing happens in *The Ski Bum*: the character of the hero's employer, a rich, big-time bore, is a blatant caricature of Joe Levine, who financed the movie. *The Ski Bum* (which is being released in New York this week) might seem wildly anti-Semitic if one failed to consider that one of the young filmmaking team is Jewish, and so are several members of the cast; probably, while doing the picture, they got so high on rage — or audacity — that things went a little out of control.

Though the audience I saw *Billy Jack* with was almost all male, it responded happily to the independent, tough-talking girls. It is a curious fact of movie history (and one that may be lost sight of) that, in general, the men always did like the independent women. It was the women who liked the sobbing and suffering ladies. (My father's favorite actresses were Joan Blondell and Barbara Stanwyck; my mother's were Helen Hayes and Ruth Chatterton.) The movie businessmen recognized what the female preferences were when they called certain pictures "women's pictures"; that meant not that they were made by women (though frequently women wrote them, and Dorothy Arzner directed a batch of them) but that they were shaped for women's tastes. They were lachrymose, masochistic, supposedly *realistic* stories about noble dames sacrificing everything for their children, or for their lovers or husbands, or sometimes even for their lover's children by his wife. And though men usually hated them, a lot of women did like them. Those sacrificial tearjerkers were often highly refined in tone, and they could seem serious and worthwhile, whereas it was very difficult to know what to do with tart, independent women except in wisecracking comedies or in men's action films, in which the shady ladies could be tough.

Though the only word for what the man did to Hepburn's aviatrix in *Christopher Strong* is "emasculation," it was perfectly well understood in 1933 that her full possibilities as a woman, as a person, were being destroyed. By the forties, however, it was standard Broadway and Hollywood practice to show that a woman of any achievement must give up whatever she was good at in order to get a man and become a real woman, which meant marriage and family *only*. At worst, there was something sick about a woman if she was successful — like Ginger Rogers as a neurotic magazine editor looking for a dominating male, in the poisonous movie of *Lady in the Dark*. The contrived, often sour endings of the Claudette Colbert and Rosalind Russell pictures were never, I think, felt as satisfactory by anybody. Those slapped-on endings in which sophisticated women had to humble themselves became more and more frequent as the men returning from the war wanted the jobs the women had been filling, but they always felt phony. The movies fell apart at the end because nobody really knew how to resolve those battles of the sexes. By the end of the sixties, there was practically nothing for women on the screen to *be* but prosties or bitches or bunnies, and, as a result, there are at present almost no women movie stars, while the male stars double up in buddy-buddy pictures. How many different kinds of prostitute could Shirley MacLaine play?

In movies, the primal scene of *Christopher Strong* has never been played out satisfactorily — at least, not from the woman's point of view. She always gives in, whether fatally, as in *Christopher Strong* or in the paste-up screwball style that provided the fake resolutions in the forties. And not solving this problem is a major factor in the gradual impoverishment of human relations on the screen since the war years. *Billy Jack*, hopeful as it is, and even though it was made by a husband-and-wife team, ducks the problem. There is no sexual relationship between Billy Jack and the teacher; they are both loners, and though they love each other, they appear to be only spiritual lovers. I suppose this is better than having them enemies, but if it's any reflection of a new mood, it's dispiriting. Movies are full of depersonalized sex, but in terms of sexual love between equals nobody's flying, both sexes are grounded.

[November 27, 1971]

Notes on New Actors, New Movies

Frank Capra destroyed Gary Cooper's early sex appeal when he made him childish as Mr. Deeds; Cooper, once devastatingly lean and charming, the man Tallulah and Marlene had swooned over, began to act like an old woman and went on to a long sexless career — fumbling, homey, mealymouthed. Can this process be reversed? It's easy to see why Richard Benjamin has been working so much. He's a gifted light romantic comedian (on the order of Robert Montgomery in the thirties), and he's physically well suited to the urban Jewish heroes who dominated American fiction for over a decade and have now moved onto the screen. Benjamin is good at miming frustration and wild fantasies, and he's giggly and boyishly apologetic in a way that probably pleases men, because it reminds them of their adolescent silliness, but he doesn't quite appeal to women. What's missing seems to be that little bit of male fascism that makes an actor like Robert Redford or Jack Nicholson dangerous and hence attractive. Benjamin needs some sexual menace, some threat; without that there's no romantic charge to his presence. There's a distinctive nervous emotionalism in his voice (there is in Deborah Kerr's, too); one isn't quite sure how to react to it, because, although his sensitivity is sometimes rich (like Miss Kerr's), it's also on the borderline of weakness. He uses his voice for tricky comic effects: he cackles when one least expects it, or lets the sound break on a word, as if his voice were still changing. (That's a borderline device, too, although Melvyn Douglas always got by with it — but only within limits. Douglas was a leading man, never a star.) When Benjamin slips into nasality — even when it's for humor — there's the danger that he'll slide

347

down into the Arnold Stang range and be sexually hopeless. Can Benjamin get by in the movies without that bit of coarseness or aggression which seems so essential to sex appeal? Fredric March did, but I can't think of many others. And now there's a new question: Can Benjamin get by if he *develops* sex appeal?

Richard Benjamin has, of course, been in demand for some roles just *because* he can project lack of confidence and suggest sexual inadequacy; he can impersonate the new movie stereotype of the American male as perennial adolescent. The Tony Perkins boyish juveniles of the late fifties are now exposed, like Art Garfunkel in *Carnal Knowledge,* in terms of their failure to become men. The new trend is to show the women as abused, deprived, and depersonalized, and an actor with sexual assurance wouldn't function right in these movies, because then there might seem to be something the matter with the woman if she wasn't having a good time. In *Diary of a Mad Housewife,* the mopey heroine is meant to be superior to her tormentors; she's given a nagging, social-climbing fool of a husband (Benjamin), and her selfish lover is played by Frank Langella, the new chief contender for the acting-in-a-mirror (or Hermann Hesse) award. The period coming up may not be the best period for actors who project sexual competence. In Paula Fox's fine novel, *Desperate Characters,* the husband is civilized and fastidious, a rather elegant man, who deeply loves his wife; in the movie version, the director, Frank Gilroy, cast an actor best known for his mad Nazi in *The Producers,* and so the reason for the woman's isolation becomes largely the brutish man she is married to, who at one point in the movie is so sexually excited by the vandalism of their home that he is moved to rape her.

•

Though directors become fairly knowledgeable about the chemistry of performers, even the greatest directors are not always in control of the effects the performers produce. I was offended for Bibi Andersson in Ingmar Bergman's *The Touch* when Elliott Gould, playing a lout, but also playing loutishly, was nuzzling her — offended that she should have to be touched by him. Gould's performance threw me out of the framework of the movie, since what was happening on the screen made me react for the actress, and not in terms of the role she was playing. Most of the women I know felt Gould's touching Bibi Andersson as a physical affront to her and recoiled in the same kinesthetic, empathic way that I did. Some men have said they felt it, too, and were embarrassed for the women they were with. At *Waterloo,* the audience broke into laughter when Rod Steiger, as Napoleon, spoke his first line, simply because he was so unmistakably Rod Steiger. Second-generation actors and actresses may throw us out of the movie because of a line reading or a camera angle that recalls their parents. Peter Fonda can't move or talk without creating an echo chamber, and he looks as if somehow, on the set of *The Grapes of Wrath,* John Carradine and Henry Fonda had mated.

•

In *Doc,* Stacy Keach presents so obdurate a face that you feel he has to consider when to let a flicker of expression through. Those who fight easy expressiveness may be actors of integrity, but they're likely to be repellent screen actors. In movies, one can accept non-actors and mediocrities, one can accept stone-faced dummies, but deliberately masked, intellectualized acting — acting by a theory — is intolerable. Keach doesn't offer himself to the camera; he fights it, and in so doing he limits the meaning of his roles and sharply limits our pleasures. Such pleasures may have as much to do with what we see in an actor as in what he consciously projects. We care more for a trace of personality than for all of Keach's serious intentions. If Richard Benjamin is too lightweight, and maybe even too *loose,* Keach turns himself into a heavyweight and is much too tight. He's so determined to give us the constricted performance he has worked out that he gives us less than most Hollywood bums do just by not caring.

•

Dustin Hoffman has become such a culture hero that one hesitates to point out that he's more relaxed and likable on TV talk shows than when he's acting. In his screen roles, he hasn't yet found the gift of moving into a part and then just going with it. I love to watch him, because he's intelligent and he has extraordinary drive and he takes us by surprise, but he isn't an intuitive actor, and we're aware of how cleverly he's playing the part. To some degree, his rapport with the audience is based on our awareness of his cleverness, and our rooting for him, but then when his dexterity fails, and he's open-mouthed — and Hoffman, like Richard Benjamin, is nasal — we have nothing to fall back on. When his role isn't funny, he's usually helplessly tense; you can see him wishing he had something to *play.*

•

Though the dream of movies as a great popular art slips further and further away as the audience grows smaller and smaller, still, every year there are a handful of really good movies and others that reveal social changes, and almost always, even in bad films, one can count on some good performances. That's probably what holds the remaining audience together: actors like Dustin Hoffman and Richard Benjamin are fun to watch. There aren't any rules about movies — except maybe the fluky ones, such as that it's impossible to get a college atmosphere on film that feels authentic, and that pictures set in ancient Egypt are always ridiculous — but one might say with some confidence that feature filmmakers who don't care about actors and acting may have some sporadic luck but they're not likely to make movies for long, because nobody is going to go to their pictures. The promising American directors are not those who try to give us a sensory overload (we get enough overload without getting it at the movies) but directors such as Robert Altman, Paul Mazursky, Jack Nicholson, Irvin Kershner, John Korty, Woody Allen, Brian De Palma, and Tom Laughlin, who are trying to find new ways for the performers to connect with the audience. They use quick-witted performers — often those trained in cabaret theatre, who can enter into the moviemaking in a different spirit from the actors who just learn their lines.

•

In the past two decades, male movie actors have carried the pictures, not only without much help from women but often without much help from the scripts and the directors. Still, they have had a rough time trying to keep some pride in themselves as actors. Every time we pick up the paper, another top-box-office actor informs us that he wants to become a director in order to do something "creative": Paul Newman, George C. Scott, Jack Lemmon, and even John Wayne and Clint Eastwood — though perhaps in their cases for other reasons. Maybe just a change? (The actresses don't want to direct, they want to write books — but that's another story.) Men — and not only American men — have always had hangups about acting; heterosexual men, in particular, tend to feel that acting is not a fit occupation, and that it doesn't fully use their abilities. One famous male star said in conversation, "I just can't say lines anymore" — meaning, I suppose, among other things, that he'd grown up. Yet few of the men stars risk more difficult roles or attempt new styles of acting, in which they might grow up as actors. The stars prefer to become directors, usually to turn out more of the same kind of movies that make actors feel like fools.

But movie acting has been loosening up, and it could be turning into a profession for smarter, more intuitive people. Some of the most inventive performances have been in flops — like the performances of Peter Bonerz, the hero of the neglected film *Funnyman*, and Barry Primus, the hero of *Been Down So Long It Looks Like Up to Me*, and William Tepper, the hero of *Drive, He Said* — and so they aren't talked about. But these put-on artists are part of a new and already taken-for-granted style of screen acting, which affects how we look at star-commodity performances. It's now difficult for us to accept the established stars in contemporary settings. We've lived for years with stars who didn't know what to do with a laugh line. (Has anyone seen Charlton Heston, for example, trying to play comedy?)

•

George Segal, who is probably the best light comedian in American movies, bridges the styles of the romantic screen stars, such as Cary Grant and Paul Newman, and the hip, loose, put-on comedy style of the sixties. He seems to be one of the few actors to find their challenge in acting, and he gives his roles solidity and some human weight — the way Spencer Tracy did but without Tracy's boring pugnacity. He's kept working for seven years, as if the old studio system were still intact, and he gets better all the time — maybe because he's never quite made it to the top box-office brackets, so he isn't image-conscious, like the million-dollar-a-picture men, whose films become high-risk corporate enterprises. Last year, he did the failed artist in *Loving,* the self-deceiving book clerk in *The Owl and the Pussycat,* and the frustrated lawyer in *Where's Poppa?,* and now he has tried, and brought off, the prodigiously difficult role of a hipster junkie in the Czech director Ivan Passer's new film — and his first to be made in this country — *Born to Win.*

Movies are so porous a mixture of intentions and accidents that when cultures are crossed the resonances may become confused. Dubbing is the most egregious example, but the resonances can go more subtly wrong, as when the locale of a story is changed, or when the director is a foreigner. In Miloš Forman's first American picture, *Taking Off,* the suburban Americans looked Czech to me and seemed to be living in the thirties, and I got a little sleepy, the way I sometimes do at Czech films, in which the rhythm of life seems too mild, too pokey. I didn't have that problem with *Born to Win;* Passer's sense of America is very sharp, and the rhythm of the picture, edited by Ralph Rosenblum, who was once a jazz musician, is active, volatile. You feel your senses are being quickened as you watch. The only way Passer reveals his foreignness is in the innocent, idealistic sincerity with which this slice-of-life film appears to be made, and in the tactful intelligence with which he spares us needles in the arm. He doesn't try to turn the audience on; it's clear that he wants to show us this junkie's soul, not his habit.

Born to Win, from a screenplay by David Scott Milton, was shot under the much better title *Scraping Bottom;* I assume that the title was changed to con audiences into thinking they were going to see an upbeat movie. But it isn't that the movie is downbeat that works against it commercially — it's that it's downbeat in a way that isn't glamorous. J, the junkie, isn't mutinous, isn't anti-establishment. J isn't even chasing freedom. The movie doesn't make him a romantic loser (which is the path to box-office success). It's like those other stories of driven men who destroy themselves — usually prizefighters, as in *Requiem for a Heavyweight*, or gangsters. Anyone can see that *Born to Win* isn't totally successful. It's the best of the addict movies, yet, like the others, it has no place to go but the too familiar down. Junkies don't get cured in contemporary movies — they don't even want to be cured — so we know everyone is doomed. And the explanations never suffice: we come out still puzzled as to why people do it to themselves. Maybe the best clue to J's character is his line "I'm a very boring guy when I'm straight." But though, in all probability, nobody will come out of *Born to Win* fully satisfied, I don't think anybody will regret having gone to see it, either.

Segal gives the most imaginatively complete performance in an American movie since Jane Fonda in *Klute*. His J, the city rat, is a smarter version of Dustin Hoffman's Ratso — not pathetic and not a simpleton. You know J isn't going to get away with anything, yet this stoolie — the lowest of the low, and not because of stupidity but because of an addict's moral vacuity and indifference — holds you. J doesn't know or care that New York City is under siege. At the bottom, things don't change that much. Yet the bottom can also be funny in a different way from any other place (as Samuel Beckett recognized), because of the insane freedom of total losers. Words come easily to this smart, funny hipster, who seems essentially harmless and yet manages to wreck everyone who gets close to him. He has an anguished but ironic and knowing face; the transitions of mood are so fast they seem never to have gone through the brain. His sense of the ridiculous includes whatever he's doing, and the glee and the horror are rolled up together; he's like Harry Ritz in agony. Like many good movie actors, Segal can be very quiet, very still; he seems able to incorporate a character and then let it come out easily, naturally — as if it had always been there in him. But he has never before attempted such a quicksilver character: J is a comedian in pain yet so shallow he forgets his own pain, a man with absolutely no sense of tomorrow or of yesterday — an absurd man seen not in the abstract setting of an absurdist play but in the lower depths of New York City.

•

If an actor has any screen presence at all, his ego usually shows: you know he thinks well of himself. (When he pushes his luck, we call it conceit.) For a while in the thirties, juvenile leads did the passive-vulnerable bit, like some of the ingénues, but that was when there were strong women to overpower them — Garbo swooping down over them and exposing her throat, and Hepburn playing tomboy to fey young men — and it doesn't work anymore. Even a juvenile like Ryan O'Neal comes on cocky-vulnerable, and when you see a non-egocentric performer, like Timothy Bottoms in *The Last Picture Show,* you know that he requires a director to bring him out — that, like the European actors who often fail over here, he doesn't have the strength of the actors who bust through no matter what. Richard Benjamin's comic persona is based on his self-confidence as an *actor.* George Segal has this cockiness, Spencer Tracy carried it to monotonous extremes, Gable wore it as his crown. It's what gives Warren Beatty his comic edge — he uses it ironically; so did Burt Lancaster and Kirk Douglas. A dull actor like Rock Hudson lacks it, and so does Gregory Peck — competent but always a little boring, a leading man disguised as a star. It's a quality that is usually described unflatteringly in women, though the only recently arrived woman star, Barbra Streisand, has got it, and I doubt if a new woman star could come up without it.

Robert Mitchum has that assurance in such huge amounts that he seems almost a lawless actor. He does it all out of himself. He doesn't use the tricks and stratagems of clever, trained actors. Mitchum is *sui generis.* There have been other good movie actors who invented for themselves without falling back on stage techniques — Joel McCrea, for one, a talented romantic comedian who became a fine, quiet, and much underrated actor. But there's no other powerhouse like Mitchum. This great bullfrog with the puffy eyes and the gut that becomes an honorary chest has been in movies for almost thirty years, and he's still so strong a masculine presence that he knocks younger men off the screen. His strength seems to come precisely from his avoidance of conventional acting, from his dependence on himself; his whole style is a put-on, in the sense that it's based on our shared understanding that he's a man acting in material conceived for puppets. He can barrel his way through, as he does in the new *Going Home,* even when the role isn't worth playing. The script, an original by Lawrence B. Marcus, is about a man who kills his wife, with their child as witness (this opening scene is bloody powerful); when he is paroled from prison thirteen years later, the obsessed boy, full of fear and hate for his father, comes to visit him. I'm sure the script looked good on paper; like the scripts — also originals — that Alan Sharp wrote for *The Hired Hand* and *The Last Run,* this Marcus script has a literate, "gritty" surface and a symmetrical structure. The trouble with these scripts is that they achieve their classicism too easily: there's nothing *under* them; they have the paper thinness of TV drama. In *Going Home,* the ominous atmosphere (Will the son do something terrible? Will the father kill the son?) is simply for its own sake; there isn't enough revelation to justify keeping us so tense. The lurid big sequences (a rape in a room full of crowing gamecocks; an Expressionistic party and fight in the old family home, now a restaurant called the Inferno) are beyond redemption, but the director, Herbert B. Leonard, has done an impressive professional job; the small towns and seashore trailer-camp locations have an authentic and lovely melancholy, and are not presented condescendingly. Still, *Going Home* is an empty suspense film that exploits its star for a fake humanity. Mitchum is forced to overdraw on himself.

[December 4, 1971]

Peter Brook's "Night of the Living Dead"

Peter Brook's *King Lear* is gray and cold, and the actors have dead eyes. I didn't just dislike this production — I hated it. The fact that it's *intentionally* gray and cold and dead doesn't redeem it; a slob of a director might have let the actors take over and some of *King Lear's* emotional poetry might have come through, but Brook has a unified vision and never lets go of the reins. There are no accidental pleasures in this movie — and, as I see it, no deliberate ones, either. I think I understand why Gloucester's eyes are plucked out in giant closeup (though I averted my own eyes); I guess I know why the black-and-white cinematography is predominantly dark gray and pale gray and why everyone is lighted in a flat, *unlighted* way, and why Cordelia is sullen and mechanical — a walking corpse, like the others. One can glimpse the intention to make Lear himself less centrifugal and to use the icy, empty landscapes (the film was shot in northern Denmark) as a metaphor for the unyielding, ungoverned universe, in which all men are pawns and there is no hope for anyone. There are no apparent light sources, and surely the dead eyes are metaphorically linked to this blind, godless desolation. The movie is all nightmare images of blindness and nothingness; Brook has retained the metaphors of *Lear* and thrown out the play. Ideas in theatre are rare, but to have a conception is not the same as having a good conception. The world's exhaustion and the light's having disappeared may open up new meanings in Shakespeare's play to us, but as the controlling metaphors in this production they don't enlarge the play, they cancel it out.

The performances are kept so dry and rigidly mannered that you don't get involved in who is who in time to catch hold of the plot strands, which are clipped short and presented in a loony, egalitarian manner, as if all the elements were of equal importance. Obviously, Brook intends to make them so, because when the several subplots have the same weight as the story of Lear and his daughters the action of the play tends to become meaningless and the characters are drained of emotional force. If Lear is not allowed to be a titanic unreasonable man, a vain, impetuous old fool who stands for all of us when he brings torment upon himself — if he is cut down to life-size, so that he no longer represents supreme human rashness — then he is merely one of us, and what happens to him becomes part of a generalized meaninglessness and despair. This *Lear* is made essentially plotless not by removing the plot (that is practically all that *remains* of the play) but by using the plot as a diagram for movement abstracted from psychological and dramatic meaning. By the time you've seized the outline, the cutting has become jaggedly mannered, with sudden shifts from one angle to another and from long shots to closeups, often while someone is speaking, and then your eyes are punished by blinding flashes that are like exploding bombs. The cutting seems designed as an alienation device, but who wants to be alienated from Shakespeare's play and given the drear far side of the moon instead? A number of critics pointed out that although Peter Brook's production of *Marat/Sade* was certainly theatrical, the play itself wasn't dramatic. Brook has managed to make this *King Lear* theatrical and to destroy the Shakespearean drama. His theatrical conception is all there onscreen, fully realized, in the first shots of the soulless people; there's no development — the movie simply grinds on from ellipsis to ellipsis. His theatrical conception kills not only the drama but most of the poetry; Shakespeare's words are a celebration of the mysteries of personality and destiny — they ring with all the meanings and emotions that this production denies. But when people with dead souls are saying Shakespeare's lines the emotional resonances die away. You may feel dead while you watch.

Dubious as the mechanism of the play always was, it had a fairy-tale grandeur, and Lear's error of judgment in disinheriting Cordelia, the youngest princess and the only one who truly loved him, had both psychological and dramatic power; now this act, too, is void of meaning — just another thing that happens, senselessly. In Shakespeare's *Lear,* lack of filial piety is a form of barbarism; when Lear's older daughters treat him with contempt once they have gained their thrones and riches, the underpinnings of civilization fall away and there is chaos. But in Brook's interpretation the chaos that comes "again" is not man returning to barbarism because of cruelty and ingratitude — he has put it there in the first frames, with those implacable faces. And so the treachery or loyalty of Lear's and Gloucester's children and friends doesn't make much difference. Everything is doomed, even before Lear's decision to disinherit the daughter he loves best; Cordelia's eyes are as dead as Goneril's and Regan's, and her fatal refusal to flatter her father is not candor but odd, unfathomable behavior. There is no tragic heroine, nor does the light in the world go out; it *is* out. Nothing matters. The movie is cruelly detached: we are allowed to feel some tenderness only when the mad Lear and the blind Gloucester — the ruined pieces of nature — meet at Dover; that is, when Brook has brought the old derelicts to Endgame. The setting might be the world's elemental basement; the northernmost part of the Jutland peninsula, where they meet, is an icy desert with Arctic winds sweeping the snow-covered dunes. If, as Jan Kott suggested, *Endgame* came out of *Lear,* what purpose does it then serve to base one's *Lear* on Beckett? Doesn't that merely reduce *Lear* to the elements Beckett transformed and made his own, and thus turn Shakespeare into imitation Beckett?

I don't think one can hate an inept production the way one can hate a production that is willfully, ideologically displeasing. I know that this means that a reviewer may attack those who dare to experiment, though tolerating incompetents and hacks for whatever pleasures may be found in their work. But what is gained by performing Shakespeare so monastically, without ever letting the actors scale an emotional peak or letting a line soar? Only in a few remaining long speeches can one still be swept up by the rhythm of Shakespeare's language. And Brook wouldn't dream of letting us have so much as a bar of music. Rasping sounds — that's what we get. The conception is resolutely joyless and unbeautiful — a *Lear* without passion, *Lear* set in a glacial desert. A merciless view of theatre is implicit in this movie: the performers are so disciplined to do exactly what the director wants that they have lost their free will, and, with it, their temperament and their excitement. This, too, is part of Brook's conception, but it's ensemble acting carried to Zombieland. You feel as if you were meant to admire the discipline for its own austere sake. Paul Scofield's Lear is world-famous, but onscreen Scofield is a freezing actor, haughtily handsome—an actor who keeps us at a distance. There is no terror in Lear's madness, because Scofield is intelligent and magisterial throughout. In the opening sequence, he takes so long to say his words that we lose the sense; after an hour, I no longer cared when I lost the sense of a line. This, I would guess, is Peter Brook's aim — to reduce Shakespeare's lines to words that no longer communicate. Only Alan Webb's Gloucester has a sneaking humanity that occasionally flickers through the stylized acting. What Brook has done in *Lear* is to kill the performers in camera terms. And in doing so he has reduced the multiplicity of elements that is the saving grace of movies. If one rejects his idea of *Lear* as an expression of cold nothingness, there are no performances, no readings, no stray images to sustain one. Peter Brook, as everybody knows, is an unspecified sort of genius, and the world keeps waiting for him to define himself. But maybe he can be defined only as an oscillator — a man with more talent than judgment. This *Lear* isn't a daring conception (one could forgive the irritating, derivative film techniques if it were) — it's a second-rate conception. Shakespeare transfers to film so extraordinarily well because his plays are open in structure, not closed in time and place. This greatest dramatist is also, as it happens, the greatest scenarist. And the greatness of Shakespeare has been like the greatness of movies: the richness of what one can find there. To have limited *King Lear* to a single idea and then to have made a movie of this limited *King Lear* is an excruciating double folly.

•

Richard Harris is mauled by a grizzly bear at the gory beginning of *Man in the Wilderness* and spends the rest of the movie dragging himself across iridescent landscapes while flashbacks reveal his past life. It's a beautiful-looking movie, photographed by Gerry Fisher, and set in the United States in 1820; the natural atmosphere is so paradisiacal that one luxuriates in it, thinking that all this must be around somewhere to have been photographed. It is, but not over here; the movie was shot in Spain.

There's always a certain fascination about the Crusoe survivor theme —

about how people manage to make it alone with nothing but their wits and skills, and how it changes them. What's best in such stories is the factual account of the way practical problems are solved. But now "the kids" are known to be "into survival" and high on mysticism, and that, I suppose, explains how *Man in the Wilderness* was born and got to be made. Directed by Richard C. Sarafian, from a sub-literate script by Jack DeWitt, the movie doesn't bother to locate the hero clearly for us, so that we might judge how far he has to go. It's all rather ethereal — a survival fantasy — and more concerned with imagery of the wilds than with his problems, though he also has a ringside seat at a circus. Enough events (murders, impalings, childbirth, and so on) take place in the wilds close to him to satisfy the heartiest voyeur lost on a camping trip. In addition, there is a mystical revenge theme: the man is sustained by the desire to avenge himself on the captain of the expedition he was with, who left him to die. The movie is supposedly based on historical documents, but everything in it seems improbable, and it's never explained why the captain (John Huston, at his most idiosyncratic), who is the Ahab-Noah of an ark being pulled across the land by mules, doesn't just put the wounded man on board instead of abandoning him. In the movie, the vengeful man and the remorseful expedition crew haunt each other, and when a crew member asks the demi-maniac captain if he thinks there's any chance that Harris could have made it on his own, Huston says, "Yes, Fogarty, he's alive. I've known all along." How? Did the birds tell him? Or did he see the last pages of the script? This kind of superstitious bilge — characters look at each other with fixed expressions, intoning lines like "It ain't natural" — was considered very artistic in twenties movies, and now it's back. In the interests of cultural sanitation, I hope young audiences guffaw it off the screen.

Richard Harris is a cheerlessly powerful actor who is sometimes magnificent, and once, in *Major Dundee,* he actually revealed a little dash and charm. But his power has become a physical resource that he exploits as mechanically as other actors turn their profiles to the camera. After you've seen him on TV going through his whole repertory of agonized expressions while singing a lachrymose ballad — he wrenches Bobby Breen songs from his gut — you know how little it signifies when he goes through the same wrenched-gut suffering in a film. I think he must recover from these scenes much faster than some of us in the audience, who come out of a movie like this feeling as if we'd been put through a wringer. *Man in the Wilderness* may be for Boy Scout heads, but I don't know where Richard Harris's head is. He hauls his surly carcass from movie to movie, being dismembered. I'd just as soon wait out his next pictures until he's finished.

•

Bedknobs and Broomsticks, from the Disney studios, a fantasy starring Angela Lansbury as an apprentice witch in Second World War England, is from time to time enjoyable. It is also, however, a bewildering index to the confusion in the movie industry and in the empire Walt Disney left behind. Starting with the title, *Bedknobs and Broomsticks* is a big, mongrel production; it combines live action and animation in some fairly long sequences and includes an elaborate ballet in a mockup of Portobello Road (inspired, one assumes, by the "Consider Yourself" street ballet in *Oliver!*), and at the end there is a sequence, perhaps influenced by some of the Russian and Central European movie fantasies, that is magical animation in a tradition different from the usual Disney work. Miss Lansbury, on a broomstick, commands a ghostly army of knights on steeds against the Nazis; her army is made up of empty armor from the local museum, and this bloodless battle has the quality of fairy-tale imagination, which is the quality so painfully absent in Disney's cartooned fairy tales. But the movie is execrably shot and edited. I've never seen worse photographic framing in a big-budget film; pieces of bodies are frequently cut off by the top of the frame or by the sides. In the Portobello Road sequence, though one can see that the choreographer, Donald McKayle, had some ideas, the dance seems to have been photographed by a passing cameraman who didn't know where to turn his lens to catch the next movement. The choppy editing in this sequence is dumbfounding; Miss Lansbury begins a dance step, then the movie cuts away for an instant, and when it returns to her she's not dancing at all, she's doing something else. It is, I guess, the most poorly put-together big dance number I've ever seen on film; I think it beats out the editing in *Song of Norway*. And the color, even in the cartoon sequences, which the Disney technicians used to make so bright and clear that kids' eyes popped open (remember the yellows in *Three Little Pigs*?), is pallid and tired-looking.

There's no logic in the style of the movie. It tries to integrate early-period Silly Symphony animation (climaxed here in a frenzied — and, I thought, ugly — animal soccer game) with a story that dribbles on so long that it exhausts the viewer before the final magical battle begins. And this story is suffused with patriotic sentimentality, circa *Mrs. Miniver,* and suffocating notions of domestic tranquillity. Miss Lansbury gives up witchcraft when she gets a man, David Tomlinson, who twinkles like a sexless pixie and touches her lips chastely as he goes off — a reprobate reformed by love and duty — to join the Army. He is escorted by a detachment of the gallant, doddering Home Guard, for an extra emotional tug. And, of course, the movie includes the Disney inevitable — this time in the shape of three lovable Cockney orphans for the reformed witch and her reformed mate to adopt. Even the kids get reformed in this compulsively moral tale. The director, Robert Stevenson, a veteran in this genre, found an appallingly simple solution to the problem of enabling Americans to understand the children's Cockney intonations: every time one of the children speaks, we get a closeup, so that our full attention is focussed on the piping little speaker and we can practically read the lips. To judge by the laugh reactions, the audience didn't miss a single childish witticism, but the visual line of the movie is impacted by all these closeups — it's as if a TV show had been cut into the movie every few seconds.

The picture also plays a subtly deranging trick on our senses; it's something I don't recall ever before seeing sustained through an entire film. Though the children are photographed in their normal proportions, and though the adults don't look distorted in close shots, whenever the adults are at a distance they are elongated. This gives Miss Lansbury the greatest stems imaginable, and when she dances in an underwater ballroom with Mr. Tomlinson she is enchantingly lanky. But the dancers in the Portobello number seem to be moving on toothpicks. Adults who take children may not be bored as much as they fear; they may find themselves fixated on the eccentricities and anomalies of this film, which is part wizardry and part unholy ineptitude.

[December 11, 1971]

The Fall and Rise of Vittorio De Sica

Twenty years ago, André Bazin wrote that "the Neapolitan charm of De Sica becomes, thanks to the cinema, the most sweeping message of love that our times have heard since Chaplin." De Sica's characters are "lit from within by the tenderness he feels for them," Bazin wrote. "Rossellini's style is a way of seeing, while De Sica's is primarily a way of feeling." Vittorio De Sica is one of those directors "whose entire talent derives from the love they have for their subject, from their ultimate understanding of it." But in the years since Bazin wrote those words De Sica's films have diminished in interest, and the routine jobs have obscured the work of his great neo-realist period. After a career in the late twenties and the thirties as a movie matinée idol — the handsome singing star of dozens of romantic musicals — De Sica had become a director, at first of highly successful light comedies and then, with the collaboration of the writer Cesare Zavattini, of a series of movies that were aesthetically revolutionary. The style that they initiated in 1942 with *The Children Are Watching Us* reached international critical recognition, after the war, with *Shoeshine,* in 1947, and then, in 1948, achieved its only financial success with the classic *The Bicycle Thief.* They followed that with the comic fantasy *Miracle in Milan,* in 1951, and, finally, later that year, the luminous, slightly flawed masterwork *Umberto D.* Commercially, *Umberto D.* was an abject failure; it didn't even get an opening in the United States until 1955. And the film was attacked by Italian government officials — which was financially crippling, because De Sica and Zavattini needed government subsidies in order to finance their projects. They gave up; they went on working together, but in the commercial cinema. Later, they made one last attempt — *The Roof,* in 1957 — but the impulse that had motivated their greatest work seemed spent, and *The Roof* was tired. It had less life than their commercial jobs, which, though star vehicles and conventional crowd-pleasers, were often crowd-pleasers in the best sense — high-spirited satirical entertainments, with that nonprofessional actress Sophia Loren, who in De Sica's hands blossomed into the most luscious comedienne the screen has ever known. In full bloom, she is a glory, yet without De Sica she is not quite so funny and her humor and beauty lack roots.

There were few so holy that they could cry "Sellout!" to Vittorio De Sica and Cesare Zavattini, who openly abandoned their hopes. Maybe they could have fought their way through if they had been younger, but De Sica was born in 1901 and Zavattini in 1902. Movies have been a young man's medium (largely, one assumes, because of the business pressures that drain an artist's energy), and De Sica had made his greatest films at an age when most good directors have their best work behind them. It may have been the mellowed emotions of this late beginner that gave that series of neo-realist films their special purity. Though those films (which used actual locations and, as actors, people who actually were what they were supposed to be) were made on aesthetic principles that appear to have been formulated by Zavattini, it was De Sica's way of feeling that provided the soul for Zavattini's theory of a direct seizure of "reality." (The films that Zavattini wrote on the same principles for other directors turned out to be rather unpleasant.) But De Sica's famous "limpidity" — the technique that one was not aware of, because all one saw was the subject made radiant — was lost when he moved into the commercial cinema. It was by means of his limpid style that he and Zavattini had extended our sense of the beauty in common experience and of the elegance of simple gestures. It was a selfless director's art, an art so transparent that we think of those De Sica films purely in terms of emotion. When we recall moments from *Shoeshine,* or Umberto D.'s voice calling "Flick," or Emma Gramatica hopping over the spilled milk in *Miracle in Milan,* we are likely, I think, to experience a poignancy so strong that it amounts to an ache, like the ache we feel when we recall moments in a D. W. Griffith film or a Chaplin comedy. Like Griffith and Chaplin, De Sica achieved images that one feels to be essences of human experience — suffering or joy turned into poetry. Bazin tried to explain this phenomenon when he said, "Poetry is but the active and creative form of love, its projection into the world." Because of De Sica's selflessness and the way he has disappeared into the subject, those great films stay almost incredibly distinct in the memory, the characters separately imprinted.

The later entertainments run together; they were often agreeable enough, but they leave few memories. *The Gold of Naples, Marriage — Italian Style, Yesterday, Today, and Tomorrow,* and a host of short-story films in big-director packages are not entirely bad, but they don't mean much to us, and, far from being limpid, they are careless, crowded, on occasion downright ugly. If De Sica became somewhat indifferent to how the commercial entertainments were made, who is to say that it mattered much? These were "lusty" films, not intended to be lingered over. Both as actor and as director, De Sica is a man of different sides. In his fifties, he became a superb ham actor in a florid tradition, but as the arm-waving lawyer defending Gina Lollobrigida in the trial for murder in *Times Gone By,* and in such movies as *Bread, Love, and Dreams, The Miller's Beautiful Wife,* and *The Anatomy of Love,* he is a different man from the restrained, civilized diplomat in *The Earrings of Madame De . . .* The hammy, extravagantly good-natured actor seems to be the director of the entertainments, which, though coarse, are not coarsely *felt.* In his crowd-pleasers, as in his refined work, De Sica is the true democrat of directors: his love of people has nothing to do with rank — he can be generous even toward the rich. His courtly tact extends to everyone, and he never swarms all over a character. The distance he keeps is an implicit homage to the dignity of the characters; he reveals more by not invading their privacy — and that takes art.

This doesn't mean, however, that one looked forward to the *next* De Sica film. He had, after all, first appeared on the screen as the boy Clemenceau in *The Clemenceau Case,* in 1915, and men of seventy don't often make good movies. (Buñuel is about the only exception who comes to mind.) De Sica's work had seemed in fairly obvious decline, as if he no longer had the energy — or perhaps the interest — to hold the complex elements of filmmaking together. And so *The Garden of the Finzi-Continis* is a beautiful surprise — a return not to neo-realism but to the limpid style of his neo-realist days.

Graceful and leisurely, *The Garden of the Finzi-Continis,* which is set in Ferrara in the Fascist period of the late thirties and early forties, is unmistakably novelistic in style, and different from anything else De Sica has ever done. The movie, from a semi-autobiographical novel by Giorgio Bassani published in Italy in 1962, is about a now vanished group of people and a vanished mood, and you can feel a novelist's sensibility in the tenuous relationships and the romantically charged decadence of the aristocratic setting. But though the relationships are tenuous, you feel that the movie is complete — that the tenuousness is an expression of the writer's obsession with this incompletely understood part of his past.

The movie not only is faithful to this obsession but validates the obsession — and without making a great to-do about it. De Sica's early films call up waves of emotion in us because the great moments are not overstated; he seems incapable of the cultural inflation that goes on in a film like *The Go-Between,* in which all that "style" is looking over our shoulders and telling us that there are deep things lurking in the empty spaces. That movie, I feel, did not validate the boy outsider's obsession. In the De Sica film — to borrow from Flip Wilson — what you see is what you get. The protagonist, Giorgio, from whose point of view we perceive the characters and events, is a middle-class Jewish-Italian student (Lino Capolicchio) who falls in love with Micòl (Dominique Sanda), the young daughter of the Finzi-Continis — rich, cultivated Sephardic Jews, descendants of the Venetian merchants who fled the Spanish Inquisition and intermarried with the leading Jewish families of Europe. Landowners with vast holdings, the Finzi-Continis live in a huge old house surrounded by a private park, with tennis courts and stables. Micòl, intelligent but imperious and contrary, and her languid, sickly brother, Alberto (Helmut Berger), live behind their garden walls in a decaying world that they haven't the strength or the will to change or to escape. It's an enchanted world for Giorgio, the middle-class outsider who is drawn into it — to play tennis when the Jews are expelled from the local tennis club, to use the Finzi-Continis' library when he can no longer use the city library. He is drawn in only part way, and obsessively, because Micòl does not return his love. Giorgio is not unlike the hero of *Goodbye, Columbus*, and the characters here, too, are predominantly Jewish, but the Finzi-Continis are the very opposite of vulgar nouveaux riches: the parents, with their distant, benevolent smiles for the young, seem detached and bloodless, the father an antiquarian preoccupied with seventeenth-century studies, the mother vague and formal. And if Giorgio, like Roth's hero, has difficulty comprehending the family's way of life, it's for the opposite reason: the Patimkins are survivors, the Finzi-Continis — assimilated to a nineteenth-century liberalism — are not. They have lost connection with the realities of Mussolini's Italy, which will soon de-assimilate them.

At the beginning of the movie, I thought that Dominique Sanda was shot like a young Garbo, and that I hadn't seen a brother and sister who were such glamorous look-alikes since Greta Garbo and Douglas Fairbanks, Jr., in *A Woman of Affairs*, the movie version of *The Green Hat*. Not that Dominique Sanda and Helmut Berger are quite in that league, but they're close enough to it to suggest the earlier pair and to be fairly dazzling. Then my reaction shifted as I realized that their relationship was reminiscent of Elisabeth (Nicole Stéphane) and Paul (Édouard Dermithe), the brother and sister in *Les Enfants Terribles*. A moment later, Micòl was reading the Cocteau novel and remarking on how chic it was. And then I understood that the connections I had been making were implicit in the scheme. If Dominique Sanda's Micòl seems to suggest both Garbo and Elisabeth, it should be recalled that Cocteau (as Francis Steegmuller explained in his biography) had Garbo in mind when he wrote Elisabeth — Garbo at eighteen, Cocteau said. And the novel *Les Enfants Terribles*, which was published in 1929, did have an unusual influence on the life style of adolescents in the thirties, who, Cocteau said, "found themselves mirrored in Paul and Elisabeth." Paul and Elisabeth were natural aristocrats by virtue of a narcissistic mixture of youth, pride, beauty — and contempt for all other values, especially self-preservation. It's apparent that Bassani (who also worked on the movie) intended Micòl and her brother to be among the mirror images. The sense of youth as an élite in *The Garden of the Finzi-Continis* is linked to Cocteau's reckless adolescents, just as the atmosphere of the youth-filled summer garden is, inevitably, Proustian.

Though Dominique Sanda's face is that of a perverse goddess, it isn't very expressive, but she has a great slouch, and if she stalks around her castle looking maybe a little more opaque than is absolutely necessary, she is nevertheless wonderfully *remote* — which is what Micòl is meant to be, since Giorgio and we never get to understand her. This novelistic approach is not, however, totally satisfying on the screen. De Sica's neo-realist films were dramatically structured so that we grasped everything there was to understand in the situation; here our point of view is Giorgio's — which is tentative, slightly bewildered. We want to perceive more than Giorgio does; we want to understand Micòl even if he doesn't. And at this level I think De Sica's fidelity to the novel becomes a limitation. Obviously, the author, looking back on the time, is fascinated by the Jewish landed gentry and their paralysis of will; the movie records Mussolini's small oppressive edicts — the gradual loss of rights — and we know where it will end. But we Americans have an aversion to watching people drift to destruction; many young Americans were furious at the suicide of the lovers in *Elvira Madigan,* and I believe they may also get angry at Micòl, lazing around putting on the same record year after year and dressing up. We want to know: Why don't they do something? But this is the elusive part of the story, which I'm afraid we must take as the given in this movie, just as the suicide was the given in *Elvira Madigan.* The fact is that these people didn't save themselves. What's unsatisfying is in the nature of the material — that it's autobiographical and historical and rather precious, and that it's a minor novel when we want the insights and explanations that a major novelist could give us. A major novelist solves the mysteries for us; Bassani dwells on what he doesn't understand. You feel that the author is more involved in his own responses — in his own style — than in the subject. And that might be a definition of decadence. It is what links Giorgio Bassani to Micòl and pale Alberto and to Cocteau's gorgeously corrupt children and to the ancestral super-elegant tribe of *The Green Hat*. This is not the highest form of art, but, as it happens, the movies of *The Garden of the Finzi-Continis* and *Les Enfants Terribles* are, in different ways, quite marvellous, and Garbo has never been more extraordinary than in *A Woman of Affairs*. In their own terms, these movies are honest. *The Go-Between* pretends to be an attack on decadence, and the style of the movie gives it the lie; these movies openly love their spoiled beautiful people.

André Bazin was right when he said that De Sica drew his art from his understanding of his subjects, and it's a happy coincidence that Bazin's supremely perceptive essays on him should be available in English for the first time — in Volume II of *What Is Cinema?* — just when *The Garden of the Finzi-Continis,* which might be an illustration of his thesis, is opening. I think the only disappointment in the film is that Vittorio De Sica is a major film artist translating to the screen a minor novel. It has provided him with his finest subject in many years, but, except in a few moments of faultless intuition, he can't transcend it. The novel is not one of those sprawling second-rate novels that a movie director can use as a skeleton; it is a true minor novel, unmistakably slender. There was no way, I think, for De Sica to give it more body — to provide a fuller psychology and a richer social context — without destroying the mysteriously lyric quality of Bassani's memories.

There is an instant toward the end that is, however, purest De Sica. When the Finzi-Continis have been arrested, Micòl and her grandmother are herded into a room with other Jews from the town, and the bewildered old lady tries to smile sociably and keep her composure. The anxious face of the dignified old lady, who a moment later crumples in tears on her granddaughter's shoulder, is one of those faces lit from within by the director's love. And at the end there is a daring stroke that raises the movie above itself: we are not shown the gas chambers, but we hear a great, full-throated cantor singing a lament for the dead, and the lament brings to earth the melancholy glamour of the Finzi-Continis.

[December 18, 1971]

Couples

Nicholas and Alexandra is as obsequiously respectful as if it had been made about living monarchs who might graciously consent to attend the first performance. The seven other movie versions of the fall of the Romanovs that have played in this country have all concentrated on that mystic voluptuary Rasputin, for the good reason that he was the most dramatic character in the story. The new Sam Spiegel production, directed by Franklin J. Schaffner, sticks to those two royally dull people. Can one make a film about a stolid, well-intentioned couple whose self-preoccupation and need to prove themselves the leaders they weren't precipitated the butchery of millions of people in a war and a revolution — can one make such a film *without irony* and expect the audience to become involved in the fate of the unfortunate couple? The picture moves in a stately progression from one fond smile they exchange to the next. Ah, yes, they care for each other — we can certainly see that. But, far from developing sympathy for them, we get so fed up with their mediocrity that we wait for their execution to liberate us from the theatre. We quickly perceive the film's point of view — that they are a decent, neurotic pair who might have been mildly happy (in a domineering-wife-and-henpecked-husband way) if only Nicholas hadn't been the head of state. But that seems to be the film's one point of view. Their lack of judgment and imagination is treated not as a horrible black joke of history — two dunces sitting on a volcano — or as a key to the eruptions but merely factually, without interpretation.

The 1932 version, featuring the Barrymores, was painfully stuffy, too, but not so epically long, and when Rasputin, after being poisoned and shot and beaten, still refused to die, there really seemed to be something vile and supernatural about him. And since it was John Barrymore playing the Romanov who, after all other measures failed, tried to choke Lionel Barrymore, done up in long, straggling whiskers as Rasputin, there was also some humor to it, especially since Lionel's Rasputin looked so much like John's Svengali of the year before that the brothers seemed to have swapped beards. The new version provides no such divertissements. Rasputin was unquestionably the funkiest monk in history, and if you're not going to interpret the historical events — if you're not basically serious anyway — why not use the one wild joker in your hand and let the audience enjoy a fantastic character? Since Rasputin (Tom Baker here) did have mesmeric gifts, why not show them? In the 1938 French version, Hárry Baur as Rasputin danced so orgiastically that the whole crazy, fetid period came alive. You could feel his powers, and they were sly and dirty; you knew why the Russian people hated him. This movie skips the triumph of that crude peasant libertine over the court; it *avoids* drama, and Rasputin's death is so badly staged that it seems not that he is hard to kill because he has so much rotten life in him but that his murderers are incompetent.

This Russian court must surely be the least scintillating court in movie history. Before seeing the movie, I had always felt sorry for the Romanov family, simply because they were powerless and helpless when they were murdered. But when one is asked to witness over three hours of Russian history with no object but to feel sorry for them one's sympathies dry up. Besides, leaden-spirited authenticity can kill sympathy fast. And is there not a calculated attempt to flatter the audience by showing the Romanovs to be one man's family in trouble — the four pretty, obedient daughters so witless a troupe of princesses they seemed to have grown up next door to Andy Hardy? It's hard to see how one can fail to be moved by a sick child on the screen, but the movie's assumption that we in the audience are more interested in the Czarevitch's hemophilia than in the way that Rasputin, who treated the boy, became a ruinous political influence stifles feelings of pity. The condescending assumption is that we're celebrity-royalty lovers who hunger for details of a sick boy's bleeding and don't care about the disintegration of a society. It's offensive to be put in the position of status-hungry voyeurs eager to partake of the home life of the dullest of the Czars; I think we're meant to revel in the imperial pomp and to identify with the little people wearing the jewelled crowns. But when the First World War and the Russian Revolution are reduced to events going on in the background of the stodgy life in the royal apartments, even if the intention isn't satirical the results become so.

Of the directors who came from TV, Franklin J. Schaffner has seemed to have the greatest sense of sweep and spectacle, and in *The War Lord*, the first three-quarters of an hour of *Planet of the Apes*, and *Patton* he showed a marvellous command of large-scale visual imagery. No one in recent years has used the wide screen more effectively. But this picture, big though its effects often are, is visually square and solemn; the compositions are head on and centered and lifeless. This may be a result of the conception or it may be the inevitable consequence of the employment of the cinematographer Freddie Young, who has worked so long for David Lean that everything he does looks static and framed for hanging.

Janet Suzman has a grave elegance as Alexandra, and one senses the presence of a fine actress, but her role is written so impersonally that we get very little insight into Alexandra's character or into what her husband sees in her. Of why he calls her "Sunny," there is no hint. Quiet, refined Michael Jayston is submerged in the character of weak Nicholas; though it may be unfair to Jayston to say so, it does seem as if the least charismatic of monarchs were being impersonated by the least charismatic of actors. For emotion, Jayston widens his tiny eyes from time to time. In minor roles, Laurence Olivier, Harry Andrews, and Alan Webb show their professional stature, but Irene Worth, like Janet Suzman, is forced to show hers mainly by the regal assurance with which she wears her gowns. The two ladies are superbly accoutred; their dresses (by Castillo) may be the only trace of art in the entire production.

The script is the heart of the trouble; it's a lame script, lamely directed. You never believe anything that's going on — not the princess exposing herself to a soldier, not the transvestite luring Rasputin. You don't even believe in the Revolution. One hesitates to blame the scriptwriter (James Goldman, with additional dialogue by Edward Bond), because in a Sam Spiegel production (this one originated in Spiegel's enthusiasm for the popular biography by Robert K. Massie) the conception may be his. There's no point in belaboring the writers for the clunky lines that get laughs; they must have heard the laughter, too, and if Lenin and Trotsky and Stalin sound as silly as ancient Greeks passing the time of day in a movie epic, how *should* revolutionaries talk in a movie in which they are walk-ons? (Michael Bryant's tight-faced Lenin is photographed so that he looks like the statues of Lenin, and this Lenin behaves like a statue.) When it is decided to concentrate on the family life of a family of dullards, how should *anybody* talk? When Nicholas of Russia asks his Alexandra "How did I go wrong?" we don't know where to point.

•

So far, it has never failed that when you're depressed after a bunch of expensive clinkers — this time after *Nicholas and Alexandra, The Gang That Couldn't Shoot Straight, $, Star Spangled Girl,* and *Happy Birthday, Wanda June* — a little picture sneaks in from left field. Renée Taylor and her husband, Joseph Bologna, are a comedy-writing team with a talent for revealing the emotional desperation of loudmouthed characters. The Bolognas' comedy is a variation on the skit style of Nichols and May, but applied to the psychological patterns of ethnic groups. They don't seek merely to entertain you with the absurdities of Jewish and Italian misbehavior; their object (possibly their unconscious object) is to find the beauty under the ugliness. It's not easy to find. That they succeed is what makes *Made for Each Other* the most satisfying comedy of the year.

There hasn't been much competition, though the first half of *Bananas* was almost up with the best of the Marx Brothers. Woody Allen's style of comedy overlaps that of the Bolognas, but he turns being Jewish into a hangup, while they satirize ethnic hangups for remedial purposes. They are perhaps the ultimate idealists among comedy writers: they want people to come clean with each other, and they assume that there is a naked honesty that can be reached. The movie is conceived as if it were an extended encounter session; its rationale is that if you tear away neurotic defenses you will get to the true person, who will be free to love. This is a less sophisticated approach than Woody Allen's gamesmanship about those defenses, but it has a romantic appeal. The Bolognas' naïve view of character could, a few movies hence, turn into soggily sentimental fake "depth," but it nevertheless gives this work unexpected sweetness. A psychological view doesn't have to be large — or sensible, either — to function in drama, especially in comedy. At this point in their writing careers, the Bolognas' belief in the dignity of psychological nakedness is what saves their work from grossness. The grossness is an omnipresent threat. The people in this movie have a lot of lungs, and they yell and stumble around and make fools of themselves, but our laughter at them isn't cruel, because it's the laughter of recognition of what — in the Bolognas' view — makes them behave like maniacs.

As a writing team, the Bolognas are a balancing act. Their comedy has the advantage of a double sexual perspective. Since their subject here is the coming together of a man and a woman (played by themselves) who haven't been able to find a way to live with themselves or anyone else, the balancing keeps the story in motion. Each character in turn messes things up and is seen through by the other. The lovers are in their thirties — Pandora Gold, a tatty, bleached-blond failed actress who tries to be sprightly, and Giggy Pinimba, a seminary dropout, a grubby misfit in personnel work. Pandora has been dumped on so many times that she looks older than she is, and Giggy is so frightened of everything that he looks younger. The background to their problems is the lunacy of their families. The Bolognas' technique is to turn psychodrama into vaudeville, to show us the comic side of suffering, but not as a put-down. The burlesque is a clarification of the characters' mechanisms — psychodrama heightened. I prefer Woody Allen's throwaway style and the jokes from out of nowhere, but he sets up comic situations, such as the courtroom scene in *Bananas,* and walks away from them, so *Bananas* doesn't build, and by the end everything has run down. *Made for Each Other* is fully worked out and grows in feeling, so that by the end the comedy has become bigger, not smaller. The clowns have become people, and the audience goes out smiling. It's Frank Capracorn updated.

The writers' attitudes are Freudian — sub-Freudian, really, since the movie accepts the neurotic person's simplified view that he has been molded by the madness of his parents — but their observation has a quirky particularity that saves them from the mechanical use of this dogma, which has become standard in TV drama. In the movie of *Lovers and Other Strangers,* for example (which they wrote and, after its purchase, lost control of), the Italian father, played by Richard Castellano, was sexually frustrated by his stony wife, who, however, enjoyed stuffing him, so he ate his way through life. So far, orthodox sub-Freud. But when his second son was getting married, the father, handing him a present of money, explained that though it might appear to be more than the first son had received, it wasn't; he had taken inflation into account, so the sums were really equal. As he awkwardly explained this, the overstuffed, sad-eyed man's feelings of love and his consideration for his sons came out in the clumsy, prosaic words. You couldn't help laughing, and yet your laughter brought you closer to him. That's the distinctive quality of the Bolognas' comic style. Though *in toto Lovers and Other Strangers* was not much more than a pleasant entertainment, it had scenes that showed a special feel for ethnic comedy and for family life. In that movie, the material was shoved into old movie formulas — the best characters de-emphasized and the ethnic tones confused by Hollywood-style casting. *Made for Each Other* is clearly not just remnants of the writers' intentions but their intentions realized.

Joseph Bologna acts "natural," and is acceptable because he handles the material so well; Renée Taylor, however, is a gifted and accomplished performer with a five-octave emotional range. She has appeared in movies before, in small roles, but she was deployed so unattractively that it was impossible to guess that she was a knocked-out original. No woman onscreen has ever done anything quite like Pandora's expression of stupefied disbelief at what a fast nothing it was after she and Giggy have had sex in his car. Her "Who Am I?" night-club routine is so rambunctiously awful and yet her face while she's doing it is so eager to please that the sequence is reminiscent of Marilyn Monroe's "That Old Black Magic" number in *Bus Stop*. Renée Taylor's greatest asset in this role is the Cinderella-like transformation of coarseness into softness. The term "vulnerability" can't be avoided here, because it is essential to the theme — which is the necessity for these two to stop protecting themselves in the clinches, to be vulnerable and to help each other to be vulnerable. The movie believes that there is a Kingdom of Heaven you get to if you open yourself to it. If *Made for Each Other* seems to belong to Miss Taylor and to be her personal triumph, it is because she expresses this theme so deeply, in her very bones, and makes you believe in it — for the duration of the movie, anyway.

Up until the fifties, although color was being used for Westerns and spectacles and musicals, comedies could be shot in black-and-white in a simple, functional manner that brought out the style of the performers. Now that the future sale of movies to TV is a prime consideration in movie financing, color is almost mandatory, yet no one seems able to find a visual style in color that helps to bring out comic values. Even our best comedies tend to look shoddy and fancy, like TV commercials, because the color and the color design aren't organic to the material. You can see the cinematographer desperately blurring a foreground here and a background there, trying for movement and pleasing tones and variety while the characters talk in bed or walk along a dirty, dark street. The simplicity and stylization of black-and-white made it easy for the director to control the situations and eliminate everything he didn't need (great comedies, such as Keaton's, often look startlingly abstract); now comedy is drowned in colors that distract from it, and the actions lose their clarity. In the case of the Bolognas, the comedy depends on the exactness of their ethnic idioms. "I'm *entitled* to be loved," Pandora says in her encounter group. There's not much that color can do for this kind of comedy (or black-and-white, either, except to allow one to listen in peace). Robert B. Bean, who directed the picture, also shot it; though he has done his best to keep his eye on the action, and has shot the picture expertly, he hasn't solved this problem. He gets some scenes to work well by using realistically tight space (a family dining room at New Year's, with the extra chairs that no one can get past; the shoebox-size night club) and the décor in the homes is blessedly uncondescending, but the busywork of razzle-dazzle effects to keep the picture from being visually monotonous is merely an acceptable style, not one that grows out of the material.

The material here is so organically developed in every other way, with characters who are emanations of the actor and actress playing them, that the movie almost qualifies as a minor comedy classic. It's when the other elements are so right that one regrets the peculiar problems of modern American color comedies. I don't think the all-purpose solution now would be to go back to black-and-white, even if there were no TV sale to worry about, and even if the large audience hadn't grown to expect color and to prefer it. A big-city comedy such as this one might seem too drab in black-and-white; it might even be intolerable, because the color helps to gloss over the urban ugliness and the caricatured urban types. Chances are that if it were made in black-and-white the cinematography would need *more* razzle-dazzle to make it visually bearable. A simplified spectrum might work for some types of comedy, or perhaps a stylization emphasizing primary colors, like the stylization Godard used in some of his sixties films — though that certainly wouldn't be right for this particular film. It may be that in emphasizing or, more exactly, exploiting grossness, the modern urban comedies have created an aesthetic problem that can't be satisfactorily solved. As comedy has become harsh and freaky, colors have become an enrichment system, yet color used as prettification is a commercial solution, not an aesthetic one. That's why *Made for Each Other* is an emotionally satisfying comedy but is not aesthetically satisfying.

[December 25, 1971]

Stanley Strangelove

Literal-minded in its sex and brutality, Teutonic in its humor, Stanley Kubrick's *A Clockwork Orange* might be the work of a strict and exacting German professor who set out to make a porno-violent sci-fi comedy. Is there anything sadder — and ultimately more repellent — than a clean-minded pornographer? The numerous rapes and beatings have no ferocity and no sensuality; they're frigidly, pedantically calculated, and because there is no motivating emotion, the viewer may experience them as an indignity and wish to leave. The movie follows the Anthony Burgess novel so closely that the book might have served as the script, yet that thick-skulled German professor may be Dr. Strangelove himself, because the meanings are turned around.

Burgess's 1962 novel is set in a vaguely Socialist future (roughly, the late seventies or early eighties) — a dreary, routinized England that roving gangs of teen-age thugs terrorize at night. In perceiving the amoral destructive potential of youth gangs, Burgess's ironic fable differs from Orwell's *1984* in a way that already seems prophetically accurate. The novel is narrated by the leader of one of these gangs — Alex, a conscienceless schoolboy sadist — and, in a witty, extraordinarily sustained literary conceit, narrated in his own slang (Nadsat, the teen-agers' special dialect). The book is a fast read; Burgess, a composer turned novelist, has an ebullient, musical sense of language, and you pick up the meanings of the strange words as the prose rhythms speed you along. Alex enjoys stealing, stomping, raping, and destroying until he kills a woman and is sent to prison for fourteen years. After serving two, he arranges to get out by submitting to an experiment in conditioning, and he is turned into a moral robot who becomes nauseated at thoughts of sex and violence. Released when he is harmless, he falls prey to his former victims, who beat him and torment him until he attempts suicide. This leads to criticism of the government that robotized him — turned him into a clockwork orange — and he is deconditioned, becoming once again a thug, and now at loose and triumphant. The ironies are protean, but Burgess is clearly a humanist; his point of view is that of a Christian horrified by the possibilities of a society turned clockwork orange, in which life is so mechanized that men lose their capacity for moral choice. There seems to be no way in this boring, dehumanizing society for the boys to release their energies except in vandalism and crime; they do what they do as a matter of course. Alex the sadist is as mechanized a creature as Alex the good.

Stanley Kubrick's Alex (Malcolm McDowell) is not so much an expression of how this society has lost its soul as he is a force pitted against the society, and by making the victims of the thugs more repulsive and contemptible than the thugs Kubrick has learned to love the punk sadist. The end is no longer the ironic triumph of a mechanized punk but a real triumph. Alex is the only likable person we see — his cynical bravado suggests a broad-nosed, working-class Olivier — and the movie puts us on his side. Alex, who gets kicks out of violence, is more alive than anybody else in the movie, and younger and more attractive, and McDowell plays him exuberantly, with the power and slyness of a young Cagney. Despite what Alex does at the beginning, McDowell makes you root for his foxiness, for his crookedness. For most of the movie, we see him tortured and beaten and humiliated, so when his bold, aggressive punk's nature is restored to him it seems not a joke on all of us but, rather, a victory in which we share, and Kubrick takes an exultant tone. The look in Alex's eyes at the end tells us that he isn't just a mechanized, choiceless sadist but prefers sadism and knows he can get by with it. Far from being a little parable about the dangers of soullessness and the horrors of force, whether employed by individuals against each other or by society in "conditioning," the movie becomes a vindication of Alex, saying that the punk was a free human being and only the good Alex was a robot.

The trick of making the attacked less human than their attackers, so you feel no sympathy for them, is, I think, symptomatic of a new attitude in movies. This attitude says there's no moral difference. Stanley Kubrick has assumed the deformed, self-righteous perspective of a vicious young punk who says, "Everything's rotten. Why shouldn't I do what I want? They're worse than I am." In the new mood (perhaps movies in their cumulative effect are partly responsible for it), people want to believe the hyperbolic worst, want to believe in the degradation of the victims — that they are dupes and phonies and weaklings. I can't accept that Kubrick is merely reflecting this post-assassinations, post-Manson mood; I think he's catering to it. I think he wants to dig it.

This picture plays with violence in an intellectually seductive way. And though it has no depth, it's done in such a slow, heavy style that those prepared to like it can treat its puzzling aspects as oracular. It can easily be construed as an ambiguous mystery play, a visionary warning against "the Establishment." There are a million ways to justify identifying with Alex: Alex is fighting repression; he's alone against the system. What he does isn't nearly as bad as what the government does (both in the movie and in the United States now). Why shouldn't he be violent? That's all the Establishment has ever taught him (and us) to be. The point of the book was that we must be as men, that we must be able to take responsibility for what we are. The point of the movie is much more *au courant*. Kubrick has removed many of the obstacles to our identifying with Alex; the Alex of the book has had his personal habits cleaned up a bit — his fondness for squishing small animals under his tires, his taste for ten-year-old girls, his beating up of other prisoners, and so on. And Kubrick aids the identification with Alex by small directorial choices throughout. The writer whom Alex cripples (Patrick Magee) and the woman he kills are cartoon nasties with upper-class accents a mile wide. (Magee has been encouraged to act like a bathetic madman; he seems to be preparing for a career in horror movies.) Burgess gave us society through Alex's eyes, and so the vision was deformed, and Kubrick, carrying over from *Dr. Strangelove* his joky adolescent view of hypocritical, sexually dirty authority figures and extending it to all adults, has added an extra layer of deformity. The "straight" people are far more twisted than Alex; they seem inhuman and incapable of suffering. He alone suffers. And how he suffers! He's a male Little Nell — screaming in a straitjacket during the brainwashing; sweet and helpless when rejected by his parents; alone, weeping, on a bridge; beaten, bleeding, lost in a rainstorm; pounding his head on a floor and crying for death. Kubrick pours on the hearts and flowers; what is done to Alex is far worse than what Alex has done, so society itself can be felt to justify Alex's hoodlumism.

The movie's confusing — and, finally, corrupt — morality is not, however, what makes it such an abhorrent viewing experience. It is offensive long before one perceives where it is heading, because it has no shadings. Kubrick, a director with an arctic spirit, is determined to be pornographic, and he has no talent for it. In *Los Olvidados*, Buñuel showed teen-agers committing horrible brutalities, and even though you had no illusions about their victims — one, in particular, was a foul old lecher — you were appalled. Buñuel makes you understand the pornography of brutality: the pornography is in what human beings are capable of doing to other human beings. Kubrick has always been one of the least sensual and least erotic of directors, and his attempts here at phallic humor are like a professor's lead balloons. He tries to work up kicky violent scenes, carefully estranging you from the victims so that you can *enjoy* the rapes and beatings. But I think one is more likely to feel cold antipathy toward the movie than horror at the violence — or enjoyment of it, either.

Kubrick's martinet control is obvious in the terrible performances he gets from everybody but McDowell, and in the inexorable pacing. The film has a distinctive style of estrangement: gloating closeups, bright, hard-edge, third-degree lighting, and abnormally loud voices. It's a style, all right — the movie doesn't look like other movies, or sound like them — but it's a leering, portentous style. After the balletic brawling of the teen-age gangs, with bodies flying as in a Western saloon fight, and after the gang-bang of the writer's wife and an orgy in speeded-up motion, you're primed for more action, but you're left stranded in the prison sections, trying to find some humor in tired schoolboy jokes about a Hitlerian guard. The movie retains a little of the slangy Nadsat but none of the fast rhythms of Burgess's prose, and so the dialect seems much more arch than it does in the book. Many of the dialogue sequences go on and on, into a stupor of inactivity. Kubrick seems infatuated with the hypnotic possibilities of static setups; at times you feel as if you were trapped in front of the frames of a comic strip for a numbing ten minutes per frame. When Alex's correctional officer visits his home and he and Alex sit on a bed, the camera sits on the two of them. When Alex comes home from prison, his parents and the lodger who has displaced him are in the living room; Alex appeals to his seated, unloving parents for an inert eternity. Long after we've got the point, the composition is still telling us to appreciate its cleverness. This ponderous technique is hardly leavened by the structural use of classical music to characterize the sequences; each sequence is scored to Purcell (synthesized on a Moog), Rossini, or Beethoven, while Elgar and others are used for brief satiric effects. In the book, the doctor who has devised the conditioning treatment explains why the horror images used in it are set to music: "It's a useful emotional heightener." But the whole damned movie is heightened this way; yes, the music is effective, but the effect is self-important.

When I pass a newsstand and see the saintly, bearded, intellectual Kubrick on the cover of *Saturday Review*, I wonder: Do people notice things like the way Kubrick cuts to the rival teen-age gang before Alex and his hoods arrive to fight them, just so we can have the pleasure of watching that gang strip the struggling girl they mean to rape? Alex's voice is on the track announcing his arrival, but Kubrick can't wait for Alex to arrive, because then he couldn't show us as much. That girl is stripped for our benefit; it's the purest exploitation. Yet this film lusts for greatness, and I'm not sure that Kubrick knows how to make simple movies anymore, or that he cares to, either. I don't know how consciously he has thrown this film to youth; maybe he's more of a showman than he lets on — a lucky showman with opportunism built into the cells of his body. The film can work at a pop-fantasy level for a young audience already prepared to accept Alex's view of the society, ready to believe that that's how it is.

At the movies, we are gradually being conditioned to accept violence as a sensual pleasure. The directors used to say they were showing us its real face and how ugly it was in order to sensitize us to its horrors. You don't have to be very keen to see that they are now in fact desensitizing us. They are saying that everyone is brutal, and the heroes must be as brutal as the villains or they turn into fools. There seems to be an assumption that if you're offended by movie brutality, you are somehow playing into the hands of the people who want censorship. But this would deny those of us who don't believe in censorship the use of the only counterbalance: the freedom of the press to say that there's anything conceivably damaging in these films — the freedom to analyze their implications. If we don't use this critical freedom, we are implicitly saying that no brutality is too much for us — that only squares and people who believe in censorship are concerned with brutality. Actually, those who believe in censorship are primarily concerned with sex, and they generally worry about violence only when it's eroticized. This means that practically no one raises the issue of the possible cumulative effects of movie brutality. Yet surely, when night after night atrocities are served up to us as entertainment, it's worth some anxiety. We become clockwork oranges if we accept all this pop culture without asking what's in it. How can people go on talking about the dazzling brilliance of movies and not notice that the directors are sucking up to the thugs in the audience?

[January 1, 1972]

Pleasing and Punishing

Hospital jokes are like Polish jokes: they're sick, and dumb as hell, and they all have the same point, but you can't help laughing at them. *The Hospital,* written by Paddy Chayefsky and directed by Arthur Hiller, is mostly one big hospital joke, and, terrible as it is in just about every way, it's one of the few enjoyable new movies. Low comedy, to be sure, but funny and lively. If one took the movie's social observations too seriously, it would be easy to be offended by the way the community-action groups who are picketing the hospital are presented. And Chayefsky cheats on the very material that gets laughs by introducing a lunatic posing as a staff doctor in order to account for much of the confusion and the killing incompetence we've been laughing at. This is false to why we laugh: probably everyone in the theatre knows that no madman is necessary to account for the foul-ups and neglect and bureaucratic impersonality in a big-city hospital. However, the movie is an exaggeration of what we know or have heard or suspect — the way farces about the Army or other institutions are — and the nut on the loose is an acceptable convention of this genre, though the director, pedestrianly sane, doesn't do too well by this nut. But the silly movie has enough verve to ride right over its weaknesses. Chayefsky uses his doctor-hero (George C. Scott) to lecture us with what sound suspiciously like the author's sentiments. And the author throws in some antique dramaturgy: the doctor is in a suicidal crisis and requires Diana Rigg, as a cool kook, to restore him to himself — and to potency.

The only thing that saves this stuff is that it is played for comedy, and Scott has such good timing he gets laughs on atrocious, youth-baiting lines. Is it possible that he is turning into a great spangled ham, who is at his best in hokum? He's brilliant in this — even when the doctor is called upon to make wretched speeches about his domestic problems and the meaning of his work. I doubt if there's another actor in the country who could carry off those speeches, but I don't think one should necessarily conclude that Scott could be great in a great role. He may be the king of the bums. He achieves these sensational effects by being so tense and high-strung that he dominates the screen; his bravura is so startling in this generally naturalistically acted piece that we're knocked out of our seats in admiration, but I can't think of very many good roles in which this kind of domination wouldn't look like hammy hokum. Luckily, it's just what Chayefsky's entertaining potboiler needs.

•

The Boy Friend might have been a lovely little movie, gently mocking the Victorian soul under the John Held, Jr., look, and with that bittersweet Jazz Age gaiety that is foolish and yet heartbreakingly winning. Sandy Wilson's show, produced first in London in 1953 and then on Broadway, with Julie Andrews, the next year, is a parody of the cheerfully imbecilic clichés of American and British musicals of the pre-twenties and twenties. The heroine, Polly, is a poor little rich girl who falls in love — on the Riviera — with a poor boy who turns out to be a lord's son incognito. To make this sort of *faux-naïf* pastiche work, one must not only point up the clichés but reactivate them, so that the audience can laugh affectionately at the lost naïveté of the outmoded plot conventions and yet still feel the romance and sweetness in them. The distancing must be very delicate, because if the production tries to make the present audience feel superior by suggesting that audiences of the past really believed in those conventions, the romance dies. If the past is merely patronized — if we're never caught up in a new tenderness toward what is being parodied, never feel a quickening of sympathy for the daydreams of the past — the show is cold camp instead of delicious camp.

Ken Russell, who made the movie version, is not an affectionate director, and even before seeing the film one knew that he radically lacks innocence, and that without innocence *The Boy Friend* was not likely to have much charm. Still, the show is basically about love of theatre, and I hoped that even if he turned it into cold camp, he might reveal some feeling for musical-comedy traditions. Though one might have guessed from his earlier movies that his desire to impress and shock was stronger than his love of theatre, I was still unprepared for what he has done to *The Boy Friend*. The theatre people in it are petty and self-centered and older than you think. The show is no longer a parody that is also love's tribute to the past; it has become the basis for a harsh anti-show-business satire.

Russell is the most recklessly eclectic movie director now at work; he tosses together styles and ideas without bothering to integrate them. He has pumped up the Sandy Wilson show with theatrical conceits that distance it several times over. The original musical is now a tacky matinée performance being put on by a seedy provincial company managed by Max Adrian and being witnessed by a Hollywood director (Vladek Sheybal), who fantasizes how he will convert it into a big movie musical, while the performers upstage each other and make whores and asses of themselves trying to capture his attention. And in enlarging the scope of the parody to include movie musicals of the thirties Russell has added a framing story in which Twiggy (making her movie début) is a mousy, gawky stage assistant who, in the tradition of *On with the Show* and *42nd Street*, goes on as Polly when the star (Glenda Jackson, in a cameo performance) breaks her leg. The movie thus gives Russell the chance to satirize impoverished, desperate-to-make-it-into-the-big-time provincial players as well as an opportunity to stage some pseudo-Busby Berkeley routines. The Sandy Wilson musical is mere grist for Russell's mill, and his wheels never stop turning. He throws in numbers presented as Polly's fantasies and as the theatre manager's dreams of how his show would look if he were staging it for a royal command performance; Russell is an imprecise satirist, and the theatre manager's fantasy life looks just like the Hollywood director's. The production is relentlessly metallic and glittering: all showing off and no generosity. It's an unusually joyless musical, and I think Russell means it to be joyless.

For a director — especially a director making a musical — to be so indifferent to what gives an audience pleasure (Russell may not consider that worth his while) suggests both enormous, confident egotism and a deficiency in ordinary good sense. To take a musical with a story and then kill the story by overelaboration, leaving a collection of musical numbers — a revue without stars — is, theatrically speaking, insanity. Audiences may enjoy musical revues without a story; I certainly do. But for a musical revue you need celebrated, or at least greatly gifted, performers. In this movie, the numbers don't have the variety that star acts provide; we keep looking at the same cast in different sets and costumes, and the film doesn't take hold emotionally. It is a revue showcase for Russell's supposed virtuosity; about midway it becomes compellingly soporific. There isn't a first-class voice in the entire movie, and we can tell how little interest Russell has in the performers from the way the only dancer we're longing to watch — the tall, gangling Tommy Tune — has his best numbers shredded by tricky camera angles. There is an almost suicidal indifference toward the audience in the way Russell fails to develop Twiggy's personality. She sings adequately and dances rather better, but her voice isn't sweet enough for the load of singing she's asked to carry, and Russell never opens her character beyond our first view of her. She needs the sort of treatment William Wyler gave Audrey Hepburn in *Roman Holiday*; we wait for the withdrawn little face to become radiant, and it never does, because Russell doesn't make her beautiful from within. Granted that Twiggy may very well not have what Audrey Hepburn proved to have, still she is appealing, and Russell does less to bring out her personality than directors customarily do with untrained children in small parts. He misses out on the tantalizing suggestiveness of Twiggy's still photos: how she seems both a publicity stunt and yet a natural phenomenon — a nymphet version of the glamour queens of the past. In the movie, her pre-pubescent figure in white satin is an almost perverse image; she has the erotic appeal of asexuality. But she isn't given enough help, and when she dances with her boyfriend (Christopher Gable) nothing happens. Gable is an abominably vacuous partner for her; there's no spark, no combustion, nothing. I don't think Russell particularly wants us to like Twiggy; he doesn't seem to give a damn about the Cinderella transformation and the romance that might have held the show together. I think his conception is quite the reverse — to have her remain a blank.

Whereas in most movie musicals we could do with less filler between numbers, in this one we learn to appreciate how useful filler is; we're famished for it. Technically, Russell's greatest deficiency is that he doesn't understand the beauty of simplicity. This movie is always doing something; it's never at peace. And a musical needs moments of repose. You don't go to a movie musical for a frenzy of activity; you go hoping that it will make you feel good, that life will become — for a few hours — an exuberant lyric. You go hoping for what Fred Astaire described in *Top Hat* — "And the cares that hung around me through the week/ Seem to vanish like a gambler's lucky streak." If there's anything we don't want when we go to a musical comedy, it's to have it turn against itself. That's probably why Russell wanted to do it this way — taking the romance out — but a mean-spirited musical is almost a contradiction in terms. Musicals, at their best, are an apotheosis of romance — the songs and dances are idealized courtship rites, formalized dreams. Musical comedy is never literally believed. There is no myth to puncture; the shows that Sandy Wilson parodied were already deliberately funny. That probably explains why Russell's interest shifted to an exposé of the performers. If he had started with corny, cheating show-business sentimentality, like the kind that Lenny Bruce epitomized in his classic routine "The Palladium," his approach might make sense, but the material he started with is so harmlessly frivolous that he seems to be debunking the performers out of sheer nastiness. Glenda Jackson, in the small part of the star Twiggy replaces, is the only one who manages both to parody the conventions and to reactivate them — maybe because with her leg in a cast she isn't required to be on the stage carrying on frenetically, like the others. Max Adrian manages to show some music-hall spunk in the "It's Never Too Late to Fall in Love" number, but he is horribly used throughout. Russell's idea of satire is to make the characters stupid or spiritually and physically ugly. The faces in heavy stage makeup are photographed in closeup, so we can see how grotesque they are; a couple of the girls — a cat-eyed, grinning brunette (Antonia Ellis) and a seductively gravel-voiced blonde (Georgina Hale) — are so good that one really resents the way the director puts them down. The intention is mean — satire without wit. The device of having the performers vie with each other for the Hollywood director's attention provides him with an excuse to show how sleazily competitive they are — they have no show-business solidarity, and the aging chorines use the stage as a casting couch. He never shows that even out of this cheap tawdriness some kind of theatrical magic may bloom. The provincial theatre is cruelly empty, with fewer people in the audience than on the stage, and those bored.

From what we can see, all Russell cares about is his own conception. And I don't think it's so hot. He mucks up the original show and doesn't work out his own ideas. (The opening is particularly bad — you feel as if you'd been flung into the middle of something.) Russell was once a ballet dancer, but he's certainly no choreographer. Most of the numbers have no polish or point, and his attempt to reproduce the airborne dance that Dave Gould devised for *Flying Down to Rio* is pathetic. Russell's airplane never gets off the ground — literally as well as figuratively. As for Busby Berkeley, his choreographic engineering was innocently lunatic, and I don't know how it could be parodied, since it was already so naïvely funny. Russell doesn't begin to understand Berkeley well enough to imitate him successfully; he misses out even on the true, homegrown Surreal madness of those routines — the permutations that have no choreographic logic, and the shifts to the utterly unexpected, like a closeup of a bird's nest, with the baby birds popping from their eggs. What Ken Russell thinks is a satire of Busby Berkeley is more like a reprise of the stage show at Radio City Music Hall.

Russell is still young and he's apparently tireless, and because of his facility and his excesses some people have become fascinated by the energy he pours into his destruction bouts against what he apparently thinks are sacred cows (though I doubt if there are any sacred cows for the American audience that now goes to movies). He attacks romanticism with a romantic vengeance. Why? Nostalgic musical-comedy parody is so little the enemy to this generation that the younger audience probably doesn't even recognize that this movie is not it but its reverse. Moviegoers are getting used to being punished; they're reconciled to taking what they can get, and an anti-nostalgic put-down still provides some songs and dances. All Russell has succeeded in doing is to kill most of the pleasure the audience might have had. Russell's future projects are reported to include the life of Sarah Bernhardt, with Barbra Streisand, and the life of Edith Piaf. The thought of how he will muck up the lives of those poor women is discouraging. In his own way, Ken Russell is as unflappable and indefatigable and as wrong-headed as a Stanley Kramer. Do the people who sell him their books take the trouble to look at his movies, or do they leave it all to their agents?

•

In what world do movie directors live that they ask us to feel sorry for a well-heeled young married woman in a well-staffed house who is hard put to it to answer a doorbell or get to a party on time? The basis for the suffering of Julie Messinger (Dyan Cannon), the heroine of Otto Preminger's *Such Good Friends*, is even more obscure than the basis for the heroine's suffering in *Diary of a Mad Housewife*. We are shown Julie's subservience to her demanding son-of-a-bitch husband (Laurence Luckinbill); we see that he exploits her (he doesn't carry packages for her, he leaves her to pay off the taxis while he strides ahead, and so on), and he's sexually indifferent to her, so that she's love-starved and sex-starved, but we never find out what she wants done about it. Why she allows herself to be used is the missing center of the story; the movie is all peripheral. We get a generalized sense that it is about the dissatisfactions of a masochist, but when Julie's husband is in the hospital and she discovers that he has been unfaithful to her with several of her friends, her only recourse seems to be to abase herself with other men. When she makes snide remarks while an impotent man works away on her, or when she services a fat doctor (James Coco), is she getting even with her husband or proving her independence or just intensifying her masochism? Like *Diary of a Mad Housewife*, this movie is caught between making the woman's whining noble and making it filthy-corrupt. Julie obviously feels that she's worthless, but there's not much drama in that unless she's wrong. Since neither the discovery of her husband's infidelity, nor his death changes her, there's no clue to what the movie is meant to be about. Her only claim on our interest is some wit — which, however, is muffled by Miss Cannon's monotone delivery.

"Sensitive" is a word that isn't often applied to Preminger; still, one is not prepared for the ugliness of the Jewish jokes here. (The sequence at the hospital in which Julie's friends and relatives who have come to give blood do business first makes the wedding-reception scene in *Goodbye, Columbus* seem almost wholesome.) The script, by Elaine May (under a pseudonym, which is no excuse), is full of that bitchiness which in movies is passed off as Manhattan chic; you're supposed to enjoy it while perceiving how depraved it is. In this movie, it's so sour it really does seem depraved. Everything in this movie does, and for the same reason — sourness. Preminger strips Burgess Meredith — not a young man — down to nothing but a book over his genitals and fails to get the intended laugh. The only time I heard any laughter was when James Coco, who was being undressed by Dyan Cannon, was wrestling to unlace a corset; Preminger squeezes Coco's fat for laughs in an imitation of the way John Avildsen gets laughs out of Allen Garfield in *Cry Uncle*. Avildsen was once Preminger's assistant; now Preminger seems to be aping his former student, though he lacks his humor. The rancid fake-smart atmosphere suggests that Otto Preminger is eager to do porno pictures but wants the prestige of a modern-woman's-sensibility picture. He might just as well go all the way; he has become too crude to do anything else.

[January 8, 1972]

Saint Cop

The movie opens on a memorial plaque in the lobby of the San Francisco Hall of Justice, and we read the words "In Tribute to the Police Officers of San Francisco Who Gave Their Lives in the Line of Duty," and then the beginning of a list of names. This is a rather strange opening for *Dirty Harry* since it isn't about the death of a police officer. The tribute, however, puts the viewer in a respectful frame of mind; we all know that many police are losing their lives. The movie then proceeds to offer a magically simple culprit for their deaths: the liberals. Actually, the opening is strange for other reasons, too. I grew up in San Francisco, and one of the soundest pieces of folk wisdom my mother gave me was 'If you're ever in trouble, don't go to the cops." I remember a high-school teacher telling me that it never ceased to amaze him that his worst students — the sadists and the bullies — landed not in jail but on the police force, though sometimes on the police force and then in jail. Even as children, San Franciscans were deeply aware of the corruption of the police — something totally ignored in this movie. *Dirty Harry* is not about the actual San Francisco police force; it's about a right-wing fantasy of that police force as a group helplessly emasculated by unrealistic liberals. The conceit of this movie is that for one brief, glorious period the police have a realist in their midst — and drive him out.

Dirty Harry is not one of those ambivalent, you-can-read-it-either-way jobs, like *The French Connection*; Inspector Harry Callahan is not a Popeye — porkpie-hatted and lewd and boorish. He's soft-spoken Clint Eastwood — six feet four of lean, tough saint, blue-eyed and shaggy-haired, with a rugged, creased, careworn face that occasionally breaks into a mischief-filled Shirley MacLaine grin. He's the best there is — a Camelot cop, courageous and incorruptible, and the protector of women and children. Or at least he would be, if the law allowed him to be. But the law coddles criminals; it gives them legal rights that cripple the police. And so the only way that Dirty Harry — the dedicated troubleshooter who gets the dirtiest assignments — can protect the women and children of the city is to disobey orders.

As suspense craftsmanship, *Dirty Harry* is smooth and trim; based on an original screenplay by Harry Fink and his wife, R.M. Fink (formerly a TV writing team, now operating out of Switzerland), with some additional writing by Dean Riesner, it was directed in the sleekest style by the veteran urban-action director Don Siegel, and Lalo Schifrin's pulsating, jazzy electronic trickery drives the picture forward. Lalo Schifrin doesn't compose music — he works on you. It would be stupid to deny that *Dirty Harry* is a stunningly well-made genre piece, and it certainly turns an audience on. But turning on an audience is a function of motor excitation that is not identical with art (though there is an overlap); if it were, the greatest artists would be those who gave us heart attacks. Don Siegel is an accomplished exciter; once considered a liberal, he has now put his skills to work in a remarkably single-minded attack on liberal values, with each prejudicial detail in place. *Dirty Harry* is a kind of hardhat *The Fountainhead;* Callahan, a free individual, afraid of no one and bowing to no man, is pitted against a hippie maniac (loosely based on San Francisco's Zodiac Killer) who is a compendium of criminal types. The variety of his perversions is impressive — one might say that no depravity is foreign to him. He is pure evil: sniper, rapist, kidnapper, torturer, defiler of all human values. Paradisiacal San Francisco supports this vision. In New York, where crime is so obviously a social outgrowth, the dregs belong to the city, and a criminal could not be viewed as a snake in paradise. But, as everyone knows, the San Francisco light and the beauty of the natural setting transform and unify the architectural chaos; even poverty looks picturesque, as in other tourist traps, and crime can be treated as a defiler from outside the society. This criminal is not one for whom we need feel any responsibility or sympathy, yet he stands for everything the audience fears and loathes. And Harry cannot destroy this walking rot, because of the legal protections, such as the court rulings on Miranda and Escobedo, that a weak, liberal society gives its criminals. Those are the terms of the film. The dirtiness on Harry is the moral stain of recognition that evil must be dealt with; he is our martyr — stained on our behalf. The content fits the form, and beautifully — hand in glove. In the action genre, it's easier — and more fun — to treat crime in this medieval way, as evil, without specific causes or background. What produces a killer might be a subject for an artist, but it's a nuisance to an exciter, who doesn't want to slow the action down. When you're making a picture with Clint Eastwood, you naturally want things to be simple, and the basic contest between good and evil is as simple as you can get. It makes this genre piece more archetypal than most movies, more primitive and dreamlike; fascist medievalism has a fairy-tale appeal.

The movie was cheered and applauded by Puerto Ricans in the audience, and they jeered — as they were meant to — when the maniac whined and pleaded for his legal rights. Puerto Ricans could applaud Harry because in the movie laws protecting the rights of the accused are seen not as remedies for the mistreatment of the poor by the police and the courts but as protection for evil abstracted from all social conditions — metaphysical evil, classless criminality. The movie shrewdly makes the maniac smart, well-spoken, and white, and in order to clear Harry of any charge of prejudice or racism he is given a Mexican partner (Reni Santoni). The audience is led to identify totally with Harry and to feel victorious because the liberals don't succeed in stopping him. He saves us this time; he slaughters the maniac who has grabbed a busload of terrified children and is slapping them around. But Harry Callahan has to defy the mayor and the police department to do it. And, in a final gesture of contempt for the unrealistic legal system, Harry throws his badge into the same waters that the killer's corpse is floating in. Harry has dirtied himself for the last time; there is no one now to save us from evil, because the liberals are running the city.

The gesture at the end is a reprise of Gary Cooper's gesture at the end of *High Noon,* but with a difference: in high-minded *High Noon,* phony in its own way, Cooper, the marshal, singlehandedly cleaned up the outlaw gang and then threw his badge on the ground in contempt for the cowardice of the townspeople, who didn't live up to the principles of the law and wouldn't help him defend it. *Dirty Harry* says that the laws were written by dupes who protect criminal rats and let women and children be tortured, and Eastwood throws his badge away because he doesn't respect the law; he stands for vigilante justice.

If you go along with the movie — and it's hard to resist, because the most skillful suspense techniques are used on very primitive emotional levels — you have but one desire: to see the maniac get it so it hurts. The movie lacks the zing and brute vitality of *The French Connection,* but it has such sustained drive toward this righteous conclusion that it is an almost perfect piece of propaganda for para-legal police power. The evil monster represents urban violence, and the audience gets to see him kicked and knifed and shot, and finally triumphantly drowned. Violence has rarely been presented with such righteous relish.

At one point, Harry catches the mass murderer, but the police — in an implausible scene that really pushes its political point — decide they can't bring him to trial, because of legal technicalities, and so they blithely release him. Although they know he has already killed several people, they don't even bother to put a tail on him. And whom do they consult before releasing him? A Berkeley law professor, of course. Such a perfect touch for the audience. Anyone who knows San Francisco knows that in the highly unlikely circumstance that a law professor were to be consulted, he would be from the University of San Francisco, a Catholic institution closer in location and nearer in heart to the S. F. Police Department — or, if not from there, from Hastings College of the Law, a branch of the University of California that is situated in San Francisco. But Berkeley has push-button appeal as the red center of bleeding-heart liberalism; it has replaced Harvard as the joke butt and unifying hatred of reactionaries. The movie is just as astute in what it leaves out: in his guise as sniper, the many-sided evil one has an impressive arsenal that includes a high-powered rifle and a machine gun. But the movie raises no question about how he was able to purchase these weapons. There is one virtuoso plot development: the maniac arranges to get himself beaten to a garish pulp, so that he can scream police brutality and pin the blame on Callahan. The San Francisco police, with their unenviable record of free-style use of the billy, should contribute to a memorial plaque for *Dirty Harry*.

On the way out, a pink-cheeked little girl was saying "That was a *good* picture" to her father. Of course; the dragon had been slain. *Dirty Harry* is obviously just a genre movie, but this action genre has always had a fascist potential, and it has finally surfaced. If crime were caused by super-evil dragons, there would be no Miranda, no Escobedo; we could all be licensed to kill, like Dirty Harry. But since crime is caused by deprivation, misery, psychopathology, and social injustice, *Dirty Harry* is a deeply immoral movie.

To excite an audience, you don't really need to believe in anything but manipulative skills — and success. If you're intelligent and work this way, you become a cynic; if you're not very intelligent, you can point with pride to the millions of people buying tickets.

•

Diamonds Are Forever starts with a full head of steam, and one expects a luxuriant, mock-sadistic good time. But a few minutes later Sean Connery, as Bond, and a villain are in a tiny elevator, lunging at each other and pounding each other with excruciatingly amplified blows; the sequence goes on and on, and the movie loses its insolent cool. The Bond pictures depend on the comic pornography of brutality; the violence has to be witty. When people are just slugging each other, as in any movie fight, the point of the picture is blunted. This movie never recovers for long. The script (by Richard Maibaum and Tom Mankiewicz) involves diamond smuggling and old Blofeld; it's a wilted affair with deep-in-the-closet bitch-fag villains. The one new character with possibilities, a billionaire Las Vegas recluse modelled on Howard Hughes, is dimly written, and played — shall we say rustically? — by Jimmy Dean. (He acts as if someone had just suggested to him that he turn actor but hadn't told him how.) The picture isn't bad; it's merely tired, and it's often noisy when it means to be exciting. Guy Hamilton directs more or less adequately, but he isn't precise enough for nonchalance — for the right, perfectly careless throwaway-joke tone. Hamilton doesn't quite parody urbanity and flippancy, because he's still struggling to achieve them. The Ken Adam sets just sit there, and the film doesn't have anything like those flamboyant sequences in the snow — the ski chase and the bobsled run — that were quite literally dazzling in *On Her Majesty's Secret Service*. What's missing may be linked to the absence of Peter Hunt, who worked on the action sequences of all the earlier Bonds, and who directed the last one; perhaps it was he who gave the series its distinctive quality of aestheticized thrills. The daring seemed *beautiful* in the earlier films — precariousness glorified. This time, even when a sequence works (that is, is both daring and funny), such as the car chase, and the battle between Connery and the black and white Amazons, it lacks elegance and visual opulence; it looks like sequences of the same kind in the Bond imitations. No doubt those of us who love the Bond pictures are spoiled, but really we've come to expect more than a comic car chase.

Customers may, however, be happy enough with what they get. *Diamonds Are Forever* has opened just at the moment when people long for a familiar, stable, unalienated hero with a capacity for enjoyment; the timing could not be better for Sean Connery to come back as Bond. He no longer wears the waxy deadpan of a sex-fantasy stud dummy; over the years he has turned the robot matinée-idol Bond into a man — himself. The foppery and the gadgetry have diminished, and the sexual conquests, too. Almost imperceptibly, Bond has lost his upper-class snobbery along with the toiletries; it's as if that snotty, enigmatic Bond disgusted Connery. His instinct was right: it's better this way, because Connery's mock-heroic presence incarnates the appeal of the series without need of the commodity accoutrements of a modern pasha — without need even of a harem. Bond doesn't seem a phony anymore.

[January 15, 1972]

Baby Machos

The Cowboys, which features one of the most torpid cattle drives since the invention of motion pictures, is an incomparable index to the confusion of values in the movie business right now. This Western epic, shaped for the family trade, is set in cattle country in 1877. John Wayne is a rancher whose hired hands desert him when there's a gold strike; unable to find men to help drive his cattle to market, he takes on eleven local schoolboys — aged nine to fifteen — and trains them during the four-hundred-mile drive. Cow*boys* — get it? The movie, which minds its language and is sexually clean as a eunuch's whistle, is sufficiently sanctimonious to have earned a GP* ("Contains material which may not be suitable for pre-teenagers") rating. It is playing at Radio City Music Hall, which was graced with an appearance by Wayne himself, who then lunched with five hundred newsboys and winners of *Cowboys* contests. It is being touted as the biggest family picture since *The Sound of Music.* One could easily think that Warner Brothers and the director, Mark Rydell, and the writers, Irving Ravetch and his wife, Harriet Frank, Jr., and William Dale Jennings (who also wrote the original novel), were in the business of corrupting minors, because this movie is about how these schoolboys become men through learning the old-fashioned virtues of killing.

It's a no-nonsense view of growing up; the *macho* cadets are well-mannered, obedient, good-boy killers. The whole world knows that Wayne is not a man to put up with any guff. Almost in passing, he cures a boy of stuttering by telling him that if he wanted to speak clearly he could, and the boy cries "Son of a bitch!" over and over with perfect articulation. Is Warners getting ready to sell holy water under the Warner Brothers–Lourdes label?

At one point along the trail, there is an encounter with a madam (Colleen Dewhurst) and her girls, and you may guess that the plot logic requires the boys to be sexually initiated as part of their transition to manhood. A look at the book on which the movie is based confirms your guess, but in the movie the whores (starlets in exquisitely laundered petticoats) are introduced and then left with nothing to do. The boys can kill and the movie gets its GP * and is booked into the Music Hall, but if they had been sexually initiated the picture would have been restricted. *One* boy getting initiated — and so tactfully that you might have thought he was taking the veil — was sufficient to get *Summer of '42* restricted; the mothers of America may not go to the movies anymore, but they are still the watchdogs of movie morality when it comes to their sons' purity. So the boys must be virginal killers; sex would make them bad, dirty boys.

In the first half of the picture, the actors seem to be planted where they speak, and there's an awesome interval before anyone replies. It feels like a long wait before overlapping dialogue will be invented. Wayne is presented as an idealized Western father figure, and his screen career as the archetypal good guy gives weight to the homely, reactionary platitudes that make this a family picture. Even when he works himself up for an oath, the final words are always genteel. He pontificates to his gruff, understanding wife — played by Sarah Cunningham, who is in the Leora Dana–Anne Revere mold: the strong women who turn understanding into a form of doughy piousness. They're *boring;* that's no service to women — and their dreary goodness certainly doesn't light up the screen. And this movie needs lighting up, because the eleven boys don't do much for it. They're Disney choirboys — clean, scrubbed nothings — so there's no dramatic or psychological preparation for the explosion of killing. The director doesn't care about the characters; he is just marking time until the mayhem. The only preparation for the explosions is in Wayne's code of honor.

Wayne's teaching is that there are good men and there are bad men; there are no crossovers and nothing in between. People don't get a second chance around him; to err once is to be doomed. Most of the bloodshed seems to be caused by his pigheadedness, but that is definitely not the movie's point of view. The boys learn their lessons so well that when Wayne is killed by rustlers they know better than to waste effort trying to bring the rustlers to justice. The movie is set up so that *they* are justice. Their faces are strong and clear-eyed as they slaughter some seventeen men; they appear to have an almost mystic union as they act in concert, infallibly, and without a glimmer of doubt or of pity. When the ex-convict villain (Bruce Dern) is trapped under his horse and pleads for help, a boy cuts one strap loose and fires a gun to frighten the horse, and the whole troupe watches with manly impassivity as the horse runs, dragging the man screaming to his death. The obscenely complacent movie invites us to identify with these good little men and to be proud of them.

There are things going on in this movie for kids that shouldn't escape notice. Some of these things — like the way that people don't die in clean kills but writhe in slow torture — may be among the reasons that this movie is expected to make money. In its way, it's innovative: the sensual pleasures of violence haven't been packaged with eternal verities before. Blood and homilies.

The confusion of values in the seedy folklore is glaringly obvious in matters of race. The Negro cook on the drive is played with peerless urbanity by Roscoe Lee Browne; with his reserves of charm to call upon, and with that deep voice rising from his great chest, Browne acts Wayne right off the screen, and without raising a bead of sweat. Not only does Browne come across as the only real actor in the movie but the cook is by far the verbal and intellectual superior of everyone else. He's wickedly, incongruously suave, like a Shakespearean ham lost in the sticks but dressing for dinner every night. If you retain any sense of humor, you may ask yourself why the *cook* isn't the father figure for the boys, particularly since it is he who devises the strategies that enable them to kill all the rustlers without loss of a boy. Parading their own lack of prejudice, the moviemakers have turned the cook into a super-black and then let Browne do his number. He's entertaining — which is better than the moviemakers deserve. And, still trying to save face, they toss in a bit of dialogue in which one of the boys informs Wayne that he is fighting-Jewish — which enables Wayne to show his patriarchal tolerance. (Another boy is an Indian — distrusted at first, but he proves himself.) As long as the movie isn't anti-Semitic or anti-Negro, the Hollywood liberals who worked on it can probably convince themselves that they have retained their image. The villains are — natch — all nondenominational whites, and they are such vipers that you hear rattles on the sound track when they are lurking nearby. Bruce Dern gives the kind of wheedling, cringing-cur ex-convict performance that disappeared for decades but is now renascent. Pro-violence, pro-revenge movies like *Dirty Harry* and *The Cowboys* require the unredeemably vicious villains of primitive melodrama. But these movies are not inconsequential melodramas; they thump for a simplistic right-wing ideology at a time when people may be ready to buy it.

Wayne says, "It's a hard life," and that's supposed to be the truth that explains why boys must learn to be killers. It's not such a hard life for the Hollywood moviemakers who are peddling this line. *The Cowboys* cost five million dollars, and most of us will never earn in a lifetime what an anxious hack director makes on a five-million-dollar movie. Mark Rydell hasn't mastered much film technique — just enough of the old show-biz one-two to raise lumps in some throats — and the violence is bloody-banal. The Hollywood hills are full of educated liberals who will make a movie glorifying the tortures at the Dacca race course and try to get it to come out right by working in a Puerto Rican love interest or a black rabbi.

[January 22, 1972]

Peckinpah's Obsession

Sam Peckinpah is the youngest legendary American director. When you see his Western movies, you feel that he's tearing himself apart, split between a compulsion to show that people are messing up their lives and an overwhelming love of the look and feel of those people rattling around in the grandeur and apparent freedom of the landscape. He is so passionate and sensual a film artist that you may experience his romantic perversity kinesthetically, and get quite giddy from feeling trapped and yet liberated. He's an artist in conflict with himself, but unmistakably and prodigally an artist, who uses images of great subtlety and emotional sophistication — the blown-up bridge of *The Wild Bunch*, with the horses and riders falling to the water in an instant extended to eternity; the exhilaration of space in *Major Dundee;* the visual tribute to the old Westerner of *Ride the High Country*, who sinks to the bottom of the frame to die; the vulture in the *The Wild Bunch* sitting on a dead man's chest and turning his squalid, naked head to stare at the camera.

Peckinpah has finally made the movie he's been working his way toward: though small in scale, and not nearly as rich or varied as parts of his earlier films, *Straw Dogs* is a complete work — a structured vision of life on film. I think Peckinpah has been honest in terms of his convictions, and in terms of those convictions it's a work of integrity, but it's not a work of major intelligence. It represents — superficially, at least — a resolution of his conflicts, but in a spiritually ugly way. His earlier films were recklessly high on beauty and excess; this time he brings everyone down. The vision of *Straw Dogs* is narrow and puny, as obsessions with masculinity so often are; Peckinpah's view of human experience seems to be no more than the sort of anecdote that drunks tell in bars. The story is a male fantasy about a mathematics professor's hot young wife (Susan George) who wants to be raped and gets sodomized, which is more than she bargained for, and the timid cuckold-mathematician (Dustin Hoffman), who turns into a man when he learns to fight like an animal. The subject of *Straw Dogs* is machismo. It has been the obsession behind most of Peckinpah's other films; now that it's out in the open, his strengths and follies are clearly visible. His intuitions as a director are infinitely superior to his thinking.

From the opening shot, of ambiguous children's games in a church cemetery, through to the close, there is no suggestion of human happiness, no frolicking animal, nothing blooming anywhere. The actors are not allowed their usual freedom to become characters, because they're pawns in the over-all scheme. The director doesn't cut loose, either; he sacrifices the flow and spontaneity and the euphoria of spaciousness that have made him a legend — but not the savagery. For the first time, he has left the West, and for the first time he has a statement to make. The film is constructed like a demonstration — a misanthropic one. Working from a script that he wrote with David Z. Goodman, he carefully plants the prejudicial details that will later pay off; there are menacing closeups and more than one superfluous reaction shot. The preparations are not in themselves pleasurable; the atmosphere is ominous and oppressive, but you're drawn in and you're held, because you can feel that it is building purposefully. The setting is a Cornish village and a lonely farmhouse on the moors that the American mathematician — he has a grant to work on celestial navigation — and his English wife have moved into. The farmhouse is singularly uninviting; no objects have been placed to catch the light or give off a glow. The landscape is barren and alien — not exactly desolate but neutral. Peckinpah is famous for the love that makes his Western landscapes expressive, but no love informs this landscape with feeling. The townspeople, who are creepy enough for a horror thriller, include a collection of stud louts who jeer at Hoffman while they snigger and smack their lips over his wife's braless sweaters. One look at her provocative walk and you know that her husband is in trouble — that he can't handle her.

The setting, the music, and the people are deliberately disquieting. It *is* a thriller — a machine headed for destruction. Hoffman, the victim of the villagers' (and the director's) contempt, is that stock figure of fun the priggish, cowardly intellectual. It's embarrassing that a man of Peckinpah's gifts should offer such stale anti-intellectualism, but one can't avoid the conclusion that Hoffman's David is meant to be a symbolic "uncommitted" intellectual who is escaping the turmoil of America. "You left because you didn't want to take a stand," his wife taunts him, while we squirm and wish she didn't represent the film's point of view. Inevitably, David discovers that he can't hide in his study, and that in the peaceful countryside nature is red in tooth and claw. The casting, however, is impeccable. Hoffman, notoriously a cerebral actor, projects thought before movement; he's already a cartoon of an intellectual. There's a split second of blank indecision before the face lights up with purpose. He never looks as if he just naturally lived in the places he's stuck into for the camera; he always seems slightly the outsider anyway, and his duck walk and physical movements are a shade clumsy. Whatever he does seems a bit of a feat — and that, I think, is why we're drawn to him. This role might almost be a continuation of his Benjamin in *The Graduate*.

The movie never explains how he and his Lolita-wife got together, and one's mind strays from the action to ask this question. We can't believe in this marriage; we feel it to be a marriage for Peckinpah's convenience. Susan George, with her smudged, pouty mouth and her smile that's also a snarl, is superlatively cast and can act, besides; she's a sex kitten here — an unsatisfied little tart, a child-wife who wants to be played with. David is even more of an ingenuous jerk than Benjamin. We don't believe it when he interrupts his wife's passionate lovemaking to wind the alarm clock; we just take it as a point being racked up. Peckinpah treats him so prejudicially that it isn't even meant to be funny when he stares in bewilderment at the joshing of the locals — as if no one in America ever indulged in coarse, dumb badinage — and it isn't played for comedy when he goes out hunting with local yokels, who leave him sitting in the brush while they go back to get at his wife. David allows himself to be humiliated for an unpleasantly long time — for so long that he becomes quite unappetizing. We're just about ready to give up on him when his car hits a half-wit (David Warner) who is trying to escape these same bullies, who are after him for molesting a teen-age girl. David shelters the half-wit in the farmhouse, and, while waiting for a doctor to arrive, is confronted by them — a childish, crazed, indiscriminately violent gang (like the most wanton degenerates among the Wild Bunch) led by a grizzle-bearded old horror who fills the screen with repulsiveness.

David knows that this gang will beat the simpleton to death, and he feels he can't turn him over. And that's when the ferocity we've been dreading, and waiting for, erupts.

He announces, "This is where I live," and he refuses to let the men come into his home; as they lay siege to the farmhouse, he destroys each of them — with grisly ingenuity — until the last one, whom his wife shoots. When he takes a knife to the first, his action comes faster than you expect, and it's startling; you're better prepared for the frenzies that follow, and although the tension mounts, you're not caught off guard again. Not surprisingly, the audience cheers David's kills; it is, after all, a classic example of the worm turning. It's mild-mannered Destry putting on his guns, it's the triumph of a superior man who is fighting for basic civilized principles over men who are presented as mindless human garbage. It's David versus Goliath, and so, of course, the audience roots for David. When the last of the louts has him pinned down, and his terrified wife, with her finger on the trigger, panics and delays, it's unbearable; your whole primitive moviegoer's soul cries out for her to fire — and then she does. You just about can't help feeling that way. You know that the response has been pulled out of you, but you're trapped in that besieged house and you want the terror to be over, and if you believe in civilization at all you want David to win. As the situation has been set up, every possibility for nonviolent behavior has been eliminated.

If all that *Straw Dogs* set out to say was that certain situations may be posited in which fighting is a moral decision, few besides total pacifists would disagree. In a sense, what the movie does is play a variation on the old question asked of conscientious objectors: "What would you do if someone tried to rape your sister?" The question asked here is "What would you do if someone tried to invade your house to kill an innocent person?" In such extreme circumstances, probably most of us would use whatever means came to hand and brain, and if we won by violence we would be glad to have won but be sickened and disgusted at the choice forced on us. We would feel robbed of part of our humanity — as soldiers even in "just" wars are said to feel. And here is where we can part company with Peckinpah, for the movie intends to demonstrate not merely that there is a point at which a man will fight but that he is a better man for it—a real man at last. The goal of the movie is to demonstrate that David *enjoys* the killing, and achieves his manhood in that self-recognition. David experiences no shock, no horror at what he has done but only a new self-assurance and pleasure. And Peckinpah wants us to dig the sexiness of violence. There is even the faint smile of satisfaction on the tarty wife's face that says she will have a new sexual respect for her husband. The movie takes not merely a non-pacifist position but a rabidly anti-pacifist position; it confirms the old militarists' view that pacifism is unmanly, is pussyfooting, is false to "nature."

And this is the stupidity and moral corruption of *Straw Dogs*. It may be necessary to be violent in order to defend your home and your principles, but Peckinpah-Patton thinks that's what makes a man a man. Yet there is also — one senses — a slight condescension on Peckinpah's part, and this relates to his anti-intellectualism: David has become as other men, has lost his intellectual's separation from the beasts, and Peckinpah's victory is in bringing him down. Another ambivalence in Peckinpah is his contempt for the brute yokels and his respect for David for using brains to kill them. In the view of the movie, the yokels deserve their deaths. Peckinpah appears to despise them for their ignorance and inefficiency, just as he despises David as unnatural and dishonest when he is pacific. The corollary of David's becoming a man is that the slutty, baby-doll wife becomes a woman when her husband learns to be man and master — which is what she wanted all along. As a woman, she is not expected to have any principles; she was perfectly willing to yield the half-wit to the mob — she doesn't have an idea in her head but sex and self-preservation. The movie is tight, and it all adds up; the male clichés come together in a coherent fantasy.

Peckinpah is a spartan director this time, but with an aesthetic of cruelty. The only beauty he allows himself is in eroticism and violence — which he links by an extraordinary aestheticizing technique. The rape is one of the few truly erotic sequences on film, and the punches that subdue the wife have the exquisite languor of slightly slowed-down motion. This same languor is present in the later slaughters; the editing is superb in these sequences, with the slowing-down never prolonged but just long enough to fix the images of violence in your imagination, to make them seem already classic and archaic — like something you remember — while they're happening. The rape has heat to it — there can be little doubt of that — but what goes into that heat is the old male barroom attitude: we can see that she's asking for it, she's begging for it, that her every no means yes. The rape scene says that women really want the rough stuff, that deep down they're little beasts asking to be made submissive. I think it's clear from the structuring of the film and the use of the mathematician to represent intellectuals out of touch with their own natures that his wife is intended to be representative of woman's nature, and that the louts understand her better than her husband does. The first rapist understands what she needs; the sodomist (this has been slightly trimmed, so that the film could get an R rating, rather than an X) terrorizes her. Another girl in the movie — the teen-ager who gets the gentle simpleton in trouble by making advances to him after David, the only other gentle person in town, rejects her — sustains the image of Eve the troublemaker. We know as we watch the teen-ager luring the simpleton that girls her age are not so hard up for boys to fondle them that they are going to play around with the village half-wit; we realize it's a plot device to get him pursued by the louts. But implicit in this recognition is that the movie is a series of stratagems to get the characters into the positions that are wanted for a symbolic confrontation. The siege is not simply the climax but the proof, and it has the kick of a mule. What I am saying, I fear, is that Sam Peckinpah, who is an artist, has, with *Straw Dogs,* made the first American film that is a fascist work of art.

It has an impact far beyond the greedy, opportunistic, fascist *Dirty Harry* or the stupid, reactionary *The Cowboys,* because — and here, as a woman, I must guess — it gets at the roots of the fantasies that men carry from earliest childhood. It confirms their secret fears and prejudices that women respect only brutes; it confirms the male insanity that there is no such thing as rape. The movie taps a sexual fascism — that is what machismo is — that is so much a part of folklore that it's on the underside of many an educated consciousness and is rampant among the uneducated. It's what comes out in David's character — what gives him that faintly smug expression at the end. Violence is erotic in the movie because a man's prowess is in fighting and loving. The one earns him the right to the other. You can see why Peckinpah loaded the dice against David at the beginning: he had to make David such a weakling that only killing could rouse him to manhood.

I realize that it's a terrible thing to say of someone whose gifts you admire that he has made a fascist classic. And in some ways Peckinpah's attitudes are not that different from those of Norman Mailer, who is also afflicted with machismo. But Mailer isn't so single-minded about it; he worries it and pokes at it and tries to dig into it. Despite Peckinpah's artistry, there's something basically grim and crude in *Straw Dogs.* It's no news that men are capable of violence, but while most of us want to find ways to control that violence, Sam Peckinpah wants us to know that that's all hypocrisy. He's discovered the territorial imperative and wants to spread the Neanderthal word. At its sanest level, the movie says no more than that a man should defend his home, but Peckinpah has not only pushed this to a sexual test but turned the defense of the home into a destruction orgy, as if determined to trash everything and everyone on the screen. The fury goes way beyond making his point; it almost seems a fury against the flesh. The title has been extracted from a gnomic passage in Lao-tse: "Heaven and earth are ruthless and treat the myriad creatures as straw dogs; the sage is ruthless and treats the people as straw dogs." That's no sage, it's a demon.

[January 29, 1972]

Killers and Thieves

In the Manson case, there was an eerie element that the public responded to. Even though we knew that Roman Polanski had nothing whatever to do with causing the murder of his wife and unborn child and friends, the massacre seemed a vision realized from his nightmare movies. And there was an element of guilt and embarrassment in this connection we made, particularly when Polanski said that the crime was being "reviewed in terms of my films." He didn't quite seem to understand why the connection was inevitable. Now it suggests either a strange form of naïveté or a divided consciousness for Polanski to complain that his *Macbeth* is being reviewed in terms of the Manson case. How else is one to look at the knives, the slain servants, the bloody, mangled babies? How else is one to listen when Lady Macduff, the one warm, human character — who is, of course, soon slain, with all those of her household — says that her husband has left his wife, his babes, and his mansion, or when she says, "I have done no harm"? The movie is full of correlations with what happened in Hollywood. One sees the Manson murders in this *Macbeth* because the director has put them there. Normally, one goes to *Macbeth* to see a famous actor; this time the actor — Jon Finch — is barely featured. Slaughter is the star of this *Macbeth*. Shakespeare's offstage corpses and murders are added to the onstage ones, and they so dominate the material that it's difficult to pay attention to the poetry. Polanski shows such literal horror — and always a shade faster than you expect, so you're not prepared — that there is no horror left to imagine.

One may think that Polanski must have been drawn to this play full of helpless victims because it gave him an opportunity to exorcise the Manson demons, and yet the film does not seem an exorcism. In the movie, the chain of violent events that Macbeth's insanely ambitious act initiates is the ordinary way that power changes hands. The film says that nothing is possible but horror and more horror, and at the end, when Macbeth the tyrant is slain, the new king's crippled, envious brother seeks out the witches, and the cycle of bloodletting is about to begin again. Once more, Jan Kott has had his influence. The effect is to cancel any depth or importance, and to send you out with nothing — no hope of peace, no belief that there could be even a period of order and justice. It's a handsome, well-acted, and intelligent production, and yet it diminishes the complexity and meaning of Shakespeare's play, and the simplification isn't satisfying. Polanski is a gothic realist; his murderous carnivals have an everyday look, with no mystery, and no exaltation, either. The murder of King Duncan does not change Macbeth or awaken anything in him. This *Macbeth* plays well; it succeeds as vivid melodrama without a trace of academicism. But it lacks imaginative power. When Polanski converts what in Shakespeare was pathology into the normal state of affairs, he gives us a horrendous vision but also a rather complacently lucid one. It's as if the riddles had all been solved. The lines have only one meaning now, and that's not what we want: we want the flow of meanings, layer upon layer; we want to be caught up in the counterpoint.

The contrasts have been removed, even physically. The movie does not, perhaps, show more slaughter than other movies, but there is nothing to balance it. It is a winter world at sunset. People cut each other up and watch, smiling, fascinated, as dogs tear a bear apart (mercifully, offscreen — the only mercy we're extended). And the conception here of a *young* Macbeth subtly diminishes our involvement — he's too callow to express Shakespeare's emotions — and the immature Lady Macbeth (Francesca Annis) lacks the enigmatic drive that is the essence of the character. Dissatisfactions and frustrations haven't had time to fester in this young couple: their actions lack resonance, their emotions are thin. Their youth makes the play less tragic and more melodramatic. In this production, we feel no pity for Macbeth, the protagonist, but only shock at what happens to his victims; we view the atrocities and we're destroyed by them, but we don't experience the drama. Shakespeare didn't write the play to tell us that life is a jungle. For the play to involve us and move us, we must see ourselves in Macbeth. The nightmare that he brings upon himself is the greatest cautionary nightmare in dramatic literature; we know that it could be ours if we took the first awful step. We know that we, too, could kill our sleep. In Polanski's version, there is no innocent sleep to kill; Macbeth is so villainously twisted throughout that it's not a matter of his yielding to his worst impulses but of his just being himself. He's so transparently evil that when his lady says he's too full of the milk of human kindness it seems a sick joke. Jon Finch is dark-eyed and devious, more lurking Cassius than conscience-shattered Macbeth; he looks like the two neurotic types of *Rope* synthesized — a sneering, scar-mouthed mixture of John Dall and Farley Granger. Polanski's Macbeth is not a man made different from other men by his crime, not a man corrupted, but a corrupt man — perhaps one could go as far as to say corrupt because he is a man. This dark vision has nowhere to go but further into gore, and that's where it goes. Surprisingly, Polanski fumbles the big scene that one looks forward to as a change of pace — Birnam Wood moving. The picture is shot in a Todd-AO 35 process and is twice as wide as it is high, and Polanski sacrifices the camouflage strategy of the moving wood to string the men with their branches across the wide horizon. It's an effect, all right, but pointless. In any case, it is perfectly clear that the effects he cares about are the brutal ones; that is his métier. Great Birnam Wood can't compete with the stabbings. I came out willing to believe Polanski hates violence, but I wish he could give some evidence of caring about something else.

•

Three happy-monkey actors — George Segal, Ron Leibman, and Paul Sand — win out over the stilted smart talk in *The Hot Rock,* a comedy thriller about the frustrations of four fraternal thieves trying to steal an elusive diamond. The fourth is Robert Redford; the others get rid of their lines, but he can't seem to throw his away (is it possible he doesn't know that the author should have?), and they cling to him and make him seem less straight man than stooge. He's still playing the cool anti-hero of year before last, and the performance has lost its fizz. He doesn't get much to work with: he mugs pain when a baby wets him, and develops gastritis to show us the hardships of a life of crime. The script, based on a novel by Donald E. Westlake, is by William Goldman, but it sounds like a script thrown together in a factory of bored collaborators. Goldman, who wrote *Butch Cassidy and the Sundance Kid,* has now turned those cleancut kidders, the train robbers of the changing West played by Paul Newman and Redford, into the New York City blundering hoods played by Segal and Redford. Once again, the crimes are slapstick, and once again the men "share" a girl. (This time, Segal is married to Redford's sister.) Goldman appears to be writing boys'-series books for the screen; this script, like the last, is a boyhood movie fantasy acted out — how you and your adolescent buddy see yourself up there fooling around on the screen in a Western or a crime caper. In Godard's *Band of Outsiders,* two boys, driving along, leap out of their car and act out a scene from an American movie in the street, get killed, and hop back in the car and drive off. Though it may not be consciously intended, there's something of the same movie-fed imagination in these Goldman scripts, in which the characters skip happily from one implausibility to the next. We understand that they aren't really meant to be outlaws or gangsters — they're nice boys playing at it — but must they try to talk sophisticated? The dialogue in this one is much worse than the hip-cute quips of *Butch Cassidy;* it gets really cheap — like a bum comic coming on on a talk show. But *Butch Cassidy,* a put-on that took its mockery seriously, kept straining toward the lyrical and the legendary. This time, the adolescent silliness isn't inflated. So after a half hour of recoiling from the failed attempts at wit one may become reconciled, because the show is cheerful and the actors are thriving maniacs.

In *Butch Cassidy,* Newman and Redford set up a competitive system of buddy-buddy smirks and shoves. Segal and Redford don't get that competitive thing going, and Ron Leibman (he was Segal's brother in *Where's Poppa?*) moves into the vacuum at the center created by Redford's glumness. My guess is that this happens partly because Goldman's fantasy world collides with that of the director, Peter Yates (whose best-known film is *Bullitt*): the hero turns out to be not Bucko Redford, the leader of the gang, but Leibman, who plays the freaky genius driver of the gang's getaway vehicles. Yates, whose career has been in the theatre and films except for a two-year interval as a racing-car driver and manager, has encouraged Leibman to release his considerable actor's energy in a demented fix on motors. His driver's zeal is not just comic frenzy, it's concentrated true love. With Leibman playing this euphoric driver and Segal playing a friendly, panicky lock picker — he has the same total immersion in a character's lunacy that he had in *Born to Win* — the picture has two actors who get carried away into clown character roles, and at the beginning Paul Sand (as a bomb wizard) is right up there, too. Sand gives promise of being that rarity, a sexy mime; he's like Harpo Marx as a stoned hipster, innocently spaced out. When he wears his hair in what appears to be his normal electric beehive, he's crazy-hip and very funny, but midway in the movie, after he escapes from prison, he goes into disguise by slicking down his hair. It's so effective a disguise that his whole personality is cancelled out. The modern meaning of hair has never before been so clearly demonstrated in a movie — though I don't know if the demonstration is intentional. Maybe Paul Sand really needs *hair*.

Yates isn't always on top of the situation; the movie is often ragged in what seem like the simplest scenes. But he has his specialty. At crucial points, the vehicles — the cars, a van, a helicopter — and their fevered driver determine whether the gang will succeed, and Yates endows the machines with a quality of vulnerability. When Leibman is piloting a helicopter — for the first time — and climbing up the sides of skyscrapers, the little chopper is like a butterfly trying to scale the walls, fluttering valiantly. You want the mock-heroic vehicles to come through and function ideally, as in a fairy tale, and they do. After we have got rather fond of the robbers as harmless sweeties, the movie tries to trick us with a scene in which they have supposedly turned against each other. We sort of know it's fake, but there's a moment when real nastiness seems to be involved, and this kills the fun; even after it turns out to be a hoax, the ugliness lingers. And at the end, when Redford finally gets his big scene — robbing a safe-deposit box at the First National City Bank at Fifty-third Street and Park Avenue — Yates doesn't quite hit the right tone, because the tension makes us nervous without compensatory pleasure. It comes out all right, though. Redford steals the diamond, and his victory is celebrated in a final burst of lyricism, in which he gets a chance to go into his adorable number. But the picture was stolen from him long before.

•

Claude Chabrol's *Le Boucher* has everything but what ultimately counts. Back in 1948, Alexandre Astruc predicted that artists would be able to express themselves in films as they do in essays or novels; he called the coming age the age of *caméra-stylo,* when directors would use the camera as writers use a pen. That is indeed how Chabrol uses his medium, and he has the grace and fluency of a master, but, unfortunately, *Le Boucher* is penmanship, not literature. In *Le Boucher,* as in *La Femme Infidèle,* there's a remarkable consistency of tone; everything seems on the same level of interest to Chabrol — the vase of flowers that balances a composition, a wedding scene, a funeral (the bride's) in the rain, the look of schoolchildren in a Cro-Magnon cave, the cinematographer Jean Rabier's Périgord landscapes. Perhaps Chabrol gives a shade more than his usual decorous, unblinking gaze to the numerous eating scenes, and there's a leg of lamb that the butcher brings to his beloved like a bouquet, but nothing in the movie is very exciting, just as nothing is boring.

You know that Chabrol knows exactly what he's doing as he shows us the beautiful loner schoolteacher (Stéphane Audran) who has been hurt in love and doesn't want to risk another hurt, and the butcher (Jean Yanne) who hated his butcher-father and went into the Army for fifteen years. And the serenely quiet village is a perfect storybook setting for murder. Everything in the movie is just about perfect. Chabrol was once the co-author of a book on Alfred Hitchcock; now his films are like a learned but slightly dense aesthete's commentaries. He provides all the elements for a thriller except the kicker. He seems to cherish the atmospheric elements without quite getting the point of them; Hitchcock used them to prepare us for something. Chabrol makes tone poems on thriller themes. The ambiguities fabricated for the come-on have become the essence; for Chabrol, the atmosphere is everything. Even the one thriller centerpiece — a corpse on a cliff above a children's picnic drips blood on a little girl and she asks if it's raining, and then the blood falls on the bun she's eating — is such a recognizable piece of Hitchcockery that it seems a homage. One can see how Chabrol thinks — he is more interested in the personalities involved in murders, and in the ambience, than in the crude simplicities of whodunit and why. But as the inscrutable characters do not have any more depth or complexity than the characters in a typical thriller, what one gets has neither the zings of a thriller nor the richness of art.

The acting, too, is remarkably even. Stéphane Audran and Jean Yanne seem unforced — incarnations rather than performers. Miss Audran (who is Chabrol's wife) has the elegance of a goddess but no range; her acting is a function of beauty, not of soul, and perhaps her husband's camera is too consciously adoring. Her beauty has become almost the subject of this film, and she isn't quite spiritual enough for that. Jean Yanne, a television talk-show host whom Godard induced to turn actor to play the aggressive, self-centered husband of *Weekend* (the man cannibalized by his luscious wife), is astutely cast here, because he suggests a man whose civilization is something put on, like a workman's Sunday clothes. But the melancholy of this unhappy pair and the perhapses that are the substance of the story — perhaps killing is the butcher's only release for his feelings, perhaps the schoolteacher might have saved him from committing murders if she had not been so fearful of a new love, and so on — are just faintly titillating hints, and the hints don't develop into recognitions. The film's point of view is so flexible that it doesn't seem to matter whether the movie is saying she could have saved him or saying nothing.

A director who uses the camera as fluently as if it were a pen may settle down (perhaps for a period) to being a minor master, turning out movies like the annual output of a detective-fiction writer. Chabrol's restrained surface blocks off the passions that cause murder, and in recent years nothing new seems to have come into his world. In film after film, one waits for Chabrol's revelations. At the end of *Le Boucher,* one doesn't feel cheated, exactly, but feels: Is that all?

[February 5, 1972]

The Messiness of Love

Love knows no honor; people in love do things that they never thought they'd do and that they've always despised other people for doing. They violate not only their own scruples but their own *style.* The shocking messiness of love, which is the subtext of so much great literature, rises to the surface in Edna O'Brien's writing, and in her original screenplay for *X Y & Zee* it has become the text. *X Y & Zee* resembles *Who's Afraid of Virginia Woolf?* but the revelations and emotional convulsions are not so dramatically structured, or so decisive; *X Y & Zee* is more like a long short story. A hollering, brawling marriage, based on the same sort of cast-iron dependencies, is picked up at a time of crisis, when the husband considers leaving the wife — Zee — for another woman, and it ends when the crisis is more or less resolved. The crisis is never *explained.* We never quite discover what brought this couple (Elizabeth Taylor and Michael Caine) together or how the marriage works or why it stops working the night the film begins, when they go to a party and the husband — a veteran philanderer — sees Stella (Susannah York) in a silvery gown. In the past, his affairs didn't disrupt the marriage; inexplicably, this one becomes more than an affair. The way nothing makes sense in love and everything gets loused up is part of Edna O'Brien's subject, and of her method. Characters aren't "worked out" to behave a certain way; the evaporation of love isn't necessarily explainable, or its renewal, either. Things change unpredictably. What is less satisfactory in the movie — and this may be the failure of the director, Brian G. Hutton — is that we must take the dependency of Zee and her husband for granted, though we don't really feel the bondage.

Reading Edna O'Brien's fiction, I've been surprised by perceptions of what I thought no one else knew — and I wasn't telling. Probably other readers react exactly the same way: she makes private shames public. But I've also been disappointed that, knowing so much, she didn't know more — that she didn't move outside the magic circle of women's emotional problems. Maybe that's why this movie seems like M-G-M forties heightened — because, essentially, it deals with the wife's fierce determination to hold on to her husband by any means. It deals, that is, with a willfully spoiled woman's living on her rapacious impulses — and this is only a few steps up from the old Joan Crawford–Rosalind Russell bitches. The gloss and corruption of this kind of "women's picture" is that love, knowing no honor, is treated not as a sloppy fact but as a triumphal statement — a battle cry in the war of the sexes. The prize defines the genre: the prize is not losing your man. It's a specialized, limited view, commercial and rubbishy, but the contestants here are entertainingly polarized — Zee the sun lover, the overdressed wife in her millionaire gypsy couture, versus the cool, restful mistress. And the dialogue has a sardonic tickle to it. There's some wildness in Edna O'Brien's playfulness and love of words; her writing isn't merely clever — it's delicate in odd, indelicate ways. Indelicacy in women artists can be like the stripping off of corsets. Edna O'Brien likes to reveal, and even though her revelations don't go deep, they're loose and free; she's so full of the wicked zest of being unfettered that there's something almost rapturous about her naughtiness. For her, writing seems another way of sowing her wild oats. Her dialogue, which is one trespass after another, is so good because there's no sense of strain: it flows. The performers in this movie — they must be greedy for lines like this — know what to do with it. The dialogue isn't hollow, like Broadway wisecracks. It sounds likely, because the wit belongs to the subject; rich, smart women who have never needed to develop their intelligence, who use their brains only to climb and to hang on to money and men, do become high-pitched and clever in this combative way. This honed edge of glitzy bitchery isn't an accomplishment, it's a dysfunctional weapon — the tic of wasted minds.

At the beginning of *X Y & Zee*, Elizabeth Taylor, peering out of blue lamé eyeshadow like a raccoon, seemed ridiculous and — well, monstrous. But as the picture went on, I found myself missing her whenever she wasn't onscreen (when Michael Caine and Susannah York were acting immaculately), and I'm forced to conclude that, monstrous though she is, her jangling performance is what gives this movie its energy. She has grown into the raucous-demanding-woman role she faked in *Who's Afraid of Virginia Woolf?* When she goes too far, she's like the blowziest scarlet woman in a Mexican movie, but she's still funny. She wears her hair like upholstery, to balance the upholstery of flesh. The weight she has put on in these last years has not made her gracefully voluptuous; she's too hard-boiled to be Rubensesque. The weight seems to have brought out this coarseness, and now she basks in vulgarity. She uses it as a form of assault in *X Y & Zee,* and I don't think she's ever before been as strong a star personality.

Elizabeth Taylor has changed before our eyes from the fragile child with a woman's face to the fabled beauty to this great bawd. Maybe child actresses don't quite grow up if they stay in the movies; maybe that's why, from ingénue-goddess, she went right over the hill. (The change in her is not unlike the change in Judy Garland.) Her Zee is a gross sensualist beyond shame or fear; possibly Zee is not really written to be as down-to-earth honest as Taylor plays her, but Taylor's all-out, let-it-bleed performance is a phenomenon — a world-famous woman changing status and, I think, maybe getting in touch with the audience in a new, egalitarian way. Her range has become even smaller. She's worst in some subdued scenes that take place in a hospital, when she droops and tries to call up that early demure beauty; she becomes flaccid — a fallen-angel-face. And she's not enough of an actress to get by with the bruised-and-hurting bit. She's got to be active and brassy and bold; she's best when she lets her gift for mimicry and for movie-colony sluttiness roll out. What she does may not be acting, exactly — I can't think of any tradition or school it fits into — but this isn't like her moldy performances in *Boom!* and *Secret Ceremony* or the anachronistic girlishness of her sweet young thing in *The Only Game in Town.* She responds to the zest in Edna O'Brien's material; you can feel her willingness to go all the way with it, and her delight at letting it all spill out. Though her voice is stronger now, she still gets shrill, and she starts so whoopingly high that the performance can't build and the viewer needs to recover. But Taylor has a talent for comic toughness; what she needs is a director to rein her in a little, to keep her from toppling over into the ridiculous and turning into a heavyweight Susan Hayward.

Brian Hutton plunges us straight into this *haut*-forties bedlam of domestic crisis. He aims each shot for the jugular. Nothing is implied, nothing suggested; everything belts you. Hutton isn't incompetent — he keeps things going by staying with the performers — but he can't redeem the hokey scenes toward the end, and he doesn't have much skill at modulation or atmosphere. We need to feel the contagion of Zee's messiness, feel how it works on her husband, driving him berserk, and how it infects

Stella, but the picture doesn't develop. It has nowhere to go, anyway, because its emotional logic has been jiggled. Had Edna O'Brien's screenplay (published in England as *Zee & Co*) been followed, the movie might have got at the insanity of passion and might have broken through the fancy "women's-picture" format by sheer sensuous force. The author pushed what's implicit in the triangle to a classic climax: the couple jointly possess Stella. The movie substitutes a makeshift ending (Zee seducing Stella and thus winning out and keeping her husband) that has no strength. Photographed in Billy Williams' ripest palette, the production is mod-harem — a cushiony London version of old studio style. I don't suppose anyone in his right mind would call *X Y & Zee* a good movie; it's more like a plush circus, and it's even got slurpy theme music. But one may remember bits of old "women's pictures" — or even a relatively recent one, like *The Chapman Report* — for a surprisingly long time; in their gaudy way, they deal with a familiar inferno.

This one has a script that enabled Elizabeth Taylor to come out. The aging beauty has discovered in herself a gutsy, unrestrained spirit that knocks two very fine performers right off the screen — and, for the first time that I can recall, she appears to be having a roaring good time on camera. Susannah York, with her corn-silk hair and her round blue eyes, seems lovely, if a bit pallid. She has a harlequin voice — she rings wonderful low notes on it — and she carries her own quiet, vulnerable atmosphere, but the character she plays is slightly withdrawn, and that is Taylor's opportunity. After Zee, in a nasty snit, describes her as soulful and always a little out of breath, Stella looks like a narcissistic moonbeam. Even Susannah York's subtle, lapidary acting begins to seem overrefined when this rowdy broad is working up one of her rages. The corn-silk Stella is no match for Zee, and York, the polished actress, is unfairly matched against Taylor, an uncontrolled actress but a cunning force of nature. One can take pleasure in Taylor's brute triumph, especially since she's working with two of the best screen performers of our time. (Michael Caine does all he can with a role that requires him to be mostly exasperated, infuriated, and exhausted.) Perhaps a loud, uncontrolled performer can always dominate a controlled performer, because the element of accident and risk, the possibility that something grotesque may be revealed, adds danger and excitement — and there is something of this in Taylor's performance here. But there is also the excitement of seeing a woman who has vast reserves of personality and who wants to come forward, who wants to make contact. There's a documentary going on inside this movie — part of it may be parallel to Edna O'Brien's theme, but part of it isn't.

It's of a woman declaring herself to be what she has become. Like everyone else, I adored the child Elizabeth Taylor, but I have never liked her as much since as in this bizarre exhibition. She's Beverly Hills Chaucerian, and that's as high and low as you can get.

[February 12, 1972]

Grinning

Cabaret is a great movie musical, made, miraculously, without compromises. It's miraculous because the material is hard and unsentimental, and until now there has never been a diamond-hard big American movie musical. The people involved must have said something like "Let's do it right — let's use the right people, let's not wreck it the way *Pal Joey* was wrecked, and *The Boys from Syracuse* and *Guys and Dolls* and *Gypsy* and *Sweet Charity* and all the rest. Maybe it won't work at the box office, maybe the movie moguls have basically been shrewd when they insisted on all the softening and spoiling and the big names in the leads, but let's do it right for once anyway." And so *Cabaret* was made, with Joel Grey as our devil-doll host — the master of ceremonies — and Liza Minnelli, in her first singing role on the screen, as Sally Bowles. And it is everything one hopes for and more; if it doesn't make money, it will still make movie history.

After *Cabaret*, it should be a while before performers once again climb hills singing or a chorus breaks into song on a hayride; it is not merely that *Cabaret* violates the wholesome approach of big musicals but that it violates the pseudo-naturalistic tradition — the *Oklahoma!–South Pacific–West Side Story* tradition, which requires that the songs appear to grow organically out of the story. That pretense used to be charming in the light musical comedies with a French-farce base, like the Ginger Rogers and Fred Astaire series, but the "organic" big show has become the white elephant of Broadway, and by the time the elephants reached the screen nothing seemed more theatrical — in the worst sense — than the clumping attempts to go into a number "naturally." It was as if there were something the matter with song and dance, as if they had to be excused by being worked into "a life situation" — or one of those damn dream ballets.

Cabaret turns the conventions of recent big-musical movies inside out: the floor show at the Kit Kat Klub is used as a prism through which we see the characters' lives. The formalized numbers are at the center of the movie — are its essence. The songs comment on the lives of Sally Bowles and the other characters from the Christopher Isherwood "Goodbye to Berlin" stories, and they interpret the period — the end of an era (Weimar) and the beginning of Nazism. With this prismatic approach, *Cabaret* totally escapes grandiosity; it's a big musical that doesn't feel like one, and the first really innovative movie musical in many years. Not only is the subject not wholesome but the tone is detached and objective.

The usual movie approach to decadent periods of history is to condemn decadence while attempting to give us vicarious thrills. Here, in a prodigious balancing act, Bob Fosse, the choreographer-director, keeps this period — Berlin, 1931 — at a cool distance. We see the decadence as garish and sleazy, and yet we see the animal energy in it, and the people driven to endure. The movie does not exploit decadence; rather, it gives it its due. The reminiscences of Brecht and Kurt Weill in Joel Grey's opening "Willkommen" and of *The Blue Angel* in Liza Minnelli's first song, "Mein Herr," help us get our bearings; reminiscence is part of the texture. The whory chorus girls displaying the piquant flesh around their garters, the Max Beckmann angles and the Edvard Munch hollows are part of the texture, too. The movie is never cynical (it may be one of the least cynical big movies ever made); it is, on the contrary, so clear-eyed that it winks at nothing. Though it uses camp material, it carries camp to its ultimate vileness — in the m.c.'s mockery of all things human, including himself. His lewd smirks, like Sally's broad, fatuous, flirtatious grins, are emblems of corruption. *Cabaret* does not merely suggest Egon Schiele's moribund, erotic figures and the rictus smiles and rotting flesh in the paintings and graphics of artists such as James Ensor and George Grosz but captures the same macabre spirit — and *sustains* it. What makes the art of such men powerful is that they help us recognize the sensual strength of decadence. When there is nothing to believe in but survival and pleasure, gaiety has a ghastly, desperate edge, but the way people still seek pleasure is testimony to something both base and fascinating. Everything seems to become sexualized. The grotesque amorality in *Cabaret* is frightening, not because it's weak but because it's intensely, obscenely alive.

The method of the movie is to embrace this life and to show us the appeal of its horror, and by this satiric embrace to put us at a distance. The detached tone makes it possible for us to observe the decay, consciously — with full awareness. You never get lost in it; you're aware of every detail — and you're also aware of the intelligence at work, keeping you aware. Fosse never slips tongue into cheek or lets the performers get moist; the movie doesn't lose its chilling tone. When the apocalyptic chill deepens, it deepens because of the precise, unhysterical direction. It's this masterly control that makes the movie biting and aesthetically exciting — so that it gets better as it goes along.

The metallic songs by John Kander, who wrote the music, and Fred Ebb, who did the lyrics, have a distinctive, acrid flavor — a taste of death on the tongue. In the smoky atmosphere, the little m.c. is both ringmaster and marionette. His professional, insidious complicity with us, the audience — his slyness and malice — makes us draw back to objectivity. He looks as if he had been born in a night club. With his rouged cheeks, yellow-stained teeth, and smeared-down patent-leather hair, Joel Grey is every tantalizingly disgusting show-biz creep one has ever seen — all the cheap comics and night-club entertainers rolled into one. He's the essence of show-biz tawdriness, and the pure-tin evil heart of the period.

Joel Grey, Bob Fosse, and Liza Minnelli are all children of show-business families, and that may be why they understand these musical numbers so shatteringly well. Liza Minnelli's exuberant, corruptible Sally, going after fame and stardom no matter what, has that persistent spark — the amoral soul of theatre. Her emerald-green fingernails are no longer just the mark of a girl who wants to be shockingly original; Sally is no longer just an innocently and adorably mad gamine, older sister to Holly Golightly. This Sally has grown claws. The m.c. has burnt out his hopes, but she has youth and drive. He presides over a sinking ship and enjoys the spiteful knowledge of how tacky it is. But Sally, at the end, beckoning us with those emerald nails, has real force. Liza Minnelli makes you believe in the cabaret as "life" because she comes fully to life only when she sings. The features that seemed too large for her face suddenly fit. Her cherry lips and unnaturally bright eyes are no longer wild makeup; they belong to her performer's face. And her movements have speed and tension. Her desperation and Sally's are fused together; when a singer is belting it out, how can one separate the performer from the role? Liza Minnelli is a fine, if slightly overeager, actress and an inventive, appealing comedienne, but only when she sings is she a star: she's charged to give all she's got.

The material has come a long way from the Isherwood stories —

through the play and movie of *I Am a Camera* to the Broadway musical *Cabaret* and this version, adapted for the screen by Jay Allen, with the assistance of Hugh Wheeler. The heightened powers of song and dance dominate the naturalistic characters (Michael York in the Isherwood-as-a-young-writer role, Marisa Berenson as a beautiful Jewish heiress, Fritz Wepper as her penniless suitor, Helmut Griem as a baron who courts both Sally and the writer) and subtly alter the meanings of the original material. When theatrical rot becomes a metaphor for a rotting period, it may also illuminate rotting theatre. If the cabaret numbers are the frame through which we see the themes and the story, the themes are also mirrored in the cabaret. And what these three children of show business may know in their bones is how true that mirror is.

There are a few minor imperfections: I could have done without the montage that involves a child, a ball, and some shrieking can-can dancers. Michael York's creamy-smooth glaze-of-youth skin looks too much like the baron's creamy-smooth skin — they seem to have come out of the same jar. (On the other hand, York's makeup after a street fight is a hilarious success.) Though York acts more simply and attractively than usual, his phrasing sounds uncannily as if he were being dubbed by James Mason. The first use of dialogue as a bridge between two sequences sticks out as a device, and a few lines are too pat. But this is nit-picking; I can see no major faults. My ideal musical would include far more dancing, but this conception doesn't allow for it, and that is hardly a fault. What dancing there is — which is mostly movement during songs — is marvellous, particularly that of Liza Minnelli and Joel Grey in the "Money" number, and of Grey and the shy gorilla lady dressed in flesh-pink tulle in the romantic soft-shoe "If You Could See Her." And there's a brief goose-stepping dance performed by helmeted chorus girls, with Grey among them in drag, that has prurient images worthy of Lautrec; Liza Minnelli, too, when she sings takes positions — the way she leads with her truculent shoulders, her small flapper-head like a predatory bird's — that suggest Lautrec's posters.

Cabaret is the only expensive American movie musical (actually, it was shot in West Germany) that takes its form from political cabaret. The political satire here might be thought to have too easy and obvious a target, but, as it works out, the associations we have with this target — from art and literature and journalism — enable the satire to function at a higher level of ironic obscenity than would be possible with a more topical subject. And the picture goes way beyond topical satire into a satire of temptations. The only number that doesn't take place in the Kit Kat Klub is a song in the open air. In a country-inn beer garden, a golden-haired, fresh-faced young boy begins to sing with the lilting sweetness of an Irish tenor. He's everything the movies have taught us to idolize — his teeth are the prettiest white teeth in the world — and as his stirring Nazi song, "Tomorrow Belongs to Me," builds relentlessly his radiant fervor transforms itself before our eyes. More typically, the movie intercuts between a slapdance on the stage inside the Klub and a beating in the street outside. The counterpoint may be a facile idea, but it is not carried out facilely. Decadence comprises so much more than any specific satirical target that the movie's cold embrace of decadence is a richly suggestive form of satire.

No one has ever made a musical that looked better than this one — photographed by Geoffrey Unsworth, and the first film produced by the Broadway producer Cy Feuer. The design and the lighting and the color are superb; the picture has the distortions and the exaggerations and the grinning vividness of Expressionist art. *Cabaret* demonstrates that when you revolt against the organic *Oklahoma!* conception of musicals you can create a new organic whole by style and imagination — if you have enough faith in the audience to do it right.

[February 19, 1972]

Literary Echoes—Muffled

Without Apparent Motive, which begins with an epigraph from Raymond Chandler, is an affectionate, unconcealed imitation of *The Big Sleep*, with Jean-Louis Trintignant in the Bogart role, and Dominique Sanda as the rich, knowing, big pussycat — the tawny-blond Lauren Bacall girl without illusions. The setting is Nice; the audience, whimpering from the pain of the bitter cold experienced while waiting in line to get into the theatre, practically swoons with pleasure at the first resplendent views of the Côte d'Azur. Philippe Labro, the director, lays his American-movie cards on the table a little too baldly when the stunning, long-stemmed Carla Gravina presents Trintignant with a whistle and quotes the familiar line from *To Have and Have Not*, but this baldness is redeeemed in a later scene involving that whistle. The French can now do better with a certain kind of laconic American thriller involving the corrupt rich than Americans can. Labro, a journalist, is a fine technician, and he has assimilated the American genre into his own style; his mind is steeped in Raymond Chandler, but the movie comes out classically French.

The shift from sunny, stucco-bungalowed southern California to the sunny baroque of Nice civilizes a detective story; the vision of corruption is still glamorously shallow, but it isn't seedy now — it has a patina. And the lithe, leggy beauties — who are probably chosen because they look like American girls — are ineffably European to us. They have the best of both worlds — long legs, sad eyes, and a mysterious chic. Labro's French outlook transforms the hardboiled into the understated, while the insolence and the giddy implausibilities are replaced by finesse and rationality. Here action doesn't stop for a song about a husband who socked his wife in the choppers; you don't enjoy yourself hugely, as you can at *The Big Sleep* — the genre has become too refined for that — but you can have a felicitous good time. Chandler said that his master, Dashiell Hammett, "gave murder back to the kind of people that committed it for reasons, not just to provide a corpse; and with the means at hand, not with handwrought duelling pistols, curare and tropical fish." The irony in the French love for Chandler and Hammett is that the French make the material so ultra-civilized — so élitist — that murders are once again committed on the fancy, curare-and-tropical-fish level, and this, also ironically, is the appeal of French thrillers to Americans staggering under the knowledge of too many murders committed with the all too vulgarian means at hand.

A series of murders "without apparent motive" are linked only by the weapon — a rifle equipped with telescopic sights and a silencer. Trintignant is the detective looking into the victims' lives in search of the motive, so he can find the killer. (Here, too, there is a difference: in this country at this time the more likely assumption would be that there was no motive linking the victims.) Trintignant, who has always gained from his elusive, submerged resemblance to Bogart, toys with the Bogart snarl-grin and makes the identification explicit; this seems a pity, but he can get by with it. So far, he's the only one who can. It takes a volatile, wary actor like Trintignant playing at half-mast; Bogart's wariness, the suggestion of ferocity under control, was what gave his low-key, slightly cute roles their tension and their special, playful, sexy charm. And not only Trintignant but most of the leading players seem to have an existence — and some depth — beyond their few minutes on the screen. That, too, is typically "French." The plot is some gimcrackery derived from an Ed McBain novel, but it creates suspense and it doesn't fizzle out. The orderly narrative suits the landscape.

Those who don't go won't miss out, but moviegoers with memories may enjoy such details as Trintignant doing a variation on his gunplay in *The Conformist,* and the reversal of the sexes in the reënactment of that last scene in *The Third Man,* when Alida Valli walked past Joseph Cotten. In a cast that includes Stéphane Audran, Sacha Distel, and Erich Segal, who plays an astrologer, Segal, though a presentable enough actor, is at a disadvantage: the audience, casually familiar with the others, has too sharp a recognition of him. His presence seems a little lurid, somehow — it fits the world of *The Big Sleep* better than the world of *Without Apparent Motive.* But he has the best single moment in the movie when, seated on a luxurious patio, he looks out and spots a sniper just an instant before the bullet reaches his heart. One flagrant lapse of style: a painting that is meant to reveal the painter's obsessed imagination is actually a commercial artist's slick job of diabolism. One touching weakness in Labro's direction: he seems quite stiff — almost embarrassed — in his handling of the crafty killer, and he's so shy and self-effacing about presenting a psychopathic woman that the movie comes to a pause. He lacks the American thriller directors' pulpy brashness about sickness. It's a fault but far from a sin.

•

There's talent and intelligence in the Australian film *Outback.* More remarkably, it has a subject — the crude comradeship among the white men in the vast desert areas, and their erratic destructiveness. It has additional interest because it records the same kind of senseless destruction that in recent American movies has been blamed on the corruptiveness of American racism and capitalist exploitation and the Vietnam war. The story is about a male schoolteacher (Gary Bond) who hates his job in Tiboonda, a flat, dusty railroad stop a thousand miles from Sydney; both sensitive and arrogant, he is repelled by the coarseness of the life. There's a stale whiff of Conrad in his feeling trapped and living on his nerves and in the atmosphere of foreboding, and this is intensified by the fact that Bond bears an unfortunate, anemic resemblance to Peter O'Toole, who played a Conrad hero and has sometimes seemed to be playing one when he wasn't. An educated doctor turned drunken, half-mad amoralist (Donald Pleasence, doing the sneeringly dirty again, but practice has made him just about perfect this time) is Conradian, too. But the teacher's attempt to escape and his ordeals provide enough narrative to hold the social material together. And much of the Conradian turbid literary self-disgust is rackingly effective on a horror-melodrama level. However, the picture's more solid strength is that, unlike the American films in which vengeful, hypocritical (usually middle-class) whites destroy mercilessly, slaughtering Indians or animals, or both, *Outback* is fair-minded. And because the mindless violence you're shown isn't attributed to what you know damned well didn't cause it, you can't shrug it off; you're stuck with it, trying to understand it, trying to figure out what, if anything, can be done about it.

The men in this sterile, parched back country are crazily hospitable; in a way that has less to do with a stranger's needs than with their own. They no sooner see a stranger than they toss him a can of beer and invite him to join them. They guzzle all day and all night; they garland themselves with the pull tabs from beer cans. It's a frontier society, but, unlike the green American frontier, without idealism, without that dream of moving "civilization" west, without a trace of culture. It's a butch boomtown society made in the image of good-natured, roughhousing, not too bright boys — life as one long beer bust. The men gamble big stakes at childish games; they can't think of anything else to do. They smash things for excitement, or brawl, or shoot anything that moves, or run it down with their cars. The red eyes of the kangaroos in the glare of the headlights — that's what you take home from *Outback*. Of course, this is a racist society, too, but the movie doesn't bother to underline that point, because it is so clear that the men are not morally destroyed by their treatment of the Aborigines; they're morally *unawakened* and they're bored — too bored to treat their environment with respect. They age but never grow up; they keep acting out adolescent rituals of virility. Their blood sport is boxing with wounded kangaroos and then slitting their throats.

The schoolteacher's snobbery about them — his finding them oppressively stupid — is, from the start, the clue to his limitations, not because he's wrong but because he enjoys feeling superior. However, his inadequacies are the focal point, and the picture goes off, I think, in staying with him throughout the process of his disintegration and self-discovery. For one thing, we don't believe in the lesson: though the melodrama requires that he come to a new understanding of himself, we experience what happens to him as total defeat. But a more serious problem is that (despite the banal photography) the semi-documentary aspects of the film are so much more vivid and authentic and original than the factitious Conradian hero that we want to see more of that material — we want to learn more. The rough white men out there in the wilderness are a new race to us. They're beasts but not villains; they're "decent" and unaware of wrongdoing — and that suggests that they are unreachable. There have been other Australian films, so it's not all new, but Ted Kotcheff, who directed this picture, and Evan Jones, who wrote it (from a novel by Kenneth Cook), have seen the life in a more objective way, almost as if they were cultural anthropologists examining a newly developed form of primitive life — the primitivism of the master race. Maybe Kotcheff didn't dare to expand this vision at the expense of the plot line, but he got on to something bigger than the plot. And, even though the movie retreats into its narrow frame, you come out with a sense of epic horror. You come out with the perception that this master race is *retarded*.

•

In his brief essay on Kafka's precursors, Borges did not suggest any Americans, but Melville's "Bartleby, the Scrivener" is a possible candidate, and a precursor, also, of Oblomov, of Dostoyevsky's underground man, and of Camus's Meursault. The shock when you first read the story may be in the recognition that Melville had this pre-vision of modern alienation back in 1853. You can't grasp how this specifically modern man was formed in that mid-nineteenth-century setting: What is he doing in that world, passively resisting, and withdrawing into a courteous, stubborn catatonia? The new English movie *Bartleby*, with John McEnery in the lead and Paul Scofield as the employer, is set in modern London, and that kills the visionary quality right off the bat. This disappointment doesn't diminish as the picture goes on, because the story is never made to belong to its new setting (the specific misery of his copyist's job no longer exists, and the substitution doesn't have the same life-wasting colorlessness; we can see from the start that a man in Bartleby's condition wouldn't be hired, and the other employees are not plausible as our contemporaries), and, since the movie is empty of detail and most of the action was obviously shot in a studio, we don't know why it has been modernized, unless on the naïve ground that it would mean more to us if we saw how modern it was.

Bartleby as a type certainly persists, and McEnery is successful in bringing the clerk up to date; McEnery suggests both the mournful, bleached-out intransigence of the character and all the wan, misfit loners, in their seat-sprung pants, who wander through the big cities. We can see that Bartleby can't depend on reflexes, that he has to think out every motion; his neck and head hang forward, expecting nothing. Melville's Bartleby was perhaps more tranquil, less distressed and fearful, than McEnery's, but this fearfulness seems right, it belongs. And Scofield's amiable, confused responsiveness to Bartleby is nicely sketched. But the original story moves logically and inexorably; there are no subplots — nothing but the movement of a wage slave toward the freedom of total negation. It's a composition in monotone; when it's padded to feature-film length it doesn't get richer, it just gets thin and loses its omniscient force. Of all stories, it is perhaps the least suited to the memory cut-ins that the director, Anthony Friedman, uses. The picture was obviously made on a shoestring and with honorable intentions, but it's tentative and lame and bland-looking. You feel that the story is being acted out but that it hasn't been made into a movie — not in the way that Alain Jessua, for example, took a similar case of withdrawal and made a film of it in *Life Upside Down*. The scene of Scofield lecturing his empty office, rehearsing what he'll say to Bartleby, is so trite it's difficult to watch the screen without blushing for all concerned. When Bartleby should be looking at brick walls, Friedman has him looking at birds and trees, as if it were the ecological destruction that he is protesting when he refuses to work. And instead of withholding the information about his having worked in the dead-letter division of the postal system, as Melville did, for the final note, the movie introduces it at the beginning and milks it throughout. The film has little to recommend it but the two actors, Melville's dialogue, and the remnants of his great, spooky conception.

•

To Die of Love, a French movie with an unconvincing air of high-minded rectitude, is a thinly fictionalized version of the Gabrielle Russier case (reported by Mavis Gallant in the "Annals of Justice" in *The New Yorker* of June 26, 1971). The movie exploits the obvious and turns what might have been a gleaming social tragicomedy into one more bathetic, sacrificial love story. Readers will recall that Gabrielle Russier, a thirty-one-year-old teacher, a woman whose thesis was on the use of the past tense in Robbe-Grillet and Nathalie Sarraute, and who did not permit her twin children to fraternize with each other or to leave their rooms without permission, fell in love with the sixteen-year-old son of two of the professors who had trained her. They were Communists, the boy a Maoist; that caused tension in the family, and when he neglected his studies for his love affair they acted like proper bourgeois and took full advantage of the laws, by which he was legally a child. They had the teacher arrested for causing a minor to leave home; caught in a round of imprisonments and trials, she committed suicide. Not the least of the ironies in the case was the unworldliness of the tiny, boyish-looking, humorless teacher and her vision of herself as a literary heroine (as Mrs. Gallant pointed out, she signed letters "Phèdre" and "Antigone"), and one of the most scandalous ironies was the use of modern psychiatry — especially "sleep cures" — to break down the boy's resistance to his parents' determination to end the attachment.

The movie barely taps any of this; it is a polemic against hypocrisy and the double standard, combined with a pedestrian attempt at a modern *Devil in the Flesh*. Annie Girardot, an elegant actress in the Edwige Feuillère–Jeanne Moreau–Emmanuelle Riva grand tradition, goes at the role like a cross between Greer Garson as a mother superior and the Maid of Orleans in love. Wtih her hair cropped like Gabrielle Russier's, she even has the coiffure of the saintly Maid, and her tears stain her cheeks, just as in Dreyer's *The Passion of Joan of Arc*. (She's actually laid out like a statue at the end.) With the heroine turned into a gallantly suffering lady, the story loses its distinctive character, and the movie, directed by André Cayatte, from a script he and Gabrielle Russier's lawyer concocted, is loaded with verisimilitude but has little of the actual story's political ambience (the affair blossomed during the student uprisings of 1968) or its social satire. Inept even at the simplest dramatic levels, Cayatte follows the lovers' itineraries and leaves out the crucial scenes that we wait for— such as how she tells the boy's parents that they are lovers. They kiss a lot whenever they're reunited, but what brought them together or what they mean to each other never emerges. (One good scene: the woman, fed up with repression, telling the boy to pour more red wine into her glass until it overflows and spreads across the restaurant tablecloth.) Annie Girardot is so assured and controlled that you don't really understand what she's doing with this kid — played by Bruno Pradal, who gives the only halfway decent performance in the movie but is used as a stand-in for Gérard Philipe. His parents are monsters who specialize in cold, malignant looks, while the rest of the adult cast is stereotyped for life-denying callousness or world-weary cynicism or impotence. The youth contingent is all open-faced, innocent goodness — just as in American movies of last year and the year before. The students are so life-enhancing they look stuffed; love is coming out their ears.

[March 4, 1972]

Alchemy

If ever there was a great example of how the best popular movies come out of a merger of commerce and art, *The Godfather* is it. The movie starts from a trash novel that is generally considered gripping and compulsively readable, though (maybe because movies more than satisfy my appetite for trash) I found it unreadable. You're told who and what the characters are in a few pungent, punchy sentences, and that's all they are. You're briefed on their backgrounds and sex lives in a flashy anecdote or two, and the author moves on, from nugget to nugget. Mario Puzo has a reputation as a good writer, so his potboiler was treated as if it were special, and not in the Irving Wallace–Harold Robbins class, to which, by its itch and hype and juicy *roman-à-clef* treatment, it plainly belongs. What would this school of fiction do without Porfirio Rubirosa, Judy Garland, James Aubrey, Howard Hughes, and Frank Sinatra? The novel *The Godfather*, financed by Paramount during its writing, features a Sinatra stereotype, and sex and slaughter, and little gobbets of trouble and heartbreak. It's gripping, maybe, in the same sense that Spiro Agnew's speeches were a few years back. Francis Ford Coppola, who directed the film, and wrote the script with Puzo, has stayed very close to the book's greased-lightning sensationalism and yet has made a movie with the spaciousness and strength that popular novels such as Dickens' used to have. With the slop and sex reduced and the whoremongering guess-who material minimized ("Nino," who sings with a highball in his hand, has been weeded out), the movie bears little relationship to other adaptations of books of this kind, such as *The Carpetbaggers* and *The Adventurers*. Puzo provided what Coppola needed: a storyteller's outpouring of incidents and details to choose from, the folklore behind the headlines, heat and immediacy, the richly familiar. And Puzo's shameless turn-on probably left Coppola looser than if he had been dealing with a better book; he could not have been cramped by worries about how best to convey its style. Puzo, who admits he was out to make money, wrote "below my gifts," as he puts it, and one must agree. Coppola uses his gifts to reverse the process — to give the public the best a moviemaker can do with this very raw material. Coppola, a young director who has never had a big hit, may have done the movie for money, as *he* claims — in order to make the pictures he really wants to make, he says — but this picture was made at peak capacity. He has salvaged Puzo's energy and lent the narrative dignity. Given the circumstances and the rush to complete the film and bring it to market, Coppola has not only done his best but pushed himself farther than he may realize. The movie is on the heroic scale of earlier pictures on broad themes, such as *On the Waterfront, From Here to Eternity,* and *The Nun's Story*. It offers a wide, startlingly vivid view of a Mafia dynasty. The abundance is from the book; the quality of feeling is Coppola's.

The beginning is set late in the summer of 1945; the film's roots, however, are in the gangster films of the early thirties. The plot is still about rival gangs murdering each other, but now we see the system of patronage and terror, in which killing is a way of dealing with the competition. We see how the racketeering tribes encroach on each other and why this form of illegal business inevitably erupts in violence. We see the ethnic subculture, based on a split between the men's conception of their responsibilities — all that they keep dark — and the sunny false Eden in which they try to shelter the women and children. The thirties films indicated some of this, but *The Godfather* gets into it at the primary level; the willingness to be basic and the attempt to understand the basic, to look at it without the usual preconceptions, are what give this picture its epic strength.

The visual scheme is based on the most obvious life-and-death contrasts; the men meet and conduct their business in deep-toned, shuttered rooms, lighted by lamps even in the daytime, and the story moves back and forth between this hidden, nocturnal world and the sunshine that they share with the women and children. The tension is in the meetings in the underworld darkness; one gets the sense that this secret life has its own poetry of fear, more real to the men (and perhaps to the excluded women also) than the sunlight world outside. The dark-and-light contrast is so operatic and so openly symbolic that it perfectly expresses the basic nature of the material. The contrast is integral to the Catholic background of the characters: innocence versus knowledge — knowledge in this sense being the same as guilt. It works as a visual style, because the Goyaesque shadings of dark brown into black in the interiors suggest (no matter how irrationally) an earlier period of history, while the sunny, soft-edge garden scenes have their own calendar-pretty pastness. Nino Rota's score uses old popular songs to cue the varying moods, and at one climactic point swells in a crescendo that is both Italian opera and pure-forties movie music. There are rash, foolish acts in the movie but no acts of individual bravery. The killing, connived at in the darkness, is the secret horror, and it surfaces in one bloody outburst after another. It surfaces so often that after a while it doesn't surprise us, and the recognition that the killing is an integral part of business policy takes us a long way from the fantasy outlaws of old movies. These gangsters don't satisfy our adventurous fantasies of disobeying the law; they're not defiant, they're furtive and submissive. They are required to be more obedient than we are; they live by taking orders. There is no one on the screen we can identify with — unless we take a fancy to the pearly teeth of one shark in a pool of sharks.

Even when the plot strands go slack about two-thirds of the way through, and the passage of a few years leaves us in doubt whether certain actions have been concluded or postponed, the picture doesn't become softheaded. The direction is tenaciously intelligent. Coppola holds on and pulls it all together. The trash novel is there underneath, but he attempts to draw the patterns out of the particulars. It's amazing how encompassing the view seems to be — what a sense you get of a broad historical perspective, considering that the span is only from 1945 to the mid-fifties, at which time the Corleone family, already forced by competitive pressures into dealing in narcotics, is moving its base of operations to Las Vegas.

The enormous cast is headed by Marlon Brando as Don Vito Corleone, the "godfather" of a powerful Sicilian-American clan, with James Caan as his hothead son, Sonny, and Al Pacino as the thoughtful, educated son, Michael. Is Brando marvellous? Yes, he is, but then he often is; he was marvellous a few years ago in *Reflections in a Golden Eye,* and he's shockingly effective as a working-class sadist in a current film, *The Nightcomers,* though the film itself isn't worth seeing. The role of Don Vito — a patriarch in his early sixties — allows him to release more of the gentleness that was so seductive and unsettling in his braggart roles. Don Vito could be played as a magnificent old warrior, a noble killer, a handsome bull-patriarch, but Brando manages to debanalize him. It's typical of Brando's daring that he doesn't capitalize on his broken-prow profile and the massive, sculptural head that has become the head of Rodin's Balzac — he doesn't play for statuesque nobility. The light, cracked voice comes out of a twisted mouth and clenched teeth; he has the battered face of a devious, combative old man, and a pugnacious thrust to his jaw. The rasp in his voice is particularly effective after Don Vito has been wounded; one almost feels that the bullets cracked it, and wishes it hadn't been cracked before. Brando interiorizes Don Vito's power, makes him less physically threatening and *deeper*, hidden within himself.

Brando's acting has mellowed in recent years; it is less immediately exciting than it used to be, because there's not the sudden, violent discharge of emotion. His effects are subtler, less showy, and he gives himself over to the material. He appears to have worked his way beyond the self-parody that was turning him into a comic, and that sometimes left the other performers dangling and laid bare the script. He has not acquired the polish of most famous actors; just the opposite — less mannered as he grows older, he seems to draw directly from life, and from himself. His Don is a primitive sacred monster, and the more powerful because he suggests not the strapping sacred monsters of movies (like Anthony Quinn) but actual ones — those old men who carry never-ending grudges and ancient hatreds inside a frail frame, those monsters who remember minute details of old business deals when they can no longer tie their shoelaces. No one has aged better on camera than Brando; he gradually takes Don Vito to the close of his life, when he moves into the sunshine world, a sleepy monster, near to innocence again. The character is all echoes and shadings, and no noise; his strength is in that armor of quiet. Brando has lent Don Vito some of his own mysterious, courtly reserve: the character is not explained; we simply assent to him and believe that, yes, he could become a king of the underworld. Brando doesn't dominate the movie, yet he gives the story the legendary presence needed to raise it above gang warfare to archetypal tribal warfare.

Brando isn't the whole show; James Caan is very fine, and so are Robert Duvall and many others in lesser roles. Don Vito's sons suggest different aspects of Brando — Caan's Sonny looks like the muscular young Brando but without the redeeming intuitiveness, while as the heir, Michael, Al Pacino comes to resemble him in manner and voice. Pacino creates a quiet, ominous space around himself; his performance — which is marvellous, too, big yet without ostentation — complements Brando's. Like Brando in this film, Pacino is simple; you don't catch him acting, yet he manages to change from a small, fresh-faced, darkly handsome college boy into an underworld lord, becoming more intense, smaller, and more isolated at every step. Coppola doesn't stress the father-and-son links; they are simply there for us to notice when we will. Michael becomes like his father mostly from the inside, but we also get to see how his father's face was formed (Michael's mouth gets crooked and his cheeks jowly, like his father's, after his jaw has been smashed). Pacino has an unusual gift for conveying the divided spirit of a man whose calculations often go against his inclinations. When Michael, warned that at a certain point he must come out shooting, delays, we are left to sense his mixed feelings. As his calculations will always win out, we can see that he will never be at peace. The director levels with almost everybody in the movie. The women's complicity in their husbands' activities is kept ambiguous, but it's naggingly there — you can't quite ignore it. And Coppola doesn't make the subsidiary characters lovable; we look at Clemenza (Richard Castellano) as objectively when he is cooking spaghetti as we do when he is garrotting a former associate. Many of the actors (and the incidents) carry the resonances of earlier gangster pictures, so that we almost unconsciously place them in the prehistory of this movie. Castellano, with his resemblance to Al Capone and Edward G. Robinson (plus a vagrant streak of Oscar Levant), belongs in this atmosphere; so does Richard Conte (as Barzini), who appeared in many of the predecessors of this movie, including *House of Strangers,* though perhaps Al Lettieri (as Sollozzo) acts too much like a B-picture hood. And perhaps the director goes off key when Sonny is blasted and blood-splattered at a toll booth; the effect is too garish.

The people dress in character and live in character — with just the gewgaws that seem right for them. The period details are there — a satin pillow, a modernistic apartment-house lobby, a child's pasted-together greeting to Grandpa — but Coppola doesn't turn the viewer into a guided tourist, told what to see. Nor does he go in for a lot of closeups, which are the simplest tool for fixing a director's attitude. Diane Keaton (who plays Michael's girl friend) is seen casually; her attractiveness isn't labored. The only character who is held in frame for us to see exactly as the character looking at her sees her is Apollonia (played by Simonetta Stefanelli), whom Michael falls in love with in Sicily. She is fixed by the camera as a ripe erotic image, because that is what she means to him, and Coppola, not having wasted his resources, can do it in a few frames. In general, he tries not to fix the images. In *Sunday Bloody Sunday,* John Schlesinger showed a messy knocked-over ashtray being picked up in closeup, so that there was nothing to perceive in the shot but the significance of the messiness. Coppola, I think, would have kept the camera on the room in which the woman bent over to retrieve the ashtray, and the messiness would have been just one element among many to be observed — perhaps the curve of her body could have told us much more than the actual picking-up motion. *The Godfather* keeps so much in front of us all the time that we're never bored (though the picture runs just two minutes short of three hours) — we keep taking things in. This is a heritage from Jean Renoir — this uncoercive, "open" approach to the movie frame. Like Renoir, Coppola lets the spectator roam around in the images, lets a movie breathe, and this is extremely difficult in a period film, in which every detail must be carefully planted. But the details never look planted: you're a few minutes into the movie before you're fully conscious that it's set in the past.

When one considers the different rates at which people read, it's miraculous that films can ever solve the problem of a pace at which audiences can "read" a film together. A hack director solves the problem of pacing by making only a few points and making those so emphatically that the audience can hardly help getting them (this is why many of the movies from the studio-system days are unspeakably insulting); the tendency of a clever, careless director is to go too fast, assuming that he's made everything clear when he hasn't, and leaving the audience behind. When a film has as much novelistic detail as this one, the problem might seem to be almost insuperable. Yet, full as it is, *The Godfather* goes by evenly, so we don't feel rushed, or restless, either; there's classic grandeur to the narrative flow. But Coppola's attitudes are specifically modern — more so than in many films with a more jagged surface. Renoir's openness is an expression of an almost pagan love of people and landscape; his style is an embrace. Coppola's openness is a reflection of an exploratory sense of complexity; he doesn't feel the need to comment on what he shows us, and he doesn't want to reduce the meanings in a shot by pushing us this way or that. The assumption behind this film is that complexity will engage the audience.

These gangsters *like* their life style, while we — seeing it from the outside — are appalled. If the movie gangster once did represent, as Robert Warshow suggested in the late forties, "what we want to be and what we are afraid we may become," if he expressed "that part of the American psyche which rejects the qualities and the demands of modern life, which rejects 'Americanism' itself," that was the attitude of another era. In *The Godfather* we see organized crime as an obscene symbolic extension of free enterprise and government policy, an extension of the worst in America — its feudal ruthlessness. Organized crime is not a rejection of Americanism, it's what we fear Americanism to be. It's our nightmare of the American system. When "Americanism" was a form of cheerful, bland official optimism, the gangster used to be destroyed at the end of the movie and our feelings resolved. Now the mood of the whole country has darkened, guiltily; nothing is resolved at the end of *The Godfather*, because the family business goes on. Terry Malloy didn't clean up the docks at the end of *On the Waterfront;* that was a lie. *The Godfather* is popular melodrama, but it expresses a new tragic realism.

[March 18, 1972]

Collaboration and Resistance

Inexplicably, despite everything — the suicidal practices of the film industry, the defeat of many people of talent, the financial squeeze here and abroad — this has been a legendary period in movies. Just since last March: *The Conformist, McCabe & Mrs. Miller, Sunday Bloody Sunday, The Last Picture Show, Fiddler on the Roof, Murmur of the Heart, The Garden of the Finzi-Continis, Cabaret, The Godfather,* and, of course, the films one may have major reservations about — the smash-bang cops-and-robbers. *The French Connection* and the controversial *A Clockwork Orange* and *Straw Dogs.* In addition: Jane Fonda's portrait of a call girl in *Klute,* George Segal's wild, comic hustling junkie in *Born to Win,* George C. Scott's bravura hamminess in *The Hospital,* the documentary-style *Derby,* the childishly primitive, touching, messed-up *Billy Jack,* the casually diverting *Skin Game,* and the comedies *Bananas* and *Made for Each Other.* A reviewer could hardly ask for more from any art, high or popular, and that list shows how far movies have gone in blurring the distinction. And now *The Sorrow and the Pity,* a documentary epic on the themes of collaboration and resistance.

The Hollywood war movies were propaganda for our side, and put us in the comfortable position of identifying with the heroic anti-Nazis. *The Sorrow and the Pity* makes us ask what we and our friends and families would actually have done if our country had been invaded, like France. Wartime France presents one of the most intricately balanced moral dilemmas imaginable, since, of all the countries occupied by the

Nazis, the French were the only people to cave in and support a regime (the Pétain government, with its capital in Vichy) that actively collaborated with Hitler. That fact has been buried from sight in France, and a legend of national heroism has been officially encouraged; the government decided that the public was "not yet mature enough" to see this film on television. "Myths," according to the Gaullist official who made the decision, "are important in the life of a people. Certain myths must not be destroyed."

The Sorrow and the Pity is both oral history and essay: people who lived through the German occupation tell us what they did during that catastrophic period, and we see and hear evidence that corroborates or corrects or sometimes flatly contradicts them. A good portion of the material is no more than informed, intelligent television interviewing; what makes the film innovative is the immediate annotation of what has just been said, and the steady accumulation of perspectives and information. As the perspectives ramify — when we see the people as they are now and, in old snapshots and newsreel footage, as they were then — we begin to get a sense of living in history: a fuller sense of what it was like to participate in the moral drama of an occupied nation than we have ever before had. When history literally becomes the story of people's lives, we can't help but feel the continuity of those lives and our own. There's nothing comparable to *The Sorrow and the Pity*. Yet the director, Marcel Ophuls, didn't need to invent a new kind of mirror to hold up to us; all he needed to do was to hold up the old mirrors at different angles.

The Second World War was heavily recorded on film, and Ophuls draws upon newsreels from several countries and also upon propaganda shorts designed to educate and inspire the citizenry. The bits are fresh — selected, it might almost seem at first, to make marginal points; even those of us who know that period on film haven't seen much of this material. A piece of Nazi newsreel shows captured black troops from the French Army as evidence of France's racial decadence; another bit, on how to recognize a Jew, shows a collection of photos, including a glimpse of an infamous poster of Ernst Lubitsch — which, it is said, broke his heart when he realized he was being used as the model of Jewish bestiality. Pétain, visiting a schoolroom, talking high-mindedly, is the model of rectitude. There are fragments that in context gain a new meaning: the viciousness of shaving the heads of the women who had slept with Germans is horrible enough without the added recognition that probably those who did the shaving had spiritually slept with the Germans themselves. Ophuls sustains a constant ironic interplay between the old film clips and the interviews with those who gave orders, those who took orders, those who suffered and survived, and those who went on as before. The period (1940–44) is so recently past that it's still possible to delve into the psychology of history: *The Sorrow and the Pity* is about the effects of character upon political action.

It's one of the most demanding movies ever made — four hours and twenty minutes of concentrated attention. Narration, titles, voice-over translations that finish quickly so you can hear the actual voices in their own languages — Ophuls employs a variety of devices to get the data to the audience, and he tries to be aboveboard, as in the matter of the voices. (You can decide for yourself whether the dubber misrepresents the person's character.) You really process information, and doing so makes you aware of how falsely the phrase is applied to the unconscious soaking up of TV commercials and banalities. You experience the elation of using your mind — of evaluating the material, and perceiving how it's all developing, while you're storing it up. There's a point of view, but judgments are left to you, and you know that Ophuls is reasonable and fair-minded, and trying to do justice to a great subject: how and why the French accepted Nazism, and then rejected what they had done, so that it was lost even from public memory. The Occupation has long been demythologized in print, and this film does not attempt to replace the printed studies; it does something different. On film it's possible to incorporate the historian's process of research — to show us the witnesses and the participants, so that we are put in the position of the investigators, seeing what they see and trying to frame some conclusions. Inevitably, the picture gets better as it goes along: the more we have to work with, the more complex our own reactions become. There's grace in Ophuls' method; he helps us to see that the issues go way beyond conventional ideas of assessing guilt — that the mysteries of human behavior in the film are true mysteries.

The cast is made up of the known, such as Pierre Mendès-France, Georges Bidault, Anthony Eden, and Albert Speer, and the unknown, who are principally from the small industrial city of Clermont-Ferrand, which the movie focusses on. Clermont-Ferrand is near Vichy and was the home base of Pierre Laval, and it is in the Auvergne, which was one of the centers of the Resistance. Those interviewed are, in their own terms, articulate and clearheaded, and are at their ease; *no one* appears to feel any guilt about past conduct. Whatever they did, they have, from what we can see, made their peace with themselves, though an upper-class Frenchman who fought alongside the Nazis in Russia appears to be almost in mourning for his duped and wasted youth. Some are less reflective and more open than we could have expected: Pétain's Minister of Youth discusses his morale-building among French children; a former Wehrmacht captain who was stationed in Clermont-Ferrand defends his right to wear his war decorations. From England, Anthony Eden, who used to look weak and foolish, suggests that anyone who did not live under the Occupation cannot judge the French. He comments on those days with great dignity and humanity: who would have expected him to age so intelligently? The heroes of the Resistance are the most unlikely people — stubborn, rebellious "misfits": a genial, though formidable, farmer, a bohemian aristocrat who at one time smoked opium, a diffident homosexual who became a British agent in France in order, he says, to prove that he was as brave as other men. They're not like the fake heroes in Hollywood's anti-Nazi movies, and they're impossible for us to project onto: we would be diminishing them if we tried. People who suffered tell stories of iniquities that we can scarcely bear to hear; others remember nothing, selectively. One man saw no Nazis and doesn't believe Clermont-Ferrand was occupied.

Were the French perhaps so passive in the Second World War because they were still depleted by their courage and sacrifices in the First World War? All sorts of speculative questions come to mind, and there are aspects of what happened in France in the early forties that I wish the film had clarified; for example, that the Germans had taken two million French prisoners of war, and that the promise of liberating these prisoners was a factor in encouraging France to fill its industrial quotas. Still . . . the French coöperation was peerless. The picture neglects to point out that the French Communists, serving the interests of Russian foreign policy (it was during the period of the Hitler-Soviet pact), were collaborationists until Hitler invaded Russia. But then the movie doesn't go into the close ties between the Catholic Church and the Vichy government, either. There are probably countless areas in which specialists would ask for more emphasis or greater detail, but that is true of almost any written work of history, and such works do not provide the psychological understanding that this film does.

We see that those who were inactive were not necessarily indifferent to the suffering of others: a sane, prosperous pharmacist sits, surrounded by his handsome children, and, without attempting to deny knowledge of what was going on, tells his reasons for remaining apolitical. They're not bad reasons — and who could call a man a coward for not having the crazy, aberrant nobility it takes to risk his life (and maybe his family)? (It's especially difficult for a woman to pass judgment, since women are traditionally exempted from accusations of cowardice. For most women, the risk of being separated from their children is a sufficient deterrent from any dangerous political acts, and who considers them immoral for that, even though they constitute a huge body of the docile and fearful?) It's only when you think of a country full of decent, reasonable people with such good reasons that you experience revulsion. The inactive, like the pharmacist, and the actual collaborators are easily accessible to the camera — perhaps more so than the resisters, because there is something special about the nature of intransigence, and maybe for that we need a literary or dramatic artist rather than a documentarian. But this film goes very far in bringing those approaches together. There may be a streak of romanticism in the way Ophuls leads us to the theory that only loners and black sheep — and workers and youth — are free enough to resist authority; I wasn't convinced, but I was charmed. I would like to know more of Louis Grave, the Maquis farmer who was betrayed by a neighbor and sent to Buchenwald: what formed this man that makes him so solid and contained, so beautifully rooted? When he tells about an old German's slipping him an apple when he was starving, you know that "documentary" has no boundaries. Louis Grave and his apple might be out of *Grand Illusion*, while Maurice Chevalier singing away becomes a little like the m.c. in *Cabaret*. We enjoy him, yet his entertainer's soul is perplexing; there's an element of the macabre in his good cheer. A German comedian entertaining troops and straining for laughs has that same macabre gaiety — the emblem of show business — but he's coarser (and German), and so less troubling. Chevalier's recurrent presence gives the film a lilt of satirical ambiguity.

It was in France during the Occupation that Simone Weil wrote, "Nothing is so rare as to see misfortune fairly portrayed. The tendency is either to treat the unfortunate person as though catastrophe were his natural vocation or to ignore the effects of misfortune on the soul; to assume, that is, that the soul can suffer and remain unmarked by it — can fail, in fact, to be recast in misfortune's image." She was writing about the *Iliad,* but she was writing about it because the Nazis, like the Greek and Trojan warriors, were modifying the human spirit by the use of force. It is the highest praise I can offer *The Sorrow and the Pity* to say that in it misfortune *is* fairly portrayed. One is left with the question of whether (and how much) the French really have been marked — in the long run — by the Nazi experience.

Screwball comedy flourished in the thirties and died of exhaustion in the forties; Peter Bogdanovich tries but fails to resuscitate it in *What's Up, Doc?* He tries in the most direct, most naïve way — not by transforming the material with a new point of view, and not by distilling it to its frivolous essence, but simply by reproducing the old plot situations and gags and characters. The result isn't effective as nostalgia, because the spirit is missing. It works only fitfully and at a rather low level — with the old gags themselves, which are sometimes funny, even when they're dragged in and sloppily executed (the way they are when they're reworked on TV). Bogdanovich's affection for old-movie comedy seems genuine, and the movie's imitativeness is too childlike to be offensive (though those whose work has been so blatantly imitated may feel differently). But the picture is ridiculous and noisy and finally depressing, because his handling of the old routines lacks the immaculate timing that made them truly comic. (Even the camerawork is insecure, and the action poorly framed.) Its chief source, *Bringing Up Baby*, with Cary Grant and Katharine Hepburn, was a lovely piece of lunacy — an extended absent-minded-professor joke, its underlying assumption being that if you repress your instincts you can get so disjointed you can forget your own name. The hero, a square pedant engaged to a bossy girl pedant, was a paleontologist, putting together the bones of a dinosaur. Katharine Hepburn was a live-animal lover, an uninhibited girl with a fluffy wild mane, and her dog ran off with one of his treasured bones. She undermined the orderly absent-mindedness of his life, and everything in the movie flowed from that. *What's Up, Doc?* takes the plot and the externals of the characters but loses that logic. It goes off every which way, restaging gags from Buster Keaton and Laurel and Hardy and W. C. Fields, plus a lot of cornball devices; for example, the Hepburn character, who should be all instinct, is now endowed with a photographic memory for the courses she took in various colleges. That joke never was very good.

Ryan O'Neal and Barbra Streisand are asked to play Cary Grant and Katharine Hepburn; they're given no other characters. O'Neal is the film's chief embarrassment as he diligently goes through the Grant motions; he can't do Grant's bewilderment, and he kills his own appeal when he tries. It took Cary Grant a long time to become Cary Grant. O'Neal's blank stares and double takes are totally on the outside — just mugging. (Dean Martin used to be able to do something close to Grant's sexy-*farceur* style; he held his head the same stiff-necked way, but his spirit was different — well oiled and always a little lewd.) Streisand comes off much better than Ryan O'Neal, because she doesn't try to be Hepburn, she does her own shtick — the rapid, tricky New Yorkese line readings. She is tanned and elegant, and she works at making brashness adorable, but she doesn't do anything she hasn't already done. She's playing herself — and it's awfully soon for that. Bogdanovich has made her glamorous in an almost ordinary glamour-queen way. She can't be made completely ordinary, because she has that archaic look and her skeptic's predatory instinct.

Streisand sings a sizzling version of "You're the Top" behind the titles, and there's a moment in the movie when the audience cheers as she starts to sing "As Times Goes By," but it's just a teaser, and it has to last for the whole movie. Why? Nothing that happens in the movie — none of the chases or comic confusions — has the excitement of her singing. When a tiger pretends to be a pussycat, that's practically a form of Uncle Tomism. Yes, she's more easily acceptable in *What's Up, Doc?* than in her bigger roles, because she doesn't tap her full talent and there is an element of possible unpleasantness, of threat, in that red-hot talent — as there is in Liza Minnelli at full star strength — which produces unresolved feelings in us. It's easy to see that those people who haven't liked Streisand before could like her this time, because here her charm has no drive. She doesn't have the cloudy look in her eyes that's part of her strangeness. But movies don't need another baby-blue-eyed plastic siren, movies need the actress who sings — the one who could bring vibrancy even to the clanking, big *Hello, Dolly!* When she and Louis Armstrong greeted each other, they were drunk on love. There's no love at that level in *What's Up, Doc?* She brings it some sex, but there's no romance in the movie (it's too stupid). And that's what *Bringing Up Baby* was — a *romance*.

What's Up, Doc? is saved intermittently by the character bits; I laughed out loud once when Sorrell Booke tripped Mabel Albertson, and again when they wrestled in a hotel corridor. Madeline Kahn is funny, although, finally, on too single a track, as the bossy fiancée, and Liam Dunn has a moment or two as a judge — another facsimile. But it's too early in the history of movies for this feeding off the past, and, as it is, there's almost nothing left; TV has picked those bones clean. It's the tragedy of TV that instead of drawing upon new experience and fresh sources of comedy it cannibalizes old pop culture. When movies do the same now, they aren't even imitating movies, they're imitating TV. The result is too infantile to be called decadent; it's pop culture for those with bad memories for pop culture, or so young they have no memories.

And there's an essential ugliness to the picture's final zinger, in which Streisand and O'Neal mock *Love Story*. It's one thing for outsiders like me to call *Love Story* a boobish movie, but when O'Neal, who starred in it (and who gave it all the conviction it had), turns around and dumps on it, and, implicitly, on the people who loved him in it, all he does is expose his own cheap, cute cynicism. Why is it so difficult for actors to say no?

[March 25, 1972]

Index

Abbott & Costello, 180
Abel, Jeanne and Alan, 324, 326; dirs., *Is There Sex After Death?*, 324–326
Act of the Heart, The, 205–206
Adalen 31, 41–42, 104
Adam, Ken, 389
Addy, Wesley, 147
Adrian, Max, 380, 382
Adventurers, The, 132–136, 148, 420
Age d'Or, L', 336
Agee, James, 133
Agnew, Spiro, 100, 420
Ah, Wilderness!, 76
Airport, 132, 136–137, 147, 173, 220, 233, 294
Akins, Zoë, 341
Albertson, Mabel, 432
Aldington, Richard, 139
Aldrich, Robert, dir., *The Legend of Lylah Clare*, 148; *The Dirty Dozen*, 315
Aleichem, Sholom, 330
Alex in Wonderland, 224–228
Alexander the Great, 49, 221
Alfred the Great, 67–68
Ali, Muhammad, 160
Alice Adams, 311
Alice's Restaurant, 5, 6, 197, 212, 215
All Quiet on the Western Front, 16, 17, 134
All the Emperor's Horses, 151
All the King's Men, 63
All the Loving Couples, 57–58
Allen, Fred, 180
Allen, Jay, 412
Allen, Seth, 56
Allen, Steve, 62
Allen, Woody, 13, 60, 62, 325, 350, 369, 370; dir., *Take the Money and Run*, 13, 60; *Bananas*, 314, 369, 370, 426
Almendros, Nestor, 266
Almond, Paul, 206; dir., *The Act of the Heart*, 205–206
Altamont, 206–208, 210, 211, 315
Altman, Robert, 94, 148, 227, 228, 277–278, 280, 282, 350; dir.: *M*A*S*H*, 92–95, 147, 185, 227, 277, 278; *Brewster McCloud*, 227–228; *McCabe and Mrs. Miller*, 277–280, 426
Ameche, Don, 82
America America, 50–52, 328, 331
America the Beautiful, 151
American Film Institute, 165
American in Paris, An, 84
American International Pictures, 18, 315, 342
Ames, Leon, 147
Amiche, Le, 113
Anatomy of Love, The, 362
Anderson, Lindsay, dir., *If . . .*, 117
Anderson, Maxwell, 95, 97
Anderson, Robert, 169, 170
Anderson Tapes, The, 285, 314
Andersson, Bibi, 28, 105, 348
Andreas-Salomé, Lou, 250–251
Andress, Ursula, 193
Andrews, Harry, 368
Andrews, Julie, 379
Andromeda Strain, The, 275–276
Angst, Richard, 19
Anhalt, Edward, 25
Anka, Paul, 109
Ann-Margret, 173, 174, 283, 284
Anne of the Thousand Days, 95–97
Annis, Francesca, 400
Anthony Adverse, 117
Antonioni, Michelangelo, 113–117, 121, 211, 308; dir., *L'Avventura*, 51, 85, 113, 121, 308, 309; *Zabriskie Point*, 113–117, 131, 211; *Blow-Up*, 113, 114, 117, 197, 231; *Le Amiche*, 113; *La Notte*, 113; *Red Desert*, 116, 252
Antrobus, John, 17
April Fools, The, 182
Arkin, Alan, 253, 254, 256, 330; dir., *Little Murders*, 253–257, 314, 330
Arlen, Richard, 200
Arlorio, Georgio, 176
Armstrong, Louis, 81–83, 85, 149, 432
Arosenius, Per-Axel, 80
Around the World in 80 Days, 15

Arrangement, The, 48–53, 252
Arzner, Dorothy, 341, 345; dir., *Christopher Strong*, 341, 342, 346
"As Time Goes By," 432
Ashcroft, Peggy, 290
Astaire, Fred, 28, 29, 84, 85, 272, 381, 409
Astor, Mary, 157
Astruc, Alexandre, 403
Attenborough, Richard, 16; dir., *Oh! What a Lovely War*, 14–17
Aubrey, James, 188, 420
Audran, Stéphane, 54, 404, 415
Avakian, Aram, 111, 112; dir., *End of the Road*, 111–112, 148
Avco Embassy Pictures, 151
Averback, Hy, 9; dir., *I Love You, Alice B. Toklas*, 9
Avildsen, John G., 384; dir., *Joe*, 148, 152–153, 313; *Cry Uncle*, 314, 325, 384; *Guess What We Learned in School Today?*, 325
Avventura, L', 51, 85, 113, 121, 308, 309
Aznavour, Charles, 106

Baby Maker, The, 157–158
Babylon Revisited, 308
Bacall, Lauren, 12, 247, 310, 413
Bacharach, Burt, 7
Badel, Alan, 135
Bainter, Fay, 310
Baker, Stanley, 193
Baker, Tom, 367
Balcony, The, 124
Balin, Marty, 211
Ballad of Cable Hogue, The, 279
Balsam, Martin, 213
Balzac, Honoré de, 422
Bananas, 314, 369, 370, 426
Band of Outsiders, 279, 402
Bankhead, Tallulah, 290, 347
Bardot, Brigitte, 308, 309
Barrie, James M., 40
Barry, John, 162, 250
Barry, Philip, 261
Barrymore, John, 25, 367
Barrymore, Lionel, 367
Barth, John, 111, 112
Bartleby, 417–418
"Bartleby, the Scrivener," 417
Bassani, Georgio, 363–366
Bates, Alan, 139, 142
Battle of Algiers, The, 176
Battle of Britain, 56
Bauer, David, 126
Baur, Harry, 367
Bazin, André, 360–362, 365–366
Bean, Robert B., 372; dir., *Made for Each Other*, 369–373, 426
Beast Must Die, The, 172

Beatles, 208, 340, 345
Beaton, Cecil, 185
Beatty, Warren, 115, 122, 123, 277–279, 353
Beau Serge, Le, 54
Beautiful and Damned, The, 32
Beck, Martha, 105–107
Beckett, Samuel, 156, 352, 356
Beckmann, Max, 410
Bed and Board, 243–245
Bed Sitting Room, The, 17, 148
Bedazzled, 10
Bedelia, Bonnie, 70
Bedknobs and Broomsticks, 359–360
Been Down So Long It Looks Like Up to Me, 350
Beethoven, Ludwig van, 198, 377
"Before the Parade Passes By," 80
Before the Revolution, 270, 272
Before Winter Comes, 329
Behold a Pale Horse, 176
Bell'Antonio, Il, 195
Belli, Melvin, 208, 209
Belmondo, Jean-Paul, 31, 270, 309
Benjamin, Richard, 347–349, 353
Benny, Jack, 61
Benton, Robert, 229, 230
Berenson, Marisa, 412
Bergen, Candice, 283–285, 312, 313
Berger, Helmut, 87, 364
Berger, Thomas, 212, 213, 236
Berggren, Thommy, 135
Bergman, Ingmar, 162, 252, 348; dir., *Shame*, 17, 298; *The Seventh Seal*, 17, 18; *The Silence*, 59; *Wild Strawberries*, 252; *Summer Interlude*, 252; *Dreams*, 252; *The Touch*, 348
Berkeley, Busby, 82, 380, 382–383
Bernhardt, Sarah, 383
Bertolucci, Bernardo, 220, 270–275; dir., *La Commare Secca*, 270; *Before the Revolution*, 270, 272; *The Conformist*, 270–275, 415, 426; *Partner*, 272–273; *The Spider's Stratagem*, 273
"Best Things in Life Are Free, The," 70
Beverly Hillbillies, The, 58, 234
Bey, Turhan, 25
Beyond the Valley of the Dolls, 147
Bibb, Porter, 208
Biches, Les, 53
Bicycle Thief, The, 361
Bidault, Georges, 428
Big Sleep, The, 413–415
Billy Budd, 170
Billy Jack, 341–347, 426
Birds in Peru, 247
Bisset, Jacqueline, 137
Björnstrand, Gunnar, 18
Black Glossary, A, 217

Black Narcissus, 139
Blackboard Jungle, 152
Blake, Nicholas, 172
Blake, Robert 77
Blondell, Joan, 345
Blood and Sand, 45
Blood of a Poet, The, 336
Blow-Up, 113 114, 117, 197, 231
Blue, Ben, 331
Blue Angel, The 410
Bob & Carol & Ted & Alice, 8–14, 225
Bock Jerry, 333
Bofors Gun, The, 89
Bogarde, Dirk, 86, 87
Bogart, Humphrey, 71, 271, 413, 414
Bogart, Paul, 299; dir., *Skin Game*, 299–300, 426
Bogdanovich, Peter, 293–296, 299, 431, 432; dir., *The Last Picture Show*, 293–297, 299, 353, 426; *What's Up Doc?*, 431–433
Boleyn, Anne, 95–97
Bolkan, Florinda, 221
Bologna, Joseph, 369–372
Bolt, Robert, 189–192
Bombay Talkie 195–196
Bond, Edward, 369
Bond, Gary, 415
Bond, Julian, 312
Bonerz, Peter, 350
Bonnes Femmes, Les, 54
Bonnie and Clyde, 6, 152, 170, 173, 212
Booke, Sorrell, 432
Boom!, 407
Boone, Richard, 49, 52, 105
Borges, Jorge Luis, 220, 273, 417
Borgnine, Ernest, 74
Born, Max, 129
Born Losers, 342
Born to Win, 314, 351–352, 402, 426
Bosch, Hieronymus, 261, 263
Bottoms, Timothy, 295, 296, 353
Boucher, Le, 403–405
Bouquet, Michel, 54
Bowery Savings Bank, 320
Boy Friend, The, 379–383
Boy Named Charlie Brown, A, 91–92
Boyer, Charles, 26
Boyle, Peter, 313
Boys from Syracuse, The, 409
Boys in the Band, The, 137–138
"Bozo Barrett," 219
Bozzufi, Marcel, 65
Bradley, Omar, 99
Bradley, Paul, 171
Bragg, Melvyn, 239, 242
Brahms, Johannes, 172, 308
Brand, Neville, 147

Brando, Marlon, 175, 177–179, 249, 322, 422–423
Brautigan, Richard, 230
Brazzi, Rossano, 190
Bread, Love, and Dreams, 362
Brecht, Bertolt, 159, 161, 410
Breen, Bobby, 358
Brennan, Eileen, 296
Bresson, Robert, 8, 307, 308; dir., *A Man Escaped*, 307
Brewster McCloud, 227–228
Brialy, Jean-Claude, 264, 266
Brice, Fanny, 84
Bricusse, Leslie, 39, 84, 196
Bride Wore Black, The, 243
Bridges, Beau, 74
Bridges, James, 157, 158; dir., *The Baby Maker*, 157–158
Bridges, Jeff, 295
Brief Encounter, 291
Bringing Up Baby, 431, 432
Bron, Eleanor, 10, 141
Bronson, Emerick, 252
Brontë sisters, 139
Brook, Peter, 354–357; dir., *Marat/Sade*, 242, 355; *King Lear*, 354–357
Brooks, Mel, 180, 226; dir., *The Twelve Chairs*, 180, 226; *The Producers*, 348
Brooks, Richard, dir., *The Happy Ending*, 148; *Blackboard Jungle*, 152; *The Professionals*, 229
Brooks Wilson Ltd., 121
"Brother, Can You Spare a Dime?", 222
Brother Sun and Sister Moon (projected), 182–183
Brown, Helen Gurley, 283
Brown, John Moulder, 162, 163
Browne, Roscoe Lee, 80, 392
Browning Version, The, 38
Bruce, Lenny, 256, 382
Bruegel, Peter, 248
Brute Force, 63
Bryant, Michael, 369
Brynner, Yul, 26
Buckley, Jr., William F., 297
Bujold, Genevieve, 95–97, 206, 301–302
Bullitt, 162, 316, 402
Buñuel, Luis, 102–103, 128, 258, 263, 307, 336, 337, 363, 376; dir., *The Milky Way*, 102–103; *L'Age d'Or*, 336; *Los Olvidados*, 376
Burgess, Anthony, 373–376
Burke, Billie, 341
Burn!, 175–180
Burnett, Carol, 251
Burroughs, William, 173
Burstyn, Ellen, 225, 227, 296
Burton, Richard, 37, 91, 95

Burton, Wendell, 33–34
Bus Stop, 29, 371
Butch Cassidy and the Sundance Kid, 5–7, 149, 173, 401, 402
Buttons, Red, 69
Byington, Spring, 284

Caan, James, 312, 422, 423
Cabaret, 409–413, 426, 430
Cacoyannis, Michael, 246, 300–305; dir., *Zorba the Greek*, 35, 246; *Stella*, 246; *The Trojan Women*, 300–305
Cactus Flower, 104, 233
Caged, 106
Cagney, James, 374
Caine, Michael, 248–249, 405, 406, 408
Calcutta, 309
Callahan, James, 126
Camelot, 26, 27, 328
Camus, Albert, 68, 417
Canadian Film Development Corporation, 171
Canalejas, Lina, 264
Candy, 147
Cannes Film Festival, 305
Cannon, Dyan, 11–13, 260, 383, 384
Capek, Karel, 312
Capolicchio, Lino, 363
Capone, Al, 424
Capra, Frank, 5, 347, 370
Captive Mind, The, 203
Carmen, 158
Carnal Knowledge, 282–285, 348
Caron, Leslie, 323
Carpetbaggers, The, 135, 420
Carradine, John, 349
Carroll, Lewis, 118
Casablanca, 65
"Casey at the Bat," 23
Cash, Johnny, 173
Cason, Barbara, 107
Cassavetes, John, 222–224; dir., *Faces*, 36, 222; *Husbands*, 222–224, *Shadows*, 223
Castellano, Richard, 371, 424
Castillo, 369
Castle, The, 220
Cat Ballou, 28
Catch-22, 146, 215, 256, 282, 283
Cates, Gilbert, 169, 170; dir., *I Never Sang for My Father*, 169–171
Cavalcade, 16
Cavett, Dick, 222
Cayatte, André, 419; dir., *To Die of Love*, 418–419
C. C. and Company, 171, 173–174
Céline, Louis-Ferdinand, 17
Central Park, 112, 185, 186, 254
Cervantes, Miguel de, 127

Chabrol, Claude, 53–54, 172, 234, 243, 307, 403–405; dir., *La Femme Infidèle*, 53–54, 172, 403; *Les Biches*, 53; *Le Beau Serge*, 54; *Les Cousins*, 54; *Les Bonnes Femmes*, 54; *This Man Must Die*, 172; *Le Boucher*, 403–405
Challis, Christopher, 187
Chamberlain, Richard, 26, 239, 242
Chandler, Raymond, 413, 414
Chaplin, Charles, 61, 93, 194, 360, 362; dir., *Shoulder Arms*, 93; *Pay Day*, 194
Chapman Report, The, 281, 408
Charge of the Light Brigade, The, 15, 17, 99, 213, 215
Charles I, 181
Charles, Ray, 85
Charly, 59
Charterhouse of Parma, The, 270
Chatterton, Ruth, 345
Chayefsky, Paddy, 27, 378, 379
Chekhov, Anton, 163
Chelsea Girls, The, 154
Chevalier, Maurice, 430
Children Are Watching Us, The, 361
Chinoise, La, 167, 272, 306
Chopin, Frédéric, 240
Chris, Marilyn, 107
Christie, Julie, 277–279
Christmas Carol, A, 196
"Christmas Trees, The," 219
Christopher Strong, 341, 342, 346
Churikova, Inna, 311
Citizen Kane, 252
Clair, René, 244
Claire's Knee, 264–267, 275, 280
Clark, Mark, 44, 45
Clark, Petula, 38, 40
Clark, Susan, 77, 300
Clarke, Shirley, 31
Clavell, James, 248, 249; dir., *The Last Valley*, 248–250; *To Sir, with Love*, 343
Clayton, Jack, dir., *Room at the Top*, 142; *The Pumpkin Eater*, 292
Clemenceau Case, The, 363
Clémenti, Pierre, 272
Cleopatra, 27
Clive, Colin, 341
Clockwork Orange, A, 373–378, 426
Cochran, Steve, 296
Cocker, Joe, 198
Cockeyed World, The, 93
Coco, James, 269, 384
Cocteau, Jean, 278, 279, 336, 364, 365; dir., *The Blood of a Poet*, 336
Cohen, Leonard, 280
Cohn, Roy, 316
Colbert, Claudette, 346
Colicos, John, 97, 260

Colonel Blimp, 16
Columbia Pictures, 176
Comden, Betty, 82
Comic, The, 60–62
Coming Apart, 36, 59, 148
Commare Secca, La, 270
Committee, The, 344
Concerto in B Flat Minor (Tchaikovsky), 241
Confession, The, 200–205
Conformist, The, 270–275, 415, 426
Connery, Sean, 104, 119, 285, 329, 388, 389
Conrad, Joseph, 138, 415–416
"Consider Yourself," 359
Constant Nymph, The, 34
Conte, Richard, 424
Cook, Kenneth, 417
Cool Hand Luke, 181
Coolidge, Calvin, 46
Cooper, Gary, 77, 347, 387
Coppolla, Francis Ford, 420, 421, 423–425; dir., *The Rain People*, 59; *The Godfather*, 420–426
Corey, Jeff, 213, 214
Cornered, 63
Cornfield, Hubert, dir., *The Night of the Following Day*, 59
Cornu, Aurora, 264
Cort, Bud, 228
Cortese, Valentina, 162
Costa-Gavras, 63–67, 200, 202–205; dir., *Z*, 63–67, 152, 154, 200, 202, 204, 316, 317, 319; *The Sleeping Car Murder*, 64; *The Confession*, 200–205
Cottage Productions, 58
Cotten, Joseph, 415
Cotton Comes to Harlem, 314
Counterfeit Traitor, The, 136
Country Girl, The, 136
"Couple of Swells, A," 82
Cousins, Les, 54
Cousteau, Jacques, 307; co-dir., *The Silent World*, 307
Coutard, Raoul, 63, 202
Coward, Noël, 16
Cowboys, The, 390–393, 398
Crane, Norma, 332
Crawford, Joan, 137, 406
Crawford, Michael, 83
Crenna, Richard, 86, 260
Crichton, Michael, 276
Crime and Punishment, 161
Cromwell, 181
Cromwell, Oliver, 181
Cronyn, Hume, 74, 229
Cross of Lorraine, The, 63
Crosse, Rupert, 75, 76
Crossfire, 63

Crowley, Mort, 137
Cry Uncle, 314, 325, 384
Cukor, George, dir., *The Women*, 137; *Pat and Mike*, 184; *The Chapman Report*, 281, 408; *My Fair Lady*, 328
Culp, Robert, 11–13
Cummings, Robert, 13
Cunningham, Sarah, 391
Curtis, Tony, 25, 67, 252
Curtiz, Michael, dir., *Casablanca*, 65
Custer, General George A., 212–216

Dall, John, 401
Dallesandro, Joe, 155, 157
D'Amico, Suso, 183
Damned, The, 86–88, 271, 272, 274
Dana, Leora, 147, 391
Dance of Death, The, 109
Daniels, Danny, 83
Daniels, William, 10
D'Antoni, Philip, 316
Dark Victory, 217
Darkness at Noon, 201
Darling, 278
Dassin, Jules, 65, 182, 246–248; dir., *Brute Force*, 63; *Promise at Dawn*, 245–248; *Rififi*, 248; *Never on Sunday*, 248
Dauphin, Claude, 26
Davenport, Nigel, 249
Davis, Bette, 71, 157, 281
Davis, Miles, 308
Davis, Ossie 299; dir., *Cotton Comes to Harlem*, 314
Day, Doris, 9, 12, 13, 227, 296
Day of the Locusts, The, 68
Dayan, Assaf, 18, 247
Dean, James, 190, 298
Dean, Jimmy, 389
De Antonio, Emile, 42–45; dir., *In the Year of the Pig*, 42–45
de Beauvoir, Simone, 36
Début, The, 311
Decae, Henri, 123
Decline and Fall of the Roman Empire, The, 189
Degermark, Pia, 118
de Laclos, Choderlos, 265
Delius, Frederick, 239
Delon, Alain, 115
"Delta Lady," 198
DeLuise, Dom, 180
De Mille, Cecil B., 127, 128, 130, 196, 274; dir., *The Sign of the Cross*, 131
De Monaghan, Laurence, 265
Deneuve, Catherine, 244
Denner, Charles, 65
Dennis, Sandy, 59
De Palma, Brian, 350; dir., *Greetings*, 314

Derby, 426
Dermithe, Édouard, 364
Dern, Bruce, 323, 391, 392
de Sade, 18–19
De Sica, Vittorio, 360–366; dir., *The Children Are Watching Us*, 361; *Shoeshine*, 361, 362; *The Bicycle Thief*, 361; *Miracle in Milan*, 361, 362; *Umberto D.*, 361; *The Roof*, 361; *The Gold of Naples*, 362; *Marriage — Italian Style*, 362; *Yesterday, Today, and Tomorrow*, 362; *The Garden of the Finzi-Continis*, 363–366, 426
Desire, 193
Desperate Characters, 348
Devil in the Flesh, 419
Devils, The, 315
Devlin, Don, 121
Dewhurst, Colleen, 390
de Wilde, Brandon, 25, 163
DeWitt, Jack, 358
Diamond, I. A. L., 187
Diamonds Are Forever, 388–389
Diary of a Mad Housewife, 314, 348, 383, 384
Dickens, Charles, 196, 420
Didion, Joan, 250–252
Diem, Ngo Dinh, 44
Dien Bien Phu, 43, 306
Dietrich, Marlene, 74, 86, 87, 193, 207, 347
Dirty Dozen, The, 315
Dirty Harry, 385–388, 392, 398
Disney, Walt, 76, 315, 345, 359
Distel, Sacha, 415
Dmytryk, Edward, 65, 135; dir., *Crossfire*, 63; *The Carpetbaggers*, 135; *The Young Lions*, 249
Doc, 349
Doctor Doolittle, 26, 120, 328
Dr. Strangelove, 99, 375
Doctor Zhivago, 188–192, 279
Doctors' Wives, 259–260, 262
Dohrn, Bernardine, 166
Dolce Vita, La, 127–131, 308
$, 369
Don Quixote, 127
Donat, Robert, 38
Donati, Danilo, 129
Donen, Stanley, dir., *Bedazzled*, 10; *Two for the Road*, 10; *Seven Brides for Seven Brothers*, 29; co-dir., *Singin' in the Rain*, 209, 322
Donner, Clive, 67–68; dir., *Alfred the Great*, 67–68
Dostoyevsky, Fyodor 142, 272, 417
Double, The, 272
Douglas, Kirk, 48–50, 52, 173, 229, 353
Douglas, Melvyn, 170, 347
Douglas, Michael, 42

Dovzhenko, Alexander, 274
Downey, Robert, dir., *Putney Swope*, 154
Downhill Racer, 45–47, 173
Downs, Johnny, 262
Dreams, 252
Dreyer, Carl, 419; dir., *The Passion of Joan of Arc*, 419
Drive, He Said, 294, 323, 350
Dubček, Alexander, 201
Duchaussoy, Michael, 172
Duck Soup, 16
Duet for Cannibals, 35–36
Duffy, 148
Dullea, Keir, 18–19, 119
Dulles, John Foster, 43, 44
Dunaway, Faye, 49, 50, 52, 213, 214, 250–253
Dunn, Liam, 432
Dunne, Irene, 312
Duvall, Robert, 423
Dux, Pierre, 65

Earhart, Amelia, 341
Earrings of Madame de ..., The, 279, 362
East Lynne, 138
East of Eden, 252
Easter Parade, 82
Eastman, Carol (pseudonyms, Adrien Joyce, Adrian Joyce), 251–252
Eastwood, Clint, 27–29, 350, 385–387
Easy Rider, 3, 4, 78, 84, 117, 147, 152, 173, 297, 298
Ebb, Fred, 411
Ecstasy, 189
Eddy, Nelson, 28
Eden, Anthony, 428, 429
Edge, The, 164, 165
Edge of Darkness, 63
Edwards, Antoinette, 107–110
Edwards, Billy, 107–110
Efron, Marshall, 325
Eggar, Samantha 104
8½, 129, 130, 225, 227
Eisenhower, Dwight D. 44, 100
Eisenhower, Mamie, 107
Eisenstein, Serge, 175, 258
"Elegance," 82
Elgar, Edward, 377
Elizabeth I, 96, 97
Ellis, Antonia, 382
Ellsberg, Daniel, 318
Elvira Madigan, 7, 41, 154, 365
Enchanted Cottage, The, 34
End of the Road, 111–112, 148
Endgame, 356
Endless Summer, The, 154
Enfants Terribles, Les (The Strange Ones), 364–365

Ensor, James, 410
Enter Laughing, 10, 61
Esalen, 13
Escape Me Never, 34
Escobedo case, 386, 388
Euripides, 300–301, 303, 304
Euro International Productions, 183
Evans, Edith, 25, 323
Evans, Robert, 183, 216

"Fabulas Panicas," 334
Faces, 36, 222
Fairbanks, Jr., Douglas, 364
Falk, Peter, 222, 224
Fanon, Frantz, 175, 258
Fantasia, 131
Fantastic Voyage, 216
Far from the Madding Crowd, 141
Farewell to Arms, A, 217
Farnham, Johnny, 59
Farrell, Sharon, 76
Farrow, Mia, 72–73
Father of the Bride, 296
Faulkner, William, 75, 76, 237, 318
Faye, Alice, 82
Fazenda, Louise, 200
F.B.I., 203
Fehmiu, Bekim, 136
Feiffer, Jules, 253–257, 282, 283
Fellini, Federico, 13, 127–132, 189, 225, 247, 274; dir., *Fellini Satyricon*, 127–132; *La Dolce Vita*, 127–131, 308; *8½*, 129, 130, 225, 227; *Juliet of the Spirits*, 129, 130
Fellini, Satyricon, 127–132
Femme Infidèle, La, 53–54, 172, 403
Fernandez, Raymond, 106, 107
Ferreux, Benoit, 306, 310
Ferzetti, Gabriel, 85–86, 204
Feu Follet, Le (The Fire Within), 308, 309
Feuer, Cy, 413
Feuillère, Edwige, 419
Fiddler on the Roof, 327–333, 426
Fields, Robert, 262
Fields, W. C., 28, 85, 183, 269, 329, 431
Film Society of Lincoln Center, 146
Finch, Jon 399, 401
Finch, Peter, 289–290
Fine Madness, A, 105, 119
Fink, Harry and R. M., 386
Finlay, Frank, 104
Finney, Albert, 196, 197
First Love, 162–163
Fisher, Eddie, 27
Fisher, Gerry, 357
Fitzgerald, F. Scott, 308, 310
Five Easy Pieces, 152, 153, 231, 251, 252
Fixer, The, 199, 200
Flanders, Michael, 324

Flaubert, Gustave, 191
Fleischer, Richard, 147; dir., *Doctor Dolittle*, 26, 120, 328; *Tora! Tora! Tora!*, 147–148; *Fantastic Voyage*, 216; *The Last Run*, 294, 353
Fleming, Victor, dir., *Gone with the Wind*, 28, 74
Flesh, 153, 157
Flicker, Ted., dir., *The President's Analyst*, 10
Flying Down to Rio, 382
Flynn, Errol, 177
Fonda, Henry, 229, 349
Fonda, Jane, 71, 280–282, 352, 426
Fonda, Peter, 78, 115, 349; dir., *The Hired Hand*, 323, 353
Forbes, Bryan, 25, 321, 323–324; dir., *The Madwoman of Chaillot*, 25–26; *Long Ago, Tomorrow*, 321–324; *The L-Shaped Room*, 323; *The Whisperers*, 323
Ford, John, 296; dir., *Tobacco Road*, 155; *Wagonmaster*, 296; *The Grapes of Wrath*, 349
Forman, Milos, 351; dir., *Taking Off*, 351
Forsythe, John 80, 190
Forth, Jane, 156
42nd Street, 380
Fosse, Bob, 410, 411; dir., *Sweet Charity*, 26, 409; *Cabaret*, 409–413, 426, 430
Fountainhead, The, 48, 386
400 Blows, The, 244, 245, 307
Fox, Paula, 348
Fox, The, 59
Fraker, William A., 162; dir., *Monte Walsh*, 162
Frank, Jr., Harriet, 76, 390
Frankenheimer, John, 199–200; dir., *The Gypsy Moths*, 52, 200; *I Walk the Line*, 199–200; *The Manchurian Candidate*, 199, 261; *Seven Days in May*, 199; *The Fixer*, 199, 200
Franklin, Aretha, 85
Frankovich, Mike, 260
Frechette, Mark, 115
Freed, Bert, 345
French Connection, The, 315–319, 385, 387, 426
Freud, Sigmund: Freudianism, 77, 108, 149, 220, 245, 247, 254, 337, 370, 371
Frey, Leonard, 331
Friedkin, William, 137, 138, 315, 317; dir., *The Night They Raided Minsky's*, 83; *The Boys in the Band*, 137–138; *The French Connection* 315–319, 385, 387, 426
Friedman, Anthony, 318; dir., *Bartleby*, 417–418
From Here to Eternity, 421

Frost, David, 200
Fuller, Samuel, 78, 297
Funny Girl, 328
Funnyman, 350
Furie, Sidney J., 173; dir., *Little Fauss and Big Halsy*, 171, 173–174
Futz, 54–57, 59, 112, 148, 241

Gabel, Martin, 229
Gabin, Jean, 329
Gable, Christopher, 242, 381
Gable, Clark, 110, 329, 353
Gaily, Gaily, 73–74
Gallant, Mavis, 418, 419
Gandhi, Mahatma, 67, 226
Gang That Couldn't Shoot Straight The, 369
Garbo, Greta 302, 313, 353, 364, 365
Garden of Delights, The, 263–264
Garden of Earthly Delights, The, 261
Gardens of the Finzi-Continis, The, 363–366, 426
Gardenia, Vincent, 255
Gardner, Ava, 28
Garfield, Allen, 325, 384
Garfunkel, Arthur, 283, 284, 348
Garland, Judy, 407, 420
Garner, James, 299–300
Garson, Greer, 38, 419
Gary, Romain, 245–247; dir., *Birds in Peru*, 247
Gatti, Marcello, 176
Gavin, John, 26
Gazzara, Ben, 222
Gelin, Daniel, 306
Genêt (Janet Flanner), 308
Genet, Jean, 124
George, Chief Dan, 213, 215
George, Susan, 394, 395
Geret, Georges, 65
Gershwin, George, 333
Gershwin, Ira, 333
Getino, Octavio, 257, 258
Getting Straight, 149–151, 236
Gibbon, Edward, 128
Gibran, Kahlil, 163
Gielgud, John, 15, 37
Gilbert, John, 196
Gilbert, Lewis, 133, 135; dir., *The Adventurers*, 132–136, 148, 420
Gilbert and Sullivan, 16
Gill, Brendan, 308
Gilliatt, Penelope, 292, 293
Gillmor, Noelle, 195
Gilroy, Frank D., 122, 348; dir., *Desperate Characters*, 348
Gimme Shelter, 206–211
Ginnes, Abram S., 74

Ginsberg, Milton Moses, 36; dir., *Coming Apart*, 36, 59, 148
Girardot, Annie, 419
Giraudoux Jean, 25
Glaser, Michael, 332
Go-Between, The 292, 363
Godard, Jean-Luc, 63 168, 209, 220, 243, 253, 259, 272, 273, 279, 306, 372, 402, 404; dir., *La Chinoise*, 167, 272, 306; *One Plus One*, 168, 209; *Weekend*, 253, 298, 404; *Band of Outsiders*, 279, 402; *Masculine Feminine*, 306
Godfather, The, 420–426
Goin' Down the Road, 171–172
Going Home, 353–354
Gold, Ernest, 35
Gold, Jack, 89; dir., *The Bofors Gun*, 89; *The Reckoning*, 89
"Gold Fever," 28
Gold of Naples, The, 362
Goldman, James, 369
Goldman, William, 6, 7, 327–328, 401–402
Gone with the Wind, 28, 74
Goodbye, Columbus, 4, 32, 218, 260, 364, 384
Goodbye, Mr. Chips, 38–41
"Goodbye to Berlin," 410
Goodman, David Z., 394
Gordon, Ruth, 186
Goring, Marius, 162
Gossett, Lou, 299
Gould, Dave, 382
Gould, Elliott, 11, 12, 93, 94, 254, 256, 348
Gould, Joe, 125
Graduate, The, 9, 10, 152, 283, 395
Grahame, Gloria, 296
Gramatica, Emma, 362
Grand Illusion, 430
Granger, Farley, 401
Grant, Cary, 351, 431
Grapes of Wrath, The, 349
Grave, Louis, 430
Gravey, Fernand, 26
Gravina, Carla, 413
Great Lie, The, 157
Great White Hope, The, 158–161
Green, Adolph, 82
Green, Nigel, 105
Green Berets, The, 316
Green Hat, The, 364, 365
Greetings, 314
Grenfell, Joyce, 269
Grey, Joel, 409–412
Grieg, Edvard, 187
Griem, Helmut, 412
Grierson, John, 251
Griffith, D. W., 149, 275, 362; dir., *Intolerance*, 319, 320; *Orphans of the Storm*, 319

444

Griffith, Hugh, 123
Gris, Juan, 299
Groom, Sam, 157
Grosz, George, 410
Groupies, 197–199
Guerre Est Finie, La, 64
Guess What We Learned in School Today?, 325
Guevara, Che, 257, 258
Guffey, Burnett, 159
Guinness, Alec, 37, 181, 185, 197, 203
Guitry, Sacha, 194
Gunsmoke, 191
Guru, The, 195
Guthrie, Arlo, 7, 197, 215
Guys and Dolls, 409
Gypsy, 409
Gypsy Moths The, 52, 200

Hackman, Gene, 47, 170, 316, 318
Hagmann, Stuart, 150; dir., *The Strawberry Statement*, 149–151
Hail, Hero!, 42
Hailey, Arthur, 136
Hair, 31, 130
Halberstam, David, 44
Hale, Georgina, 382
Hall, Conrad, 7
Hall, Peter, 193; dir., *Perfect Friday*, 193
Halprin, Daria, 115, 117
Hamilton, Edith, 305
Hamilton, Guy, 389; dir., *Diamonds Are Forever*, 388–389
Hamilton, Margaret, 227–228
Hamlet, 127
Hamlet (Richardson version), 89–91
Hammett, Dashiell 69, 414
Happy Birthday, Wanda June, 369
Happy Ending, The, 148
Hardwick, Elizabeth, 291
Hardy, Thomas, 141
Harlow, Jean, 227
Harnick, Sheldon, 333
Harris, Julie, 311
Harris, Richard, 104, 181, 357–359
Harris, Rosalind, 331
Harrison, Rex, 37
Hart, William S., 344
Harvey, Anthony, dir., *The Lion in Winter*, 37
Harvey, Laurence, 142, 182
Haver, June, 159
Hawks, Howard, 296–297; dir., *To Have and Have Not*, 235, 237, 413; *Red River*, 297; *The Big Sleep*, 413–415; *Bringing Up Baby*, 431, 432
Hayes, Helen, 137, 311, 345
Hayward, Susan, 407

Hayworth, Rita, 324
Head, Murray, 289
Healy, Ted, 318
Heath, Gordon, 26
Hébuterne, Jeanne, 54
Hecht, Ben, 73, 74
Hedren, Tippi, 192
Hee Haw, 234
Hefner, Hugh, 110
Held, Jr., John, 379
"Hello, Dolly!," 83
Hello, Dolly!, 80–85, 185, 328, 432
Hell's Angels, 174, 208–211
Hemingway, Ernest, 46
Hemmings, David, 67
Hendrix, Jimi, 198
Henreid, Paul, 26
Henry, Buck, 184, 324–325
Henry, O., 267
Henry VIII, 95, 96
Hepburn, Audrey, 71, 381
Hepburn, Katharine, 25, 184, 218, 290, 301, 302, 311, 313, 341, 346, 353, 431
Herman, Jerry, 84
Hernández, Juano, 75, 76
Hershey, Barbara, 157
Hesse, Hermann, 230, 348
Heston, Charlton, 351
Hickok, Wild Bill, 213
Higby, Mary Jane, 107
Higgins, Michael, 267
High Noon, 387
High School, 20–24
Hill, Arthur, 276
Hill, George Roy, 6; dir., *Butch Cassidy and the Sundance Kid*, 5–7, 149, 173, 401, 402; *Period of Adjustment*, 281
Hiller, Arthur, 219, 378; dir., *Love Story*, 216–220, 237, 321, 322, 432–433; *The Hospital*, 378–379, 426
Hiller, Wendy, 142
Hilsman, Roger, 44
Hilton, James, 38, 39
Hingle, Pat, 182
Hired Hand, The, 323, 353
Hiroshima, 112
Hitchcock, Alfred, 79–80, 192, 317, 404; dir., *Marnie*, 79; *Topaz*, 79–80; *Torn Curtain*, 79; *The Birds*, 192; *Strangers on a Train*, 261–262; *Psycho*, 316; *Rope*, 401
Hitler, Adolf, 87, 427, 429
Ho Chi Minh, 42, 45
Hoffman, Dustin, 72 73, 213, 215, 349, 352, 394, 395
Home for Life, 207
Honeymoon Killers, The, 105–107
Hoodlum Priest, The, 119

"Hooray for Hollywood," 227
Hope, Bob, 61
Hopkins, Anthony 91, 118
Hopper, Dennis, 148, 297–299; dir., *Easy Rider*, 3, 4, 78, 84, 117, 147, 152, 173, 297, 298; *The Last Movie*, 297–299
Hordern, Michael, 97
Horovitz, Israel, 150, 151
Horseman, Pass By, 294
Hospital, 101–102
Hospital, The, 378–379, 426
Hot Rock, The, 401–403
Hotel, 136
Hour of the Furnaces, The, 257–259
House of Strangers, 424
"How Do I Love Thee?," 162
How I Won the War, 15, 17
How to Steal a Million, 37
Howard, Sidney, 74
Howard, Trevor, 142, 190, 192
Howe, James Wong, 103, 159
Howl, 48
Hud, 173, 294–295
Hudson, Rock, 47, 225, 353
Hughes, Howard, 389, 420
Hughes, Ken, 181; dir., *Cromwell*, 181
Hughes, Mary Beth, 25
Humanité, L', 203
Humphrey, Hubert H., 43
Hunt, Peter, 85, 389; dir., *On Her Majesty's Secret Service*, 85–86, 389
Hunter, Ross, 136, 173, 285
Hurry Sundown, 59
Husák, Gustav, 203
Husbands, 222–224, 284
Hustler, The, 47
Huston, Anjelica, 18
Huston, John, 17–18, 104, 105, 358; dir., *A Walk With Love and Death*, 17–18; *Reflections in a Golden Eye*, 17, 422; *The Kremlin Letter*, 104–105; *The Treasure of Sierra Madre*, 298
Hutton, Brian G., 405, 407; dir., *X Y & Zee*, 405–409
Hutton, Lauren, 173
Hypatia, 36

I Am a Camera, 412
I Am Curious (Yellow), 18
I Ching, 230
"I Hate People," 197
"I Like Life, Life Likes Me," 197
I Love My Wife, 231, 232
I Love You, Alice B. Toklas, 9
I Never Sang for My Father, 169–171
"I Talk to the Trees," 28
I Walk Alone, 133
I Walk the Line, 199–200

Ibbetson, Arthur, 97
Ibsen, Henrik, 50, 52
Ice, 163–168
If . . ., 117
"If You Could See Her," 412
Ilf and Petrov, 180
Iliad, 430
"I'll String Along with You," 284
Imitation of Life, 131, 217
Immoral Mr. Teas, The, 58
Impossible Camera, The, 309
In the Heat of the Night, 330
"In the Region of Ice," 32
In the Year of the Pig, 42–45
Inadmissible Evidence, 89
Inheritors, The, 151
"Inside the Whale," 125
Intolerance, 319, 320
Intruder in the Dust, 75
Invasion of the Body Snatchers, 275
Investigation of a Citizen Above Suspicion, 221–222
Is There Sex After Death?, 324–326
Isherwood, Christopher, 410–412
It's in the Bag, 180
"It's Never Too Late to Fall in Love," 382
Ivan the Terrible, 242
Ivory James, 195, 196; dir., *Shakespeare Wallah*, 195; *The Guru*, 195; *Bombay Talkie*, 195–196

Jackson, Glenda, 139, 141, 239, 242, 289–291, 380, 382
Jacobi, Lou, 255
Jade, Claude, 244–245
Jagger, Mick, 112, 156, 206–211
Janssen, David, 86
Jarre, Maurice, 189
Jarrott, Charles, 96–97; dir., *Anne of the Thousand Days*, 95–97
Jayston, Michael, 368
Jefferson Airplane, 211
Jennings, William Dale, 390
Jersey, William C., 207; dir., *A Time for Burning*, 207
Jessua, Alain, 418; dir., *Life Upside Down*, 418
Jewell, Isabel, 69
Jewison, Norman, 74, 327, 330–332; dir., *Gaily, Gaily*, 73–74; *Fiddler on the Roof*, 327–333, 426; *In the Heat of the Night*, 330; *The Russians Are Coming*, 330
Joan of Arc, 311
Joanna, 151
Jodorowsky, Alexandro, 334, 337–340; dir., *El Topo* 334–340
Joe, 148, 152–153, 313

John and Mary, 72–73
Johnny Guitar, 335
Johnson, Ben, 295, 296
Johnson, Jack, 160
Johnson, Lyndon B., 43, 112, 165
Jones, Christopher, 117, 118, 189, 190, 191
Jones, Evan, 417
Jones, James Earl, 112, 158–159
Joplin, Janis, 85
Jory, Victor, 162
Joyce, James 124
Jules and Jim, 243
Juliet of the Spirits, 129, 130
Jung, C. G., 128

Kafka, Franz, 220–222, 256, 417
Kahn, Madeline, 432
Kander, John, 411
Kapoor, Shashi, 195, 196
Karina, Anna, 281
Kastle, Leonard, 106; dir., *The Honeymoon Killers,* 105–107
Kaufman, Robert, 150–151
Kaye, Danny, 25, 93
Kazan, Elia 48–53, 328; dir., *The Arrangement,* 48–53, 252; *America America,* 50–52, 328, 331; *On the Waterfront,* 152, 338, 421, 426; *Viva Zapata!,* 175; *East of Eden,* 252
Keach, Stacy, 112, 228, 349
Keaton, Buster, 61, 244, 372, 431
Keaton, Diane, 424
Keith, Brian, 74
Keller, Hiram, 130
Kellerman, Sally, 93, 228
Kelly, Gene, 82, 83; dir., *Hello, Dolly!,* 80–85, 185, 328, 423; co-dir., *Singin' in the Rain,* 209, 322
Kelly, George, 170
Kelton, Pert, 62
Kendal, Jennifer, 195
Kennedy, Burt, 149
Kennedy, Edgar, 123
Kennedy, John F., 64, 112, 207
Kennedy, Joseph P., 43
Kennedy, Robert, 31, 112
Kerkorian, Kirk, 188
Kerr, Deborah, 49, 52, 269, 347
Kershner, Irvin, 19–122, 350; dir., *A Fine Madness,* 105, 119; *Loving,* 119–122, 351; *The Hoodlum Priest,* 119; *The Luck of Ginger Goffey,* 119–120, 122
Khrushchev, Nikita, 201
Kid from Texas, The, 296
Kidd, Michael, 82
King, Allan, 107–109; dir., *A Married Couple,* 107–111
King, Martin Luther, 112, 226

King Lear, 354–357
Kings Row, 294
Kirkland, Sally, 55
Klane, Robert, 186
Klein, Robert, 184
Klute, 281–282, 285, 314, 352, 426
Kohner, Susan, 131
Kolb, Ken, 236
Koningsberger, Hans, 17
Korean war, 93
Korman, Harvey, 182
Korty, John, 350; dir., *Funnyman,* 350
Kosleck, Martin, 97
Kotch, 345
Kotcheff, Ted, 417; dir., *Outback,* 415–417
Kott, Jan, 356, 400
Kovacs, Laszlo, 298
Kramer, Larry, 140
Kramer, Robert, 164, 165, 168; dir., *Ice,* 163–168; *The Edge,* 164, 165
Kramer, Stanley, 34, 150, 216, 383; dir., *The Secret of Santa Vittoria,* 34–35; *R.P.M.,* 150
Kremlin Letter, The, 104–105
Krüger, Hardy, 35
Kubrick, Stanley, 131, 373, 374–377; dir., *Dr. Strangelove,* 99, 375; *2001,* 131; *A Clockwork Orange,* 373–378, 426
Kullers, John, 222, 224
Kurosawa, Akira, 139, 248; dir., *Throne of Blood,* 139, 336; *The Seven Samurai,* 248

La Mama, 55–57
Labro, Philippe, 413–415; dir., *Without Apparent Motive,* 413–415
Lacouture, Jean, 44
Lady in the Dark, 346
Lambrakis, Gregorios, 63–64
Lancaster, Burt, 137, 299, 353
Landlord, The, 314
Lane, Mark, 64
Lang, Fritz, 87
Lange, Dorothea, 342
Langella, Frank, 180, 348
Lansbury, Angela, 359, 360
Lao-tse, 399
Lardner, Jr., Ring, 94
Larner, Steve, 30
Last Movie, The, 297–299
Last Picture Show, The, 293–297, 299, 353, 426
Last Run, The, 294, 353
Last Valley, The, 248–250
Last Year at Marienbad, 244
Laughlin, Tom, 342–345, 350; dir., *Billy Jack,* 341–347, 426; *Born Losers,* 342
Laughter in the Dark, 41, 89

Laughton, Charles, 95
Laurel, Stan, 61
Laurel and Hardy, 431
Laval, Pierre, 428
Law and Order, 20, 23, 207
Lawrence, D. H., 57, 138–142, 191
Lawrence, Frieda, 141
Lawrence, Gertrude, 41
Lawrence, T. E., 178
Lawrence of Arabia, 192
Lazenby, George, 85
le Carré, John, 117
Leachman, Cloris, 182, 296
Lean, David, 188–192, 270, 368; dir., *Doctor Zhivago*, 188–192, 279; *Ryan's Daughter*, 188–193, 218; *Lawrence of Arabia*, 192
Leary, Timothy, 13
Léaud, Jean-Pierre, 244, 245
Leaves of Grass, 124
Lee, Michele, 61
Legend of Lylah Clare, The, 148
Lehman, Ernest, 83
Leibman, Ron, 186, 401–403
Leighton, Margaret, 25
Lelouch, Claude, dir., *A Man and a Woman*, 72, 322
LeMay, Curtis, 44, 45
Lemmon, Jack, 350; dir., *Kotch*, 345
Lenin, V. I., 203, 369
Leonard, Herbert B., 354; dir., *Going Home*, 353–354
Lerner, Alan Jay, 27, 29
Lerner, Irving, 25; dir., *The Royal Hunt of the Sun*, 24–25
Lester, Richard, 4, 15, 17, 308; dir., *Petulia*, 4; *How I Won the War*, 15, 17; *The Bed Sitting Room*, 17; *The Running, Jumping and Standing Still Film*, 17
Lettieri, Al, 424
Levant, Oscar, 424
Levine, Joseph E., 132, 136, 151, 345
Lewis, Andy and Dave, 281
Lewis, Sinclair, 44
Life, 36, 50, 111
Life Upside Down, 418
Lift to the Scaffold (Frantic), 308
Lincoln, Abraham, 161
Lincoln Center, 188
Linden, Jennie, 141
Lindfors, Viveca, 252
Lindsay, John, 313
Lion in Winter, The, 37
Lions Love, 30–31
Little Big Horn, 214
Little Big Man, 212–216, 236, 252
Little Boy Lost, 136
Little Fauss and Big Halsy, 171, 173–174
Little Murders, 253–257, 314, 330
Little Women, 198
Livesey, Roger, 91
Lloyd, Harold, 61
LoBianco, Tony, 106
Loden, Barbara, 267–269; dir., *Wanda*, 267–269
Loewe, Frederick, 27, 29
Logan, Joshua, 27, 29; dir., *Paint Your Wagon*, 26–30, 31, 328; *Camelot*, 26, 27, 328; *Bus Stop*, 29, 371; *South Pacific*, 409
Lollobrigida, Gina, 362
London, Artur, 202–204
Lonely Boy, 109
Lonesome Cowboys, 153
Long Ago, Tomorrow, 321–324
Long Day's Journey Into Night, 169
Long, Hot Summer, The, 76
Lonsdale, Michel, 309
Look Back in Anger, 90
Looking Glass War, The, 117–119, 148
Loren, Sophia, 361
Losey, Joseph, 307; dir., *The Go-Between*, 292, 363; *Boom!*, 407; *Secret Ceremony*, 407
Lost Horizon, 39
Lot in Sodom, 55, 242
Louis XVI, 123
"Louise," 185
Louise, Anita, 157
Love Machine, The, 198
Love Story, 216–220, 237, 321, 322, 432–433
Loved One, The, 4
Lovell, Dyson, 183
Lovelock, Raymond, 332
Lovers, The, 306, 308, 309
Lovers and Other Strangers, 370–371
Loves of Isadora, The, 239, 302
Loving, 119–122, 351
Lowe, Edmund, 93, 94
L-Shaped Room, The, 323
Lubitsch, Ernst, 427
Luck of Ginger Coffey, The, 119–120, 122
Luckinbill, Laurence, 383
Lumet, Sidney, dir., *The Anderson Tapes*, 285, 314
Luv, 10
Luxemburg, Rosa, 182, 203
Lydia Bailey, 177
MacArthur, General Douglas, 204
Macbeth, 139
Macbeth (Polanski version), 399–401
MacGraw, Ali, 216–219, 313
MacLaine, Shirley, 200, 346, 385
Macready, George, 147, 262
Mad, 15, 186, 325
Madame X, 217
Made for Each Other, 369–373, 426

448

Madison Square Garden, 208
Madwoman of Chaillot, The, 25–26
Magee, Patrick, 375
Magic Box, The, 16
Magic Christian, The, 123, 148
Magnani, Anna, 35, 329
Magnificent Obsession, 217
Magritte, René, 307
Magus The, 148
Mahler, Gustav, 106
Maibaum, Richard, 389
Mailer, Norman, 17, 50, 124, 222, 398
Major Dundee, 358, 393
Malcolm X, 161
Malden, Karl, 99
Malle, Louis, 306–310; dir., *Murmur of the Heart*, 305–310, 426; *The Lovers*, 306, 308, 309; *Lift to the Scaffold (Frantic)*, 308; *Zazie dans le Métro*, 308, 309; *Vie Privée*, 308; *Le Feu Follet (The Fire Within)*, 308, 309; *Viva Maria!*, 309; *The Thief of Paris*, 309; *Calcutta*, 309; *The Impossible Camera*, 309; *Phantom India*, 309; co-dir., *The Silent World*, 307
Malone, Dorothy, 296
Maltese Falcon, The, 69
Man and a Woman, A, 72, 322
Man Escaped, A, 307
Man for All Seasons, A, 95
Man in the Wilderness, 357–359
Manchurian Candidate, The, 199, 261
Mancini, Henry, 104
Manhoff, Bill, 184
Mankiewicz, Joseph L., 229; dir., *Cleopatra*, 27; *There Was a Crooked Man . . .*, 229–230; *Guys and Dolls*, 409; *House of Strangers*, 424
Mankiewicz, Tom, 389
Mann, Paul, 52, 331
Man's Blessing, A, 221
Man's Castle, A, 73
Mansfield, Katherine, 141
Manson, Charles, 375, 399
Mao Tse-tung, 418
Marat/Sade, 242, 355
Marceau, Marcel, 334
March, Fredric, 348
Marcus, Lawrence B., 353
Marnie, 79
Marooned, 86
Marquand, Christian, dir., *Candy*, 147
Marquez, Evaristo, 178
Marriage—Italian Style, 362
Married Couple, A, 107–111
Marsh, Linda, 52
Marsh, Michele, 332
Marshall, E. G., 147
Marshall, George C., 100

Marshall, Herbert, 190
Marshall, Peter, 321
Martí, José, 257
Martin, Dean, 82, 137, 431
Martin, Mary, 40
Marvin, Lee, 27–30, 162
Marx Brothers, 15, 84, 369
Marx, Groucho, 122
Marx, Harpo, 254, 402
Marx, Karl, 163; Marxism, 16, 77, 175, 176
Masculine Feminine, 306
M*A*S*H, 92–95, 147, 185, 227, 277, 278
Masina, Giulietta, 25
Mason, James, 412
Massari, Lea, 305–306, 309–310
Massie, Robert K., 369
Master Builder, The, 50
Mastroianni, Marcello, 193–195, 220–221
Matras, Christian, 103
Matthau, Walter, 81, 83, 269
Max, Peter, 222
May, Elaine, 10, 73, 269, 369, 384; dir., *A New Leaf*, 269
Mayer, Louis B., 151
Maysles, Albert and David, 206–209, 211
Mazursky, Meg, 227
Mazursky, Paul, 9–11, 14, 148, 225–227, 350; dir., *Bob & Carol & Ted & Alice*, 8–14, 225; *Alex in Wonderland*, 224–228
McAndrew, Marianne, 83
McBain, Ed, 415
McCabe and Mrs. Miller, 277–280, 426
McCambridge, Mercedes, 335
McCarthy, Eugene, 168
McCarthy, Joseph, 43, 63
McCoy, Horace, 68–70, 72
McCrea, Joel, 353
McCullers, Carson, 32
McDowell, Malcolm, 322, 374, 376
McEnery, John, 417
McGrath, Doug, 171
McGrath, Joseph, 123; dir., *The Magic Christian*, 123, 148
McGuane, Thomas, 261
McGuire, Dennis, 111
McKayle, Donald, 359
McKern, Leo, 190
McKuen, Rod, 91
McLaglen, Victor, 93, 94
McLuhan, Marshall, 24, 236
McMurtry, Larry, 293–296, 299
McQueen, Steve, 75, 76, 110, 174, 228
Medium Cool, 117
Meeker, Ralph, 199
"Mein Herr," 410
Melville, Herman, 417, 418
Men, The, 322

Mendès-France, Pierre, 428
Merchant, Vivien, 68
Mercouri, Melina, 74, 182, 245–248
Meredith, Burgess, 76, 229, 384
Metro-Goldwyn-Mayer, 51, 67, 105, 155, 188, 211, 225, 226, 406
Meyer, Russ, dir., *The Immoral Mr. Teas,* 58
Midnight Cowboy, 4, 76, 147, 152, 314
Mifune, Toshiro, 336
Miles, Sarah, 189, 190
Milestone, Lewis, dir., *All Quiet on the Western Front,* 16, 17, 134; *Edge of Darkness,* 63; *Mutiny on the Bounty,* 177
Milky Way, The, 102–103
Miller, Arthur, 50, 208
Miller, Henry, 123–127, 219
Miller's Beautiful Wife, The, 362
Milligan, Spike, 17
Mills, John, 190
Milosz, Czeslaw, 203
Milton, David Scott, 351
Mindszenty, Joseph, Cardinal, 201, 202
Minnelli, Liza, 32–34, 409–412, 432
Minnelli, Vincente, 275; dir., *An American in Paris,* 84; *On a Clear Day You Can See Forever,* 185; *Father of the Bride,* 296
"Minute Waltz," 137
Miracle in Milan, 361, 362
Miracle on 34th Street, 136
Miranda case, 386, 388
Miró, Joan, 299
Missa Luba, 175
Mitchum, Robert, 189, 190, 353, 354
Moffo, Anna, 135
Molly Maguires, The, 103–104, 159
Moment of Truth, The, 171
Mon Oncle, 245
Mondo Trasho, 130
"Money," 412
Monroe, Marilyn, 156, 209, 371
Montand, Yves, 64, 184, 202, 204
Monte Walsh, 162
Monterey Pop, 208
Montez, Maria, 25
Montgomery, General Bernard, 99, 100
Montgomery, Robert, 347
Moody, Ron, 180
Moore, Mary Tyler, 61
Moore, Robin, 316
Moran, Jim, 325
Moravia, Alberto, 270
More, Kenneth, 197
Moreau, Jeanne, 12, 115, 162, 226, 227, 308–310, 419
Moreno, Rita, 284
Morgan!, 152
Morgan, Michèle, 259

Morley, Robert, 318
Morris, Chester, 161
Morrissey, Paul, 153–156; dir., *Trash,* 153–157; *Flesh,* 153, 157
Morse, Wayne, 43
Mortimer, John, 73
Moses, Grandma, 180
Mosjoukine, Ivan, 246, 248
Most, The, 109–110
Mostel, Zero, 329
Motion Picture Academy of Arts and Sciences, 61, 136, 260
Motion Picture and the Teaching of English, The, 145
Motion Picture Association of America (M.P.A.A.), 92, 145, 171; Rating Board, 250
Mozart, Wolfgang Amadeus, 188, 292
Mr. Hulot's Holiday, 194
Mrs. Miniver, 359
Mulligan, Richard, 215
Mulligan, Robert, dir., *Up the Down Staircase,* 23; *Summer of '42,* 321, 391
Munch, Edvard, 410
Munk, Andrzej, 205
Murmur of the Heart, 305–310, 426
Murnau, F. W., 87
Murphy, Audie, 296
Mus, Paul, 44
Music Lovers, The, 238–243
Mussolini, Benito, 116, 270, 273, 364
Mussolini, Vittorio, 116
Mutiny on the Bounty, 177
My Fair Lady, 328
My Life to Live, 281
Myra Breckinridge, 147, 151

Naked Lunch, The, 173
Namath, Joe, 173–174
Napoleon Bonaparte, 348
National Council of Teachers of English, 145
National Educational Television, 20, 319, 320
Neagle, Anna, 16
Neame, Ronald, 196; dir., *The Prime of Miss Jean Brodie,* 187; *Scrooge,* 196–197
Nelson, Ralph, dir., *Charly,* 59; *Requiem for a Heavyweight,* 352
Nero, 127
Never on Sunday, 248
New Leaf, A, 269
New York Film Festival, 8, 20, 146, 272
New York Review of Sex & Politics, 57
New York Times, 8, 56, 92, 145, 150, 337, 340
New Yorker, The, 293, 308, 418
Newman, David, 229, 230

Newman, Nanette, 26, 322, 323
Newman, Paul, 6, 7, 46–47, 110, 173, 174, 182, 200, 350, 351, 401, 402
Newsweek, 154
Nhu, Mme., 44
Nicholas and Alexandra, 366–369
Nichols, John, 32
Nichols, Mike, 10, 73, 215, 282, 369; dir., *The Graduate*, 9, 10, 152, 283, 395; *Catch-22*, 146, 215, 256, 282, 283; *Carnal Knowledge*, 282–285, 348; *Who's Afraid of Virgina Woolf?*, 405, 406
Nicholson, Jack, 251, 283, 284, 347, 350; dir., *Drive, He Said*, 294, 323, 350
Night of the Following Day, The, 59
Night They Raided Minsky's, The, 83
Nightcomers, The, 422
1984, 28, 373
Niven, David, 269
Nixon, Richard, 44, 112, 162, 299
No Way to Treat a Lady, 314
Noel, Magali, 65
Noiret, Philippe, 80
Notte, La, 113
Nun's Story, The, 421
Nykvist, Sven, 162

Oates, Joyce Carol, 32
Oates, Warren, 229, 323
O'Brien, Edna, 405–408
O'Brien, Pat, 45
O'Connell, Arthur, 249
Odd Couple, The, 233
Oedipus Rex, 304
Of Mice and Men, 4
"Of This Time, of That Place," 32
O'Horgan, Tom, 54–57; dir., *Futz*, 54–57, 59, 112, 148, 241
Oh! What a Lovely War, 14–17
Oklahoma!, 29, 409, 413
Oliver!, 359
Olivier, Laurence, 15, 37, 86, 149, 159, 195, 368, 374
Olson, James, 276
Olvidados, Los, 376
On a Clear Day You Can See Forever, 185
On Approval, 194
On Her Majesty's Secret Service, 85–86, 389
On the Waterfront, 152, 338, 421, 426
On with the Show, 380
One Plus One, 168, 209
O'Neal, Cynthia, 283, 284
O'Neal, Patrick, 105
O'Neal, Ryan, 219, 296, 353, 431–433
O'Neill, Eugene, 170, 208
Only Game in Town, The, 122–123, 407
Open City, 65

Operation Mad Ball, 94
Ophuls Marcel, 427, 428, 430; dir., *The Sorrow and the Pity*, 426–430
Ophuls, Max, 279; dir., *The Earrings of Madame de . . .*, 279, 362
Orphans of the Storm, 319
Orwell, George, 125, 126, 373
Osborne, John, 90, 162
Oscar, The, 182, 259
Oscarsson, Per, 249
Oswald, Lee Harvey, 207
Othello, 159
O'Toole, Peter, 37–38, 40–41, 415
Our Town, 76
Outback, 415–417
"Over the Rainbow," 227
Owens, Rochelle, 54, 55
Owl and the Pussycat, The, 183–185, 314, 351

Pacino, Al, 422–424
Page, Genevieve, 187
Paint Your Wagon, 26–31, 328
Pakula, Alan J., 32, 34, 281, 282; dir., *The Sterile Cuckoo*, 31–34; *Klute*, 281–282, 285, 314, 352, 426
Pal Joey, 409
Palance, Jack, 162
"Palladium, The," 382
Panfilov, Gleb, 311; dir., *The Début*, 311
Panic in Needle Park, The, 305, 314
Papandreou, George, 64
Papas, Irene, 65, 96, 302–303, 305
Paramount Pictures, 84, 132, 173, 182, 216, 217, 420
Paris Review, 327
Parker, Charlie, 310
Parker, Dorothy, 327, 333
Parkins, Barbara, 105
Parsons, Estelle, 170, 199
Partner, 272–273
Pasolini, Pier Paolo, 8, 263; dir., *Pigpen*, 59
Passer, Ivan, 351; dir., *Born to Win*, 314, 351–352, 402, 426
Passion of Joan of Arc, The, 419
Pat and Mike, 184
Patton, 97–100, 368
Patton, General George, 97–99, 318
Patton III, George S., 45
Pavese, Cesare, 113
Pay Day, 194
Payne, John, 159
Peace Corps, 220, 258
"Peanuts," 91
Peck, Gregory, 63, 86, 199, 200, 353
Peckinpah, Sam, 133–135, 148, 279, 393–398; dir., *The Wild Bunch*, 133–134,

451

149, 393; *The Ballad of Cable Hogue,* 279; *Major Dundee,* 358, 393; *Ride the High Country,* 393; *Straw Dogs,* 393–399, 426
Peerce, Larry, 4, 260–262; dir., *Goodbye, Columbus,* 4, 32, 218, 260; *The Sporting Club,* 261–263
Penn, Arthur, 5, 135, 212–216; dir., *Alice's Restaurant,* 5, 6, 197, 212, 215; *Bonnie and Clyde,* 6, 152, 170, 173, 212; *Little Big Man,* 212–216, 236, 252
Perfect Friday, 193
Performance, 156, 209
Périer, François, 65
Period of Adjustment, 281
Perkins, Tony, 182, 348
Perón, Juan, 258; Peronism, 257–258
Perry, Frank, 182; dir., *Diary of a Mad Housewife,* 314, 348, 383, 384; *Doc,* 349
Perugia, Luciano, 183
Pétain, Marshal Henri, 427, 429
Petri, Elio, 220–222; dir., *We Still Kill the Old Way,* 221; *Investigation of a Citizen Above Suspicion,* 221–222
Petronius, 129
Petulia, 4
Peyton Place, 219, 295
Peyton Place (Robson movie), 294
Pham Van Dong, 45
Phantom India, 309
Philadelphia Story, The, 261
Philipe, Gérard, 259, 419
Phillips, Sian, 38, 41
Piaf, Edith, 383
Picasso, Pablo, 267
Piccoli, Michel, 80
Pickwick Papers, The, 54
Picon, Molly, 331
Pidgeon, Walter, 262
Pierson, Frank R., 117, 118; dir., *The Looking Glass War,* 117–119
Pigpen, 59
Pinter, Harold, 10, 223
Pirandello, Luigi, 207
Pirro, Ugo, 221
Pisanello, Il, 265
Pitts, ZaSu, 31
Pizza Triangle, The (A Case of Jealousy), 193–195
Planet of the Apes, 98, 368
Plautus, 219
Play It As It Lays, 250–251
Playboy, 282
Pleasence, Donald, 26, 415
Plimpton, Shelley, 197
Plumed Serpent, The, 138
Plummer, Christopher, 24, 25
Poe, James, 70

Poitier, Sidney, 75
Polanski, Roman, 399–401; dir., *Macbeth,* 399–401
Pollack, Sydney, 70; dir., *They Shoot Horses, Don't They?,* 68–72, 76, 281; *The Scalphunters,* 299
Pollard, Michael J., 173
Polonsky, Abraham, 77; dir., *Tell Them Willie Boy Is Here,* 76–78
Pontecorvo, Gillo, 175–177; dir., *Burn!,* 175–180; *The Battle of Algiers,* 176
Popcorn, 58–59
Porgy and Bess, 333
Porter, Cole, 328
Portnoy's Complaint, 219
Potter, Martin 130
Pound, Ezra, 36
Pound, Homer Shakespear, 36
Powell, Dick, 284
Power, Tyrone, 177
Pradal, Bruno, 419
Preminger, Otto, 383, 384; dir., *Hurry Sundown,* 59; *Such Good Friends,* 383–384
President's Analyst, The, 10
Presnell, Harve, 28
Pretty Maids All in a Row, 225
Previn, André, 27
Prime of Miss Jean Brodie, The, 187
Primus, Barry, 252, 350
Prisoner, The, 201, 203
Private Life of Henry VIII, The, 95
Private Life of Sherlock Holmes, The, 186–187
Producers, The, 348
Professionals, The, 229
Promise at Dawn, 245–248
Prophet, The, 337
Proud and the Beautiful, The (Les Orgueilleux), 259
Proust, Marcel, 265, 365
Psycho, 316
Pumpkin Eater, The, 292
Purcell, Henry, 377
Putney Swope, 154
Puzo, Mario, 420–421
Puzzle of a Downfall Child, 250–253

Quayle, Anthony, 97
Queen, The, 197
Queneau, Raymond, 308
Quinn, Anthony, 34–35, 59, 150, 246, 247, 329, 423
Quinn, Gordon, 207

Rabelais, François, 124
Rabier, Jean, 403
Radio City Music Hall, 42, 80, 91, 92, 324, 383, 390, 391

Rado, James, 31
Rafelson, Bob, dir., *Five Easy Pieces*, 152, 153, 231, 251, 252
Raffoul, François, 247
Ragni, Gerome, 31
Raimu, 329
Rain People, The, 59
Rainer, Luise, 73
Randolph, John, 229
Ransome, Prunella, 67
Rasputin, 366–368
Rattigan, Terence, 38–39
Ravetch, Irving, 76, 390
Ray, Aldo, 173
Razzia, 316
Reader's Digest, 253
Reagan, Ronald, 296
Rebel Without a Cause, 152
Reckoning, The, 89
Red Desert, 116, 252
Red River, 297
Redfield, William, 269
Redford, Robert, 6, 7, 45, 47, 77, 78, 88, 173, 174, 231, 347, 401–403
Redgrave, Vanessa, 195, 302
Reed, Oliver, 139, 141, 142
Reflections in a Golden Eye, 17, 422
Reid, Kate, 276
Reiner, Carl, 60–62, 185–186; dir., *Enter Laughing*, 10, 61; *The Comic*, 60–62; *Where's Poppa?*, 185–186, 314, 351, 402
Reisz, Karel, dir., *Morgan!*, 152
Reivers, The, 75–76
Renoir, Claude, 25, 135
Renoir, Jean, 149, 238, 425; dir., *Grand Illusion*, 430
Republic Pictures, 107
Requiem for a Heavyweight, 352
Resnais, Alain, dir., *La Guerre Est Finie*, 64; *Last Year at Marienbad*, 244
Revere, Anne, 391
Rey, Fernando, 316
Reynolds, Debbie, 141
Rice, Elmer, 312
Richardson, Ralph, 17, 37, 118
Richardson, Tony, 4, 15, 89, 90, 99, 213, 308; dir., *The Loved One*, 4; *The Charge of the Light Brigade*, 15, 17, 99, 213, 215; *Laughter in the Dark*, 41, 89; *Hamlet*, 89–91; *A Taste of Honey*, 187; *Tom Jones*, 308
Richthoven, A. E. V., 19
Ride the High Country, 393
Riefenstahl, Leni, 28, 207; dir., *Triumph of the Will*, 207
Riesner, Dean, 386
Riff Raff, 227
Rififi, 248

Rigg, Diana, 85, 378
Rigoletto, 273
Rilke, Rainer Maria, 251
Ritchie, Michael, 46, 47; dir., *Downhill Racer*, 45–47, 173
Ritt, Martin, 103, 104, 158, 159; dir., *The Long, Hot Summer*, 76; *The Molly Maguires*, 103–104, 159; *The Great White Hope*, 158–161; *Hud*, 173, 294–295
Ritz, Harry, 352
Riva, Emmanuelle, 419
Robbe-Grillet, Alain, 418
Robbie, Seymour, 173; dir., *C. C. and Company*, 173–174
Robbins, Harold, 133–136, 151, 420
Robbins, Jerome, 332
Roberts, Hermese E., 217
Roberts, Rachel, 260
Robinson, Edward G., 424
Robson, Mark, dir., *Peyton Place*, 294; *Happy Birthday, Wanda June*, 369
Rodd, Marcia, 254
Rodin, Auguste, 422
Roehm, Ernst, 86
Rogers, Ginger, 28, 184, 272, 296, 346, 409
Rogers, Paul, 118
Rohmer, Eric, 265–267; dir., *Claire's Knee*, 264–267, 275, 280
Rolling Stones, 58, 208–210
Roman Holiday, 381
Romand, Beatrice, 265
Romanovs, 366–368
Romeo and Juliet (Zeffirelli version), 18, 182, 219
Ronet, Maurice, 54, 308
Roof, The, 361
Room at the Top, 142
Rooney, Mickey, 60
Roosevelt, Franklin Delano, 204
Rope, 401
Rose, George, 269
Rosenberg, Stuart, 181–182; dir., *WUSA*, 181–182; *Cool Hand Luke*, 181; *The April Fools*, 182
Rosenblum, Ralph, 351
Rosi, Francesco, 171; dir., *The Moment of Truth*, 171
Ross, Herbert, 38, 183, 185, 311; dir., *Goodbye, Mr. Chips*, 38–41; *The Owl and the Pussycat*, 183–185, 314, 351; *T. R. Baskin*, 311–313
Ross, Katherine, 6, 77
Rossellini, Roberto, 361; dir., *Open City*, 65
Rossen, Robert, dir., *The Hustler*, 47; *All the King's Men*, 63
Rossetti, Dante Gabriel, 239

Rossini, G. A., 377
Rota, Nino, 422
Roth, Philip, 260, 364
Roud, Richard, 80
Royal Hunt of the Sun, The, 24–25
R.P.M., 150
Rubens, Peter Paul, 407
Rubinstein, Anton, 240
Rubinstein, Nicholas, 240
Rubirosa, Porfirio, 136, 420
Rugoff, Don, 153–154, 321
Rule, Janice, 260
Runacre, Jenny, 222
Running, Jumping and Standing Still Film, The, 17
Rush, Richard, 150–151; dir., *Getting Straight*, 149–151, 236; *The Savage Seven*, 150
Rusk, Dean, 43
Russell, Ken, 138–142, 238–243, 340, 379–383; dir., *Women in Love*, 138–142, 239; *The Music Lovers*, 238–243; *The Devils*, 315; *The Boy Friend*, 379–383
Russell, Rosalind, 346, 406
Russians Are Coming, The Russians Are Coming, The, 330
Russier, Gabrielle, 418, 419
Ryan, J. M., 121
Ryan, Mitch, 162
Ryan's Daughter, 188–193, 218
Rydell, Mark, 75, 390, 393; dir., *The Fox*, 59; *The Reivers*, 75–76; *The Cowboys*, 390–393, 398

Sacher-Masoch, Leopold van, 312
Sackler, Howard, 158–160
Safer, Morley, 45
Sahl, Mort, 10
Saint, Eva Marie, 121, 122
St. Francis of Assisi, 183
Sainte-Marie, Buffy, 175
Salesman, 208
Salisbury, Harrison, 44
Salter, James, 46
Salvatore, Renato, 65
San Francisco Film Festival, 113
Sand, Paul, 401–403
Sanda, Dominique, 162, 163, 271, 274, 363–365, 413
Sandburg, Carl, 74
Sanders, George, 105
Sandrelli, Stefania, 271
Sands, Diana, 260
Santoni, Reni, 387
Sappho, 36
Sarafian, Richard C., 358; dir., *Man in the Wilderness*, 357–359
Sargent, Alvin, 32

Sarne, Michael 151; dir., *Myra Breckinridge*, 147, 151; *Joanna*, 151
Sarraute, Nathalie, 418
Sarrazin, Michael, 71
Satie, Erik, 308
Saturday Review, 36, 377
Saura, Carlos, 263–264; dir., *The Garden of Delights*, 263–264
Savage Seven, The, 150
Scalphunters, The, 299
Schaefer, George, 260; dir., *Doctors' Wives*, 259 260, 262
Schaffner, Franklin J., 98, 367, 368; dir., *Patton*, 97–100, 368; *Planet of the Apes*, 98, 368; *Nicholas and Alexandra*, 366–369; *The War Lord*, 368
Schatzberg, Jerry, 252; dir., *Puzzle of a Downfall Child*, 250–253; *The Panic in Needle Park*, 305, 314
Schell, Maximilian, 162, 163, 262; dir., *First Love*, 162–163
Schiele, Egon, 242, 410
Schifrin, Lalo, 182, 386
Schine, G. David, 316
Schisgal, Murray, 10
Schlesinger, Jr., Arthur, 43
Schlesinger, John, 4, 290, 292, 293, 424; dir., *Midnight Cowboy*, 4, 76, 147, 152, 314; *Far from the Madding Crowd*, 141; *Darling*, 278; *Sunday Bloody Sunday*, 289–293, 424, 426
Sciascia, Leonardo, 221
Scofield, Paul, 37, 357, 417, 418
Scola, Ettore, 194; dir., *The Pizza Triangle*, 193–195
Scorpio Rising, 87
Scott, George C., 97–99, 350, 378, 379, 426
Scott, Lizabeth, 313
Screen Stories, 216
Scrooge, 196–197
Seaton, George, 136; dir., *Airport*, 132, 136–137, 147, 173, 220, 233, 294; *Miracle on 34th Street*, 136; *Little Boy Lost*, 136; *The Country Girl*, 136; *The Counterfeit Traitor*, 136
Seberg, Jean, 27–29, 137
Second City, 10
Secret Ceremony, 407
Secret of Santa Vittoria, The, 34–35
Segal, Erich, 216–219, 415
Segal, George, 120–122, 183–186, 351–353, 401, 402, 426
Segall, Bernardo, 122
Semple, Jr., Lorenzo, 261
Semprun, Jorge, 64, 202
Sennett, Mack, 195
Setlowe, Rick, 113
Seven Brides for Seven Brothers, 29

Seven Days in May, 199
Seven Samurai, The, 248
Seventh Seal, The, 17, 18
Shadows, 223
Shaffer, Peter, 24
Shaft, 314, 316
Shakespeare, William, 24, 49, 90, 127, 181, 354, 356, 357, 399, 400
Shakespeare Wallah, 195
Shame, 17, 298
Sharif, Omar, 190, 248, 249
Sharp, Alan, 353
Shaw, George Bernard, 84, 156
Shaw, Robert, 24, 119
Shearer, Norma, 137, 157, 216–217
Shebib, Don, 171; dir., *Goin' Down the Road,* 171–172
Shepherd, Cybill, 296
Sheybal, Vladek, 380
Shoeshine, 361, 362
Shoot the Piano Player, 92, 243
Shoulder Arms, 93
Siegel, Don, 386; dir., *Invasion of the Body Snatchers,* 275; *Dirty Harry,* 385–388, 392, 398
Sign of the Cross, The, 131
Signoret, Simone, 142, 202, 204
Silence, The, 59
Silent World, The, 307
Silent Years, The, 319–321
Silliphant, Stirling, 151
Simon & Garfunkel, 23
Sinatra, Frank, 209, 271, 420
Singin' in the Rain, 209, 322
"Skating in Central Park," 219
Skerritt, Tom, 94
Ski Bum, The, 345
Skin Game, 299–300, 426
Slansky, Rudolph, 201, 202, 204
Sleeping Car Murder, The, 64
Slick, Grace, 85, 210
Small, Neva, 332
Smith, Maggie, 15
"Snow Frolic," 219
"So Long, Dearie," 83
Solanas, Fernando, 257, 258; dir., *The Hour of the Furnaces,* 257–259
Solinas, Franco, 176
Son of Fury, 177
Song of Norway, 187, 242, 359
Song to Remember, A, 187, 240
Song Without End, 187
Sons and Lovers, 142
Sontag, Susan, 18, 35, 36; dir., *Duet for Cannibals,* 35–36
Sorrow and the Pity, The, 426–430
Sound of Music, The, 27, 84, 187, 219, 328, 330, 390

South Pacific, 409
Southern, Terry, 9, 111, 123, 218
Sparv, Camilla, 45, 47
Speer, Albert, 428
Spider's Stratagem, The, 273
Spiegel, Sam, 366, 369
Sporting Club, The, 261–263
Stafford, Frederick, 80
Stairway to Heaven, 16
Stalin, Joseph, 112, 201, 369; anti-Stalinism,, 203
Stang, Arnold, 348
Stanwyck, Barbara, 345
Stapleton, Maureen, 137
Star!, 26, 328
"Star-Spangled Banner, The," 228, 325
Star Spangled Girl, 369
Start the Revolution Without Me, 123
Steagle, The, 314
Steegmuller, Francis, 364
Stefanelli, Simonetta, 424
Steiger, Rod, 330, 348–349
Stein, Joseph, 332
Steiner, Max, 104
Stella, 246
Stéphane, Nicole, 364
Stephens, Robert, 186–187
Steppat, Ilse, 86
Sterile Cuckoo, The, 31–34
Stern, Isaac, 328, 332
Stevens, George, 122; dir., *The Only Game in Town,* 122–123, 407; *Vivacious Lady,* 184; *Alice Adams,* 311
Stevens, Stella, 28
Stevenson, Robert, 360; dir., *Bedknobs and Broomsticks,* 359–360
Stine, Harold E., 94
Stolen Kisses, 243, 244
Stoler, Shirley, 106
Stone, Andrew, 187; dir., *Song of Norway,* 187, 242, 359
Stone, Robert, 182
Stone Promotions, 208
Storm, Gale, 296
Storm Warning, 296, 297
Strange, Billy, 19
Stranger, The, 68, 193
Strangers on a Train, 261–262
Strauss, Richard, 239
Stravinsky, Igor, 242, 304
Straw Dogs, 393–399, 426
Strawberry Statement, The, 149–151
Streisand, Barbra, 80–85, 149, 183–185, 353, 383, 431–432
Strick, Joseph, 123–127; dir., *Tropic of Cancer,* 123–127; *The Balcony,* 124; *Ulysses,* 124
Strindberg, August, 109

Sturges, John, 86; dir., *Marooned*, 86
Sturges, Preston, 255
Subject Was Roses, The, 122
Such Good Friends, 383–384
Sullivan, Barry, 77
Summer Interlude, 252
Summer of '42, 321, 391
Sun Also Rises, The, 217
Sunday Bloody Sunday, 289–293, 424, 426
Sundowners, The, 18
Susskind, David, 65
Sutherland, Donald, 93, 94, 123, 206, 224–227, 254, 281–282
Suzman, Janet, 368, 369
Swan Lake, 235, 243
Sweet Charity, 26, 409
Sweet Smell of Success, 252, 318
Swift, Jonathan, 221
"Sympathy for the Devil," 210

Take the Money and Run, 13, 60
Taking Off, 351
Taradash, Daniel, 260
Taste of Honey, A, 187
Tate, Sharon, 152, 167, 339
Tati, Jacques, 308; dir., *Mr. Hulot's Holiday*, 194; *Mon Oncle*, 245
Taylor, Delores, 341, 342
Taylor, Elizabeth, 112–123, 296, 297, 405–409
Taylor, Renée, 369–372
Tchaikovsky, Nina, 239
Tchaikovsky, Peter Ilich, 239–243
Teaching Film Custodians, 145
Telephone Book, The, 325
Tell Them Willie Boy Is Here, 76–78
Temaner, Gerald, 207
Teorema, 9
Tepper, William, 350
Terry, Ellen, 84
Thalberg, Irving, 216–217
That Certain Woman, 157
"That Old Black Magic," 371
"Theme from *Love Story*," 219
Theodorakis, Mikis, 64
There Was a Crooked Man ..., 229–230
There's a Girl in My Soup, 231, 235
"They Call the Wind Maria," 28
They Shoot Horses, Don't They?, 68–72, 76, 281
Thief of Bagdad, The, 320
Thief of Paris, The, 309
Thing, The, 275
Third Man, The, 415
This Man Must Die, 172
Thompson, Robert E., 70
Three Little Pigs, 359
Three Stooges, 31, 180, 198

Throne of Blood, 139, 336
Thulin, Ingrid, 86, 87
Tidyman, Ernest, 316
Tierney, Gene, 177
Tiger Makes Out, The, 10
Time, 8
Time for Burning, A, 207
Times Gone By, 362
Titicut Follies, 20, 21
Tito, Marshal, 201
To Die of Love, 418–419
To Have and Have Not, 235, 237, 413
To Sir, with Love, 343
Tobacco Road, 155
Tolan, Michael, 73
Tolkien, J. R. R., 60, 230
Tom Jones, 308
Tomlinson, David, 359, 360
"Tomorrow Belongs to Me," 413
Top Hat, 381
Topaz, 79–80
Topo, El, 334–340
Topol, 328–330
Tora! Tora! Tora!, 147–148
Torn, Rip, 36, 126
Torn Curtain, 79
Touch, The, 348
Toulouse-Lautrec, Henri de, 412
Tra Donne Sole, 113
Tracy, Spencer, 184, 227, 351, 353
Trash, 153–157
T. R. Baskin, 311–313
Treasure of Sierra Madre, The, 298
Trial, The, 220
Trilling, Lionel, 32
Trintignant, Jean-Louis, 65, 270–271, 273, 274, 413–415
Tristan, Dorothy, 111
Triumph of the Will, 207
Trojan Women, The, 300–305
Tropic of Cancer, 123–127
Trotsky, Leon, 369; Trotskyism, 201
Trotter, John Scott, 91
True Detective, 106
True Grit, 149
Truffaut, François, 243–245, 307; dir., *Shoot the Piano Player*, 92, 243; *Jules and Jim*, 243; *The Wild Child*, 243, 245; *The Bride Wore Black*, 243; *Stolen Kisses*, 243, 244; *Bed and Board*, 243–245; *The 400 Blows*, 244, 245, 307
Trujillo, Rafael, 135
Truscott, John, 30
Tucker, Larry, 9–10, 14, 148, 225–227
Tune, Tommy, 381
Turgenev, Ivan, 162, 163
Turner, Lana, 284
Tushingham, Rita, 17

Twain, Mark, 124
Twelve Chairs, The, 180, 226
Twentieth Century-Fox, 100, 148
Twenty Million Sweethearts, 284
Twiggy, 59, 380–382
Two for the Road, 10
2001, 131

U.C.L.A., 5, 171
Ulysses, 124
Umberto D., 361
United Artists, 177
Universal Pictures, 91
Unsworth, Geoffrey, 413
Up in Arms, 93
Up the Down Staircase, 23
Ure, Mary, 119
Uris, Leon, 79
Ustinov, Peter, dir., *Billy Budd*, 170

Vadim, Roger, 222, 225; dir., *Pretty Maids All in a Row*, 225
Valli, Alida, 415
Van Devere, Trish, 185
Van Dyke, Dick, 60
Van Runkle, Theodora, 52
Varda, Agnès, 30; dir., *Lions Love*, 30–31
Variety, 113, 124, 219, 322
Vassilikos, Vassili, 63
Vaughn, Robert, 262
Vie Privée, 308
Vietnam, 14, 42–45, 147, 163, 179, 215, 216, 249, 415
V.I.P.s, The, 136
Visconti, Luchino, 86, 87, 271, 272; dir., *The Damned*, 86–88, 271, 272, 274; *The Stranger*, 68, 193
Vitti, Monica, 194, 195
Viva, 31
Viva Maria!, 309
Viva Zapata!, 175
Vivacious Lady, 184
Vogel, Mitch, 75
Volonte, Gian Maria, 221
von Meck, Mme., 239, 240
von Sydow, Max, 105
Vonnegut, Jr., Kurt, 230

Wagner, Robert, 47
Wagonmaster, 296
Walk with Love and Death, A, 17–18
Walker, Robert, 261
Wallace, Irving, 420
Waller, Fats, 85
Walsh, Raoul, 78
Wanda, 267–269
"Wand'rin' Star," 29
War Lord, The, 368

Warhol, Andy, 13, 31, 153–157, 197; dir., *Lonesome Cowboys*, 153; *The Chelsea Girls*, 154
Warner Brothers, 105, 299, 343, 390
Warner, David, 89, 193, 395
Warner, Jack, 119
Warshow, Robert, 425
Waterloo, 348
Watson and Webber, 242; dirs., *Lot in Sodom*, 55, 242
Wayne, David, 276
Wayne, John, 174, 229, 350, 390–393
We Still Kill the Old Way, 221
Webb, Alan, 357, 368
Weekend, 253, 298, 404
Weil, Simone, 430
Weill, Kurt, 410
Weld, Tuesday, 199, 223
Welles, Orson, 105; dir., *Citizen Kane*, 252
Wepper, Fritz, 412
Wertmuller, Lina, 183
West, Mae, 183
West, Nathanael, 68
West Side Story, 328, 409
Westlake, Donald E., 401
Weston, Jack, 269
Wexler, Haskel, dir., *Medium Cool*, 117
What Is Cinema? (Vol. II), 366
What Price Glory, 93
What's Up, Doc?, 431–433
Wheeler, Hugh, 412
Where's Poppa?, 185–186, 314, 351, 402
Whisperers, The, 323
White, David, 151
White, Pearl, 184
White, Ruth, 76
Whiting, Leonard, 24
Whitman, Walt, 274
Whitmore, James, 147
"Who Am I?," 371
Who Is Harry Kellerman and Why Is He Saying Those Terrible Things About Me?, 314, 323
Who's Afraid of Virginia Woolf?, 405, 406
Widerberg, Bo, 41–42; dir., *Elvira Madigan*, 7, 41, 154, 365; *Adalen 31*, 40–42, 104
Wilcox-Horne, Collin, 157
Wild Angels, The, 84
Wild Bunch, The, 133–134, 149, 393
Wild Child, The, 243, 245
Wild One, The, 152
Wild Strawberries, 252
Wilde, Cornel, 62, 240, 242
Wilder, Billy, 186–187; dir., *The Private Life of Sherlock Holmes*, 186–187
Wilder, Gene, 123
Williams, Billy, 408

Williamson, Nicol, 37, 88–91
Willis, Gordon, 112, 122, 254
"Willkommen," 410
Wilson, Angus, 150
Wilson, Flip, 85, 149, 363
Wilson, Sandy, 379, 380, 382
Windy Day, 91
Winn, Kitty, 305
Winters, Jonathan, 85, 329–330
Winters, Shelley, 109
Wise, Robert, 275, 276; dir., *Star!*, 26, 328; *The Sound of Music*, 27, 84, 187, 219, 328, 330, 390; *The Andromeda Strain*, 275–276; *West Side Story*, 328, 409
Wiseman, Frederick, 20, 24, 101, 207, 295; dir., *Law and Order*, 20, 23, 207; *High School*, 20–24; *Titicut Follies*, 20, 21; *Hospital*, 101–102
Without Apparent Motive, 413–415
WNET, 319, 320
Wolsey, Cardinal, 97
Woman of Affairs, A, 364, 365
Women, The, 137
Women in Love, 138–142, 239
Wood, Charles, 17
Wood, Natalie, 11–13
Woodlawn, Holly, 155–157
Woodstock, 208
Woodward, Joanne, 59, 181, 182
Woolf, Virginia, 36, 188, 291
World War I, 15, 189, 368, 429
World War II, 40, 45, 86, 99, 100, 146, 216, 359, 427, 429
Worth, Irene, 369
Wright, Jenny Lee, 222
WUSA, 181–182
Wyler, William, 381; dir., *How to Steal a Million*, 37; *Roman Holiday*, 381
Wynter, Dana, 137

X Y & Zee, 405–409

Yanne, Jean, 172, 404
Yates, Peter, 73, 402, 403; dir., *John and Mary*, 72–73; *Bullitt*, 162, 316, 402; *The Hot Rock*, 401–403
Yesterday, Today, and Tomorrow, 362
Yordan, Philip, 24
York, Michael, 67, 412
York, Susannah, 69, 189, 405, 406, 408
Yorkin, Bud, 123; dir., *Start the Revolution Without Me*, 123
Young, Freddie, 368
Young, Gig, 70
Young, Loretta, 73
Young Lions, The, 249
"You're the Top," 432
Yulin, Harris, 112

Z, 63–67, 152, 154, 200, 202, 204, 316, 317, 319
Zabriskie Point, 113–117, 131, 211
Zanuck, Darryl F., 83, 151
Zavattini, Cesare, 361–362
Zazie dans le Métro, 308, 309
Zee & Co., 408
Zeffirelli, Franco, 182, 183, 272; dir., *Romeo and Juliet*, 18, 182, 219; *Brother Sun and Sister Moon* (projected), 182–183
Zinnemann, Fred, 176; dir., *Oklahoma!*, 29, 409, 413; *The Sundowners*, 18; *A Man for All Seasons*, 95; *Behold a Pale Horse*, 176; *The Men*, 322; *High Noon*, 387; *From Here to Eternity*, 421; *The Nun's Story*, 421
Zionism, 201
Zola, Emile, 267
Zorba the Greek, 35, 246
Zwerin, Charlotte, 206